SUPERVISION
Key Link to Productivity

Sixth Edition

Leslie W. Rue
Professor of Management and holder of the
Carl R. Zwerner Chair of Family Owned Enterprises
College of Business Administration
Georgia State University

Lloyd L. Byars
Professor of Management and Director of Undergraduate Programs
School of Management
Georgia Institute of Technology

Irwin
McGraw-Hill

Boston   Burr Ridge, IL   Dubuque, IA   Madison, WI   New York   San Francisco   St. Louis
Bangkok   Bogotá   Caracas   Lisbon   London   Madrid
Mexico City   Milan   New Delhi   Seoul   Singapore   Sydney   Taipei   Toronto

Irwin/McGraw-Hill

*A Division of The **McGraw·Hill** Companies*

SUPERVISION: KEY LINK TO PRODUCTIVITY

This book is printed on acid-free paper.

2 3 4 5 6 7 8 9 0 DOW/DOW 9 3 2 1 0 9

ISBN 0–256–27173–9

Vice president and editorial director: *Michael W. Junior*
Publisher: *Craig S. Beytein*
Sponsoring editor: *Karen M. Mellon*
Editorial assistant: *Jade Emrich*
Marketing manager: *Kenyetta Giles*
Project manager: *Denise Santor-Mitzit*
Production supervisor: *Debra R. Benson*
Designer: *Jennifer McQueen Hollingsworth*
Cover illustrator: *Gerald Bustamante*
Supplement coordinator: *Nancy Martin*
Compositor: *Shepherd, Inc.*
Typeface: *10/12 ITC Century*
Printer: *R. R. Donnelley & Sons Company*

Library of Congress Cataloging-in-Publication Data

Rue, Leslie W.
    Supervision, key link to productivity / Leslie W. Rue, Lloyd L.
Byars.—6th ed.
      p.   cm.
    Includes bibliographical references and indexes.
    ISBN 0–256–27173–9
    1. Supervision of employees.   I. Byars, Lloyd L.   II. Title.
HF5549.R7825   1999   98–20986
658.3′02—dc21

http://www.mhhe.com

DEDICATION

To very important people in our lives

Harriet and Bill Rue

Henry and Lula Byars

Bob and Tweetie Schwefel

Contents in Brief

SECTION I
Foundations of Supervision   1

CHAPTER 1 The Supervisor's Job   2
CHAPTER 2 Making Sound and Creative Decisions   23
CHAPTER 3 Improving Your Communication Skills   44
CHAPTER 4 Ethics and Organization Politics   63
CHAPTER 5 Managing Your Time   79

SECTION II
Planning and Organizing Skills   97

CHAPTER 6 Supervisory Planning   98
CHAPTER 7 Organizing and Delegating   121
CHAPTER 8 Understanding Work Groups   143
CHAPTER 9 Productivity and Methods
                    Improvement   161

SECTION III
Staffing Skills   183

CHAPTER 10 Obtaining and Developing Employees   184
CHAPTER 11 Appraising Employee Performance   208
CHAPTER 12 Understanding Equal Employment
                    Opportunity   229
CHAPTER 13 Understanding Unions   250

SECTION IV
Human Relations Skills   269

CHAPTER 14 Motivating Today's Employee   270
CHAPTER 15 Leading Employees   289
CHAPTER 16 Handling Conflict   308
CHAPTER 17 Coping with Change and Stress   323
CHAPTER 18 Counseling Employees   345

SECTION V
Controlling Skills   363

CHAPTER 19 Supervisory Control and Quality   364
CHAPTER 20 Improving Productivity Through Cost
                    Control   388
CHAPTER 21 Safety and Accident Prevention   407
CHAPTER 22 Discipline and Grievance Handling   427

GLOSSARY   447
NAME INDEX   455
COMPANY INDEX   457
SUBJECT INDEX   458

Contents

SECTION I
Foundations of Supervision   1

CHAPTER 1   The Supervisor's Job   2

What Is Supervision?   3

Who Is a Supervisor?   4

Where Do Supervisors Come from?   5

The Functions of Supervision   5

    Key Reasons for Supervisory Success   8

**The Changing Nature of the Supervisor's
Environment   10**

    Changes in Information Availability   10

    Changes in Outlook toward the Work Environment   10

Supervision: Key Link to Productivity   14

Skill-Building Applications   17

INCIDENT 1–1: Promotion into Supervision   17

INCIDENT 1–2: Not Enough Time to Supervise   17

EXERCISE 1–1: Understanding the Job of a Supervisor   18

EXERCISE 1–2: Required Attributes of a Supervisor   20

EXERCISE 1–3: The Supervisor's Personal Inventory   20

EXERCISE 1–4: Understanding Diversity   22

Selected Supervisory and Related Periodicals   22

CHAPTER 2   Making Sound and Creative Decisions   23

Decision Making versus Problem Solving   24

Recognition and Timeliness of the Decision   25

Steps in the Decision-Making Process   26

    Step 1: Be Alert to Indications and Symptoms of
    Problems   26

    Step 2: Tentatively Define the Problem   26

    Step 3: Collect Facts and Redefine the Problem if
    Necessary   27

    Step 4: Identify Possible Alternatives   27

    Step 5: Gather and Organize Facts Concerning Identified
    Alternatives   28

    Step 6: Evaluate Possible Alternatives   29

    Step 7: Choose and Implement the Best Alternative   29

    Step 8: The Follow-Up   30

Group Decision Making   30

Practical Traps to Avoid When Making Decisions   32

    Trap 1: Making All Decisions BIG Decisions   32

    Trap 2: Creating Crisis Situations   33

    Trap 3: Failing to Consult with Others   33

    Trap 4: Never Admitting a Mistake   33

    Trap 5: Constantly Regretting Decisions   33

    Trap 6: Failing to Utilize Precedents and Policies   33

    Trap 7: Failing to Gather and Examine Available Data   34

    Trap 8: Promising What Cannot Be Delivered   34

    Trap 9: Delaying Decisions Too Long   34

Making Creative Decisions   34

    The Creative Person   34

    Improving Personal Creativity   35

    Establishing and Maintaining a Creative Climate   35

    Barriers to Organizational Creativity   37

Skill-Building Applications   41

INCIDENT 2–1: A Second Chance?   41

INCIDENT 2–2: Bad Times at Quality Shoe   41

EXERCISE 2–1: Lost at Sea   42

EXERCISE 2–2: Assessing Your Creativity   43

CHAPTER 3   Improving Your Communication Skills   44

What Is Communication?   45

Interpersonal Communication   45

    Poor Listening Habits   46

    Lack of Feedback   48

    Differences in Perception   48

    Misinterpretation of Words   49

    Poor Example Set by the Supervisor   50

    Lack of Interest by the Receiver   50

Improving Your Communication Skills   51

Oral Skills   51

Writing Skills   52

Nonverbal Communication   52

Communicating with Your Boss   54

Organizational Communication   54

Handling Meetings   55

Giving Instructions   56

Dealing with the Grapevine   57

Skill-Building Applications   60

INCIDENT 3–1: "I Told You . . ."   60

INCIDENT 3–2: Shutdown at Glover Manufacturing   60

EXERCISE 3–1: Meanings Are in People   61

EXERCISE 3–2: Perception Test   61

EXERCISE 3–3: Reading Comprehension   61

EXERCISE 3–4: Your Listening Ratio   62

CHAPTER 4   Ethics and Organization Politics   63

Ethics in the Workplace   64

Codes of Ethics   65

Setting the Tone   66

Areas Requiring Ethical Conduct by Supervisors   67

Loyalty   67

Human Relations   67

Overt Personal Actions   67

Dealing with Dishonest Employees   68

Building a Supervisory Power Base   69

Organization Politics   70

How to Keep Your Boss Happy   70

Socializing with Other Members of the Organization   72

Skill-Building Applications   75

INCIDENT 4–1: Additional Expenses?   75

INCIDENT 4–2: The Date   75

EXERCISE 4–1: Where Do You Stand?   76

EXERCISE 4–2: Evaluate Your Ethics   77

CHAPTER 5   Managing Your Time   79

Typical Time Wasters   80

Understanding Your Job   81

Analyzing Your Time   81

Planning Your Time   82

Optimizing Your Work Routine   84

Establishing Good Work Habits   85

Think Time   90

Skill-Building Applications   93

INCIDENT 5–1: Not Enough Time   93

INCIDENT 5–2: Plan for a Day   93

EXERCISE 5–1: Are You Using Your Time Effectively?   94

EXERCISE 5–2: Time Trap Identification   95

EXERCISE 5–3: Time Management Assumptions   95

SECTION II
Planning and Organizing Skills   97

CHAPTER 6   Supervisory Planning   98

How the Organization Plans   99

The Supervisor and Strategic Planning   100

The Supervisor's Role in Planning   101

The What and How of Supervisory Planning   101

Objectives versus Goals   103

Setting Objectives   103

Action Planning   105

Contingency Plans   106

Policies, Procedures, and Rules   107

Policies   107

Procedures   108

Rules   108

Common Supervisory Planning Activities   108

Providing Information for High-Level Planning   109

Developing a Budget   109

Improvement Programs   109

Human Resource Needs   109

Production Planning   109

Management by Objectives (MBO)   112

Skill-Building Applications   118

INCIDENT 6–1: A Plan for Productivity Improvement   118

INCIDENT 6–2: What Should I Do Next?   118

EXERCISE 6–1: Personal Objectives   119

EXERCISE 6–2: Identifying Personal Goals   119

EXERCISE 6–3: Drawing a CPM Logic Network   119

CHAPTER 7   Organizing and Delegating   121

The Organization Structure   122

    Organization Charts   122

    Departmentation   122

    Authority and the Supervisor   123

    Line versus Staff Authority   124

    Centralized versus Decentralized Authority   125

    Power and the Supervisor   126

    Responsibility and the Supervisor   126

Principles of Supervision Based on Authority   127

    Parity Principle   127

    Exception Principle   127

    Unity of Command Principle   128

    Scalar Principle   128

    Span of Control Principle   128

Delegating Authority and Responsibility   129

    How to Delegate   130

    Why People Are Reluctant to Delegate   131

    Tasks That Can't Be Delegated   133

    Practical Tips for Effective Delegation   134

Skill-Building Applications   139

INCIDENT 7–1: Where Do You Start?   139

INCIDENT 7–2: A Hectic Day   139

EXERCISE 7–1: Minor Errors   140

EXERCISE 7–2: "In-Basket"   141

EXERCISE 7–3: Promotion Role Play   141

EXERCISE 7–4: Delegation Quiz   142

CHAPTER 8   Understanding Work Groups   143

Formal Work Groups   144

    Quality Circles   146

Informal Work Groups   146

    Characteristics of Informal Work Groups   148

    Informal Work Group Leadership   150

Group Pressures on Individuals   151

Supervision and Informal Work Groups   152

    Getting the Informal Work Group to Work with You instead of against You   153

Skill-Building Applications   159

INCIDENT 8–1: Jokes on the Night Shift   159

INCIDENT 8–2: A New Job   159

EXERCISE 8–1: Crash Project   160

EXERCISE 8–2: Characteristics of Effective Work Groups   160

CHAPTER 9   Productivity and Methods Improvement   161

Kaizen Philosophy for Improvement   163

Methods Improvement and the Supervisor   164

    Employee Fears   164

    Establishing the Proper Climate   165

Benefits of Methods Improvement   165

Systematic Methods Improvement   166

    Stage 1: Plan—Where and How to Make Improvements   166

    Stage 2: Do—Try Out the Improvements   169

    Stage 3: Check—Evaluate the Results   171

    Stage 4: Act—Take Action and Fine-Tune   171

Time Study   171

Skill-Building Applications   176

INCIDENT 9–1: Who Works Harder?   176

INCIDENT 9–2: The Lines at Sam's   176

EXERCISE 9–1: Improving Your Exam Performance   176

EXERCISE 9–2: Processing Customers   177

Appendix   178

    Flow-Process Chart   178

    Layout Chart   179

SECTION III
Staffing Skills   183

CHAPTER 10   Obtaining and Developing Employees   184

Recruiting Qualified Personnel   185

    Job Analysis   185

    Job Posting and Bidding   187

    Advertising   187

    Employment Agencies   187

    Internship and Co-Op Programs   188

    Employee Referrals   188

Selecting Personnel   188

    Who Makes the Selection Decision?   188

    The Selection Process   188

Legal Implications in Recruiting and Hiring New Employees 197

Orienting the New Employee 198

Training Employees 200

Steps in Training Employees in Job Skills 202

Get the Trainee Ready to Learn 202

Break Down the Work into Components and Identify the Key Points 202

Demonstrate the Proper Way the Work Is to Be Done 202

Let the Trainee Perform the Work 202

Put Trainees on Their Own Gradually 203

Skill-Building Applications 206

INCIDENT 10–1: Hiring a New Employee 206

INCIDENT 10–2: Lake Avionics 206

EXERCISE 10–1: The Layoff 207

EXERCISE 10–2: OJT 207

CHAPTER 11 Appraising Employee Performance 208

What Is Performance? 209

Job Descriptions and Job Specifications 211

Performance Appraisal Defined 212

Performance Appraisal Methods 213

Graphic Rating Scale 214

Essay Appraisals 214

Checklist 214

Forced-Choice Rating 216

Critical-Incident Appraisals 216

Work-Standards Approach 216

Ranking Methods 217

Management by Objectives (MBO) 218

Frequency of Performance Appraisals 218

Supervisor Biases in Performance Appraisals 219

Overcoming Biases in Performance Appraisals 219

Conducting Performance Appraisal Interviews 220

Preparing for Your Own Performance Appraisal Interview 221

Handling the Poor Performer 222

Skill-Building Applications 226

INCIDENT 11–1: Lackadaisical Manager 226

INCIDENT 11–2: The New Auditor 226

EXERCISE 11–1: Developing a Performance Appraisal System 227

EXERCISE 11–2: Who Are Normal Employees? 228

CHAPTER 12 Understanding Equal Employment Opportunity 229

What Are Protected Groups? 230

Effects of Discrimination 231

Antidiscrimination Laws That Affect Organizations 231

Title VII of the Civil Rights Act of 1964 231

Title VI 232

Equal Pay Act 232

Education Amendments Act 232

Age Discrimination in Employment Act 232

Affirmative Action 232

Veterans Readjustment Act 232

Rehabilitation Act of 1973 233

Americans with Disabilities Act (ADA) 233

Civil Rights Act of 1991 234

Other Antidiscrimination Legislation 235

Enforcement Agencies 237

Interpretation and Application of Title VII and Affirmative Action 237

Title VII of the Civil Rights Act of 1964 237

History of Affirmative Action Programs 239

Effect of Antidiscrimination Laws on the Supervisor 240

Hiring Practices 240

Job Assignments 241

Performance Evaluation and Upward Mobility 241

Disciplinary Action 242

A Positive Approach to Equal Employment Opportunity and Affirmative Action 242

Preventing Sexual Harassment in the Workplace 244

Skill-Building Applications 248

INCIDENT 12–1: This Is a Man's Job 248

INCIDENT 12–2: Affirmative Action 248

EXERCISE 12–1: Affirmative Action Debate 249

EXERCISE 12–2: Legal Issues in Equal Employment Opportunity 249

CHAPTER 13   Understanding Unions   250

Differing Philosophies of Unions and Management   251

Development of Labor Law   251

Structure of Labor Unions   254

Reasons for Joining Unions   256

Union Organization Drive   257

Collective Bargaining   257

    Negotiation of the Contract   257

    Administering the Contract   258

Supervisor's Responsibility to the Employer and the Union   259

Supervisory Responsibilities and Unions   259

    Working with the Steward   261

    During Collective Bargaining   261

    Administering the Contract   261

    During a Strike   262

Skill-Building Applications   266

INCIDENT 13–1: Working with Trudy   266

INCIDENT 13–2: Wildcat Strike   266

EXERCISE 13–1: What Have You Learned?   266

EXERCISE 13–2: Contract Negotiations   267

EXERCISE 13–3: How Do You Rate as a Business Negotiator?   268

SECTION IV
Human Relations Skills   269

CHAPTER 14   Motivating Today's Employee   270

What Is Motivation?   271

Understanding People   272

Basic Motivation Theories   272

    Traditional Theory   272

    Need Hierarchy Theory   273

    Achievement-Power-Affiliation Theory   276

    Motivation-Maintenance Theory   277

    Preference-Expectancy Theory   278

    Reinforcement Theory   279

What Can the Supervisor Do?   280

    Make the Work Interesting   280

    Relate Rewards to Performance   281

    Provide Valued Rewards   281

    Treat Employees as Individuals   281

    Encourage Participation and Cooperation   281

    Provide Accurate and Timely Feedback   282

Job Satisfaction   282

Skill-Building Applications   287

INCIDENT 14–1: No Extra Effort   287

INCIDENT 14–2: The Secure Employee   287

EXERCISE 14–1: Money as a Motivator   288

EXERCISE 14–2: Motivation-Maintenance Theory   288

CHAPTER 15   Leading Employees   289

Power, Authority, and Leadership   290

Formal versus Informal Leaders   291

Leadership Characteristics   292

    Self-Confidence   292

    Mental and Physical Endurance   292

    Enthusiasm   292

    Sense of Responsibility   292

    Empathy and Good Human Relations   292

Basic Styles of Leadership   293

    Supportive or Directive?   294

How Do the Different Styles of Leadership Relate?   295

Picking the Best Style   298

    Fiedler's Contingency Approach   298

Leader Attitudes   299

Leadership and Morale   300

Implications for Today's Supervisors   301

Skill-Building Applications   304

INCIDENT 15–1: Jealousy at the Bank   304

INCIDENT 15–2: Promises You Can't Keep   304

EXERCISE 15–1: Insubordination?   305

EXERCISE 15–2: Situational Approach to Leadership   305

EXERCISE 15–3: Test Your Leadership Style   305

CHAPTER 16   Handling Conflict   308

What Is Conflict?   309

Positive and Negative Aspects of Conflict   310

Types of Conflict in Organizations   310

Intrapersonal Conflict   310

Interpersonal Conflict   313

Structural Conflict   314

Political Conflict   315

Managing Conflict   315

Skill-Building Applications   320

INCIDENT 16–1: Trouble in the Claims Department   320

INCIDENT 16–2: Ingram Manufacturing Company   320

EXERCISE 16–1: Conflict over Quality   321

EXERCISE 16–2: Secretarial Problems   321

CHAPTER 17   Coping with Change and Stress   323

Change and the Supervisor   324

Reactions to Change   325

Resistance to Change   326

Fear of the Unknown   326

Threat to Job or Income   327

Fear that Skills and Expertise Will Lose Value   327

Threats to Power   327

Inconvenience   327

Threats to Interpersonal Relations   327

Reducing Resistance to Change   328

Build Trust   328

Discuss Upcoming Changes   328

Involve the Employees   329

Make Sure the Changes Are Reasonable   329

Avoid Threats   329

Follow a Sensible Time Schedule   330

Implement the Changes in the Most Logical Place   331

The Five Ws and an H   331

Lewin's Three-Step Model for Change   331

Managing Stress   332

Types of Job-Related Stress   332

Organizational Guidelines for Managing Stress   333

Personal Guidelines for Managing Stress   333

The Family and Medical Leave Act of 1993   334

Skill-Building Applications   338

INCIDENT 17–1: A New Boss   338

INCIDENT 17–2: Getting Rid of Bart   338

EXERCISE 17–1: Preparing for Resistance to Change   339

EXERCISE 17–2: Truth and Misconceptions about Stress   339

EXERCISE 17–3: Measuring Your Level of Stress   340

EXERCISE 17–4: Life Events Causing Stress   342

CHAPTER 18   Counseling Employees   345

When and Why to Counsel   346

Counseling Techniques   347

Directive versus Nondirective Counseling   347

Steps in the Counseling Interview   347

Career Counseling   348

Supervising Troubled Employees   349

How the Troubled Employee Affects the Organization   350

Help from the Organization   350

Detecting the Troubled Employee   351

Confronting the Troubled Employee   351

Aiding and Evaluating Recovery   353

Employee Assistance Programs   354

Legal and Union Demands   354

Problem Employees   356

Skill-Building Applications   360

INCIDENT 18–1: Changes in an Employee's Behavior   360

INCIDENT 18–2: Smoking in the Stockroom   360

EXERCISE 18–1: What Is the Problem?   361

EXERCISE 18–2: How Do You Rate as a Career Counselor?   361

EXERCISE 18–3: Who Is Right?   362

SECTION V
Controlling Skills   363

CHAPTER 19   Supervisory Control and Quality   364

Steps in the Controlling Process   365

Establishing Performance Standards   365

Monitoring Performance   366

Taking Corrective Action   366

Tools for Supervisory Control   367

Budgets   367

Written Reports   368

Personal Observation   369

Electronic Monitors   369

Management by Objectives   369

Supervisory Control in Practice   369

Quality and the Supervisor   370

Why Insist on Quality?   370

Who Is Responsible for Quality?   370

Quality Assurance   371

Total Quality Management   371

Other Quality Standards   373

Quality Guidelines   375

The Malcolm Baldrige National Quality Award   376

Types of Quality Control   376

Inventory Control   377

Just-in-Time Inventory Control   379

Skill-Building Applications   383

INCIDENT 19–1: The Assuming Supervisor   383

INCIDENT 19–2: High-Quality Toys   383

EXERCISE 19–1: Controlling Production   384

EXERCISE 19–2: Assessing Quality   385

Appendix   386

Managing Inventories   386

Independent versus Dependent Demand Items   386

Inventory Considerations for Independent Demand Items   386

Managing Inventories for Dependent Demand Items   387

CHAPTER 20   Improving Productivity through Cost Control   388

The Supervisor's Role in Cost Reduction and Control   389

Establishing the Proper Environment   389

Figuring Costs   390

Cost Budgets   391

Cost-Reduction Strategies   393

Cost-Reduction Resources   394

A Nine-Step Plan for Cost Reduction   395

Cost Areas That Frequently Cause Problems   397

Overtime   397

Absenteeism   398

Tardiness   399

Employee Theft   400

Materials Handling   401

Why Do Employees Sometimes Fear Cost Reduction?   401

Skill-Building Applications   405

INCIDENT 20–1: A Recommendation for Cutting Costs   405

INCIDENT 20–2: Here We Go Again   405

EXERCISE 20–1: Preparing a Cost Report   405

EXERCISE 20–2: Cost Overruns   406

EXERCISE 20–3: Comparing Costs   406

CHAPTER 21   Safety and Accident Prevention   407

The Supervisor's Responsibility for Safety   408

The Cost of Accidents   409

The Causes of Accidents   411

Personal Acts   411

Physical Environment   412

Accident-Proneness   412

How to Measure Safety   413

The Safety Program   414

Organizational Strategies for Promoting Safety   414

How the Supervisor Can Prevent Accidents   415

Violence in the Workplace   418

Occupational Safety and Health Act (OSHA)   419

The Supervisor and OSHA   421

Hazard Communications Standard   421

Skill-Building Applications   425

INCIDENT 21–1: The Safety Inspection   425

INCIDENT 21–2: No One Listens   425

EXERCISE 21–1: Potential Safety Problems   426

EXERCISE 21–2: National Safety   426

CHAPTER 22   Discipline and Grievance Handling   427

A Positive Approach to Discipline   428

How Does the Supervisor Maintain Good Discipline?   429

Applying the Discipline Procedure   429

Predisciplinary Recommendation   431

Administering Formal Discipline   432

Minimizing Grievances   435

Recommendations for Pregrievance Settlement   **437**

Handling the First Step of the Grievance Process   **438**

Handling Later Steps in the Grievance Process   **440**

Discipline in Nonunionized Organizations   **440**

Skill-Building Applications   **443**

INCIDENT **22–1:** You're Fired!   443

INCIDENT **22–2:** Keys to the Drug Cabinet   443

EXERCISE **22–1:** Mock Arbitration   444

EXERCISE **22–2:** Discipline in a Nonunionized Business   445

GLOSSARY   447

NAME INDEX   455

COMPANY INDEX   457

SUBJECT INDEX   458

Preface

We are both very happy that this book has gone into six editions. We feel that the clear writing style and the practical emphasis of this text are its most popular features. Many professors tell us that their students—many of whom are already practicing supervisors—often keep *Supervision* as a handbook and reference even after the class is over.

Another enduring feature of *Supervision* is its emphasis on productivity. Since 1982, when the first edition was published, productivity has remained a major concern of today's managers and government leaders. Time, experience, and research have all shown that the supervisor can have a significant impact on an organization's productivity. This edition builds on the previous edition's emphasis on total quality management (TQM), the Kaizen philosophy, and other approaches directly related to productivity.

As with earlier editions, we have stressed real-world applications seen from the supervisor's viewpoint by using numerous and varied examples throughout the text and in the end-of-chapter materials. Each chapter begins with a Supervision Dilemma, which is a realistic example related to the chapter topic. The same example is revisited at the end of the chapter in the Solution to the Supervision Dilemma. Also in keeping with the practical nature of this text, we have several Supervision Illustrations in each chapter. These illustrations contain real-life incidents or news stories that further shape the chapter focus. Each chapter includes review questions, as well as several skill-building questions. In addition, a Skill-Building Applications section at the end of each chapter contains two incidents and at least two experiential exercises.

Organization of the Sixth Edition

After a substantial reorganization of the fourth edition and additional work on the fifth, this edition is a refinement of a proven successful text. We have continued to organize the materials based on the skills necessary to successfully supervise. We feel that this is a very practical and academically sound approach. This edition is arranged in five major sections:

> Section I: Foundations of Supervision
> Section II: Planning and Organizing Skills
> Section III: Staffing Skills
> Section IV: Human Relations Skills
> Section V: Controlling Skills

Section I provides a foundation necessary to embark on the practice of supervision. The topics covered span all supervisory jobs. Specific topics include the supervisor's job, decision making, communication, ethics and organizational politics, and managing your time.

Section II stresses the planning and organizing skills that today's supervisors must possess to be successful. Chapters are devoted to supervisory planning, organizing and delegating, understanding work groups, and improving methods.

Section III emphasizes the important role that all supervisors play in the staffing process. Obtaining and developing people, appraising performance, equal employment, and unions are all explored in this section.

Section IV is devoted to exploring the multitude of human relations skills that are necessary for successful supervision. Motivation, leadership, handling conflict, dealing with change and stress, and counseling are all discussed at length.

Section V discusses the different controlling approaches that are available to help supervisors. Control concepts, quality, cost control, safety and accident prevention, and discipline are presented in this section.

We have attempted to write this book considering the needs of teachers, students, aspiring supervisors, and practicing supervisors. We have tried to arrange the concepts and materials to appeal to each of these groups. Naturally, we welcome any ideas and suggestions that might improve the book.

Acknowledgments

We are indebted to our families, friends, colleagues, and students for the assistance we have received. Unfortunately, space limitations allow us to name only a few. We give special thanks to the following reviewers, who provided many helpful comments during the preparation of the sixth edition: Steve Floyd, Manatee Community College; James P. Orr, Southern Illinois University; Smita Oxford, Texas A & M University; Elliot F. Porter, Los Angeles Trade Technical College; Greg Saboe, Des Moines Area Community College; Gene Stewart, Brookhaven College; Margene Sunderland, Fayetteville Technical Community College; and Dan Underwood, Inver Hills Community College.

Special thanks are extended to sponsoring editor Karen Mellon and project manager Denise Santor-Mitzit of Irwin/McGraw-Hill. Sincere appreciation is extended to Charmelle Todd for her typing and editing support.

Foundations of Supervision

SECTION OUTLINE

1 The supervisor's job

2 Making sound and creative decisions

3 Improving your communication skills

4 Ethics and organization politics

5 Managing your time

The Supervisor's Job

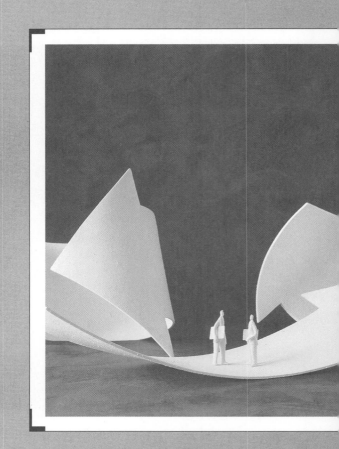

LEARNING OBJECTIVES

After studying this chapter, you should be able to:

1. Define supervision.

2. Describe the work of a supervisor.

3. Present the types of skills necessary to perform the job of supervision.

4. State the key reasons for supervisory success.

5. Explain the glass ceiling concept.

6. Describe guidelines for managing diversity in the workforce.

SUPERVISION DILEMMA

Global Insurance is a worldwide company with several thousand employees. Jane Harris and John Lewis are employees in one of the company's claims-processing offices. Both have been with the company for approximately six years. This morning, their department head, Les Thomas, gave Jane and John a big shock. He asked both of them if they would like to become supervisors in the claims-processing office. Les explained that two of the supervisors in the department were being promoted and that he needed two new supervisors. Les also stated that he felt that Jane and John would make good supervisors because they knew the job and knew the people in the department. Les asked both of them to think it over and let him know their decisions the next day. Later, John saw Jane at lunch and they began discussing the possibilities of the new jobs. However, both of them agreed that they had never given much thought to being a supervisor. Both wondered just what that would entail.

WHAT IS SUPERVISION?

LEARNING OBJECTIVES

LEARNING OBJECTIVES

Supervision is defined in this book as the first level of management in the organization and is concerned with encouraging the members of a work unit to contribute positively toward accomplishing the organization's goals and objectives. This means that the supervisor does not do the operative work but sees that it is accomplished through the efforts of others.

Although the definition is simple, the job of supervision is quite complex. The supervisor must learn to make good decisions, communicate well with people, make proper work assignments, delegate, plan, train people, motivate people, appraise performance, and deal with various specialists in other departments. The varied work of the supervisor is extremely difficult to master. Yet mastery of supervision is vital to organizational success because supervisors are the management persons that most employees see and deal with every day.

The names used to describe supervisory jobs vary from industry to industry. What might these supervisors' titles be?
Daniel Bosler/Tony Stone Images, Ken/Chernus/FPG International, J. Greenberg/The Image Works

FIGURE 1.1   Partial Organization Chart from Exodus

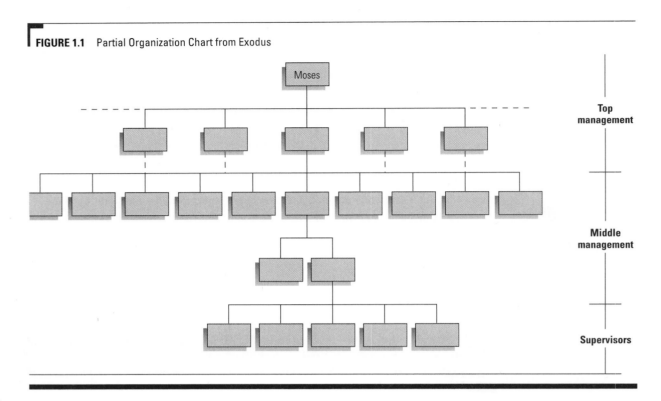

WHO IS A SUPERVISOR?

The need for supervision dates back to biblical times. When Moses was attempting to lead the people of Israel from Egypt to the Promised Land, his father-in-law, Jethro, advised him as follows:

> Find some capable, godly, honest men who hate bribes and appoint them as judges, 1 judge for each 1,000 people; he in turn will have 10 judges under him, each in charge of 100; and under each of them will be 2 judges, each responsible for the affairs of 50 people; and each of these will have 5 judges beneath him, each counseling 10 persons.

Figure 1.1 shows the form of organization suggested to Moses. It contains the three levels of management that exist in most organizations. The top management of private enterprise organizations usually includes the chairman of the board, the president, and the senior vice presidents. This level of management establishes the goals and objectives of the organization and the policies necessary to achieve them. Middle management includes all employees below the top-management level who manage other managers. A supervisor's boss is normally classified as a middle manager. Middle management develops the departmental objectives and procedures necessary to achieve the organizational goals and objectives.

FIGURE 1.2 Supervisory Job Titles	
Assistant cafeteria manager	Records and documents supervisor
Assistant credit supervisor	Records and materials supervisor
Crew leader	Shift supervisor
Employment supervisor	Supervisor for secretarial services
Head nurse	Supervisor of budget and cost control
Lead person	Supervisor of word processing
Meter routing supervisor	Training and safety supervisor
Office manager	Training supervisor
Powerhouse mechanic foreman	Utility foreman
Receiving and warehousing supervisor	Welding foreman

The final level of management includes supervisors. Supervisors manage operative employees—those who physically produce an organization's goods and services. Many names are used to describe the people who supervise. These names vary from industry to industry. Figure 1.2 lists some of the names given to supervisory jobs in different types of organizations. Regardless of the name, a supervisor is the manager who serves as the link between operative employees and all other managers.

WHERE DO SUPERVISORS COME FROM?

The vast majority of new supervisors are promoted from the ranks of operative employees. Employees with good technical skills and good work records are the ones who are normally selected by management for supervisory jobs.

However, it should be noted that good technical skills and a good work record do not necessarily make a person a good supervisor. In fact, sometimes these attributes can act adversely to productive supervisory practices. As will be seen later in this chapter, other skills are also required to be an effective supervisor. Officers of labor unions are sometimes chosen for supervisory jobs. Because union officers are elected, it can be assumed that the voting employees view them as having some leadership abilities. Thus, they are a source of supervisory talent. Another source is new college graduates. Many organizations place such graduates in supervisory jobs after a brief training period.

Figure 1.3 shows a normal progression into supervision. A person who gets into supervision does not necessarily stop progressing. It is possible to rise from supervision to the top of the organization. In fact, developing the skills required for supervision prepares a person for higher levels of management.

THE FUNCTIONS OF SUPERVISION

The complex work of supervision is often categorized into five areas, called the **functions of management** or the **functions of supervision.** These functions are planning, organizing, staffing, leading, and controlling.

FIGURE 1.3

Progression of Jobs into
Supervision

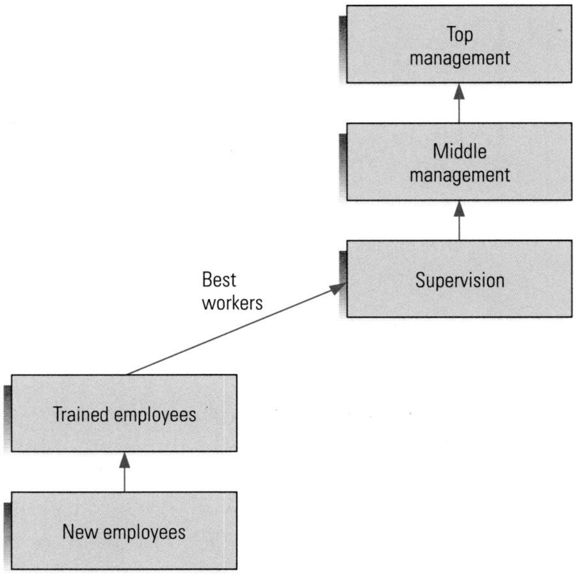

3 LEARNING
OBJECTIVES

Planning involves determining the most effective means for achieving the work of the unit. Generally, planning includes three steps:

1. Determining the present situation. Assess such things as the present condition of the equipment, the attitude of employees, and the availability of materials.
2. Determining the objectives. The objectives for a work unit are usually established by higher levels of management. Thus, this step is normally done *for* the supervisor.
3. Determining the most effective way of attaining the objectives. Given the present situation, what actions are necessary to reach the objectives?

Everyone follows these three steps in making personal plans. However, the supervisor makes plans, not for a single person, but for a group of people. This complicates the entire process.

Organizing involves distributing the work among the employees in the work group and arranging the work so that it flows smoothly. The supervisor carries out the work of organizing through the general structure established by higher levels of management. Thus, the supervisor functions within a general structure and is usually given specific work assignments from higher levels of management. The supervisor then sees that the specific work assignments are done.

Staffing is concerned with obtaining and developing good people. Since supervisors accomplish their work through others, staffing is an extremely important function.

Leading involves directing and channeling employee behavior toward the accomplishment of work objectives and providing a workplace where people can be motivated to accomplish the work objectives.

FIGURE 1.4

Relative Amounts of Time
Spent on the Functions of
Management by the Three
Levels of Management

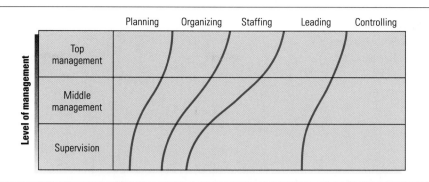

Controlling determines how well the work is being done compared with what was planned. Basically, this involves measuring actual performance against planned performance and taking any necessary corrective action.

Figure 1.4 indicates the relative amounts of time that each level of management devotes to the functions of management. Note that supervisors spend the largest portions of their time on the leading and controlling functions. The other functions are not necessarily less important, but they usually take less of the supervisor's time. The supervisor must perform all of the functions in order to be successful. For instance, organizing is difficult without a plan. Good employees obtained through staffing will not continue to work in a poorly planned, poorly organized work environment. Furthermore, it is very difficult to lead people if planning, organizing, and staffing are not done properly. Thus, the five functions of supervision can be viewed as links in a chain. For the supervisor to be successful, each of these links must be strong. (See Figure 1.5.) It is also important to remember that the

FIGURE 1.5

The Chain of Supervisory
Functions

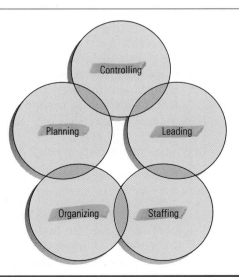

FIGURE 1.6

Mix of Skills Required at Different Management Levels

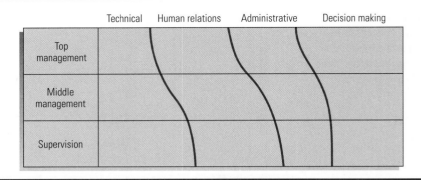

supervisory functions do not involve a sequential process, but generally occur simultaneously.

The supervisor's work can also be examined in terms of the types of skills required. Four basic types of skills have been identified:

1. **Technical skills** refer to knowledge about such things as machines, processes, and methods of production.
2. **Human relations skills** refer to knowledge about human behavior and to the ability to work well with people.
3. **Administrative skills** refer to knowledge about the organization and how it works—the planning, organizing, and controlling functions of supervision.
4. **Decision-making** and **problem-solving skills** refer to the ability to analyze information and objectively reach a decision.

It is generally agreed that in most organizations supervisors need a higher level of technical, human relations, and decision-making skills than of administrative skills. The mix of skills needed changes as a person moves up the managerial ladder. Figure 1.6 illustrates this concept. This does not imply that a supervisor needs more technical skills than a top manager, but that a supervisor needs more technical skills relative to human behavior, administrative, and decision-making skills. A supervisor who is ambitious and wishes to move up in the organization must develop all four types of skills. Supervision Illustration 1–1 describes some of the work performed by supervisors and managers at Harley-Davidson.

Key Reasons for Supervisory Success

Supervisors are successful for many reasons. However, five characteristics are important keys to supervisory success:

1. *Ability and willingness to delegate.* Most supervisors are promoted from operative jobs and have been accustomed to doing the work themselves. An often difficult, and yet essential, skill that such supervisors must develop is the ability or willingness to delegate work to others.

SUPERVISION ILLUSTRATION 1–1

WORK OF SUPERVISORS AND MANAGERS AT HARLEY-DAVIDSON

Harley-Davidson, Inc., the Milwaukee-based company, is the only U.S. company to regain market dominance from the Japanese in the past decade and the only remaining U.S. manufacturer of motorcycles.

How did they do this? Employee involvement is one of the answers. For example, managers and supervisors at the Tomahawk, Wisconsin, facility of Harley-Davidson, which makes painted Fiberglas parts for bikes, set out to answer questions such as: If the plant were perfect, how would the customer-supplier relationship work? As a supplier of parts to Harley assembly plants, how should Tomahawk communicate with its internal customers? Action plans then helped them focus on ways to improve their product, as well as customer service.

This process, part of a "sociotechnical" change that also involved redesigning some jobs and production processes, produced impressive results in less than one year. The plant reduced its quality problems dramatically, reduced its work-in-process time (the time it takes for a product to make its journey through the plant) from two-and-a-half days to less than 16 hours, and reduced float (the average time a bike in production is pulled off the line to wait for a part from the Tomahawk plant) from 22 days to less than two.

Source: Adapted from Chris Lee, "Followership: The Essence of Leadership," *Training,* January 1991, pp. 33–34. For more information on Harley-Davidson, visit its Web site at:
www.harley-davidson.com/home

---

2. *Proper use of authority.* Some supervisors let their newly acquired authority go to their heads. It is sometimes difficult to remember that the use of authority alone does not get the support and cooperation of employees. Learning when not to use authority is often as important as learning when to use it.

3. *Setting a good example.* Supervisors must always remember that the work group looks to them to set the example. Employees expect fair and equitable treatment from their supervisors. Too many supervisors play favorites and treat employees inconsistently. Government legislation has attempted to reduce this practice in some areas, but the problem is still common.

4. *Recognizing the change in role.* People who have been promoted into supervision must recognize that their role has changed and that they are no longer one of the gang. They must remember that being a supervisor may require unpopular decisions. Supervisors are the connecting link between the other levels of management and the operative employees and must learn to represent both groups.

5. *Desire for the job.* Many people who have no desire to be supervisors are promoted into supervision merely because of their technical skills. Regardless of one's technical skills, the desire to be a supervisor is necessary for success in supervision. That desire encourages a person to develop the other types of skills necessary in supervision—human relations, administrative, and decision-making skills.

The five characteristics discussed above are not the only ones necessary for supervisory success, but they are certainly some of the most important.

THE CHANGING NATURE OF THE SUPERVISOR'S ENVIRONMENT

Anyone who reads a newspaper recognizes that rapid changes are occurring in lifestyles, resources, information availability, and the work environment. These changes influence the supervisor. This section reviews some of these changes and examines their impact on the supervisor.

Changes in Information Availability

Because of the increasing sophistication of communication systems and the rapid increase in the use of computers, new data and information are being provided at an accelerating rate. For example:

- Between 6,000 and 7,000 scientific articles are written each day.
- Scientific and technical information now increases 13 percent per year, which means that it doubles every 5.5 years.
- By the year 2000, the volume of scientific and technical information will be significantly greater than its size in 1996.

The rapid increase in information availability increases technological change. Increases in information availability and technological change require supervisors to have increased technical skills. Furthermore, these changes require more skilled and trained employees. This then increases the importance of the supervisor's role in training. Higher levels of skill and training require new approaches to motivation and leadership. Thus, the supervisor needs more skill in the human relations area.

Changes in Outlook toward the Work Environment

Some forecasters predict that there will be more emphasis on the quality of work life in the future. The factors that can improve the quality of work life include:

1. Safe and healthy working conditions.
2. Opportunity to use and develop individual capabilities.
3. Opportunity for personal and professional growth.
4. Work schedules, career demands, and travel requirements that do not regularly take up family and leisure time.
5. The right to personal privacy, free speech, equitable treatment, and due process.

Because some of these factors fall within the scope of supervision, changes affecting them will have a direct impact on the supervisor's job.

Managing diversity.   One of the more prevalent changes in today's work environment is the increasing diversification of the workforce. Diversity of the workforce encompasses many different dimensions, including sex, race, religion, age, and types of disability. Compared to a workforce that historically consisted of white males, today's workforce is very diverse, and this diversity is projected to increase.

FIGURE 1.7

Workforce Entrance
Projections for the
Year 2000

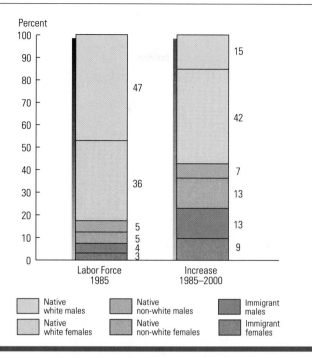

Source: William B. Johnston and Arnold E. H. Parker. *Workforce 2000: Work and Workers for the 21st Century*, Indianapolis, Ind.: Hudson Institute Inc., 1987, p. 95.

The widely referenced study, *Workforce 2000*, published in 1987 by the Hudson Institute and undertaken by a grant from the Employment and Training Administration of the U.S. Department of Labor, projected that only one-third of the workforce in the year 2000 will be native-born, white males.[1] Figure 1.7 shows the projected percentages of new entrants to the total workforce that will represent each of the shown entities in the year 2000. It is also projected that three-fifths of all women over 16 will work in the year 2000 and that almost two-thirds of the people entering the workforce in the 1990s will be women.[2] Just this one dimension of diversity has many ramifications for organizations. Child care, spouse relocation-assistance programs, pregnancy-leave programs, flexible hours, and stay-at-home jobs are all directly affected by the increase of women in the workforce.

Non-Caucasians are projected to constitute 29 percent of labor-force entrance during the 1990s. In addition, some 600,000 legal and illegal immigrants are expected to enter the United States each year. Of these numbers, two-thirds are expected to join the workforce. In addition to the possibility of their limited educational background, immigrant employees are likely to have language, attitude, and cultural problems. Organizations must begin now to successfully integrate these people into their workforces. A survey published by the Olsten Corporation in 1992 emphasizes that these changes will apply to small business as well as to large. Nearly half of the small companies (less than $50 million in annual sales) responding to the survey reported increases in the number of women and racial minorities among their employees during the past five years.[3]

SUPERVISION ILLUSTRATION 1-2

WOMAN WITH A MISSION

Barbara Samson, a 24-year-old graduate of the University of Florida with a telecommunications degree, does not take no for an answer; she takes it as a challenge. Thus did a young novice launch a highly successful telephone company in Tampa, Florida. Intermedia Communications of Florida sells long-distance service to business customers. Samson had heard numerous complaints about how expensive and unreliable businesses found it to connect to their long-distance carriers through the local phone companies. Solution: Build a network to bypass the local phone lines and give customers a cheaper alternative.

Though most entrepreneurial endeavors are capital intensive, Samson began with $50,000 and a $450,000 loan. This was not much considering the task before her: compete with the Baby Bells. By the time the first fiber-optic line was laid, venture capitalists had raised an additional $18 million. According to Samson, "We had to prove ourselves every step of the way." Her philosophy is to sell service first, then lay cable. The strategy seems to be working. Among her first and top customers are General Mills, Florida state government offices in Tallahassee, and Merrill Lynch. From her company's small beginnings in 1989, revenues soon mushroomed; 1995 revenues reached $42 million.

Intermedia is now the largest competitive-access provider in the Southeast, with 480 miles of fiber-optic cable. In Florida its network connects 350 buildings in five major cities. It recently acquired fiber networks in Cincinnati; Raleigh/Durham; Huntsville, Alabama; and St. Louis. With its hard-charging spirit, Intermedia has won business away from AT&T, BellSouth, GTE, and others. Hard work, dreams, and a youthful, entrepreneurial spirit sometimes do pay off!

Source: Adapted from Toddi Gutner Black, "Women with a Mission," *Forbes,* September 25, 1995, pp. 172, 174. For more information about *Forbes* magazine, visit its Web site at:
www.forbes.com

---

5 LEARNING OBJECTIVES

One of the most significant issues facing women and minorities in management is the **glass ceiling**—a reference to a level within the managerial hierarchy beyond which very few women and minorities advance. Much emphasis is expected to be placed by both the government and business during the 1990s on breaking this glass ceiling. Supervision Illustration 1–2 describes how one woman has broken the glass ceiling.

Almost everyone has heard the phrase "the graying of America." By the year 2000, it is projected that the average age of employees will climb from 36 today to 39.[4] This will be accompanied by an 8 percent drop in the number of young employees between 16 and 24 years old. This age increase and drop in the entering labor pool will have a mixed effect. The older workforce will likely be more experienced, reliable, and stable but also less adaptable to change and retraining. One direct result of this trend is that retirement age is already increasing. A variety of work alternatives such as flexible benefits, sabbatical leaves, job sharing, and part-time work may become necessary to hire and hold good employees.

Guidelines for managing diversity. Diversity management has been defined as "the process by which a company (or manager, human resource department, or any individual) incorporates the dissimilarities of its workforce into the decision-making process in order to motivate, direct, lead, organize, plan, and staff more efficiently."[5] From an overall viewpoint, supervisors must get away from the tradition of fitting employees into a single corporate mold. Everyone will not look and act the same. New policies must be created to explicitly recognize and respond to the unique needs of individual employees. Specifically, there are certain guidelines that today's supervisors should follow for supervising within and among a diverse workforce:[6]

6 LEARNING OBJECTIVES

1. *Focus on observable behavior.* Don't jump to conclusions but instead focus on actual observations. Resist saying things like "There goes Mary again" or "Joe looks like he hasn't heard a thing I said for the last two hours."

2. *Avoid stereotyping.* One suggestion is to use people's names even when thinking about them. It's easy to stereotype people when they're thought of in terms of "types," but it's hard to do so when using an individual's name. For example, think "What can I expect from Tom?" as opposed to "What can I expect from them?"

3. *Evaluate output, not input.* Results are what counts. Don't worry about minor habits and idiosyncracies, especially when the work is getting done.

4. *Don't make assumptions about nonstandard behavior.* Begin with the fact that a nonstandard behavior is different but not necessarily inappropriate. Remember the old saying, "There is more than one way to skin a cat."

5. *Provide feedback based on observations.* Let employees know how you see certain behaviors or events. Often others don't perceive things the way the supervisor does. Don't dismiss dysfunctional behavior as either improvable or deliberately manifest. Often the person's perception is simply different and, in the absence of feedback to the contrary, he or she will continue to think so.

6. *Don't tolerate nonbehavioral assumptions from anyone.* Regardless of how unpopular it might be at the time, confront any form of stereotyping. One approach is to point out that the accuser is really describing behavior that everyone in the workplace engages in to some extent.

7. *Test your own behaviors.* Ask employees for feedback to determine what effects your own behaviors have on others and look for what you might do to improve.

Greater diversity can be expected to create certain specific challenges but also some important contributions. Communication problems are certain to occur. This includes misunderstandings among employees and supervisors. There may also be a need to translate verbal and written materials into several languages. Additional training, including remedial work in very basic skills such as writing and problem solving, will be necessary. Organizational factionalism can be expected to increase. This will require that increasing amounts of time be dedicated to dealing with special-interest and advocacy groups.

In addition to creating the above challenges, greater diversity also presents new opportunities. Diversity contributes to creating an organization culture more tolerant of different behavioral styles and wider views. This often leads to better business decisions. Another potential payoff is a greater responsiveness to diverse groups of customers.

The increasing diversification of the workforce is fact. Not only are the demographics of today's workforce different, but so are its attitudes, expectations, and needs. Learning to effectively supervise a diverse workforce should be viewed as an investment in the future.

SUPERVISION: KEY LINK TO PRODUCTIVITY

Successful supervision requires the knowledge of, and ability to use, a multitude of skills. The primary measure used in determining a supervisor's success or failure is the productivity of the supervisor's work unit. This book is designed to provide the skills necessary for successful supervision. Practice in applying these skills can be gained by answering the discussion questions, studying the incidents described at the end of each chapter, and completing the exercises also provided at the end of each chapter.

This book is organized into five basic sections:

Section I   Foundations of Supervision
Section II   Planning and Organizing Skills
Section III   Staffing Skills
Section IV   Human Relations Skills
Section V   Controlling Skills

Section I—Foundations of Supervision—is designed to develop a foundation for the development of supervisory skills. Understanding the job of supervision, making sound and creative decisions, improving communication skills, understanding the need for ethics, dealing with organization politics, and managing one's time and career are discussed. These should provide a necessary foundation for studying the skills of supervision.

Section II—Planning and Organizing Skills—analyzes the supervisor's role in planning, organizing, and delegating work. Understanding the nature and importance of both formal and informal work groups is also discussed. Finally, methods improvement (or work simplification) is examined as a means to get more and better output at a lower cost in a shorter time period.

Section III—Staffing Skills—examines the supervisor's role in obtaining and developing good people. Topics such as appraising employee performance, understanding equal employment opportunity, and dealing with unions are discussed.

Section IV—Human Relations Skills—discusses human behavior and how a supervisor must have the ability to work well with people. Motivating and leading employees, handling conflict, coping with change and stress, and counseling employees are discussed in this section.

Section V—Controlling Skills—describes the supervisor's role in determining how well the work is being done compared with what was planned. Topics such as supervisory control and quality; improving productivity through cost control; safety and accident prevention; discipline; and grievance handling are all described in detail.

SOLUTION TO THE
SUPERVISION
DILEMMA

By studying this chapter, Jane and John have learned that supervision is the first level of management in an organization and is concerned with encouraging the members of a work unit to contribute positively toward accomplishing the organization's goals. They have learned what work a supervisor performs. Planning, organizing, staffing, leading, and controlling (pp. 5–7) are the five forms of work that a supervisor must perform. They have also learned that four basic types of skills are required to do the work of supervision (p. 8). These are technical skills, human relations skills, administrative skills, and decision-making and problem-solving skills. Finally, they have learned five reasons why supervisors are successful (pp. 8–9). If they are to be good supervisors, they must understand the work of supervision, master the skills necessary to perform that work, and consistently apply the elements necessary for supervisory success.

SUMMARY

The purpose of this chapter is to give the reader a clear understanding of what supervision involves. The chapter also discusses several reasons why supervisors are successful.

1. *Define supervision.*   Supervision is defined in this book as the first level of management in the organization and is concerned with encouraging the members of a work unit to contribute positively toward accomplishing the organization's goals and objectives.

2. *Describe the work of a supervisor.* The work of a supervisor is often categorized into five areas: planning, organizing, staffing, leading, and controlling. Planning involves determining the most effective means for achieving the work of the unit. Organizing involves distributing the work among the employees in the work group and arranging the work so that it flows smoothly. Staffing is concerned with obtaining and developing good people. Leading involves directing and channeling employee behavior toward the accomplishment of work objectives. Controlling determines how well the work is being done compared with what was planned.

3. *Present the types of skills necessary to perform the job of supervision.* Four basic types of skills have been identified. Technical skills refer to knowledge about such things as machines, processes, and methods of production. Human relations skills refer to knowledge about human behavior and to the ability to work well with people. Administrative skills refer to knowledge about the organization and how it works. Decision-making and problem-solving skills refer to the ability to analyze information and objectively reach a decision.

4. *State the key reasons for supervisory success.* Five key reasons for supervisory success are ability and willingness to delegate, the proper use of authority, setting a good example, recognizing the change in role, and desire for the job.

5. *Explain the glass ceiling concept.* The glass ceiling concept refers to a level within the organizational hierarchy beyond which very few women and minorities advance.

6. *Describe guidelines for managing diversity in the workforce.* The guidelines are as follows:

   Focus on observable behavior.

   Avoid stereotyping.

   Evaluate output, not input.

   Don't make assumptions about nonstandard behavior.

   Provide feedback based on observations.

   Don't tolerate nonbehavioral assumptions from anyone.

   Test your own behaviors.

   Expect feedback.

REVIEW QUESTIONS

1. What is supervision?
2. What are three general levels of management?
3. Give five names (or job titles) of supervisors.
4. Name three sources that organizations can use when seeking to fill supervisory positions.
5. What are the five functions of management that a supervisor performs?
6. Outline the four classifications of skills necessary to do supervisory work.
7. Identify five characteristics that make supervisors successful.
8. What is the impact of the following changes on supervision?
   a. Changes in information availability.
   b. Changes in outlook toward the work environment.
9. Explain the glass ceiling concept.
10. What are seven guidelines for managing diversity?

SKILL-BUILDING QUESTIONS

1. "A good supervisor in a manufacturing plant could be a good supervisor in a bank." Discuss.
2. Do you think that supervision can be learned through books and study or only through experience? Why?
3. Do you think that the best worker also makes the best supervisor? Why or why not?
4. "A good supervisor should be able to do any job that he or she supervises better than any of the operative employees." Discuss your views on this statement.

REFERENCES

1. William B. Johnston and Arnold H. Parker, *Workforce 2000: Work and Workers for the 21st Century*, Indianapolis, Ind.: Hudson Institute, 1987.
2. Robert W. Goddard, "Work Force 2000," *Personnel Journal*, February 1989, p. 68.
3. Ellyn E. Spragins, "The Diverse Workforce," *Inc.*, January 1993, p. 33.
4. Goddard, "Work Force 2000," p. 67.
5. David S. Gold, "Managing Diversity . . . Defined," in *Managing Diversity*, vol. 1, no. 2 (Jamestown, N.Y.: Jamestown Area Labor Management Committee, 1992), p. 3.
6. These guidelines are adapted from Alan Weiss, "Understanding Behavior in Managing Diversity," in *Managing Diversity*, vol. 1, no. 2 (Jamestown, N.Y.: Jamestown Area Labor Management Committee, 1992), pp. 6–7.

ADDITIONAL READINGS

Bielous, Gary A. "Five Things Supervisors Must Never Say to Subordinates," *Supervision*, November 1995.

Buhler, Patricia. "Managing in the 90's" [Self-Management Techniques], *Supervision*, September 1996.

———. "Scanning the Environment: Environmental Trends Affecting the Workplace," *Supervision*, March 1997.

Hardy, Marc. "In Pursuit of Management Mastery: Making Mistakes Meaningful" [The Importance of People Skills], *Supervision*, July 1996.

Painter, Charles. "Effective Supervision for the New Supervisor," *Supervision*, August 1995.

Perican, John. "Casually Yours" [Shortcomings of Supervision], *Supervision*, September 1996.

SKILL-BUILDING APPLICATIONS

Incident 1–1

Promotion into Supervision

Roy Thomas has been with the Rebco Manufacturing Company for 15 years. He joined Rebco right after his high school graduation and has been with the company ever since.

Ten years ago, Rebco became unionized and Roy was one of the people primarily responsible for its unionization. He helped the organizer from the Teamsters Union plan the union election campaign. He helped get the local union established after the election and then served as its president for its first three years. After that, he continued to serve in various capacities with the local union. Two years ago, he was again elected for a three-year term as its president.

Over the years, Roy has developed a reputation for being firm but fair with the management of Rebco. He is well respected by both the members of the union and the management of Rebco.

Roy was quite shocked when he was recently called into the plant manager's office for the following discussion.

Bill Lindsay (Plant Manager): Good to see you, Roy.

Roy: Yeah, it's good to see you, Bill, especially when we're not arguing over a problem. I hope you didn't call me here for that.

Bill: No, Roy, I didn't. In fact, I called you here to talk about something else entirely. Some of our older supervisors are retiring shortly, as you know, and we would like you to consider becoming a supervisor.

Roy: A supervisor—you've got to be kidding! I've fussed and fought with you and the other managers around here for 10 years. Now you want me to join you. How would the employees react?

Bill: That's just it, Roy. We think they would be pleased. After all, they've elected you president of the local twice already. You've got their respect. A good supervisor just needs to know how to handle people, and you sure know how to do that.

Roy: I just don't know, Bill. Give me a couple of days to think about it.

Questions (Explain your answers in writing.)

1. Do you think Roy would be a good supervisor?
2. What qualities does Roy possess that support your answer?
3. Do you agree with Bill Lindsay's statement that "a good supervisor just needs to know how to handle people"?
4. What do you think the reaction of the employees would be if Roy accepted the job?

Incident 1–2

Not Enough Time to Supervise

Len Massey is a supervisor in a large fire and casualty insurance company. He is in charge of a group of clerical workers who review policies and endorsements, calculate commissions, and maintain records. Before his promotion to supervisor, Len himself was a clerical worker in the department. It was largely due to his reputation as the best worker in the department that he was promoted. "If Len did the work," his co-workers said, "it is right."

This reputation has carried over into Len's supervisory practices. Everything coming out of his group is perfect. In fact, Len rechecks in detail all the work coming out of his group to ensure that it is accurate. It is not unusual for him to turn work back to one of his employees several times until it is perfect. Len's employees quickly recognized his eye for detail and his checking and rechecking of their work. One of them was recently overheard to say, "I don't really worry about accuracy in my work too much, because if I make an error, I know Len will catch it."

Last week, at Len's annual performance evaluation, his boss, Pam Levine, said that Len was spending too much time on detail work and not enough time on supervision. In fact, she said that he must start spending more time in supervision and less time in doing the work of others. Len's response to Pam was, "People in my unit don't seem to care about sloppy work, and since I'm responsible, I feel obligated to check it before it goes out."

Questions

1. Is Pam Levine right?
2. What does Len need to know about supervision?
3. What do you think of the reasons given for Len's promotion?

Exercise 1–1

Understanding the Job of a Supervisor

Exhibit 1.1 gives a job description for a maintenance supervisor in a manufacturing company. From this job description, classify the duties and responsibilities as to whether they are planning, organizing, staffing, leading, or controlling.

Also identify the specific skills of supervision—technical, human relations, administrative, and decision making that are described in this job description.

EXHIBIT 1.1
Position of Maintenance Supervisor

Basic Purpose
To supervise the maintenance activity through the implementation of a preventive maintenance program and an ongoing maintenance repair program for the facility, vehicles, production maintenance, and process equipment.

Duties and Responsibilities
1. Plans and implements effective procedures and policies for the maintenance department to ensure that all equipment, facilities, and utilities are in an acceptable state of repair.
2. Coordinates with vendors, suppliers, and contractors the installation of new equipment or equipment processes.
3. Establishes, with direction from the plant manager, priorities of all maintenance activities through a work order procedure.
4. Supervises all daily activities of the maintenance department through subordinates to ensure completion of assigned projects that will result in the least amount of machine downtime.
5. Monitors completion of maintenance projects to ensure that safety and quality standards are met.
6. Approves all requisitions relating to new and replacement parts, supplies, machinery, and equipment for the maintenance department.
7. Provides technical knowledge and expertise to solve problems of a mechanical, electrical, or hydraulic/pneumatic nature.
8. Develops and maintains responsible labor/management relations consistent with the labor agreement, including representing the company in certain grievances.
9. Schedules and assigns hourly personnel to maintain good housekeeping for the facility grounds and administrative offices.

Organizational Relationships
This position reports to the manager/engineering and maintenance and indirectly to the plant manager. Coordinates work with all service and production departments.

Position Specifications
Must possess 8 to 10 years' experience in maintenance, engineering, or related fields. Prefer minimum of 3–5 years' supervisory experience. Must be familiar with each of the following areas: boilers, air compressors, heating, and air-conditioning, plumbing, welding, carpentry, electrical/electronic equipment, pneumatic hydraulics, and heavy manufacturing equipment.

Source: Adapted from John D. Ulery, *Job Descriptions in Manufacturing Industries* (New York: American Management Associations, 1981), pp. 120–21.

SUPERVISOR
RIGHTS-OF-WAY AND LAND

ABC is a diversified energy company making important contributions in the pursuit of new energy resources around the world. A position of Supervisor—Rights-of-Way and Land is currently available at ABC's Houston location.

A college education is required, with a degree preferably in business, law, or engineering. Strong experience in pipeline right-of-way work is required with a minimum of three years of right-of-way field experience. Additional experience must include a minimum of five years of general right-of-way office experience, with a heavy supervisory background in right-of-way. The responsibilities will include supervising the acquisition of right-of-way and the settlement of claims; following litigations; and conducting and coordinating contact with the state and local authorities. The ability to negotiate and prepare amendatory, alteration, and relocation agreements is mandatory.

ABC offers competitive salaries, a comprehensive employee benefits program, and a variety of career challenges. If interested, send résumé and salary history to:

P.O. Box 000
An equal opportunity employer
Principals Only!

WEEKEND PRODUCTION SUPERVISOR

XYZ Corporation, a smoke-free environment and manufacturer of soft contact lenses and solution-related products, has an immediate opening for a Weekend Production Supervisor. This individual must be able to plan, organize, and control staffing, equipment, and facilities in an efficient manner within budgetary guidelines. This includes being held accountable for the quality and quantity of products produced, compliance with CGMP and OSHA standards, and guiding the department toward achieving departmental and company goals and objectives. BS/BA and one year production supervisory experience required. Solid background in highly technical production environment. Good written and oral communication skills. Must work weekends (11:00 PM to 11:00 AM), and a minimum of one additional day per week is required. We regret that we are unable to respond to all inquiries. We will only respond to those candidates selected for an interview.

Qualified applicants should forward résumé with salary requirements to:

XYZ
Corporation
P.O. Box 000

ACCOUNTING
A/R SUPERVISOR

Progressive company with high-volume receivables department is looking for a sharp individual with accounts receivable supervisory experience. Excellent starting salary and benefits. If you are a motivated self-starter, respond with salary history to Box 000.

SUPERVISING

Senior Auditor: Plan, direct, and conduct audits for client operations. Review and prepare corporate tax returns, develop budget forecast and analysis, and develop and improve accounting systems. Must have Bachelor's in Accounting for Business Administration with two years' experience in job or as Analyst or Accountant. Hours 9:00 AM–5:00 PM, Monday–Friday, overtime as needed. Those qualified, résumé to P.O. Box 000

SUPERVISOR &
SALES MANAGER

French-owned, U.S.-based corporation seeks National Supervisor & Sales Engineer to supervise and coordinate the U.S. marketing and distribution efforts. Experience in the processes of importation of European products into the United States as well as fluency in written and spoken French are required. Applicants must have four years' experience in the stone products industry as well as six years' experience in construction supervision and sales of stone products. Send résumé to: P.O. Box 000

Exercise 1–2

Required Attributes of a Supervisor

1. From the supervisory jobs described in the ads on the previous page, choose the one that is most attractive to you.
2. Form into groups of four or five with others who selected the same job as you.
3. Develop a group list of required and desirable skills for the job.
4. Present and defend your group's list before the entire class.

Exercise 1–3

The Supervisor's Personal Inventory

The following inventory has helped many supervisors determine to what extent their behaviors or practices contribute to difficulties for their employees. The items below represent important supervisor behaviors and practices that build positive work relationships. Rate yourself and your company on each item, giving yourself one (1) point if the item rarely applies, two (2) points if it sometimes applies, and three (3) points if it applies to you most of the time.

	Rating Scale		
	Applies Rarely 1	Applies Sometimes 2	Applies Most of Time 3
1. Know my job	•	•	•
2. Know my employees' jobs	•	•	•
3. Know my company's objectives and standard procedures	•	•	•
4. Convey my objectives and procedures to my employees	•	•	•
5. Define my objectives and procedures clearly	•	•	•
6. Try to resolve those objectives and procedures that are in conflict	•	•	•
7. Establish clear performance standards	•	•	•
8. Convey performance standards to my employees	•	•	•
9. Insist that performance standards are met	•	•	•
10. Try to improve substandard performance	•	•	•
11. Set standards for myself and follow them	•	•	•
12. My employees know what to expect from me	•	•	•
13. Avoid self-centeredness	•	•	•
14. Am employee-centered	•	•	•
15. Know my employees' strengths and weaknesses	•	•	•
16. Keep my employees well informed on matters affecting them	•	•	•
17. Keep channels of communication open	•	•	•
18. Actively lead, direct, and control employees when necessary	•	•	•
19. Allow my employees to lead and control themselves when they are able to	•	•	•

	Rating Scale		
	Applies Rarely 1	Applies Sometimes 2	Applies Most of Time 3
20. Avoid unjust criticism	•	•	•
21. Criticize employees in private	•	•	•
22. Give credit when it is earned	•	•	•
23. Commend employees publicly	•	•	•
24. Avoid taking credit for things my employees did	•	•	•
25. Show respect toward employees	•	•	•
26. Command respect from employees by my conduct	•	•	•
27. Discipline fairly	•	•	•
28. Discipline only when needed	•	•	•
29. Back employees to fullest when they are right	•	•	•
30. Refuse to back employees when they're wrong even though such refusal may lessen my popularity	•	•	•
31. Delegate as far down the line as possible	•	•	•
32. Value my employees' input	•	•	•
33. Provide opportunities to get employee input	•	•	•
34. Use the input I receive	•	•	•
35. Encourage employees to develop their sense of responsibility and initiative	•	•	•
36. Use my authority appropriately	•	•	•
37. My employees have pride in their accomplishments	•	•	•
38. Actively try to build esprit de corps	•	•	•
39. Practice what I preach	•	•	•
40. Recognize my shortcomings	•	•	•
41. Compensate for my shortcomings	•	•	•
42. Retain my sense of humor in dealings with employees	•	•	•
43. Admit my errors when I'm wrong	•	•	•
44. Apply the same standards of conduct and performance to men and women	•	•	•
45. Continually strive to improve myself and my company	•	•	•

Scoring: Total all your points for the 45 items. If you scored 125 or above, your supervisory behaviors and company practices promote positive work relationships. If you scored between 100 and 124, some of your behaviors/practices may contribute to difficulties with employees, but no urgency for change is indicated unless one or more items scored very low. If you scored between 75 and 99, probably many of your behaviors/practices contribute to difficulties with employees, and you should ask yourself what you can do to improve the low scoring items. If you scored below 75, improving your overall supervisory behaviors/practices should be a high priority for you.

Regardless of your score, the awareness that comes from taking such an inventory is the prerequisite for self-improvement. Your inventory results can serve as the basis for eliminating managerial blind spots and creating a personal development plan to ensure that the impact of your behaviors and practices is a positive one.

Source: Adapted from Gary W. Hobson, "Eliminating Managerial Blind Spots," *Supervision,* August 1990, pp. 16–17.

Exercise 1–4

Understanding Diversity

As a part of communicating that an organization is truly committed to supporting a highly qualified and diverse workforce, supervisors should take every opportunity to demonstrate the use of non-sexist language.

A. In this vein, try and identify a nonsexist word to use in place of each of the following words that may carry a sexist connotation:

Man-hours	Waiter/Waitress
Girl Friday	Watchman
Layout man	Repairman
Salesman	Man-made
Foreman	Spokesman
Policeman	Draftsman

B. List additional words or terms that you think might carry a sexist connotation.

SELECTED SUPERVISORY AND RELATED PERIODICALS

This list provides the reader with the names of the more commonly referenced supervisory and related periodicals.

Academy of Management Review
Administrative Management
Arbitration Journal
Business Horizons
Business Week
California Management Review
Forbes
Fortune
Harvard Business Review

Human Resource Management
Journal of Business
Mangement Review
Management Solutions
Management Today
Personnel Journal
Personnel Administrator
Supervision
Supervisory Management
The Wall Street Journal (newspaper)
Training and Development Journal

CHAPTER

2

Making Sound and Creative Decisions

LEARNING OBJECTIVES

After studying this chapter, you should be able to:

1. Discuss the importance of recognition and timeliness in decision making.

2. State the steps followed in the scientific method of decision making.

3. Name several potential advantages and disadvantages of group decision making.

4. List several traps that supervisors frequently fall into when making decisions.

5. Discuss the role that the supervisor plays in establishing a creative environment.

6. Describe several group-oriented techniques that can be employed by supervisors to encourage creativity.

7. Itemize some of the more frequently encountered barriers to organizational creativity.

SUPERVISION
DILEMMA

> Since the first day that Jane Harris accepted the supervisor's job, she has been con-
cerned about the many tough decisions she has had to make. Just this morning, for example, Jerry Krzyzanowski, one of her employees, requested a change in the vacation
schedule. Jerry had received a last-minute invitation to go on a Canadian hunting trip
as his uncle's guest. Jerry considered this "the chance of a lifetime." The problem is
that three other members of the department have already been approved for vacation
during the same week that Jerry requested. Even with Jerry on hand, the department
would be operating with a skeleton crew.

Jane has also been concerned about her apparent inability to come up with, and
implement, new ideas. It seems to Jane that most of her employees are perfectly happy
to do things the way they have been done for years. Last week, when she asked Jerry
Krzyzanowski if he had considered reviewing the procedures for filing completed
claims, Jerry replied, "Why change? It's worked well up to now."

Among the primary factors that distinguish supervisors from operative employees are the level and types of decisions that they must make. A supervisor must
be concerned with how a decision might affect his or her employees and the organization. An operative employee, in contrast, is primarily concerned with
how a decision affects him or her individually.

In fact, a supervisor's skill in making decisions is often a key factor in the
kind of evaluation and rewards (promotion, money, assignments, etc.) that he
or she receives. Moreover, a supervisor's decision-making ability will ultimately
contribute to the success or failure of the organization.

Figure 2.1 gives some examples of both expected and unexpected decisions that a supervisor might face. Although the supervisor generally
has more time to deal with expected decisions than with unexpected decisions, this does not necessarily mean that expected decisions are easier
to make or less critical. For example, a supervisor's recommendation to hire
or not to hire a job applicant could have serious ramifications for a long time
to come.

DECISION MAKING VERSUS PROBLEM SOLVING

The terms *decision making* and *problem solving* are often confused and therefore need to be clarified. **Decision making,** in its narrowest sense, is the
process of choosing from among various alternatives. A *problem* is any deviation from some standard or desired level of performance. **Problem solving,**
then, is the process of determining the appropriate responses or actions necessary to alleviate a problem. Problem solving necessarily involves decision making, since all problems can be attacked in numerous ways and the problem
solver must decide which way is best. On the other hand, not all decisions involve problems (such as a person sorting fruit and vegetables). However, from
a practical perspective, most supervisory decisions do involve solving or at
least avoiding problems.

FIGURE 2.1

Examples of Expected and Unexpected Decisions

Expected (Anticipated) Decisions

1. Recommendation concerning the hiring of a new job applicant.
2. Salary and promotion recommendations.
3. Approval of vacation requests.
4. Assignment of a new piece of equipment.

Unexpected (Unanticipated) Decisions

1. An employee requests next Friday off to attend a Shriners' convention.
2. An employee who doesn't seem to get along with others in the department requests a transfer.
3. A piece of major equipment is malfunctioning but still operable—should it be shut down until it is repaired?
4. An employee expresses fear of a new machine and refuses to work on it.
5. Three employees call in sick today. What adjustments must be made to meet production schedules?

RECOGNITION AND TIMELINESS OF THE DECISION

LEARNING OBJECTIVES

Recognizing the need to make a decision is a natural prerequisite to making a sound decision. Timeliness is also critical to a sound decision. Some supervisors always seem to make decisions on the spot, others tend to take forever in deciding even a simple matter, and still others just seem to ignore matters requiring decisions by acting as if the problems don't exist. The supervisor who takes pride in making quick decisions also runs the risk of making bad decisions. Failure to gather and evaluate available data, to consider employees' feelings, and to anticipate the impact of the decision can result in a very quick but poor decision. Just as risky, of course, is the other extreme—the supervisor who listens to the problem and promises to get back to the employee but never does. Nearly as bad is the supervisor who gets back to the employee—but only after an inordinate amount of time. There are other familiar types: The supervisor who never seems to have adequate information to make a decision, the supervisor who frets and worries over even the simplest decisions, and the supervisor who refers everything to the boss.

All of the types described above are either overconcerned or underconcerned about making a decision. They show little regard for the timing and quality of the decision. Especially when the situation involves some unpleasant matter (such as whether to fire an employee), it is common for the supervisor to make a quick decision and thus get rid of the problem or to ignore the problem and hope that it will go away. These are natural human reactions. The successful supervisor has learned to resist such reactions and to make decisions with a proper concern for their timeliness.

Knowing when to make a decision is complicated by the fact that different decisions must be made within different time frames. For example, a supervisor would generally have much more time in deciding on promotion recommendations than in deciding what to do when three employees call in sick.

Unfortunately, there is no magic formula that tells a supervisor when a decision should be made or how long it should take. The supervisor has to develop an awareness for the importance of properly timing decisions.

The supervisor should also understand the relationship between properly timing decisions and being decisive. Decisiveness is a necessary characteristic of a good supervisor. Avoiding a decision or putting off a decision can result in worse circumstances than making a questionable but timely decision. However, being decisive does not mean making a decision in the least amount of time. Being decisive means making a decision in a reasonable amount of time.

STEPS IN THE DECISION-MAKING PROCESS

Once the supervisor has recognized the need to make a decision, there are things that he or she can do to affect the quality of the decision. Most successful supervisors use some type of systematic and logical approach to making decisions. The following steps, based on the scientific method, are recommended for making decisions:

2 LEARNING OBJECTIVES

1. Be alert to indications and symptoms of problems.
2. Tentatively define the problem.
3. Collect facts and redefine the problem if necessary.
4. Identify possible alternatives.
5. Gather and organize facts concerning identified alternatives.
6. Evaluate possible alternatives.
7. Choose and implement the best alternative.
8. Follow up.[1]

Each step is discussed in the following paragraphs. It should be noted that these steps are not always sequential. As new facts become available, for example, the decision maker might be required to loop back to Step 2 or Step 3.

Step 1: Be Alert to Indications and Symptoms of Problems

Being alert to indications and symptoms of problems is an integral part of recognizing the need to make a decision (which was discussed in the preceding section). All too often supervisors tend to brush off or ignore indicators and symptoms of problems. Supervisors should constantly be cognizant of any changes that might indicate a potential problem.

Step 2: Tentatively Define the Problem

Frequently, the hardest part of making a decision is defining just what the decision problem is. It is very difficult for a supervisor to make a sound decision about anything unless the exact nature of the problem is known. For example, suppose a certain machine operator is producing an unacceptably high number of rejects. Is the problem due to the machine, the operator, the raw material, or some other factor? Similarly, an employee complains about the workplace being too hot. Is the temperature set too high? Does the employee just

FIGURE 2.2	Symptoms:	What has alerted you to the problem?
Factors to Aid in Defining the Problem		How did you recognize the problem?
		What is wrong?
		Have there been any obvious changes?
	Location:	Where are the symptoms occurring?
	Time:	When did you discover the symptoms?
		How long have they existed?
	Extent:	How severe does the problem appear to be?

FIGURE 2.3	Symptoms:	Weekly report on number of rejects showed inordinately high number.
Defining the Problem	Location:	Machine 27, operated by E. B. Wilcox (Shift 1), S. A. Lopez (Shift 2), and Q. T. Thomas (Shift 3).
	Time:	High rejects began appearing on Wednesday of previous week and continued throughout the week.
	Extent:	Number of rejects is running about three times the norm for that machine.

prefer a cooler temperature? Is something wrong with the air conditioner? Or is the employee just a complainer?

Many supervisors find it difficult to distinguish between the symptoms of the problem and the problem itself. As a result, a supervisor may treat the symptoms and not the problem. Treating the symptoms is usually a short-term solution at best. For example, suppose your car has a faulty generator, which in turn causes the battery to run down. If you treat the symptom and replace the battery, you will have solved the problem only for a very short time. At this stage, supervisors should do their best to define the problem based on the identified indicators and symptoms.

Step 3: Collect Facts and Redefine the Problem if Necessary

After the problem has been tentatively defined, based on the initial indicators and symptoms, a supervisor should then collect pertinent data and facts.

Figure 2.2 presents four factors that, when systematically addressed, can help define most problems. The responses to each of these factors should be recorded in writing to help the supervisor maintain objectivity. Figure 2.3 analyzes the factors of a problem concerning an unacceptable number of rejects. By pinning down and identifying the symptoms, the location, the time, and the extent of the problem, the supervisor can usually get a much better grasp of what the problem really is. If a supervisor finds that he or she has several problems, then the problems should be prioritized and addressed in order.

Step 4: Identify Possible Alternatives

Once the problem has been clearly defined, possible alternatives can be identified. Obviously, any decision is only as good as the best of the alternatives that are considered. One common pitfall in identifying possible alternatives is

FIGURE 2.4

General Questions for Gathering Facts about Alternatives

- Does company (organization) policy have anything to say about the decision at hand?
- Has a similar situation occurred in the past? If so, what was done?
- What are the costs involved?
- How will this decision affect productivity? work procedures? employee morale?

considering only obvious alternatives or alternatives that have been used previously. With such an approach, many viable alternatives may not even be considered. As a general rule, the more alternatives generated, the better the final solution. There is a tendency among many supervisors to stop looking for alternatives once they have identified one or two that seem acceptable. A good rule of thumb is to try to generate at least four alternatives.

Asking for the opinions of others who may know something about the problem can be helpful in generating alternatives. The supervisor may become so involved in a particular problem that he or she overlooks alternatives obvious to a person who is not as close to the problem.

Suppose that in defining the reject problem explained in Figure 2.3, the supervisor concluded that the difficulty was a faulty machine. Possible alternatives might include:

1. Repair the machine.
2. Replace the machine with a reconditioned one.
3. Replace the machine with a new but identical model.
4. Replace the machine with a new, more modern model.

Step 5: Gather and Organize Facts Concerning Identified Alternatives

After the problem and possible alternatives have been identified, the next step is to gather and organize facts that are relevant to the various alternatives. It is difficult, if not impossible, to make sound decisions without the pertinent facts. At the same time, however, a supervisor rarely has all of the facts that he or she would like. Of course, the timeliness of the decision has a major impact on how much data to gather and analyze. Successful supervisors learn to make decisions based on the available facts plus those that can be obtained within a reasonable amount of time and at a reasonable cost. Figure 2.4 lists some general questions that might be addressed in this phase.

It should be mentioned that today's supervisor can be faced with too much information instead of not enough. Computers and modern technology have made information overload a real problem for many supervisors. This occurs when the supervisor receives irrelevant reports, computer printouts, and memos. It is not unusual for a simple and useful report to evolve into a large report with very little useful information. The problem facing the supervisor then is to sort out the relevant from the irrelevant information. Thus, organizing the available facts can be a difficult task.

TABLE 2.1

Sample Format for
Evaluating Alternatives

Alternative	Time Required to Implement (days)	Estimated Costs ($)	Favorable Points	Unfavorable Points
A. Repair machine	15	2,000	Employees are familiar with the machine; it has proved itself.	Might break down again soon; not as fast as new machine; takes longer to fix.
B. Replace with reconditioned machine	8	4,500	Same as old machine; no training necessary.	Reconditioned machine may not last as long as new one; not as fast as some new models.
C. Replace with new but identical machine	5	6,000	Same as old machine; no training necessary; likely to last a long time.	Relatively expensive.
D. Replace with new, more modern machine	5	7,000	Fastest machine available; likely to last a long time.	Most expensive; operator will require some training.

Step 6: Evaluate Possible Alternatives

Once the facts have been gathered and organized, the next step is to evaluate each of the alternatives. Generally, this involves a comparison of their costs, the time required to implement them, and their expected end results, and an evaluation of how the alternative would affect other areas of the business. Using the collected data, the supervisor should project what would happen if each of the alternatives were implemented. How long would this take? How much would it cost? What would be the favorable and unfavorable outcomes? It is usually helpful to develop a system for recording the evaluations in some written form. Table 2.1 shows a sample format. Such an approach provides much more objectivity than a simple mental evaluation of the alternatives. It permits all of the alternatives to be compared at the same time, and it uses the same categories of information in evaluating all those alternatives.

Step 7: Choose and Implement the Best Alternative

Choosing the best or most desirable alternative is not always as easy as it seems. Certainly, this step is made easier if the previous steps in the decision-making process were thorough. After the costs, time, and potential outcomes have been evaluated, the decision still requires some judgment and even willpower on the part of the supervisor. While some alternatives can usually be eliminated as soon as the data have been collected, others may require a closer look. In such situations, the supervisor draws on experience, intuition, and suggestions from others in making the final choice. Caution is necessary to prevent personal biases and prejudices from influencing the decision.

It is not unusual for the supervisor to select the best of the alternatives being considered even if none of them appears to be satisfactory. The tendency here is to select an alternative and thus get the decision out of the way. In essence, completing the decision becomes more important than the decision itself. In such situations, a viable alternative that should be considered is to do nothing. This alternative gives the supervisor time to go back and seek additional alternatives.

After the final decision has been made, the supervisor should take the necessary steps to implement it. These steps include assigning responsibilities, communicating the timetable to be followed, outlining the types of control to be used, and identifying potential problems. Experience has shown that employees (and people in general) are much less resistant to a decision when they understand the why, when, and what of the decision. When communicating the decision to the affected parties, the supervisor should explain why the decision was necessary, why the specific alternative was chosen, what actions are required, and what results are expected.

Step 8: The Follow-Up

The final phase of the decision-making process is to evaluate the outcomes of the decision. The basic questions to be answered are: Did the decision achieve the desired results? If not, what went wrong? Why? The answers to these questions can be of great help in a similar future situation. Unfortunately, many people have a tendency to stick with a decision even when it begins to be apparent that it is not going to work well. The key is to learn from the past and apply this knowledge to future decisions.

GROUP DECISION MAKING

Everyone is familiar with the old saying that two heads are better than one. This saying holds true in many decision situations. There are many advantages to involving the members of the work group in the decision process. The most obvious advantage is that with several people participating, there are more resources to call upon. This usually results in the generation of more and better alternatives. An equally important advantage is that the participation of group members in decisions results in their commitment to the decisions that are made. People more readily accept decisions in which they have participated than those that are forced upon them. If people participate in reaching a decision, they usually feel a commitment to make it work. The value of involving group members extends beyond the final decision. A more complete understanding of what alternatives were considered and how each was evaluated can be of enormous help in getting the group to accept change. This is especially true if those who must implement the change are the ones who participated in the decision.

FIGURE 2.5

Positive and Negative
Aspects of Group
Decision Making

Positive Aspects of Group Decision Making
1. The sum total of the group's knowledge is greater.
2. The group generally develops a much wider range of alternatives.
3. Participation increases the acceptability of the decision to the group.
4. Group members better understand why a decision was made.

Negative Aspects of Group Decisions
1. Group decisions take more time.
2. The phenomenon of groupthink may occur.
3. One individual may dominate or control the group.
4. Pressures to conform may inhibit group members.
5. Competition may become overly intense among group members.
6. Groups have a tendency to accept the first potentially positive alternative.

Group decisions can be very advantageous in certain situations. However, group decisions have drawbacks that make individual decisions preferable in other situations. In general, groups that are not knowledgeable or organized will usually not make good decisions. And because group decisions almost always require more time, an individual decision is generally best when there is a critical time limitation. Another drawback to group decisions is the possibility that groupthink might occur. **Groupthink** occurs when the drive to achieve consensus among group members becomes so powerful that it overrides independent, realistic appraisals of alternative actions. In other words, the group becomes more interested in achieving consensus than in making the best decision. As a result of groupthink, criticism is suppressed and conflicting opinions are inadequately considered. A further potential problem with group decisions is the possibility that one person may dominate and control the group. It is also possible that pressure to conform may inhibit certain group members. Yet another possibility is that competition within the group may develop to such an extent that winning becomes more important than the issue itself. A final hazard of group decisions is the tendency of groups to accept the first potentially positive solution and give little attention to other alternatives. Rather than depending on a simple majority rule, effective groups go out and gather more information if the group is not convinced that they have reached a good solution.

In summary, group decisions are generally preferable where avoiding mistakes is of greater importance than speed. Figure 2.5 summarizes the positive and negative aspects of group decision making. One way to enhance the effectiveness of group decision making is to provide preparatory training for employees concerning the process.

Group participation in decision making is not an all-or-nothing proposition. The degree of participation can vary widely from situation to situation. A common approach is for the supervisor to set certain limitations on the decision before turning it over to the group. Another approach is for the supervisor to reserve the right to modify or reject the group's decision. Still another approach is to have the group assist in the generation and evaluation of alternatives but not in the final selection of an alternative. Whatever approach is used, the supervisor must always be honest with the group and not mislead it as to what its

3 LEARNING OBJECTIVES

SUPERVISION ILLUSTRATION 2–1

SOFTWARE SOLICITS INPUT FROM OTHERS

Milagro Systems, Inc., is a software company located in Austin, Texas, that has developed and marketed a set of computer programs and tools known as Knowledge Networks. Knowledge Networks are a means of deliberately setting up systems and processes in order to rapidly collect knowledge from individuals and then immediately use it for the benefit of other decision makers across the organization. The overall purpose of Knowledge Networks is to allow decision makers to explore issues, bring ideas to the surface, discover new insights, learn from others, be better informed to make decisions, and end up with complete documentation of all the assumptions.

According to Milagro, the Knowledge Networks are simple to use and effective when:

- The decision makers believe that others might have solutions to suggest.
- The decision makers feel free to ask for help.
- The decision makers are willing to share information.
- The decision makers want to acknowledge others for their intellect.

Information on how to access Knowledge Networks can be found by E-mailing Milagro Systems at the following address: info:@milagro.austin.tx.us.

Sources: Amy Doan, "Intranet Tools Foster Teamwork," *InfoWorld,* January 13, 1997, p. 48, and
http://milagro.austin/tx/us/knownet/index.html

---

role will be. The supervisor who asks for the group's input but never uses it is quickly recognized. Everyone is familiar with the supervisor who asks for the group's opinion and then does exactly what he or she wants to do anyway.

The Japanese have successfully used group decision making for years. Under the Japanese system, employees are involved through a form of collective decision making in which employees participate in decisions that affect them. Supervision Illustration 2–1 discusses some new software designed to assist decision makers in soliciting inputs from others.

PRACTICAL TRAPS TO AVOID WHEN MAKING DECISIONS

Many supervisors have a tendency to fall into one or more traps in making decisions. This section outlines some of these traps and offers some suggestions for avoiding them.

Trap 1: Making All Decisions BIG Decisions

Everyone has run into the supervisor who treats every decision as if it were a life-and-death issue. Such a supervisor spends two hours deciding whether to order one or two boxes of rubber bands. This approach wastes much of the supervisor's time. It also keeps the employees confused; they have a hard time distinguishing between the important and not so important issues. As a result of this approach, the really important problems may not receive proper attention because the supervisor becomes bogged down in unimportant matters. This type of supervisor must learn to allocate an appropriate amount of time to each decision, based on its relative importance.

Trap 2: Creating Crisis Situations

Some supervisors seem to delight in turning all decision situations into crisis situations. A true crisis occurs when a decision must be made under extreme time constraints. In actuality, very few crises occur naturally. What usually happens is that the supervisor transforms a normal situation into a crisis situation. Even when a true crisis does occur, such as the breakdown of a major piece of equipment or an accident, the supervisor must learn to remain calm and think clearly. It is a good habit to always ask yourself, "How much time do I really have to make this decision?" It is easy and even natural to assume that you have less time than you actually do.

Trap 3: Failing to Consult with Others

The advantage of consulting others in the decision-making process was discussed earlier in this chapter. Yet some supervisors are reluctant to consult others. They fear that asking for advice will make them look incompetent. Many supervisors, especially new ones, are under the impression that they should know all the answers and that to ask someone else for advice would be admitting a weakness. These are natural tendencies and should be recognized as such. Successful supervisors learn to put good sense and their reasoning ability ahead of ego.

Trap 4: Never Admitting a Mistake

No one makes the best decision every time. If a supervisor makes a bad decision, it is best to admit this and do what is necessary to correct the mistake. The worst possible course is to try to force a bad decision into being a good decision. For example, suppose you buy a used car. After you have owned the car for a couple of months, it becomes apparent that the car is a lemon. It would probably be much better to admit the mistake and get rid of the car, even at a loss, than to pretend that the decision was a good one and continue to pour more money into the car. Again, the natural tendency is to not admit mistakes.

Trap 5: Constantly Regretting Decisions

Some supervisors may admit their mistakes but seem to be forever regretting their decisions—the good ones as well as the bad ones. These people always want to change the unchangeable. A typical sentence of theirs starts with the words "I sure wish I had . . ." Once a decision has been made and is final, don't brood over it. Remember, very few decisions are totally bad; some are just better than others. Often, a supervisor who spends time dreaming about "what ifs" will not have enough time to implement the current decisions.

Trap 6: Failing to Utilize Precedents and Policies

Why reinvent the wheel? If a similar decision situation has occurred in the past, supervisors should draw on that experience. If a certain situation seems to be constantly recurring, it is usually useful to implement a policy covering the situation. For example, it is wise to have a policy covering priorities for vacation time. Also, supervisors should keep abreast of current organizational policies. These can often help in decision situations.

Trap 7: Failing to Gather and Examine Available Data

Supervisors often ignore or fail to utilize available factual information. One common reason for this is that some degree of effort is normally required to gather and analyze data. In other words, it is easier to utilize only the data already on hand. A related problem is separating the facts from gossip and rumor. The general tendency is to believe only what one wants to believe and not to consider the facts.

Trap 8: Promising What Cannot Be Delivered

Supervisors sometimes make commitments when they don't have the necessary authority. Similarly some supervisors make promises that they know they can't keep. This is usually done to make the decision-making process easier for the supervisor. Also, supervisors may view such commitments and promises as ways of getting subordinates to go along with decisions. Such an approach almost always comes back to haunt the supervisor. The best approach is to promise no more than can be delivered.

Trap 9: Delaying Decisions Too Long[2]

As discussed in an earlier section of this chapter, many supervisors tend to put off making a decision "until we have more information." Timeliness is often critical and even good decisions can be ineffective if delayed too long. It is rare that any supervisor ever has all the information he or she would like. The key is for supervisors to know when they have adequate information.

MAKING CREATIVE DECISIONS

Being creative does not necessarily mean coming up with revolutionary ideas. It does mean taking a fresh and uninhibited approach when making decisions and not being restricted by what has been done in the past. From a supervisory standpoint, being creative relates not only to the personal ideas of the supervisor but also to the climate that the supervisor develops. Creative supervisors not only have new ideas but also elicit new ideas from their employees. The supervisor sets the creative tone; if he or she encourages creativity, the employees sense this and act accordingly.

The Creative Person

People tend to think of themselves and others as being creative or not creative. But being creative is not an all-or-nothing characteristic. Everyone can be creative to some extent. Creativity is not a mysterious power given to a select few. Typically, the person who believes "creativity is not my bag" has never tried to

FIGURE 2.6
Characteristics of
Creative People

- Creative people tend to be bright rather than brilliant.
- Creative people have a youthful curiosity throughout their lives.
- Creative people are emotionally expressive and sensitive to the world around them and the feelings of others.
- Creative people tend to have a positive self-image; they feel good about themselves.
- Creative people have the ability to tolerate isolation.
- Creative people are nonconformists.
- Creative people often have thrill-seeking tendencies.
- Creative people are persistent.

Source: Andrew J. DuBrin, *Human Relations: A Job-Oriented Approach,* 4th ed. (Englewood Cliffs, N.J.: Prentice Hall, 1988), p. 105.

use his or her creative powers. Figure 2.6 lists some general characteristics of people who tend to excel in creativity.

Improving Personal Creativity

Unfortunately, most creativity is suppressed in the growing-up process. In fact, studies have shown that by the age of 40 the average adult retains only about 2 percent of the creativity that he or she possessed at age 5.[3] The key to improving personal creativity is unlocking the untapped creative potential that most people possess.

One aid to being creative is to concentrate. Think of only one problem or subject at a time, and strive to get as many different ideas as you can. Forget about whether they are practical or not. The initial step is to get a number of ideas. The evaluation of each idea takes place later. It is important that you use your subconscious brain. To do this, rest your conscious mind when you feel tired. The subconscious brain then takes over and reviews and relates thoughts that the conscious mind produced. This is commonly called "sleeping on the problem." In addition, be persistent. Keep trying. Useful ideas seldom result from the first attempts. You may well go over many ideas before you discover the one best suited to the situation. Finally, implement the idea. This can be a difficult step. It has been said that the most difficult task in the world is to drive an idea through the skull of a human being.

Establishing and Maintaining a Creative Climate

5 LEARNING OBJECTIVES

Every supervisor is responsible for the type of environment that he or she creates. Just how does the supervisor go about developing a creative environment? First and foremost, supervisors must demonstrate that they value creativity. All too often, supervisors pay lip service to creativity while rejecting any and all suggestions for doing things differently. Employees judge supervisors by what they do, not by what they say. Almost everyone has at one time or another approached the boss with a new idea only to be flatly rejected or ignored. This does not have to happen many times before employees "get the picture" and quit coming up with new ideas. On the other hand, the supervisor who reinforces creativity continues to get new ideas from employees. Group decision making, which was discussed earlier in this chapter, is one method of encouraging creativity among employees. Several other methods are discussed in the following sections.

6 LEARNING OBJECTIVES

Brainstorming. **Brainstorming** is an approach that involves presenting a problem to a group of people and then allowing the group to develop ideas for solutions. The basic approach is to encourage all participants to suggest any and all ideas that come to mind. The ideas may be wild and seemingly impractical, but they may lead to a creative solution. To encourage the free flow of ideas, no criticisms of suggested solutions are allowed at first. Only after all ideas have been presented and recorded does the group begin to evaluate them. Ideally, a brainstorming session should last from 45 minutes to an hour. The problem should not be discussed before the session. A small room and conference table should be used to encourage free communication. After the problem has been presented, a response should be sought from each participant. If an individual offers a suggestion, it is recorded. A person who does not have a suggestion merely says "pass." This process is repeated around the table a number of times until everyone passes. Such a procedure allows everyone an equal chance to participate and it prevents a few people from dominating the process.

Brainstorming is most applicable to simple decision problems requiring creative ideas. Naming a new product or service, coming up with a new use for a product, and identifying new ways to reduce wasted time are examples of situations where brainstorming might be effective. Supervision Illustration 2–2 describes an electronic-assisted method for brainstorming.

SUPERVISION ILLUSTRATION 2–2

BRAINSTORMING IN THE 1990s

Some organizations are now using electronic methods for brainstorming. For example, Fayetteville Technical Community College in Fayetteville, North Carolina, has a Team Focus Room which has computers positioned around a large screen. After team members have been presented with a problem, they enter their responses on keyboards that are hidden under a glass top. The responses are then projected on a screen with a reference number that does not indicate who typed in the response. Members can respond immediately to any response that appears on the screen. As the responses appear on the screen, they are also fed to a computer printer and can be picked up after the problem-solving session.

The Team Focus Room can be used by local businesses for a fee. Many business users have stated that the use of the room is well worth the cost because it enables them to get better results faster and cheaper. Some business users have even stated that the Team Focus Room enabled them to produce better results in one day than they might otherwise have obtained in five days!

Source: Margene E. Sunderland, Fayetteville Technical Community College, Fayetteville, North Carolina. For more information about Fayetteville Community College, visit its Web site at: www.uncfsu.edu

Brainwriting.   Under this approach, group members are presented with a problem situation and then asked to jot down their ideas on paper without any discussion. The papers are not signed. The group members then exchange the papers with others, who build on the ideas and pass the papers on again until all have had an opportunity to participate.

Input-output scheme.   This technique was developed by General Electric for use in solving energy-related problems. The first step under this method is to describe the desired output; the next step is to list all possible combinations of inputs that could lead to the desired output. After the list of possible inputs has been exhausted, the group discusses and prioritizes the desirability of the different possibilities. This process continues until eventually one input emerges as the preferred approach.

Barriers to Organizational Creativity

7 LEARNING OBJECTIVES

Many organizations and supervisors have created numerous barriers that inhibit organizational creativity. Usually, but not always, these barriers have been established unintentionally, yet their effect is to discourage creativity among employees. Some of the more frequently encountered examples of organizational creativity barriers are:[4]

Fear of failure. The simple fear of failure prevents many people from ever trying anything creative.

Premature criticism. Premature criticism and judgment of new ideas can quickly cause people to shy away from creative ideas.

The supervisor's shadow. Some supervisors create an environment that encourages employees to try to anticipate the way the boss is thinking. This discourages individual creativity.

Distractions and interruptions. Creative thinking is enhanced by quiet and uninterrupted periods of thinking time.

Protection of the status quo. Creative ideas often affect the status quo, and those who challenge the status quo often meet with criticism, lack of support, and threatened self-esteem.

Hierarchical idea filter. The more hierarchical levels an idea must pass through to be implemented, the greater the chances of its being distorted or lost.

Appropriated ideas. Some supervisors take credit for ideas that actually originated with one or more subordinates. This appropriation naturally discourages subordinates from generating new ideas.

Lack of support. Creative ideas are enhanced when they are supported by the supervisor and fellow employees.

Excessive togetherness. Excessive togetherness saps individuality and promotes consensus ideas that are rarely creative.

SOLUTION TO THE
SUPERVISION
DILEMMA

Jane appears to have recognized the need to make decisions as a supervisor (pp. 25–26). If she is not already doing so, it would benefit her to get in the habit of using the scientific method to work through decisions. The major advantages of the scientific method are that it is systematic and objective (pp. 26–30).

As for coming up with and implementing better ways of doing things, Jane should try some of the approaches suggested in this chapter. First and foremost, she should concentrate on creating the proper climate to encourage new ideas (pp. 35–36). At a minimum, this means giving every suggestion a fair hearing. If a suggestion is workable, Jane should implement it and give the employee credit. If a suggestion is unworkable, she should take the time to explain why it won't work.

Next, Jane should utilize group decision making whenever possible. This might result in more creative solutions, and it would almost certainly increase the employees' acceptance of the decisions reached. Brainstorming, brainwriting, and the input-output scheme are all techniques that might be tried as appropriate opportunities present themselves (pp. 36–37).

SUMMARY

This chapter emphasizes the importance of decision making for successful supervision. It describes the scientific method for making decisions and discusses several traps to avoid when making decisions. The chapter also gives particular attention to establishing a climate that encourages creative decisions.

1. *Discuss the importance of recognition and timeliness in decision making.* Recognizing the need to make a decision is a natural prerequisite to making a sound decision. Timeliness is also critical to a sound decision. Good decision makers realize that different decisions must be made within different time frames.

2. *State the steps taken in the scientific method of decision making.* The scientific method of decision making is composed of the following steps: (1) be alert to indicators and symptoms of problems; (2) tentatively define the problem; (3) collect facts and redefine the problem if necessary; (4) identify possible alternatives; (5) gather and organize facts; (6) evaluate possible alternatives; (7) choose and implement the best alternative; and (8) follow up.

3. *Name several potential advantages and disadvantages of group decision making.* Potential advantages of group decision making include: (1) the sum total of the group's knowledge is greater; (2) the group generally develops a much wider range of alternatives; (3) participation increases the acceptability of the decision to the group; and (4) group members better understand why a decision was made.

Potential disadvantages of group decision making include: (1) it takes more time; (2) groupthink may occur; (3) one individual may dominate or control the group; (4) pressures to conform may inhibit group members, (5) competition may become overly intense among group members; and (6) groups have a tendency to accept the first potentially positive alternative.

4. *List several traps that supervisors frequently fall into when making decisions.* Among the traps that supervisors frequently fall into when making decisions are: (1) making all decisions *big* decisions, (2) creating crisis situations, (3) failing to consult with others, (4) never admitting a

mistake, (5) constantly regretting decisions, (6) failing to utilize precedents and policies, (7) failing to gather and examine available data, and (8) promising what cannot be delivered.

5. *Discuss the role that the supervisor plays in establishing a creative environment.* The supervisor sets the creative tone; if he or she encourages creativity, the employees sense this and act accordingly.

6. *Describe several group-oriented techniques that can be employed by supervisors to encourage creativity.* Brainstorming is an approach that involves presenting a problem and then allowing the group to develop ideas for solutions. Only after all ideas have been presented and recorded are any criticisms or evaluations of ideas allowed. In brainwriting, group members are asked to jot down on paper their ideas relating to a problem. Without

discussion, the unsigned papers are then exchanged. The recipients build on the ideas and pass the papers until all have had an opportunity to participate. The input-output scheme first requires group members to describe the desired output of a problem. The next step is to list all possible combinations of inputs that could lead to the desired output. These possibilities are then evaluated until one emerges as the most preferred.

7. *Itemize some of the more frequently encountered barriers to organizational creativity.* The more frequently encountered barriers to organizational creativity include: fear of failure, premature criticism, the supervisor's shadow, distractions and interruptions, protection of the status quo, hierarchical idea filter, appropriated ideas, lack of support, and excessive togetherness.

REVIEW QUESTIONS

1. Give at least three examples of expected decisions and unexpected decisions that a supervisor might face.

2. Name the steps in the scientific approach to making decisions.

3. Why is it usually a good idea to generate several alternatives when making a decision?

4. Discuss both the positive and the negative aspects of group decision making.

5. Name and briefly discuss several traps that supervisors frequently fall into when making decisions.

6. List several characteristics of creative people.

7. Briefly describe the following techniques for encouraging creativity: brainstorming, brainwriting, the input-output scheme.

8. List several potential barriers to organizational creativity.

SKILL-BUILDING QUESTIONS

1. Do you think that the same general approach used in making organizational decisions should be used when making personal decisions? Why or why not?

2. Supervisor Bill Quane recently presented a decision situation to the members of his work group in order to get their input. Much to his dismay, he found considerable disagreement concerning

the decision. At present, he is not sure what to do. What do you think he should do? Why?

3. As a supervisor faced with many decisions, how would you know which decisions should be made immediately and which should not be made immediately?

4. "Very little creativity is required in supervision." Discuss.

REFERENCES

1. These steps were delineated by Margene E. Sunderland, Fayetteville Technical Community College, Fayetteville, North Carolina.
2. Thanks to Elliott F. Porter of Los Angeles Trade Technical College for the inclusion of this trap.
3. Richard L. Bencin, "How to Keep Creative Juices Flowing," *International Management*, July 1983, p. 26.
4. This list of barriers is summarized from Bencin, "How to Keep Creative Juices Flowing," pp. 27–28.

ADDITIONAL READINGS

Beaubien, Elaine. "Brainstorming Rules," *Executive Excellence*, August 1997.

Doan, Amy. "Intranet Tools Foster Teamwork," *InfoWorld*, January 13, 1997.

Jones, Michael. "Getting Creativity Back into Corporate Decision Making," *Journal for Quality & Participation*, January/February 1997.

Wachtel, George S. "The Idea Doctor Is In," *Bank Marketing*, September 1997.

SKILL-BUILDING APPLICATIONS

Incident 2–1

A Second Chance?

Word came down to the office supervisor, Jill Clark, that the Bright-Star Company had decided to computerize its billing, payroll, and inventory systems. The Bright-Star Company had always demonstrated concern for its employees, and this instance was no exception. Jill was instructed to tell her employees that no one in the department would be laid off because of the computer.

Learning to operate the new computer required a six-week training period. The first two weeks were spent at the computer company's facilities and the last four at Bright-Star under the supervision of the computer company's training personnel. Those employees who learned to operate the new computer would receive a 20-cents-per-hour raise.

After consulting with her boss, Jill decided that the fairest thing to do would be to offer the computer training to the seven employees whose jobs would be eliminated by the new computer. Four of them accepted the offer. The other three declined, saying that they thought the change would be too great for them. Of the four who accepted, three had been with the company more than 10 years. The fourth had five years' service. Since five people were needed to operate the computer, another employee was selected from the department to receive the computer training. The employees who declined the training were to be transferred to other work in the department at the same pay. This would work out quite well, because two other department employees were coming up for retirement within the next four months.

The training period went very well, and the computer was successfully implemented on schedule. About six months later, however, and without much warning, sales for the company began to slow drastically. Jill soon received word to lay off five of the department's employees. None of the computer operators would be affected by the layoffs since the computer would continue to be used. Among those to be laid off by Jill was Barbara Peters. Barbara had been with Bright-Star seven years and was one of the employees who turned down the computer training. Within a few minutes of receiving her layoff notice, Barbara went to Jill's desk.

Barbara: I've been here over seven years, and I need my job. You know my husband left me with three children to support.

Jill: I understand. Don't forget, I also have children.

Barbara: I hear that none of the computer operators will be laid off. Let me have a shot at one of those jobs. After all, I have over seven years with the company.

Jill: Barbara, you know you are not qualified for that. Anyway, you had your chance and didn't want any part of it. I'm simply following company policy, which states—and I quote— "When it is necessary to reduce our labor force, seniority shall apply, providing performance and skill are equal."

Barbara: *Seniority* is the key word. You and I both know that I could learn to operate the computer in a few days. Originally, the idea scared me. But after seeing it in operation, I know I could catch on in no time. Jill, you owe me a second chance.

Questions

1. Do you think that the original decision regarding the selection of computer operators was fair? Justify your answer.
2. Do you think that Jill should reconsider her decision to lay off Barbara? Why or why not?
3. What alternatives are available to Jill, and which one would you choose?

Incident 2–2

Bad Times at Quality Shoe

Mack Moller was supervisor of the production department of the Quality Shoe Company. He received a call from the general manager informing him that production must be cut back 20 percent due to declining sales. Mack knew that this also meant that labor costs must be cut by approximately 20 percent. His problem was deciding where to make the cuts. Fortunately (as Mack saw it), Quality Shoe was not unionized. This gave him much more freedom to make decisions than he would have had if Quality were unionized. Some of the obvious alternatives were a layoff of employees based on seniority, a reduction of the hours worked by all employees, or a layoff of employees based on performance evaluations. Cutbacks were rare at Quality, and Mack knew that the current situation could cause a few waves if not properly handled.

Mack had recently attended a supervisory seminar on group and creative decision making and had been quite impressed. He decided that this would be an excellent opportunity to try out some of the ideas he had learned. He strolled out on the floor and stopped at Ralph Russell's workstation. Ralph had been at Quality almost 15 years, and Mack knew that he was well respected by all the production employees.

Mack: Ralph, we've got a problem. I just received word from the boss that production and labor must be cut by 20 percent.

Ralph: I've suspected that something like that might happen with the economy in a nosedive and everything else that is going on.

Mack: Ralph, I'd like you to get everybody in the department together [a total of 16 people] and discuss among yourselves how you think the cuts should be made. Once you reach agreement, let me know—but not later than day after tomorrow! Try to come up with something creative.

Ralph: OK, Mack, but can't you give us some general guidelines to go by?

Mack: I guess I could, Ralph, but for starters I'd like to see what you come up with on your own.

Ralph: Just how much weight will our decision carry? We don't want to spend a lot of time on this if our ideas aren't going to count for anything.

Mack: As long as it's reasonable, I'll implement it in its entirety.

Questions

1. What do you think of Mack's approach to solving his problem?
2. How would you go about the task if you were Ralph?
3. What do you think Mack should do if he doesn't think that the group's decision is reasonable?

Exercise 2–1

Lost at Sea

This exercise is designed to demonstrate the value of group decision making. The exercise requires that you first make a set of decisions individually and then repeat the same decisions using a group format.

You are adrift on a private yacht in the South Pacific. Because of a fire of unknown origin, much of the yacht and its contents have been destroyed. The yacht is now slowly sinking. Your location is unclear because critical navigational equipment was destroyed and you and the crew were distracted trying to bring the fire under control. Your best estimate is that you are approximately 1,000 miles south-southwest of the nearest land.

Below is a list of 15 items that are intact and undamaged after the fire. In addition to these articles, you have a serviceable rubber life raft with oars large enough to carry yourself, the crew, and all the items listed below. The total contents of all survivors' pockets are a package of cigarettes, several books of matches, and five one-dollar bills.

Your task is to rank the 15 items below in terms of their importance to your survival. Place the number 1 by the most important item, the number 2 by the second most important, and so on through number 15, the least important.

—Sextant
—Shaving mirror
—Five-gallon can of water
—Mosquito netting
—One case of U.S. Army C rations
—Maps of the Pacific Ocean

—Seat cushion (flotation device approved by the Coast Guard)

—Two-gallon can of oil-gas mixture

—Small transistor radio

—Shark repellent

—20 square feet of opaque plastic

—One quart of 160-proof Puerto Rican rum

—15 feet of nylon rope

—Two boxes of chocolate bars

—Fishing kit

After everyone has completed the above rankings, your instructor will divide you into groups. Your group is to then rank the same items, using a group consensus method. This means the ranking for each of the 15 survival items *must* be agreed upon by each group member before it becomes part of the group decision. Consensus is difficult to reach. Therefore, not every ranking will meet with everyone's complete approval. As a group, try to make each ranking one with which all group members can at least partially agree. Here are some guidelines to use in reaching consensus:

1. Avoid arguing for your own individual judgments. Approach the task on the basis of logic.

2. Avoid changing your mind if the change is only to reach agreement and to avoid conflict. Support only solutions with which you are able to agree at least somewhat.

3. Avoid "conflict-reducing" techniques such as majority vote, averaging, or trading.

4. View differences of opinion as a help rather than a hindrance in decision making.

After you have completed your individual and group decisions, be prepared to discuss the following questions:

1. Were your group decisions better than your individual decisions? Why or why not?

2. Did any individual tend to dominate your group? If so, how could this situation have been better managed?

Source: Adapted from John E. Jones and J. William Pfeiffer, eds., *The 1975 Annual Handbook for Group Facilitators* (La Jolla, Calif.: University Associates, Inc., 1975).

Exercise 2–2

Assessing Your Creativity

Most of us believe we are more creative than we really are. Take a maximum of four minutes each on solving the following three problems.

1. Draw four straight lines connecting the dots in the diagram below without lifting your pencil (or pen) off the paper. You are permitted to cross a line, but you cannot retrace any part of a line.

2. What do the following words have in common (other than that they are all in the English language)?

calmness

canopy

deft

first

sighing

stun

3. Place 10 circles of the same size in five rows with four circles in each row.

After you have attempted each of the above problems, be prepared to discuss the following questions:

1. Why do you think these "simple" problems were difficult for you?

2. Do you think grade-school children tend to do better or worse than adults on problems such as these? Why?

CHAPTER 3

Improving Your Communication Skills

LEARNING OBJECTIVES

After studying this chapter, you should be able to:

1. Define communication.
2. Describe the interpersonal communication process.
3. Explain the concept of feedback in the communication process.
4. Define perception.
5. Define semantics.
6. Discuss guidelines for conducting effective meetings.
7. Explain the importance of the grapevine in organizations.

SUPERVISION
DILEMMA

John Lewis hadn't really thought about the importance of communication until after the conversation he had just completed with one of his best workers, Eva Sampson. John had given Eva an assignment and thought that he had clearly communicated the date when he wanted it completed. However, the assignment was not completed by that date because Eva thought she had more time than John had given her. What was the source of this communication failure, and how could it have been avoided?

It has been estimated that communication occupies between 50 percent and 90 percent of a supervisor's time. It has also been estimated that as much as 70 percent of organizational communications fail to achieve their purpose. Thus, a supervisor's communication skills can greatly affect his or her performance. The purpose of this chapter is to provide information for improving communication skills.

WHAT IS COMMUNICATION?

1 LEARNING
OBJECTIVES

Numerous definitions exist for the term *communication*. Communication occurs in many forms, ranging from face-to-face conversation to written messages to the more subtle forms involving facial expressions and body movements. In this book, **communication** is defined as the process by which information is transferred from one source to another source and is made meaningful to the involved sources. Supervisors must communicate with individual employees, the employees as a work group, the boss, and other individuals and groups in the organization.

In organizations, communication can be viewed from at least two perspectives. Communication between individuals is called **interpersonal communication.** Communicating within the formal organization structure (committee meetings, reports, memos, suggestion systems, etc.) is called **organizational communication.** The two forms of communication overlap in that interpersonal communication is often a part of organizational communication. For the purposes of this chapter, however, they are discussed separately. Supervision Illustration 3–1 illustrates an organizational communication system at American Airlines.

INTERPERSONAL COMMUNICATION

2 LEARNING
OBJECTIVES

Interpersonal communication involves the transmission and reception of verbal and nonverbal messages between two people. The basic purpose of interpersonal communication is to transmit ideas, thoughts, or information to someone else so that you are understood and so that you understand the response. Figure 3.1 is a diagram of the dynamic and interactive nature of the interpersonal communication process.

SUPERVISION ILLUSTRATION 3–1

Sᴜɢɢᴇsᴛɪᴏɴ Sʏsᴛᴇᴍ ᴀᴛ Aᴍᴇʀɪᴄᴀɴ Aɪʀʟɪɴᴇs

After nearly six years, the employee suggestion program at American Airlines, Inc., IdeAAs in Action, has produced total savings of nearly $250 million to date. In 1991, nearly 48,700 ideas were submitted, producing enough savings—$58.6 million—to purchase a Boeing 757 for the Dallas-based carrier. The first nine months of 1992 produced 33,000 ideas and $38.9 million in savings.

American uses a point system in its suggestion program. Employees can redeem their points for gift certificates to more than 25 stores, merchandise from an employee gift shop, or gifts from the Achievers Book of Awards that includes more than 3,000 items, including a grand piano.

Employees get 15 percent of the first-year savings in points. If the suggestion is an intangible idea, they get 15,000 credit points—the equivalent of $75. There is no cap on how much an employee can earn in one year, except that the maximum credit per idea is 7.5 million credit points (the equivalent of $37,500) for an idea that generates more than $247,000 in savings in one year. In 1991, American awarded 48 maximum credit awards.

Source: Adapted from Michael A. Verespej, "Suggestion Systems Gain New Lustre," *Industry Week,* November 16, 1992, p. 18. For more information on American Airlines, visit its Web site at:
www.americanair.com

As can be seen from Figure 3.1, an event or condition generates an idea, thought, or information. The desire to share information or to inform another person provides the need to communicate. The supervisor then creates a message and transmits it both verbally and nonverbally. This message is perceived and interpreted by the receiver. It should stimulate the receiver to create a reply message expressing a response to the initial message or a reaction to it. If the supervisor responds to this reply message, the process is repeated. Many factors often interfere and cause failures in this process. Some of these are discussed in the following sections.

Poor Listening Habits

Good interpersonal communication skills involve not only sending messages but also receiving them. Listening is the primary method of receiving messages. Unfortunately, many people are not very good listeners. Research has shown that the average person retains only about 25 percent of what he or she hears.

Effective listening is not a natural skill for most people. One factor that influences how well a person listens is the attitude of the listener toward the sender. For example, most people tend to listen more closely to their boss than to their subordinates. Respect for the sender and the belief that the receiver will benefit from the message definitely increase listening retention. Posture, personal mannerisms, and method of speaking can also affect listening retention.

Effective listening habits can be developed. Below are some tips to improve listening skills:

1. Relax and clear your mind if someone is speaking, so that you're receptive to what he or she is saying.

FIGURE 3.1

Interpersonal
Communication Process

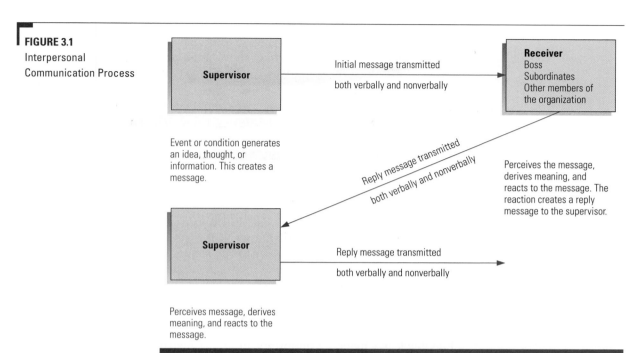

FIGURE 3.1

Interpersonal
Communication Process

Supervisor

Initial message transmitted
both verbally and nonverbally

Receiver
Boss
Subordinates
Other members of
the organization

Event or condition generates
an idea, thought, or
information. This creates a
message.

Reply message transmitted
both verbally and nonverbally

Perceives the message,
derives meaning, and
reacts to the message. The
reaction creates a reply
message to the supervisor.

Supervisor

Reply message transmitted
both verbally and nonverbally

Perceives message, derives
meaning, and reacts to the
message.

2. Never assume that you've heard correctly because the first few words have taken you in a certain direction. Most listening mistakes are made by people who hear only the first few words of a sentence, finish the sentence in their own minds, and miss the rest.

3. Don't tune out a speaker just because you don't like his or her looks, voice, or general demeanor. Stay open to new information. Concentrate on what is being said.

4. Part of listening is writing down things that are important. You should always have a piece of paper, a pencil, a notebook, or a card in your pocket. Throughout the day, many important things are discussed whose details you don't remember by the close of business. How many of you have found a phone number with no name attached in your handwriting on a scrap of paper? So take notes to listen, to remember later, and to document if necessary.

5. People often say one thing and mean something else. As you grow in your listening sophistication, it is important to listen for *intent* as well as *content.* Watch as you listen. Be sure that the speaker's eyes, body, and face are sending signals consistent with the speaker's voice and words. If something sounds out of sync, get it cleared up. Many people are afraid of looking foolish if they ask for clarification because doing this may make it seem that they weren't paying attention. But it is better to have the speaker repeat a message on the spot than to set off a chain reaction of misunderstanding.

6. Human communication goes through three phases: reception (listening), information processing (analyzing), and transmission (speaking). When you overlap any of those, you may short-circuit the reception (listening) process. Try to listen without *over*analyzing. Try to listen without interrupting the speaker.

7. A major failing of people in listening is simple distraction. To listen correctly, you must be able to reprioritize immediately. The second you hear sound coming toward you, focus and say to yourself, "This is important." Keep your eye on the speaker. Don't fiddle with pens, pencils, papers, or other distractions.[1]

Lack of Feedback

LEARNING OBJECTIVES 3

Communication is a two-way process. For the process to be effective, information must flow back and forth between the sender and the receiver. The flow of information from the receiver to the sender is called **feedback.** Feedback can be verbal or nonverbal. Limited feedback decreases the time required in the communication process. However, it also decreases the accuracy of communication and the degree of confidence that the listener has in its accuracy. Thus, feedback takes more time but significantly improves the quality of communication.

Feedback is especially important in giving instructions. One tip is to ask the listener to explain what has been communicated instead of asking if the communication was understood. Asking if the message was understood places the listener on the defensive. The tendency then is to say yes even if the message was unclear. People can also paraphrase the message they feel that they have received from the sender. A person could say, "Here is what I think you are telling me. Is this correct?"

Differences in Perception

LEARNING OBJECTIVES 4

Perception refers to how people view situations. Experience, personality, and method of communication affect a person's perception. Because these factors differ, each person's perception is unique. This explains why two people can view the same situation in entirely different ways and why a message may be received and interpreted in a manner entirely different from what was intended.

Examine Figure 3.2 and answer the following questions:

1. In Figure 3.2(a), describe the physical characteristics and age of the woman you see.
2. In Figure 3.2(b), which shape is larger?
3. In Figure 3.2(c), which line—AX, CX, CB, or XD—is the longest?

About 60 percent of the people viewing the picture in Figure 3.2(a) for the first time see a young, attractive, and apparently wealthy woman. About 40 percent see an old, ugly, and apparently poor woman. Figure 3.3 clarifies the profiles of the two women. In Figure 3.2(b), both shapes are the same size. In Figure 3.2(c), all of these four lines are the same length.

Obviously, if differences exist in how physical objects are perceived, the potential for differences in perception in interpersonal communication is even

FIGURE 3.2

Examples for
Demonstrating
Differences in Perception

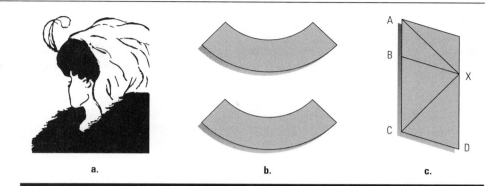

a.   b.   c.

Source: (a) Edwin G. Boring, "New Ambiguous Figure." *American Journal of Psychology,* July 1930, p. 444. Also see
Robert Leeper, "A Study of a Neglected Portion of the Field of Learning—the Development of Sensory Organization,"
Journal of Genetic Psychology, March 1935, p. 62. Originally drawn by cartoonist W. E. Hill and published in *Puck,*
November 8, 1915. (b) and (c) Gregory A. Kimble and Normal Gamezy, *General Psychology* (New York: Ronald Press,
1963), pp. 324–25.

FIGURE 3.3

Pictures of Young
and Old Woman

Source: Robert Leeper, "A Study of a Neglected Portion of the Field of Learning—the Development of Sensory
Organization," *Journal of Genetic Psychology,* March 1935, p. 62.

greater. Differences in perception can occur between younger and older employees, college graduates and noncollege graduates, supervisors and subordinates, and supervisors and their bosses. The supervisor should never assume
that his or her actions and words will be perceived exactly as they were intended. In fact, it is probably safer to assume that they will *not* be perceived as
they were intended. Feedback is the most effective method for reducing differences in perception.

Misinterpretation of Words

5 LEARNING
   OBJECTIVES

Semantics is the study of the meaning of words and symbols. Words have
meaning only in terms of how they are perceived and understood by people. Facial expressions, hand gestures, and voice inflection influence the understanding of words.

Two general problems tend to arise in semantics that influence the interpersonal communication process. First, some words and phrases can have

FIGURE 3.4

Interpretations of the
Word *Fix*

An Englishman visits America and is completely awed by the many ways we use the word *fix*. For example:

1. His host asks him how he'd like his drink fixed. He means *mixed.*
2. His hostess calls to everyone to finish their drinks because dinner is all fixed. She means *prepared.*
3. As he prepares to leave, he discovers that he has a flat tire and calls a repairman who says he'll fix it immediately. He means *repair.*
4. On the way home, he is given a ticket for speeding. He calls his host, who says, "Don't worry, I'll fix it." He means *nullify.*
5. At the office the next day, he comments on the cost of living in America, and one of his colleagues says, "It's hard to make ends meet on a fixed income." He means *steady* or *unchanging.*
6. Later, he remarks that he doesn't know what to do with his college diploma. A colleague says, "I'll fix it on the wall for you." He means *attach.*
7. He has an argument with a co-worker. The latter says, "I'll fix you." He means *seek revenge.*
8. Another co-worker remarks that he is in "a fix." He means *condition* or *situation.*
9. He meets a friend at his apartment who offers to "fix him up" with a young woman. You know what that means.

multiple interpretations (as shown in Figure 3.4, the word *fix* can be used in many ways). In addition, some groups of people develop their own technical language, which may not be understood by outsiders. For example, doctors, lawyers, and government and military employees often use abbreviations and acronyms that only they understand.

Since words are the most common method of interpersonal communication, they must be carefully chosen and clearly defined. Again, the use of feedback can reduce failures in interpersonal communication that result from semantics.

Poor Example Set by the Supervisor

One reason for supervisory failure is the setting of a poor example. Setting a poor example can also cause communication failure. The theory of "Do what I say, not what I do" is unfortunately subscribed to by many supervisors. Supervisors communicate not only with words but also with their actions. It is natural for employees to watch closely the actions of their supervisors. Thus, if a supervisor says one thing and does another, interpersonal communication is likely to fail. Empathy (placing yourself in the other person's position) is the key to overcoming this communication failure.

Lack of Interest by the Receiver

Lack of interest or attention by the receiver can result in interpersonal communication failures. Effective listening generally assumes that the receiver is interested in what the sender has to say. But if the receiver is not interested, what can the sender do?

It is always helpful for the supervisor to show how a particular communication affects the receiver. When people receive a message, they sometimes wonder, "Why do I need to know this?" The supervisor who addresses this question at the start is more likely to raise the receiver's interest level. Eliminating unnecessary messages can also help raise receiver interest.

IMPROVING YOUR COMMUNICATION SKILLS

Failure by the supervisor to develop good communication skills—oral, written, and nonverbal—can also cause many communication breakdowns. Many supervisors use statements such as "I am not a public speaker" or "I never could write very well" as excuses for communication weaknesses. The desire to be a supervisor should carry with it the desire to overcome one's weaknesses in these areas. This section directly relates to improving a supervisor's oral, written, and nonverbal communication skills.

Oral Skills

Most people have little trouble carrying on a conversation one-on-one. A supervisor does a great deal of one-on-one communicating when giving job instructions, disciplining employees, answering questions, and communicating with the boss. Every supervisor needs to ensure that he or she is specific in all communications, especially in oral communication. Some helpful hints for improving one-on-one verbal communication skills are:

1. Determine in advance the purpose of the conversation.
2. Organize your thoughts before you begin talking. Some supervisors tend to talk on and on with little organization to their thoughts.
3. Listen to what the other party has to say.
4. Ask for feedback from friends concerning their perception of your one-on-one verbal skills. A word of caution: Don't be hurt if they point out weaknesses. Learn from the feedback.
5. If possible, tape-record yourself during a one-on-one session. Listen to your voice and eliminate such phases as "you know" and other personalized expressions that detract from your communication effectiveness.

Speaking before groups or leading conferences is a much bigger problem for most supervisors. In fact, it has been estimated that fear of public speaking is one of the most common fears of people in general. Top management and middle management often receive formal training in public speaking. Unfortunately, this is not the case for supervisors. However, these useful tips will improve your public speaking skills:

1. Speak before groups whenever you can. Nothing overcomes the fear of public speaking better than experience.
2. Practice giving a talk before your family, friends, or even a mirror.
3. Ask for feedback from your practice audience.

4. Tape your presentation and listen to your own voice. Eliminate such phrases as "you know" and phrases that result in too many "aahs."

5. Always remember that your audience is *not* against you. In fact, your audience wants you to do a good job. Have you ever listened to someone make a speech and hoped that he or she would do a poor job? More than likely you have not: *Your audience is pulling for you.*

Writing Skills

The supervisor's writing skills are most frequently used to communicate within the formal organization. Memos, written disciplinary actions, and reports require effective writing skills. Some hints for improving your writing skills are:

1. Outline your thoughts on paper before writing the final copy. An outline gives you the opportunity to look at the organization of your presentation. Does the presentation flow smoothly? Are there logical transitions between major points?

2. Get feedback on your writing. Again, don't take negative feedback personally. Learn from it.

3. Practice writing whenever you can.

4. Read periodicals. (Some periodicals related to supervision are listed at the end of Chapter 1.) After reading an article, analyze whether it was logically organized and think about what you would have done differently.

Figure 3.5 provides some suggestions on when to use oral instead of written communication.

Nonverbal Communication

Nonverbal communication involves body movements, facial expressions, gestures, or even silences that communicate messages. Nonverbal communication can totally change the meaning of verbal communication. In fact, a great deal of interpersonal communication is done nonverbally. For example, if a supervisor is continually yawning or looking out the window during a discussion with an employee, the employee may interpret this to mean that the supervisor isn't interested.

Nonverbal messages can also be communicated by the environment within which the communication process occurs and by a person's appearance. For example, certain kinds of furniture arrangements appear to improve the effectiveness of the communication process more than do other kinds. When a desk separates a supervisor and an employee, tension tends to increase. This may be desirable when the supervisor is giving a directive or disciplining an employee. However, it is not desirable on all occasions. Finally, through such factors as dress, hair style, and personal adornments, appearance communicates important nonverbal messages. Sloppy, unkempt clothes and hair on a supervisor do not contribute to an effective work environment.

Some suggestions for the effective use of nonverbal communication are:

1. Know the most frequent methods of nonverbal communication that you use. Repetitive uses of nonverbal communication can be very distracting. Again, the best method of learning this is through feedback from friends and peers.

FIGURE 3.5	Method of Communications	Situations	
Situations for Using Oral versus Written Communications		**Most Effective**	**Least Effective**
	Oral communication by itself	1. Reprimanding employees 2. Resolving work-centered disputes	1. Communicating information regarding future employee action 2. Communicating information of a general nature 3. Communicating a company directive or order 4. Communicating information about an important company policy change 5. Communicating with your boss about work problems 6. Promoting a safety campaign
	Written communication by itself	1. Communicating information requiring future employee action 2. Communicating information of a general nature	1. Communicating information requiring immediate action 2. Commending an employee for noteworthy performance 3. Reprimanding an employee for poor performance 4. Settling work-related disputes
	Oral, then written communication	1. Communicating information requiring immediate action 2. Communicating company directives or orders 3. Communicating information about an important policy change 4. Communicating with your boss about work-related problems 5. Promoting a safety campaign 6. Commending an employee for noteworthy performance	

Source: Dale Level, Jr., "Communication Effectiveness Method and Situation," *Journal of Business Communication,* Fall 1972, pp. 19–25.

2. Remember that your personal appearance communicates messages to employees.
3. Do not artificially use nonverbal communication. Hand movements that do not coincide with your verbal expressions are distracting.

COMMUNICATING WITH YOUR BOSS

One of the most important people that the supervisor communicates with is his or her boss. This communication usually occurs on a face-to-face basis, and it sometimes occurs through written memos. Knowing what to communicate to the boss is essential. However, too many supervisors consider it essential that the boss know everything. This is *not* true. The boss doesn't want to discuss time-consuming problems that the supervisor should be solving. The following guidelines are offered to assist in knowing what should be communicated to the boss:

1. Understanding your authority and responsibility helps in knowing what to communicate. The concepts of authority, responsibility, and delegation are discussed in detail in Chapter 7.
2. Exceptions to work rules and policies should always be discussed with the boss.
3. Controversial situations should be discussed. For instance, suspending an employee for tardiness should be discussed with the boss.
4. Factors that positively or negatively affect production should be discussed. Frequently, supervisors want to communicate only positive happenings to the boss—and good news should certainly be reported. However, bad news should never be withheld from the boss. It is better for the boss to hear bad news from you than to hear it from someone else.

ORGANIZATIONAL COMMUNICATION

The formal structure of an organization establishes formal channels of communication. Normally, this so-called chain of command is to be followed because bypassing a member on the chain can lead to serious difficulties. For example, a bypassed member may not know the latest status of an important matter, work already scheduled may be disrupted, and orderly communication may give way to confused, haphazard communication. However, emergencies arise in which a person must be bypassed because he or she cannot be located and quick action is necessary. In such cases, it is advisable to explain the situation to the bypassed person as soon as possible. There are no precise answers as to when the chain of command should be short-circuited. But the key to effective organizational communication is to ensure that bypassed members understand *why* they were bypassed and that they feel secure in their jobs. Bypassing a member of the chain of command should not occur regularly.

Organizational communication also involves such things as formal meetings, reports, memos, electronic (E-mail) systems, and voice mail. Guidelines for effective writing have already been discussed. One word of caution should be given about the distribution of memos and reports. Too many memos and re-

---

SUPERVISION ILLUSTRATION 3–2

COFFEE TALKS AT HEWLETT-PACKARD

Duane Hartley is general manager of the Hewlett-Packard (H-P) microwave instruments division. The upheaval in the computer business hit H-P hard. Despite painful downsizing that affected 6,800 of its employees, H-P has preserved much of its culture of divisional autonomy.

Duane Hartley's work schedule is filled with "coffee talks," informal chats between senior management (who want to keep everyone up-to-date on corporate goals and the progress toward them) and employees (who want to voice their gripes and fears). At these sessions, Hartley shares all kinds of informa-

tion: the profitability of the division and its contribution to overall profitability for H-P, market share, and candid results of the employee satisfaction survey. He also reports on current corporate strategy. Questions from the employees demonstrate a high degree of sophistication. At the end of the sessions, several employees always remain behind to talk to Hartley about their problems.

Hartley maintains offices at two of his division's plants, both of them partitioned cubbyholes erected in the middle of the room. When employees encounter him, they invariably call him by his first name.

Source: Adapted from John Hacy, "Managing in the Midst of Chaos," *Fortune,* April 5, 1993, pp. 38–48. For more information on Hewlett-Packard, visit its Web site at:
www.hp.com

---

ports can create an excess of paperwork—which can itself be a communication problem. Unfortunately, the supervisor is often on the receiving end of too many reports and memos. In this situation, the supervisor must decide which reports or memos are important and which are relatively unimportant. Reading the important information first and the relatively unimportant information during slack times helps manage the problem of information overload. The supervisor should not contribute to the problem by sending memos or reports to people who should not receive them. The practice of sending copies to noninvolved people is much too common in today's organizations. Supervision Illustration 3–2 shows how one manager handles organizational communication.

Handling Meetings

6 LEARNING OBJECTIVES

Before a meeting is scheduled, a supervisor first needs to ask himself or herself the following question: "Is the meeting necessary or can another means of communication be used in place of the meeting?" If meetings are to be held, the effective handling of meetings is an important skill for the supervisor to develop. Most meetings should have a specific agenda that is closely followed. If the agenda of a meeting is given in advance to each of the participants, everyone can be prepared to discuss its items. A specific time period should be allocated for the meeting. All of these suggestions keep the meeting from dragging out and accomplishing very little. Each person at the meeting should be encouraged to participate, but the supervisor should not allow certain members to dominate the meeting. Lengthy remarks should be politely curtailed. The supervisor should lead the meeting and actively participate in the discussion but should be careful not to dominate the meeting. The meeting should begin and end at its scheduled time. Written summaries of the results of the meeting should be given to each participant as quickly as possible. Figure 3.6 summarizes these key guides for conducting effective meetings.

FIGURE 3.6

Guides for Conducting
Effective Meetings

1. A specific agenda should be prepared and given in advance to each participant in the meeting. The agenda should specify which items require preparation by the participants. Prepared participants make for a more effective meeting, as time is more effectively used and the need for follow-up meetings is eliminated.
2. A specific time period should be established for the meeting.
3. The meeting should begin and end on time.
4. Each member should be encouraged to participate.
5. No member should be allowed to dominate the meeting.
6. The supervisor should actively participate but should not dominate the meeting.
7. Lengthy remarks should be politely curtailed.
8. Written summaries of the results of the meeting should be given to each participant as quickly as possible.

The effective handling of meetings is an important skill for the supervisor to develop.
Walter Hodges/Tony Stone Images

Giving Instructions

Another situation faced by all supervisors that requires effective communication skills is giving instructions. How often have you given what you considered to be perfectly clear instructions—only to have them incorrectly interpreted? This is often a problem for supervisors since they spend a significant portion of their time giving instructions. The following suggestions for effectively giving instructions should be helpful to supervisors:

1. Instructions should be made as short and simple as possible. In order to provide clear, concise instructions, the supervisor should plan and organize his or her thoughts before giving instructions.

2. The supervisor should explain not only what is to be done but also why the instructions are being given.

3. The supervisor should ask employees to repeat the instructions in their own words and should *not* ask if they understand what was said. Asking people if they understand what was said places them on the defensive and reduces communication.

Dealing with the Grapevine

The **grapevine** is the informal communication system resulting from casual contacts between friends or acquaintances in various organization units. All organizations have a grapevine, and that grapevine exists not only among operative personnel but also among supervisors, middle management, and top management. In fact, supervisors and other levels of management are often very active participants in the grapevine.

Obviously, much information gets communicated in the organization through the grapevine. Some of it is accurate, and some of it is inaccurate. If a supervisor obtains information through the grapevine and knows that it is true, the supervisor should call a meeting to acknowledge the truthfulness of the information. If the information is false and is disrupting the work environment, the supervisor should call a meeting to correct the information. Supervisors should be extremely careful not to criticize everything communicated through the grapevine because doing so can damage their credibility. This is especially true if the information communicated or even a portion of it is accurate. The following suggestions for dealing with the grapevine should also be followed:

1. The grapevine should be viewed as a permanent part of the formal organization structure and should be used to improve communication within the organization.

2. Supervisors should know what information the grapevine is communicating and why that information is being communicated.

3. Supervisors should seek accurate information so that the messages they communicate through the grapevine are correct.

4. False information in the grapevine should be corrected by the supervisor by calling a meeting of employees and providing the accurate information.

SOLUTION TO THE SUPERVISION DILEMMA

Eva's misunderstanding of John's message illustrates a breakdown in the interpersonal communication process. Eva received John's message, interpreted it, and acted on it. However, the message that Eva received was not the message that John intended to send. This may have happened because of poor listening on Eva's part or because John did not get feedback from Eva to ensure that the message he transmitted was the one she received. Several suggestions for improving listening skills are given on pp. 46–47. John should be aware of the tips for receiving feedback on p. 48. He should also review the situations for using oral versus written communications on p. 53. Perhaps he should have put his instructions to Eva in writing.

SUMMARY

This chapter explores one of the most important supervisory skills—communication. Information is provided on interpersonal communication, feedback, perception, conducting effective meetings, and dealing with the grapevine.

1. *Define communication.* Communication is the process by which information is transferred from one source to another source and is made meaningful to the involved sources.

2. *Describe the interpersonal communication process.* Interpersonal communication occurs between individuals. It is an interactive process in which a person attempts to attain meaning and respond to it. It involves sending and receiving verbal and nonverbal messages.

3. *Explain the concept of feedback in the communication process.* Feedback is the flow of information from the receiver to the sender. For communication to be effective, information must flow back and forth between the sender and the receiver.

4. *Define perception.* Perception refers to how individuals process messages. Perception of the received information is modified by the individual's personality, previous experience, and other factors.

5. *Define semantics.* Semantics is the study of the meaning of words and symbols. Because of the possibility of misinterpretation, words must be carefully chosen and clearly defined for effective communication.

6. *Discuss guidelines for conducting effective meetings.* A meeting is the best means for dealing with the problem at hand, and a specific agenda should be prepared in advance and given to each participant in the meeting. A specific time period should be established for the meeting, and the meeting should begin and end on time. Each member should be encouraged to participate. No member should be allowed to dominate the meeting. The supervisor should actively participate but should not dominate the meeting. Lengthy remarks should be politely curtailed. Written summaries of the results of the meeting should be given to each participant as quickly as possible.

7. *Explain the importance of the grapevine in organizations.* The grapevine is the informal communication system that overlaps the formal organization structure. Although generally not sanctioned by management, the grapevine exists in all organizations.

REVIEW QUESTIONS

1. What is communication?
2. What is interpersonal communication?
3. Give five reasons why interpersonal communications fail.
4. What is perception? semantics?
5. Give some guidelines for helping a supervisor improve the following communication skills:
   a. Oral
   b. Written
   c. Nonverbal
6. What things should be communicated to the boss?
7. Give some guidelines for handling effective meetings.
8. Give several suggestions that are useful when giving instructions.
9. What are some suggestions for dealing with both true and false information in the grapevine?

SKILL-BUILDING QUESTIONS

1. "The boss should be told only good news, not bad." Discuss your views on this statement.
2. Do you feel that the grapevine usually carries false information?

3. Poor communication is blamed for too many other organization problems. Discuss.
4. "Watch what I do, not what I say." Should a supervisor make a practice of following this philosophy? Why or why not?

REFERENCE

1. Roger Ailes with Jon Kraushar, *You Are the Message* (Homewood, Ill.: Dow Jones-Irwin, 1988), pp. 50–51.

ADDITIONAL READINGS

Darragh-Jeromos, Peggy. "A Suggestion System That Works for You," *Supervision*, November 1996.

Lindo, David K. "Supervisors Must Speak Up. (Relationship of Supervisors with Subordinates)," *Supervision*, February 1996.

Moore, Jere N., Jr. "Supervisors Learn to Listen to Employees," *Supervision*, April 1996.

Ramsey, Robert D. "Voice Mail Etiquette," *Supervision*, March 1996.

Waddell, Janet R. "You'll Never Believe What I Heard. (Gossiping at Work)," *Supervision*, August 1996.

Weiss, W. H. "Getting Connected Electronically: The Internet," *Supervision*, January 1996.

SKILL-BUILDING APPLICATIONS

Incident 3–1

"I Told You . . ."

Bruce Hobbs hung up the phone. The call had been from his boss, Judy Tinsley. She informed him that she had just received the weekly accounts payable report, which was prepared in his department, and that she had several problems with it.

Bruce immediately called John Logan, the employee in his department who was responsible for preparing the report. He asked John to come to his office immediately. The following conversation occurred:

Bruce: Judy just called and said there are several errors in the weekly accounts payable report.

John: I checked it carefully, and I'm certain I can explain . . .

Bruce [*interrupting John.*]: I don't need an explanation. I told you no reports were to go out of here without my approval.

John: Well, I certainly haven't heard you say that.

Bruce: Maybe that's the problem—you just don't listen.

John: I do listen. You told us to check with you on any reports with which we had questions or concerns. I checked over the accounts payable report, and there were some last-minute changes that caused some increases, but they can be explained.

Bruce: Didn't you feel you should check with me about those changes?

John: No, because I understood them.

Bruce: Well, let me make it clear. From now on, I want to see all reports before they leave this office.

Questions

1. What went wrong?
2. How could the situation have been handled differently?
3. What do you think of Bruce's solution?

Incident 3–2

Shutdown at Glover Manufacturing

Art Gleason, supervisor of the winding department at Glover Manufacturing, had a long discussion with Sam Rawlings, one of his best employees. The conversation went as follows:

Sam: Art, I feel I need to let you know what's going on out on the floor.

Art: What is it, Sam?

Sam: Well, the word is out that there's going to be a big layoff. In fact, most people say we're going to cut back from three shifts to one shift. People are really upset.

Art: If that's true, I haven't heard anything about it.

Sam: People are also saying that there have even been discussions among the management team about closing the entire plant and moving the operation to the South. People realize that management was pretty upset about the union organizing campaign last year. Even though most of us voted against the union, we understand management really resented the fact that an election was held.

Art: Sam, let me check into this. I'll let you know what I find out.

Art immediately went to his boss, Clint Chaplin. The following conversation occurred:

Art: Clint, I hear from the grapevine that we may be cutting back to one shift. I also hear that there's talk about Glover moving its entire operation to the South. Have you heard anything about it?

Clint: Yeah, I hear that the rumor mill is really going. However, I can assure you that we are not going to move. The discussions on cutting back are only tentative and are entirely dependent on the economy.

Art: Good, I'll go back and straighten out the false impressions my people have.

Clint: Don't do that. Let them worry a little bit. After all, we really sweated out that union election. Let's let them sweat a little bit.

Questions

1. How would you handle the situation?
2. Was the grapevine accurate?
3. What message does Clint's attitude communicate about his feelings toward the employees of Glover? Answer this question in writing.

Exercise 3–1

Meanings Are in People

1. Write down the maximum number of people you feel could live in a town and have the town be described as being small.
2. Write down the minimum number of people that you feel could live in a town and have the town be described as being large.
3. The instructor will collect this data and help you draw some conclusions.

Exercise 3–2

Perception Test

1. In 1963, if you went to bed at 8 o'clock at night and set the alarm to get up at 9 o'clock the next morning, how many hours of sleep would this permit you to have?
2. If you have only one match and enter a room in which there is a kerosene lamp, an oil stove, and a wood-burning stove, which would you light first? _____
3. Some months have 30 days; some have 31. How many have 28 days?
4. If a doctor gave you three pills and told you to take one every half hour, how long would they last? _____
5. A man builds a house with four sides, and it is rectangular in shape. Each side has a southern exposure. A big bear comes wandering by. What color is the bear?

6. I have in my hand two U.S. coins that total 55 cents in value. One is not a nickel. Please bear that in mind. What are the two coins? _____
7. Divide 30 by ½ and add 10. What is the answer? _____
8. Take two apples from three apples and what do you have? _____
9. An archaeologist found some gold coins dated 34 B.C. How old are they?
10. How many animals of each species did Moses take aboard the ark with him?

Exercise 3–3

Reading Comprehension

Time limit: five minutes

Directions

1. Read everything before doing anything.
2. Put your name in the upper-right-hand corner of this page.
3. Draw a line under the word *page* in number 2.
4. On the bottom of this page add the numbers 7,165 and 9,867.
5. Draw a line under your first name.
6. On the back of this page, multiply the number of people in the room by four.
7. If you are the first person to get this far, announce loudly, "I'm through with the first seven."
8. How many quarters in three half-dollars?
9. Draw a circle around your answer to number 8.
10. Write today's date in the lower-right-hand corner of this page.
11. Divide the sum of your answer to number 4 by three.
12. Draw a triangle around your answer to number 11.
13. Say in a quiet voice, "I'm just about through and I am capable of following directions very well."
14. Now that you have read all of the directions, do only numbers 1 and 2.

Exercise 3–4

Your Listening Ratio

Do you talk more than you listen? Rate yourself on the talk/listen ratio chart. Then ask two family members or two friends to score you. If employed, have two co-workers score you.

Check the line of the ratio best representing the percent of the time you generally:

Talk	Listen	
10	90	_____
20	80	_____
30	70	_____
40	60	_____
50	50	_____
60	40	_____
70	30	_____
80	20	_____
90	10	_____

Compare your self-assessment with the way others rated you. If there are major discrepancies in the scores, the more accurate numbers are the ones reflecting how others view you. Their perception is what's real.

In general, though, you should strive to listen 60 to 70 percent of the time and talk 30 to 40 percent. The reason for this bias toward listening is that most people listen but don't really *hear*. We therefore need to overcompensate—and listen more—to improve our comprehension.

Source: Roger Ailes with Jon Kraushar, *You Are the Message* (Homewood, Ill.: Richard D. Irwin, 1988), pp. 45–46.

CHAPTER 4

Ethics and Organization Politics

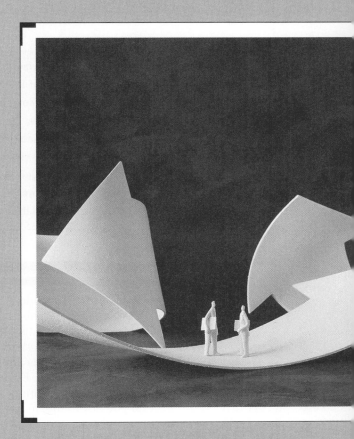

LEARNING OBJECTIVES

After studying this chapter, you should be able to:

1. Define ethics and discuss what behaviors are considered unethical in the workplace.

2. Discuss codes of ethics and the role they can play in encouraging an ethical workplace.

3. Discuss the role that supervisors play in setting the ethical tone of an organization.

4. Identify the major areas that require ethical conduct by supervisors.

5. Outline the steps the supervisor should follow when dealing with a dishonest subordinate.

6. Describe five types of power and discuss how a supervisor can positively increase his or her power base.

7. Define organization politics.

8. Discuss several guidelines that supervisors should follow when socializing with other members of the organization.

SUPERVISION
DILEMMA

Jane Harris, a supervisor at Global Insurance Company, was caught off guard during lunch with a group of fellow supervisors. Some of them said they were able to slip away for a couple of hours each week to tend to personal business. Jane listened in a state of disbelief. How could these supervisors steal time from the company and not expect their subordinates to do the same? What upset Jane was that they seemed to think nothing of it—to view it as accepted behavior. The real kicker came when one of the supervisors bragged that he had always been able to get a little extra money by padding his expense account. Jane left lunch wondering what the world had come to. Were ethics a thing of the past?

1 LEARNING
OBJECTIVES

Ethics are standards or principles of conduct that govern the behavior of an individual or a group of individuals. Ethics are generally concerned with moral duties or with questions relating to what is right or wrong. The behaviors of supervisors, what goals they seek, and what actions they take are all affected by ethics. In any given situation, what a supervisor perceives as "right" naturally affects his or her actions and the actions of the employees.

Moral standards are the result of social forces and human experiences over hundreds of years. For example, society condemns cheating, lying, and stealing. However, the application of ethics is an individual consideration. Do you or do you not follow moral standards when dealing with others? Are you aware of a moral code and, if so, how do you interpret it?

Differences in awareness and interpretation of ethical standards create many problems. To illustrate, when does an action leave the sphere of honorable self-interest and become personal dishonesty? Does the fact that a person was not disciplined for a certain action make it acceptable?

All too often, actions are justified based on the means used or on the ends accomplished. That is, do we hold an act to be morally right on the basis of the means used or on the basis of the end result? One might reason, for example, that the act of lying is acceptable if it achieves positive results. Conversely, one might consider any action that employs ethical means to be perfectly justifiable regardless of the outcome.

ETHICS IN THE WORKPLACE

One problem in talking about business ethics is that there is no unanimity as to what is ethical and what is unethical. Little disagreement exists with regard to flagrant ethical violations such as embezzlement or stock fraud. Views become clouded, however, with regard to less obvious ethical questions, such as whether it is ethical to take longer than necessary to do a job or to engage in a few minutes of personal business on company time. Figure 4.1 lists several common practices that often involve questions of ethics in the workplace. Blaming or taking advantage of an innocent co-worker, divulging confidential information, falsifying reports, claiming credit for someone else's work, padding an expense account, and pilfering company materials and supplies are behaviors that are generally considered to be unethical.

FIGURE 4.1
Ethically Questionable
Behaviors

Using company services for personal use. N
Padding an expense account. N
Calling in sick to take a day off. ?
Authorizing a subordinate to violate company rules. N
Pilfering company materials and supplies. N
Accepting gifts/favors in exchange for preferential treatment. N
Giving gifts/favors in exchange for preferential treatment. N
Taking longer than necessary to do a job. ?
Divulging confidential information. N
Doing personal business on company time. ?
Concealing mistakes. N
Passing blame for errors to an innocent co-worker. N
Claiming credit for someone else's work. N
Falsifying time/quality/quantity reports. N
Taking extra personal time (late arrivals, longer lunch hours and breaks, early departures). ?
Not reporting others' violations of company policies and rules. ?
Copying copyrighted computer software. N
Hiring a key employee from a competitor. ?
Dating someone who works for you. ?

A recent study involving 1,324 employees found that unethical acts are widespread in the U.S. workplace.[1] The study found that 56 percent felt under pressure to act unethically or illegally on the job; 48 percent reported that they had engaged in one or more unethical and/or illegal acts in the previous year. Five percent of this same sample confessed to lying or deceiving supervisors on a serious matter.

CODES OF ETHICS

LEARNING OBJECTIVES

One concrete action that can be taken to encourage ethical standards is to establish a code of ethics. A **code of ethics** is a written statement of principles that should be followed in the conduct of business. A code of ethics typically addresses such topics as ethical standards, questionable payments, meals, gifts, purchasing policies, and employee involvement in political campaigns and noncorporate political activities. Ideally, a code of ethics is comprehensive and addresses issues applicable to all areas of the organization.

If a code of ethics is to help mold the ethical environment of the organization, it must be communicated to all employees. The code can be communicated through company mailings, bulletin board postings, employee handbooks, and general announcements. Many organizations require all new employees to sign a form confirming that they have read the company's code of ethics. Even more important than the method of communication is that the code be actively supported by all levels of management. Support for the code of ethics must start at the top of the organization and filter down through all levels. Employees must perceive that managers at all levels believe in and adhere to the code of ethics. If a comprehensive code of ethics does not exist, supervisors can clearly communicate their ethical expectations through their actions and personal behaviors.

SETTING THE TONE

3 LEARNING OBJECTIVES

Although ethical behaviors of supervisors do not often make newspaper headlines, situations that test their ethics arise almost daily. Where it exists, a code of ethics provides the framework within which supervisors must act. However, numerous situations not specifically covered by a code of ethics often arise. In these situations, supervisors need to use individual judgment. It is often these judgments that most influence employee ethics. The supervisor must set the example. Subscribing to the theory of "Do what I say, not what I do" doesn't work. Employees are much more impressed by what supervisors do than by what they say. Employees' notions as to what is acceptable and not acceptable are largely based on the supervisor's actions. If employees perceive a supervisor as being slightly unethical or dishonest, they are likely to feel that similar behavior on their part is acceptable. For example, if the employees have reason to believe that the supervisor is "borrowing" things from the storeroom, they may not see anything wrong with their doing the same thing. On the other hand, some employees may still feel that doing this is wrong and thus lose respect for the supervisor.

The supervisor's general attitude toward ethics can greatly affect the ethics of the employees. The supervisor's failure to take corrective action in certain situations can also affect the ethical behavior of the employees. They often interpret such failures as condoning or giving tacit approval. Supervision Illustration 4–1 describes how Levi Strauss and Company has attempted to integrate ethics into the everyday decisions made by its managers.

SUPERVISION ILLUSTRATION 4-1

VALUES-BASED ETHICS

Compliance-based approaches to business ethics are often designed by corporate lawyers and are based on rules and regulations. The goal of compliance-based programs is to prevent, detect, and punish legal violators. Managers at Levi Strauss and Company tried this approach and found that it didn't serve them very well. They concluded that ethical conduct cannot be forced but rather that it is a function of the collective attitudes of employees.

Levi Strauss and Company replaced its compliance-based approach with a values-based approach. This approach combines functional values with individual responsibility and accountability. This current approach to ethics is based on six ethical principles: honesty, promise keeping, fairness, respect for others, compassion, and integrity. This approach is put into practice by first identifying which of these principles applies to a particular business decision that might come up. Management then determines which internal and external stakeholders' ethical concerns should influence their business decisions. Before a decision is made, information on stakeholder issues is gathered and possible recommendations are discussed with "high influence" stakeholder groups, such as shareholders, employees, customers, and members of local communities.

Source: Robert D. Haas, "Business Ethics," *Executive Excellence,* June 1997, pp. 17–18. For more information about Levi Strauss and Co., visit its Web site at: **www.levi.com**

AREAS REQUIRING ETHICAL CONDUCT BY SUPERVISORS

LEARNING OBJECTIVES

Many areas of supervision require ethical conduct (some were listed in Figure 4.1). Most of these areas can be grouped into three general categories: (1) loyalty, (2) human relations, and (3) overt personal actions.

Loyalty

The category of loyalty has to do with where a supervisor's loyalties lie. Does the supervisor place personal interests ahead of everything else, or is he or she dedicated to the goals and needs of the employees, the organization, the family, or others? Regardless of the supervisor's leadership qualities, communication skills, or general knowledge, his or her personal influence will not be effective unless the employees view the stated objectives positively. Supervisors who are perceived as being interested only in themselves and their futures will have difficulty in getting the full cooperation of employees. Employees may ask themselves, "Would this supervisor destroy another person's career in order to advance?"

Human Relations

This category centers on a supervisor's concept of fairness. It is concerned with how the supervisor treats other people, especially subordinates. Ethics play a major role in determining how a supervisor treats subordinates. Is the supervisor consistent in the way that he or she deals with different subordinates, or does the supervisor play favorites? Are all of the supervisor's interpersonal dealings honest, or does he or she have a tendency to "talk behind people's backs"? Does the supervisor deceive his or her peers in order to make them look bad? Is the supervisor genuinely interested in the careers of subordinates?

Overt Personal Actions

The category of overt personal actions includes all of the other actions taken by a supervisor that may reflect his or her ethics. Those actions may be internal or external to the organization. Behavior inside the company would include such things as not circumventing organizational policy. External actions would include such things as how supervisors handle themselves in the community.

Figure 4.2 gives several examples under each category of the ethical conduct required of supervisors. Supervision Illustration 4–2 describes some games used by companies to teach ethics to their employees.

FIGURE 4.2

Examples of Ethical Conduct Required of Supervisors

Loyalty	Human Relations	Overt Personal Actions
Has concern for employee welfare.	Deals honestly with employees.	Doesn't cut corners to save time.
Has concern for company welfare.	Shows empathy when appropriate.	Is concerned with employee safety.
Has concern for employee families.	Objectively evaluates employees.	Never tries to cheat the company out of something.
Takes credit only when deserved.	Fairly disciplines employees.	Is well thought of in the community.

SUPERVISION ILLUSTRATION 4–2

ETHICS BOARD GAMES

Citicorp has developed a sophisticated board game, called The Work Ethic, to teach business ethics to its 90,000 employees worldwide. Citicorp's objectives are to communicate the corporate ethical culture to employees and encourage ethical behavior through subtle peer pressure. The game board is divided into four levels: entry level, supervisor, manager, and senior manager. Ethical dilemmas and four possible solutions to each are presented to the players. The consequences of decisions become more serious at higher levels. No solution is perfect and so changes can be made to make any of the choices more acceptable. Based on the answers chosen, participants win or lose points, lose a turn, or get fired for just cause (kicked out of the game).

The Work Ethic has been translated into Spanish, Portuguese, French, German, Flemish, and Japanese.

After reviewing The Work Ethic, managers at Martin Marietta Corporation created their own game called Gray Matters. Gray Matters adapts controversial, real-world situations and creates responses that appeal to a variety of people. Players cannot debate the situations presented, only the appropriateness of the answers provided. Points are awarded for each of the different answers. Depending on the answers chosen and the associated points awarded, players move up or down the "company progression ladder."

Sources: Karin Ireland, "The Ethics Game," *Personnel Journal,* March 1991, pp. 72–75, and Phillip Barnhart, "The Ethics Game," *Training,* June 1993, pp. 65–67. For more information about Citicorp, visit its Web site at:
www.citicorp.com

DEALING WITH DISHONEST EMPLOYEES

LEARNING OBJECTIVES

The U.S. Department of Commerce estimates that employees steal $40 billion to $50 billion every year from American businesses. How does the supervisor deal with dishonest employees? Because the relationships involved differ, situations with dishonest subordinates are sometimes handled differently from those dealing with peers and other managers.

With regard to subordinates, the supervisor must first recognize the problem and then build a case. For various reasons, supervisors are often reluctant to admit to problems involving dishonest employees. Some supervisors believe that bringing such a problem into the open would be bad for morale. Others mask the problem by arguing that "everybody does it." The problem is compounded if the dishonest employee has been with the company a long time and has a good work record. Whatever the case, such an employee should be confronted and dealt with appropriately. The supervisor must gather proof of the employee's dishonesty. This does not mean taking the word of others; it means carefully documenting the available evidence. For example, if an employee is suspected of stealing from the supply cabinet, care should be taken to document what was missing, the times it was missed, and the employee's whereabouts at those times. Once the supervisor is confident of the facts, he or she should confront the employee and follow the disciplinary system. The keys here are (1) recognize the problem, get the facts, and document the case; (2) confront the employee; and (3) follow the established disciplinary system.

FIGURE 4.3

Types of Power

Coercive power	Based on fear, the employee does what is required to avoid punishment or some other negative outcome. The disciplinary policies of organizations generally are based on this type of power.
Reward power	Based on the ability of one individual to provide rewards, either intrinsic or extrinsic, for compliance with this individual's wishes.
Legitimate power	Based on an individual's position in the organization; thus, when joining an organization, a person accepts the fact that the boss's orders are to be carried out.
Expert power	Based on the special skill, expertise, or knowledge that a particular individual possesses.
Referent power	Based on the personal characteristics of an individual that make others want to associate with him or her; exemplified by the charismatic individual who has traits that allow that person to control situations.

The general approach followed in dealing with dishonest peers and other managers is similar to the one followed in dealing with dishonest subordinates. Since the relationships involved are significantly different, however, some deviation from this approach may be necessary. Moreover, you may not be in a position to deal directly with the problem. For example, if you suspect that a supervisor in another area is dishonest, you may never be in a position to prove or disprove your suspicions. In this case, you should deal cautiously with that supervisor and alert your boss as to your suspicions. When dealing with dishonest peers and other managers, it is in most cases better to report your suspicions and findings to your boss and let him or her confront those involved.

Supervisors should be aware that the usual tendency in dealing with dishonest employees is to do nothing and hope that the problem will go away. Unfortunately, the problem rarely goes away; it usually gets worse.

BUILDING A SUPERVISORY POWER BASE

Power is the ability to get others to respond favorably to instructions and orders. Put another way, power is the ability to command and get others to do what you ask. The use of or desire for power is often viewed negatively in our society because power is often linked with the capacity to punish. While there are some negative types of power, there are also several very positive types. Fortunately, not everybody seeks or enjoys equal degrees of power. However, every supervisor needs some amount of power. Supervisors who have built a broad power base can more readily get employees' attention and cooperation and are more likely to be respected by higher-level managers.

6 LEARNING OBJECTIVES

Figure 4.3 describes five basic types of power. In light of these different types of power, there are many positive things that supervisors can do to increase their power base in a positive manner.

Gain the respect of subordinates.   Gaining the respect of subordinates goes a long way toward building a power base. If your subordinates respect you, they will stand up for you in a crisis—they will give you active support when you need it. Others in the organization will interpret the support as a sign of power. Being competent and doing your job well is one of the best ways to gain the respect of subordinates.

Be "in good" with your boss.   A certain amount of power goes with being in good with your boss. Subordinates and peers treat you with a certain respect if they know you have a close relationship with your supervisor. A preceding section discussed ways "to keep your boss happy."

Get people obligated to you.   Another way of building a power base is to get others obligated to you. Politicians have used this method for many years. However, its use can easily border on the unethical. For example, a supervisor might be tempted to bribe an employee with a good pay raise in exchange for support on certain matters. The supervisor should help other people, but should not do this merely for personal benefit.

Seek responsibility.   **Responsibility** is accountability for reaching objectives, using resources properly, and adhering to organizational policy. Supervisors can gain power by seeking and accepting responsibility. The key here is to aggressively seek out additional responsibility rather than waiting for it to come. Peers and subordinates will automatically bestow a certain degree of power on the supervisor who has considerable responsibility.

ORGANIZATION POLITICS

LEARNING
OBJECTIVES
7

Organization politics refer to the practice of using means other than merit or good performance for bettering your position or gaining favor in the organization. Organization politics include such things as trying to influence the boss, trying to gain power, and trying to gain a competitive edge over your peers. Many people often associate sneaky, devious, or unethical behavior with the phrase "organization politics." However, this is not necessarily the case. There are many forms of organization politics that are not sneaky, devious, or unethical. Only when an individual pursues self-interest to the detriment of others or the organization does the behavior becomes unethical. When viewed in this light, almost any approach to organization politics can be ethical or unethical, depending on how it is used. Because organization politics are a reality in organizations, supervisors should understand them and know how to use them in a positive and ethical manner.

How to Keep Your Boss Happy

Almost all employees want to keep their bosses happy—and supervisors are no exception. Supervisors want to keep their bosses happy for many understandable reasons. A very obvious reason is to keep from getting fired. Even if your boss doesn't fire you, life can become pretty miserable if he or she doesn't like you. Knowing that your relationship with your boss is not good will keep you in constant fear of being fired or, at least, not being treated fairly. And you can be pretty sure that you won't be a prime candidate for promotion! A poor relationship with your boss also means that you will probably not receive much coaching and counseling. This in itself can greatly hinder your progress.

Know your boss.   The first step in keeping your boss happy is to know him or her. It is hard to keep a person happy if you don't know something about what makes that person tick. Answering the following questions will give you a better insight into your boss. It can also help you anticipate his or her actions.

> To whom does your boss report?
>
> What are your boss's primary responsibilities?
>
> What are your boss's chief successes, and when did they take place?
>
> What are some recent failings that are bothering him or her?
>
> Who are your boss's enemies?
>
> Who are your boss's friends?
>
> What is the extent of your boss's authority?
>
> What responsibilities and authority has your boss delegated?
>
> What are your boss's major concerns?
>
> On what basis is your boss being evaluated?
>
> What does your boss regard as good performance?
>
> On what basis is your boss evaluating you?[2]

Be loyal.   Loyalty is a trait that all bosses admire. You can demonstrate your loyalty to your boss in a variety of ways. One good way is to defend the boss when he or she is being criticized. You can do this, even if you don't agree with the boss 100 percent, by pointing out probable reasons why the boss did whatever he or she did. A sure way to demonstrate disloyalty is publicly criticizing your boss. Regardless of how careful you try to be, such comments always seem to get back to the boss. Seemingly insignificant things often influence a boss's interpretations of loyalty. These include attendance at company functions and parties, willingness to work overtime and on Saturdays, and general enthusiasm. For example, a good performer who genuinely cares for the company may be branded by a boss as disloyal simply because he never attends company parties.

Show respect for your boss.   This doesn't mean that you have to bow and scrape at your boss's feet. It does mean that you should use common sense in your dealings with your boss. Be on time for meetings and conferences; talk and listen in a respectful manner; and use respectful gestures when in the boss's presence. In addition, exhibit a general attitude of respect toward your boss and his or her position. If you have occasion to disagree, do so in a tactful and respectful manner.

Seize opportunities to make your boss look good.   In the usual course of events, many opportunities arise for you to make your boss look good. Take full advantage of them. When appropriate, praise your boss to top management.

Be prepared in meetings to explain things that your boss might be asked, especially when you may know more about the details. Another suggestion is to head off problems that may be brewing for your boss or your department.

Avoid antagonizing other departments.   Don't contribute to poor relations with other departments. This is especially necessary if your boss must interact with those departments. You want your boss to think of you as someone he or she can trust in dealings with other departments. Antagonizing other departments only makes things more difficult for both you and your boss. Learn to reconcile differences among departments; undertake positive actions to keep problems from growing.

Insist on feedback.   One easy way to get on the bad side of your boss is to make a mistake and not know it. When this happens, it is easy to innocently repeat the mistake. Don't depend solely on formal performance appraisals for feedback. Create an environment that encourages your boss to tell you how you're doing. Take advantage of opportunities for informal discussions with the boss. For example, when your supervisor visits your area, ask for his or her opinion on how you handled a recent situation. As a part of this process, you must know how to accept negative feedback. Don't get angry or huffy when you get it; be grateful for your boss's honest evaluation.

Help take the load off your boss.   Actively look for ways in which you can help take some of the load off your boss. Don't make the boss have to ask you every time he or she wants something done. Ask what you can do! Volunteer solutions to problems. Strive to be viewed as a problem solver and not a problem creator. Don't continually talk about how bad things are. Talk about what has been accomplished.

SOCIALIZING WITH OTHER MEMBERS OF THE ORGANIZATION

Should the supervisor socialize with subordinates? Should the supervisor socialize with superiors? What tack should be taken by the person who is promoted to supervisor over former peers with whom he or she has frequently socialized (as a member of the bowling team, a softball team, and so forth)? Such questions, sooner or later, confront almost every supervisor. There are no hard-and-fast answers. However, these general guidelines should be followed:

1. Don't be overly eager to socialize with subordinates or superiors. Let things take their normal course.
2. Use common sense. Don't do anything while socializing that will later cause problems (such as getting highly intoxicated at a party at your boss's house). The supervisor who does not use common sense when socializing with superiors or subordinates is surely courting trouble.
3. Be yourself. Don't try to put on a false front to impress your boss or other superiors.
4. Don't try to use your rank when socializing with subordinates.
5. Don't make any work-related promises to subordinates while socializing.
6. Don't date or become romantically involved with subordinates.

SOLUTION TO THE
SUPERVISION
DILEMMA

**It appears that Global Insurance Company (Jane's company) could benefit from estab-
lishing a code of ethics (pp. 65–66). Such a code should clearly address the issues that
confronted Jane (co-workers' tending to personal business on company time and
padding expense accounts). Once the code has been developed, it should be communicated to all of Global's employees. Jane should now have a much better understanding
of what actions are generally considered unethical.**

**Jane's peers are committing clearly unethical actions and Jane has recognized
this problem. She should gather her facts and document her case to whatever extent
she can. If Jane feels comfortable, she should personally confront her peers about their
ethical behavior. Otherwise, she should present the evidence to her boss, Joyce Logan,
and let her confront them (pp. 68–69).**

SUMMARY

This chapter discusses the importance that
ethics and organization politics play in the life of
the supervisor. It offers numerous guidelines to
assist supervisors in dealing with ethical questions and to enhance their understanding of organization politics.

1. *Define ethics and discuss what behaviors
   are considered unethical.* Ethics are
   standards or principles of conduct that
   govern the behavior of an individual or a
   group of individuals. Ethics are generally
   concerned with moral duties or with
   questions relating to what is right or
   wrong. Blaming or taking advantage
   of an innocent co-worker, divulging
   confidential information, falsifying
   reports, claiming credit for someone
   else's work, padding an expense account,
   and pilfering company materials and
   supplies are generally considered unethical
   behaviors.

2. *Discuss the role that supervisors play
   in setting the ethical tone of an
   organization.* As the final link between
   management and operative employees,
   supervisors play a major role in setting the
   ethical tone of the organization. Employees
   look to their supervisors for cues as to
   what is considered ethical behavior and
   what is not.

3. *Identify the major areas that require ethical
   conduct by supervisors.* Most of the areas
   requiring ethical conduct by supervisors can
   be grouped into three general categories:
   (1) loyalty, (2) human relations, and
   (3) overt personal actions.

4. *Outline the steps the supervisor should
   follow when dealing with a dishonest
   subordinate.* When dealing with a dishonest
   subordinate, the supervisor should
   (1) recognize the problem, get the facts,
   and document the case; (2) confront the
   employee; and (3) follow the established
   disciplinary system.

5. *Define organization politics.* Organization
   politics refer to the practice of using
   means other than merit or good
   performance for bettering your position or
   gaining favor in the organization. Because
   organization politics are a reality in
   organizations, supervisors should
   understand them and know how to use
   them in a positive and ethical manner.
   Organization politics include such things as
   trying to influence the boss, trying to gain
   power, and trying to gain a competitive edge
   over your peers.

6. *Recount several things that the supervisor
   can do to help keep the boss happy.* The
   supervisor can help keep the boss happy

by knowing the boss, being loyal to the boss, showing respect for the boss, making the boss look good, getting along with people in other departments, insisting on feedback from the boss so as to avoid mistakes, and taking some of the load off the boss.

7. *List five types of power.* Five types of power are: coercive, reward, legitimate, expert, and referent.

REVIEW QUESTIONS

1. What are ethics?
2. Give several examples of behaviors that most people would consider unethical.
3. What are codes of ethics, and why are they desirable?
4. What are three major areas that require ethical conduct by supervisors?
5. Define organization politics.
6. List several things that you can do to help keep your boss happy.
7. Briefly define the five major types of power.
8. What are some tactics that are often used to gain a competitive edge on peers?
9. Outline the basic guidelines that the supervisor should follow when socializing with superiors and subordinates.

SKILL-BUILDING QUESTIONS

1. Do you think that most people consider their personal ethical standards to be higher than those of their peers? Explain.
2. At a recent retirement party, a supervisor with 30 years of service boasted, "I've never played politics in my job." Do you think this is possible, and even if it is, do you think it is desirable?
3. Suppose your boss asked you to do something that you considered unethical. Would you do it? If not, how would you handle the situation?
4. What are your personal views regarding socializing with superiors? with subordinates?

REFERENCE

1. "Unethical Acts Rampant, U.S. Study Finds," *Worklife Report*, 1997, p. 18.
2. Adapted from Perry, Pascarella, "How Can I Keep the Boss Happy," *Industry Week*, October 3, 1975, pp. 38–39.

ADDITIONAL READINGS

"Walking the Line," *Health Care Supervisor*, March 1997.

Driscoll, Dawn-Marie, and W. Michael Hoffman. "Spot the Red Flags in Your Organization, *Workforce*, June 1997.

Ramsey, Robert D. "Are Ethics Obsolete in the 90s?" *Supervision*, February 1996.

SKILL-BUILDING APPLICATIONS

Incident 4–1

Additional Expenses?

Principals

Steve Logan—resident accounts supervisor for United Electric Company in Midland. Steve is 26 years old and is considered to have a bright future at United. He has been a supervisor for two months.

Jack Moore—district manager in Midland for United Electric. Jack is 41 and has been in his present job nine years. His district, Midland, has strong political influence in the company since the current president of United Electric was raised in Midland. Jack is Steve's boss.

Chester ("Chet") Orr—division manager for United. He is 61 years old and is located at company headquarters about 30 miles from Midland. Chet is Jack's boss and also a close personal friend of the president of United.

At 8:30 AM on Monday morning, Steve Logan was preparing to leave Jack Moore's office after planning the week's activities.

Steve: Oh, I almost forgot. As soon as I have my monthly expense voucher typed, I'll send it to you for signature so it can be forwarded to accounting.

Jack: I'm glad you mentioned that. I've been meaning to talk to you about your voucher this month. I have about $100 worth of items I want you to include on your voucher. My voucher is really loaded this month, and it would look bad to submit an extremely high amount—especially in light of the recent emphasis on personal expenses. It's really no big deal. Anyway, I'm the only one who has to sign it. When you get your check back, you can give me the extra $100. Here's an itemized list of my expenses that should be added to your expense report. Also, don't forget that we're supposed to go to lunch with Chet Orr today at 12 o'clock sharp.

Steve leaves Jack's office with the itemized list in his hand. During the morning, Steve gives

much thought to Jack's request. He doesn't like the idea, but Jack is the boss. At about 11 AM, Jack calls Steve on the intercom and says he can't make the lunch with Chet because the local congressman is making an unscheduled visit to the Midland office. Jack asks Steve to take Chet to lunch and give him his regrets and to tell Chet that he will see them after lunch around 2 PM. Chet shows up at noon, and he and Steve leave for lunch.

Questions

1. If you were Steve, would you say anything to Chet about Jack's request? Why or why not?
2. How would you handle the situation with Jack if you were Steve?

Incident 4–2

The Date

Jim's Perceptions

It's been almost six months since Jim came to work at the downtown branch as an assistant branch manager for the First National Bank. Over this time period Jim has become fed up with the whole place. In his college days and during the period when he served as a supervisory trainee, things were a lot better. He was meeting new people and learning new things. Also, he didn't have to take "orders" from anyone.

However, since he worked at the downtown branch things have gone downhill from Jim's perspective. Jim thinks that his branch manager, Louise, takes herself and her work too seriously. Jim also believes that she goes out of her way to pick on him and that she assigns him menial jobs from time to time.

On several occasions when Louise has seen Jim having lunch with the tellers, she asked him "not to be too friendly toward them since you're now in supervision." She stated that Jim should be more "professional."

A few minutes ago Louise asked Jim to meet with her at 1 o'clock. During lunch break, the head teller informed Jim that this morning Louise had overheard some of the tellers say that he was out on a date with Patty—the newest teller—the previous evening.

Louise's Perceptions

Ever since Jim arrived—about six months ago—Louise has been concerned about his attitude. Given his excellent academic record and his apparent intelligence, Louise is very surprised about his job performance. She can find no fault with the quantity or quality of Jim's work, but does find fault with his entire attitude and professionalism. This morning, for example, Louise found out that Jim was out on a date last night with Patty, the newest teller.

It is now 1 o'clock and Jim is entering Louise's office.

Questions

1. What do you think Louise should say to Jim?
2. Do you think that it is unethical for Jim to date a teller? Why or why not?

Exercise 4–1

Where Do You Stand?

Read the following descriptions, and then decide how you would respond to each of the situations described. Be prepared to justify your position in a class discussion.

Situation 1: Family versus Ethics*

Jim, a 56-year-old supervisor with children in college, discovers that the owners of his company are cheating the government out of several thousand dollars a year in taxes. Jim is the only employee in a position to know this. Should Jim report the owners to the Internal Revenue Service at the risk of endangering his family's livelihood, or should he disregard the discovery in order to protect his family's livelihood?

Situation 2: The Roundabout Raise

When Mary asks for a raise, her boss praises her work but says that the company's rigid budget won't allow any further merit raises for the time being. Instead, her boss suggests that the company "won't look too closely at your expense accounts for a while." Should Mary take this as authorization to pad her expense account on the ground that she would simply be getting the money that she deserves through a different route, or should she ignore this opportunity to obtain a "roundabout raise"?

Situation 3: The Faked Degree

Bill has done a sound job for over a year, but his boss learns that he got the job by claiming to have a college degree, although he actually never graduated. Should the boss dismiss him for submitting a fraudulent résumé, or should the boss overlook the false claim since Bill has otherwise proved conscientious and honorable and since making an issue of the degree might ruin Bill's career?

Situation 4: Sneaking Phone Calls

Helen discovers that a fellow employee regularly makes about $100 a month worth of personal long-distance telephone calls from an office telephone. Should Helen report the employee to the company or disregard the calls on the grounds that many people make personal calls at the office?

Situation 5: Cover-Up Temptation

Bill discovers that the chemical plant in which he works as supervisor is creating slightly more water pollution in a nearby lake than is legally permitted. Revealing the problem will bring considerable unfavorable publicity to the plant, hurt the lakeside town's resort business, and create a scare in the community. Solving the problem will cost Bill's company well over $100,000. Outsiders are unlikely to discover the problem. The violation poses no danger to people; at most, it will endanger a small number of fish. Should Bill reveal the problem despite the cost to his company, or should he view the problem as little more than a technicality and disregard it?

Situation 6: E-Mail Messages

Juan, a recent college graduate, spends about an hour a day writing E-mail messages to his college classmates. In spite of this practice, Juan's performance is at least average if not better. Should Juan's boss, Ruth, confront Juan about his misuse of company time?

*These situations are adapted from Roger Richles, "Executives Apply Stiffer Standards than Public to Ethical Dilemmas," *The Wall Street Journal*, November 3, 1983, p. 33.

Exercise 4–2

Evaluate Your Ethics

How will you act in situations that test your honesty and acceptance of rules, regulations, and codes of behavior?

That depends on the values you use to frame your approach to life and to work, says Paul Mok, president of Training Associates, a consulting firm.

Mok, with a doctorate in psychology and 20 years' experience advising corporations, says that most of us operate from one or more of four basic value sets, which are especially apt to surface during stress. He contends the key to predicting how someone will react under ethical pressure is discovering what his or her dominant values are. Mok developed a test, called SPOT (Situational Perceptions–Observations Test), to help in that discovery. Here is a sample from that test.

To identify your dominant value set(s) assign the numbers 4, 3, 2, and 1 to each set of four phrases that are shown to complete the eight self-descriptive statements below. Use 4 for the response that best describes you; 3, next most like you; 2, next; and 1, least like you.

1. In relating to a boss, I may:
   a. Express a lack of concern if a lack of concern is expressed to me.(S)
   b. Convey impatience with ideas that involve departures from procedures.(R)
   c. Show little interest in thoughts and ideas that show little or no originality or understanding of the company.(I)
   d. Tend to get impatient with lengthy explanations and direct my attention to what needs to be done right now.(C)

2. When circumstances prevent me from doing what I want, I find it most useful to:
   a. Review any roadblocks and figure out how I can get around them.(C)
   b. Rethink all that has happened and develop a new idea, approach, or view of my job.(I)
   c. Keep in mind the basics, pinpoint the key obstacles, and modify my game plan accordingly.(R)
   d. Analyze the motivations of others and develop a new "feel" for those around me.(S)

3. If I must deal with an unpleasant customer, I would probably try to:
   a. Clarify the problem and explore the alternatives.(R)
   b. Highlight in plain language what I want, need, or expect the customer to do.(C)
   c. Explain the "big picture" and how the situation relates to it.(I)
   d. Express empathy by putting myself in his or her shoes.(S)

4. In terms of things like personal phone calls on the job, a company should probably:
   a. Be understanding of the employees if they don't overdo it.(S)
   b. Make the rules clear and see that employees follow them.(R)
   c. Do what is best for company profits.(C)
   d. Explore company policies that are consistent with personal needs.(I)

5. If a friend told me he was "padding" the expense account for $10, I would probably:
   a. Advise the person not to; that he or she is stealing and should not do it.(R)
   b. Figure this is common practice even if it isn't right.(I)
   c. Figure each person is trying to survive the best he can.(C)
   d. Try not to be judgmental and see if I could help.(S)

6. If I have done something that goes against company policy and procedures, I probably:
   a. Would have done so to help others in the company.(S)
   b. Would be upset and need to reexamine my actions.(R)
   c. Would have done so to get results in the most practical way.(C)
   d. Would consider how the policies and procedures could be modified in the future.(I)

7. When I start a new job, I feel it is preferable to:
   a. Learn what is expected—what the rules are—and follow them.(R)
   b. See where the company is and what its orientation really is.(I)
   c. Make a name for myself based on competitive results.(C)
   d. Make friends and show I am a "regular" person.(S)

8. When co-workers take shortcuts, my actions will probably depend on:
   a. Whether the co-workers are good friends or not.(S)
   b. Whether they knew the rules; if they didn't, I would explain them.(R)
   c. Whether their actions would hurt me and my department.(C)
   d. Whether such shortcuts would significantly affect results.(I)

After each statement is a letter—S, R, I, or C. Make a column for each of the four letters, place your numbers (1 to 4) for each statement in the appropriate column, and total the figures. The category in which you scored highest corresponds to your primary value set; the second highest score shows your back-up system.

▪ **S:** Socially oriented values are characterized by deep concern for the welfare of others. Someone meeting this profile might not see a conflict in stealing company resources to help indigent people.

▪ **R:** Rational values center on commitment to rules and regulations. A rationalist might be indecisive in a crisis not covered by specific rules or procedures.

▪ **I:** Individualistic values are expressed in autonomous thinking and the belief that people should evaluate rules rather than obey them blindly. Under stress, an individualist may become rigid and dogmatic, ignoring others and putting his or her cause above the established codes.

▪ **C:** Competitive values are typical of someone motivated by the desire "to win the game." If this means bending the rules or cutting corners, so be it.

Source: Reprinted by permission, *Nation's Business,* August 1987. Copyright 1987. U.S. Chamber of Commerce.

CHAPTER 5

Managing Your Time

LEARNING OBJECTIVES

After studying this chapter, you should be able to:

1. Identify several common time wasters.

2. Analyze how you actually spend your time on the job.

3. Discuss how to plan your time.

4. Discuss how to optimize your work routine.

5. Identify several areas that typically have a high potential for better time utilization.

6. Discuss the importance of "think time."

SUPERVISION
DILEMMA

Although he has been in his supervisory job for only a relatively short time, John Harris is beginning to feel that there are not enough hours in the day. Meetings, paperwork, unscheduled visitors, and telephone calls seem to take up his entire day. Furthermore, rushing from one thing to another leaves John totally exhausted at the end of the day. He has also noticed that he is becoming much more irritable at home.

John recently observed one of his fellow supervisors preparing a "to do" list for the next day's activities. John wondered if he should be making a similar list and if there were any other techniques or tips that he should know about.

All of a supervisor's work is performed within time constraints. A supervisor may know the best way to handle a particular situation but may not have the time to do all that is necessary. No matter how knowledgeable and motivated supervisors are, their ability to manage time affects how successful they will be.

TYPICAL TIME WASTERS

1   LEARNING OBJECTIVES

Time is wasted in numerous ways. The following are some of the more common ways in which supervisors waste time:

- Telephone interruptions.
- Visitors dropping in without appointments.
- Meetings, both scheduled and unscheduled.
- Reading nonessential E-mail.
- Crisis situations for which no plans were possible.
- Lack of objectives, priorities, deadlines.
- Cluttered desk and personal disorganization.
- Involvement in routine and detail that should be handled by others.
- Attempting too much at once and underestimating the time it takes to do it.
- Failure to set up clear lines of authority and responsibility.
- Inadequate, inaccurate, or delayed information from others.
- Indecision and procrastination.
- Lack of, or unclear, communication and instruction.
- Inability to say no.
- Lack of standards and progress reports that enable the supervisor to keep track of developments.
- Fatigue.

Obviously, not all of these time wasters can be eliminated. However, many of them can be either eliminated or reduced by applying sound supervisory practices. This chapter offers suggestions for eliminating some of these typical time wasters and for becoming a better manager of time.

UNDERSTANDING YOUR JOB

The ability to manage time makes any job easier, improves performance on the job, and reduces on-the-job stress. Higher levels of management often recognize this ability as a reason for advancement.

To manage time effectively, a supervisor must first have a thorough understanding of exactly what he or she is expected to do. Have you ever known a supervisor who spent an inordinate amount of time performing all the wrong tasks? As elementary as this may seem, a great many supervisors do not have a clear picture of what is expected of them. Numerous studies have shown that employees and their bosses often have a different understanding of the employee's job. Because of this, people often expend considerable time and effort performing a host of related and/or inconsequential tasks that are neither required nor appreciated by the boss. How much more effective it would be to channel that time and energy accomplishing tasks that had been mutually determined by you and your boss. A good suggestion is for every supervisor and his or her boss periodically (at least once per year) to outline in writing what each perceives to be the major expectations of the supervisor's job. After each party has written down his or her expectations of the job, these lists should be exchanged and then discussed. Following this procedure should make it easier to reach a mutual agreement concerning the basic job expectations. The results of this process should then be reflected in the written job description of the supervisor's job.

Resolving any misunderstandings that surface here can reduce the possibility of conflict and can result in time savings. Once supervisors have a clear understanding of their job duties they should attempt to use time as efficiently as possible in carrying them out.

ANALYZING YOUR TIME

2 LEARNING OBJECTIVES

To manage time efficiently and effectively, supervisors must first have a clear understanding of exactly how their time is being spent. Then they can establish priorities for the various tasks and duties that make up their jobs, strive to improve their work habits, and eliminate needless effort.

A time inventory is the same thing as a time budget. Analyzing the workday to see how time is being spent is as sensible as analyzing expenditures to see how money is being spent. In preparing a budget, one often discovers that money is being wasted on needless expenditures or low-priority items while important needs are being ignored. A similar discovery may be made when a time budget or inventory is prepared. Supervisors are often shocked to find that much of their time is being wasted or spent on low-priority items.

There are several ways to prepare a time inventory. One of the best ways is to keep a daily log. This log should briefly note each task you performed, the names of the other people who were directly involved in each task, and where the task was performed. It is best to make these log entries every few hours. If you wait until the end of the day, you may have trouble recalling everything that went on during the day. Figure 5.1 illustrates a very abbreviated example of a time caddy that can be used to prepare a time inventory. Feel free to

FIGURE 5.1

Time Caddy

Time	Monday	Tuesday	Wednesday	Thursday	Friday
8:00–9:00					
9:00–10:00					
10:00–11:00					
11:00–12:00					
Lunch					
1:00–2:00					
2:00–3:00					
3:00–4:00					
4:00–5:00					

design and use any form that captures the needed information. Do not attempt to analyze the data as you are recording them. The log should be kept over a period long enough to ensure that a representative sample of your use of time has been recorded. A two-week period is usually sufficient.

Naturally, you should try to pick a time period that you think will best reflect your normal duties. (For example, you would probably not want to use a period immediately following a vacation.) At the end of the recording period, you should carefully analyze the data to determine just how your time is being spent. A good approach is to divide the data into a manageable number of appropriate categories. Sample categories include telephone, meetings with subordinates, meetings with suppliers, office paperwork, and observing the work flow. Almost always, supervisors are surprised at how much or how little time they are spending in certain areas. From this analysis, they can identify changes they might want to make in allocating their time.

PLANNING YOUR TIME

3 LEARNING OBJECTIVES

Many successful supervisors make a daily "to do" list of things to be accomplished. The key to preparing an effective "to do" list is to get in the habit of preparing it at the same time each day—usually at the end of the preceding or beginning of the current day. When composing your list, don't concern yourself with priorities because this may restrict your thinking. First, simply record everything that needs to be done as the thoughts come to you. After you have exhausted this process, go back and prioritize the different tasks. The following scheme is useful for prioritizing different work activities:

Must do first	1
Must do	2
Desirable to do	3
Can wait	4

Table 5.1 gives an example of priority rankings. After you have inventoried your time and prioritized your work activities, you can then schedule your day.

	Ranking	Activity
TABLE 5.1 Priority Setting of Work Activities	2	Read interoffice mail.
	4	Read brochures received through the mail.
	2	Answer interoffice mail.
	3	Read supervisory journal.
	3	Lunch.
	4	Personal telephone call.
	2	Telephone call to personnel department to check on an employee's vacation days.
	1	Schedule overtime for the weekend.
	2	Safety meeting with all subordinates.
	1	Grievance meeting in boss's office with grievant.
	4	Return a telephone call from an office machines salesperson.
	2	Prepare employee performance evaluation for an interview that is to be conducted in two weeks.

This involves more than simply superimposing your list on a time caddy or a personal planner. Among other things, consider your personal energy pattern and try to match your periods of peak effectiveness throughout the day with the degree of sensitivity or difficulty of the tasks to be performed. For example, your number-one priority may be a delicate negotiation requiring your peak mental abilities. If you are generally a slow starter in the mornings but build up momentum toward midday, you may want to arrange for that number-one priority negotiation at 10:00 or 11:00, rather than at 8:00 AM. Schedule tasks with somewhat lower priorities that require less demanding mental concentration at the earlier time. Supervision Illustration 5–1 provides some interesting information regarding the peak productive times of day for American employees.

In specifying more precisely *when* during the day you expect to perform each task, it is necessary to estimate the approximate amount of time required. This forces a degree of preliminary planning and organizing that helps overcome the inertia in getting a task started. Furthermore, the fact that a specific time has been assigned for each task throughout the day causes a supervisor to be more time conscious, and this seems to reinforce self-discipline.

Finally, a time caddy permits you to look a week ahead and reserve time for prior commitments. Thus, planning for each day's activities can take into account blocks of time previously committed, and thereby avoid future conflicts.

Many supervisors use a "follow-up" or "tickler" filing system to help manage their priorities. With such a system, issues are placed in a chronological file under the date that some future action needs to be taken. For example, if a certain letter needs to be sent out on the 15th of next month, a copy of the letter would be placed in a file that would be automatically reviewed on that date. Computer software programs are also available for helping

---

SUPERVISION ILLUSTRATION 5–1

PRODUCTIVITY PEAK

America's employees reach their peak of productivity in the middle of the morning, while they are least productive during the afternoon, according to a nationwide survey of leading corporations. The survey was initiated by Accountemps. Here are the results of the survey conducted for Accountemps by a major independent research firm:

Most Productive Time

Early morning	23%
Midmorning	66
Late morning	7
Early afternoon	1
Midafternoon	0
Late afternoon	0
Don't know	3

Least Productive Time

Early morning	10%
Midmorning	0
Late morning	0
Early afternoon	12
Midafternoon	6
Late afternoon	67
Don't know	5

"Management should view the substantial impact the time of day appears to have on employee productivity as a significant factor in planning and scheduling," said Accountemps vice president Robert Glass. The human resources directors of 100 of America's 1,000 largest corporations participated in the survey. Accountemps, which has 130 offices on three continents, is a division of Robert Half International Inc.

Source: Sanford Teller Communications, *Supervision,* September 1988, p. 11. For more information about Accountemps, visit its Web site at: **www.accountemps.com**

---

manage time priorities. Software programs designed to help manage individual time priorities and personal business are known as personal information managers (PIMs). Supervision Illustration 5–2 provides more information about PIMs.

OPTIMIZING YOUR WORK ROUTINE

4   LEARNING OBJECTIVES

As you try to implement your work schedule, you may note a pattern of failures to meet the schedule. The pattern may provide a clue as to the source of the trouble or the disruption responsible for the failures. For example, Don Gorecki blocks off an hour each morning from 10:00 to 11:00 for answering the mail, but after numerous attempts to dictate replies to correspondence, finds that he invariably ends up doing most of the task after everyone has gone home and the telephone quits ringing. By that time, however, his secretary has also left and the dictaphone tape has to wait until the next day before any transcription can be accomplished. In fact, it isn't until the next day's mail arrives that replies to the previous day's mail are sent out. By then, Don is running at least a day behind.

In studying his dilemma, Don decides to carve out for himself a quiet hour each day—the time between 10:00 and 11:00 AM. During this time, he asks not to be disturbed except for emergencies. He would never ask his secretary to lie by telling people he is not in, but simply instructs her to say, "I'm sorry but Mr. Gorecki is tied up right now. Can he call you back within the hour?" Most

---

SUPERVISION ILLUSTRATION 5–2

PERSONAL INFORMATION MANAGERS

Personal information managers (PIMs) allow users to do all their organizing right on the screen of their personal computer; some can even be linked to handheld computers. The basic features of most PIM programs include (1) a computerized Rolodex, date book, notepad, time sheet, and expense form; (2) electronic mail or messaging systems; and (3) tickler files to alert the user of meeting times and client follow-ups.

Recently the basic capabilities of PIMs have been expanded so that users can share their calendars over the World Wide Web with co-workers around the globe.

Other trends include auto-fill features to make data entry faster and easier, calling number identification support for instant contact information on incoming calls, and better links to electronic organizers. The most important aspect when selecting any PIM is matching it to the way you work; if you don't use it, even the fanciest is worthless.

Some of the software companies that have PIMs include Microsoft Corporation, Lotus Development Corporation, Symantec, MicroLogic, Janna Contact, Maximizer Technologies, and Now Software.

Sources: "Getting Organized", *Fortune: Technology Buyer's Guide Supplement,* Winter 1997, pp. 112–13; "What's New in Organizers," *Fortune: Technology Buyer's Guide Supplement,* Winter 1997, pp. 114–16. For more information about *Fortune* magazine, visit its Web site at: **www.fortune.com**

people, including the boss, will generally accept this response if Don is conscientious and develops a reputation for returning those calls as promised. The secretary soon learns to arrange notices of telephone calls in the order of priority for return, not necessarily in chronological order of receipt. The boss, for example, may have been the last to call but the secretary senses from the tone of his voice that he should be the first to be called back. During this quiet hour, Don is virtually uninterrupted in dictating replies to incoming correspondence; by 11:00 he gives the tape to his secretary, who transcribes it and has the letters back to him for signature and in the mail before the close of business that day.

Similar situations may be obvious, as you periodically check to see whether you might combine compatible activities, such as those with similar physical locations or similar routines. In this way you can save time—by working more wisely instead of just longer or harder.

ESTABLISHING GOOD WORK HABITS

When one stops to consider the letters, reports, memos, telephone calls, meetings, visitors, and reading material that the average supervisor is faced with each day, it is not hard to see that he or she could spend the entire day on communication alone. Communication is an important part of the supervisor's job. Still, there are many ways in which a supervisor can manage the time spent on the communication process.

5 LEARNING OBJECTIVES

Paperwork.   It is rare when a supervisor is not swamped with paperwork. Most supervisors must keep certain employee records, prepare or assist in preparing various reports, write letters and memos, and stay current by reading newsletters, magazines, and trade journals.

One suggestion for dealing with paperwork is to categorize it as you go through it. Basically, there are three classes of paperwork:

1. Requires action by the supervisor.
2. Needs reading, passing on to someone else, or filing.
3. Needs to be discarded.

Class 3 can be discarded and the paper can be recycled immediately. Classes 1 and 2 must be handled more carefully, but there are also effective means of dealing with such items. A goal is to handle each piece of paper only once; do not set it aside until you have completed the necessary action. When it is not possible to complete the necessary action, such as with a very large task, at least take some action before putting the paper aside.

Letters and memos.   Letters and memos are the most common types of communication requiring action by the supervisor. As suggested in the previous section, action should be taken on a letter without putting the letter down. Handwritten responses on the bottom of a letter are usually acceptable. Use form letters for responses whenever possible. Use E-mail. Send E-mail messages only to those with a definite need; sending E-mail messages to everyone wastes the time of individuals who must read and discard these messages.

If you have a secretary, consider the use of a dictating machine. Giving dictation directly to your secretary wastes time because it ties up two people at the same time on the same letter or memo. Furthermore, many letters and memos can be answered directly by your secretary if the secretary has enough information. Delegating the authority to answer certain letters and memos increases a secretary's job scope and can be a source of motivation to the secretary. Learn to view your secretary as your business partner and not as your servant! Finally, you can often use the phone instead of sending a letter.

Report writing.   Many of the suggestions for handling letters and memos also apply to report writing. Plan the report completely before you start writing. Use a word processor or a dictating machine whenever possible. Keep the report as short as possible while covering the material that needs to be covered. Also, write the report for the reader. Big words and long sentences may impress the reader but may not get the message across.

Filing.   Almost everyone has computer files or a filing cabinet full of material that will never be looked at again. Knowing what to save and what to throw away is not easy. When deciding whether something should be filed, answer the following questions:

1. Is this on my "useful filing" list?
2. How can I get this information if I ever need it and it isn't in my files?
3. How (exactly) am I going to use this piece of paper within the next 12 months?[1]

After answering these questions, the supervisor can better decide whether to file something. If the information can easily be recaptured and the supervisor does not anticipate using the information in the intermediate future, it should ordinarily be discarded. Filing unneeded documents clutters up files and makes

Plan a report completely before you start writing.
Jim Whitmer/FPG International

it harder to locate needed documents. One additional suggestion is to go through and clean out the files at least once a year. Throw away material that you haven't used during the year.

Reading material.   We all have a stack of reading material that we intend to read "one of these days." Unfortunately, that day never comes, and the stack just gets higher and higher. One way to lessen this problem is to improve your reading skills. If your organization offers a seminar on reading skills, ask to attend it. Also, many local colleges and universities offer courses to help improve reading skills.

Another suggestion for handling reading materials is to scan the table of contents or the major headings. If either one of these looks interesting, you might read some or all of the material. Otherwise, you should probably throw it away.

Meetings.   Effective ways of handling meetings were discussed in Chapter 3. Important points that should be reemphasized here are that all unnecessary meetings should be discouraged and that supervisors should not allow their time to be wasted by others during meetings. Whether conducting a meeting or merely attending, make sure that the agenda is followed and that discussions relate to the topic.

Telephone.   The telephone can either save or waste a lot of time. Too many supervisors allow the telephone to run their day. If you have a secretary, have the secretary hold your calls when you are attending an important meeting or

TABLE 5.2 Tips for Better Time Utilization with the Telephone	1. Be available for outside calls only at certain times.
	2. Bunch your outgoing calls to avoid interrupting yourself.
	3. Place outgoing calls according to the other person's best times.
	4. Develop an awareness of long-winded calls and learn to get off.
	5. Have an agenda ready before making a call.
	6. Hang up on hold calls for another party.
	7. Where possible, have someone screen your calls.
	8. Use conference calls when feasible.

working on an important problem. When you are on the phone for business reasons, realize that the time of two people is being tied up. Be polite, but make your point and get off the phone. Nothing is wrong with telling a caller in a polite manner that you have to get off the phone. Table 5.2 lists these and several other tips to help you manage your telephone time. Supervision Illustration 5–3 provides some interesting facts regarding American executives and their use of the telephone.

Visitors.   Supervisors often have expected and unexpected visitors. Salespeople are a common example. Visitors can monopolize precious time. One time saver here is to establish a policy of seeing only visitors who have made an appointment. Let the scheduled visitor know how much time you have allowed for that visit. Then stick to that time. If visitors you don't want to see do get to you, don't let them seat themselves comfortably in your office. As soon as you see them coming, get up and meet them at your door. Talk to them standing up. This communicates that you don't expect the visit to last long. Table 5.3 summarizes several tips for managing visitor interruptions.

Procrastination.   Two primary causes of procrastination by supervisors are complexity and fear. Supervisors are often overwhelmed by projects that seem complex, because they just don't know where to start. Fear causes procrastination when a supervisor must deal with an unpleasant task, such as disciplining an employee. All too often, supervisors think that a huge block of time must be available to them before they start work on a complex project. The key is to break the project down into smaller tasks and then to get started on these smaller tasks. When this occurs, most supervisors find that the project appears far less overwhelming.

Because valuable time and energy are often wasted by jumping from project to project, supervisors should use deadlines. These provide wanted and needed targets and assist in getting the work accomplished. Such tasks as work orders and reports carry their own deadlines, but others do not. Supervisors should assign dates for the completion of those that don't. This helps supervisors to schedule time better and to accomplish all projects on a timely basis.

SUPERVISION ILLUSTRATION 5–3

Wasted Telephone Time

Recent information shows that American executives are wasting at least four workweeks each year on unproductive or unnecessary telephone calls. That's the finding of a nationwide survey developed by Motivational Systems, a corporate management development and sales training organization. The survey was conducted among vice presidents of 200 of the nation's 1,000 largest corporations.

When asked: "What percent of the average executive's working day is spent on the telephone?" the answer was an overall average of 29 percent. Based on a nine-hour executive workday, this translates to 14.5 full weeks on the phone each year. The respondents were also asked: "What percent of the time that executives spend on the telephone

is wasted or unproductive?" The average answer was 28 percent. Twenty-eight percent of 14.5 weeks equals slightly over four full weeks that are spent on wasted or unproductive calls each year by the average executive!

Furthermore, in another survey conducted in 1993 by Officeteam, a division of Robert Half International Inc., it was discovered that American executives waste an average of an additional 15 minutes per day on hold, resulting in two more weeks per year that an executive wastes on the telephone. Even though an executive may have little or no control over being placed on hold, this time can be used productively, e.g., organizing files, writing "to do" lists, or cleaning up the work area.

Source: Sanford Teller Communications, "Executives Waste One Month a Year on Telephone Calls," *Supervision,* May 1990, p. 12; Jennifer L. Laabs, "Executives on Hold," *Personnel Journal,* February 1994, pp. 18, 20. For more information about Motivational Systems, visit its Web site at: **www.msitrain.com**

TABLE 5.3

Tips for Handling Visitor Interruptions

1. Set time limits for visits and stick to them.
2. Set the agenda early in the conversation.
3. Meet visitors outside your door.
4. Confer while standing.
5. Do not place chairs in your office so that they are inviting to people passing by.
6. Do not place items such as candy dishes on your desk as they invite visitors.
7. If a visitor becomes seated, get up from your seat to signal the end of the conversation.
8. Where feasible, have someone screen visitors.
9. Use the conference room or the other person's office so you can leave when you wish.
10. Reserve certain hours for visitors.

The tendency is to hope that unpleasant tasks will go away. Unfortunately, they generally don't go away and they often get worse if you try to avoid them. It is usually much better to deal with an unpleasant task than to try to avoid it.

Delegating work.   Proper delegation is a major key to the supervisor's effective use of time. Doing work that a subordinate should handle is a most serious time waster of supervisors. Delegation frees a supervisor to perform the more important tasks of supervision. It also teaches subordinates to think for themselves, to make decisions, and to function effectively. Because of its importance, delegation is covered extensively in Chapter 7.

THINK TIME

LEARNING OBJECTIVES

Thinking is a natural human activity. The secret of doing something well is to spend some quiet time thinking about it. Supervisors should reserve a fixed place and time for thinking. This helps ensure that time to think has priority. To begin your thinking time, scan the areas you deal with. Give preference to those areas that you feel have some potential for improvement. Make no attempt to find the solution or improvement at this stage. It may come later—either spontaneously or after concentration. During this initial stage, you should merely try to identify the areas. Next, select an area that needs improvement. Concentrate on this area. Look into various elements of this area without being concerned about whether the solutions that occur to you are feasible. Jot down your thoughts and ideas. If no solution is forthcoming, proceed to the next identified area and repeat the process for that area. You will find that ideas for solutions in one area trigger ideas for solutions in another area. Out of all this, tentative answers will emerge. They may result from logical handling of your thoughts and ideas, but more likely they will emerge when you least expect them—early in the morning when you arise, late at night while you are listening to music, or while you are watching a sporting event. Thinking helps achieve solutions to problems that would not be possible otherwise.

SOLUTION TO THE
SUPERVISION
DILEMMA

John, like most supervisors, is experiencing the frustrations that result from interruptions of a planned work schedule. Meetings, paperwork, uninvited visitors, and telephone calls can all disrupt a schedule. John should now have a heightened awareness of the requirements for time management, and this in itself should be helpful to him. As a start, he should analyze how he spends his work time by keeping a daily log for a couple of weeks (pp. 81–82). Then he should analyze the data he has gathered and determine the areas in which he is spending too much time and those in which he is not spending enough time. On this basis, he should make the necessary adjustments in his work schedule (pp. 82–84). He should also attempt to implement many of the time management tips discussed on pages 85–90.

⌐ SUMMARY

This chapter introduces and discusses the topic of time management. It presents several tips for managing your time and improving your work habits.

1. *Identify several common time wasters.* The following are some of the more common ways in which time is wasted: telephone interruptions; visitors dropping in without appointments; unproductive meetings; reading nonessential E-mail; unnecessary crisis situations; lack of objectives, priorities, and deadlines; personal disorganization; overinvolvement in routine matters; attempting too much at once and underestimating the time it takes to do it; unclear lines of responsibility and authority; inadequate, inaccurate, or delayed information from others; indecision and procrastination; unclear communication; inability to say no; lack of standards and progress reports; and fatigue.

2. *Analyze how you actually spend your time on the job.* One of the best ways to analyze how you spend your time is to keep a daily log for two weeks. Every few hours, you should briefly note each task that you performed, the names of the people who were directly involved in the task, and where the task was performed. At the end of the data collection period, you should carefully analyze the data and compare your findings with the requirements of the job. You will probably discover that you are spending too much time in some areas and not enough in others.

3. *Discuss how to plan your time.* One key to preparing your time is to use a daily "to do" list. A daily "to do" list should be prepared at

the same time each day, usually at the end or beginning of the day. When composing the list, don't be concerned with priorities, but record the activities as they come. After you have exhausted this process, go back and prioritize each activity. The next step is to superimpose your prioritized list on a time caddy. This step requires you to estimate how long each task will take and to specify when during the day you expect to perform each task.

4. *Discuss how to optimize your work routine.* A good way to improve your work routine is to notice any patterns of failure that might be regularly occurring (for example, you are continually late in getting your correspondence out). Once you become aware of these patterns, you can then look for ways to combine compatible activities and thus save time.

5. *Identify several areas that typically have a high potential for better time utilization.* The following areas typically have a high potential for better time management: (1) handling paperwork; (2) writing letters, memos, and reports; (3) filing; (4) dealing with reading material; (5) handling meetings; (6) managing the telephone; (7) dealing with visitors; (8) overcoming the natural tendency to procrastinate; and (9) delegating work.

6. *Discuss the importance of "think time."* One secret of doing something well is to spend some quiet time thinking about it. Because "think time" is not built into the schedules of most supervisors, they should reserve for themselves a fixed place and time for thinking.

REVIEW QUESTIONS

1. Name several of the most frequently encountered time wasters.
2. What is a time inventory?
3. What factors should be covered in a daily time log?
4. What is a "to do" list?
5. Describe a scheme for prioritizing activities on a "to do" list.
6. Identify three classes of paperwork.
7. What questions should be answered in determining whether to file a report or letter?
8. Give some guidelines for better time utilization of the telephone.
9. List several tips for handling visitor interruptions.

SKILL-BUILDING QUESTIONS

1. "My boss determines how I spend my time, and I don't really have much control over it." Discuss how you feel about this.
2. "The problem with time management is that you never know when a crisis is going to occur." How would you respond to this statement?
3. Respond to the following statement: "If I could just get rid of my telephone, I would not have any problems managing my time."
4. Suppose that the most productive time of your boss is early morning and that this is your least productive time. What problems might this cause you? How might you deal with these problems? Can you think of any opportunities that this situation might present?

REFERENCE

1. Donna Niksch Douglas and Merrill E. Douglas, "Timely Techniques for Paperwork Mania," *Personnel Administrator*, September 1979, p. 21.

ADDITIONAL READINGS

Farrant, Don. "A New Look at Time Leaks," *Supervision*, May 1997.

Reynolds, James E. "The 10 Best Tools for Organizing Your Life (at Last)!" *Money*, August 1997.

Van de Vliet, Anita. "Beat the Time Bandits," *Management Today*, May 1997.

SKILL-BUILDING APPLICATIONS

Incident 5–1

Not Enough Time

Bill Thompson, supervisor of the computer data processing center, was involved in a minor car accident this morning and arrived 25 minutes late for work. As he entered his office, the telephone rang. It was Lewis Wiley, head of cost accounting, who said that there must have been some error in processing the last cost data since what he received yesterday afternoon makes no sense. He asked Bill to check into the matter and call him back.

While Bill was talking with Wiley, Bruce White, head of quality control, walked into his office. As soon as the telephone conversation ended, Bruce asked, "When am I going to get the quality reports for last week? I know you're busy, but the reports were due day before yesterday. I need them because we're having trouble in assembly." Bill said that the reports should be ready. He asked Bruce to wait a minute and walked out to the processing area, looking for his assistant, Clifford Sommer. Not seeing Cliff, he asked a programmer where Cliff was. "Haven't seen him, Mr. Thompson." Bill asked, "Have the quality reports for last week been finished?" The programmer replied, "I don't know; Martha would know. I'll ask her for you." "Good, let me know right away. I'll be in my office." Several minutes later, Martha entered Bill's office and reported that the quality reports had not been processed yet. Bill then told Bruce that he would gather the data and get it on the computer right away. "I'll see that you get the reports this afternoon," he promised.

Bill started to prepare the data for running the quality reports. After spending nearly an hour searching through stacks of papers and cards, he had the data lined up fairly well. He was then interrupted by a telephone call from the receptionist: "A Mr. Elmer McCall from Eureka Computer Company is here to see you. He said he has an appointment at 12:00 noon for lunch." "An appointment with me at 12:00," said Bill as he fingered his calendar but found no note of any such appointment. "Well, tell him I can't see him for 20 minutes or so." Bill returned to work on the quality reports, got them ready to run, and then turned the job over to the computer group leader with instructions to process the reports that afternoon and deliver them in person to Bruce White.

The visit with McCall was social. McCall simply wanted to know if everything was working OK with the Eureka installation. Upon Bill's return to the office about 2:10 PM, a telephone call reminded him that the production committee meeting was in process and asked whether he was coming right over to it. "Yes, I'm on the way now," replied Bill. Actually, he had forgotten about the meeting. It lasted till 4:00 PM; Bill was drowsy and thought it quite dull. On the way back to his office, Bill stopped to ask Bruce if he had received the quality reports. "Not yet," Bruce replied. Bill hurried back to his office to expedite work on the reports.

Questions

1. In your opinion, what is Bill's difficulty?
2. What suggestions do you feel are in order for Bill? Discuss.

Incident 5–2

Plan for a Day

Frances S. Russell is assistant general manager and sales manager for Webb Enterprises. At the moment, this self-styled perfectionist is sitting up in bed, checking her TTD (things to do) sheet for tomorrow. The TTD itemizes her daily activities, placing them on an exact time schedule. Never one to browbeat subordinates, Russell has her own special way of reminding people that time is money. Ever since the days when she was the best salesperson the company ever had, she had worked harder than the rest. It had paid off, too, because in only two years (when old Charlie retired), she was the heir apparent to the general managership. As this thought crossed Russell's mind, her immediate pride was replaced with a nagging problem. Where was she going to find the time to do all the things her position required? She certainly couldn't afford to just maintain the status quo. Then her mind forced her to plan tomorrow's activities and the problem was pushed into the background for future consideration. (Following is a portion of Russell's well-planned day.)

TTD—OCTOBER 16th

7:15   Breakfast with Johnson (Purchasing). Get information on his cataloging system. Maybe combine with sales department and avoid duplication.

8:30   Meeting with Julie (asst. sales manager). Tell her exactly how the sales meeting for out-of-state representatives should be conducted. Caution—she's shaky on questions.

9:15   Discuss progress on new office procedures manual with Charlie (general manager). (He's irritated because I've dragged my heels on this. Let him know I've got Newman working on the problem.)

9:45   Assign Pat Newman the job of collecting data (and sample copies) regarding office manuals in other companies in our industry. Set up a system for her to use in analysis.

10:45   Call on Acliff Printing. A potentially big customer. [As Russell jotted down some information on this client, she reflected that it was a shame no one else on her staff could really handle the big ones the way she could. This thought was pleasing and bothersome at the same time.]

12:00   Lunch with J. Acliff (reservations at Black Angus).

3:00   Meet with Frank Lentz (advertising assistant) and check his progress on the new sales campaign. [Russell thought about Lentz's usual wild ideas and hoped that he had followed the general theme and rough sketches she had prepared.]

7:30   Chamber of Commerce meeting. (Look up Pierce Hansen—he may be able to help on the Acliff account.)

Questions

1. What problems do you see concerning Russell's effectiveness as a manager?

2. Assuming you were Charlie, the general manager, what solutions would you recommend?

Exercise 5–1

Are You Using Your Time Effectively?

Take no more than 10 minutes to answer the following 10 questions. Answer each question carefully, and be prepared to argue in favor of your response. Your instructor will tell you how to score your responses.

	True	False
1. It's best to begin work with the task that worries you most.	____	____
2. A good way to accomplish more is to do two jobs at once (e.g., sign letters and take phone calls).	____	____
3. Answer correspondence by giving your ideas to your assistants. Let them write the letters.	____	____
4. Invite visitors to sit down in a chair on the opposite side of your desk.	____	____
5. The best way to handle "in-basket" material is to sort it so you can do the most important jobs first.	____	____
6. After delegating a job to a subordinate, check with him/her frequently on progress.	____	____
7. It's discourteous to refuse to take phone calls.	____	____

8. Don't review routine reports. Give this job to an assistant. ____ ____

9. It's useless and time-consuming to write a plan for your day's activities. ____ ____

10. Schedule regular staff meetings to discuss common business. ____ ____

Source: Ted Pollock, "A Personal File of Stimulating Ideas and Problem Solvers," *Supervision*, May 1991, p. 24. Reprinted by permission of *Supervision*, The National Research Bureau, Inc., 424 North Third St., Burlington, Iowa 52601–5224.

Exercise 5–2

Time Trap Identification

Identify and list all those activities that you feel currently consume inordinate portions of your time. Consider primarily repetitive activities. You should be able to develop a list of at least five or more activities.

After identifying your time traps, *rank* them in the order of their significance to you.

Select the three most significant time traps and list them on a clean sheet of paper. Then indicate what specific actions you might take to overcome each of these traps. For each suggested action, list any problems that you think might be encountered. Why do you think that you have not previously implemented these actions?

Exercise 5–3

Time Management Assumptions

The following list contains 10 common assumptions concerning time management. Check whether you believe each statement is true or false. Be honest with yourself!

	True	False
1. If you really look, you can probably find many ways to save time.	____	____
2. Being busy and active is the best way to get the most done.	____	____
3. Time problems can usually be solved by working harder.	____	____
4. "If you want it done right, you'd better do it yourself" is still the best advice.	____	____
5. Finding the problem is easy—it's finding the solution that is difficult.	____	____
6. Most of the ordinary day-to-day activities don't need to be planned—and you probably can't plan them anyway.	____	____
7. Managers who concentrate on doing things efficiently are also the most effective managers.	____	____
8. A good way to reduce time waste is to look for shortcuts in managerial functions.	____	____
9. Managing time better is essentially a matter of reducing the time it takes to accomplish various tasks.	____	____
10. No one ever has enough time.	____	____

Source: This exercise is adopted from Merrill E. Douglass, "Test Your Assumptions about Time Management," *The Personnel Administrator*, November 1976, pp. 12–15.

Planning and Organizing Skills

SECTION OUTLINE

6 Supervisory planning

7 Organizing and delegating

8 Understanding work groups

9 Productivity and methods improvement

CHAPTER 6

Supervisory Planning

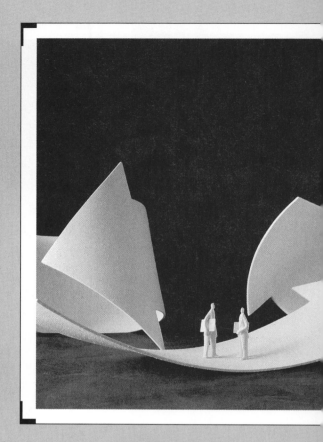

LEARNING OBJECTIVES

After studying this chapter, you should be able to:

1. Describe how an organization plans.

2. Describe the supervisor's role in the overall planning system of the organization.

3. Discuss the steps involved in the supervisory planning process—with special emphasis on setting objectives.

4. Discuss the role of contingency plans.

5. Differentiate among organizational policies, procedures, and rules.

6. List several common supervisory planning activities.

7. Understand the basic elements of a management by objectives (MBO) system.

SUPERVISION
DILEMMA

After Jane Harris had been in her new supervisory job for only a few months, she realized the importance of meeting deadlines. This first came home to her when she missed a promised deadline on a large batch of claims. Joyce Logan, her department head, had phoned her on a Friday and asked if she could expedite a large batch of claims for a preferred customer. With little forethought, Jane promised to get them out by the following Tuesday. Due to some unexpected problems with office equipment, she did not get the claims out until late the next Thursday. When a similar incident occurred only a few weeks later, Joyce called her in and discussed the importance of setting objectives and meeting agreed-upon deadlines. Jane decided that she had better learn how to plan her workload more effectively.

The supervisor must plan his or her work if it is to be done effectively, properly, and on time. The supervisor's failure to plan can result in lost time, wasted materials, poor use of equipment, and misuse of space. The supervisor must also understand how his or her plans fit into the overall planning scheme of the organization.

HOW THE ORGANIZATION PLANS

1 LEARNING OBJECTIVES

Ideally, all levels of management within an organization develop plans. Plans developed at higher levels of management involve many people and resources and may be very complex. Such plans frequently deal with long-range time spans. A plan orchestrated by the top management of an organization is usually called a **strategic or corporate plan.** Although top management has the primary responsibility for developing the strategic plan, many levels of managers, including supervisors, are involved in the development of the plan.

Once the strategic plan has been developed, specific plans for the different parts of the organization are derived from it. This is done by starting at the higher-level organization units and working down to the lower units. For most organizations, this means starting with the highest-level divisions or departments and then developing plans for successively lower levels of the organization. The key is for each lower-level plan to be based on the plan at the next-higher level. This does not mean that plans are developed by higher levels of management and forced on lower levels. It does mean that lower-level plans are developed by managers at their respective levels based on the plans of higher levels. As the planning process moves down to lower levels in the organization, it becomes narrower in scope and covers shorter time spans. Furthermore, as plans cascade downward through the organization, they become more specific and detailed in nature. At the supervisory level, most plans have relatively short time spans and are very application oriented. In fact, most supervisory planning deals with time periods of a month or less. Figure 6.1 illustrates how supervisory planning relates to other levels of planning.

FIGURE 6.1   The Relationships among Corporate, Divisional, and Supervisory Plans

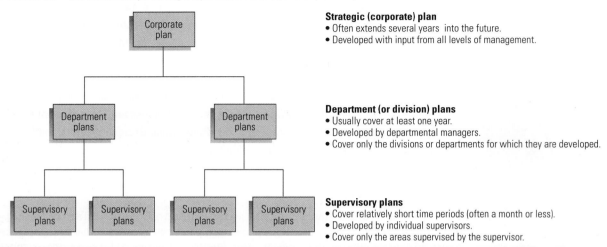

Strategic (corporate) plan
- Often extends several years into the future.
- Developed with input from all levels of management.

Department (or division) plans
- Usually cover at least one year.
- Developed by departmental managers.
- Cover only the divisions or departments for which they are developed.

Supervisory plans
- Cover relatively short time periods (often a month or less).
- Developed by individual supervisors.
- Cover only the areas supervised by the supervisor.

The Supervisor and Strategic Planning

2 LEARNING
OBJECTIVES

Strategic management is the process of developing strategic plans and keeping them current as changes occur internally and in the environment. It is through the strategic management process that top management determines the long-run direction and performance of an organization by ensuring careful formulation, proper implementation, and continuous evaluation of plans. Although orchestrated by top management, successful strategic management involves many different levels in the organization, including supervisors. For example, top management may solicit inputs from all levels of management when formulating top-level plans. Once top-level plans have been finalized, different organizational units may be asked to formulate plans for their respective areas. A proper strategic management process helps ensure that plans throughout the different levels of the organization are coordinated and mutually supportive.

Unfortunately, many managers think that strategic management is just for top managers and of little concern for supervisors.[1] As discussed in the preceding paragraph, *successful* strategic management necessarily involves managers at *all levels*, including supervisors. In addition to that necessity, there are additional benefits to supervisors. Engaging in the strategic management process allows supervisors to see the "big picture" by viewing the organization as an integrated whole. A positive outcome of this exposure is that supervisors develop more conceptual skills and better decision-making skills. Not only does this better prepare supervisors to make daily decisions but also it prepares them to move up in the organization.

An additional benefit of supervisors being involved in the strategic management process is that it fosters a long-range orientation. Because much of a supervisor's work focuses on the short range, this involvement can be a broadening and beneficial experience.

THE SUPERVISOR'S ROLE IN PLANNING

3 LEARNING OBJECTIVES

Supervisory plans are derived from the plans of higher levels of management. Usually, the planning information that comes from upper management is general in nature. For example, upper management may establish production objectives. However, only rarely are these objectives accompanied by a detailed plan for reaching them. Such a plan must be developed by the supervisor. Developing a detailed plan involves answering the following questions: What must be done? Why must it be done? Where should it be done? Who should do it? How should it be done? In essence, supervisory plans operationalize the plans of higher management.

Successful planning for the entire organization involves gathering information from all levels. It is a common practice for the supervisor to provide information to upper-level managers for their use in planning. For example, supervisors are often asked by middle- and upper-level managers to contribute information about future human resource and equipment requirements. Such exchanges between supervisors and upper-level managers keep the supervisors informed and make plans more practical and workable. When gathering information for upper levels of management or for input into their own plans, supervisors often involve their employees in the process.

Figure 6.2 presents a model of the supervisory planning process. The different parts of the model are discussed in the following sections.

THE WHAT AND HOW OF SUPERVISORY PLANNING

Planning is concerned, not with future decisions, but with the future impact of today's decisions. When planning, a supervisor should think about how today's decisions might affect future actions. **Planning** is the process of deciding what objectives to pursue during a future time period and what to do to achieve those objectives. As previously discussed, a supervisor's objectives are usually derived from the plans of higher levels of management. In fact, it is not unusual for a supervisor's objectives to be spelled out by higher levels of management. These objectives are usually broadly defined, however, and require further refinement by the supervisor.

Once the objectives have been established, the second phase of the planning process involves deciding what must be done to achieve them. Supervisory planning involves developing the details of how objectives are to be achieved.

FIGURE 6.2

Supervisory Planning
Process

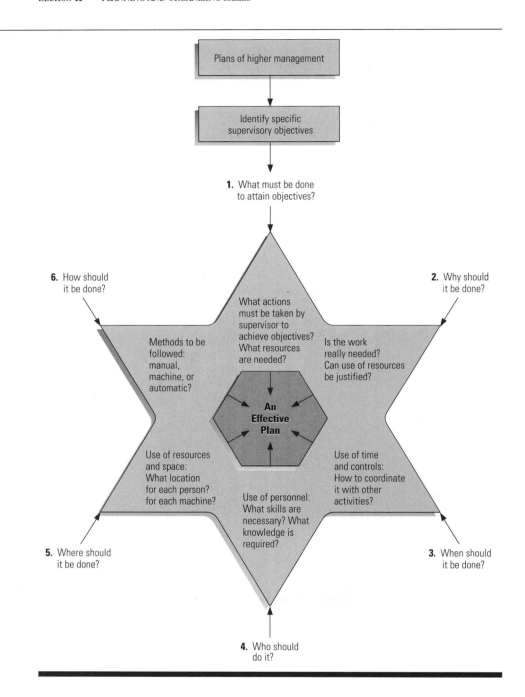

Some people regard the objective-setting process as separate from the planning process. In their view, planning is determining *how* to achieve a given objective or set of objectives. Whether or not the objective-setting process is viewed as an integral part of the planning process, objectives must be established before the planning process can be completed. Obviously, it is not possi-

FIGURE 6.3

Different Levels of
Objectives

Corporate-Level Objective
To increase corporatewide sales by 20 percent for the current fiscal year.
International Division's Objective
To increase sales in the international division by 25 percent for the current fiscal year.
Production Department's Objective
To increase production of the department by 20 percent for the current fiscal year.
Production Supervisor's Objective
To produce 300 units of model B within the next 20 working days.

ble for a supervisor to formulate a course of action for reaching an objective if he or she does not know what the objective is.

Objectives versus Goals

An objective is a statement of a desired measurable result of what is to be achieved. When objectives are viewed in this way, the terms **objectives** and **goals** are interchangeable. Some authors and practitioners, however, distinguish between objectives and goals. These people usually view goals as broader, more encompassing, and longer range than objectives. They believe that objectives can be stated very concisely and in measurable terms. In this book, the terms *goals* and *objectives* will be used interchangeably. Instead of referring to objectives as a subset of goals, we will refer to different levels of objectives. Figure 6.3 illustrates several levels of objectives.

Setting Objectives

Objectives enable the supervisor to focus directly on the targets to be reached within a given period. A supervisor's success depends largely on having a clear understanding of objectives. Similarly, a supervisor must be able to communicate these objectives to the employees who will actually perform the tasks necessary to achieve them.

Objectives should be clear, concise, quantifiable, and measurable whenever possible. They should be detailed enough so that employees understand exactly what is expected. They should span all significant areas of the department. This usually means that several objectives must be set. The problem with a single objective is that it is often achieved at the expense of other desirable objectives. For example, a supervisor may go all out to achieve a production objective even if this means lowering quality.

At the supervisory level, objectives typically deal with quantity, quality, cost, personnel, and safety. For example, a supervisor may have the objective of increasing the department's production by 10 percent over the next 90 days. How objectives are set at the supervisory level and how they are stated can have a great deal to do with how successful a supervisor may be in reaching them. Objectives that have the best chance for success have certain characteristics. Some of the important characteristics are described below:

The objective-setting process should involve those responsible for achieving the objectives. Whenever feasible, supervisors should consult with and involve their employees in the objective-setting process. This does not mean that employees should actually set the objectives but that they should be given an opportunity to express their opinions and provide inputs. Most employees want to be asked for their opinions and suggestions. Objectives that are simply announced by the supervisor are less likely to be achieved than objectives that employees have helped formulate. Another good reason for involving employees is that they frequently have valuable information to contribute. Being near to, and actually performing, the work provides insight and practical experience that the supervisor may not have. However, it is not always possible to involve employees in the objective-setting process. For example, the supervisor's time frame may not allow for it. However, it is a practice that can be used in many circumstances and can be very beneficial to the supervisor and the organization.

Objectives should be written.   Written objectives have several potential advantages over unwritten objectives. They usually receive more attention than unwritten objectives. They tend to be updated on a more regular basis than unwritten objectives. And unlike unwritten objectives, they provide a permanent record.

Objectives should be measurable and understandable.   Generally, objectives should be expressed in quantitative terms and include a stated time frame for completion. Avoid the use of such words as *maximize* and *minimize*. The objective of minimizing costs is commendable but not measurable. How does a supervisor ever know if costs have been minimized? In reality, the only way to truly minimize costs is to have zero costs! A much better way of stating the objective of minimizing costs would be, for example, "to reduce costs by 5 percent by the end of next quarter."

Objectives should be challenging but realistic.   Some people think that objectives should be set just slightly higher than what can be attained. The thought here is to keep the employee stretching and to avoid the letdown that might occur once the objective has been reached. One problem with this approach is that it takes only a short time for employees to figure out that the objective is unattainable. This can quickly demotivate employees. On the other hand, most people are turned on, not off, when they reach a challenging goal. The key is for the objective to be challenging and realistic. Employees should be required to stretch, but the objective should be within their capabilities.

Objectives should be regularly updated.   All too often, objectives are not regularly reviewed and updated. Pursuing outdated objectives wastes resources. Objectives should be reviewed periodically. Those that are no longer of value should be discarded. Others will need revising in light of recent changes.

Objectives should be assigned priorities.   Objectives are of differing importance. Both the supervisor and employees should know an objective's relative importance. Everyone should know which objective is most important and which is least important. Then, if problems occur, everyone will be able to budget time accordingly. Prioritizing objectives does not involve deciding *how* the various objectives will be reached. It does involve establishing their relative im-

FIGURE 6.4

Examples of How to
Improve Work Objectives

Poor:	To maximize production.
Better:	To increase production by 10 percent within the next three months.
Poor:	To reduce absenteeism.
Better:	To average no more than three absent days per employee per year.
Poor:	To waste less raw material.
Better:	To waste no more than 2 percent of raw material.
Poor:	To improve the quality of production.
Better:	To produce no more than 2 rejects per 100 units of production.

FIGURE 6.5

Typical Areas of
Supervisory Objectives

1. Production or output:
   Usually expressed as number of units per time period.
   Example: Our objective is to average 20 units per hour over the next year.
2. Quality:
   Usually expressed as number of rejects, number of customer complaints, amount of scrap.
   Example: Our objective is to produce fewer than 10 rejects per week for the next six months.
3. Cost:
   Usually expressed as dollars per unit produced or dollars per unit of service offered.
   Example: Our objective is for the cost of each widget produced to average less than $5.00 over the next three months.
4. Human resources:
   Usually expressed in terms of turnover, absenteeism, tardiness.
   Example: Our objective is to average less than three days of absenteeism per employee per year.
5. Safety:
   Usually expressed in terms of days lost due to injury.
   Example: Our objective is to reduce the number of days lost due to injury this year by 10 percent.

portance. Deciding how the objectives will be achieved is part of action planning, which is discussed in the next section.

Figure 6.4 presents examples of how some poorly stated objectives might be better stated. Figure 6.5 shows some typical areas in which a supervisor might set objectives.

Action Planning

Once the objectives have been set and prioritized, the supervisor must decide how they will be achieved. This phase of the planning process is called **action planning.** When developing an action plan, a supervisor must answer the following questions:

1. What must be done? Precisely what actions must be taken to reach the stated objectives? Are there any viable alternatives? The supervisor must be sure that all of the actions taken contribute to the accomplishment of the objectives.

FIGURE 6.6

Abbreviated Action Plan

Supervisory Objective: To average 20 units per hour over the next year.

1. What must be done? Provide a complete rebuild of both milling machines.
2. Why must it be done? Both milling machines have been experiencing unplanned and costly downtime.
3. When should it be done? The rebuild on milling machine A should begin before the end of the month. The rebuild on milling machine B should begin as soon as the work on A has been completed.
4. Who should do it? Both machines should be rebuilt by our departmental maintenance team headed by Juan Perez.
5. Where should it be done? Both machines should be rebuilt by removing the necessary parts at their current locations.
6. How should it be done? The maintenance crew should remove those parts needing to be replaced or repaired. Replacement parts can be ordered from the manufacturer. Parts needing to be repaired can either be handled internally or sent to the manufacturer if necessary.

2. **Why must it be done?** This question serves as a check on question 1. Are the actions taken necessary? Can the use of resources be justified?

3. **When should it be done?** The supervisor must decide how to coordinate the necessary actions with other activities. Dates and times should be selected and coordinated.

4. **Who should do it?** The supervisor must decide what skills and abilities are required. Once this has been accomplished, the appropriate human resources must be identified.

5. **Where should it be done?** This question is closely related to question 4. Where will the necessary people and equipment be located?

6. **How should it be done?** What methods and procedures will be used? Can existing procedures be used, or must new ones be developed?

By addressing each of these questions, the supervisor can work out the details of exactly how to proceed. This process can also help identify potential problems. Figure 6.6 provides an example of an abbreviated action plan.

CONTINGENCY PLANS

LEARNING OBJECTIVES

Regardless of how thorough the supervisor's plans are, there will always be things that go wrong. What goes wrong is often beyond the control of the supervisor. For example, a machine may break down or the arrival of a new piece of equipment may be delayed. When such things happen, the supervisor must be prepared with a backup, or contingency, plan. **Contingency plans** address the "what-ifs" of the supervisor's job. Contingency planning gets the supervisor in the habit of being prepared and knowing what to do if something does go wrong. Naturally, contingency plans cannot be prepared for all possibilities. What the supervisor should do is identify the most critical assumptions of the

---

SUPERVISION ILLUSTRATION 6–1

Contingency Planning at Southwest National Bank

Regardless of which part of an organization develops and coordinates a contingency plan, it is important for all functions to work together in designing and testing the contingency plan. Judith Johnston, manager of security and disaster recovery for Southwest National Bank, believes that interdepartmental cooperation is critical to the bank's contingency plans for handling disaster. Southwest Bank's contingency plans for disaster recovery also involve extensive cross-training of employees and the active participation of senior managers.

Even with the increasing amount of attention being paid to disaster recovery planning, it sometimes takes a minor incident to bring the meetings, plans, and exercises to life. For Southwest Bank, the value of contingency planning was demonstrated when the bank lost its telephone service for a day. Because Southwest had a contingency plan in place, employees shifted into a response mode and started operating with cellular phones. Even though it was a minor incident, it showed that there is substance to having a thorough contingency plan.

Source: "Getting People Involved," *Risk Management,* September 1996, p. 56. For more information about Southwest National Bank visit its Web site at: **www.bud.stocksmart.com**

---

current plan and then develop contingencies for problems that have a reasonable chance of occurring. A good approach is to examine the current plan from the point of view of what could go wrong. Ideally you can identify a set of indicators to look for so as to know when you should initiate the contingency plan. The supervisor should discuss contingency plans with subordinates and other supervisors who would be affected by them. Supervision Illustration 6–1 emphasizes the importance of involving employees in the contingency planning process.

POLICIES, PROCEDURES, AND RULES

5 LEARNING OBJECTIVES

Whenever supervisors engage in planning, they must take into account existing policies, procedures, and rules. Policies, procedures, and rules are designed to aid managers at all levels in carrying out their day-to-day activities.

Policies

Policies are broad, general guidelines to action. Policies usually do not dictate exactly how something should be done, but they do set the boundaries within which it must be done. A major purpose of policies is to ensure consistency in the decisions and actions taken throughout the organization.

Policies exist at all levels of an organization. A typical organization has some policies that relate to the entire organization and some policies that relate only to certain parts of the organization. For example, "This company will always try to fill vacancies at all levels by promoting present employees" is a policy that relates to the entire organization. On the other hand, "The public relations department will respond to all customer complaints in writing" is a policy that relates only to a single department.

FIGURE 6.7

One Company's Procedure for Responding to a Written Customer Complaint

Step 1:   All written customer complaints will be forwarded to the customer relations department within 24 hours of receipt.

Step 2:   Upon receipt of a written complaint, the customer relations department will respond in writing to the customer within 48 hours.

Step 3:   One copy of the response will be forwarded to any individuals directly affected by the complaint or response.

Step 4:   One copy of the complaint and response will be filed in the customer relations department and maintained for five years.

Policies define the limits within which supervisors must operate. A company policy of trying to fill vacancies by promoting present employees does not dictate who should be promoted, but it does require that present employees be given preference. A supervisor charged with making a recommendation for filling a vacancy must abide by this policy. It is the supervisor's responsibility to make sure that his or her employees are aware of and understand the policies that relate to them.

Procedures

A **procedure** is a series of related steps or tasks performed in sequential order to achieve a specific purpose. In other words, procedures define in step-by-step fashion how a recurring activity should be accomplished. Well-established and formalized procedures are often known as **standard operating procedures (SOPs).**

Major advantages of procedures are that they achieve a degree of uniformity in how things are done and lessen the need for decisions. Figure 6.7 presents sample procedures that have been developed to support a company policy of responding to all customer complaints in writing.

Rules

Rules require that specific and definite actions be taken or not taken with respect to given situations. For example, "No smoking in the building" is a rule. Rules leave little room for interpretation of what is to be done or not done. Unlike policies, they permit no flexibility or deviation. Unlike procedures, rules do not necessarily specify sequence. Also, rules usually involve a single action or lack of action whereas procedures involve a sequence of actions.

COMMON SUPERVISORY PLANNING ACTIVITIES

6 LEARNING OBJECTIVES

The previous sections examined the overall framework of supervisory planning. Within this framework, supervisors regularly engage in certain specific planning activities. Some of the most common planning activities performed by supervisors are considered next.

Providing Information for High-Level Planning

As discussed earlier in this chapter, upper-level management planners often ask supervisors for certain information. For example, supervisors are often called upon to provide estimates of their human resource and equipment needs.

Developing a Budget

A **budget** is a statement of expected results or requirements expressed in financial or numerical terms. While the monitoring and administration of a budget is part of the control function, the preparation of a budget is a planning activity.

Ideally, a supervisor plays a very active part in developing the budget for his or her area of responsibility. A common approach is to have the supervisor propose the initial budget for the department and then discuss it with the manager at the next higher level. Naturally, the supervisor must be able to justify the proposal and be willing to consider modifications suggested by upper management. This approach has the advantage of producing a realistic final budget that is thoroughly understood by the supervisor. A very important outcome of this approach is that supervisors are committed to the budgets because they had a role in their formulation. Once a budget has been prepared, it can be used very effectively as a control device (this is discussed further in Chapter 19).

Improvement Programs

Improvement programs that often involve supervisors include cost-reduction programs and programs aimed at improving safety, quality, methods, and housekeeping. Maintenance programs can be viewed as a type of improvement program. Successful improvement programs do not just happen; they must be carefully planned. Several types of improvement programs are discussed in detail in later chapters.

Human Resource Needs

Projecting and providing for the human resource needs of the department requires careful planning. Included in this planning activity is the determination not only of staffing needs but also of things such as vacation scheduling and leaves of absence. In many instances, supervisors plan for unexpected absences by maintaining an auxiliary list of part-time employees who can be called in on short notice.

Production Planning

Production planning primarily involves determining the necessary materials, facilities, and human resources. The production plan is the crucial link between the demand for a company's products or services and its ability to supply those products or services at the right time for a reasonable cost. Resource allocation, routing, and scheduling are three of the most common production planning activities performed by supervisors.

Resource allocation—the efficient allocation of people, materials, and equipment to meet objectives—is an important production planning activity.
Steve Weber/Tony Stone Images

Resource allocation.   **Resource allocation** refers to the efficient allocation of people, materials, and equipment so as to successfully meet the objectives that have been established. Resource allocation determines what work will be performed by what person and/or machine and under what conditions. The materials needed must be determined and ordered. The work must be distributed to the different workstations. Human resource requirements must be determined and time requirements established for each stage of the production process.

Routing.   **Routing** involves determining the best sequence of operations. Its purpose is to make optimum use of the existing equipment and human resources through careful assignment of resources. However, the desired level of output and the available mix of equipment and human resources place constraints on the sequence of operations. Although a route may appear to be fixed because of certain physical limitations, it should always be carefully analyzed. Flowcharts and other graphic devices are often used to help detect and eliminate inefficiencies in routes. Flowcharts are discussed in some detail in Chapter 9.

Scheduling.   **Scheduling** develops the precise timetable that is to be followed in producing products or services. It involves determining not how long a job will take but when the work will be performed. The purpose of scheduling is to help assure that the work is synchronized and completed within certain time limits. Scheduling is of course much easier if a thorough job has been done in analyzing the product or service route. Also, when scheduling it is sometimes easier for a supervisor to work backward from a due date.

SUPERVISION ILLUSTRATION 6–2

AUTOMATED ROUTING AND SCHEDULING AT DOMINO'S

Domino's Pizza, the $2.5 billion national pizza delivery chain has greatly reduced its annual transportation costs by implementing Manugistics routing and scheduling software. The company has 18 distribution sites which must deliver food ingredients and supplies to 4,256 stores several times a week. Using a computer with Manugistics to aid in transportation planning for its 160-truck fleet was a big change for Domino's. Before, Domino's had used push pins, string, and huge wall maps as its routing tools. Before automation, Domino's routing philosophy was to run the same route every day. Automated routing and scheduling permits a more strategic approach, including zone routing and grouping of stores based on actual demand.

The Manugistics software delivered quick returns to Domino's. Across its entire distribution network, Domino's slashed an estimated 1 million miles in the first year following automation. The truck fleet has also been reduced.

Source: Kelly Hayes Madden, "Software Drives Down Transportation Costs," *Distribution,* February 1997, pp. 50–52. For more information about Domino's Pizza, visit its Web site at:
www.dominos.com

Determining and implementing priorities is a major part of scheduling. The supervisor may be told which items have high priorities and which have low priorities, or the supervisor may be required to develop this information.

Anticipating lost time is a requirement of scheduling. Many supervisors try to schedule every minute of every working day. Such overscheduling can cause problems if a machine breaks down or if an employee is absent. At the same time, underscheduling can lead to idle equipment and personnel. Successful supervisors must learn to anticipate and schedule for the unexpected. Supervision Illustration 6–2 describes how Domino's Pizza has greatly reduced the routing and scheduling costs of its supply fleet.

Gantt charts.   Numerous types of tools have been developed to help visualize and simplify scheduling. Most of these tools are adaptations of the **Gantt chart.** With a Gantt chart, the activities to be performed are usually shown vertically and the times required to perform them are usually shown horizontally. By plotting these activities and their respective times, the scheduler can visually determine when to schedule each activity. Figure 6.8 shows a Gantt chart for scheduling customer orders through an assembly department.

CPM and PERT.   The Gantt chart concept of identifying the work to be done and graphing it against time provided the foundation for more advanced scheduling methods known as networking methods. CPM (critical path method) and PERT (program evaluation and review technique) are two of the most popular of these methods. Both were developed in the late 1950s. CPM and PERT result in a graphic network representation of the things to be done. The graphic network is composed of activities and events. An **activity** is the work necessary to complete a particular event; it usually consumes time. An **event** denotes a point in time; the occurrence of an event signifies the completion of all activities leading up to it. All activities originate and terminate at events. Activities are normally represented by arrows in a network; events are represented by circles. The dashed arrows, called **dummies,** show the dependent relationships

FIGURE 6.8

Gantt Chart for Scheduling Orders through an Assembly Department

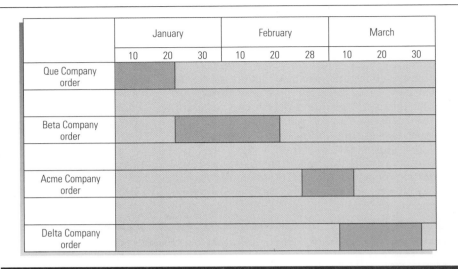

among activities. They denote that the starting of an activity or a set of activities depends on the completion of another activity or set of activities.

Figure 6.9 shows the series of activities required to build a house as represented by a Gantt chart and by CPM and PERT. CPM and PERT methods have two distinct advantages over the Gantt chart: (1) They note explicitly the dependencies of the activities on each other (for example, the dry wall in a house cannot be put up until all the electrical rough-in has been completed); and (2) they show the activities in greater detail. Both of these advantages would help a supervisor in scheduling.

The path through the network that has the longest duration (based on a summation of estimated individual activity times) is referred to as the *critical path*. If any activity on the critical path lengthens, the entire sequence of events lengthens. Thus, the activities on the critical path should be watched most closely by the scheduler.

The major difference between CPM and PERT centers on the activity time estimates. CPM is used to schedule activities whose durations are known with some degree of certainty. PERT is used when the activity durations are more uncertain and variable.

MANAGEMENT BY OBJECTIVES (MBO)

LEARNING OBJECTIVES

Management by objectives (MBO) is a style of supervising that has its roots in the planning function. MBO is based on the premise that establishing personal objectives elicits employee commitment, which in turn leads to performance.

After the supervisor's objectives have been set (as discussed earlier in this chapter), his or her attention is focused on establishing objectives for each employee. Under MBO, each employee has a part in determining work objectives and the means for achieving them. The supervisor and an employee jointly agree upon what the employee's work objectives will be and how they should be pursued. The key to success here is a genuine exchange of ideas between

FIGURE 6.9

Comparison of a Gantt Chart and CPM or PERT Chart for Building a House

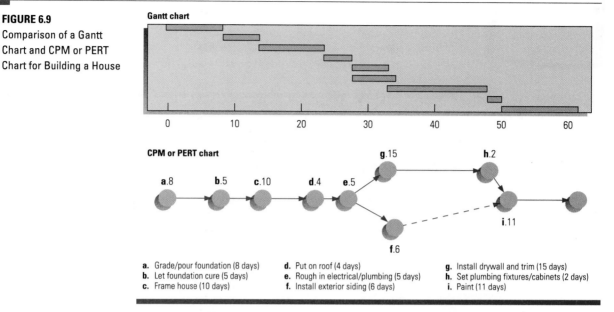

Gantt chart

CPM or PERT chart

a. Grade/pour foundation (8 days)
b. Let foundation cure (5 days)
c. Frame house (10 days)
d. Put on roof (4 days)
e. Rough in electrical/plumbing (5 days)
f. Install exterior siding (6 days)
g. Install drywall and trim (15 days)
h. Set plumbing fixtures/cabinets (2 days)
i. Paint (11 days)

FIGURE 6.10

Guidelines for Setting Individual Objectives

1. Adapt your objectives to the overall mission of the organization.
2. Quantify your objectives when possible.
3. Make your objectives challenging but realistic.
4. Establish reliable performance reports and milestones.
5. Put your objectives in writing, using clear and concise statements.
6. Limit your objectives to the most relevant key result areas.
7. Communicate your objectives to your employees.
8. Review your objectives with your superiors and employees to ensure consistency.
9. Modify your objectives as conditions and priorities change.
10. Do not continue to pursue objectives that become obsolete.

Source: Adapted from Anthony P. Raia, *Managing by Objectives* (Glenview, Ill.: Scott, Foresman, 1974), p. 67.

the supervisor and the employee. After the work objectives and the means for achieving them have been agreed upon, the employee is allowed considerable freedom in pursuing the work objectives. In effect, the employee is free to act within the constraints of what has been agreed upon. The emphasis is on the results that are achieved.

One of the most difficult aspects of an MBO system is deciding in what areas to set objectives. A helpful approach is for the individual to answer the following questions: How would I most like to be evaluated on my job? What things or areas should my boss look at to evaluate my performance? The answers to these questions usually identify the areas in which objectives should be set. Difficulty in answering the questions indicates that the individual may not thoroughly understand the job. Figure 6.10 provides some additional tips for setting individual objectives.

FIGURE 6.11

Basic Elements of an MBO System

1. Individual objectives are set jointly by the employee and the supervisor.
2. Individual employees are periodically evaluated and receive feedback from the supervisor concerning their performance.
3. Individual employees are evaluated and rewarded by the supervisor on the basis of objective attainment.

FIGURE 6.12

MBO at the Supervisory Level

Essential Elements	Persons Involved	Basis for Action
Set objectives for supervisor ↓	Supervisor and supervisor's boss	Objectives of higher management
Set objectives for employees ↓	Supervisor and respective employees	Objectives of supervisor
Periodic progress reviews ↓	Supervisor and respective employees	Objectives for respective employees
Reward employees based on objective attainment	Supervisor and respective employees	Objectives for respective employees

Periodic progress reviews are an essential ingredient of MBO. In these reviews, the employee is provided with direct feedback on actual performance as compared to planned performance (objectives). The manner in which such feedback is given is important. If the supervisor gives the feedback in a downgrading or hostile fashion, performance may be reduced. The important thing is to let the employee know how he or she is doing and to identify areas where the supervisor might provide help. The supervisor acts as a counselor and problem solver *with* the employee, not to the employee. Usually, it is recommended that feedback be provided formally at least two or three times each year. One major advantage of using MBO is that it makes the performance appraisal process more objective.

A final requirement of MBO is that the employees be rewarded on the basis of objective attainment. This means that employee rewards are directly linked to the results attained as measured by the agreed-upon objectives. MBO can work only when employees believe rewards are dependent on results.

Thus, for an MBO system to be successful, three minimum requirements must be met: (1) Individual objectives must be jointly set by the supervisor and the employee; (2) employees must be periodically and regularly evaluated; (3) employees must be rewarded based on objective attainment. Most MBO systems that have failed have fallen short on one or more of these requirements. For example, a supervisor might set objectives for employees and then ask the employees if they agree with the objectives. This is not *jointly* setting the objectives. Another example is the supervisor who does a good job of jointly setting the employees' objectives and periodically evaluating the employees but then gives everyone an equal across-the-board pay raise.

MBO is most effective when it is used at all levels of the organization. When this is done, the objectives at each level should contribute to achieving the objectives at the next-higher level. However, a supervisor can implement MBO in his or her department even if it doesn't exist at other levels. In either case, MBO will not succeed on its virtues alone. It must have the full attention of the supervisor and the employees; it must be thoroughly understood by everyone involved; and it must be given adequate time to succeed. It is not at all unusual for an MBO system to require up to a year for successful implementation. Figure 6.11 reiterates the basic elements of an MBO system. Figure 6.12 summarizes how the MBO process works at the supervisory level.

SOLUTION TO THE SUPERVISION DILEMMA

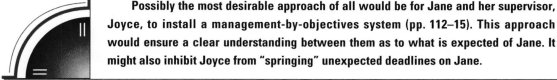

Jane has obviously had problems setting objectives and meeting deadlines in her new job as a supervisor. All indications are that she has a tendency to set or agree to deadlines with little thought as to what will be required to meet them. Jane should learn the importance of not being a "yes person." Before she arbitrarily accepts additional assignments, she should think through each individual request. Even where she has no choice but to agree to a deadline (for example, her boss assigns one), there are helpful attitudes to take. She must realize that a deadline is a type of objective. In this light, she should make sure that the deadline meets the characteristics of a well-stated objective (pp. 104–5).

Jane's current method of planning her daily schedule does not allow for much flexibility, and consequently she has difficulty accommodating unexpected situations. Once a deadline has been agreed upon and clearly stated, Jane should develop an action plan for meeting it. This can be accomplished by addressing the questions listed on pp. 105–6 and/or by following the model presented in Figure 6.6.

Possibly the most desirable approach of all would be for Jane and her supervisor, Joyce, to install a management-by-objectives system (pp. 112–15). This approach would ensure a clear understanding between them as to what is expected of Jane. It might also inhibit Joyce from "springing" unexpected deadlines on Jane.

SUMMARY

This chapter emphasizes the importance of planning to the supervisory process. The chapter contains a discussion of the basic steps in planning and a model of the supervisory planning process. Several of the most commonly encountered supervisory planning activities are discussed, with particular emphasis on management by objectives (MBO).

1. *Describe how an organization should plan.* A strategic plan is developed by top management. Once the strategic plan has been developed, specific plans for the different parts of the organization are derived from it. As the planning process moves down to subsequently lower levels in the organization, it becomes narrower in scope and covers shorter time spans.

2. *Describe the supervisor's role in the overall planning system of the organization.* Supervisory plans are derived from the plans of higher levels of management. Usually, the planning information that comes down to the supervisor is of a general nature, and the supervisor is charged with developing detailed action plans for reaching agreed-upon objectives.

3. *Discuss the steps involved in the supervisory planning process, with special emphasis on setting objectives.* Planning is the process of deciding what objectives to pursue during a future time period and what to do to achieve those objectives. Thus, the first step in the planning process is to establish objectives and the second step is to decide what must be done to achieve these objectives. Objectives should be written, measurable, understandable, challenging, and realistic.

4. *Discuss the role of contingency plans.* When things don't go exactly according to plan, supervisors must be prepared with a backup, or contingency, plan. Contingency plans address the "what-ifs" of the supervisor's job; they get the supervisor in the habit of being prepared if something does go wrong.

5. *Differentiate among organizational policies, procedures, and rules.* Policies are broad, general guidelines to action. A procedure is a series of related steps or tasks performed in chronological order to achieve a specific purpose. Rules require that specific and definite actions be taken or not taken with respect to given situations.

6. *List several common supervisory planning activities.* Common supervisory planning activities include the following: providing information for high-level planning, developing a budget, implementing improvement programs, preparing paperwork and reports, projecting and providing for the human resource needs of the department, engaging in production planning, and implementing a management-by-objectives system.

7. *Understand the basic elements of a management-by-objectives (MBO) system.* The basic elements of an MBO system are that individual objectives are jointly set by the supervisor and the employee, employees are periodically and regularly evaluated, and employees are rewarded based on objective attainment.

REVIEW QUESTIONS

1. Explain the strategic management process and the role that supervisors play in the process.
2. What time span do most supervisory plans cover?
3. Name and briefly discuss six characteristics that should be sought when developing objectives.
4. What is action planning? What six questions should be addressed in action planning?
5. What is a contingency plan?
6. Define and distinguish among policies, procedures, and rules.
7. Name five specific planning activities in which supervisors commonly engage.
8. What are the differences between resource allocation and scheduling?
9. What is routing, and what does it do?
10. What is a Gantt chart?
11. What are CPM and PERT?
12. What are the basic elements of an MBO system?

SKILL-BUILDING QUESTIONS

1. Discuss the following statement: "Planning is something that supervisors should do when they don't have anything else to do."
2. Comment on the following: "Planning is concerned with the future implications of today's decisions and not with decisions to be made in the future."
3. Why do you think that supervisors often have a hard time determining how their plans and activities fit into the overall scheme of things for the organization? Would strategic management help with this problem? Why or why not?
4. Research has shown that more than half of the attempts to install MBO have failed. What do you think might be some reasons for this high failure rate?

REFERENCE

1. Patricia Buhler, "Managing in the 90's," *Supervision*, March 1994, p. 7.

ADDITIONAL READINGS

Buhler, P. "Strategic Management: A Process for Supervisors Organizationwide," *Supervision*, March 1994.

Hecht, Françoise. "The Aha! Factor," *Director*, July 1997.

Tilley, Kate. "Contingency Planning Key for Business Interruption," *Business Insurance*, December 16, 1996.

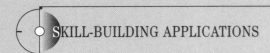

SKILL-BUILDING APPLICATIONS

Incident 6–1

A Plan for Productivity Improvement

The management of the Kleetop Corporation had been concerned about the productivity of the machine shop for some time. During the past few years, it had tried numerous things in hopes of improving the situation. These included a study of work standards, implementation of a piece-rate system, and shop improvements such as a new acoustic ceiling, new fluorescent lighting, and repainted walls. None of these things had any appreciable effect on productivity.

Last fall, Grady Cole became supervisor of the machine shop upon the retirement of Tom McCall. After he had been in his new job for a few weeks, he began working on a new plan for improving the productivity of the machine shop. Grady's plan was to have each employee establish his or her own productivity goal for the next six months. That goal was then to be submitted to Grady for approval. Under this plan, Grady would have the final say concerning the goal. The plan called for Grady to meet once a month with each employee to discuss how the employee was progressing toward his or her goal. A major purpose of these meetings would be to identify problems and to devise methods for overcoming them. Furthermore, Grady's plan called for each employee to receive one honor point for each month that he or she reached the designated productivity goal. At the end of the six-month period, each employee would receive a $50 bonus for each point earned.

Grady's boss, Al Kowalski, was skeptical of the plan. After all, nothing that had been tried had worked. Also, Al suspected that everyone would try to set unacceptably low goals. Finally, after much pleading by Grady, Al agreed to let him try the plan for six months. Then the results of the plan would be evaluated and a decision about whether to continue it would be made. Grady was convinced that the plan would work.

Just before the plan was officially implemented, Grady held a series of meetings to explain it to his employees. Most of them thought it was a good idea. However, a few of the more senior employees questioned its value.

Questions

1. Do you think Grady's plan will work if it is implemented as described above? Why or why not?
2. Can you think of any ways in which Grady's plan might be improved?
3. What do you think are the chances that Grady's plan will enjoy initial successes and then slowly lose the group's interest as the newness wears off? Give reasons for your response.

Incident 6–2

What Should I Do Next?

Kim Allred is relatively new as a supervisor, having been promoted only two months ago. Before her promotion, she had worked for the company for seven years as a sales specialist in office equipment. There is no doubt that she is a whiz at selling office equipment. Because of her accepted expertise in the field, it was natural for her to be promoted when the supervisory opening in office equipment sales became available.

Yesterday, Kim received a memo from her boss, Ed Jackson, stating that all departmental plans for the next fiscal year were due by the end of the month, which was 10 days away. She immediately went into a panic. She had never prepared a formal plan, and she had no idea what was required. After worrying over the matter for a day, Kim decided that the best thing to do would be to ask Ed for some guidelines.

Kim: Ed, yesterday I received your memo regarding next year's plan. I've never prepared a formal plan, and frankly, I don't even know where to start.

Ed: Calm down, Kim. I apologize for forgetting that this is your first go-around in the planning process. What I am looking for is a plan for attaining the objectives that we agreed upon for your department last month. In other words, the ABC's of how you plan to accomplish each objective.

Kim: In other words, you want a written explanation of just how I expect to accomplish each objective. Just how detailed should this plan be, and what format are you looking for?

Questions

1. How would you answer Kim's questions if you were Ed Jackson?

2. How would you go about preparing this plan if you were Kim Allred? (Suggest a framework for Kim to follow.)

3. Do you think Kim's initial reaction to the planning process was unusual? Why or why not?

Exercise 6–1

Personal Objectives

Assume that you are scheduled to graduate from college or a trade school in three months. Develop a list of personal objectives that you would like to achieve within one year after you graduate (try to come up with at least five). After you have established your objectives, prioritize them with regard to their importance to you. Then take your top two objectives and formulate a written action plan for achieving them. What do you think are the weakest parts of your plan?

Be prepared to discuss your plan with the class.

Exercise 6–2

Identifying Personal Goals

Please complete each of the assignments below as you come to them. (Do not read through the entire exercise and then begin filling in your answers.)

Assume you have just won $3 million (after taxes) in a state-sponsored lottery. List five things you would do or buy in the next six months.

1. _____
2. _____
3. _____
4. _____
5. _____

Assume you have just been told by your doctor you have six months to live, but you will feel relatively good until the end. List five things you would do or accomplish in the next six months.

1. _____
2. _____
3. _____
4. _____
5. _____

Now go back and circle any item on each list that has nothing to do with money or how long you will live. Which of these goals could you accomplish now, even without the lottery money or the fear of dying in six months? Could you accomplish some of these goals by some straightforward modification of your actual situation?

Exercise 6–3

Drawing a CPM Logic Network

Based upon the following narrative description of a project, draw a CPM logic network that accurately shows the natural dependencies among the activities involved. Be prepared to share your network with the class.

The Sheffield Manufacturing Company is considering the introduction of a new product. The first step in this project will be to design the new product. Once the product is designed, a prototype can be built and engineers can design the process by which the product will be produced on a continuous basis. When the prototype is completed, it will be tested. Upon completing the process design, an analysis will be made of the production cost per unit for the new product. When the prototype testing and the production cost analysis are both finished, the results will be submitted to an executive committee which will make the final go-ahead decision on the product introduction and establish the price to be charged. Assuming that the committee's decision is positive, several steps can be taken immediately. The marketing department will begin designing sales literature. The production department will obtain the equipment to be used in the manufacture of the new product, hire the additional personnel needed to staff the process, and obtain an initial stock of raw materials. After sales literature has been designed, it will be printed. The new equipment obtained for the production process will have to be modified slightly. The production personnel will be trained as soon as the equipment modifications are complete, all necessary personnel have been hired, and the initial stock of materials has been obtained. When the printing of the sales literature is completed and the production personnel have been trained, the sales literature will be distributed to the salespersons and the product introduction will be considered complete.

Questions

1. What specific benefits do you think that a CPM network would provide on this project?
2. What information does the CPM network that you created provide that would not be provided by a Gantt chart of the same project?

CHAPTER 7

Organizing and Delegating

LEARNING OBJECTIVES

After studying this chapter, you should be able to:

1. Define departmentation and describe several ways it is implemented in organizations.

2. Understand the difference between authority and responsibility and between line and staff personnel.

3. Explain the concept of centralized versus decentralized authority.

4. Define empowerment and explain how it can be encouraged.

5. Identify and describe several principles of supervision based on authority.

6. Recount the basic steps in the delegation process.

7. Discuss why supervisors are often reluctant to delegate authority.

8. Describe some supervisory tasks that can't be delegated.

9. Describe several tips for making delegation more effective.

SUPERVISION
DILEMMA

Prior to his promotion, John Harris had often said and had heard other employees say, "We need to get organized around here." Now that he is a supervisor, John wants to do his best to ensure that his employees won't feel this way. He also remembers the many times when he had more than one supervisor telling him what to do. Since becoming a supervisor, John has discovered that getting things organized is not an easy job. For instance, the other day John asked one of his employees, Lou Berry, to get an order out to a preferred customer. When John checked on the order three days later, he found that nothing had been done. John wondered where he had gone wrong in delegating this task to Lou.

Organizing is the grouping of activities necessary to achieve common objectives. Organizing also involves the assignment of each grouping to a manager with the authority necessary to supervise the people performing the activities. Thus, delegation of authority is a major part of the organizing function. Both organizing and delegating are duties that a successful supervisor must master.

THE ORGANIZATION STRUCTURE

The organization structure results from the grouping of work activities and the assignment of each grouping to a manager. Generally, this structure is developed by upper levels of management. However, it is important that the supervisor know and understand the makeup of the total organization. The supervisor must be familiar with the job that the entire organization is meant to do and with the role that each part of the overall organization plays in doing that job. This familiarity helps the supervisor understand the job, work with other supervisors, and know what to delegate.

Organization Charts

An organization chart uses a series of boxes connected with one or more lines to graphically represent the organization's structure. Each box represents a position within the organization, and each line indicates the nature of the relationships between the different positions. The organization chart not only identifies specific relationships but also provides an overall picture of how the entire organization fits together. As organizations become larger and more complex, it becomes increasingly difficult to represent all of the relationships accurately.

Departmentation

① LEARNING OBJECTIVES

Departmentation is the grouping of activities into related work units. Departmentation is the method most often used to structure the organization. Departments can be formed on the basis of work function, product or service, geographic area, customer, or time. **Functional departmentation** occurs when organization units are defined by the nature or function of the work. Under functional departmentation, jobs requiring similar skills are grouped together. A sales department, an accounting department, and a personnel department are

The Hard Rock Cafe is an example of an organization with
geographic departmentation.
John Coletti/Stock Boston

examples of functional departments. Under *departmentation by product or
service*, all the activities necessary to produce and market a product or service
are under a single manager. Many retail stores are organized along these lines,
having a hardware department, a furniture department, and so forth. **Geographic departmentation** occurs most frequently in organizations with operations or offices that are physically separated from each other. A company with
regional offices uses geographic departmentation. In *departmentation by customer*, a company might have one department for retail customers and one for
wholesale or industrial customers. *Departmentation by time or shift* may be
used by organizations that work more than one shift.

Most organizations do not use the same type of departmentation at all levels. Figure 7.1 shows a sales organization that is departmentalized on a different basis at each level.

Authority and the Supervisor

Authority is the right to issue directives and expend resources. The lines of
authority are established by the organization structure and link the various organization units together. The authority of supervisors is determined by upper
levels of management and implemented through the organization structure. The
amount of authority given to supervisors varies with the situation. Thus, some

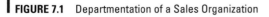

FIGURE 7.1   Departmentation of a Sales Organization

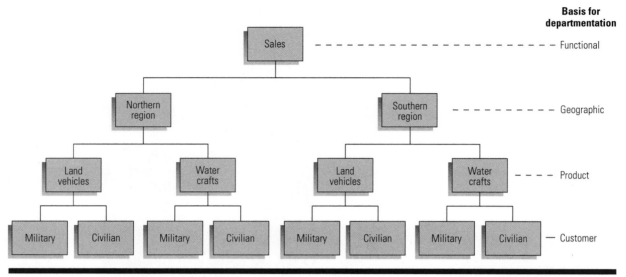

supervisors may be given much more authority than others. Almost all supervisors, however, have some authority to make work assignments. Additionally, supervisors often have the authority to organize the work unit within broad guidelines.

Line versus Staff Authority

Within the organization structure are two major types of authority: line and staff. **Line authority** is based on the supervisor-employee relationship. With line authority, there is a direct line of authority from the top to the bottom of the organization structure. Line managers and line employees are directly involved in producing and marketing the organization's goods or services. For example, assembly-line supervisors are line managers in that they are directly involved in producing the organization's goods.

Staff authority is used to support and advise line personnel. Staff employees are generally specialists in a particular field. For example, employees in the personnel department are normally considered to have staff authority since their authority is normally limited to making recommendations to line personnel.

Most organizations today have both line and staff. This means that they have both managers with line authority and managers with staff authority. The largest number of supervisors are usually line managers.

Line and staff conflict.   The presence of both line managers and staff managers sometimes creates conflict. Some staff specialists resent the fact that they may be only advisers to line personnel and have no real authority over the line. At the same time, line managers, knowing they have final responsibility for the product or service, are often reluctant to listen to staff advice. Many staff specialists think they should not be in a position of having

---

SUPERVISION ILLUSTRATION 7–1

DECENTRALIZATION AT HARLEY-DAVIDSON

In the 1980s, the Harley-Davidson Motor Company faced serious challenges from Japanese companies like Honda, Suzuki, and Yamaha. The company overcame these challenges under the direction of a very strong hierarchical, centralized leadership. Under that structure, the company expanded its manufacturing capability and became more customer-focused. Lines of private-brand riding and fashion apparel for the entire family were developed and a whole new retail look for dealers to market these products was designed.

Today Harley-Davidson is moving toward becoming a more decentralized organization. President and chief executive Richard F. Teerlink, who is leading this move, believes that this type of organizational structure and process will better support individual growth and excellence and develop interdependence and cross-functional collaboration. The new structure not only allows but encourages managers and supervisors to be more involved in the decision-making process at all levels.

Source: Clyde Fessler, "Rotating Leadership at Harley-Davidson: From Hierarchy to Interdependence," *Strategy and Leadership,* July–August 1997, pp. 42–43. For more information about Harley-Davidson, visit its Web site at: **www.harley-davidson.com**

---

to sell their ideas to the line. They believe the line managers should openly listen to their ideas. If the staff specialist is persistent, the line manager often resents even more that the staff "always tries to interfere and run my department." The staff specialist who does not persist often becomes discouraged because "no one ever listens."

Centralized versus Decentralized Authority

3 LEARNING OBJECTIVES

Limitations are placed on the authority of any position. **Centralization and decentralization** refer to the degree of authority delegated by top management. This is usually reflected in the numbers and kinds of decisions made by middle and supervisory management. The more decisions made by middle and supervisory management, the more decentralized the organization is said to be. Organizations are never totally centralized or totally decentralized but fall along a continuum ranging from highly centralized to highly decentralized. From the supervisor's perspective, the more freedom the supervisor has to make decisions, the more decentralized the organization tends to be. Supervision Illustration 7–1 describes how Harley-Davidson has recently become a more decentralized organization.

4 LEARNING OBJECTIVES

Empowerment.   **Empowerment** is a form of decentralization that involves giving employees substantial authority to make decisions. Under empowerment, supervisors express confidence in the ability of employees to perform at high levels. Employees are also encouraged to accept personal responsibility for their work. In situations where true empowerment takes place, employees gain confidence in their ability to perform their jobs and influence the organization's performance. One result of empowerment is that employees demonstrate more initiative and perseverance in pursuing organizational goals. Supervision Illustration 7–2 describes how Disney World has empowered its frontline employees.

SUPERVISION ILLUSTRATION 7-2

EMPOWERMENT AT DISNEY WORLD

While many managers talk about empowerment, few actually practice it. More times than not, managers don't really understand what empowerment is. True empowerment means that employees have the authority to bend and break the rules to do whatever it takes to take care of the customer. Unfortunately, many managers think that empowerment is giving employees the authority to make a decision to take care of the customer—as long as the action they take follows the rules, policies, and procedures of the organization.

Disney World represents the epitome of empowerment in that employees are thoroughly trained and then given the authority to do whatever is necessary to deal with problems on the spot in order to make customers happy. If a supervisor at Disney World sees a frontline person "giving away the store, he'll usually wait and talk it over with him later," says James Poisant, former manager of business seminars at Disney World. "It's OK if a guest gets away with something. The alternative is that we could be wrong, and that could cost us a fortune. An aggrieved guest would tell everyone he knows that Disney is cheap. Occasionally, we'll take a hit, but that's OK."

Source: John Tschohl, "Empowerment: The Key to Customer Service," *Nation's Restaurant News,* August 11, 1997, p. 40. For more information about Disney World, visit its Web site at:
www.disney.com

Power and the Supervisor

Many supervisors confuse power with authority. The terms are related, but they mean different things. As defined in Chapter 4, **power** is the ability to get others to respond favorably to instructions and orders. Power is personal in that it is a function of the person's ability to get others to act. As defined earlier, authority is the right to command and expend resources. Authority is positional in that it goes with a given position or title. A person holding a position automatically has the authority that goes with a position as long as he or she maintains that position.

Authority and power usually accompany each other. Thus, a supervisor who has a certain degree of authority usually has certain powers that go along with the authority. Almost all successful supervisors are able to get their employees to follow their lead.

Responsibility and the Supervisor

Responsibility is accountability for reaching objectives, using resources properly, and adhering to organizational policy. Once you accept responsibility, you become obligated to perform the assigned work. A certain degree of responsibility is inherent in every supervisory job. Put another way, it is almost impossible to hold a supervisory job and have no responsibility. Responsibility and supervision go hand in hand. The term *responsibility* as defined above should not be confused with the term *responsibilities* as used in defining job duties. When used to define job duties, **responsibilities** refer to the things that make up the supervisor's job. Figure 7.2 lists some typical supervisory responsibilities.

FIGURE 7.2
Typical Supervisory
Responsibilities

1. Assign specific duties to each employee.
2. Determine the amount of work to be accomplished by each employee.
3. Transfer employees within your department.
4. Authorize overtime.
5. Answer questions about time standards.
6. Make suggestions for improvements in work procedures.
7. Work with appropriate staff groups to develop and implement better work methods.
8. Counsel employees.
9. Process grievances with shop stewards.
10. Participate in drawing up departmental budgets.
11. Authorize repair and maintenance work.
12. Maintain production records.

PRINCIPLES OF SUPERVISION BASED ON AUTHORITY

Because the proper use of authority is a key to successful supervision, numerous related principles have been developed. These five principles should be viewed as guides to assist the supervisor, not as laws to be followed without exception.

Parity Principle

5 LEARNING OBJECTIVES

The **parity principle** states that authority and responsibility must coincide. The supervisor must give employees the authority they need to do their jobs. At the same time, employees can be expected to accept responsibility only for those areas within their authority. In other words, if an employee is to assume certain responsibilities, then the supervisor must give the employee sufficient authority to meet those responsibilities. Delegation of authority does not come naturally to most supervisors; yet, it is critical to success. Delegation of authority is discussed at length later in this chapter.

Exception Principle

The **exception principle** (also known as *management by exception* and closely related to the parity principle) states that supervisors should concentrate their efforts on matters that deviate from the norm and let their employees handle routine matters. The idea is that supervisors should not become bogged down by insignificant and routine matters. The exception principle can be violated by insecure employees who refer everything to their supervisor because they are afraid to make decisions. It can also be violated by supervisors who continue to make decisions that have supposedly been delegated. The following example illustrates how the exception principle might be effectively used. Assume that it normally takes one week to replenish raw materials when they are ordered and that the company uses approximately 100 units of raw material per week. A supervisor might instruct an employee to reorder whenever the raw material inventory falls to a level of 300 units. Furthermore, the supervisor might instruct the subordinate to notify him or her if the raw material level ever reaches 100 units so that steps could be taken to avoid a stockout. Thus, the supervisor would become involved only in those exceptional cases when the raw material inventory dropped to 100 units.

Unity of Command Principle

The **unity of command principle** states that an employee should have one and only one immediate boss at a given time. In situations where employees are shared (such as small companies), an employee should report to only one manager on any one task for which he or she is responsible. The difficulty of serving more than one boss has been recognized for thousands of years. Recall that in the Sermon on the Mount, Jesus said, "No man can serve two masters." Experts have speculated that violations of the unity of command principle account for almost one-third of the human relations problems in industry. Such a violation occurs when two or more supervisors tell an employee to do different things at the same time. This places the employee in a no-win situation. Regardless of what the employee does, one supervisor will be dissatisfied. Violation of the unity of command principle is usually caused by unclear lines of authority and poor communication.

Scalar Principle

The **scalar principle** states that authority flows one link at a time from the top of the organization to the bottom. The scalar principle is also referred to as the **chain of command.** Violations of the scalar principle occur when one or more links in the chain of command are bypassed. For example, suppose Jerry goes directly above his immediate boss, Ellen, to her boss, Charlie, for permission to take an early lunch break. Believing the request to be reasonable, Charlie approves it. Later, Charlie discovers that the other two people in Jerry's department had also rescheduled their lunch breaks, so that the department was unstaffed from 12:30 to 1:00 PM. Had Ellen not been bypassed, this problem could have been avoided. The problem arose not because Charlie was incapable of making a good decision, but because he lacked the information needed to make such a decision.

A common misconception is that every action must painfully progress through every link in the scalar chain. The key is to use common sense. A superior who has a need to know should be involved. On the other hand, purely informational requests can usually be met without going through a superior.

Span of Control Principle

The **span of control principle** (also called the *span of management*) refers to the number of employees a supervisor can effectively manage. For years, the span of control was thought to be five to seven. However, practitioners experienced many situations in which this was not the case. For example, a department of 50 claims processors all doing the same work would not require 8 to 10 supervisors. Recently, the principle of the span of control has been revised to state that a supervisor's span depends on several factors: the complexity of the jobs, the variety of the jobs, the proximity of the jobs, the quality of the people

	Factor	Description	Relationship to Span of Control
FIGURE 7.3 Factors Affecting the Span of Control	Complexity	Job difficulty	Inverse*
	Variety	Number of different types of jobs being managed	Inverse
	Proximity	Physical closeness of jobs being supervised	Direct**
	Quality of employees	General quality of employees being supervised	Direct
	Ability of supervisor	Ability to perform supervisory duties	Direct

* As the factor of complexity (or variety) increases, the span of supervision decreases.
** As the factor of proximity (or quality) increases, the span of supervision increases.

filling the jobs, and the ability of the supervisor. *Complexity* refers to the difficulty of the jobs being supervised. Naturally, more complex jobs lower the span of control. *Variety* refers to the number of different types of jobs being managed; the more varied the jobs, the lower the span of control. *Proximity* has to do with the physical closeness of the jobs. If all the employees are working in one room, the span of control is greater than it would be if they were spread all over the building or city. *Quality of the employees* refers to the fact that some people require closer supervision than do others. The *ability of the supervisor* refers to the skill of the supervisor. Thus, in situations where employees are engaged in simple, repetitive operations in close proximity, the span of control can be very large. In situations involving highly diversified work, the span of control might be as low as three or four.

While much thought is given to ensuring that a supervisor's span is not too large, the opposite situation is often overlooked. It is easy for situations to develop in which too few employees are reporting to a supervisor. Such situations can lead to an inefficient organization. Figure 7.3 summarizes the factors affecting the span of control.

DELEGATING AUTHORITY AND RESPONSIBILITY

Failure to delegate is probably the most frequent reason that supervisors fail in their jobs. Delegation is an art. Unfortunately, it does not come naturally for many people. In its most common use, **delegation** refers to the delegation of authority. To delegate authority means to grant or confer authority from one person to another. Generally, authority is delegated to assist the receiving party in completing his or her assigned duties. For example, a supervisor may give employees the authority to organize their own work as long as they meet certain production requirements.

There is much debate about the delegation of responsibility. Some people say that you can delegate responsibility; others say that you can't. A close analysis of the issue generally reveals that the debate is more a communication problem than a misunderstanding of the concepts involved. Those who say that responsibility cannot be delegated contend that supervisors can never shed their job responsibilities by passing them on to their employees. Those who say that responsibility can be delegated point out that supervisors can certainly make their employees responsible for certain actions. Both parties are correct! Supervisors can delegate responsibility in the sense of making their employees responsible for certain actions. However, this delegation does not make supervisors any less responsible to their bosses. Thus, delegation of responsibility does not mean abdication of responsibility by the delegating party. Responsibility is *not* like an object that can be passed from individual to individual. Suppose a claims supervisor for a life insurance company decides to delegate to the claims investigators the responsibility for investigating all claims within a 60-day limit. The claims supervisor can certainly make the claims investigators responsible (accountable) for meeting this target. At the same time, however, the claims supervisor is no less responsible for the investigation of claims.

How to Delegate

6 LEARNING OBJECTIVES

Successful delegation involves three basic steps: (1) assigning work to the different employees in the work group, (2) creating an obligation (responsibility) on the part of each employee to perform the duties satisfactorily, and (3) granting permission (authority) to take the actions necessary to perform the duties. Thus, successful delegation involves the delegation of both authority and responsibility.

Assigning work.   The first step in assigning work is to identify what work should be delegated. A good way for a supervisor to identify which tasks should be delegated is to utilize a time log as discussed in Chapter 5. By recording and then analyzing a time log, a supervisor can often identify tasks that can and should be delegated. Once a supervisor has determined which tasks should be delegated, he or she must then decide which subordinates should handle each task. The supervisor should look upon this as a process of matching the available human resources with the task requirements. The key to success when assigning work is to make the best use of the skills and resources available. Therefore, supervisors must be well acquainted with the skills of their employees. Other factors that must be considered when making work assignments include:

1. The personal relationships involved.
2. The effect on others.
3. The attitudes of the affected parties.
4. Company policies that might be applicable.
5. Applicable provisions of a union contract (such as seniority).
6. Safety considerations.

Once the supervisor has decided how the work will be assigned, this information must be clearly communicated to the employees. It is important to note that the assignment of work involves telling employees *what* to do, not *how* to do it. Giving employees a certain amount of freedom as to how their job will be done creates an environment in which initiative and ideas are welcomed. Obviously, the degree of freedom allowed will vary with the specific work assignment. All too often, supervisors stifle employee creativity by demanding that everything be done exactly as prescribed by the supervisor. Most employees are all too happy to please, and thus any trace of creativity quickly disappears.

Creating an obligation (responsibility).   Supervisors sometimes expect employees to seek and assume responsibility that they have not been asked to assume. Some supervisors engage in a game with their employees: "I know what I want Joe to do, but I'm not going to tell him." The reasoning here is that if Joe is ambitious enough, he will figure out exactly what the supervisor wants. In other words, the supervisor looks upon assignments as if they were tests to separate the more ambitious employees from the less ambitious employees. However, it makes a lot more sense and gets better results to simply tell an employee what is expected. Only after the employee has a clear understanding of what is expected can feelings of responsibility be created. These feelings of responsibility are influenced by the manner in which the supervisor arrives at and communicates expectations. For example, a supervisor who solicits the thoughts and ideas of employees is much more likely to foster feelings of responsibility. Unfortunately, many supervisors act like dictators when assigning work and then wonder why they don't evoke feelings of responsibility. Feelings of responsibility cannot be ordered by another person; they must come from within the individual.

Granting permission (authority).   Granting permission to take certain actions necessary to perform the assigned duties is often the most difficult part of delegating. Many supervisors think that once responsibility has been established, the employees should then ask for the necessary authority. This approach gives only the authority that is specifically sought by the employee. But why not empower employees so that they can better perform their jobs? As discussed earlier in this chapter, empowerment involves giving subordinates substantial authority to make decisions. The keys to successfully empowering employees are to express confidence in their abilities to perform at high levels, designing jobs so that employees have considerable freedom, setting meaningful and challenging goals, applauding good performance, and encouraging employees to take personal responsibility for their work.

Why People Are Reluctant to Delegate

7   LEARNING OBJECTIVES

Many supervisors are promoted into their supervisory positions from the ranks of the operative employees. The move from operative employee to supervisor involves some differences that can affect the new supervisor's ability to delegate. An operative employee's performance is, for the most part, an individual function. In other words, an operative employee's performance is not normally dependent on anyone else. The performance of a supervisor, however, is almost totally dependent on the performance of others—namely his or her subordinates. Problems occur when the new supervisor does not fully realize this difference and, rather than concentrating on the functions of supervision, tries to do everyone else's job. The supervisor may think that the way to look good is to ensure that everyone's job is done right. This is a very natural trap to fall into. It is also the basis for most of the reasons why supervisors are reluctant to delegate.

If you want anything done right, do it yourself. Many supervisors subscribe to the old saying "If you want anything done right, do it yourself!" This attitude shows that the supervisor does not understand the supervisory process. It also indicates that the supervisor has done a poor job of selecting and training his or her employees. Supervisors who attempt to do it all themselves or to prove that they are superior operative workers spend a great deal of time on nonsupervisory tasks—and then they do not have time to perform their supervisory tasks.

The question is not whether the supervisor can do the job better but whether the employee can do it in an acceptable manner. If an employee can do the job satisfactorily, then the employee should be assigned the job and left alone to do it. It is sometimes helpful for the supervisor to look at the situation from a return on investment (*ROI*) standpoint. If the employee (who is paid less money per hour than the supervisor) can do the job in an acceptable manner, then the organization is getting more for its money than if the supervisor does it.

It is easier to do it myself. Supervisors often say that it is easier for them to do the job than to explain it to their employees. While this may be true in some cases, it usually represents a very shortsighted view. It may be easier for the supervisor to do the task the 1st time or even the 5th time around, but is it easier still on the 20th or the 50th time? In other words, although some investment of the supervisor's time may be required to train employees to do the job, this is usually the best approach. If a supervisor continually finds that an employee just can't seem to learn the task, the supervisor should carefully examine the hiring and training practices being used.

Fear of an employee looking too good. Some supervisors are inhibited from delegating by the fear that they might be replaced by an employee who looks too good. Such fears are totally unfounded for good supervisors. As mentioned previously, a supervisor's performance is, for the most part, a reflection of the employee's performance. If a supervisor's employees look good, the supervisor looks good. If the employees look bad, the supervisor looks bad. Experience has also shown that a truly outstanding employee will eventually move ahead regardless of the supervisor's actions. Under these circumstances, the supervisor might easily live to regret any actions taken to stifle that employee's work performance.

The human attraction for power. Most people like the feel of power. Many supervisors get considerable satisfaction from having the power and authority to grant or not grant certain requests. A supervisor should realize that these feelings are natural and that it may take some conscientious effort to overcome them. The key is to learn to get satisfaction by accomplishing things through others.

FIGURE 7.4

Reasons Why Supervisors
Are Reluctant to Delegate

1. If you want anything done right, do it yourself.
2. It is easier to do it myself.
3. Fear of an employee looking too good.
4. The human attraction for power.
5. More confidence in doing the detail work.
6. Preconceived ideas about employees.
7. Desire to set the right example.

More confidence in doing detail work.   Some supervisors feel much more confident when doing detail and operative work than when performing their supervisory functions. Most people have some fear of the unknown and tend to shy away from it. Thus, it is understandable that a new supervisor would feel much more confident doing those things that he or she did successfully in the past. The behavior is likely to occur if the new supervisor has initial setbacks in performing the supervisory functions. Discouraged supervisors often attempt to immerse themselves in their old duties. Closely related to this problem is the supervisor who wants to do things because he or she has *always* done them. In either case, the end result is a failure to delegate.

Preconceived ideas about employees.   Sometimes supervisors erroneously jump to conclusions about the capabilities of employees. For example, a supervisor might form a negative opinion about an employee's ability based on one occurrence. This occurrence may be very unrepresentative of the employee— or the supervisor may be unaware of the facts surrounding the circumstances. Yet another possibility is for supervisors to base an opinion of employees on secondhand information. Such information may come from other supervisors, employees, or personal acquaintances, and it may be very inaccurate. Naturally, if a supervisor believes that an employee lacks ability, that supervisor will be reluctant to delegate to that employee.

Desire to set the right example.   Most supervisors want to set a good example for their employees. The problem, however, is to decide what a good example is. Some supervisors think that to set a good example they must be busy—or at least look busy—all the time. Such supervisors hoard work that should be delegated. A similar type of supervisor is the one who enjoys being a martyr. An example is the supervisor who thinks that he or she must always be the last one to leave the office or plant: "This place would fall apart if I didn't work here." Supervisors of this kind also tend to hoard work and not delegate. Figure 7.4 summarizes the reasons why supervisors are reluctant to delegate.

Tasks That Can't Be Delegated

8 LEARNING OBJECTIVES

While the problem of overdelegation is not common, it can occur. The quality and type of employees greatly affect what can be delegated. However, certain things normally should not be delegated.

Planning activities.   Planning activities (which were discussed in the last chapter) include deciding what objectives to pursue and how to achieve them. These activities also include the routing and scheduling of people and materials. While it is desirable to actively involve employees in planning activities, the supervisor should retain primary authority and responsibility for them. Although a supervisor may (and should) delegate certain parts of the planning process, he or she should retain authority for the coordination and finalization of plans.

Assigning work.   The assignment of work should also be controlled by the supervisor. As with planning activities, parts of this process may and probably should be delegated, but the supervisor should retain overall control.

Motivational problems.   Creating the proper work environment to enhance employee motivation is primarily the responsibility of the supervisor. This does not imply that employees do not play a significant part in their own motivation. However, it does imply that the supervisor will always have a strong influence on the work environment, which in turn affects employee motivation.

Counseling employees.   The supervisor normally should not delegate the counseling of employees regarding job-related issues. However, when an employee needs personal counseling or technical information that might better be supplied by a staff person, the supervisor should refer the employee to the proper source.

Resolving conflict situations.   Whenever a conflict arises between two or more employees, the supervisor should assist in resolving the conflict. This does not mean that the supervisor should personally resolve the conflict, but that the supervisor should see that the involved parties resolve it.

Tasks specifically assigned to the supervisor.   It is generally not a good idea to delegate tasks or assignments that upper management expects the supervisor to do personally (such as serving on a committee).

Supervision Illustration 7–3 provides insights from several top executives about what can and can't be delegated.

Practical Tips for Effective Delegation

9 LEARNING OBJECTIVES

Some specific things can be done to make it easier to delegate:

1. Know your employees' abilities. Become familiar with their major strengths and weaknesses by observing their work, discussing problems when they arise, and reviewing past performance appraisals.
2. Don't be afraid of overdelegating. Many supervisors don't delegate enough for fear of delegating too much.

SUPERVISION ILLUSTRATION 7–3

WHAT CAN AND CAN'T BE DELEGATED

When asked, "How much do you delegate and which details do you consider indispensable?" top executives from several companies provided the following insights:

A. Malachi Mixon, Chief Executive Officer, Invacare

> "One thing I don't delegate is firing. I've always terminated executives myself rather than delegate the job. Some say give it to the vice president of human resources and let him handle it. It's tempting to delegate those kinds of human-emotion situations, but I don't think it's right. You've got to face up to your own judgment of executives."

Vincent Orza, President, Eateries Inc.

> "I respond personally to all of the complaints from customers who write or call us. They're often surprised to hear back from the president and ask why I'm calling back and not one of my people.

> "Some say: 'Oh it's not that important.' "I tell them: 'You did me a favor and I want you to eat here again.' And I'm the guy who can get it fixed quicker than anyone else."

Kendrick Melrose, Chief Executive Officer, The Toro Co.

> "I have some pet things—like the use of the Toro brand name. If some marketing manager wants to use the Toro brand and I don't like it, I'll say no. If I see something connected to the brand, I'll jump in."

Joseph Liemandt, Chief Executive Officer, Trilogy Development Group

> "To help make delegation easier, I put together a framework: If you can delegate a task to somebody who can do it 75 percent to 80 percent as well as you can today, you delegate it immediately."

Source: Scott Bistayi, "Delegate or Not? *Forbes,* April 21, 1997, pp. 20–22. For more information about *Forbes,* visit its web site at: **www.forbes.com**

---

3. Practice good communication skills when delegating. Give clear instructions and check that the employee understands what has been delegated.

4. Minimize overlap of authority. Establish clearly defined levels of authority. Avoid duplication of effort.

5. Give employees some freedom in deciding how to implement their authority. Delegate what to do, not how to do it.

6. Assign related areas of authority and responsibility to each individual. Try to make sure that the different assignments given to each individual are as closely related as possible.

7. Once you have delegated, let the employee take over. Don't rush in at the drop of a hat to straighten things out. Before giving assistance, make sure the employee has had a fair chance.

8. Don't expect perfection the first time. The question is not "Was the job done perfectly?" but "Was the job done in an acceptable manner?"

SOLUTION TO THE
SUPERVISION
DILEMMA

Looking back at John's apparently unsuccessful delegation to Lou, let us see what John could have done differently. First, we must determine whether the task was one that should have been delegated. Based on the limited available information and reviewing the list of tasks that should not be delegated (pp. 133–34), we see no reason to believe that the task should not have been delegated. Having determined this, we must investigate the manner in which John attempted the delegation. Reviewing the basic steps in the delegation process (pp. 130–31), we find that John did assign the task to Lou; however, Lou may not have been the best person for this task. John was probably not successful in creating an obligation on Lou's part. In merely telling Lou what he wanted done, John did not go far enough. He should have clearly communicated his expectations to Lou and involved Lou in jointly establishing a due date for completion of the task. This would most likely have enlisted Lou's commitment to the task. John should also have clearly outlined the limits of Lou's authority.

SUMMARY

This chapter begins with a discussion of organization structure and of the role played by authority in establishing an organization structure. Five principles of supervision based on authority are discussed. The importance of delegation to the supervisory process is emphasized, and guidelines for successful delegation are presented.

1. *Define departmentation and describe several ways it is implemented in organizations.* Departmentation is the grouping of activities into related work units. Departmentation can be implemented on the basis of work function, product or service, geographic area, customer, or time.

2. *Understand the difference between authority and responsibility and between line and staff personnel.* Authority is the right to issue directives and expend resources. Responsibility is accountability for reaching objectives, using resources properly, and adhering to organizational policy. Line personnel are directly involved in producing and marketing the organization's goods or services. Staff personnel support and advise line personnel.

3. *Explain the concept of centralized versus decentralized authority.* Centralization and decentralization refer to the degree of authority delegated by top management. The more decisions made by middle and supervisory managers, the more decentralized the organization is said to be.

4. *Define empowerment and explain how it can be encouraged.* Empowerment is a form of decentralization that involves giving subordinates substantial authority to make decisions. The keys to successfully empowering employees are expressing confidence in their abilities to perform at high levels, designing jobs so that employees have considerable freedom, setting meaningful and challenging goals, applauding good performance, and encouraging employees to take personal responsibility for their work.

5. *Identify and describe several principles of supervision based on authority.* The parity principle states that authority and responsibility must coincide. The exception principle states that supervisors should concentrate their efforts on matters that

deviate from the norm and let their employees handle routine matters. The unity of command principle states that an employee should have one and only one immediate boss. The scalar principle states that authority flows one link at a time from the top of the organization to the bottom. The span of control principle refers to the number of employees a supervisor can effectively manage and is dependent on several factors: the complexity, variety, and proximity of the jobs being supervised; the quality of the employees; and the ability of the supervisor.

6. *Recount the basic steps in the delegation process.* Successful delegation involves three basic steps: (1) assigning work to the different employees in the work group, (2) creating an obligation to perform the duties satisfactorily on the part of each employee, and (3) granting authority to take the actions necessary to perform the duties.

7. *Discuss why supervisors are often reluctant to delegate authority.* Supervisors may be reluctant to delegate for the following reasons: (1) fear that they are the only ones who can do the job right; (2) a belief that it is easier to do the job themselves; (3) fear of having an employee look too good; (4) their own attraction to power; (5) more confidence in doing their own detail work; (6) preconceived ideas about employees; and (7) a misconceived desire to set the right example.

8. *Describe some supervisory tasks that can't be delegated.* The quality and type of employees greatly affect what can be delegated. However, the following tasks should normally not be delegated: planning activities, assigning work, motivation work, counseling employees, resolving conflict situations, and tasks specifically assigned to the supervisor.

9. *Describe several tips for making delegation more effective.* These specific things can be done to make it easier to delegate: (1) know your employees' abilities; (2) don't be afraid of overdelegating; (3) practice good communication skills when delegating; (4) minimize overlap of authority; (5) give employees some freedom in deciding how to implement their authority; (6) assign related areas of authority and responsibility to each individual; (7) once you have delegated, let the employee take over; and (8) don't expect perfection the first time.

REVIEW QUESTIONS

1. What is departmentation? What are the different types of departmentation?
2. Define *authority*. What is the difference between line authority and staff authority?
3. What is meant by centralized versus decentralized authority?
4. Define *empowerment*. What are some things a supervisor can do to foster an environment that encourages empowerment?
5. Define *power*. What is the difference between power and authority?
6. Define *responsibility*. Can authority and responsibility be delegated?
7. What is the parity principle?
8. What is the exception principle?
9. What is the unity of command principle?
10. What is the scalar principle?
11. What is the span of control principle?
12. What are the three basic steps involved in delegation? Briefly discuss each.
13. State seven reasons why supervisors are reluctant to delegate authority.
14. Name six general categories of things that should usually not be delegated.
15. Discuss several tips that can help a supervisor delegate.

SKILL-BUILDING QUESTIONS

1. If you were planning to give a 10-minute talk to your employees on the topic of delegation, what would you say? Give your answer in outline form.

2. Some supervisors contend that the art of delegation either comes naturally or never comes. Do you agree with this contention? Why or why not?

3. How does the concept of empowerment relate to delegation? Do you think that successful delegation depends on subordinates being empowered?

4. "The scalar principle creates so much red tape and slows down activity to such an extent that it creates more problems than it solves." Do you agree or disagree with this statement? Support your answer.

ADDITIONAL READINGS

Beaubien, Elaine. "Legendary Leadership," *Executive Excellence*, September 1997.

Bielous, G. A. "The Transition from Worker to Supervisor: Five Common Mistakes," *Supervision*, February 1994.

McConnell, Charles R. "Delegation vs. Empowerment: What, How, and Is There a Difference?" *Health Care Supervisor*, September 1995.

Pollock, Ted. "Don't Let Emotions Prevent You from Delegating," *Supervision*, March 1996.

SKILL-BUILDING APPLICATIONS

Incident 7–1

Where Do You Start?

Carl was a hard-working supervisor. He had enough personnel in his organization to accomplish the workload, but in spite of this, his work was rarely done on time. One day, Carl excused himself from his boss's staff meeting, stating that he had to get back to the job. Roger, his boss, decided to spend the next morning with him.

When Roger arrived the next morning, Carl was talking on the phone and at the same time, signing some forms. He interrupted the phone conversation and called to the secretary, "Mary, these forms are signed."

While still talking on the same phone call, Carl then thrust the signed forms toward Mary as she entered. His movement pushed the disorderly pile of papers off the corner of his desk. The papers were scattered on the floor by a breeze through an open window, and Mary began to pick them up. Carl shouted, "I'll think about it and call you back, Oliver." Then he said to Mary, "Don't pick them up, you'll just mix them worse." He scooped up a paper that was on the desk and handed it to the chief, "There is Don Pitt's idea of how to save about half the time we spend on processing. Wish we had time to try it out. What do you think of it?"

Mary came back in. "Bill Evans wants to know if he can start on the priority job right now," she said. "Tell him to wait," Carl replied. "I haven't time to finish training him, and I just can't trust him to start a job that important without checking it myself."

While Carl was picking up the fallen papers and sorting them, Mary brought in some forms. "You just signed those on the line for the president's signature, so I typed them over."

"Too much to do," muttered Carl, glancing at Roger as he signed. "If you're signing them now, I'll take them to the president right away," said Mary, reaching. "I'll take them," replied Carl, "the President might want to ask me about them."

Carl explained to Roger, "Don and Bob can't do a thing till I run these through. I'll be right back." He dashed off, but was back in a minute.

Questions

1. Do you think Carl is highly motivated? Is he a good supervisor?
2. What do you think are Carl's major problems?
3. What suggestions would you make to Carl?

Incident 7–2

A Hectic Day

Francis S. Russell is a supervisor for the Tri Cities Country Club. At the moment, this self-styled perfectionist is sitting up in bed, checking his TTD sheet for tomorrow. The TTD (Things to Do) itemizes his daily activities, placing them on an exact time schedule. Never one to browbeat subordinates, Russell had his own special way of reminding people that time is money. Ever since the days when he was the best waiter the club ever hand, he had worked harder than the rest. It had paid off, too, because in only two years (when old Charlie retired), he was the heir apparent to the general manager of the club. As this thought crossed Russell's mind, his immediate pride was replaced with a nagging problem. Where was he going to find the time to do all the things his position required? He certainly couldn't afford to just maintain the status quo. Then his mind forced him to plan tomorrow's activities, so the problem was pushed into the background for future consideration. (Below is a portion of Russell's well-planned day.)

TTD—October 16th

7:15 Breakfast with Johnson (the tennis pro) about information on his cataloging system for the club's tennis shop.

8:30 Meeting with Henry (assistant club manager). Tell him exactly how the annual meeting for the membership should be set up. Caution—he's shaky on questions.

9:15   Discuss progress on new office procedures manual with Charlie (general manager).

[He's irritated because I've dragged my heels on this. Let him know I've got Newman working on the problem.]

9:45   Assign Pat Newman the job of collecting data and sample copies regarding office manuals in other clubs. Set up a system for him to use in analysis.

10:45   Call on Roger Bradshaw, a very influential board member, and solicit his support on the proposed budget.

[As Russell jotted down some information on Bradshaw, he reflected that it was a shame no one else on his staff could really handle the big shots the way he could. This thought was pleasing and bothersome at the same time.]

12:00   Lunch with Roger Bradshaw at the club.

3:00   Meet with Frank Lentz, a new board member, and check his progress on the new membership campaign.

[Russell thought about Lentz's usual wild ideas and hoped that he had followed the general theme and rough sketches he had prepared.]

7:30   Chamber of Commerce meeting. Look up Pierce Hansen—a friend and club member. He may be able to help secure Bradshaw's support on the budget.

Questions

1. Do you think Russell is highly motivated? Is he a good supervisor?

2. What problems do you see concerning Russell's effectiveness as a supervisor?

3. Assuming that you are Charlie, the general manager, what solutions would you recommend?

Exercise 7–1

Minor Errors

Recently, you have noticed that one of the staff members on the same level as your boss has been giving you a hard time concerning reports that you submit to him. In reviewing your recent reports, you have discovered a few minor errors that you should have caught, but in your opinion they are not significant enough to warrant the kind of criticism you've been receiving.

Your boss and this particular manager have a history of bad relations, which may be one reason for the manager's criticism.

As you think about how to best handle the situation, you consider these alternatives:

Questions

1. Talk to the manager in private and ask him why he is being so critical.

2. Do nothing. This situation is probably temporary, and bringing undue attention to it will only make matters worse.

3. Since your boss may get involved, discuss the situation with him and ask for his advice on what to do.

4. Simply work harder to upgrade the reports. Make sure that there will be nothing to criticize in the future.

5. Discuss the situation with your boss, but minimize or "play down" the problem by letting him know that you feel that constructive criticism of this type is usually healthy.

Other alternatives may be open to you, but assume that these are the only ones you have considered.

Without discussion with anyone, decide which of these approaches you would take now. Be prepared to defend your choice.

Exercise 7–2

"In-Basket"

Imagine yourself in the role of supervisor of a shoe store. You have two assistant or shift managers, who also sell on the floor but have authority only when you are not present, and seven salesclerks, who work various schedules on the floor. The store is not unionized.

You have just arrived back from three days at the company headquarters and are faced with the following list of items in your in-basket:

1. Two applications for jobs (no positions open right now).
2. A note to call Mary (salesclerk) about vacation schedule.
3. A notice that the mall will be changing hours for the upcoming holiday and requesting notice of store plans.
4. A customer complaint regarding product quality.
5. Four shipping receipts indicating that about 130 pairs of shoes have been delivered and need to be stocked.
6. Bids from three companies responding to requests for bids on a cash register system (each store chooses its own).
7. A notice from the fire department of an impending inspection.
8. A note that the rest room is out of order.
9. Notice from the company headquarters that a holiday sale will begin soon.
10. Five advertisements and two catalogs from various vendors.

You should decide to "act on" or "delegate" each of the 10 items. After you have made these decisions, your instructor will assign you to a group with two or three other students. The group will then decide as a group which items should be "acted on" or "delegated."

Questions

These questions should be addressed both individually and by the group:

1. Which tasks are supervisory in nature and which are operational in nature?
2. How does each task compare to the list of tasks that can't be delegated on pages 133–34?
3. For those tasks that you chose not to delegate, were you influenced by any of the reasons listed in Figure 7.4?

Be prepared to discuss your answers with the class.

Exercise 7–3

Promotion Role Play

Your instructor will ask some of you to role-play either the president or the prospective supervisor of sales in the following scenario:

The assistant supervisor of sales for the ABC Company has been in that job for six months. Due to poor sales over the past 18 months, the sales supervisor (the assistant's boss) has just been fired. The president of ABC then offers this job to the assistant sales supervisor, subject to the following stipulations:

▪ You cannot increase the advertising budget.
▪ You must continue to let Metro-Media, Inc., handle the advertising.
▪ You cannot make any personnel changes.
▪ You will accept full responsibility for the sales for this fiscal year (which started two months ago).

The role play will simulate a meeting between the president and the assistant sales supervisor to discuss the offer. You can make any reasonable assumptions you think are necessary to play the role assigned to you.

Exercise 7–4

Delegation Quiz

This exercise is most applicable for students who are currently employed. If you are not currently employed, think of your most recent employment as you complete the quiz.

	Yes	No
1. Do you spend more time than you should doing detail work that others could do?	____	____
2. Do employees often interrupt you with questions and problems on their projects?	____	____
3. Are you still concerned with activities and problems on their projects?	____	____
4. Do you take work home regularly?	____	____
5. Do you work longer hours than your employees?	____	____
6. Are you making decisions that should be made at the level of your employees?	____	____
7. Do you feel you should be able to answer any question your boss asks you on any project in your shop?	____	____
8. Do you have trouble meeting deadlines?	____	____
9. Do you have trouble establishing and maintaining priorities?	____	____
10. Is your in-box often full?	____	____
11. Are you expecting to call your office or to have them call you?	____	____

If you answered yes to only one of these, chances are you're an excellent delegator. If you had two to four yes answers, you can improve. If you had five or more, you should place a high priority on improving your delegating.

CHAPTER 8

Understanding Work Groups

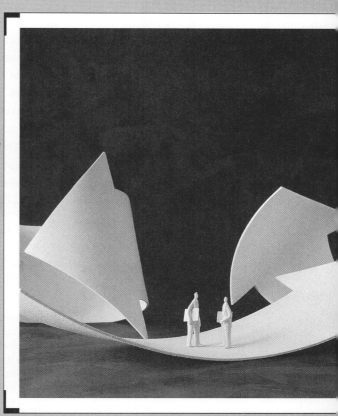

LEARNING OBJECTIVES

After studying this chapter, you should be able to:

1. Compare formal and informal work groups.

2. Describe the role of the supervisor as a linking pin.

3. Describe a quality circle.

4. Explain group norm, group cohesiveness, and group conformity.

5. State some important conclusions regarding informal work group leadership.

6. Discuss how you can get the informal work group to work with you instead of against you.

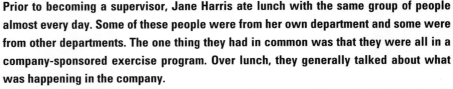

Prior to becoming a supervisor, Jane Harris ate lunch with the same group of people almost every day. Some of these people were from her own department and some were from other departments. The one thing they had in common was that they were all in a company-sponsored exercise program. Over lunch, they generally talked about what was happening in the company.

Jane realized that in her work unit there was also a small group of people who always seemed to be doing things together. However, something bothered Jane about this group. The group sometimes seemed to have a negative effect on the work of her unit.

Belonging to groups is an inherent part of everyone's life. In fact, much of human behavior can be understood by looking at the group within which the behavior occurred. The following quote describes the effect of one group on an individual:

> Joe Marm was a young second lieutenant serving in South Vietnam. In the fall of 1965, he grabbed up two side arms and a pile of grenades and ran up a hill alone. He attacked and destroyed a machine-gun nest, killing eight Viet Cong. Afterward, Lieutenant Marm was recommended for the Congressional Medal of Honor for his heroic actions. When asked why he had made the attack on his own, Marm replied, "What would the fellows have thought of me if I had been afraid to do it?"[1]

Group pressures also affect the actions of individuals in the workplace. Groups can contribute either positively or negatively to the organization's goals. To be effective, supervisors must understand the nature of groups and how to work with them.

One of the more significant studies that demonstrated the effects of groups in organizations was conducted at the Hawthorne Plant of Western Electric in Cicero, Illinois. In this study, the researchers first lowered the level of illumination, expecting productivity to decrease. To their surprise, productivity increased. Next, they altered such variables as rest periods, the length of the workday, and noise. Production still increased. The researchers concluded that other factors besides the physical environment affected worker productivity. One of these factors was the influence of informal work groups.

FORMAL WORK GROUPS

1 LEARNING OBJECTIVES

Basically, there are two types of groups in organizations—formal and informal work groups. **Formal work groups** result primarily from the organizing function of management. As discussed in Chapter 7, **organizing** is the grouping of activities necessary to achieve common objectives. The organization structure results from the assignment of work activities to work groups and the assignment of each work group to a manager or supervisor. The group of people who report to a supervisor is a formal work group. All of the supervisors who report to a particular manager are another formal work group.

Rensis Likert described managers and supervisors in an organization as linking pins because each manager or supervisor has overlapping group mem-

FIGURE 8.1 Linking-Pin Concept

Linking pin

Middle manager

Supervisor

Work group

Work group

Work group

Operative employees

FIGURE 8.2

Suggestions for Building a Team

1. Establish a working environment that the employees consider fair and equitable.
2. Practice participation—listen to the employees' ideas, and get the employees involved in planning.
3. Show the employees that you, the supervisor who represents upper levels of management, also see issues from the employees' side.
4. Attempt to gain acceptance as the group's leader.

2 LEARNING OBJECTIVES

berships in two formal work groups. The supervisor must represent both management and the operative employees. Figure 8.1 illustrates this concept. Likert feels that organizations can be effective only when each employee is a member of one or more work groups that have a high degree of loyalty, interact well with each other, and have high performance goals.[2] The supervisor should consciously attempt to build these qualities within a formal work group. Much of the material presented in this book is directed toward achieving this type of formal work group. Developing a formal work group of this kind is referred to as "building a team" or "developing a team spirit." Figure 8.2 offers four suggestions for building a team spirit within the formal work group.

First, supervisors must establish working environments that are considered fair and friendly. This cannot be done solely by supervisors; all levels of management must contribute. However, if supervisors do not establish such environments in their work units, the contributions of higher levels of management will be wasted. Second, allowing the employees to participate in working out changes and keeping the employees informed about what is taking place also help build team spirit. Effective supervisors attempt to see and understand issues from the employees' point of view. Supervisors need to be careful here. Supervisors who always side with the employees and take an "it's us against them" attitude can create a negative environment. The point is *not* to side with the employees against management but to attempt to understand issues from the employees' point of view. Finally, supervisors should strive, within reason, to gain acceptance as the groups' leaders. Certainly, supervisors have formal authority that higher levels of management have delegated to them. However, formal authority does not guarantee effective leadership. Leadership is discussed in more detail in Chapter 15.

Quality Circles

3 LEARNING OBJECTIVES

One use of a formal work group is the quality circle, which originated in Japan. A **quality circle** is composed of a group of employees (usually from 5 to 15 people) who are members of a single work unit, section, or department. The unit's supervisor or manager is usually included as a member of the quality circle. These employees have a common bond; they perform a similar service or function by turning out a product, part of a product, or a service. Membership in a quality circle is almost always voluntary. The basic purpose of a quality circle is to discuss quality problems and to generate ideas that might help improve quality.

A quality circle usually begins by exposing the members to specialized training relating to quality. Meetings of a quality circle are normally held once or twice per month and last for one to two hours. After the initial training, a quality circle begins by discussing specific quality problems that are brought up either by management representatives or by the circle members. Staff experts may be called upon by the circle as needed. As with other forms of participative management, the underlying objective of quality circles is to get employees actively involved. The success of a quality circle is largely dependent on the management team. Management's commitment and support help create commitment and support from employees. Currently, the concept of quality circles is being used to provide continuous improvement in production and service quality within many organizations. In fact, the term *quality circle* has been replaced in many organizations by **continuous improvement teams.** Supervision Illustration 8–1 illustrates a form of quality circle at GE.

INFORMAL WORK GROUPS

Overlapping the formal work groups in organizations are **informal work groups** that are not defined by the organizing function. All organizations have informal work groups. Informal work groups are just as important in the organization as formal work groups. They can greatly affect an employee's motivation, both positively and negatively. Thus, effective supervisors must learn to work with informal work groups.

When people are brought together in a work environment, they interact in performing their duties. From these contacts, and from other areas of common interest, friendships emerge. Friendships, mutual interests, and the satisfaction of social needs are three reasons why informal work groups form. Furthermore, employees get a strong sense of security from membership in informal work groups because such groups usually have a strong sense of loyalty and share common values. In general, informal work groups develop to satisfy

---

SUPERVISION ILLUSTRATION 8–1

GENERAL ELECTRIC'S "WORK-OUT" PROGRAM

At General Electric, employees at all levels participate in the company's Work-Out program. Effective since 1990, the program is used to empower employees by allowing them to work together in groups over a period of three days to resolve certain company problems.

The corporatewide Work-Out program has been effective at GE. Not only have employee–management relations improved, but managers have become more people oriented while employees have been given more power in the company's decision-making process.

A typical Work-Out accomplishes the following tasks in just three days:

Day One

- 40 to 100 diverse employees selected by management arrive.
- The top manager gives the group specific problems to solve.

- The top manager leaves.
- The group breaks up into smaller groups; each group is responsible for one issue.

Days One and Two

- The groups brainstorm for ideas.

Day Three

- The top manager returns and hears every idea proposed.
- The top manager makes on-the-spot decisions, either "yes," "no," or "I need more information."

By giving its employees the opportunity to work together, GE has increased production and improved the company as a whole. Very recently, suppliers and customers have been invited to participate in Work-Outs. This has also proved to be very successful, giving the company perhaps another viewpoint on certain company issues.

Source: Adapted from Joseph D'O'Brian, "GE's 'Work-Outs' Change Role of Management," *Supervisory Management,* January 1994, p. 6. For more information on General Electric, visit its Web site at:
www.gec.com

---

many of the basic needs of people. Employees can satisfy safety, social, ego, and self-actualization needs through membership in informal work groups.

Most people enjoy giving and receiving recognition; they also enjoy the sense of belonging that comes from the exchange of feelings. Emotional support and a sense of belonging are two reasons why informal work groups form. Such groups also assist the individual in solving specific problems and protect the individual from his or her mistakes.

Physical working conditions also contribute to the formation of informal work groups. People who work close to one another are almost forced to interact. The arrangement of desks, furniture, offices, equipment, and work flows can either encourage or discourage the formation of informal work groups. Generally, a work environment that enables employees to interact socially increases the likelihood of informal work groups. This is one reason why organizations sometimes put partitions around clerical workers. However, as any supervisor knows, putting up partitions doesn't stop informal work groups from forming.

The style of leadership used by a particular supervisor can influence the formation of informal work groups. For example, the informal work groups that develop under an autocratic supervisor and those that develop under a participative supervisor would probably be entirely different.

In summary, the reasons for the formation of informal work groups in organizations are diverse. The important point for the supervisor to remember is that informal work groups overlap formal work groups and can have a significant impact on performance.

Characteristics of Informal Work Groups

When people begin to work together, cliques tend to form. Certain people are drawn together by common interests. Likes and dislikes of certain employees for other employees emerge. Efforts are made by certain employees to get to know other employees. All of these outcomes are typical of the initial stages in the formation of an informal work group. Once informal work groups have been formed, they seem to take on a life of their own. Over time, most informal work groups develop certain characteristics and a set way of doing things.

4 LEARNING OBJECTIVES

Group norms. A **group norm** is an understanding among group members concerning how those members should behave. An informal work group may, for example, play a joke or trick on all new employees. It may also establish certain performance or production standards that its members are not expected to exceed. Unfortunately, those standards may be below what management feels they should be. The practices described in this book and the guidelines mentioned earlier in this chapter should help foster pro-organization norms. However, a factor that determines whether the norms of an informal work group are followed by its members is the group's cohesiveness.

Group cohesiveness. **Group cohesiveness** refers to the degree of attraction or stick-togetherness of the group. Cohesiveness is very important to the group because it largely determines whether the group's members will adhere to the group's norms or will pursue their own individual norms. The greater the group cohesiveness, the more the individual members will conform to group norms. For example, it is extremely difficult for a supervisor to raise the production norm of a highly cohesive group—even if the norm is very low.

The cohesiveness of informal work groups is influenced by many factors. The size of the group is one factor. Group cohesiveness decreases as the size of the group increases. It is impossible to set an upper limit on the size of informal work groups. Generally, however, if an informal work group becomes larger than 20, subgroups begin to form. Thus, informal work groups usually don't have more than 15 or 20 members. Of course, smaller informal work groups are very common.

The success and status of the informal work group also influence group cohesiveness. Informal work groups that have succeeded in achieving their goals are more cohesive than those that have not succeeded. The process reinforces itself in that success breeds cohesiveness, which in turn breeds more success

These advertising agency co-workers have formed an informal work group.
Jean-Claude LeJeune

and more cohesiveness. Informal work groups with a higher status have more cohesiveness than those with a lower status. Numerous factors determine the status of certain work groups. Among these factors are skill requirements (skilled versus unskilled employees), the type of work performed (the more dangerous or the more financially rewarding the work, the higher the status), the degree of supervision required (the less the supervision required, the higher the status), and the opportunities for promotion (some groups develop a reputation for having many promotion opportunities).

Pressures from outside the group, the stability of membership in the group, the ease of communication, and physical isolation can either increase or decrease cohesiveness. For example, if the informal work group views management as a threat, the group's cohesiveness will increase to offset the threat. If the membership of the informal work group is stable, the group's cohesiveness increases because its members can get to know one another better, can learn the group norms better, and can learn how to behave according to the norms. Work flows and office layouts designed to reduce conversation tend to reduce group cohesiveness. The geographical or physical isolation of a group tends to increase its cohesiveness. Figure 8.3 summarizes the major factors that can increase group cohesiveness. Figure 8.4 describes how to decrease group cohesiveness.

An important point to know about group cohesiveness is that it can have either positive or negative effects. A highly cohesive informal work group whose goals are compatible with the organization's goals can result in above-average productivity. Of course, the opposite is also true.

FIGURE 8.3
Increasing Group
Cohesiveness

1. Smaller groups tend to have more cohesiveness. When a group becomes too large (generally larger than 20), subgroups begin to form.
2. The success and prestige of the group increase cohesiveness. Groups that are successful in achieving their goals are more cohesive. Higher-status groups are also more cohesive.
3. Physical isolation from other groups increases group cohesiveness.
4. The group becomes more attractive for individuals who gain prestige or status within the group.
5. Cohesiveness is higher under conditions where group members are in cooperative relationships than under conditions where there is competition among group members.
6. When group members can fulfill more needs through participating in the group, the attraction of the group increases.
7. When the group is attacked from the outside, its cohesiveness usually increases as its members deal with the external threat. When the group shares a common fate as a result of external attack, the reaction is usually to focus the group's resources on protecting the group. The response to an outside threat is reflected in the statement, "United we stand, divided we fall."

Source: Reproduced by permission from *Human Relations in Organizations* by Dan L. Costley and Ralph Todd. Copyright © 1978, West Publishing Company. All rights reserved.

5 LEARNING OBJECTIVES

Informal Work Group Leadership

Some of the more important conclusions regarding informal work group leadership are:

1. The group selects the leader—and the leader may change, depending on the needs of the group at a particular time.
2. The person selected as the leader is the one whom the group sees as being the most capable in helping it achieve its goals.
3. The person selected as the leader generally has strong communication skills.

If an informal work group exists in a supervisor's formal work group, the supervisor must learn to work with its leader. The supervisor should not feel that he or she is a failure as a leader just because the informal work group also has a leader. The supervisor should recognize that the other person is filling a need of the informal work group. The supervisor should not resent the role of the informal leader. The supervisor should respect that role and solicit the informal leader's support. But the supervisor should always remember the delicate position of the informal leader. The informal leader must answer to the group, and the group can take away the informal leader's position on very short notice.

FIGURE 8.4
Decreasing Group
Cohesiveness

1. When interpersonal conflict results from members' disagreements over ways to achieve group goals or solve group problems, the attractiveness of the group will decrease. Members of highly cohesive groups may often have disagreements, but they try to eliminate the disagreements quickly.

2. If participation in the group results in unpleasant experiences for an individual, the attractiveness of the group will decrease. When group activities result in embarrassment for an individual, the individual's attraction to the group is usually reduced.

3. If membership in the group places limits on participation in other activities or groups, cohesiveness may be lowered. In other words, if the group restricts its members' activities outside the group, the attraction of the group may decrease.

4. If conditions exist in the group that prevent or restrict effective communication, cohesiveness will decrease. Reduced communication may result if some members are too dominating or if some members are unpleasant or obnoxious in their communication behavior.

5. Cohesiveness may be reduced if members feel the group's activities involve too great a personal risk. The risk could be physical danger or psychological threats. Risk could involve engaging in group activities that members regard as illegal or immoral. It could also involve group actions in an organization that the individual feels might result in getting disciplined or fired.

6. If the evaluation of the group by respected outsiders becomes negative, the group can become unattractive to its members.

Source: Reproduced by permission from *Human Relations in Organizations* by Dan L. Costley and Ralph Todd. Copyright © 1978, West Publishing Company. All rights reserved.

GROUP PRESSURES ON INDIVIDUALS

Group conformity.   **Group conformity** is the degree to which the members of the group accept and abide by the norms of the group. Informal work groups seek to control the behavior of their members for many reasons. One reason the group desires uniform, consistent behavior from each member is so that other members can predict with reasonable certainty how the individual member will behave. This certainty is necessary in order to achieve some degree of coordination in working toward the group's goals. On the other hand, groups are organizations in and of themselves; as a result, conformity is often required to maintain the group. Individualistic behavior among group members can threaten the survival of the group by causing internal dissension. Individual members tend to conform to group norms under the following conditions:

1. When the norm is consistent with the personal attitudes, beliefs, and behavioral predispositions of the members.

2. When—despite the norm being inconsistent with the personal attitudes, beliefs, or behavioral predispositions—strong pressures to comply are exerted by the group, and the rewards of complying are valued or the sanctions imposed for noncompliance and viewed as being unimportant.

FIGURE 8.5
Cards in Experiment

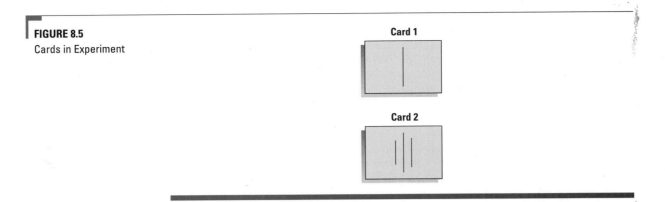

One study of the influence of group pressures on individuals placed college students in groups of seven to nine people.[3] Group members were told they would be comparing lengths of lines on white cards. Figure 8.5 shows the cards and lines. The subjects in the study were then asked to pick the line on the second card that was identical in length to the line on the first card.

In the experiment, all but one member of each group were told to pick one of the two wrong lines on card 2. In addition, the uninformed member of the group was positioned to always be one of the last individuals to respond. Under ordinary circumstances, mistakes on the line selection occur less than 1 percent of the time. However, in this experiment, the uninformed member made the wrong selection in 36.8 percent of the trials.

An uninformed member confronted with only a single individual who contradicted the choice continued to answer correctly in almost all trials. When the opposition was increased by two, incorrect responses increased to 31.8 percent.

The experiment demonstrated that the group's behavior affected the behavior of the individual members; although some individuals remained independent in their judgments, others acquiesced on almost every judgment. Over all, group pressure caused individuals to make incorrect judgments in more than one-third of the cases. The experiment also showed that the more the members that disagreed with the individual, the more likely the individual was to succumb to the judgment of the group.

SUPERVISION AND INFORMAL WORK GROUPS

Too many supervisors view informal work groups only negatively. As mentioned earlier, however, such groups can have positive effects. Figure 8.6 summarizes some of the potential benefits from informal work groups. To realize those benefits, the supervisor must be aware of the impact of informal work groups on individuals. Figure 8.7 lists several key factors that the supervisor should keep in mind when dealing with informal work groups.

FIGURE 8.6
Potential Benefits from
Informal Work Groups

1. Informal work groups blend with the formal organization to make a workable system for getting work done.
2. Informal work groups lighten the workload for the manager and fill in some of the gaps in that manager's abilities.
3. Informal work groups provide satisfaction and stability to the organization.
4. Informal work groups provide a useful channel of communication in the organization.
5. The presence of informal work groups encourages managers to plan and act more carefully than they would otherwise.

Source: Keith Davis, *Human Behavior at Work,* 7th ed. (New York: McGraw-Hill, 1985).

FIGURE 8.7
Key Factors in Dealing
with Informal Work
Groups

1. Participation in groups is a basic source of social need satisfaction for employees.
2. Informal groups try to protect their members and provide security. They try to protect their members from perceived threats from management.
3. Groups develop communication systems to provide information that members want. If management does not provide the information employees want, the informal group will try to obtain it.
4. Both formal and informal groups obtain status and prestige within an organization. Groups may use their status and prestige as a power base to influence others in the organization.
5. Groups develop and enforce norms for the behavior of members. The group norms may be supportive of management or may work against management objectives.
6. The more cohesive a group is, the more control it has over the behavior of its members. The highly cohesive group can produce high achievement of organizational goals. But it can work just as effectively against organizational objectives when it opposes management.
7. Both formal and informal groups within an organization establish roles that affect the activities and responsibilities of members. Accepting role responsibilities in an informal group may require that an individual violate the role expectations of management.

Source: Reproduced by permission from *Human Relations in Organizations* by Dan Costley and Ralph Todd. Copyright © 1978, West Publishing Company. All rights reserved.

6 LEARNING
OBJECTIVES

Getting the Informal Work Group to Work with You instead of against You

As mentioned earlier in this chapter, the informal work group can have very positive benefits if its goals are compatible with the organization's goals. Obviously, some causes of negative work group behavior are outside the supervisor's control. However, a number of causes are within the supervisor's control. The purpose here is to summarize some of the factors that can encourage an informal work group to contribute positively. Some of these factors were also presented earlier as aids in developing a team spirit in the formal work group.

Communicate openly. Most employees want to know what is happening in the organization—especially about things that will affect them. It is often said that informal work groups resist change. The statement is only partially true, however. Groups do resist changes that are going to affect them negatively. They are also likely to resist changes when they are not certain how the changes will affect them.

Keeping the members of the informal work group informed helps create the feeling that they are an accepted part of the organization and are needed. Keeping the lines of communication open also lets the supervisor quickly know about small problems before they develop into large problems. Moreover, since employees want to know what is going on, if the supervisor doesn't keep them informed, they will find out from others.

Encourage group participation in decision making. Allowing the group to participate in decisions that will affect it is very helpful in getting it to work positively with the supervisor. In Chapter 2, suggestions were offered on methods to use in getting group participation in decision making.

Respect the informal leader. Specific suggestions for dealing with the informal leader have already been made. These suggestions need to be followed if the supervisor is to get the support of the informal work group.

Remove production obstacles. The list of potential production obstacles is quite long. Among those obstacles are excess paperwork, improper maintenance, material shortages, ineffective policies and procedures, and poor working conditions. The best way to identify production obstacles is to ask the employees or the informal work group leader. Informal work groups appreciate a supervisor who is concerned and works toward removing performance obstacles. Even though the supervisor may not be able to remove all of the obstacles, he or she should keep the group informed about what is being done.

Practice constructive discipline. Chapter 22 will outline several suggestions for applying positive disciplinary procedures. If the informal work group feels that the supervisor is being unfair to one of its members, the supervisor will not get the support of the group.

Be sensitive to individual needs. It is important to remember that groups in organizations are made up of individuals. These individuals have their own likes, dislikes, needs, and wants. The supervisor should attempt to develop an understanding of each individual's needs. Supervising people as individuals and attempting to help them satisfy their individual needs are steps toward winning over the group to which they belong.

Set a good example and be consistent. A supervisor must always remember that the members of the informal work group watch the supervisor's actions. The age-old saying "Actions speak louder than words" is very true for the

FIGURE 8.8
Guidelines to Promoting
Positive Contributions
from Informal Groups

1. Communicate openly.
2. Encourage group participation in decision making.
3. Respect the informal leader.
4. Remove production obstacles.
5. Practice constructive discipline.
6. Be sensitive to individual needs.
7. Set a good example and be consistent.
8. Attempt to provide group rewards.
9. Support the group when possible.
10. Set achievable goals for your work unit.

supervisor. Supervisors whose behavior sets a poor example are very unlikely to get cooperation from the informal work group. Inconsistent behavior also contributes to negative behavior by the informal work group. For example, a supervisor who is demanding of one person in the group but lenient toward another person is unlikely to get support from the group.

Attempt to provide group rewards.   This suggestion may not be totally under the control of the supervisor. Some organizations have devised group incentive programs to help get group support. Praising the group when it deserves praise is an effective means of getting group support.

Support the group when possible.   If the supervisor supports the informal work group in its legitimate claims to higher levels of management, the group is likely to give its support to the supervisor in return. However, it is important not to develop a feeling among the employees that the supervisor is one of the gang and that "it is us against them." The supervisor is a member of the management team, and employees must know and respect this. Still, presenting and supporting legitimate employee concerns is a very effective way of getting support from the informal work group. The removal of performance obstacles is one area where the supervisor can effectively support employee concerns.

Set achievable goals for your work unit.   People are generally motivated to achieve a goal that they feel can be accomplished. On the other hand, if they feel they can't reach a goal, they generally can't and won't. Informal work groups behave in a similar fashion. They will not work toward unrealistic goals. Soliciting participation from the group when setting goals helps get its support in achieving goals.

Figure 8.8 summarizes these 10 guidelines for promoting positive contributions from informal work groups. Supervisory Illustration 8–2 gives an interesting approach to building teamwork.

SUPERVISION ILLUSTRATION 8-2

ZEN AND THE ART OF TEAMWORK

Chicago Bulls coach Phil Jackson has built a career on being different. From his Grateful Dead decal on the lamp in his office to his readings of poetry to his team before playoff games, his approach to management is a philosophy based partly on Zen Buddhism and partly on team building. Team building and Zen Buddhism, according to Jackson, delivered three back-to-back NBA championships to Chicago as of 1995.

When asked the obvious question of what Zen has to do with managing, Jackson replies, "Whether on the court or off, what I call for in my people is full awareness and attention." "That's what Zen is really all about—waking up and being mindful," says the coach. With this philosophy, individuals come to police themselves; they take responsibility for their own actions.

Does this altered consciousness have any benefits? Jackson believes the players (or any team members) learn how to subjugate themselves to the needs of the team. Many nights Michael Jordan might score 50 points, but the team might lose. High individual performance but poor team performance is not what winning is all about, whether in professional sports or in business.

To motivate individuals to do their best, Jackson recommends that the manager understand which side of the person to appeal to, materialistic or spiritual. Phil Jackson prefers the spiritual, wherein individuals surrender their own egos, so that the end result is bigger than the sum of its parts. If you can also impress on the team members that they all need to grow for the team to be successful, the sum of the parts is an expanding concept.

Finally, Jackson advocates that the manager create a balance between structure and freedom. Structure provides a foundation so that the individual and the team do not lose their focus, and freedom gives them the ability to act and to create. Picture the difference between five fingers working independently and five fingers working in concert as a hand. Modern managers will learn that by following Jackson's concepts, coordination and action will be the end result and winning will come naturally.

Source: Adapted from Ron Lieber, "Zen and the Art of Teamwork," *Fortune,* December 25, 1995, p. 218. Reprinted by permission of Fortune © 1995 Time, Inc. All Rights Reserved. For more information on the Chicago Bulls, visit their Web site at:
www.nba.com/bulls

SOLUTION TO THE SUPERVISION DILEMMA

Jane has learned that informal work groups exist in all organizations and that effective supervisors must work with these groups. She has learned why informal work groups exist (pp. 146–48) and what some of their characteristics are (pp. 148–49). Informal work groups always attempt to get their individual members to conform to group norms. Jane has learned that informal work groups can have positive effects in an organization. She has also learned that she can get the informal work group in her department to work with her instead of against her by communicating openly, encouraging group participation in decision making, respecting the informal leader, removing production obstacles, practicing constructive discipline, being sensitive to individual needs, setting a good example and being consistent, attempting to provide group rewards, supporting the group when possible, and setting achievable goals for her work unit (pp. 153–55).

SUMMARY

Groups can either contribute positively or negatively toward achieving an organization's goals. The purpose of this chapter is to help the supervisor understand the nature of groups and how to work with them.

1. *Compare formal and informal work groups.* Formal work groups result primarily from the organizing function of management. Overlapping the formal work groups in organizations are informal work groups that are not defined by the organizing function.

2. *Describe the role of the supervisor as a linking pin.* Supervisors have memberships in overlapping groups and should serve to link these groups to the total organization. Supervisors serve as the link between management and the operative employees.

3. *Describe a quality circle.* A quality circle is a group of employees who are members of a work unit and whose basic purpose is to discuss quality problems and generate ideas that might improve quality.

4. *Explain group norm and group cohesiveness.* A group norm is an understanding among group members concerning how those members should behave. Group cohesiveness refers to the degree of attraction or stick-togetherness of the group.

5. *State some important conclusions regarding informal work group leadership.* The group selects the leader— and the leader may change, depending on the needs of the group at a particular time. The person selected as the leader is the one whom the group sees as the most capable in helping it achieve its goals. The person selected as the leader generally has strong communication skills.

6. *Discuss how you can get the informal work group to work with you instead of against you.* You can get the informal work group to work with you instead of against you in these ways: communicate openly, encourage group participation in decision making, respect the informal leader, remove production obstacles, practice constructive discipline, be sensitive to individual needs, set a good example, be consistent, attempt to provide group rewards, support the group when possible, and set achievable goals for your work unit.

REVIEW QUESTIONS

1. Define the two types of groups that exist in all organizations.
2. Give four ways to develop a team spirit within the formal work group.
3. What is a quality circle?
4. What are some reasons why informal work groups form?
5. What is a group norm?
6. What is group cohesiveness?
7. What factors affect group cohesiveness?
8. What are some potential benefits of informal work groups?
9. Outline several considerations that can help encourage the informal work group to work with the supervisor.

SKILL-BUILDING QUESTIONS

1. "Informal work groups cause more harm than good." Discuss your views on this statement.

2. "Most good, high-producing employees don't belong to informal work groups." Discuss.

3. Do you feel that a supervisor can be part of an informal work group that contains employees who work for the supervisor? Discuss.

4. Suppose you were recently made supervisor of a highly cohesive work group that has established unacceptably low production norms. How would you go about changing this situation?

REFERENCES

1. Taken from *The New York Times*, November 17, 1966.

2. Rensis Likert, *New Patterns of Management* (New York: McGraw Hill Book Company, 1961), p. 104.

3. Solomon Asch, "Opinions and Social Pressure," *Scientific American*, November 1955, pp. 31–34.

ADDITIONAL READINGS

Bishop, James Wallace, and K. Dow Scott. "How Commitment Affects Team Performance." [Employee Commitment], *HRMagazine*, February 1997.

Buhler, Patricia. "Group Membership," *Supervision*, May 1994.

Hoevemeyer, Victoria A. "How Effective Is Your Team?" *Training and Development*, September 1993.

Van Auken, Phillip M. "Do You DARE to Be a Team?" [Dependancy, Accountability, Reward, Empowerment], *Supervision*, January 1997.

———. "Harnessing Group Dynamics for Greater Productivity," *Supervisory Management*, January 1992.

Williams, Bill. "Ten Commandments for Group Leaders," *Supervisory Management*, September 1992.

SKILL-BUILDING APPLICATIONS

Incident 8–1

Jokes on the Night Shift

Mary Keen is supervisor of nursing on the night shift at the Parkview Memorial Hospital. She has been supervisor for almost three years. There are 22 nurses on the night shift. A group of eight nurses have always been very close to one another. Their leader is Gwen Anderson, an exceptionally friendly and talkative person. She is an excellent nurse. All eight nurses in the group have been at the hospital longer than Mary. They are well respected by the doctors and the rest of the hospital staff.

When a new nurse comes on the night shift, Gwen and the group have their normal routine of jokes and tricks that they play. Generally, it is taken in good spirits by the new person.

In the past couple of months, however, the tricks and jokes have gotten out of hand, in Mary's view. In fact, two new nurses have resigned after only a short time on the job. One of the reasons given was the jokes and tricks that Gwen and the group were constantly playing.

Mary decided to talk to Gwen about the situation. After presenting her concerns, Mary asked Gwen what she thought. Gwen said, "You know our group works hard. A little fun now and then breaks the tension and constant pressure of looking after patients. People who can't take the jokes don't belong here anyhow."

Two weeks later, two more new nurses walked into Mary's office and said, "We're resigning." When Mary asked them why, they said, "We consider nursing to be a serious business and don't appreciate all the jokes and tricks that go on around here." Both nurses intended to express their concerns to the hospital administrator.

Questions

1. What should Mary do?
2. Do you agree with Gwen?
3. How can Mary change the attitude of the informal work group? (Answer this question in writing.)

Incident 8–2

A New Job

Mike Ponder reported early to his new job as supervisor of the records department in the tax assessor's office of Yankton City. Mike was really excited because he was fresh out of college and anxious to use some of the techniques he had learned in business school. Sam McDonald, head of the tax assessor's office, introduced Mike to the employees of the records department and asked Don Ashley, a 20-year employee in the department, to show Mike the ropes.

Don was very cooperative. He worked with Mike for the first two weeks, explaining the technical aspects of the work. It was also very apparent to Mike that Don was the informal leader in the records department. People came to him with their questions and discussed their personal problems with him.

Throughout his first month, Mike felt very uneasy about his working relationship with his employees. They continued to go to Don with their problems and quite frankly ignored Mike.

One day, Mike asked Randy Wallace to have lunch. Randy was a records department employee of about the same age as Mike. At lunch, the conversation went as follows:

Mike: Randy, I need your help.

Randy: On what?

Mike: The people in the records department just aren't accepting me as their boss. They seem to feel that I am an outsider to the group. In fact, they look to Don more than they look to me.

Randy: Well, I guess you know that most of us feel that Don should have been made supervisor.

Mike: No, I didn't know that.

Randy: Well, we did. Most of us were pretty upset when they brought in an outsider.

Questions

1. Are the group's feelings normal?
2. How would you suggest that Mike go about gaining the group's confidence?
3. What role can Don play in helping Mike? Should Mike ask for Don's help?

Exercise 8–1

Crash Project

You are told that you and your work group have two weeks to implement a new program. You feel that you and your employees would virtually have to work around the clock to implement the program in that time. Morale has always been high in your group, but you know that some of your people just don't like overtime. As you think about how to handle the situation, you consider these alternatives.

1. Tell your group, "The company is being pretty unreasonable about this—I don't see what the big rush is. But it's going to be done, so let's all pitch in and help, shall we?"
2. Tell your group, "I have told Bob Smith [your boss] that I have a superb group of people and that if anyone in the company could get the job done, we could."
3. Tell the group, "My job is on the line—and if you want me around for a while, you will have to make a heroic effort."
4. Tell your group, "I don't want to hear any griping. This is the nature of the job, and anyone who feels that he or she can't devote the extra time had better start looking for another job."
5. Tell the group, "The job must be done. Can you offer any suggestions on how it can be completed within the deadline?"

Other alternatives may be open to you, but assume that these are the only ones you have considered. *Without discussion with anyone*, decide which of these approaches you would take. Be prepared to defend your choice.

Exercise 8–2

Characteristics of Effective Work Groups

You have been a member of many groups in your lifetime. Some of these groups include both formal and informal groups. Examples of such groups might include your Sunday school class, your neighborhood playmates when you were younger, your soccer or baseball team, and the employees at your summer job. No matter whether it is a formal or informal group, everyone has been a member of a group. Some of the groups have been quite effective and some have been quite ineffective.

Recall the most effective and the most ineffective groups of which you have been a member. Prepare a description of the characteristics of both groups. Be prepared to make a five-minute presentation of these characteristics.

CHAPTER 9

Productivity and Methods Improvement

LEARNING OBJECTIVES

After studying this chapter, you should be able to:

1. Explain the three major components of organizational productivity.

2. Define the Kaizen philosophy for improvement.

3. Describe the supervisor's role in a work-methods improvement program.

4. Discuss the benefits of work-methods improvement.

5. Present a systematic approach for improving work methods.

6. Distinguish between time study and motion study.

John Harris returned from the accounting department. He was really impressed with the efficiency of those people! Everything always seemed to be in such perfect order over there. Nothing ever seemed to be out of place. The employees seemed to follow precise methods. John was sure that the accounting department had to be the most efficient in the company. All of this made him wonder why his department couldn't be just as efficient. After all, what had impressed him was not the efficiency of the equipment but the efficiency of the people. John had heard a lot of talk about productivity and work-methods improvement, but he really didn't know what it was all about. Maybe now was the time to find out.

Productivity may be defined as units of output per employee hour. Historically, the United States has enjoyed very high productivity relative to other countries. However, in the post-Vietnam era, this nation's previously unchallenged lead in productivity has been diminishing when compared to many other nations. Because increasing productivity is a key to competing at the local, national, and international levels, management and labor leaders both publicly urge high productivity in the workforce. Unfortunately, many employees interpret this urging only as a plea to work harder.

1 LEARNING OBJECTIVES

As shown in Figure 9.1, productivity is the result of three separate major components—efficiency of technology, efficiency of labor, and the effectiveness of management. *Technology* as defined here includes new and improved methods, new ideas, inventions, and innovations, as well as new and improved materials. Efficiency of labor is a function of the general level of services offered and the motivation to work. *Services* as used here includes health, education, research, and other support provided for the employees. Given high efficiencies of technology and labor, these inputs must be effectively combined by *management* if high productivity is to result. Thus, productivity is not simply a matter of making employees work longer and harder. The desire to work, which is often referred to as the work ethic, must not be absent; however, it represents only one of several requirements for high productivity.

It has been said that the real meaning of productivity is "to produce more with the same amount of human effort."[1] This statement is based on the fact that, over the long run, far greater gains in productivity have come from efficiency of technology and effective management than from efficiency of labor. For example, the average factory employee in the United States currently produces more than six times as much in an hour as that employee's grandfather produced around 1900 and with less effort in most cases.[2]

Supervisors, as the first level of management, can have a significant impact on all three major components of productivity. Chapter 2 discussed ways that supervisors might encourage innovative and creative ideas.

FIGURE 9.1 Determinants of Productivity

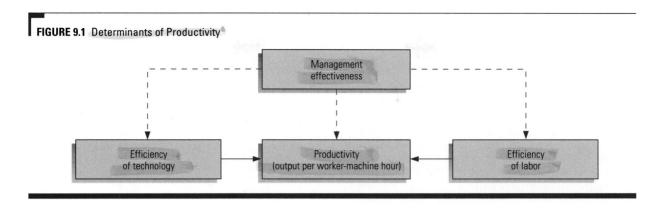

Chapter 14 discusses what supervisors can do to motivate their employees. This chapter focuses on what supervisors can do in the area of work-methods improvement.

KAIZEN PHILOSOPHY FOR IMPROVEMENT

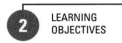

LEARNING OBJECTIVES

Because of intensified world competition, there has been increased emphasis placed on improvements of all types within today's organizations. **Kaizen** is a philosophy for improvement that originated in Japan and that has recently enjoyed widespread adoption throughout the world. The word *Kaizen* comes from two Japanese words: *Kai*, meaning "change," and *zen*, meaning "good."[3] Hence, Kaizen literally means "good change," and in today's context it describes a process of continuous and relentless improvement. Kaizen is not based on large technical leaps but on the incremental refining of existing processes. Kaizen is basically a system of taking small steps to improve the workplace. Kaizen is based on the belief that the system should be customer driven and involve all employees through systematic and open communication. Under Kaizen, employees are viewed as the organization's most valued asset. This philosophy is put into practice through teamwork and extensive employee participation. In summary, Kaizen applies the principles of participatory management toward incremental improvement of the current methods and processes. Kaizen does not focus on obtaining new and faster machines but rather on improving the methods and procedures used in the existing situation.

The single biggest waste in many companies is overproduction or producing more than needed.[4] Kaizen emphasizes direct communication with customers to clearly ascertain their order and scheduling needs and, thus, to keep inventories to a minimum. This requires open communication among many levels of employees. Supervision Illustration 9–1 describes how Kaizen programs have paid off for several companies.

SUPERVISION ILLUSTRATION 9–1

KAIZEN PAYS OFF

According to a recent study by TBM Consulting Group Inc., companies employing Kaizen production systems experienced a 6.6 percent jump in productivity in 1995, as compared to a 3.9 percent increase among companies not using Kaizen. The companies that responded to the survey represented four continents from Kuantan, Malaysia, to Sao Paulo, Brazil, to Raunheim, Germany, to Hot Springs, Arkansas. Aerospace manufacturers, automotive companies, and service-sector firms were among those responding to the survey. Survey respondents also reported the following results from their Kaizen programs:

- 73% reduced overtime as a result of increased employee productivity.

- 63% reported reduced lead times on product production.
- 63% were able to hold down or decrease product pricing.
- 61% experienced increased market share.
- 39% reduced the time required to launch new products.
- 38% used freed-up employees to work on improvement activities elsewhere in the plant.
- 33% dismissed temporary employees.

Source: Laura Struebing, "Kaizen Pays Off for Manufacturers," *Quality Progress,* April 1997, p. 16. For more information about Kaizen systems visit the Kaizen Institute Web site at:
www.gembakaizen.com

METHODS IMPROVEMENT AND THE SUPERVISOR

3   LEARNING OBJECTIVES

The best method for performing a task is a combination of how the human body is used, the arrangement of the workplace, and the design of the tools and equipment. **Work-methods improvement** is used to find the most efficient way to accomplish a given task. *Methods engineering* and *work simplification* are other terms referring to the same process. An old saying, "Work smarter, not harder," sums up the objective of work-methods improvement.

A methods improvement program should be concerned with finding the best ways of performing a task or a group of tasks. Although this involves eliminating *unnecessary* work, it need not mean that the scope of the task or job should be restructured. The objective is not to make the task or job as simple as possible, but to increase efficiency by eliminating unnecessary work and by optimally structuring necessary work.

Employee Fears

When undertaking any type of methods improvement program, supervisors should always give proper attention to the affected employees. Many employees believe that any form of methods improvement necessarily translates into more effort for the same pay. This belief, coupled with employees' natural resistance to any change, can create a negative attitude toward any methods improvement program. The previously discussed Kaizen philosophy provides an excellent method for creating a positive attitude toward methods improvement. The Kaizen philosophy directly involves employees in determining what improvements should be tried. Under the Kaizen philosophy, most suggested work improvements come from the employees themselves.

Establishing the Proper Climate

In addition to following the general approach of the Kaizen philosophy, supervisors can take several specific actions to encourage methods of improvements by employees. First and foremost, employees must be given the tools and know-how for simplifying work. While many methods improvements are based on common sense, certain available tools can greatly aid in the process of making such improvements. Second, employees must be motivated to make methods improvements. A supervisor can create an improvement-oriented atmosphere by actively listening to and following up on employee suggestions and by rewarding employees for methods improvements. On the other hand, employees quickly detect whether the supervisor is reluctant to listen to or try out suggested ideas. If a supervisor is not a true believer in methods improvements, employees will not be motivated to make such improvements.

The supervisor should set the example. He or she should never lose sight of the fact that most work methods can be improved. The key is to concentrate on the areas with the greatest potential for payoffs. Supervisors should actively participate in methods improvement, periodically talk up methods improvement with employees, and encourage employees to attend methods improvement training programs. In the final analysis, employees will react to their perceptions of the supervisor's attitude. If they believe that methods improvement is important to the supervisor, it will be important to them. If they believe that methods improvement is not important to the supervisor, it will probably be unimportant to them.

BENEFITS OF METHODS IMPROVEMENT

4 LEARNING OBJECTIVES

The benefits of methods improvement can be significant. Among the potential benefits are reduced costs, higher productivity, reduced delays, higher quality, reduced waste, improved safety, and satisfied employees. The magnitude of the benefits can be quite large even for very simple tasks. For example, the management pioneer Frederick W. Taylor increased the productivity of a man manually unloading pig iron from a rail car by almost 300 percent (from 12 tons per day to almost 48 tons per day). Taylor achieved equally impressive improvements in the simple task of shoveling coal. By closely studying the methods involved and designing a special shovel to fit the shoveler's physical characteristics, Taylor significantly increased the shoveler's productivity.

The benefits of methods improvement today are not limited to industrial or manufacturing organizations. Service organizations can apply the principles of methods improvement as effectively as industrial organizations can. For example, methods improvements can be made in the processing of customers through a cafeteria or of patients through a doctor's office. Efficiency of operations that results from work-methods improvement is one of the factors most responsible for McDonald's success as the world's largest fast-food chain (see Supervision Illustration 9–2). Methods improvement can glean substantial benefits for almost any organization.

Tasks with repetitive operations usually have a potential for substantial methods improvement.
Brown Brothers

Supervisors, other managers, employees, consumers, owners, and society in general all benefit from methods improvement (see Figure 9.2). Methods improvement can make jobs more satisfying to employees, especially if the employees have participated in working out the changes. It can also increase employee safety. The increased productivity and lower costs resulting from methods improvement reflect positively on the various levels of management. Consumers and society in general benefit from the cost savings achieved by methods improvement, which may be passed on in the form of lower prices or more goods and services. Owners or investors benefit from the increased profits resulting from methods improvement.

SYSTEMATIC METHODS IMPROVEMENT

LEARNING
OBJECTIVES

Regrettably, many supervisors look on methods improvement as something that occurs naturally. They base this belief on the assumption that any tasks warranting methods improvement are generally obvious. However, this is often not the case. With methods improvement, as with almost any other endeavor, a systematic approach produces the best results. The PDCA Cycle, also referred to as the Shewhart Cycle or the Deming Circle, is an approach to methods improvement that has enjoyed considerable success. PDCA stands for the four stages that the cycle comprises: Plan, Do, Check, and Act. Each of these stages is discussed below.

Stage 1: Plan—Where and How to Make Improvements

The first step is to plan where and how to make improvements. As discussed previously, most work methods can be improved. Still, it makes good sense to direct your methods improvement efforts to those areas that have the highest

---

SUPERVISION ILLUSTRATION 9–2

METHODS PLANNING AT MCDONALD'S

The main function of each McDonald's hamburger outlet is the fast delivery of a consistently high-quality product in a clean facility. One of the keys to McDonald's phenomenal success is the detailed facility layout and the well-planned methods used. Storage and preparation spaces are designed specifically for the existing mix of products, which discourages the owner from supplementing the menu. All products are prepackaged and premeasured to ensure uniformity. Food is cooked on equipment designed to make an optimum amount without waste. McDonald's even uses a special wide-mouthed scoop to fill a bag with exactly the right amount of french fries. The scoop prevents costly overfilling but creates an impression of abundance. The facilities and methods are planned in such detail that employee discretion is virtually eliminated and everything is positioned for a reason. For example, the french fries were situated not only to be accessible to the employees but also to catch the attention of customers and, it is hoped, entice them to order some. The size of the fryer used to cook the french fries is neither too large to cook too many at once (which would allow them to become soggy) or so small as to require frequent and costly frying.

Source: Theodore Levitt, "Production-Line Approach to Service," *Harvard Business Review,* September–October 1972, p. 41. For more information about McDonald's visit its Web site at:
www.mcdonalds.com

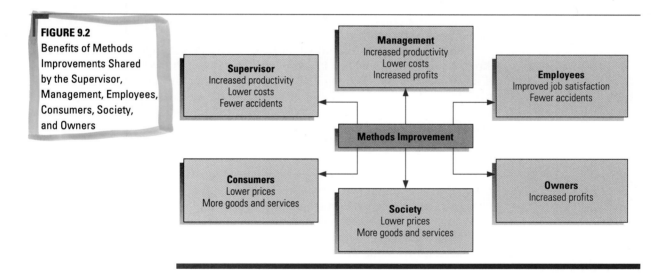

FIGURE 9.2
Benefits of Methods Improvements Shared by the Supervisor, Management, Employees, Consumers, Society, and Owners

likelihood of producing the greatest results. Determining those areas is not always easy. First, talk to other supervisors and to your employees. Find out where they think that improvements can be made. There are certain other indicators that supervisors should look for and recognize. The key is to consciously look for them. Usually fruitful areas for methods improvement are tasks involving a lot of people, where waste or scrap is high, materials are expensive, and labor costs are high. Tasks with repetitive operations also usually have a potential for substantial methods improvement. Other indicators of such a potential include production or customer bottlenecks, extensive overtime, excessive delays, and employee boredom.

FIGURE 9.3

Indicators of Tasks with a High Potential for Gain from Methods Improvements

1. Greatest workload.
2. Relatively long time to complete.
3. Great physical activity required.
4. High relative cost in work hours, machine utilization, or space.
5. Poor quality being produced.
6. Excessive waste or scrap or unused services.
7. Production bottlenecks.
8. High accident rates.
9. Excessive delays.
10. Large amount of repetition involved.
11. Employee boredom.

Identifying tasks needing methods improvement.   One good way to recognize work methods needing improvement is to periodically review output and budget data. Out-of-line costs, slow service, unmet production schedules, excessive waste, and high accident rates usually show up in these data. A good approach is to develop a priority list of tasks targeted for methods improvement. The methods used in each task on the list can then be improved as time and resources permit. Figure 9.3 itemizes indicators that can help identify tasks for methods improvement.

Another recommendation is that tasks be looked at in terms of their three chronological components: (1) preparation for doing the work, (2) actual doing of the work, and (3) cleaning and putting up of supplies and equipment. Tasks involving a considerable amount of preparation and cleanup are usually excellent candidates for methods improvement. Any time saved on these tasks can be used to do more productive work.

Seeking the ideas of employees both on an individual and a group basis can be very fruitful in identifying tasks to be improved. The people who actually perform the tasks often have the best ideas about where improvements can be made. It is the supervisor's responsibility to solicit employee inputs. All too often, supervisors depend on employees voluntarily offering their suggestions.

A final recommendation is that the beginning and ending of a task selected for methods improvement be clearly defined. This will limit the scope of the methods improvement study as well as the specific tasks to be studied.

Analyzing the task.   After a task has been selected for improvement, the task must be analyzed to determine how it is currently being performed. Once you have identified the steps of the task as it is currently being done, those steps need to be evaluated. The necessity of each step should be questioned. Why is it necessary? What would be the cost of eliminating it? (The flow-process chart described in the appendix to this chapter can be used to help spot inefficiencies and eliminate unnecessary job steps.) Each of the questions in Figure 9.4 should be addressed for each job step. As each step is questioned, pertinent notes, including the type of action required, should be recorded on the flow-process chart. Remember, the overriding purpose of this step is to identify inefficient work and wasted motions.

FIGURE 9.4

Questions to Be
Addressed at Each Step
of the Procedure Being
Flowcharted

Overall Question

WHY is this step necessary? Can it be eliminated?

Specific Questions

WHAT is being done? Have all of the steps been included? Does this step serve a
    purpose? Does this step contribute to the end result?

WHERE is the step being done? Should it be done at some other place?

WHEN should this step be done? Is the best sequence being used? Should this step
    be moved ahead or back?

WHO should do this step? Who can do it most easily? Is the right person doing it?

HOW is this step being done? Is there an easier way? Can it be done better with
    other equipment? Can it be simplified?

As a result of the questioning in each job step, many possibilities for improving the work methods may have surfaced. Each of these possibilities must be examined to determine which possibilities should be pursued. Improvements generally emerge from the questions asked in Figure 9.4. Others become apparent when the completed flowchart is studied.

Recall that the best method for performing a task is a function of (1) the use of the human body, (2) the arrangement of the workplace, and (3) the design of the tools and equipment. It is often possible to make improvements in one or more of these components and in the manner in which they are put together. Improvements can usually be made by eliminating, combining, rearranging, and simplifying the stages of the task. Logically, only some of the improvements that emerge can be used; the objective is to determine which of the suggested improvements are the best. When developing or evaluating work methods, the principles of motion economy (discussed in the next paragraph) should always be considered. At this point, it is wise to seek the ideas and opinions of the employees currently performing the task, and to keep them apprised of what is happening. This later facilitates implementing the changes selected.

Principles of motion economy.   In the early 1900s, Frank Gilbreth and Lillian Gilbreth developed the first principles relating to the conservation of body motions. Referred to as principles of motion economy, these principles concern the use of the human body, the arrangement of the workplace, and the design and use of equipment. Over the years, they have been refined and expanded. Figure 9.5 presents the most widely accepted list of basic principles of motion economy. It should be noted that these principles are concerned not only with completing the task as quickly as possible but also with conserving the energy of the employees, thus reducing fatigue.

Stage 2: Do—Try Out the Improvements

Stage 2 involves trying out the improvements developed in Stage 1. This may require obtaining approval from the boss. Even when approval is not required, it is usually wise to keep the boss informed as a new method or procedure is being developed. Care must be taken in presenting and justifying a proposal. An

FIGURE 9.5 Principles of Motion Economy

These 22 rules or principles of motion economy may be profitably applied to manufacturing and service work alike. Although not all of them are applicable to every operation, they do form a basis or a code for improving the efficiency of and reducing the fatigue in manual work.

Use of the Human Body	Arrangement of the Workplace	Design of Equipment
1. The two hands should begin as well as complete their motions at the same time.	9. There should be a definite and fixed place for all tools and materials.	17. The hands should be relieved of all work that can be done more advantageously by a jig, a fixture, or a foot-operated device.
2. The two hands should not be idle at the same time except during rest periods.	10. Tools, materials, and controls should be located close to and directly in front of the operator.	18. Two or more tools should be combined whenever possible.
3. Motions of the arms should be made in opposite and symmetrical directions and should be made simultaneously.	11. Gravity feed bins and containers should be used to deliver materials close to the point of use.	19. Tools and materials should be prepositioned whenever possible.
4. Hand motions should be confined to the lowest classification with which it is possible to perform the work satisfactorily.	12. Drop deliveries should be used whenever possible.	20. Where each finger performs some specific movement, such as in typewriting, the load should be distributed in accordance with the inherent capacities of the fingers.
5. Momentum should be employed to assist the worker wherever possible, and it should be reduced to a minimum if it must be overcome by muscular effort.	13. Materials and tools should be located to permit the best sequence of motions.	21. Handles, such as those used on cranks and large screwdrivers, should be designed to permit as much of the surface of the hand to come in contact with the handle as possible. This is particularly true when considerable force is exerted in using the handle. For light assembly work, the screwdriver handle should be so shaped that it is smaller at the bottom than at the top.
6. Smooth continuous motions of the hands are preferable to zigzag motions or straight-line motions involving sudden and sharp changes in direction.	14. Provisions should be made for adequate conditions for seeing. Good illumination is the first requirement for satisfactory visual perception.	
7. Ballistic movements are faster, easier, and more accurate than restricted (fixation) or "controlled" movements.	15. The height of the workplace and the chair should preferably be arranged so that alternate sitting and standing at work are easily possible.	22. Levers, crossbars, and handwheels should be located in such positions that the operator can manipulate them with the least change in body position and with the greatest mechanical advantage.
8. Rhythm is essential to the smooth and automatic performance of an operation, and the work should be arranged to permit easy and natural rhythm wherever possible.	16. A chair of the type and height to permit good posture should be provided for every worker.	

Source: R. M. Barnes, *Motion and Time Study: Design and Measurement of Work*, 6th ed. (New York: John Wiley & Sons, 1968). Copyright © 1968, reprinted by permission of John Wiley & Sons, Inc.

acceptable proposal includes a brief description of what the proposal will accomplish, how it will work, how much it will save, what it will cost, and what effect it will have on employees.

The improvement must then be put into operation. Acceptance of the improvement and cooperation of the affected employees are mandatory. Employees tend to resist change if they have not been involved in the change process. Therefore, employees should be involved as much as possible in any methods improvement program. Any proposed changes should be carefully explained, along with the reasons for them. Ideas for implementing a change should be actively solicited from the employees. The affected employees must receive thorough training in the improved method and on any new equipment.

Stage 3: Check—Evaluate the Results

This stage involves evaluating the results of the "do" stage. Did the changes result in significant improvements? What worked and what did not work? Where appropriate, statistical analysis is used to evaluate the effectiveness of the change.

Stage 4: Act—Take Action and Fine-Tune

The final stage requires action on the conclusions from Stage 3. Appropriate fine-tuning and corrective actions are taken. Once the fine-tuning has been accomplished the entire cycle is repeated.

Successful implementation of the PDCA Cycle depends on a balanced emphasis on each of the four stages. Such emphasis requires that the methods improvement person or team plan only as much as they can do, do only as much as they can check, check only as much as they can act upon, and act upon only as much as can be planned. The cycle then repeats itself. Table 9.1 contains a summary of each stage in the PDCA Cycle. Supervision Illustration 9–3 describes how the PDCA Cycle has been successfully implemented in one part of Digital Equipment Corporation.

TIME STUDY

LEARNING
OBJECTIVES

Time study is the analysis of a task to determine the elements of work required to perform it, the order in which these elements occur, and the times required to perform them effectively. The objective of a time study is to determine how long it should take an average person to perform the task in question. Time study is not the same as motion or methods study. Motion or methods study is concerned with determining the most efficient way of doing a task or job. Time study is concerned with *how long* it should take to do the task or job under ordinary conditions. Time study goes further than motion study by determining the actual time necessary to do the task. The time necessary to perform a task or a group of tasks is called the *standard time.* A time study makes allowances for employee fatigue and rest breaks when establishing a

TABLE 9.1

The PDCA Cycle

NOTE: Address each phase of the PDCA Cycle before beginning an improvement project and again at the start of each pass through the cycle.

Plan:
- What do we hope to gain (be specific)?
- What is the scope of this project?
- What can we *do, check,* and *act* on this project?
- How much should be *done* before *checking* the results, how much should be *checked* before *acting* on conclusions, and how much should be *acted* upon before *planning* the next cycle?
- What constraints are involved? How long should each step take?
- Who should be involved?
- Plan the change or activity.
- Allot time, money, personnel, and authority for the project.
- What should be measured? How? When?

Do:
- Perform the activity identified in the *plan* stage, preferably in a small-scale study.
- Hold meetings. Get suggestions.
- Train those involved in the necessary skills.
- Make changes.
- Collect and analyze data.

Check:
- What was the result of the *do* phase?
- Is it what we expected?
- Monitor the effects, checking for side effects and backsliding.
- Interpret the results. What conclusions can be inferred?
- What do these conclusions mean to this process?
- If the *do* was a process change, did it result in an improvement?
- Results from statistical analysis in this *check* stage influence the *act* stage.

Act:
- Act on conclusions from the *check* phase.
- Should we continue working on this process?
- Collect more data?
- Get more suggestions?
- If the *do* was a process change for the better, standardize it.
- Adopt the change, refine it, or abandon it.
- How should we change the process now?
- Run through the cycle again, possibly under different environmental conditions.

Source: Reprinted with the permission of APICS, Inc., "SPC, Process Improvement, and the Deming PDCA Circle in Freight Administration," *Production and Inventory Management Journal,* James C. Benneyan and Alan D. Chute, First Quarter 1993, p. 36.

standard. Therefore, a standard time represents the average time, including allowances for rest and fatigue, required to produce one unit of output. The primary use of time study is to provide standards to which employee performance can be compared. Most employee incentive programs use standard times for determining expected output. For example, the time-study method might be used to determine how many units a machine operator should be able to produce in an hour.

SUPERVISION ILLUSTRATION 9–3

PDCA WORKS AT DIGITAL'S FREIGHT ADMINISTRATION

Digital Equipment Corporation's U.S. Freight Administration is charged with auditing, paying, and allocating invoice charges for all freight shipments within the United States. The Freight Administration is comprised of 15 employees who manage the processing of 1.5 million transactions per year involving some 650 freight carriers. The annual cost of operating the Freight Administration is roughly $2 million.

Beginning in July 1990, the PDCA Cycle was applied in an effort to improve the efficiency of the Freight Administration. After the PDCA Cycle had been applied for only 10 months, the percentage of default invoices was reduced from 27.3 percent to 21.4 percent. By using the PDCA Cycle, new insights into the root causes of old process problems were also discovered.

The potential future direct savings of removing these old problems have been estimated to exceed $1 million per year. Additional expected benefits include increasing productivity, improving control, and providing more accurate and timely data for transportation analysis.

Source: Adapted from James C. Benneyan and Alan C. Chute, "SPC, Process Improvement, and the Deming PDCA Circle in Freight Administration," *Production and Inventory Management Journal,* First Quarter, 1993, p. 40. For more information about Digital Equipment Corporation visit its Web site at: **www.digital. com**

Although the exact method may vary with the practitioner, time study involves six basic steps.

1. Breaking the task down into its elemental steps, each of which is then timed. (For example, what motions does a computer operator go through?)
2. Determining which elements are essential for completion of the task. (Which motions are essential and which motions, if any, can be eliminated?)
3. Determining the operating time actually required for each essential element. (How much time does it take to do each of the essential motions? A stopwatch may be used to determine the time requirements of the various motions.)
4. Determining the operation time for the total task by adding the operating times of all the essential elements. (Add up the times arrived at in step 3.)
5. Determining the extra time allowances necessary for rest and fatigue. (Naturally, this depends on the operating time arrived at in step 4.)
6. Determining the standard time for the task by adding the required operating time and the extra time allowances. (Add the results of steps 4 and 5.)

If a methods study has already been completed, a time study would involve only steps 3 through 6 because the methods study would already have determined the essential elements required to do the task.

It should be noted that all work standards should be periodically monitored and evaluated. Changes in technology, equipment, materials, and methods can all require that standards be reevaluated.

SOLUTION TO THE
SUPERVISION
DILEMMA

Even though John has realized for some time that his department is not as efficient as it could be, he has not known how to go about making work-methods improvements. After studying this chapter, John should understand the Kaizen philosophy and implement the PDCA approach to methods improvement (pp. 163 and 166–71). Following this approach, John should first identify the tasks to be improved. The indicators outlined in Figure 9.3 should provide him some insights as to where to begin. He might also ask his employees for their ideas as to where methods improvement might be made. Once he has selected those tasks that have the greatest potential for methods improvement, he should pick two or three for analysis.

The current methods being used should be scrutinized. Questions regarding what, where, when, why, who, and how should be addressed for each of the tasks being analyzed. This step provides yet another opportunity for involving employees. The answers to these questions should suggest methods improvements that might be made. The next stage involves trying out the suggested improvements. This may involve obtaining approval from John's boss, Joyce Logan. The third stage involves evaluating the results of the "do" stage. The fourth and final stage requires action on any conclusions drawn from the "check" stage. In following the PDCA Cycle, John has learned the value of following a systematic approach and of involving his employees in the process.

SUMMARY

This chapter begins with a basic discussion of the major factors that affect an organization's productivity. The chapter discusses and explains the benefits of the supervisor's role in a work-methods improvement program. It presents a systematic approach to work-methods improvement.

1. *Explain the three major components of organizational productivity.* The three major components of organizational productivity are (1) efficiency of technology, (2) efficiency of labor, and (3) effectiveness of management.

2. *Describe the Kaizen philosophy for improvement.* Kaizen literally means "good change." In today's context, Kaizen describes a process of continuous and relentless improvement. Kaizen is not based on large technical leaps of innovations but on the incremental refining of existing processes.

3. *Describe the supervisor's role in a work-methods improvement program.* The supervisor plays a major role in methods improvement programs. Employees react to their perceptions of the supervisor's attitude. If they believe that methods improvement is important to the supervisor, it will be important to them. If they believe that methods improvement is not important to the supervisor, it will probably not be important to them. Also, the supervisor's vantage point places him or her in a position to spot areas that need methods improvement. Most supervisors have both close contact with the work and an overall view of what is going on.

4. *Discuss the benefits of work-methods improvement.* Reduced costs, higher productivity, reduced delays, higher quality, reduced waste, improved safety, and more satisfied employees are among the potential benefits of methods improvement.

5. *Present a systematic approach for improving work methods.* The PDCA Cycle presents a systematic approach for improving work methods. The PDCA Cycle consists of four major stages: (1) Plan, (2) Do, (3) Check, and (4) Act. Successful implementation of the PDCA Cycle requires a balanced emphasis on each of the four stages.

6. *Distinguish between time study and motion study.* Time study is the analysis of a task to determine the elements of work required to perform it, the order in which the elements occur, and the time required to perform them effectively. Motion study is concerned with determining the most efficient set of motions required to do a given task.

REVIEW QUESTIONS

1. Define *productivity* and describe the three major components of productivity.
2. Explain the concept of *Kaizen.*
3. What is the objective of work-methods improvement?
4. Name at least six potential benefits of improved work methods.
5. Name several indicators of tasks with a high potential for gain from work-methods improvements.
6. Briefly describe the PDCA Cycle.
7. What is the difference between motion study and time study?

SKILL-BUILDING QUESTIONS

1. The Kaizen philosophy has received much praise for its successes (see Supervision Illustration 9–1). What do you think is really different about the Kaizen approach?
2. If your boss asked your opinion of methods improvement, what would you say?
3. Some people argue that methods improvement is too old-fashioned for today's work environment. How would you respond to this argument?
4. Do you think that methods can be improved without making the task boring? Explain your answer.

REFERENCES

1. Richard C. Gertenberg, "Productivity: Its Meaning for America," *Michigan Business Review,* July 1972, p. 2.
2. Ibid., p. 5.
3. Vivienne Walker, "Kaizen—The Art of Continual Improvement," *Personnel Management,* August 1993, pp. 36–38.
4. Gary S. Vasilash, "Walking the Talk of Kaizen at Freudenberg-NOK," *Production,* December 1993, pp. 66–71.

ADDITIONAL READINGS

Culpan, Refik, and Orsay Kucukemiroglu. "A Comparison of U.S. and Japanese Management Styles and Unit Effectiveness," *Management International Review,* vol. 33, 1993.

Deming, W. Edwards. *Out of the Crisis.* Cambridge, Mass.: Massachusetts Institute of Technology, Center for Advanced Engineering Study, 1986.

Kronemer, Alexander. "Productivity in Industry and Government, 1973–94", *Monthly Labor Review,* November 1996.

Maynard, Roberta. "A Company Is Turned Around through Japanese Principles," *Nation's Business,* February 1996.

Sheridan, John H. "Kaizen Blitz," *Industry Week,* September 1, 1997.

SKILL-BUILDING APPLICATIONS

Incident 9–1

Who Works Harder?

Mike Hannah was driving in to work when the local newscaster began to talk about the latest national productivity figures: "National productivity has turned upward in the United States. After falling from 2.5 percent growth in the 1960s to 1.9 percent in the 1970s and 0.7 percent in the 1980s, recent figures have grown to 1.6 percent." Mike wondered why newspeople were always concerned about productivity figures. This reminded Mike of a short article he had recently run across related to productivity. The article stated that employees today were able to produce almost 10 times as much as their grandparents produced. This statement had puzzled Mike ever since he had read it. The confusing part was that Mike was fairly certain that today's employees certainly don't work 10 times as hard as their grandparents worked. In fact, Mike suspected that today's employees work less hard than their grandparents. Mike also was concerned that if productivity continued to increase indefinitely, eventually most people would be without a job.

Questions

1. Why should productivity be important to Mike?
2. Is it possible for today's employees to be almost 10 times as productive as their grandparents? Explain your answer.
3. How would you respond to Mike's concern about continued productivity increases?

Incident 9–2

The Lines at Sam's

Sam Baker owns and manages a cafeteria on Main Street in Dawsonville. Sam has been in business for almost two years. During his two years of operation, Sam has identified several problems that he has not been able to solve. One major problem is that a line always seems to develop at the checkout register during the rush hour. Another problem is that customers are constantly complaining that the employees take too much time to serve the customers as they go down the line. A third problem that has been disturbing Sam is the frequency with which the cafeteria runs out of "choice dishes." The final problem perplexing him is that every Sunday at noon, when a large crowd arrives after church, Sam's invariably runs short of seating space.

Sam had worked at other food establishments for 15 years before he opened his cafeteria, and most of them experienced similar problems. In fact, these and other related problems have come to be expected and are therefore accepted practice for the industry. After all, Sam's former boss used to say, "You can't please everybody all the time." Sam is wondering if he should take the industry's position and just accept these problems as an inherent part of the business.

Questions

1. From a methods improvement viewpoint, what suggestions would you make to Sam?
2. How might Sam implement Kaizen at his cafeteria?

Exercise 9–1

Improving Your Exam Performance

The purpose of this exercise is to apply the PDCA Cycle to how you prepare for your class exams. Using anticipated and actual exam scores as a measure of quality, apply the PDCA Cycle to improving your performance on future exams. After analyzing each exam that you have taken so far this term, plan how you might improve your performance. Implement your planned improvements in preparing for your next exam. After you get the results of your exam, evaluate how well your planned improvements worked. Based on these results, make adjustments wherever needed and repeat the cycle for the next exam.

1. Do you think the PDCA Cycle helped improve your performance? Why or why not?
2. Can you think of any other applicants for the PDCA Cycle in your role as a student?

Exercise 9–2

Processing Customers

Almost everyone has visited both a McDonald's and a Wendy's restaurant. McDonald's restaurants have a number of different lines and cash registers across the counter. Wendy's restaurants, on the other hand, have one line and one cash register and the line moves down the counter from the cash register to pick up the food and drinks. Both of these customer-processing systems appear to work for their respective companies, yet they are substantially different.

1. Which customer processing system do you like best? Why?
2. From a methods improvement viewpoint, what advantages and disadvantages can you identify for each system?
3. From a methods improvement viewpoint, can you think of any improvement that could be made to either system? If so, explain it.

APPENDIX

Flow-Process Chart

A **flow-process chart** is a graphic representation of the steps in a task. It includes basic data such as distances traveled, quantities, and time required. Basically, flowcharts show the individual operations, sequences, and movements required to perform a task. On most flow-process charts, the successive steps of the selected task are arranged vertically in chronological order. Each step is briefly described on a separate line of the chart and then, through the use of symbols, classified as an operation, transportation, inspect, delay, or storage. These classifications are defined in detail in Exhibit 9.1.

Exhibit 9.2 shows a flow-process chart for the requisition of petty cash. First, the general data in the upper portion of the form must be supplied, followed by a brief description of each step of the procedure being charted (see the left-hand column). The details should be clear and specific, and the steps should be listed in the sequence in which they occur. After all of the steps have been listed, each step is assigned the appropriate symbol in the right-hand column of the form. This is accomplished by drawing a line from each appropriate symbol to the next.

EXHIBIT 9.1
Symbols and Classifications Used in a Flow-Process Chart

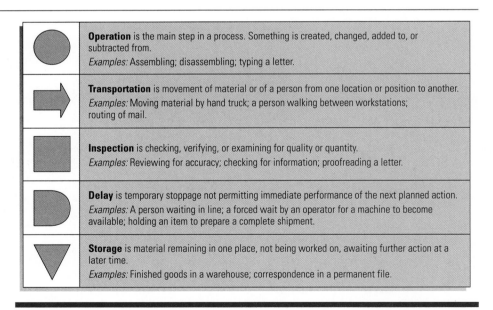

●	**Operation** is the main step in a process. Something is created, changed, added to, or subtracted from. *Examples:* Assembling; disassembling; typing a letter.
➡	**Transportation** is movement of material or of a person from one location or position to another. *Examples:* Moving material by hand truck; a person walking between workstations; routing of mail.
■	**Inspection** is checking, verifying, or examining for quality or quantity. *Examples:* Reviewing for accuracy; checking for information; proofreading a letter.
D	**Delay** is temporary stoppage not permitting immediate performance of the next planned action. *Examples:* A person waiting in line; a forced wait by an operator for a machine to become available; holding an item to prepare a complete shipment.
▽	**Storage** is material remaining in one place, not being worked on, awaiting further action at a later time. *Examples:* Finished goods in a warehouse; correspondence in a permanent file.

At this point, the flow-process chart has been used only to gather the facts about the way the task is currently being done. The flow-process chart must now be used to help analyze and question each of these facts.

Layout Chart

A **layout chart** is a sketch of a facility that shows its physical arrangement and the major flows of work through it. Sometimes a layout chart is called a *movement chart*. Specifically, a layout chart shows (1) the location of equipment and machines, (2) the spatial relationship of related workstations, (3) the walking distance required to get the work completed, and (4) the flow of the work from one location to another. The purpose of a layout chart is to help the user determine the optimal physical layout in view of known restrictions. The restrictions may be such things as facility size, facility shape, and

EXHIBIT 9.2

Flow-Process Chart for
Requisition of Petty Cash

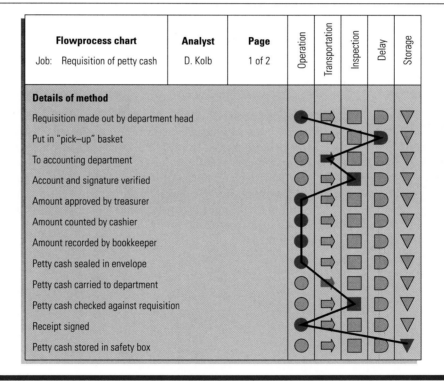

Flowprocess chart Job: Requisition of petty cash	Analyst D. Kolb	Page 1 of 2	Operation	Transportation	Inspection	Delay	Storage
Details of method							
Requisition made out by department head			●	⇨	□	D	▽
Put in "pick–up" basket			○	⇨	□	●	▽
To accounting department			○	⬛	□	D	▽
Account and signature verified			○	⇨	■	D	▽
Amount approved by treasurer			●	⇨	□	D	▽
Amount counted by cashier			●	⇨	□	D	▽
Amount recorded by bookkeeper			●	⇨	□	D	▽
Petty cash sealed in envelope			●	⇨	□	D	▽
Petty cash carried to department			○	⬛	□	D	▽
Petty cash checked against requisition			○	⇨	■	D	▽
Receipt signed			●	⇨	□	D	▽
Petty cash stored in safety box			○	⇨	□	D	▼

Source: Elias M. Awad, *Systems Analysis and Design* (Homewood, Ill.: Richard D. Irwin, 1979), p. 113. © by Richard D. Irwin, Inc. Reprinted by permission.

EXHIBIT 9.3
Principles of Physical
Layout

1. The work flow should follow straight lines without undue backtracking and cross-tracking.

2. Individuals having frequent contact should be located near each other.

3. Files, cabinets, records, and other materials should be located for the convenience and ready access of those who use them.

4. Surplus furniture and equipment should be removed to provide space for other purposes.

5. The allocation of space should be in keeping with the requirements of the work—that is, the best-lighted and -ventilated space should be used for work requiring the closest attention and concentration.

6. The layout should facilitate supervision.

7. The layout should allow for proper security precautions.

8. Individuals using the same equipment should be grouped together.

9. Individuals who receive visitors or are required to maintain outside contacts should be located near entrances.

10. The building characteristics should be studied to make certain that they can accommodate heavy and bulky equipment and equipment of unusual size, such as safes and conveyor belts.

Source: Adapted from Department of the Army Pamphlet 5–4–2, November 15, 1973, p. 8–1.

equipment size. When work flows are shown visually, poor arrangement often becomes much more obvious. In addition to studying the work flows, the principles presented in Exhibit 9.3 should be followed. These principles provide general guidelines for improving a layout.

The size and detail of layout charts can vary greatly, depending on the facility involved. Large charts can be used to show the general layout of a facility. Smaller-scale charts can be used to show a portion of the facility (such as an office or an assembly area). Exhibit 9.4 shows an example of a layout chart for a restaurant.

EXHIBIT 9.4 Layout Chart for a Restaurant

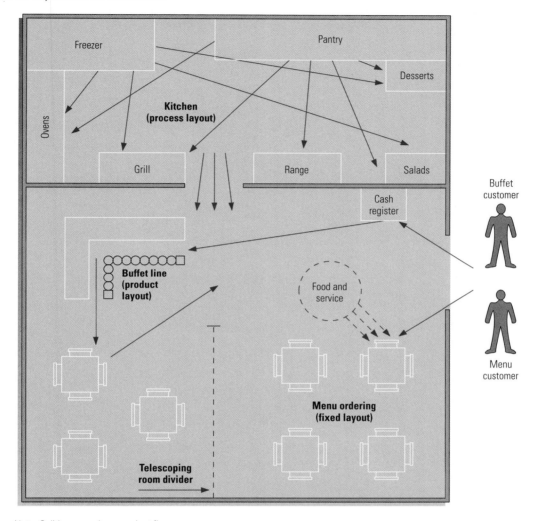

Note: Solid arrows show product flows.

Source: Richard J. Schonberger and Edward M. Knot, Jr., *Operations Management,* 4th ed. (Homewood, Ill.: R. D. Irwin, Inc., 1993), p. 720.

Staffing Skills

SECTION OUTLINE

10 Obtaining and developing employees

11 Appraising employee performance

12 Understanding equal employment opportunity

13 Understanding unions

Obtaining and Developing Employees

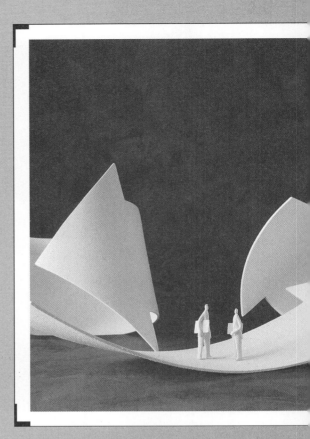

LEARNING OBJECTIVES

After studying this chapter, you should be able to:

1. Define recruiting, selection, orientation, and training.

2. Define job analysis, job description, and job specification.

3. Describe the steps in the selection process.

4. Understand the legal implications in recruiting and hiring new employees.

5. Discuss the supervisor's role in the orientation process.

6. Outline the steps in training employees in job skills.

SUPERVISION DILEMMA

Jane Harris knew when she took the supervisor's job that two of her employees would be leaving in approximately three months. One resigned to go back to school, and the other resigned because of a planned move to the West Coast. They were both good employees, and Jane wanted to be sure to replace them with equally qualified people. Because Jane wanted these replacements to get off to a good start once they were hired, she had recently started to think about how to train new employees. In fact, she felt that now might be a good time to give everyone in the department a short training program on claims processing.

1 LEARNING OBJECTIVES

One of the basic forms of work that a supervisor does is staffing. The **staffing function** of supervision is concerned with obtaining and developing qualified people. Since supervisors accomplish their work through the efforts of others, they find it very important to obtain good people. The major activities of the staffing function are recruiting, selecting, orienting, and training. **Recruiting** involves seeking and attracting qualified candidates for job vacancies. The purpose of **selection** is to choose the best person for the job from those candidates. **Orienting** is the process of introducing new employees to the organization, their work unit and their jobs. **Training** involves the acquisition by employees of the skills, information, and attitudes necessary for improving their effectiveness. Supervisors may not be primarily responsible for all of the staffing activities, but they are usually involved in one or more of them. Thus, if supervisors are to be effective in the staffing function, they must understand each of these activities. The purpose of this chapter is to acquaint the supervisor with the activities and procedures of the staffing function.

RECRUITING QUALIFIED PERSONNEL

Recruiting involves seeking and attracting qualified candidates for the job vacancies. Normally, the supervisor does not have the primary responsibility for recruiting. This is generally done by the human resources department. However, the supervisor assists the human resources department in the recruiting function. For recruiting to be effective, the requirements of the job must be defined as precisely as possible, regardless of whether the job is already in existence or is newly created.

Job Analysis

2 LEARNING OBJECTIVES

Job analysis involves determining the pertinent information relating to the performance of a specific job. Generally, a job analysis determines the skills, personality characteristics, educational background, and training that are necessary to perform a job. Job analysis *does not* study the person who is doing the job. It examines the job and its requirements.

A questionnaire is often used in performing a job analysis. Figure 10.1 shows some sample questions of such a questionnaire. The supervisor often completes the job analysis questionnaire on the jobs that he or she is supervising.

FIGURE 10.1

Partial Job Analysis
Questionnaire

Job Analysis Information Format

Your job title _____   Code _____ Date _____
Class title _____   Department _____
Your name _____   Facility _____
Superior's title _____   Prepared by _____
Superior's name _____   Hours worked   AM _____   AM _____
                                                        to
                                                   PM _____   PM _____

1. What is the general purpose of your job?

2. What was your last job? If it was in another organization please name it.

3. To what job would you normally expect to be promoted?

4. If you regularly supervise others, list them by name and job title.

5. If you supervise others, please check those activities that are part of your
   supervisory duties.

   _____ Hiring   _____ Coaching   _____ Promoting
   _____ Orienting   _____ Counseling   _____ Compensating
   _____ Training   _____ Budgeting   _____ Disciplining
   _____ Scheduling   _____ Directing   _____ Terminating
   _____ Developing   _____ Measuring performance _____ Other _____

6. How would you describe the successful completion and results of your work?

7. *Job Duties.* Please briefly describe WHAT you do and, if possible, HOW you do it.
   Indicate those duties you consider to be most important and/or most difficult.

   a. *Daily Duties*

   b. *Periodic Duties* (Please indicate whether weekly, monthly, quarterly, etc.)

   c. *Duties Performed at Irregular Intervals*

8. *Education.* Please check the blank that indicates the educational *requirements* for
   the job, not your *own* educational background.

   a. ____ No formal education required   e. ____ 4–yr college degree
   b. ____ Less than high school diploma   f. ____ Education beyond under–
   c. ____ High school diploma or equivalent   graduate degree and/or
   d. ____ 2–yr college certificate or   professional license
            equivalent

List advanced degrees or specific professional license or certificate required.

Please indicate the education you had when you were placed on this job.

Source: Richard L. Henderson, *Compensation Management,* rev. ed., 1979, pp. 148–49. Reprinted with permission of Reston Publishing Company, Inc., a Prentice Hall Company, 11480 Sunset Hills Road, Reston, Virginia.

FIGURE 10.2

Information Contained
in a Job Description
and a Job Specification

Job Description
General description of job
Examples of work performed
Job Specification
Experience and training
Education
Knowledge, skills, and abilities

Even when the questionnaire is filled out by someone else, it is normally reviewed and approved by the supervisor.

The end results of a job analysis are a job description and a job specification. A **job description** is a written portrayal of a job and the types of work required by the job. A **job specification** gives the qualifications necessary to perform the job. A job specification gives the supervisor the standards for screening employees. Only after the job analysis, job description, and job specification have been completed can successful recruiting occur. Figure 10.2 shows the types of information contained on a job description and a job specification.

Job Posting and Bidding

Job posting is the posting of notices of available jobs in central locations throughout the organization. This is done to make employees aware of job vacancies. Electronic mail (E-mail) systems and bulletin boards are used for job posting. In addition, many employers are now listing positions on the Internet. The posted notice normally gives the job title, the rate of pay for the job, and the qualifications necessary to perform the job. Interested employees contact the human resources department. After initial screening by the human resources department, qualified applicants are usually interviewed by the supervisor. In most circumstances, the final choice for the job is left up to the supervisor.

Job bidding is closely related to job posting. In **job bidding,** employees bid on a job based on seniority, job skills, or other qualifications. In unionized organizations, specific job bidding and job posting procedures are normally spelled out in the union contract.

Advertising

A widely used method of obtaining operative personnel is through the "Help Wanted" ads. The human resources department normally screens all applicants obtained from ads. Again, the supervisor interviews the most qualified applicants and normally makes the final hiring decision.

Employment Agencies

Some organizations recruit from state employment agencies. These agencies are operated in most cities with a population of 10,000 or more. Since individuals must register with the state employment service before receiving unemployment compensation, these agencies generally have up-to-date lists of unemployed persons. Contacts with state employment agencies are normally handled by an organization's human resources department.

Private employment agencies are sometimes used in hiring certain skilled personnel, such as computer operators and secretaries. Private agencies charge a fee for their service. Users of a private agency should know in advance the exact fees that are to be charged and how those fees are to be paid.

One advantage of using employment agencies is that the applicants may be already screened for the hiring organization. Many businesses now rely on agencies to provide temporary employees to meet seasonal demands. Businesses can thus preview the work of temporary employees and then decide if it would be beneficial to offer them a permanent position. At any rate, using temporaries enables a business to reduce labor costs because it reduces the number of full-time employees.

Internship and Co-Op Programs

Many firms use the Cooperative Education Departments of local colleges for recruitment of students. Under cooperative education, the student works for a business for a quarter/semester and then goes to school for a quarter/semester. Internship programs normally involve work for a student during the summer. Under both an internship and co-op program, the business can see the work of potential employees before they are hired permanently.

Employee Referrals

The present employees of an organization often become involved in the recruiting process. Recruiting through employees' referrals is normally informal and by word of mouth. For example, an employee might tell a neighbor about a job opening. One drawback to recruiting in this way is that it may lead to the formation of cliques, especially if employees recommend only their close friends and relatives.

SELECTING PERSONNEL

The purpose of the selection process is to choose individuals who are most likely to succeed from those who have been recruited. Supervisors are normally directly involved in selecting personnel for their departments.

Who Makes the Selection Decision?

In most large organizations, the human resources department does the initial screening of applicants, with the immediate supervisor making the final selection decision. This relieves the supervisor of the time-consuming responsibility of screening clearly unqualified applicants. It is not unusual for the supervisor to make the final selection, subject to the approval of higher levels of management.

The Selection Process

3 LEARNING OBJECTIVES

The steps used in the selection process vary from organization to organization. Figure 10.3 summarizes the general steps. These steps are not necessarily followed in full for each and every job.

FIGURE 10.3 Steps in the Selection Process

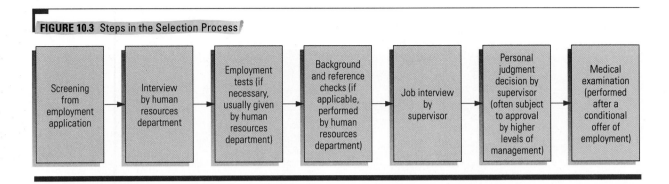

Step 1: Screening from the employment application.   A person who applies for an operative job usually completes an employment application form. Figure 10.4 shows a typical form. Employment forms are screened by the human resources department to eliminate unqualified people. Different forms are often used for clerical, technical, supervisory, and other major job groupings. Employment application forms should be designed so that they do not discriminate against certain groups. For example, questions about sex, age, race, religion, education, arrest record, and credit rating, which may not be job related, can result in charges of discrimination.

Step 2: Interview by human resources department.   After the initial screening of employment application forms, applicants are interviewed by a specialist from the human resources department. This interview is used to eliminate additional unsuitable and unqualified applicants. The interview is also used to fully explain the job and its requirements and to answer any questions that the applicant may have about the job.

Step 3: Employment tests.   Testing is a commonly used tool in medium and large organizations. It is one of the more controversial parts of the selection process because test scores are one of the most frequently used methods for predicting whether a person will perform well in a job. Of course, this prediction may or may not be correct. The law requires that there be a proven relationship between scoring high on the test and performing better on the job.

Many types of tests are used in the selection process. Among the more frequently used types are aptitude, psychomotor, job knowledge, proficiency, interest, and psychological tests. **Aptitude tests** measure a person's capacity or potential ability to learn and perform a job. **Psychomotor tests** measure a person's strength, dexterity, and coordination. **Job knowledge tests** measure the applicant's job-related knowledge. **Proficiency tests** measure how well the applicant can do a sample of the work that is to be performed. **Interest tests** are designed to determine how a person's interests compare with the interests of successful people in a specific job. **Psychological tests** measure personality characteristics.

Another type of test that can be used for screening job applicants is the polygraph test. The **polygraph,** popularly known as the lie detector, is a device that records physical changes in the body as the test subject answers a series of

FIGURE 10.4 A Typical Employment Application Form

Employment application			
Name	Last	First	Middle	Social security number
Local telephone		Business telephone	Other telephone
Present address		City	State	Zip code
Position desired		Are you legally eligible to work in the U.S.A.?	WPM typing	WPM shorthand
Minimum salary	Are you employed?	Notice required?	May we contact present employer?	Date available

Education

School name	Complete address	Month/Year from	Month/Year to	Major area of study	Grade average	Graduation Date	Degree

Employment history (list current or most recent employment first)

Employer company name	Type of business	Mailing address Street City State Zip	From Mth/Yr	To Mth/Yr	Your position	Your supervisor	Salary	Reason for leaving

Work references

Name	Complete residence address	Business address	Telephone	Occupation	Years known

Name relatives and/or spouse employed by the XYZ company	Relationship	Where employed

Have you been convicted of a crime? (exclude minor traffic if fined $50 or less)	☐ Yes ☐ No If yes explain	Reason Place Date Disposition

In case of emergency notify	Name	Phone	Address

Who referred you?	☐ Walk-in	☐ Employee referral	☐ Employment agency	☐ Newspaper ad	☐ Other

Describe additional skills, knowledge, or abilities relating to position sought

Interviewed by	I have read and understand the provisions on the reverse side of application. I certify all information given by me is correct.
	Signature	Date

XYZ Company is an equal employment opportunity organization and is an equal opportunity/affirmative action employer in compliance with TITLE VII and other civil rights laws.

FIGURE 10.4—continued

In making this application for employment I understand that an investigative report may be made whereby information is obtained through personal interviews with third parties, such as family members, business associates, financial sources, friends, neighbors, or others with whom I am acquainted. This inquiry would include information as to my character, general reputation, personal characteristics, and mode of living, whichever may be applicable. I have the right to make a written request within a reasonable period of time for a complete and accurate disclosure of additional information concerning the nature and scope of the investigation.

Regular employees: All employees employed for a period greater than three months serve the first six months on a provisional basis to provide the organization an opportunity to evaluate the employee's performance. Should the work not be satisfactory, the employee will be notified in writing prior to the completion of the six-month provisional period, and the employee may be terminated at that time without right of appeal.

All regular employment is subject to a satisfactory personal and financial background investigation, and all prospective employees must meet the standards of medical and physical fitness prescribed for the position to which he or she is being appointed.

Temporary employees: All employees employed for a period of three months or less may be terminated at any time without notice. All temporary employment is stipulated to be subject to reevaluation without prior notice to include possible change of location and function. Temporary employees are paid for hours worked and are not eligible for the special benefits given to regular employees.

Disqualification of applicants: An applicant or employee will be disqualified from employment for any of the following reasons:
- Any false statement of material fact on application
- Conviction of a crime involving moral turpitude unless pardoned

An applicant or employee may be disqualified from employment for any of the following reasons:
- Addiction to the use of alcohol or prohibited drugs which interferes with job performance
- Membership within the last ten (10) years in an organization advocating the violent overthrow of the government of the United States

questions. The polygraph records fluctuations in blood pressure, respiration, and perspiration on a moving roll of graph paper. On the basis of the recorded fluctuations, the polygraph operator makes a judgment as to whether the subject's response was truthful or deceptive.

The use of a polygraph test rests on a series of cause-and-effect assumptions: stress causes certain physiological changes in the body; fear and guilt cause stress; lying causes fear and guilt. The use of a polygraph test assumes that a direct relationship exists between the subject's responses to questions and the physiological responses recorded on the polygraph. However, the polygraph itself does not detect lies; it only detects physiological changes. The operator must interpret the data that the polygraph records. Thus, the real lie detector is the operator, not the device.

Serious questions exist regarding the validity of polygraph tests. Difficulties arise if a person lies without guilt (a pathological liar) or lies believing the response to be true. Furthermore, it is hard to prove that the physiological responses recorded by the polygraph occur only because a lie has been told. In addition, some critics argue that the use of the polygraph violates fundamental principles of the Constitution: the right of privacy, the privilege against self-incrimination, and the presumption of innocence. As a result of these questions and criticisms, Congress passed the Employee Polygraph Protection Act of 1988 that severely restricts the commercial use of polygraph tests. Those exempt from this restrictive law are (1) all local, state, and federal employees (however, state laws can be passed to restrict the use of polygraphs); (2) industries with national defense or security contracts; (3) businesses with nuclear power–related contracts with the Department of Energy; and (4) businesses and consultants with access to highly classified information.

Private businesses are also allowed to use polygraphs under certain conditions: when hiring private security personnel; when hiring persons with access to drugs; and during investigations of economic injury or loss by the employer.

In the past few years, there has also been a proliferation of drug-testing programs. Such programs have been instituted not only to screen job applicants but also to test current employees for drug use. It has been estimated that about 20 percent of the Fortune 500 companies have either instituted drug-testing programs or are contemplating their institution.

Numerous lawsuits have been filed to contest the legality of such programs. Generally, a drug-testing program is on stronger legal ground if it is limited to job applicants. Furthermore, current employees should not be subjected to drug testing on a random basis. A probable cause for drug testing, such as a dramatic change in behavior or a sudden increase in accident rates, should be established before testing. In addition, the results of drug testing should be protected to ensure confidentiality.

Generally, supervisors are not responsible for administering tests. These are normally administered by the human resources department. They should be used with other data on the applicant as an aid in the selection process and not as the sole deciding factor. Supervision Illustration 10–1 shows excerpts from three pre-employment tests.

Step 4: Background and reference checks.   Background and reference checks usually fall into three categories: personal, academic, and past employment. Contacting personal and academic references is generally of lim-

---

SUPERVISION ILLUSTRATION 10–1

EXCERPTS FROM PRE-EMPLOYMENT TESTS

1. Job-specific skills test. Custom-designed for a certain job. For example, Scheig Associates created one for Boeing to use in hiring 40 workers for its on-site day care center.

You see a child bite another child. Do you:

a. Make a mental note of the behavior and record it later.

b. Wait to see if the behavior continues tomorrow.

c. Record behavior in notebook.

d. Report behavior verbally to director.

2 Honesty test. Most popular among retailers, this test is often given to entry-level employees.

Does stealing a pencil or other small item hurt a big corporation?

Do you think everyone steals something once in a while?

3. Leadership test. This version of a psychological test was developed by Hagberg Consulting Group for use in hiring CEOs and other high-level executives.

What are some common misconceptions about you?

Source: Adapted from Ellen Neuborne, "Employers Score New Hires," *USA Today,* July 9, 1997. For more information about *USA Today,* visit its Web site at: **www.usatoday. com**

---

ited value, because few people will list someone as a reference unless they feel that that person will give them a positive recommendation. Previous employers are in the best position to supply the most objective information. However, the amount and type of information that a previous employer is willing to divulge varies. Normally, most previous employers will provide only the following information—-yes or no to the question if this applicant worked there, what the employee's dates of employment were, and what position he or she held.

If a job applicant is rejected because of information in a credit report or another type of report from an outside reporting service, the applicant must be given the name and address of the organization that developed the report. The reporting service is *not* required by law to give the person a copy of his or her file, but it *must* inform the person of the nature and substance of the information. Supervision Illustration 10–2 describes potential hazards in reference checking.

Step 5: Job interview by the supervisor.   The previous four steps in the selection process are generally conducted by the human resources department. In Step 5, the supervisor becomes actively involved in the selection process. The purpose of the job interview is to use all of the information obtained in the previous steps and determine the best person for the job.

Interviews can be either structured or unstructured. In a **structured interview,** the supervisor knows in advance what questions are going to be asked, asks the questions, and records the results. Structured interviews have the advantages of providing the same information on all interviewees, ensuring that all questions are covered with all interviewees, and minimizing the personal biases of the supervisor.

SUPERVISION ILLUSTRATION 10-2

HAZARDS IN REFERENCE CHECKING

When a Houston insurance salesman was fired from his job, he hired an investigator to find out why. Posing as a prospective employer, the investigator made some calls to the salesman's former managers. When he asked them for a reference, the managers described the former employee as a "classic sociopath," "a zero," and "lacking in scruples." The fired employee sued the firm and won $1.9 million for libel and slander.

After a sales representative was fired from NEC Electronics, Inc., an article concerning the termination appeared in *Microelectronic News,* an electronic-industry newsletter.

The article stated that the employee had misused funds and mismanaged his office. NEC Electronics reprinted the article and sent it to its regional sales offices. The former employee sued the company for breach of contract, wrongful termination, and defamation. He won the case, and a California jury awarded him $60.2 million in compensatory and punitive damages.

With an increase in litigation resulting from statements about former employees, most companies will only verify the last position held and dates of employment for former employees.

Source: Adapted from "Recruitment in the 90s Supplement," *Personnel Journal*, August 1994, pp. 22–24. For more information about the *Personnel Journal,* visit its Web site at:
www.workforceonline.com

Unstructured interviews have no definite checklist of questions or preplanned strategy. Such questions as "Tell me about your previous job" are asked. Much more participation by the interviewee is required in the unstructured interview.

Other types of interviewing techniques exist, but the supervisor will generally use a structured interview. The primary problem with interviews is that in an interview it is easy for the supervisor to become favorably or unfavorably impressed with the applicant for the wrong reasons.

Several common pitfalls are encountered in the interviewing process. One such pitfall is the evaluation of job applicants on the basis of personal biases. Supervisors, like all people, have such biases, but the supervisor should be careful not to let them play a role in the interviewing process. For example, the supervisor should not reject a qualified male applicant just because he has long hair.

Closely related to the pitfall of personal biases is the pitfall of the halo effect. The **halo effect** occurs when the supervisor allows a single, prominent characteristic of the interviewee to dominate judgment of all other characteristics. For instance, it is easy to ignore the other characteristics of a person who has a pleasant personality. However, merely having a pleasant personality does not necessarily mean that the person will be a good employee.

Overgeneralizing is another common pitfall. The supervisor should remember that the interviewee is under pressure during the interview and may become very nervous. Thus, the interviewee may not behave in exactly the same way on the job as during the interview.

Certain things can be done to overcome many of the pitfalls in interviewing. First, the supervisor should review all of the information that has been obtained in the previous steps of the selection process. Next, the supervisor should develop a plan for the interview. If a structured interview is to be used,

Structured interviews help to provide the same information on all interviewees, ensure that all questions are covered with all interviewees, and minimize the supervisor's biases.
Billy E. Barnes/Stock Boston

the supervisor should write down all of the questions that are to be asked. The plan should include room arrangements. Privacy and some degree of comfort are important. If a private room is not available, the interview should be conducted in a place where other persons are not within hearing distance. The supervisor should also attempt to put the applicant at ease. The supervisor should *not* argue with the applicant or attempt to put the applicant on the spot. Engaging in a brief conversation about a general topic of broad interest or offering the applicant a cup of coffee can help ease the tension. The supervisor should always keep in mind, however, that the primary goal of the interview is to get information that will aid in the selection decision. Finally, notes should be taken to ensure that the facts obtained from the interview are not forgotten.

Employment interviewing is subject to legal considerations. Figure 10.5 gives a summary of some questions that can and cannot be asked in an employment review.

Step 6: Selection decision by the supervisor.   At this point, all of the data from the previous steps in the selection process should be used. The supervisor should remember that in some cases none of the applicants may be satisfactory. The supervisor should not feel obligated to hire one of the applicants if none of them has the necessary qualifications. If this occurs, the job should be redesigned, more money should be offered to attract more qualified candidates, or some other action should be taken.

Finally, the supervisor should remember that in most cases the decision to hire a person is subject to the approval of his or her own supervisor. Following the suggestions offered in this chapter should help ensure that the best person is selected and that his or her own supervisor will agree with the decision.

FIGURE 10.5 Interviewing Guidelines

Item	Prohibited Information (cannot be used to disqualify candidates)	Lawful Information (can be used to disqualify candidates)
Age	Age, birth certificate. Inquiries for the purpose of excluding persons between 40 and 70. Inquiries as to date of graduation from college or high school to determine age.	Whether candidate meets minimum age requirements or is under 70. Requirement that candidate submit proof of age after hired. Whether candidate can meet the terms and conditions of the job in question.
Arrest record	Inquiries related to arrest.	None.
Conviction record	Inquiries regarding convictions that do not relate to performing the job under consideration.	Inquiries about actual convictions that relate reasonably to performing a particular job.
Credit rating	Inquiries concerning charge accounts, credit rating, etc., that do not relate to performing the job under consideration.	Inquiries about credit rating, charge accounts, etc., that relate reasonably to performing the job in question.
Education	Disqualification of candidate who does not have a particular degree unless employer has proven that the specific degree is the only way to measure candidate's ability to perform the job in question.	Inquiries regarding degrees or equivalent experience. Information regarding courses relevant to a particular job.
Handicaps	General inquiries that would elicit information about handicaps or health conditions unrelated to job performance.	Whether candidate has any disabilities that would prevent him or her from performing the job. Whether there are any types of jobs for which candidate should not be considered because of a handicap or health condition.
Marital and family status	Child care problems, unwed motherhood, contraceptive practices, spouses' preferences regarding job conditions. Inquiries indicating marital status, number of children, pregnancy. Any question directly or indirectly resulting in limitation of job opportunity in any way.	Whether candidate can meet the work schedule of the job. Whether candidate has activities, responsibilities, or commitments that may hinder meeting attendance requirements. (Should be asked of candidates of both sexes.)
Military record	Discharge status, unless it is the result of a military conviction.	Type of experience and education in service as it relates to a particular job.
Name	Inquiries to determine national origin, ancestry, or prior marital status.	Whether candidate has ever worked under a different name.
National origin	Lineage, ancestry, descent, mother tongue, birthplace, citizenship. National origin of spouse or parents.	Whether candidate is legally eligible to work in the United States.
Organizations	Inquiries about membership to determine the race, color, religion, sex, national origin, or age of candidates.	Inquiries that do not elicit discriminatory information.

FIGURE 10.5—concluded

Item	Prohibited Information (cannot be used to disqualify candidates)	Lawful Information (can be used to disqualify candidates)
Race or color	Complexion, color of skin. Height or weight where it is not related to the job.	None.
Religion	Religious preference, affiliations, denomination.	Whether candidate can meet work schedules of the job with reasonable accommodation by employer if necessary.
Sex	Sex of applicant, where sex is not a bona fide occupational qualification (BFOQ).	Sex of applicant, where sex is a BFOQ (i.e., the physical characteristics of one sex are necessary to perform the job).
Work experience	None.	Candidate's previous job-related experience.

Source: Reprinted from *Boomerang II: A Management Training Program in Equal Employment Opportunity*, 1984. Used with permission from Leopold & Associates, Chicago, Ill, pp. 119–20.

Step 7: Medical examination.   Many organizations require a person to take a medical examination. Medical examinations should take place after a conditional offer of employment. The medical exam is given not only to determine the person's eligibility for group life, health, and disability insurance but also to determine whether the person is physically capable of doing the job. Arrangements for the medical exam are usually handled by the human resources department.

LEGAL IMPLICATIONS IN RECRUITING AND HIRING NEW EMPLOYEES

4   LEARNING OBJECTIVES

Government legislation has had a significant effect on recruiting and hiring new employees. Major legislation in this area is reviewed here to give the supervisor a better understanding of the legal responsibilities. These laws are described in more detail in Chapter 12. The purpose of all these laws—and court interpretations of these laws—is to ensure that the decision to hire or not hire a person is job related. This decision cannot be based on non–job-related factors.

Title VII of the Civil Rights Act of 1964 and amendments to this act make it illegal to hire, fire, pay, or take other management actions on the basis of race, color, religion, national origin, or sex. The decision to hire must be based on the person's ability to do the job and *not* on non–job-related factors. This requirement is a direct result of the Civil Rights Act.

The **Age Discrimination in Employment Act of 1968** and amendments to this act make it illegal to discriminate against individuals over 40 years of age.

The **Rehabilitation Act of 1973** protects handicapped people. Many jobs can be effectively performed by handicapped people. The purpose of this act is to ensure that these people are not refused a job merely because of their handicap if the handicap does not affect their ability to do the job.

In May 1990, Congress approved the **Americans with Disabilities Act (ADA),** which gives the disabled sharply increased access to services and jobs.

In October 1991, Congress approved the **Civil Rights Act of 1991,** which was designed to reverse several Supreme Court decisions of 1989 and 1990 that had been viewed as limiting equal employment opportunity and affirmative action.

Much controversy surrounds one government requirement—affirmative action programs. Under **affirmative action programs,** organizations establish objectives for hiring a certain percentage of women and racial minorities. For example, an organization might set as an objective that 20 percent of its newly hired employees be women. Notice that this does *not* mean that unqualified women must be hired. The purpose of these programs is merely to ensure that women and racial minorities are *not* discriminated against in organizations. In other words, these groups must be given the same opportunity as white males. Laws and court cases relating to affirmative action and equal employment opportunity will be discussed in more detail in Chapter 12.

ORIENTING THE NEW EMPLOYEE

Orientation is concerned with introducing the new employee to the organization and the job. Orientation is not a one-time obligation, but an ongoing process. During the hiring process, most people learn the general aspects of the job and the organization. This usually includes such things as the job duties, working conditions, and pay.

Once the employee has been hired, the orientation program begins. Both the supervisor and the human resources department are involved in this program. In large organizations, the supervisor and the human resources department usually share the orientation responsibilities. If the organization has no human resources department, or has only a small one, the supervisor is generally responsible for conducting the orientation. Figure 10.6 summarizes the information that should be covered in the orientation program. Figure 10.7 shows what information is usually covered by the supervisor if a human resources department is involved.

Too many supervisors give little, if any, attention to the orientation process. A poor orientation program can quickly sour a new employee's attitude toward the job and the organization. Most people come to a new job with a positive attitude. However, if a new employee is made to feel unimportant by the lack of an orientation program, this attitude can quickly change. New employees will receive some type of orientation from either their fellow workers or the supervisor. Good, well-planned orientation programs reduce job learning time, improve attendance, and lead to better performance.

In summary, it is essential that the supervisor have a checklist of the items to be covered in the orientation. The supervisor should also provide an opportunity for questions from the new employee.

FIGURE 10.6

Information to Be Covered in Orientation by the Supervisor if There Is No Human Resources Department

1. A welcome.
2. Objectives and philosophy of the organization.
3. An explanation of the organization's operations and levels of authority and of how these relate to each other.
4. A brief history of the organization.
5. What is expected of the new employee: attitude, reliability, initiative, emotional maturity, and personal appearance.
6. Job functions and responsibilities.
7. Introduction to the department and fellow workers.
8. General office practice and business etiquette.
9. Rules, regulations, policies, and procedures.
10. Why the organization needs the new employee.
11. City, state, and federal laws, if applicable.
12. Skill training.
13. Performance evaluation criteria.
14. Promotional opportunities.
15. Conditions of employment, punctuality, attendance, conduct, hours of work, overtime, termination.
16. Pay procedures.
17. Benefits, salary, job security, insurance, recreational facilities, employee activities, rest periods, holidays, vacation, sick leave, leave of absence, tuition refund, pension.
18. Safety and fire prevention.
19. Personnel policies.
20. Functions of management.
21. Techniques for learning.
22. Encouragement.

Source: Adapted from Joseph Famularo, *Handbook of Personnel Forms, Records, and Reports* (New York: McGraw-Hill, 1982), pp. 136–40.

FIGURE 10.7

Information to Be Covered in Orientation by the Supervisor if There Is a Human Resources Department

1. Welcome the new employee.
2. Introduce the new employee to other employees in the work unit.
3. Familiarize the new employee with his or her job functions and responsibilities.
4. Explain the nature of the work and its relationship to the work of co-workers and that of the work unit as a whole.
5. Discuss policies on performance and conduct.
6. Familiarize the employee with the physical surroundings.
7. Discuss safety and fire prevention.
8. Review job performance criteria.

TRAINING EMPLOYEES

Training involves the acquisition of skills, concepts, rules, or attitudes by employees in order to increase their performance. The supervisor's primary role as a trainer falls in the area of **on-the-job training (OJT)** or in the area of job rotation. OJT is usually given by the supervisor or a senior employee. The employee is shown how the job is performed and then actually does it under the trainer's supervision. The major disadvantage of OJT is that the pressures of the workplace can cause the supervisor to either neglect the employee or give haphazard training. The major advantage of OJT is that the new employee is doing productive work and learning at the same time.

An old, yet still effective, system for giving OJT is the *job-instruction-training (JIT)* system. Figure 10.8 outlines the JIT system.

FIGURE 10.8

Steps in the JIT System

Determining the Training Objectives and Preparing the Training Area

1. Decide what the trainee must be taught so that he or she can do the job efficiently, safely, economically, and intelligently.
2. Provide the right tools, equipment, supplies, and material.
3. Have the workplace properly arranged, just as the employee will be expected to keep it.

Presenting the Instruction

Step 1: Preparation of the trainee.

    A. Put the trainee at ease.

    B. Find out what the trainee already knows about the job.

    C. Get the trainee interested in and desirous of learning the job.

Step 2: Presentation of the operations and knowledge.

    A. Tell, show, illustrate, and question to put over the new knowledge and operations.

    B. Instruct slowly, clearly, completely, and patiently, one point at a time.

    C. Check, question, and repeat.

    D. Make sure the trainee understands.

Step 3: Performance tryout.

    A. Test the trainee by having him or her perform the job.

    B. Ask questions, beginning with why, how, when, or where.

    C. Observe performance, correct errors, and repeat instructions if necessary.

    D. Continue until the trainee is competent in the job.

Step 4: Follow-up.

    A. Put the trainee on his or her own.

    B. Check frequently to be sure the trainee follows instructions.

    C. Taper off extra supervision and close follow-up until the trainee is qualified to work with normal supervision.

Source: Adapted from War Manpower Commission, *The Training within Industry Report* (Washington, D.C.: Bureau of Training, 1945) p. 195.

In **job rotation,** sometimes called **cross-training,** an employee learns several jobs and performs each job for a specific length of time. When cross-training has been given, the task of a person who is absent or leaves can be readily performed by others. Other benefits of job rotation include team building and individual skill development.

Regardless of the type of training used, there are several common pitfalls that the supervisor should avoid. Lack of reinforcement is a common error in training. An employee who is praised for doing a job correctly is likely to be motivated to do it correctly again. Too many supervisors only point out mistakes. Praise and recognition of a trainee can be a very effective means for reinforcing his or her learning. Too many supervisors tell people, "I'll let you know if you aren't doing the job right." However, people also want to know when they *are* doing the job right. Feedback about progress is critical to effective learning. Setting standards of performance for trainees and measuring their performance against the standards encourages learning.

"Practice makes perfect" definitely applies to the learning process. Too many supervisors try to explain the job quickly and then expect the trainee to do it perfectly the first time. Having trainees perform a particular job or explain how to perform a job maintains their concentration and facilitates learning. Repeating a job or task several times also helps. Learning is always helped by practice and repetition.

Frequently, supervisors have preconceived and inaccurate ideas about what certain people or groups of people can or can't do. A supervisor should realize that different people learn at different rates. Some learn rapidly and some learn slowly. The pace of the training should be adjusted to the trainee. A supervisor shouldn't expect everyone to pick the job up right away. Also, if a person is not a fast learner, this does not mean that the person will always be a poor performer. The supervisor should take the attitude that all people can learn and want to learn.

Several other methods are also used to train employees. These include vestibule training, apprenticeship training, classroom training, and programmed (or computer-assisted) instruction. Generally, the human resources department has the primary responsibility for conducting these types of training efforts. Supervisors may be asked to serve as trainers in any of these types of programs.

In **vestibule training,** the trainee uses procedures and equipment similar to those of the actual job, but located in a special area called a vestibule. Trainees are taught by skilled persons and are able to learn the job at their own speed without the pressures of production schedules. **Apprenticeship training** involves supervised training and testing for a minimum time period and until a minimum skill level has been reached. Formal **classroom training,** probably the most familiar type of training, involves lectures, movies, and exercises. Portions of orientation programs, some aspects of apprenticeship training, and safety programs are usually presented in a classroom setting. In **programmed instruction,** after material has been presented in text form, the trainee is required to read and answer questions relating to the text. A current extension of programmed instruction is **computer-assisted instruction (CAI).** Here a computer displays the material and processes the student's answers. In addition, Internet courses of instruction are available.

STEPS IN TRAINING EMPLOYEES IN JOB SKILLS

6 LEARNING OBJECTIVES

Supervisors are often required to train employees to perform the skills required in a particular job. Summarized next are five relatively simple steps that should be followed.

Get the Trainee Ready to Learn

The desire to learn comes from the trainee. The supervisor cannot force a person to want to learn. But the supervisor can show an interest in the person and point out why it is advantageous to learn to perform a particular job. Talk with the trainee. Find out something about her or his experience, ambitions, likes, and dislikes. Explain the importance of the job, why it will mean much to the person, and why it must be done correctly. Develop trainees' interest in wanting to learn; then they will be easy to teach.

Break Down the Work into Components and Identify the Key Points

This breakdown consists of determining the parts making up the total work. In each part, something is accomplished to advance the work toward completion. The operations breakdown can be viewed as a detailed road map that helps guide the trainee through the entire work cycle in a rational, easy-to-understand manner, without injury to the trainee or damage to the equipment.

A key point is any directive or information that helps a person perform a work component correctly, easily, and safely. Key points are the "tricks of the trade." Giving them to the trainee reduces the teaching time. Observing and mastering the key points help the trainee acquire the needed skill and perform the work effectively.

Work components and key points supply definite advantages. They clearly set forth the instruction pattern, they reduce the teaching time and simplify learning efforts, and they prevent costly errors. In addition, they foster technical improvements in the way the work is accomplished.

Demonstrate the Proper Way the Work Is to Be Done

Simply telling a person how to do a particular task is usually insufficient. You have to *tell and show*. How to perform work seems difficult when we merely hear it described—and some work is not easy to describe. Do a little at a time, pausing to point out the components and the key points. Let the trainee ask questions. Be reasonably certain that a component is fully understood before going on to the next step. However, no matter how carefully you demonstrate, the trainee may not be able to perform the work for these reasons: (1) if he was standing in front of you in order to see, he viewed the work done backwards (it is recommended that the instructor and the trainee be side by side and facing the same way); and (2) he has not physically gone through the steps.

Let the Trainee Perform the Work

The trainee is now ready to try doing the job under your guidance. At each component, let the trainee tell you what she is going to do. If she is correct, permit her to proceed. If not, correct her mistake and then permit her to proceed. Give the trainee encouragement when she is progressing correctly. Be firm in any corrective action that must take place. Be patient. Realize that mistakes will occur but that these are valuable because they reveal the trainee's learning difficulties and where the trainee hasn't learned. By letting the trainee perform the work, you not only find out quickly what the trainee has learned and gain an insight into her ability to perform the work; you also give the trainee some sense of satisfaction of accomplishment.

Put Trainees on Their Own Gradually

When you are reasonably sure that trainees can do the work, let them go ahead without you. But return periodically—perhaps four times the first day—to answer any questions and to see if all is going well. Above all, don't turn trainees loose and forget them. A trainee is going to have important questions, and he or she will feel better knowing that you are around to help and that you have an interest in the progress made.

SOLUTION TO THE SUPERVISION DILEMMA

Jane has learned the steps in the job-instruction-training system (JIT) (p. 200). She has also learned that a supervisor should avoid several common pitfalls in order to make a new employee's training experience more meaningful. Lack of reinforcement is a common error in training. Praise and recognition can be very effective means for reinforcing a trainee's learning. Learning is always helped by practice and repetition. Finally, supervisors frequently have preconceived and inaccurate ideas about what certain people or groups of people can or can't do. Such ideas can either help or hinder a trainee's development. Jane has also learned the five steps in training employees to perform job skills (pp. 202–3). She should incorporate these steps into all of the training she does.

SUMMARY

This chapter describes the supervisor's role in recruiting, selecting, and training employees. It also presents specific information on orienting and training employees.

1. *Define recruiting, selection, orientation, and training.* Recruiting involves seeking and attracting qualified candidates for job vacancies. The purpose of selection is to choose the best person for the job from those candidates. Orientation is the process of introducing new employees to the organization, their work unit, and their jobs. Training involves the acquisition by employees of the skills, information, and attitudes necessary for improving their effectiveness.

2. *Define job analysis, job description and job specification.* Job analysis involves determining the pertinent information relating to the performance of a specific job. A job description is a written portrayal of a job and the types of work required by the job. A job specification gives the qualifications necessary to perform the job.

3. *Describe the steps in the selection process.* Basically, there are seven steps in the selection process. These steps are not necessarily followed in full for each and every job. The seven steps are: screening from the employment application, interview by human resources department, employment tests, background and reference

checks, job interview by the supervisor, selection decision by the supervisor, and a medical examination.

4. *Understand the legal implications in recruiting and hiring new employees.* Several laws have had a significant effect on recruiting and hiring new employees. Title VII of the Civil Rights Act of 1964 and amendments to this act make it illegal to hire, fire, pay, or take other management actions on the basis of race, color, religion, national origin, or sex. The Age Discrimination in Employment Act of 1968 and amendments to this act make it illegal to discriminate against individuals over 40 years of age. The Rehabilitation Act of 1973 protects handicapped people. The Americans with Disabilities Act (ADA) gives the disabled sharply increased access to services and jobs. The Civil Rights Act of 1991 was designed to reverse several Supreme Court decisions of 1989 and 1990

that had been viewed as limiting equal employment opportunity and affirmative action.

5. *Discuss the supervisor's role in the orientation process.* Orientation is concerned with introducing the new employee to the organization and the job. In large organizations, the supervisor and the human resources department usually share the orientation responsibilities. If the organization has no human resources department, or has only a small one, the supervisor is generally responsible for conducting the orientation.

6. *Outline the steps in training employees in job skills.* The five steps in training employees in physical skills are: get the trainees ready to learn; break down the work into components and identify the key points; demonstrate the proper way the work is to be done; let the trainees perform the work; and put the trainees on their own gradually.

REVIEW QUESTIONS

1. Define the following terms:
   a. Recruiting
   b. Selection.
   c. Orienting.
   d. Training.
2. What is a job analysis? What role does it play in recruiting and selecting employees?
3. What are four methods of recruiting?
4. Who usually makes the final selection decision for operative employees?
5. What are the seven steps in the selection process?

6. Describe the purpose of the following government legislation:
   a. Civil Rights Act of 1964.
   b. Age Discrimination in Employment Act of 1968.
   c. Rehabilitation Act of 1973.
   d. Americans with Disabilities Act (ADA).
   e. Civil Rights Act of 1991.
7. What is an affirmative action program?
8. Outline some of the information that should be covered in an employee orientation program.
9. Give several tips that can help a supervisor in training employees.

SKILL-BUILDING QUESTIONS

1. "The best way to train employees is to put them on the job immediately and let them learn from their mistakes." Discuss your views on this statement.

2. "A company should be able to hire whomever it wants, without government intervention." Discuss how you feel about this.

3. What are some questions you would ask a job applicant in a structured job interview?

4. "Some people just don't want to learn anything new." Discuss.

ADDITIONAL READINGS

Brown, W. Stephen. "Failing to Train and Coach New Hires Is Failing to Manage," *Supervision*, March 1995.

Buhler, Patricia. "Recruitment: A Partner in Creating a Competitive Advantage." [Managing in the 90s], *Supervision*, June 1996.

Libes, Stewart C. "The Audition." [Employee Hiring], *Supervision*, January 1996.

Lissy, William E. "Interviewing Job Applicants under the ADA." [Americans with Disabilities Act of 1990], *Supervision*, March 1995.

———. "Lie Detector Tests," *Supervision*, October 1995.

Lousig-Nont, Gregory M. "Seven Deadly Hiring Mistakes," *Supervision*, January 1997.

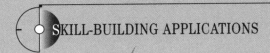

SKILL-BUILDING APPLICATIONS

Incident 10–1

Hiring a New Employee

John Arrington went to a meeting of all the supervisors in his company. The purpose of the meeting was to outline the company's new recruitment and selection program. John didn't pay much attention through most of the meeting because, as a supervisor, he had never really been involved in this process. The human resources department had always sent him his new employees.

However, about three-fourths of the way through the meeting, Tom Jackson, the human resources director, stated that one significant change in the new policy was that supervisors would now interview each job applicant. The human resources department would continue to screen applicants and would send five qualified people for any job opening in the supervisor's department. The supervisor would then interview each person in depth and make a recommendation to the human resources department. In fact, the supervisor would be required to rank the people from 1 to 5 (1 being the first choice for hiring and 5 being the last choice). Tom said that in most cases the human resources department would hire the supervisor's first choice. He explained that the change was being made because in the past supervisors had complained about not having enough input into who was hired in their departments.

John recognized what this change meant for him. He had two job openings in his department that needed filling immediately.

Questions

1. How can John prepare himself for his new responsibilities?
2. What do you think of the company's new procedure?
3. What problems might arise under the new procedure?

Incident 10–2

Lake Avionics

Sandra Hall is a new employee in the assembly department of Lake Avionics. On the day she started, Ken Williams, her supervisor, took her around and introduced her to all of the 28 employees in the department. He then took her to his office and handed her the following documents: company policy and procedures manual, a booklet on company fringe benefits, a booklet describing the company's products, and a copy of the assembly department's work rules. He told Sandra to read over the documents and said that he would be back in two hours to answer any questions she might have.

When Ken came back, Sandra told him that she had no questions about the documents he had given her. Ken then took Sandra back to the assembly area and discussed her job with her. He explained that her job required her to perform about 20 different operations. His description lasted about 10 minutes. Ken then told Sandra that he would be tied up for the rest of the day and that Greg Larson, a 15-year employee, would go over the details of the job with her.

Greg assured Sandra that she could do the work and told her to just watch him for the rest of the morning. After lunch, Greg told Sandra to try her hand at doing the job. However, she became confused about how the parts were assembled and asked Greg to show her again. Greg said, "You'll just have to learn the hard way. That's the way I did it. Learn from your mistakes."

By the late afternoon Sandra was thoroughly demoralized. She just didn't seem to be getting the hang of the assembly operation. Shortly before quitting time, Greg came by and said, "Don't get down on yourself. Now you have learned the wrong way to do it. Tomorrow morning, I'll show you some short cuts that will make the job much easier."

Questions

1. What do you think of Sandra's training program?
2. How do you think Sandra feels about her new job?

Exercise 10–1 ✓

The Layoff

Two years ago, your organization experienced a sudden increase in its volume of work. At about the same time, it was threatened with an equal employment opportunity suit that resulted in an affirmative action plan. Under this plan, additional women and minority members have been recruited and hired.

Presently, the top level of management in your organization is anticipating a decrease in volume of work. You have been asked to rank the clerical employees of your section in the event a layoff is necessary.

Below you will find biographical data for the seven clerical people in your section. Rank the seven people according to the order in which they should be laid off, that is, the person ranked first is to be laid off first, and so forth.

Burt Green: White male, age 45. Married, four children; five years with the organization. Reputed to be an alcoholic; poor work record.

Nan Nushka: White female, age 26. Married, no children, husband has a steady job; six months with the organization. Hired after the affirmative action plan went into effect; average work record to date. Saving to buy a house.

Johnny Jones: Black male, age 20. Unmarried; one year with organization. High performance ratings. Reputed to be shy—a "loner"; wants to start his own business some day.

Joe Jefferson: White male, age 24. Married, no children but wife is pregnant; three years with organization. Going to college at night; erratic performance attributed to work/study conflicts.

Livonia Long: Black female, age 49. Widow, three grown children; two years with the organization. Steady worker whose performance is average.

Ward Watt: White male, age 30. Recently divorced, one child; three years with the organization. Good worker.

Rosa Sanchez: Hispanic female, age 45. Six children, husband disabled one year ago; trying to help support her family; three months with the organization. No performance appraisal data available.

1. What criteria did you use for ranking the employees?
2. What implications does your ranking have in the area of affirmative action?

Exercise 10–2

OJT

Assume that you are the training supervisor of a large, local retail company. The company has seven department stores in your city. One of your biggest problems is adequately training new salesclerks. Because salesclerks represent your company to the public, the manner in which they conduct themselves is highly important. Especially critical aspects of their job include knowledge of the computerized cash register system, interaction with the customers, and knowledge of the particular products being sold.

1. Design a three-day orientation/training program for new salesclerks. Be sure to outline the specific topics (subjects) to be covered and the techniques to be used.
2. Specify what methods could be used to evaluate the success of the program.

Appraising Employee Performance

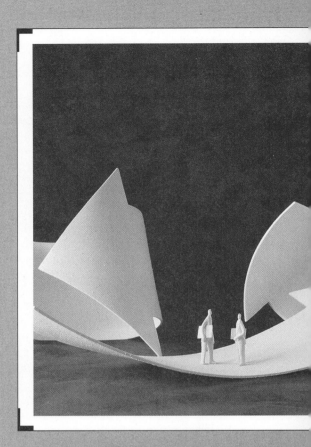

LEARNING OBJECTIVES

After studying this chapter, you should be able to:

1. Define performance.
2. Define performance appraisal.
3. List and describe the eight major performance appraisal methods.
4. Discuss the common errors in making performance appraisals.
5. Explain how to conduct performance appraisal interviews.

John Lewis has just been informed by the human resources department that it is time to conduct performance appraisals of his employees. Prior to becoming a supervisor, John had always felt uncomfortable during his performance appraisal. He had always felt that he was on the defensive. Now that he is a supervisor, he doesn't want his employees to feel the same way. However, John knows that some of his employees deserve an unfavorable appraisal. He certainly isn't looking forward to those sessions.

Appraising employee performance is one of the most difficult and important parts of the supervisor's job. **Performance appraisal** is a process that involves communicating to an employee how well he or she is performing the job and also, ideally, involves establishing a plan for improvement. All supervisors are constantly making judgments about the contributions and abilities of their employees. For example, supervisors may conclude that some employees show initiative, whereas others have a great deal of ability but must be constantly pushed.

Performance appraisals are handled in most organizations in one of two ways. Informal appraisals occur in all organizations, and many small businesses have informal appraisal systems. Under such a system, no formal procedures, methods, or times are established for conducting performance appraisals.

If a supervisor conducts appraisals informally, the employee will be given a general impression of how the supervisor feels about his or her performance. In all too many cases, such appraisals are conducted only when the employee has made a mistake. As a result, employees often develop negative feelings about this type of performance appraisal.

The other way of handling performance appraisals is to have a formal appraisal system. Under such a system, procedures, methods, and times are established for conducting appraisals. The basic purpose of this chapter is to describe formal performance appraisal systems.

It is important to note that formal appraisal systems contain an informal element. For example, general comments that a supervisor makes about an employee's performance are a type of informal performance appraisal. Supervisors must realize that any comment made by a supervisor about an employee's performance is viewed by the employee as a form of performance appraisal. Thus, the supervisor must use informal reviews to reinforce good performance and discourage poor performance. Supervision Illustration 11–1 describes one approach to performance appraisal.

WHAT IS PERFORMANCE?

LEARNING
OBJECTIVES

Performance refers to how well an employee is fulfilling the requirements of the job. Basically, the quality of an employee's performance is determined by a combination of three factors—effort, ability, and direction. **Effort** refers to how hard a person works. **Ability** is concerned with the person's capability. **Direction** refers to how well the person understands what is expected on the

---

SUPERVISION ILLUSTRATION 11-1

360-DEGREE FEEDBACK

A comprehensive way to evaluate employee feedback is through 360-degree feedback. It is used by some of the most successful companies in America, including UPS, AT&T, Amoco, General Mills, and Procter & Gamble. Traditionally, companies evaluate employee performance by relying almost exclusively on supervisor ratings that generally follow two types: measuring personality characteristics and technical abilities or appraisal by objectives. The first type of evaluation is usually in the form of a questionnaire with the evaluator ultimately making a subjective judgment. The second type of evaluation places emphasis on the achievement of recognized goals rather than personal characteristics.

With 360-degree feedback, a person's job performance is evaluated by his or her immediate supervisor as well as other individuals who have either direct or indirect contact with the person's work. The person also conducts a self-assessment of his or her performance. Co-workers also evaluate the person. Additionally, subordinates, customers, clients (internal as well as external), and anyone else who has contact with the person make an evaluation. Thus, a full circle (360 degrees) of evaluations is made by those people above, below, inside, outside, and anywhere in between. These evaluations are typically made by having all of the above mentioned individuals complete a lengthy, anonymous questionnaire.

Source: Adapted from Marc Marchese, "Industry: The Poser of the 360-Degree Feedback," *Pennsylvania CPA Journal,* December 1995. For more information on UPS, visit its Web site at:
 www.ups.com. For AT&T, visit **www.att.com**. For Amoco, visit **www.amoco.com**. For General Mills, visit **www.general-mills.com**. For Procter & Gamble, visit **www.pg.com**

FIGURE 11.1

Factors That Determine the Quality of Performance

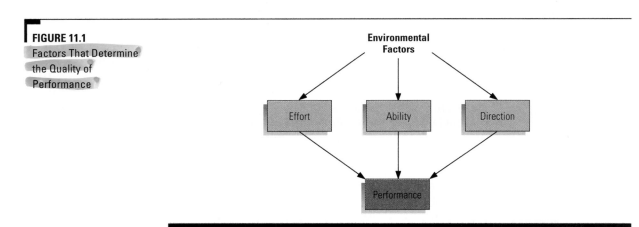

job. Figure 11.1 illustrates these relationships. Performance is often confused with effort. Although a person's performance is somewhat dependent on effort, it should be measured in terms of the results achieved, not in terms of the effort expended.

An employee's performance can be influenced by certain environmental factors that are not under the employee's direct control. Such factors include inadequate work facilities and equipment, restrictive policies that affect the job, lack of cooperation from other people and departments, and even luck. One job of the supervisor is to work with other levels of management to eliminate environmental factors that can negatively affect the performance of employees.

For certain types of jobs, such as that of the high
school teacher shown here, the level of performance
can be difficult to measure objectively.
Lionel Delevingne/Stock Boston

To obtain an acceptable level of performance, all three of the factors that determine the quality of performance must be present to some extent. If an employee puts forth a great deal of effort, has above-average ability, but lacks a good understanding of the job, the probable result would be unsatisfactory performance. If an employee understands what is expected on the job, works very hard, but lacks the ability to do the job, his or her performance would probably also be poor. Finally, if an employee has good ability, understands the job, but is lazy and exerts little effort, his or her performance is also likely to be poor. It should be pointed out that an employee who is weak in one of the performance factors can compensate for that weakness by being strong in one or both of the other factors. For example, you may have known an employee who didn't have excessive ability but was a high performer because he or she knew the job well and worked extra hard.

The key to obtaining good performance, therefore, is to encourage effort by employees, to develop their ability, and to clearly communicate what they are expected to do on the job. A supervisor can use several means to ensure that employees are properly directed. Two of the best are carefully developed job descriptions and performance appraisal systems.

JOB DESCRIPTIONS AND JOB SPECIFICATIONS

Job descriptions and job specifications were introduced in Chapter 10. A job description states the characteristics of a job and the types of work that are

FIGURE 11.2

Sample Job
Description Form

Salaried Position Description

Position _____   Position no. _____

Reports to _____   Effective date _____

Division _____

Approved by _____

General description of the job _____

_____

Types of work performed in the job _____

_____

---

performed in the job. Figure 11.2 presents a sample job description form. A job specification gives the qualifications necessary to perform a job. It states the experience, training, education, knowledge, skills, and abilities necessary to do the job.

A job description and job specification result from a **job analysis,** which is the process of determining, through observation and study, the pertinent information regarding a specific job. In most large organizations, job analyses, job descriptions, and job specifications are developed by the human resources department. However, the supervisor plays a key role in their development by providing much of the necessary information to the human resources department. In small organizations, supervisors may actually develop job descriptions and job specifications for the jobs under their authority. If called upon to develop job descriptions and job specifications, a supervisor should carefully study each job to ensure that it is described accurately. The supervisor should remember that the overriding purpose of a job description is to communicate to the employee what he or she is expected to do on the job. Thus, clearly communicating an accurate job description to the employee is the first step in the performance appraisal process.

PERFORMANCE APPRAISAL DEFINED

LEARNING
OBJECTIVES

Performance appraisal is a process that involves communicating to an employee how well the employee is performing the job and also, ideally, involves establishing a plan for improvement. Performance appraisals are used for many purposes in organizations. Among these purposes are wage and salary administration, promotions or demotions, transfers, layoffs, discharges, counseling with employees, and human resources planning. Performance appraisal systems have three principal purposes: (1) to improve employee performance in the present job, (2) to prepare employees for future opportunities that may arise in the organization, and (3) to provide a record of employee performance

FIGURE 11.3

Benefits of a Sound
Performance Appraisal
System to the
Organization, the
Supervisor, and the
Employee

Benefits to the Organization

1. Provides an evaluation of the organization's human resources.
2. Gives the organization a basis for making future human resources decisions.
3. Increases the potential of the organization's present human resources for meeting the present and future needs of the organization.
4. Improves employee morale.

Benefits to the Supervisor

1. Provides the supervisor with a clearer picture of the employee's understanding of what is expected on the job.
2. Gives the supervisor input into each employee's development.
3. Improves the productivity and morale of the supervisor's employees.
4. Helps the supervisor identify capable replacements for higher-level jobs within the supervisor's work unit.

Benefits to the Employee

1. Allows the employee to present ideas for improvement.
2. Provides the employee with an opportunity to change his or her work behavior.
3. Lets the employee know how the supervisor feels about his or her performance.
4. Assures the employee of regular and systematic reviews of performance.

that can be used as a basis for future management decisions. Many of the benefits that result from a sound performance appraisal system are outlined in Figure 11.3.

PERFORMANCE APPRAISAL METHODS

Ideally, performance appraisals should be directly related to job success. However, locating or creating satisfactory measures of job success can be difficult. There are many jobs for which performance measures can be developed but with a greater degree of difficulty (for example, evaluating the job performance of a high school teacher or a staff specialist). In addition, job performance is often influenced by factors outside the employee's control. For example, the performance of a machine operator is partially influenced by the age and condition of the equipment. For these reasons and others, performance appraisals are often based on personal characteristics and other subjective factors. Among the personal characteristics that are frequently used in performance appraisal systems are integrity, dependability, attitude, initiative, and judgment.

Numerous problems exist in performance appraisal systems based on personal characteristics. One problem is that supervisors often resist such systems. The major reason for their resistance is that systems of this type place the supervisor in the position of being a judge with the employee being the defendant. Another problem is that such systems tempt the supervisor to favor close friends and associates. Because it is natural to see favorable characteristics in friends, the supervisor may never realize that favoritism is influencing his or her appraisals. Despite the problems, performance appraisal systems based on personal characteristics and subjective evaluations are still in widespread use.

The most frequently used performance appraisal methods are:

1. Graphic rating scale.
2. Essay appraisals.
3. Checklist.
4. Forced-choice rating.
5. Critical-incident appraisals.
6. Work-standards approach.
7. Ranking methods.
8. Management by objectives (MBO).

Upper levels of management usually decide which type of performance appraisal system an organization will use. Ideally, the supervisor should have some input into that decision. However, the success or failure of any performance appraisal method is largely determined by the supervisor's use of the method. This section describes the various performance appraisal methods.

Graphic Rating Scale

With the **graphic rating scale,** the supervisor is asked to evaluate an individual on such factors as initiative, dependability, cooperativeness, and quality of work. Figure 11.4 gives an example of a typical form used in a performance appraisal system of this kind. The graphic rating scale is one of the most widely used performance appraisal methods. One of the biggest problems with its use is that many supervisors have a tendency to evaluate everyone a little above average. However, this method does give the same information on all employees and it is relatively inexpensive to develop.

Essay Appraisals

Essay appraisals require the supervisor to write a series of statements about an employee's past performance, potential for promotion, and strengths and weaknesses. One problem with the essay appraisal is that the length and content of the written statements can vary considerably from supervisor to supervisor. In addition, this method depends on the writing skills of the supervisor. For these reasons, it is difficult to compare essay appraisals made by different supervisors.

Checklist

With the **checklist**, the supervisor does not actually evaluate but merely records performance. The supervisor checks yes or no responses on a series of questions concerning the employee's performance. Figure 11.5 gives some typical questions. The principal advantage of this method is that it is easy to use. The scoring key for the checklist is usually kept by the human resources department, which computes the relative rating of the employee. Individuals with high scores are rated as better employees than those with low scores.

Performance Evaluation

Employee's name _____ Title _____

Department: _____

Select the symbol that best describes the employee's performance in each factor and check the appropriate box on the right side of the form. Cross out parts of the definition that do not apply. Add to definitions to make them more meaningful.

Exceeds Job Requirements   E   Meets Job Requirements   M   Needs Improvement   N

E   M   N

1. **Quality of work.** Accuracy, neatness, and thoroughness of work. Economy of time and materials. Care of equipment used.   ☐ ☐ ☐

2. **Quantity of work.** Productive output. Speed and consistency of output.   ☐ ☐ ☐

3. **Dependability.** Follows instructions. Exercises good judgment, punctuality, attendance, and safety habits.   ☐ ☐ ☐

4. **Cooperation.** Extent to which employee cooperates with other employees and departments.   ☐ ☐ ☐

5. **Versatility.** Resourceful in handling assignments and solving problems. Versatile in application of knowledge and skills.   ☐ ☐ ☐

6. **Planning.** Ability to plan for immediate and long–range assignments. Sets realistic goals and timetables.   ☐ ☐ ☐

7. **Initiative.** Diligent work habits. Strong sense of responsibility.   ☐ ☐ ☐

8. **Leadership.** Inspires confidence, productivity, and teamwork. Fair and consistent use of discipline.   ☐ ☐ ☐

9. **Write-in factors.** Use any factor not listed that may apply.   ☐ ☐ ☐

_____

_____

10. **Overall evaluation.** Summary of all relevant factors regarding employee's performance.   ☐ ☐ ☐

Supervisors are generally not aware of the values associated with each question; but since they can figure out the positive and negative aspects of the questions, bias can be introduced into their answers. Furthermore, assembling the questions is a difficult job. Another drawback of this method is that a different set of questions must be assembled for most job categories.

		Yes	No
FIGURE 11.5	1. Does the employee produce work that meets quality standards?	____	____
Sample Checklist	2. Does the employee have a thorough knowledge of the job?	____	____
Questions	3. Does the employee work without detailed instructions?	____	____
	4. Does the employee assist others when his or her work has been completed?	____	____

Forced-Choice Rating

The **forced-choice rating** method requires the supervisor to choose which of two statements is either most (or least) applicable to the employee being reviewed. The supervisor is required to choose between both favorable and unfavorable statements. Figure 11.6 gives some examples of statements that might appear in a forced-choice rating method.

Under the forced-choice rating method, the supervisor is not given the weights or scores assigned to each statement. Due to the nature of the questions, the supervisor usually cannot determine which answer is best. The human resources department or a member of higher management applies the weights and develops a score. Again, employees with higher scores are rated as better than those with lower scores. The forced-choice rating method attempts to eliminate bias by forcing the supervisor to choose between statements that are not obviously distinguishable. The biggest drawback of this method is that it can frustrate supervisors. In addition, the cost of developing the form may be high.

Critical-Incident Appraisals

With **critical-incident appraisals,** the supervisor keeps a written record of unusual incidents that show both positive and negative actions by an employee. The employee is then evaluated based on actual behavior. When this method is used, the employee being evaluated should always be given a chance to state his or her views on each incident. This also provides the employee with an opportunity to establish an understanding of the behavior that the supervisor is seeking.

For this method to be effective, the supervisor must record pertinent incidents as they occur. This can be time-consuming and burdensome. Another drawback is the strong tendency to record or stress primarily negative incidents.

Work-Standards Approach

With the **work-standards approach,** attempts are made to establish objective measures of an employee's work performance. An example of a work standard for production workers is the number of pieces produced per hour. A salesperson's quota is another type of work standard. Work standards for professional, staff, and clerical workers are much more difficult to define. Generally speaking, work standards should reflect the "normal output of a normal person." They attempt to answer the question "What is a fair day's work?" Thus,

FIGURE 11.6

Sample Questions for a
Forced-Choice Rating
Method

From each set of statements, choose the one statement that best describes the
employee being evaluated.

1. Keeps work up-to-date.
2. Approaches problems with an open mind.

1. Uses sick leave to excess.
2. Takes little interest in the job.

1. Organizes work well.
2. Produces work that meets quality standards.

the work-standards approach is used more frequently for operative workers in
production jobs than for other types of employees.

The major advantage of the work-standards approach is that it bases the
performance appraisal on factors that are generally more objective than those
used in other methods. To be effective, of course, the standards must be fair
and the employees must view them as being fair.

Ranking Methods

The most commonly used ranking methods are alternation ranking, paired-
comparison ranking, and forced-distribution ranking. Under **alternation ranking,** a supervisor's employees are listed down the left side of a sheet of paper.
The supervisor then chooses the most valuable employee, crosses this name off
the list, and places it at the *top* of the column on the right side. The supervisor
then selects and crosses off the name of the least valuable employee and places
it at the *bottom* of the right-hand column. The supervisor then repeats this
process for all the names on the left side. The listing of names on the right side
gives the supervisor a ranking of his or her employees from most valuable to
least valuable.

Under **paired-comparison ranking,** the supervisor again lists his or her
employees' names down the left side of a sheet of paper. The supervisor then
evaluates the performance of the first employee on the list against the performance of the second employee on the list. If the supervisor feels that the performance of the first employee is better than that of the second employee, he
or she places a checkmark by the first employee's name. The first employee is
then compared to each of the other employees. In this way, the first employee
is compared with all the other employees on the list. The process is repeated
for each of the other employees. The employee with the most checkmarks is
evaluated to be the most valuable employee, and the employee with the least
checkmarks is evaluated to be the least valuable. The major problem with the
paired-comparison method is that it becomes unwieldy when a large number of
employees are being compared.

Under **forced-distribution ranking,** the rater compares the performance
of employees and places a certain percentage of employees at various performance levels. This method assumes that the performance level in a group of
employees will be distributed according to a bell-shaped, or "normal," curve.
Figure 11.7 illustrates how the method works. The rater is required to rate 60

FIGURE 11.7
Forced-Distribution Curve

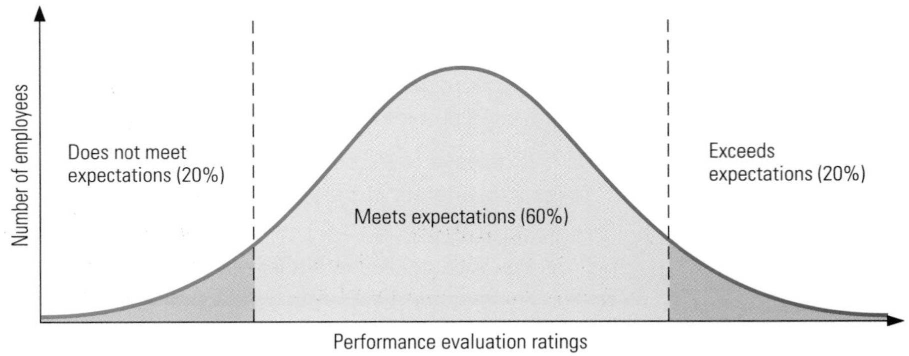

percent of the employees as meeting expectations, 20 percent as exceeding expectations, and 20 percent as not meeting expectations.

One problem with forced-distribution ranking is that a bell-shaped distribution of performance may not be applicable to small groups of employees. With such groups, even if the distribution approximates a normal curve, it is probably not a perfect curve. This means that some employees will probably not be rated accurately if forced-distribution ranking is used. Also, this method is dramatically different from the other methods in that it makes each employee's performance evaluation a function of the performance of other employees in the job. In addition, none of the ranking methods explain or quantify the differences between employees. In fact, the difference between the top employee and the one at the bottom of the list may only be time and maturity factors.

Management by Objectives (MBO)

Management by objectives (MBO) was introduced and discussed as a means of planning in Chapter 6. MBO is also used as a performance appraisal method and is similar to the work-standards approach. With MBO, the supervisor and the employee jointly agree on what the employee's work objectives will be and how they will be accomplished. The employee is then allowed considerable freedom in accomplishing the work objectives. The employee's performance appraisal is based on the degree to which the work objectives are accomplished.

FREQUENCY OF PERFORMANCE APPRAISALS

There seems to be no consensus on the question of how frequently performance appraisals should be conducted. The answer seems to be as frequently as is necessary to let employees know how they are doing. Many organizations require a formal performance appraisal at least once a year. However, most employees want to know how well they are doing more often than once a year. Therefore, it is recommended that the supervisor do at least two or three reviews each year in addition to the formal annual performance appraisal.

A supervisor should be aware of the necessity for more frequent appraisals for new employees or employees who are being retrained. These informal appraisals can be very effective in the development process of these employees.

SUPERVISOR BIASES IN PERFORMANCE APPRAISALS

Several common supervisor biases have been identified in performance appraisals. **Leniency** is the grouping of ratings at the positive end instead of spreading them throughout the performance scale. **Central tendency** is the rating of all or most employees in the middle of the scale. Leniency and central tendency errors make it difficult if not impossible to separate the good performers from the poor performers. In addition, such errors make it difficult to compare ratings from different raters. For example, it is possible for a good performer who is rated by a manager committing central tendency errors to receive a lower rating than that of a poor performer who is rated by a manager committing leniency errors.

Another common bias in performance appraisals is the **halo effect.** This occurs when supervisors allow a single prominent characteristic of an employee to influence their judgment on each of the items in the performance appraisal. A frequent result is that the employee being evaluated receives approximately the same rating on every item.

Personal preferences and prejudices can also cause errors in performance appraisals. Supervisors with biases or prejudices tend to look for employee behaviors that conform to their biases. Appearance, social status, dress, race, and sex have influenced many performance appraisals. Supervisors have also allowed first impressions to influence later judgments of an employee. First impressions are only a sample of behavior; however, people tend to retain these impressions even when faced with contradictory evidence later.

OVERCOMING BIASES IN PERFORMANCE APPRAISALS

As can be seen from the above discussion, the potential for biases in performance appraisals is great. One approach to overcoming these biases is to make refinements in the design of appraisal methods. For example, it could be argued that the forced-distribution method of performance appraisal attempts to overcome the biases of leniency and central tendency. Unfortunately, because refined instruments frequently do not overcome all the obstacles, it appears unlikely that refining appraisal instruments will totally overcome errors in performance appraisals.

A more promising approach to overcoming biases in performance appraisals is to improve the skills of raters. Suggestions on the specific training that should be given to raters are often vague, but they normally emphasize that raters should be given training to observe behavior more accurately and judge it fairly. At a minimum, raters should receive training in (1) the performance appraisal method(s) used by the company, (2) rater biases and causes of those biases, (3) the importance of the rater's role in the total appraisal process, (4) the use of performance appraisal information, and (5) the communication skills necessary to provide feedback to the employee.

CONDUCTING PERFORMANCE APPRAISAL INTERVIEWS

5 LEARNING OBJECTIVES

Appraising the employee's performance is only half of the supervisor's job in performance appraisal systems. The other half is communicating the appraisal to the employee. The purposes of communicating the performance appraisal are to (1) provide the employee with a clear understanding of how the supervisor feels the employee is performing the job, (2) clear up any misunderstandings about what is expected, (3) establish a program of improvement, and (4) improve the working relationship between the supervisor and the employee.

Effective performance appraisal interviews are the result of good planning by the supervisor. Whatever form or method is used, considerable time and thought should be given to completing the form. The form should not be completed in the few minutes before the interview. When feasible, the employee should be given at least a week's notice of the upcoming appraisal.

A private room or office should be used, interruptions should be held to a minimum, and the confidential nature of the information should be explained to the employee. The performance appraisal interview is not the time to tell the employee off. You are trying to make the job easier for the employee and to help him or her become a happier and more productive employee. Figure 11.8 gives some questions that the supervisor should consider before discussing the performance appraisal with the employee.

In addition to the steps outlined above, most organizations require that the employee and supervisor sign the performance evaluation form, acknowledging that the appraisal interview has been conducted and that the employee has read the evaluation. Ideally, the employee should be given a copy of the evaluation.

When conducting performance evaluations, it is extremely important that the supervisor be specific so that people know exactly what they are doing well and what needs improvement. In addition, it should be remembered that the performance review should be a two-way learning experience. The supervisor should ask for feedback from the employee as to how the supervisor might improve his or her own performance. Figure 11.9 presents a suggested set of specific steps to be followed when conducting an employee performance review.

FIGURE 11.8

Questions That the Supervisor Should Consider Prior to the Performance Appraisal Interview

1. What are the specific good points on which you will compliment the employee?
2. What are the specific improvement points you intend to discuss?
3. What reactions do you anticipate? How do you intend to handle these reactions?
4. Can you support your performance appraisal with adequate facts?
5. What specific help or corrective action do you anticipate offering?
6. What is your approach for gaining acceptance of your suggested corrective action?
7. What follow-up action do you have in mind?

FIGURE 11.9

Steps in the Performance
Appraisal Interview

Performance Review Discussion

Employee's name _____

Date of discussion _____

Introduction
- Put employee at ease.
- Purpose: Mutual discussion of how things are going.

Employee's view
- How does he/she view job and working climate?
- Any problems?
- Suggestions for changes, improvement?

Supervisor's view of employee's performance
- Summary statement only.
- Avoid comparisons with others.

Behavior desirable to continue
- Mention one or two items only.

Opportunities for improvement
- No more than one or two items.
- Do not present these opportunities as "shortcomings."
- Keep the suggestions work related.

Performance improvement plan
- Plan should be employee's plan.
- Supervisor merely tries to help and counsel.

Future opportunities
- Advancement possibilities?
- Future pay increase possibilities?
- Warning for poor performer.

Feedback from employee on supervisor's suggestions for performance changes, improvements.
- Any problems?

Questions
- Any general concerns?
- Close on constructive, encouraging note.

Source: Adapted from "The Annual Performance Review Discussion—Making It Constructive," by Herbert H. Meyer, reprinted with permission of *Personnel Journal,* Costa Mesa, California. All rights reserved. Copyright © October 1977.

PREPARING FOR YOUR OWN PERFORMANCE APPRAISAL INTERVIEW

Like your employees, you as supervisor also receive performance appraisals. You probably also have some of the same feelings that your employees have before the appraisal is conducted. Figure 11.10 offers some suggestions on how to prepare for your own performance appraisal session. You can also give

FIGURE 11.10

Suggestions for the Supervisor Preparing for His or Her Own Performance Appraisal

1. Using whatever form or method is used by your boss, evaluate your own performance.
2. Outline the ways in which your boss can help you do your job better.
3. Determine any additional training that you feel you need in order to do your job better.
4. Suggest any changes (reports, procedures, etc.) that would make you more effective in your job.
5. Develop a program for your self-improvement and discuss it with your boss.
6. Outline your long-range plans. Where would you like to be? How are you preparing to get there?

these suggestions to your employees in advance of their performance appraisal so that they will be better prepared. Remember, regardless of which side of the fence you are on, a performance appraisal should be a learning, growing experience.

HANDLING THE POOR PERFORMER

Supervisors are frequently faced with the common problem of what to do about the poor performer. There may be a number of causes for the employee's poor performance. Improper placement, poor training, poor communication, and lack of motivation are common causes of poor performance. Supervision Illustration 11–2 describes problems that can develop from inadequate performance appraisals.

SUPERVISION ILLUSTRATION 11–2

PERFORMANCE EVALUATION OF THE POOR PERFORMER

A recent arbitration case illustrates some considerations in performance evaluation of the poor performer. An employee was moved to a different job after 21 years of service without any significant performance problems. The employee was in the new job for two years, during which period she had three different supervisors. Although the supervisors had expressed concerns about her performance and developed plans of action to provide her training, performance evaluations, and feedback, they neglected to follow through with these plans. In addition, the employee did not get along well with her assigned trainers, which hampered the instruction she received in the new job.

The employee was put on a 30-day probation that called for her termination if she did not improve her job performance. When she failed to meet her supervisor's expectations during this period, she was discharged. She filed a grievance protesting her discharge. The arbitrator did not award any back pay to the employee but directed management to reinstate her for a 12-week probationary period. He directed management to make sure that the employee received proper training and close performance monitoring during the 12-week probationary period.

Source: Adapted from William E. Lissy, "Labor Law for Supervisors: Incompetence," *Supervision,* July 1996. For more information about labor law topics, visit the U.S. Department of Labor at its Web site: **www.dol.gov.**

The supervisor's alternatives in dealing with the poor performer are (1) improve the employee's performance to an acceptable level; (2) transfer the employee to a job that better fits his or her abilities; (3) demote the employee to a job that he or she can handle; or (4) if unable to accomplish any of these possibilities, attempt to terminate the employee. Of course, these alternatives are influenced by government regulations and by whether the organization is unionized. The supervisor should make careful preparation for any action that is to be taken, document all steps, and work closely with the human resources department.

A supervisor who has decided that an employee's performance is unacceptable should plan for an immediate interview with the employee. Putting off or delaying the interview is unfair to both the employee and the organization. Delaying the handling of the poor performer may also increase the chance of litigation when action is finally taken. Figure 11.11 outlines the main points that the supervisor should cover with a poor performer during this interview.

It is also important to note that an employee's poor performance may be caused by personal problems. Managing employees with personal problems is covered in depth in Chapter 18.

FIGURE 11.11

How to Conduct a Performance Appraisal Interview with a Poor Performer

1. Attempt to create a setting in which the employee feels encouraged to share his or her views and listen to what you have to say.
2. Be firm but fair.
3. Let the employee know exactly where he or she is weak and how to make improvements.
4. Get the employee to participate in setting goals for the present job.
5. If a transfer seems in order, get the employee to participate in setting goals for the new job.
6. Reach an agreement on what is to be achieved and the deadline for achieving it.
7. Emphasize your availability for future talks, and encourage the employee to come to you if problems remain or develop.

SOLUTION TO THE
SUPERVISION
DILEMMA

John has learned that the best thing a supervisor can do is to be well prepared. John is now better prepared to handle performance appraisals because he now knows more about the various kinds of performance appraisal methods (pp. 217–18). He also knows the potential errors that can occur in conducting performance appraisals—leniency, central tendency, and the halo effect (p. 219). His anxiety about conducting performance appraisals is understandable. Most supervisors experience some anxiety about doing this. When conducting performance appraisals, it is extremely important that John be specific so that his employees know exactly what they are doing well and what needs improvement. Finally, John has learned a number of ways to handle the poor performers in his work group (pp. 222–23).

SUMMARY

The purpose of this chapter is to explain the importance of performance appraisals. Various methods used for conducting performance appraisals are described. Suggestions for conducting performance appraisals are also given.

1. *Define performance.* Performance refers to the degree to which an employee is accomplishing the tasks that make up his or her job.

2. *Define performance appraisal.* Performance appraisal is a process that involves determining and communicating to an employee how well he or she is performing the job and also establishing a plan for improvement.

3. *List and describe the eight major performance appraisal methods.*
   a. The graphic rating scale requires the rater to assess an employee on such factors as quality of work, dependability, cooperativeness, and initiative.
   b. The essay appraisal requires the rater to describe an employee's performance in written narrative form.
   c. The checklist requires the rater to answer yes or no to a series of questions concerning the employee's behavior.
   d. The forced-choice rating method requires the rater to choose between a series of statements describing how an employee carries out the duties and responsibilities of the job.
   e. The critical-incident appraisal method requires the rater to keep a written record of unusual incidents involving job behaviors as they occur. The recorded incidents should illustrate both satisfactory and unsatisfactory performance of the employee being rated.
   f. The work-standards approach involves setting a standard or expected level of output and then comparing each employee's performance to that standard.
   g. Ranking methods (alternation ranking, paired-comparison ranking, and forced-distribution ranking) require that the rater compare the performance of an employee with the performance of other employees.
   h. Management by objectives consists of the supervisor and the employee jointly agreeing on what the employee's work objectives will be and how they will be accomplished. The employee is allowed considerable freedom in accomplishing the work objectives. The employee's performance appraisal is based on the degree to which the work objectives are accomplished.

4. *Discuss the common errors in making performance appraisals. Leniency* is the grouping of ratings at the positive end instead of spreading them throughout the performance scale. *Central tendency* is the rating of all or most employees in the middle of the performance scale. The *halo effect* occurs when managers allow a single prominent characteristic of an employee to influence their judgment on each of the separate items in the performance appraisal.

5. *Explain how to conduct performance appraisal interviews.* When feasible, the employee should be given at least a week's notice of the upcoming appraisal. Considerable time and thought should be given to completing the performance appraisal form. A private room or office should be used for the interview, interruptions should be held to a minimum, and the confidential nature of the information should be explained to the employee. The supervisor should consider some specific questions before discussing the performance appraisal with the employee.

REVIEW QUESTIONS

1. What is an informal performance appraisal system? What is a formal performance appraisal system?
2. What is performance?
3. What factors determine the quality of an employee's performance?
4. What is a job description?
5. What is a performance appraisal?
6. Describe the following performance appraisal methods:
   a. Graphic rating scale.
   b. Essay appraisal.
   c. Checklist.
   d. Forced-choice rating.
   e. Critical-incident appraisal.
   f. Work-standards approach.
   g. Ranking methods.
   h. Management by objectives.
7. What are some questions that the supervisor should consider prior to the performance appraisal interview?
8. What are some factors that the supervisor should consider in preparing for his or her own performance appraisal?
9. Discuss several points that the supervisor should cover with a poor performer in a performance appraisal interview.

SKILL-BUILDING QUESTIONS

1. Most supervisors do a good job of handling performance appraisals. Discuss your views on this statement.
2. Do you feel that conducting performance appraisals once a year is enough? Discuss.
3. Which performance appraisal method do you feel is most effective? Support your answer.
4. Why do you think that most supervisors do not look forward to appraising their employees?

ADDITIONAL READINGS

Faidley, Ray A. "Performance Essentials: Alignment + Standards + Commitment," *Supervision*, May 1996.

Lebediker, Jeremy. "The Supervisor as a Coach: 4 Essential Models for Setting Performance Expectations," *Supervision*, December 1995.

Lissy, William E. "Performance Appraisals Can Be a Weapon for Employees," *Supervision*, March 1997.

Pell, Arthur R. "Evaluation Interviews," *Managers Magazine*, August 1995.

Pollock, Ted. "Ready for That Appraisal?" *Supervision*, February 1995.

Taylor, Glenn L., and Martha N. Morgan. "The Reverse Appraisal: A Tool for Leadership Development," *Quality Progress*, December 1995.

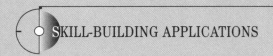
SKILL-BUILDING APPLICATIONS

Incident 11–1
Lackadaisical Manager

Plant manager Paul Dorn wondered why his boss, Leonard Hech, had sent for him. Paul, who thought Leonard had been tough on him lately, was slightly uneasy at being asked to come to Leonard's office at a time when such meetings were unusual. "Close the door and sit down, Paul," invited Leonard. "I've been wanting to talk to you."

After preliminary conversation was completed, Leonard said that because Paul's latest project was finished, he would receive the raise he had been promised on its completion.

Leonard went on to say that since it was time for Paul's performance appraisal, they might as well do it now. Leonard explained that the performance appraisal was based on four criteria: (1) amount of high-quality merchandise manufactured and shipped on time; (2) quality of relationships with plant employees and peers; (3) progress in maintaining employee safety and health; and (4) reaction to the demands of top management. The first criterion had a relative importance of 40 percent, and the rest had a weight of 20 percent each.

Paul received an excellent rating on the first item. Shipments were at an all-time high, quality was good, and few shipments had arrived late. On the second item, Paul also was rated excellent. Leonard said that plant employees and peers related well to Paul, labor relations were excellent, and there had been no major grievances since Paul became plant manager.

However, on attention to employee safety and health matters, the evaluation was below average. His boss stated that no matter how often he bugged Paul about improving housekeeping in the plant, he never seemed to produce results. Leonard also rated Paul below average on meeting demands from top management. He explained that Paul always answered yes to any request and then disregarded it, going about his business as if nothing had happened.

Seemingly surprised at the comments, Paul agreed that perhaps Leonard was right and he should do a better job on these matters.

As weeks went by, Leonard noticed little change in Paul. He reviewed the situation with an associate. "It's frustrating. In this time of rapid growth, we must make constant changes in work methods. Paul agrees, but can't seem to make people break their habits and adopt more efficient ones. I find myself riding him very hard these days, but he just calmly takes it. He's well liked by everyone. But somehow, he's got to care more about safety and housekeeping in the plant. And when higher management makes demands he can't meet, he's got to say, 'I can't do that and do all the other things you want, too.' Now he has dozens of unfinished jobs because he refuses to say no."

As he talked, Leonard remembered something Paul had told him in confidence once. "I take Valium for a physical condition I have. When I don't take it, I get symptoms similar to a heart attack. But I only take half as much as the doctor prescribed." Now, Leonard thought, I'm really in a spot. If the Valium is what is making him so lackadaisical, I can't endanger his health by asking him to quit taking it. And I certainly can't fire him. Yet, as things stand, he really can't implement all the changes we must have to fulfill the goals we set for the next two years.

Questions

1. What would you do if you were in Leonard's place?
2. What could have been done differently during the performance appraisal session?
3. What method was used in communicating the performance appraisal?

Incident 11–2
The New Auditor

About six months ago, Ray Knight was hired as a construction auditor for the Poole Construction Company. Construction auditing involves keeping track of the costs for each construction project and informing the project manager if costs of any type are getting out of hand. Ray has had over 10 years' experience as a construction auditor. There are three construction auditors at

Poole, and they all report to the accounting manager, Tom Langford.

After spending many hours interviewing applicants for the construction auditor job, Tom has selected Ray. Ray had impressed Tom as being a dedicated person with an eye for detail. Although Ray had worked for six different organizations in the past 10 years, Tom knew that this was not all that unusual in the construction industry. Ray had also impressed Tom with his sincerity.

Shortly after Ray was hired, problems began to develop. Ray became very short-tempered and irritable with the project managers when they didn't accept his advice on how to control certain costs on their projects. Furthermore, Tom has detected several mistakes in Ray's work that a person of his experience should not be making.

Tom feels that Ray's problems at work result from his attitude. Most of the project managers at Poole Construction did not attend college, whereas Ray graduated from the state university with a degree in accounting. In fact, some of the project managers have told Tom that Ray never lets them forget that he has a college degree and that they do not.

Ray is coming up for his six months' performance evaluation. Tom is still convinced that Ray can be a good auditor if he can just change his attitude. Poole Construction does not have a formal performance evaluation system, but it does require that a review of each new employee be conducted at the end of six months. This review determines whether the employee becomes a permanent employee or is to look for employment elsewhere.

Questions

1. If you were Tom, what would you do?
2. If you could extend Ray's probationary period for six more months, what would you do in the performance evaluation meeting to prepare you for the evaluation that would occur six months later?

Exercise 11–1

Developing a Performance Appraisal System

A large public utility has been having difficulty with its performance evaluation program. Under this program, all operating and clerical employees are evaluated semiannually by their supervisors.

The form that the supervisors have been using for 10 years is given in Exhibit 11.1. The form is scored as follows: Excellent = 5; Above average = 4; Average = 3; Below average = 2; and Poor = 1. The scores for each factor are entered in the right-hand column, and these scores are totaled for an overall evaluation score.

In the procedure used, each supervisor rates each employee on July 31 and January 31. The supervisor discusses the rating with the employee and then sends the rating to the human resources department. Each rating is placed in the employee's human resources file. If promotions come up, the cumulative ratings are considered at that time. The ratings are also supposed to be used as a check when raises are given.

The system was designed by Joanna Kyle, who retired as the human resources supervisor two years ago. Her replacement was Eugene Meyer. Meyer graduated 15 years ago with a degree in commerce from the University of Texas. In the past 15 years, he's had a variety of experience, mostly in utilities. For about five of those years, he did human resources work.

Meyer has been reviewing the evaluation system. The employees have a mixture of indifferent and negative feelings about it. An employee survey has shown that about 60 percent of the supervisors fill the forms out, give about three minutes to each form, and send them to the human resources department without discussing them with their employees. Another 30 percent do a little better. They spend more time completing the forms but communicate about them only briefly and superficially with their employees. Only about 10 percent of the supervisors seriously try to do what was intended.

Meyer has also found out that the forms have rarely been used for promotion or pay raise decisions. Because of this, most of the supervisors have felt that the evaluation program was a useless ritual. Where he had been previously employed, Meyer had seen performance evaluation as a much more useful experience, which included giving positive feedback to employees, improving future employee performance, developing employee capabilities, and providing data for promotion and compensation.

Meyer has not had much experience with the design of performance evaluation systems. He feels that he should seek advice on the topic.

EXHIBIT 11.1

Performance Evaluation Form

Performance Evaluation

Supervisors: When you are asked to do so by the human resources department, please complete this form on each of your employees. The supervisor who is responsible for 75 percent or more of an employee's work should complete this form on him or her. Please evaluate each factor separately.

Factor	Rating					Score
Quality of work	Excellent	Above average	Average	Below average	Poor	_____
Quantity of work	Poor	Below average	Average	Above average	Excellent	_____
Dependability of work	Excellent	Above average	Average	Below average	Poor	_____
Initiative at work	Poor	Below average	Average	Above average	Excellent	_____
Cooperativeness	Excellent	Above average	Average	Below average	Poor	_____
Getting along with co-workers	Poor	Below average	Average	Above average	Excellent	_____
					Total	_____

Supervisor's signature _____

Employee name _____

Employee number _____

Write a report summarizing your evaluation of the strengths and weaknesses of the present performance appraisal system. Recommend some specific improvements or data-gathering exercises to develop a better system for Meyer.

Exercise 11–2

Who Are Normal Employees?

Assume your company has just adopted the form shown in Exhibit 11.1 for its performance evaluation system. Assume further that your company has also instituted a policy that every manager's performance appraisals must conform to the bell-shaped curve shown below. Using this curve, a supervisor who has 10 employees would have one that would be ranked as excellent, one that would be ranked above average, six that would be ranged average, one that would be ranked as below average, and one that would be ranked as unsatisfactory.

Prepare a 10-minute presentation summarizing the problems, advantages, and disadvantages of using such a system.

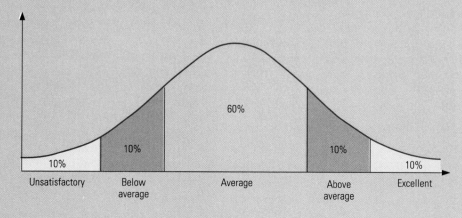

CHAPTER

12

Understanding Equal Employment Opportunity

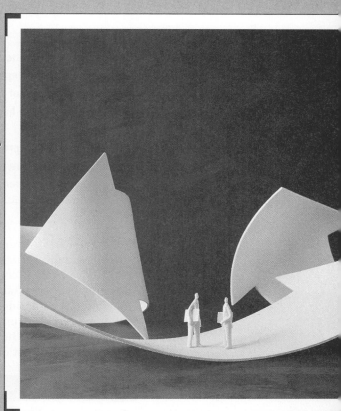

LEARNING OBJECTIVES

After studying this chapter, you should be able to:

1. Define protected groups.

2. Describe antidiscrimination laws that affect organizations.

3. Identify the major federal enforcement agencies for equal employment opportunity.

4. Define employment parity, occupational parity, and systemic discrimination.

5. Define affirmative action.

6. Define sexual harassment.

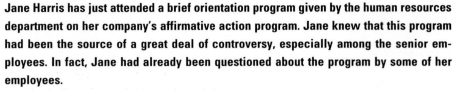

Jane Harris has just attended a brief orientation program given by the human resources department on her company's affirmative action program. Jane knew that this program had been the source of a great deal of controversy, especially among the senior employees. In fact, Jane had already been questioned about the program by some of her employees.

The orientation program made Jane much more aware of her responsibilities under the program. However, she felt that she needed additional information if she was going to give the program more than lip service.

A heightened awareness of equality issues and concerns has brought about sweeping antidiscrimination laws affecting organizations. All levels of management have been affected by these laws. The supervisor, however, probably has the greatest potential for violating them. Thus, it is crucial for supervisors to stay abreast of antidiscrimination laws. The supervisor is involved, directly or indirectly, in most of the decisions affected by antidiscrimination laws. These decisions concern hiring, job assignments, wages and salaries, performance evaluations, promotions, layoffs, recalls, discipline, and discharges. Laws prohibiting discrimination are not entirely new. The Civil Rights Acts of 1866 and 1870 and the Equal Protection Clause of the 14th Amendment were early laws that prohibited discrimination. However, enforcement of these and other antidiscrimination laws within organizations is much more recent. In addition, the laws are constantly changing, so it becomes more essential that the supervisor find ways to stay current.

WHAT ARE PROTECTED GROUPS?

Usually, a discussion of discrimination assumes that women and African Americans are the groups that have been affected by discrimination. Although women and African Americans do constitute the two largest groups that discrimination has affected, they are by no means the only groups. Other, less obvious, forms of discrimination have also occurred. There is evidence that managers and supervisors have made decisions based on assumptions about such groups as short people, overweight people, singles, young married women of childbearing age, people without children, and people without cars. However, it is no longer legal to use most non-job-related factors for making decisions affecting people in organizations.

1 LEARNING OBJECTIVES

For the purposes of this chapter, race, color, sex, age, religion, national origin, and mental and physical handicaps identify the classifications of people that are called **protected groups.** A person's classification into a group by one of these characteristics means that he or she is protected from discrimination in organizations. For example, a supervisor cannot refuse to give a person a particular job assignment just because the person happens to fall into one of these classifications. The assignment of jobs must be determined by ability to do or learn to do the job and must not be influenced by sex, race, or any other non-job-related factor.

EFFECTS OF DISCRIMINATION

Most people are aware of the effects of discrimination. Examining the human resources makeup of most large organizations generally shows the results of past discrimination. The jobs with authority are held primarily by white males. This is not the result of discrimination only; it is also the result of past inequalities in education.

The primary legislation controlling equal employment opportunity was enacted during the 1960s and early 1970s. That employment discrimination still exists is shown by statistics on unemployment, underemployment, and incomes. For example, women (who are the largest protected group) continue to be employed primarily in the same industries as they have been in the past: service industries, wholesale and retail trade, and the public service sector. The gap between the incomes of women and men who work full time continues to be large—and it is widening. Furthermore, even though the situation has been changing, the percentage of African Americans and Hispanics in supervisory and management positions is still relatively small.

ANTIDISCRIMINATION LAWS THAT AFFECT ORGANIZATIONS

2 LEARNING OBJECTIVES

Many antidiscrimination laws affect organizations. Supervisors sometimes wrongly assume that antidiscrimination policy is an attempt by higher management to favor certain groups. However, most organizational policy on this matter is based on present laws as interpreted by the courts. Management, including supervisors, is responsible for upholding all antidiscrimination laws affecting the organization.

The number of employees and the amount of business that the organization does with the federal government determine which of these laws affect the organization. The following paragraphs provide a brief description of the most important laws and court orders dealing with discrimination.

Title VII of the Civil Rights Act of 1964

Title VII of the Civil Rights Act of 1964, as amended by the Equal Employment Opportunity Act of 1972, has been the source for the greatest number of complaints concerning discrimination. This law prohibits discrimination based on race, color, religion, sex, or national origin in any term, condition, or privilege of employment. This law applies to all private employers of 15 or more people, all public and private educational institutions, all state and local governments, all public and private employment agencies, labor unions with 15 or more members, and joint labor-management committees for apprenticeships and training. This law established and gave the Equal Employment Opportunity Commission (EEOC) the power (1) to investigate job discrimination complaints, (2) to mediate an agreement between the parties to eliminate discrimination when such a complaint is found to be justified, and (3) to take court action to enforce the law when necessary.

Title VI

Title VI of the 1964 Civil Rights Act prohibits discrimination based on race, color, or national origin in all programs or activities that receive federal financial aid in order to provide employment. Although this law does not prohibit sex discrimination, some federal agencies prohibit sex discrimination by their own regulations.

Equal Pay Act

The Equal Pay Act was passed in 1963 and was later amended by Title IX of the Education Amendments Act of 1972. This law requires that all employers covered by the Fair Labor Standards Act (and others included in the 1972 extension) provide equal pay to men and women who perform work that is similar in skill, effort, and responsibility. In general, the Fair Labor Standards Act applies to individuals employed in interstate commerce or in organizations producing goods for interstate commerce and covers base pay as well as opportunities for overtime, raises, bonuses, commissions, and other benefits. The employer is also responsible for ensuring that all fringe benefits be equally available to all employees. Offering and paying higher wages to women and minorities in order to attract these groups are also illegal. Under this law, the only justification for paying a man more than a woman for doing the same job is differences in levels of seniority, responsibility, or skill.

Education Amendments Act

Title IX of the Education Amendments Act of 1972 extended coverage of the Equal Pay Act of 1963. Title IX prohibits gender discrimination against the employees or students of any educational institution receiving financial aid from the federal government.

Age Discrimination in Employment Act

The Age Discrimination in Employment Act was enacted in 1967 and amended in 1978. This law prohibits discrimination against people 40 years of age and older in any area of employment. This law applies to employers of 20 or more people. The law prohibits using age as a factor for making employment decisions.

Affirmative Action

Executive Order 11246 was issued in 1965 and amended by Executive Order 11375 in 1967. The order requires federal contractors and subcontractors to have affirmative action programs. The purpose of these programs is to increase employment opportunities for women and minorities in all areas of employment. The order further requires that employers with federal contracts or subcontracts of $50,000 or more and 50 or more employees develop and implement written affirmative action programs. These programs are monitored by the Office of Federal Contract Compliance (OFCC) of the U.S. Department of Labor.

Veterans Readjustment Act

The Vietnam-Era Veterans Readjustment Act of 1974 requires that federal government contractors and subcontractors take affirmative action to hire and pro-

Recent legislation requires employers to provide reasonable accommodations to disabled individuals.
David Young Wolff/Tony Stone Images.

mote Vietnam veterans and disabled veterans. Such contractors and subcontractors with contracts of $10,000 or more must list all suitable job openings with state employment services. Such contractors and subcontractors with contracts of $50,000 or more and 50 or more employees are required to have written affirmative action programs for Vietnam veterans and disabled veterans.

Rehabilitation Act of 1973

The Rehabilitation Act of 1973, which was amended in 1977, prohibits employers from denying jobs to individuals merely because of a handicap. The law defines a handicapped person as one who has a physical or mental impairment that significantly limits one or more major life activities. This law applies to government contractors and subcontractors with contracts in excess of $2,500. The act requires contractors to make reasonable and necessary accommodations to enable qualified handicapped people to work as effectively as other employees.

Americans with Disabilities Act (ADA)

In May 1990, Congress approved the **Americans with Disabilities Act (ADA),** which gives the disabled sharply increased access to services and jobs. Under this law, employers may not:

- Discriminate in hiring and firing against persons qualified for a job.
- Inquire whether an applicant has a disability, but may ask about ability to perform a job.

FIGURE 12.1

Who Is Disabled?

The Americans with Disabilities Act forbids bias in the workplace and in public accommodations against people with physical and mental impairments. Among the most common disabilities:

Hearing impairments	23.3 million
Visual impairments	7.5 million
Speech impairments	2.3 million
Arthritis	30.8 million
Epilepsy	1.2 million
Missing limbs	1.2 million
Partial or complete paralysis	1.4 million

Source: President's Commission on Employment of People with Disabilities and *USA Today,* July 22, 1993, p. 1.

- Limit advancement opportunity.
- Use tests or job requirements that tend to screen out the disabled.
- Participate in contractual arrangements that discriminate against the disabled.

Employers must also provide reasonable accommodations to the disabled, such as making existing facilities accessible, providing special equipment and training, arranging part-time or modified work schedules, and providing readers for the blind. Figure 12.1 lists the most common disabilities. Employers do not have to provide accommodations that impose an undue hardship on business operations.

Civil Rights Act of 1991

The **Civil Rights Act of 1991** permits women, minorities, persons with disabilities, and persons belonging to religious minorities to have a jury trial and sue for punitive damages of up to $300,000 if they can prove that they are victims of intentional hiring or workplace discrimination. The law covers all employers with 15 or more employees. Prior to the passage of this law, jury trials and punitive damages were not permitted except in intentional discrimination lawsuits involving racial discrimination. The law places a cap on the amount of damages a victim of nonracial, intentional discrimination can collect. The cap is based on the size of the employer: $50,000 for companies with 15 to 100 employees; $100,000 for companies with 101 to 200 employees; $200,000 for companies with 201 to 500 employees; and $300,000 for companies with more than 500 employees.

A second aspect of this act was concerned with the burden of proof for companies with regard to intentional discrimination lawsuits. In a series of Supreme Court decisions beginning in 1989, the Court began to ease the burden-of-proof requirements on companies. Several of these decisions are described later in this chapter. This act, however, requires that companies must provide evidence that the business practice that led to the discrimination was not discriminatory but was job-related for the position in question and consistent with business necessity.

Other Antidiscrimination Legislation

Discrimination in employment has also been prohibited by court rulings under the Civil Rights Acts of 1866 and 1870 and the Equal Protection Clause of the 14th Amendment. Discrimination because of race, religion, and national origin has also been found to violate rights guaranteed by the National Labor Relations Act. Many state and local government laws prohibit employment discrimination. Discrimination by an employer may lead to court action under any one or more of the laws and executive orders mentioned above.

Figure 12.2 provides a summary of all significant equal employment opportunity laws and executive orders related to equal employment opportunity. Executive orders are issued by the president of the United States to give direction to governmental agencies. Supervision Illustration 12–1 describes an interesting court decision regarding equal employment opportunity.

FIGURE 12.2 Summary of Equal Opportunity Laws and Executive Orders

Laws	Year	Intent	Coverage
Equal Pay Act	1963	Prohibits sex-based discrimination in rates of pay for men and women working in same or similar jobs.	Private employers engaged in commerce or in the production of goods for commerce and with two or more employees; labor organizations.
Title VII, Civil Rights Act (as amended in 1972)	1964	Prohibits discrimination based on race, sex, color, religion, or national origin.	Private employers with 15 or more employees for 20 or more weeks per year, educational institutions, state and local governments, employment agencies, labor unions, and joint labor-management committees.
Executive Order 11246	1965	Prohibits discrimination on the basis of race, sex, color, religion, or national origin; requires affirmative action regarding these factors.	Federal contracts and subcontractors with contracts in excess of $10,000. Employers with 50 or more employees.
Executive Order 11375	1967	Prohibits sex-based wage discrimination.	Government contractors and subcontractors.
Executive Order 11478	1967	Superseded Executive Order 11246 and modified some of the procedures under the previous orders and regulations.	

FIGURE 12.2—continued

Laws	Year	Intent	Coverage
Age Discrimination in Employment Act (ADEA)	1967	Prohibits discrimination against individuals who are 40 years of age and older.	Private employers with 20 or more employees for 20 or more weeks per year, labor organizations, employment agencies, state and local governments, and federal agencies with some exceptions.
Rehabilitation Act, as amended	1973	Prohibits discrimination against the handicapped and requires affirmative action to provide employment opportunity for the handicapped.	Federal contractors and subcontractors with contracts in excess of $2,500, organizations receiving federal financial assistance, and federal agencies.
Vietnam-Era Veterans Readjustment Assistance Act	1974	Prohibits discrimination in hiring disabled veterans with 30 percent or more disability rating, veterans discharged or released for a service-connected disability, and veterans on active duty between August 4, 1964, and May 7, 1975. Also requires of certain employers written affirmative action plans.	Federal contractors and subcontractors with contracts in excess of $10,000. Employers with 50 percent or more employees and contracts in excess of $50,000 must have written affirmative action plans.
Pregnancy Discrimination Act (PDA)	1978	Requires employers to treat pregnancy like any other medical condition with regard to fringe benefits and leave policies.	
Immigration Reform and Control Act	1986	Prohibits hiring of illegal aliens.	Any individual or company.
Americans with Disabilities Act	1990	Increases access to services and jobs for disabled.	Private employers with 15 or more employees.
Civil Rights Act	1991	Reversed several Supreme Court decisions and allows juries to award punitive damages for job bias related to sex, religion, or disability.	Private employers with 15 or more employees; employees of U.S. Senate; employees of the White House; high-ranking state and local government employees.

SUPERVISION ILLUSTRATION 12-1

EQUAL RISKS AT JOHNSON CONTROLS

Some assembly-line workers at the Johnson Controls battery plant in Milwaukee used torches to heat the lead that formed posts for batteries and, in the process, inhaled oxide from the melting lead. Since lead is toxic, particularly to fetuses, Johnson Controls in 1982 imposed a mandatory protection policy for women of child-bearing age. They could either prove that they were sterile or be forced to change jobs.

Seven women challenged this "fetal-protection" policy in court. In 1991, the Supreme Court ruled in favor of the women. The Court unanimously struck down Johnson Controls' mandatory exclusion of fertile women from hazardous jobs. In an interpretation of the Civil Rights Act of 1964, which prohibits sex discrimination in the workforce, the Court stated that decisions about the welfare of future children must be left to the parents who conceive, bear, support, and raise them rather than to the employers who hire those parents.

For more information about Johnson Controls, visit its Web site at:
www.jci.com

ENFORCEMENT AGENCIES

There are two major federal enforcement agencies for equal employment opportunity. These are the **Equal Employment Opportunity Commission (EEOC)** and the **Office of Federal Contract Compliance (OFCC).** In the past, enforcement activities were conducted by many agencies. The trend has been toward consolidation of these activities. It is probable that more consolidation will occur in the future, perhaps with one agency performing all enforcement activities.

INTERPRETATION AND APPLICATION OF TITLE VII AND AFFIRMATIVE ACTION

Knowing the laws and executive orders covering antidiscrimination helps avoid court actions. However, the intricacies of the laws and various interpretations by the courts may confuse even the best-intentioned person. It is impossible to discuss in this chapter all the details, interpretations, and exceptions affecting employers with regard to these laws. In fact, new interpretations are still emerging. However, some of the more important details are discussed in the following paragraphs.

Title VII of the Civil Rights Act of 1964

Title VII of the Civil Rights Act has probably been more fully interpreted by the courts than any of the other antidiscrimination laws. The courts have decided that whether the employer *intended* to discriminate is not an important factor. They have decided that employment practices denying opportunities to persons protected by Title VII are illegal no matter what the employer's intent. For instance, an employer who requires a college degree for a certain job may be required to show that the college degree is both job-related and an accurate predictor of success in the job. This is because requiring a college degree may have an adverse impact on certain groups (such as women and African Americans) protected by Title VII.

There are very few exceptions to Title VII. As has been discussed, nearly all organizations are covered to some degree by antidiscrimination laws. For years after the Civil Rights Act was passed, employers were still trying to get the courts to uphold traditional employment practices. One of the more notable cases was the airlines' demand that due to customer preference, flight attendants be female and fall within a certain weight range. The courts have not upheld these restrictions. As is apparent, there are now male flight attendants as well as less rigid weight requirements. Nearly every industry has been affected by Title VII and subsequent court rulings. Jobs have opened up to women and minorities and even to men that 20 years ago would have been off limits.

The few exceptions to Title VII that do exist have been interpreted very narrowly by the courts. It is difficult to justify discrimination by business necessity, as allowed by the law. The employer must prove that the discrimination is essential to the safety, efficiency, and operation of the business and that no alternatives exist. State laws that may have contributed to discriminatory practices in the past have also been ruled by the courts to be superseded by Title VII. Title VII allows for sex discrimination only where sex is a bona fide occupational qualification (BFOQ). This exception has been very narrowly interpreted by the courts, which have limited its application to persons such as actors, models, rest room attendants, and security guards in a maximum-security prison. Title VII does not provide for the use of race or color as a BFOQ. Age may be considered a BFOQ where there is concrete evidence that it is a job-related factor and a business necessity. Age may be a BFOQ where public safety is involved, as with airline pilots or interstate bus drivers.

Another exception to Title VII is discrimination based on a bona fide seniority or merit system. Not all seniority and merit systems qualify under this exception. Seniority or merit systems that exclude protected groups from benefits are not valid exceptions. Seniority or merit systems that perpetuate past discriminatory practices are illegal. This is true even if there is no present discriminatory intent or practice.

Contractual agreements between the union and the employer are not legal or binding if they violate antidiscrimination laws. Clauses that limit certain jobs to one group or pay one group more for equal work are not binding. Contract negotiations must be opened as soon as this type of discrimination is discovered.

4 LEARNING OBJECTIVES

Two methods can be used by the EEOC to determine whether discrimination against a protected group has occurred. These methods are called (1) employment parity and (2) occupational parity. **Employment parity** exists when the proportion of protected employees employed by an organization equals the proportion in the organization's relevant labor market. **Occupational parity** exists when the proportion of protected employees employed in various occupations in the organization is equal to their proportion in the organization's relevant labor market. Large differences in either occupational or employment parity are called **systemic discrimination.** When systemic discrimination exists, the employer is usually required to engage in affirmative action.

History of Affirmative Action Programs

Of all the requirements concerned with discrimination, affirmative action programs are by far the most controversial. Affirmative action programs are required of certain federal contractors and subcontractors and may also be required of employers who have been found to have engaged in discriminatory hiring practices or systemic discrimination. Some employers and individuals mistakenly refer to equal employment opportunity as affirmative action. The elimination of hiring practices that have an adverse impact on protected groups is not affirmative action. **Affirmative action** refers to an employer's attempt to balance its workforce in all job categories with respect to sex and race in order to reflect the same proportions as those of its general labor market. Under an affirmative action plan, an employer prepares goals and timetables for the achievement of a balanced representation. When minorities and women achieve employment and occupational parity in organizations, affirmative action programs will no longer be necessary.

Affirmative action has resulted in several discrimination suits. The first real test case in this area was the Bakke case of 1978. Allan Bakke, a white male, brought suit against the medical school of the University of California at Davis. Bakke charged that he had been unconstitutionally discriminated against when he was denied admission to the medical school while some minority applicants with lower qualifications were accepted. The Supreme Court ruled in Bakke's favor but at the same time upheld the constitutionality of affirmative action programs.

In 1984, in a case involving Memphis, Tennessee, and its fire department, the Supreme Court ruled that the fire department could not insulate African Americans from layoffs and demotions under its affirmative action plan. The ruling indicated that when hard economic times hit and layoffs were necessary, employers could not be forced to scrap seniority plans favoring white men in order to protect "affirmative action" gains by minorities and women.

During the latter part of the 1980s, the Supreme Court rendered several decisions viewed by some advocates as being negative toward affirmative action programs. In *City of Richmond* v. *J. A. Crosan Company*, the Court ruled in 1989 that state and local governments must avoid racial quotas and must take affirmative action steps only to correct well-documented examples of past discrimination. Also, in 1989, the Court ruled in *Wards Cove* v. *Atonio* that employers can use evidence of a legitimate reason for a business practice as defense against statistics showing minorities were victims of discrimination. In *Martin* v. *Wilks*, the Court also ruled in 1989 that white employees could bring reverse-discrimination claims against court-approved affirmative action plans. It is interesting to note that the Civil Rights Act of 1991 reversed both of these Supreme Court decisions.

Most affirmative action programs concentrate on racial and ethnic minorities and women. Religious and national origin minorities have not benefited nearly as much from such programs. As more organizations representing these minorities press for changes, employers may be forced to develop affirmative action programs for these groups.

Quotas for hiring minorities and women are not required by law. However, written goals are required under affirmative action guidelines. Opponents of affirmative action programs feel that written numerical goals force inflexible,

5 LEARNING OBJECTIVES

unreasonable demands on employers. They also feel that as a result of such goals, employers strive for a numerical result rather than the primary goal of equal employment opportunity. Proponents of affirmative action, however, argue that written affirmative action goals are like any other organizational goal to which quantitative measures are applied. Only when an employer consistently fails to reach its goals or when there is evidence that the employer has not acted in good faith will the enforcement agency step in to impose goals. By striving to eliminate discrimination within the organization, management can usually avoid court action and costly penalties.

It is important to note at this point that there is a significant difference between equal employment opportunity and affirmative action programs. Equal employment opportunity laws were enacted and remain in existence to prevent discrimination in the workplace. On the other hand, affirmative action's focus is to provide current opportunities to those members of groups who were previously denied access to employment and its concomitant training and development programs. In addition, recent trends in states such as California have been directed at stopping affirmative action programs in educational institutions.

EFFECT OF ANTIDISCRIMINATION LAWS ON THE SUPERVISOR

As mentioned earlier, antidiscrimination laws affect all levels of management. Developing policies to comply with these laws is imperative. Although these policies are formulated at the upper level of management, they are implemented at the middle and supervisory levels.

Hiring Practices

It is a well-known fact that the hiring policies and practices of employers may not discriminate against any person because of race, color, religion, national origin, sex, or age. Most government contractors and subcontractors are also legally required to provide equal employment opportunity to handicapped persons. Some supervisors are surprised to find how these requirements affect traditional hiring methods.

Obtaining information on a person prior to hiring has been affected by antidiscrimination laws. Certain questions have been explicitly prohibited by the courts. The burden of proof is on the employer to show that the information requested is being obtained for nondiscriminatory purposes, such as reports on affirmative action. As discussed earlier, non-job-related factors that have an adverse effect on the hiring of protected groups have been ruled illegal by the courts.

Employment application forms that solicit non-job-related information may result in charges of discrimination. The employer must then show that the data were not used to discriminate against a protected group. It is probably better in the long run for employers to remove questions concerning this type of information from their application forms.

Testing is another hiring practice that has received adverse attention. The courts have ruled that alternative hiring procedures are preferable to testing. Any test that adversely affects the employment opportunity of protected groups must be professionally validated. *Validation* means that the results of the test are proved to be a significant predictor of an applicant's ability to perform job-related tasks. A good test is not only valid but also reliable. General intelligence and aptitude tests have been found invalid in many cases.

It is not suggested that all tests are unfair or result in discrimination. If a test provides an impartial way to identify qualified applicants, it reduces the use of more subjective judgments that can easily result in discrimination. For example, suppose it is determined that a particular computer-programming position requires knowledge of a certain computer language. It would be not only legal but also wise to test job applicants for knowledge in this language.

Interviews can also result in discrimination. It is imperative that the supervisor in any job interview be willing to evaluate an applicant on ability and potential. The supervisor must be aware of the actual job requirements and not use unrelated criteria as a basis for a decision. It is easy for the supervisor to overstep the legal bounds in questioning a job applicant. Therefore, questions relating to these topics should be carefully worded and used. Figure 10.5 in Chapter 10 provides some guidelines for questions that can be asked in a job interview. It is further suggested that the supervisor discuss with the boss or the human resources department the questions that he or she intends to ask a job applicant.

As has been implied, the best way to select an individual for a job is to use job-related factors. If supervisors are making the final selection decision, they should make certain that the decision is based on job-related factors. Making selection decisions on the basis of non-job-related factors excludes not only members of the protected groups but talented members of all groups. As can be seen, the supervisor can play a key role in making nondiscriminatory hiring decisions.

Job Assignments

Fairness in hiring does not by itself result in fairness on the job. Most jobs have pleasant and unpleasant tasks associated with them. For the supervisor to assign the more popular or pleasant tasks to one group of employees may result in charges of discrimination. For instance, asking female employees to perform more of the clerical tasks than are performed by the male employees in the same job may result in charges of discrimination. However, charges of reverse discrimination may also result when employers hire people from the protected groups for a job but do not require them to perform all the tasks of that job. For example, if a woman is hired as a packager and one of the job requirements is to lift 30-pound boxes, she should be required to do the lifting just like everyone else. If not, the male employees may charge the supervisor with reverse discrimination.

Performance Evaluation and Upward Mobility

Subjective performance evaluations can also result in discriminatory practices. Performance appraisals based on subjective criteria such as attitude, appearance, maturity, ambition, and personality are easily influenced by personal bias. Therefore, supervisors should always attempt to evaluate employees objectively.

Supervisors play an important part in the advancement opportunities of their employees. Traditionally, only certain groups of employees were thought to have advancement potential. This generally led to the promotion of white males; members of the protected groups were often not even considered for promotion. Employers today are sometimes required to evaluate their methods of promoting employees. They must look for objective, job-related factors in making promotion decisions. Supervisors may even be asked to recommend a certain percentage of women, minorities, or handicapped employees for promotion.

The supervisor must make an effort to consider all subordinates for advancement. The supervisor's evaluation must be objective and related to the job for which the employee is being considered. Even widely accepted policies such as promotion from within may be found to be discriminatory. If an organization is composed primarily of white males, promoting from within might have an adverse impact on the protected groups.

Disciplinary Action

Discipline must be based on objective considerations. Discipline for subjective considerations, such as appearance, should be avoided. Discipline must be thoroughly documented for all employees. Negligence in this area is often the reason for losing a discrimination case.

The standards for determining disciplinary action must be the same for all employees. As with hiring practices, seemingly neutral standards may have an adverse effect on a particular group. For example, a discharge due to an employee's arrest might be considered a violation of Title VII because it might be discriminating against one of the protected groups. Reverse discrimination charges may result when a woman or a member of a minority group is not discharged for an offense warranting discharge.

Disciplinary action against an employee for filing a Title VII complaint is illegal. In the case of a discharge, this type of discrimination will usually result in reinstatement with back pay. It is also illegal to threaten, pressure, or harass an employee into resigning, simply because the employee has filed a Title VII complaint. Management must encourage, rather than discourage, employees to voice their complaints within the organization. Encouraging an atmosphere of openness and maintaining a reputation of acting fairly on complaints reduce the possibility of charges.

A POSITIVE APPROACH TO EQUAL EMPLOYMENT OPPORTUNITY AND AFFIRMATIVE ACTION

The previous discussion consisted primarily of guidelines to help the supervisor avoid EEO complaints. The last part of this chapter discusses a positive approach for guiding the supervisor through equal employment opportunity and affirmative action programs.

Most people realize that a large number of people have not been utilized or have been underutilized in the past. The opportunity now exists for employing these people more fully. Organizations can benefit from this new reservoir of talent. In all of the protected groups, there are people who are

FIGURE 12.3

Suggestions for Creating a Positive EEO Environment

1. Be aware of the legal and regulatory requirements of EEO and affirmative action that affect your organization.
2. Be aware of your organization's policies and practices that have resulted from EEO and affirmative action regulation.
3. Learn to recognize and eliminate stereotyping and preconceptions in your expectations of women and minorities.
4. Provide clear, challenging, and achievable expectations for all of your subordinates.
5. Provide training, support, and encouragement that fit individual needs.
6. Be aware of and sensitive to issues that commonly arise in workforces comprising different groups.
7. Help facilitate the socialization of new employees.
8. Communicate with your employees to minimize isolation and maximize the contribution of all employees.
9. Provide adequate feedback on performance of all employees.
10. Avoid the extremes of "overprotection" and "abandonment" in dealing with protected group members.

Source: "Some Aspects of the Supervisor's Role in Affirmative Action," by Daniel H. Reigle, copyright November 1978, reprinted with permission of *Personnel Journal,* Costa Mesa, California. All rights reserved.

not capable of doing the job. However, EEO and affirmative action do not require employers to hire unqualified employees. In fact, establishing and using job-related factors for employment decisions allows only the most qualified to be employed and to advance within the organization. This means that the persons hired and advanced should be the ones who are most capable of performing the job.

Equal employment opportunity will benefit not only the organization but also society. Past discrimination has prevented certain segments of society from finding employment, especially meaningful employment.

Managers of today's organizations must provide positive leadership toward the goal of equal employment opportunity just as they provide positive leadership in achieving all other goals. Supervisors have a major impact on the achievement of this goal. It is necessary for supervisors to be fully aware of EEO and affirmative action goals. Supervisors must communicate these goals in a positive way to their subordinates. As with any organizational goal, the supervisor's attitude is important to the achievement of these goals. A negative or passive attitude will most likely result in problems for the supervisor and the organization. Figure 12.3 gives some suggestions that should help the supervisor in creating a positive EEO environment.

Finally, it cannot be stressed enough that EEO and affirmative action do not require an employer to hire unqualified employees. Their purpose is simply to give protected groups a fair and equal chance to obtain a position. The person must still be qualified and is expected to perform and produce on the job. EEO and affirmative action are not designed to protect unqualified applicants or poor performance by employees.

PREVENTING SEXUAL HARASSMENT IN THE WORKPLACE

LEARNING OBJECTIVES

On March 11, 1980, the EEOC published guidelines on sexual harassment in the workplace. The EEOC has taken the position that the Civil Rights Act prohibits such harassment, just as it prohibits harassment based on race, religion, and national origin.

Unwelcome sexual advances, requests for sexual favors, and other verbal or physical conduct of a sexual nature are considered sexual harassment under the following conditions:

1. Submission to such conduct is made either explicitly or implicitly a term or condition of an individual's employment.
2. Submission to or rejection of such conduct by an individual is used as the basis for employment decisions affecting that individual.
3. Such conduct has the purpose or effect of unreasonably interfering with an individual's work performance or creating an intimidating, hostile, or offensive work environment.

Organizations are considered responsible for the acts of their managers and supervisors regardless of whether the specific acts complained of were authorized or even forbidden by the employer and regardless of whether the employer knew or should have known of their occurrence. With respect to conduct between nonmanagerial employees, an employer is responsible for acts of sexual harassment where the employer knows or should have known of the conduct, unless the employer can show that it took immediate and appropriate corrective action.

Prevention is the best tool for the elimination of sexual harassment. The following suggestions are offered to assist the supervisor in preventing sexual harassment in the workplace:

1. Affirmatively raise the subject in employee meetings.
2. Express strong disapproval.
3. Describe the disciplinary actions that will be taken against employees guilty of sexual harassment.
4. Take appropriate disciplinary action when an act of sexual harassment occurs.
5. Inform employees of their right to raise sexual harassment claims.

Supervisors should not be reluctant to take action on sexual harassment claims. Normally, the human resources department is available to provide guidance and assistance on problems of this nature. However, it is important to remember that immediate and appropriate action must be taken by the supervisor. Supervision Illustration 12–2 describes a court ruling on sexual harassment at Jacksonville Shipyards, Inc.

SUPERVISION ILLUSTRATION 12-2

PINUPS IN THE WORKPLACE

Ms. Lois Robinson, a welder at Jacksonville Shipyards, Inc., said she was constantly bombarded by sexual comments from her male co-workers. She said that pinup calendars, pictures of close-ups of nude women, and other sexually explicit photos appeared throughout the workplace. And she alleged she was harassed by managers after complaining about the presence of the pictures.

The company disputed Ms. Robinson's description of the work environment and said it was not liable for any acts that might have created the allegedly hostile environment. However, U.S. Federal Judge Melton disagreed with the company and ruled that

the company bore responsibility because managers had condoned the harassment and in some cases had hung up their own pornographic pinups. In addition, he said that the company did not adequately investigate harassment complaints and that its handling of complaints had deterred the reporting of incidents.

The judge ordered the company to institute a comprehensive sexual harassment policy written by the National Organization of Women (NOW) Legal Defense and Education Fund. That policy bans the display of such pictures, including images of nude men, even in private offices within the workplace.

Source: Adapted from Amy Dockser Marcus and Ellen Joan Pollock, "Pinups at Work Place Violate Harassment Law, Judge Rules," *The Wall Street Journal*, January 23, 1991, p. B 2. For more information about NOW, visit its Web site at:
www.now.org

SOLUTION TO THE SUPERVISION DILEMMA

First, Jane has learned the definition of protected groups. Next, Jane has obtained information on all of the significant antidiscrimination laws that affect organizations. These laws are Title VII and Title VI of the Civil Rights Act, the Equal Pay Act, the Age Discrimination in Employment Act, the Veterans Readjustment Act, the Rehabilitation Act, the Americans with Disabilities Act, and the Civil Rights Act of 1991. Jane now knows that the Equal Employment Opportunity Commission (EEOC) and the Office of Federal Contract Compliance (OFCC) enforce equal employment opportunity legislation. She also knows what affirmative action means (p. 239). Jane has learned that supervisors have a major impact on the implementation and achievement of equal employment opportunity goals and that they must communicate these goals to their subordinates in a positive way (pp. 242–43). Finally, Jane has learned what she can do to help prevent sexual harassment in the workplace (p. 244).

SUMMARY

This chapter identifies the groups in organizations that have been most affected by discrimination. The effects of antidiscrimination legislation on the supervisor are discussed. A positive approach to equal employment opportunity and affirmative action is also presented.

1. *Define protected groups.* Race, color, sex, age, religion, national origin, and mental and physical handicaps identify the classifications of people that are called protected groups.

2. *Describe antidiscrimination laws that affect organizations.* Title VII of the Civil Rights Act prohibits discrimination based on race, color, religion, sex, or national origin. Title VI of the Civil Rights Act prohibits discrimination based on race, color, or national origin in all programs or activities that receive federal financial aid in order to provide employment. The Equal Pay Act requires employers to provide equal pay to men and women who perform work that is similar in skill, effort, and responsibility. The Age Discrimination in Employment Act prohibits discrimination against people over 40 years of age in any area of employment. The Veterans Readjustment Act requires that federal government contractors and subcontractors take affirmative action to hire and promote Vietnam veterans and disabled veterans. The Rehabilitation Act prohibits employers from denying jobs to individuals merely because of a handicap. The Americans with Disabilities Act gives the disabled sharply increased access to services and jobs. The Civil Rights Act of 1991 reversed several Supreme Court decisions, and allows juries to award employees punitive damages for discrimination based on sex, religion, or disability.

3. *Identify major federal enforcement agencies for equal employment opportunity.* The two major federal enforcement agencies are the Equal Employment Opportunity Commission (EEOC) and the Office of Federal Contract Compliance (OFCC).

4. *Define employment parity, occupational parity, and systemic discrimination.* Employment parity exists when the proportion of protected employees employed by an organization equals the proportion in the organization's relevant labor market. Occupational parity exists when the proportion of protected employees employed in various occupations in the organization is equal to their proportion in the organization's relevant labor market. Large differences in either occupational or employment parity are called systemic discrimination.

5. *Define affirmative action.* Affirmative action refers to an employer's attempt to balance its workforce in all job categories with respect to sex and race in order to reflect the same proportions as those of its general labor market.

6. *Define sexual harassment.* Unwelcome sexual advances, requests for sexual favors, and other verbal or physical conduct of a sexual nature are considered sexual harassment if submission to such conduct is (1) made either explicitly or implicitly a term or condition of employment, (2) is used as the basis for employment decisions affecting that individual, or (3) has the purpose or effect of measurably interfering with an individual's work performance or creating an intimidating, hostile, or offensive work environment.

REVIEW QUESTIONS

1. Define the term *protected group*.
2. What determines which of the antidiscrimination laws affect a particular organization?
3. Describe the following antidiscrimination laws:
   a. Title VII of the Civil Rights Act.
   b. Title VI of the Civil Rights Act.
   c. Equal Pay Act of 1963.
   d. Title IX of the Education Amendments Act.
   e. Age Discrimination in Employment Act.
   f. Executive Order 11246 as amended by Executive Order 11375.
   g. Veterans Readjustment Act of 1974.
   h. Rehabilitation Act of 1973.
   i. Americans with Disabilities Act.
   j. Civil Rights Act of 1991.
4. Define the term *BFOQ*.
5. What is systemic discrimination?
6. What does the term *affirmative action* mean?
7. Give some suggestions for creating a positive EEO and affirmative action environment.
8. What is sexual harassment?

SKILL-BUILDING QUESTIONS

1. Discuss the effects of discrimination on organization performance.
2. "The use of tests in hiring results in more objective evaluations of prospective employees." Discuss your view on this statement.
3. "The supervisor's primary objective should be to avoid making mistakes in employment decisions that can lead to EEO complaints." Discuss your view on this statement.
4. "Organizations should be allowed to hire anyone they choose." How do you feel about this statement? Discuss.

ADDITIONAL READINGS

Evans, Barbara Ryniker. "Don't Get Left Behind: The New Rules on Family and Medical Leave," *Supervision*, March 1995.

Lissy, William E. "Harassment vs. Free Speech," *Supervision*, February 1996.

———. "Supreme Court Ruling on Age Discrimination," *Supervision*, September 1996.

———. "Waiver of Discrimination Claims Upheld," *Supervision*, November 1996.

Pulich, Marcia Ann, and Jackie Wenkman. "Supervising Employees with Disabilities," *Supervision*, March 1995.

Zachary, Mary-Kathryn. "Handling Religious Expression in the Workplace," *Supervision*, December 1996.

SKILL-BUILDING APPLICATIONS

Incident 12–1

This Is a Man's Job

Bill, Wally, and Jerry each have over 15 years' seniority in the maintenance department of the Elson Company. The maintenance department has 20 skilled employees—10 electricians, 5 plumbers, and 5 millwrights. Bill, Wally, and Jerry are electricians. They are all highly dependable and well-respected employees.

Several months ago, Angela Collins was hired as an electrician in the maintenance department. It became obvious rather quickly that Bill, Wally, and Jerry did not want her in the maintenance department. They told other people in the department, "Angela can't do the work and was only hired because she is a woman." The three of them conducted a campaign emphasizing Angela's shortcomings, getting into arguments with her, and urging other people to complain about her work to Ken Allen, supervisor of the maintenance department.

After several weeks of this, Bill, Wally, and Jerry asked for a meeting with Ken. At the meeting, they contended that Angela was not carrying her share of the load and that they were tired of doing her work. They said that if Angela didn't leave, they would. They told Ken that it was very easy for a skilled electrician to find a job.

Questions

1. How would you handle the situation? Be specific.
2. Do you feel that Angela has been given a fair chance?

Incident 12–2

Affirmative Action

Allen Russell is attending a supervisory development program offered by his company, Southeastern Gas Company. This is an honor for Allen because only a few supervisors were selected for the program each year. The program consists of two sessions, each lasting a week. The first session consists mostly of classroom training, with very little audience participation.

At the end of the first session, the human resources director of Southeastern, Larry Rankin, announced that each of the participants in the program would be required to make a 30-minute presentation to the group during the second session. He stated that the presentation should be of interest to supervisors at Southeastern and that each person would be graded on his or her presentation. Larry asked that the participants each contact him with their topic within two days.

Allen knew that if he wanted to move up at Southeastern, it was important that he do a good job in his presentation. After thinking it over, Allen decided to talk about Southeastern's affirmative action program and the supervisor's role in that program. When Allen gave Larry his topic, Larry was delighted. He told Allen, "You know, the affirmative action program is very important, and I believe that most of our supervisors don't understand their role in it. I'll be looking forward to hearing your presentation."

Questions

1. Do you think that most supervisors understand their role in affirmative action programs? Explain.
2. If you were Allen, what points would you cover in the presentation? Develop an outline of your presentation.

Exercise 12–1

Affirmative Action Debate

Break the class into teams of four to five students. Each team should prepare to debate one of the following statements:

1. The federal government should not require affirmative action programs for private enterprise organizations that are federal contractors or subcontractors.
2. Affirmative action programs have been very helpful to minorities and women. Private enterprise organizations should be required to have affirmative action programs.

After the debate, the instructor should list on the board the points made by each team and discuss the issues involved.

Exercise 12–2

Legal Issues in Equal Employment Opportunity

Break the class into teams of two to three students. Each team should then be given the following assignment:

Go to the library and review several recent legal cases involving equal employment opportunity. Prepare a report for presentation in class concerning the facts, issues, and current status of the cases. Each team should make a 5- to 10-minute presentation of its findings.

CHAPTER
13

Understanding Unions

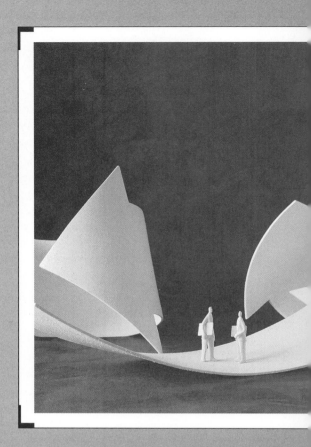

LEARNING OBJECTIVES

After studying this chapter, you should be able to:

√ **1.** Describe the differing philosophies of unions and management.

2. Discuss significant labor laws.

3. Describe four main types of union organizations.

√ **4.** Define collective bargaining.

√ **5.** Define strike, slowdown, sit-down strike, and wildcat strike.

SUPERVISION
DILEMMA

John Lewis had been a member of the union prior to becoming a supervisor, but he had never been very active in union activities. When John became a supervisor, his boss, Les Thomas, gave him a copy of the union contract and suggested that he read it over. Shortly thereafter, Les went over the contract with John and answered the questions John asked about his authority under the contract.

However, several things still bothered John. For one thing, it seemed to him that the contract reduced his authority. Furthermore, Les had told John that the contract was expiring in two months and that there might be a strike. For these reasons, John felt that he needed to know more about unions.

Approximately 12 million employees in the United States are represented by labor unions. In a unionized organization, the supervisor is the primary link between the organization and the union members. The supervisor's first responsibility is to uphold the interests of management. At the same time, the supervisor must fulfill the contractual obligations of management and see that the union fulfills its obligations.

The legal requirements and restraints in unionized organizations are many and complex. Knowing how these requirements and restraints affect organizations is essential to good supervision. Understanding the purpose and structure of labor unions also helps the supervisor manage within a unionized organization.

DIFFERING PHILOSOPHIES OF UNIONS AND MANAGEMENT

1 LEARNING OBJECTIVES

Unions and management operate on two conflicting philosophies. Generally, the union philosophy is that the management has exploited labor in the past and continues to do so. Unions usually believe that management is more interested in making a profit than in furthering the welfare of its employees. Unions maintain that profits are produced by employees' work and that employees should be well compensated to reflect their input.

Management usually looks unfavorably on unions. It feels that unions are attempting to take over decisions that should be reserved for management. Management often feels that unions foster inefficiency and reduce profits. Management also feels that unions strive to gain power for themselves and to divide the employees' loyalty. Management usually maintains that its interests are identical with the interests of its employees. If employees are to prosper, then the organization must prosper.

DEVELOPMENT OF LABOR LAW

The first U.S. unions began as organizations of skilled workers as early as 1790. These unions sought to eliminate competition by banding together people in the same craft. Their members restricted competition by agreeing among themselves to keep the skills of their craft a secret except to a very few. The early unions were generally held to be illegal.

SUPERVISION ILLUSTRATION 13–1

STRIKE AT COLORADO FUEL AND IRON COMPANY (CFI)

The Colorado Fuel and Iron Company (CFI) owned about 300,000 acres of mineral-rich land in southern Colorado. This geographical insulation helped enable CFI to impose rather primitive conditions over its 30,000 workers. Most of the workers lived in company-owned camps located 10 to 30 miles from any big towns. Within the camps, unsanitary conditions led to 151 persons contracting typhoid in 1912 and 1913. Wages were paid in a currency valid only in company stores.

These conditions sparked union-organizing activity. The United Mine Workers (UMW) demanded an eight-hour day, enforcement of safety regulations, removal of armed guards, and abolition of company currency. The company refused to negotiate on these issues.

Thus, in September 1913, up to 10,000 workers at Colorado Fuel and Iron Company went on strike. After the strike began, tensions rose quickly. CFI hired a large number of guards from outside the state, armed them, and paid their salaries.

Violence erupted almost immediately. First, a company detective and a union organizer were killed. A few days later, CFI troops broke up a strikers' mass meeting and killed three workers. Vengeful miners then killed four company men. Governor Ammons called out the National Guard to protect all property and those people who were still working.

On April 20, 1914, a major battle erupted between the strikers and the National Guardsmen. The fire that resulted led to the deaths of two women and 11 children. Several battles occurred over the next several days until, finally, on April 28, 1914, several regiments of federal troops were called in to end the war.

Source: Adapted from Graham Adams, Jr., *Age of Industrial Violence, 1910–1915* (New York: Columbia University Press, 1966), pp. 146–75. For more information about the United Mine Workers, visit its Web site at:
www.access.digex.net/~miner/index.html

2 LEARNING OBJECTIVES

In 1842, the Supreme Court of Massachusetts ruled that it was not illegal to belong to a union but that strikes and boycotts by unions might be illegal. In the late 19th century and the early 20th century, two federal laws were passed that inhibited the formation of unions. The first of these laws, the **Sherman Antitrust Act of 1890,** made it illegal to restrain trade. This law was originally thought to apply to businesses only. However, the Supreme Court decided that a union applying a national boycott against a company's products was in restraint of trade.[1] Thus, the Sherman Antitrust Act was applied against unions and restricted their growth. The *Clayton Act*, passed in 1914, was at first considered pro-union. It stated that labor unions were *not* to be considered in restraint of trade under the Sherman Antitrust Act. However, court interpretations of this law determined that a union engaged in a strike or boycott activity could be in restraint of trade. In addition, yellow-dog contracts and injunctions were used to restrict unions. A **yellow-dog contract** is an agreement between an employee and management that, as a condition of employment, the employee will not join a labor union. An **injunction** is a court order to prohibit certain actions. For example, management could obtain injunctions to prohibit unions from striking. Supervision Illustration 13–1 describes how union activity sometimes has resulted in violence.

During the 1920s and 1930s, public sentiment became more pro-union. As the Industrial Revolution progressed, employers had less need for skilled craft employees and more need for semiskilled or unskilled employees. Semiskilled and unskilled employees lacked the job security that the skilled employees had. They were much easier to replace and much more dependent on management. Because management was not always fair in its treatment of these employees, they began to push for legislation to support their rights. The bad economic times that began during the early 1930s also stimulated pro-union laws.

The first of the pro-union laws was the *Norris-La Guardia Act of 1932*. This act made yellow-dog contracts illegal and made it more difficult for employers to obtain injunctions. It also gave all employees the right to organize and bargain with their employers. The act did not, however, make it mandatory for employers to bargain with unions.

In 1935, Congress passed the *National Labor Relations Act (Wagner Act)*. This act was considered to be the workers' Magna Carta. It *required* employers to bargain collectively with the union. It also created the **National Labor Relations Board (NLRB),** which is responsible for supervising union elections and investigating unfair labor practices. The National Labor Relations Act led to increased power and growth of unions.

As America moved from the depressed economy of the 1930s to a boom economy during World War II, unions realized that they could demand very high wages and benefits. Furthermore, there were no laws requiring unions to bargain in good faith with employers. Because of rapid inflation and the sometimes crippling effect of a union's refusal to bargain, the Labor-Management Relations Act **(Taft-Hartley Act)** was passed in 1947. This act upheld the right of employees to unionize, but it also broadened management's rights and prohibited unfair labor practices on the part of both unions and management. The act also prohibited **closed shops.** That is, it prohibited a union from requiring that a person be a member of the union before he or she could be hired by an employer. The act did allow union shops. In a **union shop,** the union can require an employee who has been working for a specified period of time to become a member. However, the act also allowed individual states to pass laws prohibiting union shops. Twenty-one states now have such laws. These laws are called **right-to-work laws.**

The **Labor-Management Reporting and Disclosure Act (Landrum-Griffin Act)** was passed in 1959. This act is primarily concerned with the protection of the rights of individual union members. For example, it permits union members to sue their unions and it requires that any increase in union dues be approved by a majority of the members (on a secret ballot).

More recent legislation concerning unions has primarily affected government employees. In 1962, *Executive Order 10988* was issued. This order recognized the rights of federal government employees to join unions and bargain collectively. However, it prohibited strikes and it prohibited making union membership a condition of employment. *Executive Order 11491*, issued in 1968, gave the U.S. secretary of labor the authority to supervise union elections and investigate unfair labor practices in the public sector. Figure 13.1 summarizes the major laws and executive orders that have affected unions and organizations.

FIGURE 13.1

Laws and Executive Orders Affecting Unions and Organizations

Law	Year Enacted
Sherman Antitrust Act	1890
Clayton Act	1914
Norris-La Guardia Act	1932
National Labor Relations Act (Wagner Act)	1935
Labor-Management Relations Act (Taft-Hartley Act)	1947
Labor-Management Reporting and Disclosure Act (Landrum-Griffin Act)	1959
Executive Order 10988	1962
Executive Order 11491	1968

FIGURE 13.2

Historical Dates in the Labor Movement

Year	Event
1792	First local union—Philadelphia Shoemaker's Union
1833	First city federation—New York, Philadelphia, Baltimore
1850	First national union—International Typographical Union
1869	Knights of Labor—first attempt to form a federation of unions
1886	Formation of American Federation of Labor (AFL)
1938	Formation of Congress of Industrial Organizations (CIO)
1955	Merger of the AFL and the CIO

STRUCTURE OF LABOR UNIONS

3 LEARNING OBJECTIVES

The four main types of union organizations are (1) federations of local, national, and international unions; (2) national and international unions; (3) city or statewide federations of local unions; and (4) local unions. Figure 13.2 gives some historical dates in the formation of these types of union organizations.

The AFL–CIO (American Federation of Labor–Congress of Industrial Organizations) is a federation of local, national, and international unions that represents close to 80 percent of all union members in the United States. Its present organization structure is shown in Figure 13.3. Its basic policies are set and its executive council is elected at a national convention that is held every two years. Each national and international union sends delegates to the national convention. The number of delegates from each union is determined by the size of its membership. Local unions that are directly affiliated with the AFL–CIO can send only one delegate.

Most national and international unions are organized similarly to the AFL–CIO. They have a periodic national convention at which each local union is represented in proportion to its membership. The convention elects an executive board, which is responsible for conducting the operations of the national or international union.

FIGURE 13.3

Organization Structure of the AFL–CIO

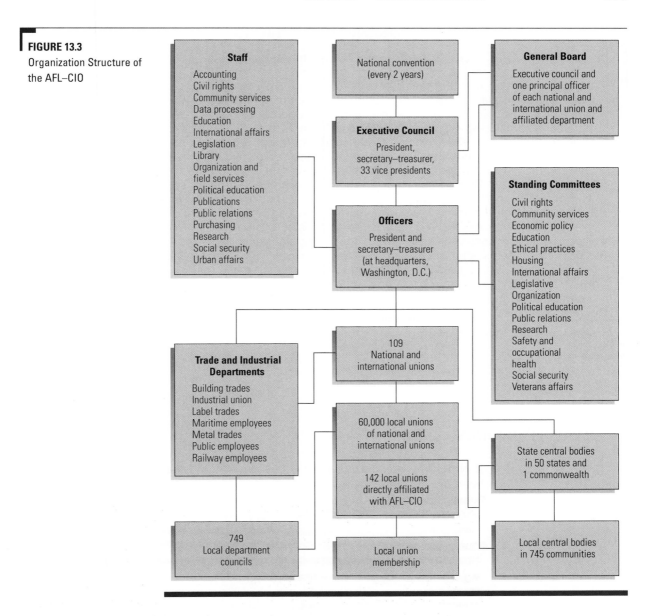

The city or statewide federations are composed of, and supported by, the local unions. These federations promote the interests of labor in the area they serve.

Most local unions operate under a national or international union. However, an independent local union can join the AFL–CIO without belonging to a national or international union. As a rule, the membership of a local union elects officers who carry on its activities. These officers normally conduct union business in addition to working at their regular jobs. They generally receive no pay from the union for their union activities. Larger local unions hire full-time paid personnel to carry out their activities. In most cases, the local union depends heavily on the staff of its national or international union for assistance in handling contract negotiations, strikes, and important grievances.

SUPERVISION ILLUSTRATION 13–2

UNIONS TARGET NONTRADITIONAL INDUSTRIES

A decline in union membership has caused union leaders to plan aggressive recruitment campaigns aimed at nontraditional membership sources, including women, doctors, and immigrant workers. In 1960, women made up 18 percent of union membership, compared with approximately 40 percent in 1997. The AFL–CIO has hired Karen Nussbaum, former head of the Department of Labor's Women's Bureau, to launch the union's Working Women's Department. AFL–CIO vice-president Linda Chavez-Thompson will lead a 20-city tour to discuss women's labor issues, and a three-day conference will be held in Washington to outline a "working-women's agenda" and strategies for organizing.

With the advent of managed care, more doctors (43 percent) work as employees. The Federation of Physicians and Dentists has more than 3,000 members, and the Union of American Physicians and Dentists has about 5,000. The AFL–CIO has formed the National Guild for Health Care Providers of the Lower Extremities to represent podiatrists.

The New York City Central Labor Council, backed by the AFL–CIO and other unions, has initiated a drive to recruit immigrants on an industry-by-industry basis. In Los Angeles, nine AFL–CIO unions launched a campaign aimed at the largely immigrant manufacturing sector. Known as the Los Angeles Manufacturing Action Project, it targets 300,000 workers for organizing.

Source: Adapted from Maureen Minehan, "Unions Target Nontraditional Industries," *HRMagazine,* June 1997, p. 272. For more information about the AFL–CIO, visit its Web site at:
www.aflcio.org

REASONS FOR JOINING UNIONS

It should be recognized that people join unions even when management has been fair in dealing with its employees. Some of the more important reasons for joining unions are purely economic. These are (1) higher wages, (2) greater job security, (3) better fringe benefits, and (4) more clearly defined procedures for advancement (normally, seniority). People also join unions for many other reasons. These reasons include (1) better working conditions; (2) more meaningful work; (3) fairer rules and procedures for determining promotions, discipline, and so on; (4) opportunity to be recognized, respected, and heard on issues; (5) opportunity to complain formally; and (6) the wish to belong to an organization of people with similar needs and desires.

Most members of unions join them for positive reasons. Some employees, however, join unions because they must do so in order to continue their employment. Even in states having right-to-work laws, many employees feel pressured into joining the union. These employees would prefer not to join the union for various reasons; among them are (1) the employee wants to progress into management and therefore identifies more with management than with the union; (2) the employee feels that the union protects the mediocre worker and does not support the merit reward system; (3) the employee wants to avoid loss of income through union dues or strikes; and (4) the employee distrusts the union. Supervision Illustration 13–2 describes several new groups that are being targeted for union membership.

UNION ORGANIZATION DRIVE

The union organization drive is usually started by the employees of the organization. For one or more of the reasons previously discussed, a group of employees determines that a union is desirable. A representative of a national or international union is then asked by this group to visit the company and solicit members. The union must obtain signed authorization cards from at least 30 percent of the employees before a representation election can be called. Such an authorization card states that the employee desires representation by a specific union. When 30 percent of the employees sign authorization cards, the union may request a representation election through the National Labor Relations Board (NLRB).

The NLRB must first determine what the bargaining unit is (which employees the union will represent) and whether the authorization requirement has been fulfilled. If it has, a secret-ballot election is then conducted. If the union receives a simple majority of the votes cast, it becomes the exclusive bargaining representative of the employees within the bargaining unit. That is, the union represents all of the employees whose work classification places them within the unit that the union covers. The union must represent all of the employees within that unit, whether or not they are union members. It should be noted that the union does *not* have to receive a majority of the votes of all the employees in the bargaining unit. It only has to receive a majority of the votes cast.

COLLECTIVE BARGAINING

 LEARNING OBJECTIVES

Collective bargaining is the process by which a contract or an agreement is negotiated, written, administered, and interpreted. The contract is a legal document that covers a specified period of time, usually two to five years. It represents the joint labor-management understanding as to the terms and conditions of employment.

The length and terms of labor agreements vary considerably, but certain provisions are nearly always included. Figure 13.4 lists common provisions of a union contract as well as rights that are usually reserved for management. It is generally assumed that management possesses any rights not specifically given to the union by the contract.

Negotiation of the Contract

The labor contract is produced by a process called **negotiation.** The course of negotiations varies, but it usually takes place in several phases. In the first phase, both labor and management present their initial demands. At this point, the demands of each party are usually not acceptable to the other party. In the second phase, the parties discuss the individual issues. As a result of concessions and the resolution of some issues, the negotiation comes to center on a few key issues. These key issues are usually not resolved until the strike deadline approaches. The reason for the delay is that both parties hold out as long as possible. The cost and uncertainty of a strike, however, generally force

FIGURE 13.4

Common Provisions of a
Union Contract

Primary Provisions of a Labor Contract

1. Management rights.
2. Union rights to represent certain employees.
3. Job classifications and related wages and hours.
4. Benefits.
5. Grievance procedure.
6. Seniority stipulations.
7. Duration of the contract.

Secondary Provisions of a Labor Contract

1. Production standards.
2. Working conditions.
3. No-strike clauses.
4. Plant rules.
5. Discipline procedures.
6. Wage reopening clauses.
7. Subcontracting.

Management Rights

1. Right to control and direct the workforce.
2. Determination of the equipment to be used.
3. Decisions on hiring and firing.
4. Determination of which products and services will be provided.

them to a compromise. Over 98 percent of all negotiations end in settlement without a strike.

Sometimes the parties use a neutral person to help resolve the disputed issues. This person, called a **mediator** or **conciliator,** may come in during any phase of the bargaining process. The mediator works with both parties in an effort to get them to reach agreement on a contract. A mediator can only offer suggestions for coming to a bargaining agreement. The mediator's suggestions are in no way legally binding. The mediator's services are seldom required by law, but those services often prevent a strike from occurring.

The National Labor Relations Act requires that both parties bargain in good faith. **Good-faith bargaining** has been interpreted as the sincere intention to negotiate differences and to seek an agreement acceptable to both parties. If one party charges the other with not bargaining in good faith, the NLRB must judge whether the words and actions of the parties represented good-faith bargaining.

Administering the Contract

Once agreement has been reached on the issues, a contract is drawn up. The contract is a legal document that can be upheld by a court of law. Court actions on labor contracts occur infrequently. Most disagreements during the contract period are resolved through the grievance procedure. Strikes seldom occur during the contract period and are usually considered to be illegal if they do.

The collective bargaining process does not end when the contract has been drawn up. The administration of the contract is an important part of that process. For example, the contract may provide that an employee can be disciplined for just cause. To fulfill this provision, management must develop a system of discipline that supervisors must follow. Management (including the supervisor) also carries out the collective bargaining process by interpreting the contract and settling complaints and grievances. Most labor contracts provide for a grievance procedure that usually ends in final and binding **arbitration**. This means that if the union and management cannot reach an agreement on a grievance, a neutral person is asked to decide the issue. This neutral person, called an *arbitrator*, is chosen by mutual agreement of the parties. The arbitrator's decision is final and must be adhered to by the parties. The supervisor's role in administering the contract is discussed at length in a later section of this chapter.

SUPERVISOR'S RESPONSIBILITY TO THE EMPLOYER AND THE UNION

In a unionized organization, the supervisor has a dual responsibility. The supervisor's first responsibility is, of course, to the employer. As a member of management, the supervisor must work toward achieving good productivity. As a member of management, the supervisor must also help uphold the commitments of management under the contract. The union holds the organization responsible for the supervisor's actions or lack of action in dealing with it and its members. The Labor-Management Relations Act, passed in 1947, outlines some unfair labor practices that the supervisor is legally required to avoid. These include (1) restraining employees from forming or joining a union, (2) trying to influence the labor organization, (3) discriminating against union members, and (4) discriminating against an employee for participating in a charge against the employer under the Labor-Management Relations Act.

A union can be either friendly or antagonistic toward management. This friend-or-foe relationship is partially determined by how well the supervisor does his or her job. The supervisor's relationship with the union begins during the union organization drive and continues during the negotiation and administration of the contract. The supervisor must fulfill his or her responsibilities during these phases of the union relationship. The next section of this chapter is designed to help the supervisor do this.

SUPERVISORY RESPONSIBILITIES AND UNIONS

Most organizations feel that keeping the union out is best. Many organizations pride themselves on treating their employees so well that they do not need or desire union representation. However, if a union begins an organization drive, the supervisor is in an extremely precarious situation. In this situation, the supervisor's actions are restricted by law.

Supervisors are free to give their views, arguments, or opinions about unions. However, they are forbidden to use threats, reprisals, or promises of benefits to get employees to choose or not to choose union representation.

FIGURE 13.5	Illegal:	If the union gets in, your hours will be cut.
Legal and Illegal	Legal:	If we were under a contract similar to the one that this union has with our competitor, you would probably have your hours cut and layoffs.
Statements by a		
Supervisor in a Union	Illegal:	If the union is elected, your wages and benefits will be cut.
Organizing Campaign	Legal:	The law requires the company to bargain in good faith with the union; but this means that the benefits you receive after the union gets in may be less than those you have now or that you may get the same benefits but arranged differently. If the benefits are rearranged, the new formula may favor employees other than those in your group.
	Illegal:	You will lose your right to deal directly with management if the union gets in.
	Legal:	This union negotiates contracts in which it is the sole spokesman for employees on grievance matters.

Source: Adapted from F. L. Sullivan, "Union Organizing in the 1980s; A Guide to the Law in Union Organizing," *Supervisory Management,* August 1982, pp. 24–25.

Knowing what to say and what not to say can be tricky. There is often a fine line between whether a statement is legal and whether it is illegal. Figure 13.5 gives some examples of legal and illegal statements. It is important to remember that the organization's human resources department is available for assistance in resolving any questions that the supervisor may have in this area.

In summary, supervisors should observe the following guidelines during a union organization drive: (1) consult higher management before dealing with officials of the union; (2) avoid arguing with employees over unionization; (3) do not threaten or bribe an employee directly or indirectly with regard to joining the union; (4) be very careful not to discriminate against any employee who is involved in the unionization attempt; and (5) do not change wages or fringe benefits during the unionization attempt.

The supervisor should also be on the lookout for unfair labor practices by the union. The union cannot force employees to participate in its activities. Complaints against the union may be filed with the NLRB.

During an organization drive, supervisors frequently feel bewildered or hurt by the employees' attempt to unionize. Many supervisors see this attempt as a reflection on their leadership skills. But—as discussed previously—there are numerous other reasons why employees attempt to unionize.

If a union is successful in becoming the employees' representative, the supervisor must accept the situation. The supervisor must then learn to lead within the restraints set by the union. There is much more flexibility within those restraints if the union and the organization develop a good relationship. The supervisor's relationship with the union is established primarily through the employees and the union steward. The **union steward** is both an employee of the organization and a union official. A supervisor who deals openly and fairly with employees and the union steward promotes a good relationship with the union.

Working with the Steward

It is difficult for the supervisor to regard the steward as anything other than an adversary. As the union's watchdog, the steward must be constantly aware of how the supervisor is administering the contract. Sometimes the steward initiates a grievance. The relationship between the supervisor and the steward may be especially difficult if the steward works for the supervisor in performing his or her normal work duties. Nevertheless, it is to the supervisor's advantage to develop a good relationship with the steward. Showing respect for the steward's position is essential in developing a good relationship. The following suggestions should also help foster a good relationship with the steward.

First, keep the steward informed. A supervisor who tries to sneak changes through without the steward's knowledge is likely to have a grievance filed. It is much wiser for the supervisor to inform the steward and thus avoid unnecessary time-consuming grievances. Many times, the steward can help work out little problems before they develop into grievances.

Second, show that you understand and appreciate the difficulty of the steward's job. The steward must serve two leaders—as a good employee and also as a good union official. The supervisor should not be more lenient with the steward than with the other employees; but showing consideration for the steward's position is helpful.

Third, show the steward that you are willing to compromise, but be careful to compromise only on issues within your authority. For instance, the supervisor might agree not to discipline an employee for tardiness because of problems beyond the employee's control. However, the supervisor should not agree to consult the union before using discipline for tardiness. And the supervisor must get the boss's permission before making any exceptions to the contract.

During Collective Bargaining

Usually, the supervisor is not directly involved in the negotiation of the contract. The supervisor is consulted, however, for information that affects the negotiation. The supervisor must be prepared for this vital contingency. By keeping careful records over the contract period on decisions concerning discipline, promotions, and any problems encountered in administering the contract, the supervisor can provide valuable information during the negotiation.

Administering the Contract

By necessity, there are many general provisions in the labor contract. It is the supervisor's job to equitably interpret such provisions. As discussed earlier, the supervisor often sets the tone for the entire union-management relationship. If, during the contract period, the supervisor has been less than fair in interpreting and administering the provisions of the contract, the union will be more inclined to hold out for more specific language in the next negotiation. This can lead to drawn-out negotiations that are more likely to end in a strike. The end result can be a loss of needed flexibility in the contract.

Strikes usually occur between contracts and are caused by the inability of the parties to reach an agreement.
Agence France Presse/Corbis-Bettmann

The supervisor is responsible for seeing that the entire contract is followed. Most supervisors find that it simplifies their jobs to have contract clauses covering overtime, seniority, promotions, and rates of pay. However, supervisors sometimes ignore contract provisions covering such matters as length of coffee and lunch breaks and cleanup time. But if supervisors, for example, allow their employees to take 10 minutes more for lunch than is given in the contract, this can be interpreted as an agreement to change the contract. The supervisor must therefore be sure to act on all provisions of the contract in order to keep them alive.

During a Strike

5   LEARNING OBJECTIVES

Strikes usually occur between contracts and are caused by the inability of the parties to reach an agreement on a new contract. In a **strike,** employees leave their jobs and refuse to come back to work until a contract has been signed. Employees also use other means to show their dissatisfaction. Sometimes they continue to work but reduce their output. This is called a **slowdown.** Staying on the job but refusing to work at all is called a **sit-down**

FIGURE 13.6

Checklist for Handling
Wildcat Strikes

1. Stay on the job.
2. Notify higher management by telephone or messenger.
3. Carefully record the events as they happen.
4. Pay strict attention to who the leaders are and record their behavior.
5. Record any lack of action by union officials.
6. Report all information as fully and as soon as possible to higher management.
7. Encourage employees to go back to work.
8. Ask union officials to instruct employees to go back to work.
9. Don't discuss the cause of the strike.
10. Don't make any agreements or say anything that might imply permission to leave work.
11. Make it clear that management will discuss the issue when all of the employees are back at work.

strike. Strikes, slowdowns, and sit-down strikes are generally illegal during the term of a contract.

There is very little that the supervisor can do to resolve a strike. It is the responsibility of the negotiating team to reach an agreement as quickly as possible.

Even though strikes are normally illegal during the contract period, some strikes do occur at that time. A strike in which employees leave their jobs and refuse to work during the contract period is called a **wildcat strike.** Wildcat strikes occur for many reasons. Many times, they are the result of mishandled grievances. The supervisor is vitally involved in reducing the chances of a wildcat strike. Fair and intelligent administering of the contract reduces the chances of wildcat strikes, slowdowns, or sit-down strikes.

If a wildcat strike does occur, it is the supervisor's responsibility to determine who the leaders are and to encourage them and the other striking employees to return to work. It is usually undesirable to discipline all of the striking employees. Management generally deals more harshly with the leaders than with the followers.

In order to get the employees to go back to work, supervisors should encourage them to abide by the contract. They should encourage employees to use the grievance procedure to settle their differences and should also instruct the union officials to encourage employees to go back to work. Supervisors should not discuss the cause of the strike with the strikers. They should also never make any agreement with the strikers or make any statement that can be interpreted as permission to leave the job. A simple statement such as "Go back to work or go home!" could be interpreted as permission to leave the job. The supervisor should make it clear that management is willing to meet and discuss the problem as soon as all of the employees are back at work. A checklist of suggested supervisory actions during a wildcat strike is provided in Figure 13.6.

SOLUTION TO THE SUPERVISION DILEMMA

John has learned about the differing philosophies of unions and management and about the development of labor law (pp. 251–54). He has also learned why people do or do not join labor unions (p. 256). He now knows that union organization drives are usually started by the employees of an organization and that during such a drive his responsibilities are to consult with higher management before dealing with officials of the union, to avoid arguing with employees over unionization, not to threaten or bribe employees directly or indirectly with regard to joining the union, not to discriminate against any employee who is involved in the unionization attempt, and not to change wages or fringe benefits during that attempt (p. 260). John has also learned what his role is in administering the union contract and in dealing with a strike (pp. 261–63).

SUMMARY

The purpose of this chapter is to develop an understanding of the purpose and structure of labor unions. Furthermore, the legal requirements and restraints in unionized organizations are explained.

1. *Describe the differing philosophies of unions and management.* The union philosophy is that management has exploited labor in the past and continues to do so. Unions usually believe that management is more interested in making a profit than in furthering the welfare of its employees. Management usually looks unfavorably on unions. It feels that unions are attempting to take over decisions that should be reserved for management.

2. *Discuss significant labor laws.* The Sherman Antitrust Act made it illegal to restrain trade, and the Supreme Court ruled that this act applied to unions. The Clayton Act stated that labor unions were not to be considered in restraint of trade. However, the Court ruled that a union engaged in a strike or boycott activity could be in restraint of trade. The Norris-La Guardia Act made yellow-dog contracts illegal and made it more difficult for employers to obtain injunctions. The National Labor Relations Act (Wagner Act) required employers to bargain collectively with unions and created the National Labor Relations Board (NLRB). The Labor-Management Relations Act (Taft-Hartley Act) upheld the right of employees to unionize, but it also broadened management's rights and prohibited unfair labor practices of both unions and management. The Labor-Management Reporting and Disclosure Act (Landrum-Griffin Act) is primarily concerned with the protection of the rights of individual union members. Executive Order 10988 recognized the rights of federal government employees to join unions and bargain collectively. Executive Order 11491 gave the U.S. secretary of labor the authority to supervise union elections and investigate unfair labor practices in the public sector.

3. *Describe four main types of union organizations.* The four main types of union organizations are (1) federations of local, national, and international unions; (2) national and international unions; (3) city or statewide federations of local unions; and (4) local unions.

4. *Define collective bargaining.* Collective bargaining is the process by which a contract or an agreement is negotiated, written, administered, and interpreted.

5. *Define strike, slowdown, sit-down strike, and wildcat strike.* Strikes usually occur when employees leave their jobs and refuse to come back to work until a contract has been signed. A situation in which employees continue to work but reduce their output is called a *slowdown.* A situation in which employees stay on the job but refuse to work at all is called a *sit-down strike.* A situation in which employees leave their jobs and refuse to work during the contract period is called a *wildcat strike.*

REVIEW QUESTIONS

1. What are yellow-dog contracts? What are injunctions?
2. Describe four laws that affect the union movement.
3. What are the four main types of union organizations?
4. Give four reasons for joining a union.
5. What is collective bargaining?
6. Give at least 10 provisions that a contract might cover.
7. What is the function of a mediator or conciliator? of an arbitrator?
8. Give five rules that should be followed by the supervisor who is faced with a union organizing attempt.
9. What is a strike? a slowdown? a sit-down strike?
10. Give some guidelines for handling a wildcat strike.

SKILL-BUILDING QUESTIONS

1. The union and management philosophies outlined in this chapter are in conflict. Which philosophy do you agree with, and why?
2. Why is it important for the supervisor to be fair in following the contract?
3. Can the supervisor single out employees who are less active in the union for preferred job assignments? Why or why not?
4. "Stewards are impossible to work with, and communication between the supervisor and the steward should be avoided." Discuss your views on this statement.

REFERENCE

1. *Loewe* v. *Lawlor*, 208 U.S. 274 (1900).

ADDITIONAL READINGS

Deshpande, Satish P. "Union Certification Elections in Hospitals," *Labor Studies Journal*, Fall 1996.

Fairley, Peter. "Labor Reenergized: Companies Divided on Response," *Chemical Week*, November 27, 1996.

Lissy, William E. "High-Tech Changes and Union Policies," *Supervision*, December 1994.

Magenau, John M., and Raymond G. Hunt. "Police Unions and the Police Role," *Human Relations*, October 1996.

Ross, Sherwood. "Labor's Saints and Unreformed Sinners," *Journal of Commerce and Commercial*, December 23, 1996.

Shine, D. Bruce. "Can the NLRB Help Cinderella and Little Orphan Annie?" *Labor Law Journal*. November 1996.

SECTION III   STAFFING SKILLS

SKILL-BUILDING APPLICATIONS

Incident 13–1

Working with Trudy

Jane Eason is new in her job as supervisor of the word processing section at the city government of Monroe. Fifteen people work in Jane's unit, and all of them are members of the American Federation of Government Employees (AFGE).

Trudy Sullivan works for Jane and is also a union steward for the AFGE. In her capacity as union steward, Trudy often has to leave her job as a word processor operator and go to other departments to handle employee complaints and grievances.

Jane has gotten along well with Trudy in the short time she has known her and wants to maintain this relationship. Yesterday, however, an awkward situation came up. Trudy informed Jane that Sue Ellison, another word processor operator in Jane's section, had approached her about filing a grievance against Jane. Jane knew exactly what it was about. Just three days ago, Jane had given Sue a written warning about her tardiness. Sue had felt that the written warning was unfair.

Trudy and Jane discussed the situation. Jane had hoped that Trudy would agree with her and not file the grievance. Much to Jane's surprise, however, Trudy didn't agree with her and informed her that she would be receiving a formal grievance that day. Jane really felt strange about justifying her actions to Trudy. After all, Trudy also worked for her.

Questions

1. Do you feel that this situation is unusual in unionized organizations?
2. If you were Jane, how would you handle the situation?

Incident 13–2

Wildcat Strike

Frank Wozniak, supervisor of the maintenance department of Grayson Manufacturing, was facing a real problem. His employees were discussing walking out of the plant on a wildcat strike. They weren't upset with Frank; they were considering the action out of sympathy for the employees in another department. These employees had walked out about 30 minutes ago and had sent word back into the plant asking Frank's people to join them.

The walkout had occurred because John Hanks, the supervisor of the other department, had fired an employee for supposed drinking on the job. Frank's people said that the guy had really been fired because Hanks disliked him and that no bottle had been found. They also said that Hanks was antiunion and had fired the guy right on the spot. Frank asked his men not to walk out until he could check out the story. They agreed to wait for 30 minutes.

Frank immediately called Linda Peterson, the human resources manager of Grayson. She confirmed Frank's worse fears. According to Linda, everything his employees had told him about Hanks was true.

Questions

1. How should Frank handle the situation?
2. What should the company do?

Exercise 13–1

What Have You Learned?

The following are excerpts from a speech made by Frederick W. Taylor in 1911.

> If any of you will get close to the average workman in this country—close enough to him so that he will talk to you as an intimate friend—he will tell you that in his particular trade if, we will say, each man were to turn out twice as much work as he is now doing, there could be but one result follow; namely, that one-half the men in his trade would be thrown out of work . . .
>
> This doctrine is preached by almost every labor leader in this country, and is taught by every workman to his children as they are growing up; and I repeat, as I said in the beginning, that it is our fault more than theirs that this fallacy prevails . . .

While the labor leaders and the workmen themselves in season and out of season are pointing out the necessity of restriction of output, not one step are we taking to counteract that fallacy; therefore, I say, the fault is ours and not theirs.

C. Jackson Grayson, speaking as chairman of the American Productivity Center in Houston, warned that if management and labor cannot make their relationship less adversarial, "then we won't get the full long-term kick in productivity that we desperately need."

Looking at Taylor's and Grayson's remarks, which were made approximately 73 years apart, one has to wonder what we have learned. Do you think that Taylor's position is equally applicable today? Be prepared to justify your answer. Do you feel that unions and management are too adversarial? Are unions needed today? Be prepared to defend your answer.

Sources: Frederick W. Taylor, "The Principles of Scientific Management," in *Scientific Management: First Conference at the Amos Tuck School* (Norwood, Mass.: Plimpton Press, 1912), pp. 23–24, and "The Revival of Productivity," *Business Week*, February 13, 1984, p. 100.

Exercise 13–2

Contract Negotiations

You will be put on a team of three to four students. Each team in the class will be required to negotiate a contract for a company or a union.

The company's wage scale, $5.80 per hour, compares favorably with most firms in its area but is about 8 percent below those firms that employ workers of equivalent skill. Wages have not increased in proportion to cost-of-living increases over the past three years.

At the last bargaining session, the company and union took the following positions:

1. *Hospital and medical plan*
   Past contract: Company paid one-fourth of cost, employee paid remaining three-fourths.
   Union: Demanded company pay full cost.
   Company: Refused to pay more than one-fourth.

Proportion of company payment				
Company 1/4	2/4	3/4	4/4	Union
0	20,000	40,000	60,000	

Increase in total dollar value per year

2. *Wages*
   Past contract: $5.80 per hour
   Union: Demanded an increase of 60 cents per hour.
   Company: Refused outright.

Cents increase per hour

Company 0	10	20	30	40	50	60	Union
0	31,200	62,400	93,600	124,800	156,000	187,200	

Total dollar value per year

3. *Sliding pay scale to conform to cost of living*
   Past contract: Pay scale is fixed through the term of the contract.
   Union: Demanded pay increases in proportion to increases in the cost of living.
   Company: Rejected outright.

Company	No	Yes	Union
	0	120,000	

Total dollar value per year

4. *Vacation pay*
   Past contract: Two weeks paid vacation for all workers with one year service.
   Union: Wants three weeks paid vacation for workers with 10 years of service.
   Company: Rejected.

Company	2weeks/ 1 year	3 weeks/ 20 years	3 weeks/ 15 years	3 weeks/ 10 years	Union
	0	10,000	20,000	30,000	

Total dollar value per year

Each week on strike (10 minutes of negotiations in the exercise) costs the company $40,000 in lost profits and the workers $40,000 in lost wages.

1. Negotiate the above contract issues with another team (as assigned by your instructor).

2. At the end of negotiations, your instructor will summarize the beginning, ending, and costs for each negotiation.

Source: *Supervision*, May 1991, p. 13. Courtesy of International and Domestic Negotiating Institute.

Exercise 13–3

How Do You Rate as a Business Negotiator?

"It's important for people to know how they feel about negotiating before they get involved in a business negotiation," says Dr. Eugene Mendonsa, director of the International and Domestic Negotiating Institute in Red Bluff, California.

To get a feeling for how you rate as a business negotiator, Mendonsa offers this short quiz. He cautions that people should answer the questions honestly to get a true profile. Give the questions a rating of 0, 1, 2, 3, 4, or 5. Zero means the statement is totally incorrect and five means the statement is totally correct.

1. I think luck has a lot to do with whether or not I get a good deal. _____

2. It's easy for me to get angry when disagreements arise in a business negotiation. _____

3. I feel uncomfortable negotiating with people of higher status. _____

4. I normally don't ask probing questions that might cause embarrassment. _____

5. Sometimes I have a problem thinking fast on my feet when the pressure gets intense. _____

6. I don't get too friendly with my opponents during a business negotiation. _____

7. I would feel uncomfortable making an extremely low offer for something that is probably worth much more. _____

8. It is important to me that most of my opponents like and accept me. _____

9. I'd rather deal with a general manager than a company president. _____

10. Helping my opponent to "save face" is not particularly important. _____

11. Where I happen to end up sitting at a business negotiation is not that important to me. _____

12. My business negotiating counterparts are usually honest and fair. _____

13. If I encounter rudeness or hostility, I wouldn't show my counterparts much courtesy. _____

14. I feel uncomfortable getting into a confrontation during a business negotiation. _____

15. I am more frank and open than tactful and discreet. _____

16. I would never negotiate prices in a department store. _____

17. I feel uncomfortable with long silences during a business negotiation. _____

18. I never get emotional or irritated in a business negotiation, not even when I am provoked. _____

19. I normally don't know much about my counterparts until the actual business negotiating starts. _____

20. I don't find it that beneficial to do a lot of advanced preparations for a normal business negotiation. _____

Add up your score:
0 to 15   = Superstar!
16 to 30 = Good business negotiator
31 to 45 = OK, but a lot to learn
46 plus = You shouldn't be negotiating business deals unless you get some proper training.

"Most business negotiations sour because of errors that are made in the process. People either don't know what to do, don't remember what to do, are afraid or get angry. But with a little work and determination, most people can improve their business negotiation abilities dramatically," concludes Mendonsa.

Source: *Supervision*, May 1991, p. 13. Courtesy of International and Domestic Negotiating Institute.

Human Relations Skills

SECTION OUTLINE

14 Motivating today's employee

15 Leading employees

16 Handling conflict

17 Coping with change and stress

18 Counseling employees

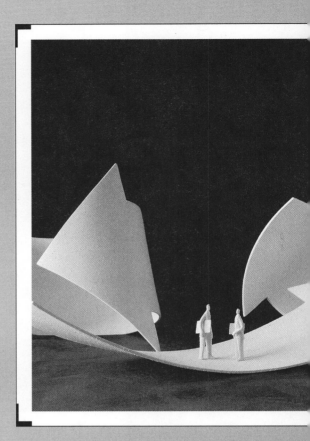

CHAPTER 14

Motivating Today's Employee

LEARNING OBJECTIVES

After studying this chapter, you should be able to:

1. Define motivation.
2. Define the traditional theory of motivation.
3. Explain the hierarchy of needs.
4. Discuss the motivation-maintenance theory of motivation.
5. Discuss the preference-expectancy theory of motivation.
6. Explain reinforcement theory.
7. State several things that the supervisor can do to affect employee motivation.

SUPERVISION
DILEMMA

In recent weeks, Jane Harris has noticed that whenever she enters the office, several of her employees appear to be loafing or involved in gossipy conversations. In Jane's opinion, they just don't seem to be working very hard. A quick review of the human resources records verified another suspicion—absenteeism and tardiness have increased in recent months. Jane is baffled. Just two months ago, everyone received an 11 percent pay raise. In addition to this, the facilities of her department have been recently refurbished. What else could the employees possibly want?

"Nobody wants to work like they did in the good old days." "Half the problems we have around here are due to a lack of personal motivation." "Workers just don't seem to care." Such sentiments are often expressed by today's supervisors. However, motivating employees is not a new problem. Much of the pioneering work in the field of management, which took place early in this century, was concerned with motivation. One can even find examples showing motivation problems existed back in biblical times.

WHAT IS MOTIVATION?

1   LEARNING OBJECTIVES

Numerous definitions can be found for the word *motivation*. Often included in these definitions are such words as *aim, desire, end, impulse, intention, objective,* and *purpose.* The word *motivation* actually comes from the Latin *movere,* which means "to move." In today's organizations, **motivation** means getting people to exert a high degree of effort on their job. A motivated employee is an employee who tries hard. The key to motivation, then, is getting employees to want to do a job. In this light, motivation is not something that the supervisor does *to* an employee. Rather, motivation is something that must come from within an employee. The supervisor can, however, create an environment that encourages motivation on the part of employees. This is the context in which the supervisor motivates employees.

Motivation can best be understood using the following sequence of events:

Needs → Drives or motives → Accomplishment of goals

In this sequence, needs produce motives, which lead to the accomplishment of goals. Needs are caused by deficiencies, which can be either physical or mental. For instance, a physical need exists when a person goes without sleep for a long period. A mental need exists when a person has no friends or no meaningful relationships with other people.

Motives produce action. Lack of sleep (the need) activates the physical changes of fatigue (the motive), which produce sleep (the accomplishment of the goal). The accomplishment of the goal satisfies the need and reduces the motive. When the goal is reached, balance is restored. Other needs soon arise, however, and the sequence repeats itself.

UNDERSTANDING PEOPLE

Every supervisor knows that some people are easier to motivate than others. Why is this true? Are some people simply born more motivated than others? No person is exactly like any other person. Each individual has a unique personality and makeup. Thus, because people are different, it stands to reason that different factors are required to motivate different people. Yet many supervisors often expect all employees to react in a similar manner.

Not all employees expect or even want the same things from their jobs. People work for different reasons. Some people work because they have to work; they need money to pay their bills. Others work because they want something to occupy their time. Some people work for extra money—to buy something they would not otherwise be able to afford. Other people work so that they can have a career and its related satisfactions. In light of the many different reasons why people work, it is *not* logical to expect the same things to motivate everyone.

When attempting to understand the behavior of an employee, the supervisor should always remember that people do things for a reason. The reason may be imaginary, inaccurate, distorted, or unjustifiable, but it is real to the individual. The reason, whatever it may be, must be identified before the supervisor can understand the employee's behavior. All too often, the supervisor disregards an employee's reason for a certain behavior as being unrealistic or based on inaccurate information. Such a supervisor responds to the employee's reason by saying, "I don't care what he thinks—that is not the way it is!" Supervisors of this kind will probably never understand why employees behave as they do.

Yet another consideration in understanding the behavior of employees is the concept of the self-fulfilling prophecy, also known as the **Pygmalion effect.** This concept refers to the tendency of an employee to live up to the supervisor's expectations. In other words, if the supervisor expects an employee to succeed, the employee usually will succeed. Of course, the opposite is also true. If the supervisor expects an employee to fail, the employee will usually fail.

All in all, humans are very complex beings. Different things motivate different people. Today's supervisor must recognize these differences and learn to deal with them. Supervision Illustration 14–1 describes a unique approach to motivation that is used by one company.

BASIC MOTIVATION THEORIES

Several basic theories of employee motivation have been developed. The most widely recognized theories are discussed below.

Traditional Theory

2 LEARNING OBJECTIVES

The **traditional theory** of motivation evolved from the work of Frederick W. Taylor and the scientific management movement in the early 1900s. Taylor's ideas were based on his belief that most reward systems were not designed to

---

SUPERVISION ILLUSTRATION 14–1

MOTIVATION THROUGH RESPECT

Motivation is a concern at Leone Ackerly's residential maid service in Marietta, Georgia. Her firm, Mini Maid Inc., has mostly women employees in their 20s with little education and few skills. Most come to the job having grown up on welfare and many have been abused or battered. Partly for those reasons, Ackerly's management philosophy since she began her business 24 years ago has been based on one principle: respect. She has learned, she says, that many of her employees have never known respect and that getting it changes them for the better.

"Most employers look at them with disdain and don't expect them to stay. As a result, they come to Mini Maid feeling that this is just a job and a paycheck," says Ackerly. "But we ask them to look at us as their partners in a team effort. We tell them, 'This is what we give you; this is what you give us.' Right off the bat, the new employees feel that they are an important part of our company. What happens at this point is that they begin to listen."

Source: Adapted from Roberta Maynard, "How to Motivate Low-Wage Workers," *Nation's Business*, May 1997, pp. 35–39. For more information on *Nation's Business,* visit its Web site at:
www.nationsbusiness.org

---

reward a person for high production. Taylor felt that the output of highly productive people would decrease when they discovered that they were receiving basically the same compensation as people who produced less. Taylor's solution was quite simple. He designed a system whereby individuals were compensated according to their production.

One of Taylor's problems was determining reasonable standards of performance. Taylor solved this problem by breaking jobs down into components and measuring the time necessary to accomplish each component. In this way, he was able to establish standards of performance "scientifically."

Under Taylor's reward system, one rate was paid for units produced up to the standard, but once the standard was reached, a significantly higher rate was paid not only for the units above the standard but for all of the units produced during the day. Thus under Taylor's system, employees could significantly increase their pay by exceeding the standard.

The traditional theory of motivation is based on the assumption that money is the primary motivator of people. Under this assumption, financial rewards are directly related to performance in the belief that employees will work harder and produce more if these rewards are great enough.

Need Hierarchy Theory

The **need hierarchy theory** is based on the assumption that employees are motivated to satisfy a number of needs and that money can satisfy, directly or indirectly, only some of these needs. The need hierarchy theory is based largely on the work of the psychologist Abraham Maslow.

Maslow felt that five levels of needs exist within individuals and that these need levels relate to one another in the form of the hierarchy shown in Figure 14.1.

FIGURE 14.1

Maslow's Need Hierarchy

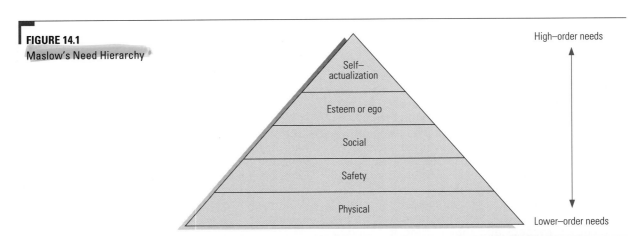

High–order needs

Self–actualization

Esteem or ego

Social

Safety

Physical

Lower–order needs

The **physical needs** are basically the needs of the human body that must be satisfied in order to sustain life. These needs include food, sleep, water, exercise, clothing, shelter, and so forth. The **safety needs** are concerned with protection against danger, threat, or deprivation. Since all employees have, to some degree, a dependent relationship with the organization, the safety needs can be critically important. Favoritism, discrimination, and arbitrary administration of organizational policies are actions that arouse uncertainty and therefore affect the safety needs.

The third level of needs is the social needs. The **social needs** include love, affection, and belonging. Such needs are concerned with establishing one's position relative to that of others. They are satisfied by the development of meaningful personal relations and by acceptance into meaningful groups of individuals. Belonging to organizations and identifying with work groups are ways of satisfying the social needs in organizations.

The fourth level of needs is the **esteem needs**. These needs include both self-esteem and the esteem of others. Maslow contended that all people have needs for the esteem of others and for a stable, firmly based, high evaluation of themselves. The esteem needs are concerned with the development of various kinds of relationships based on adequacy, independence, and the giving and receiving of indications of self-esteem and acceptance.

The highest-order needs in Maslow's hierarchy are **self-actualization** and **self-fulfillment:** the needs of people to reach their full potential in terms of their abilities and interests. Such needs are concerned with the will to operate at the optimum and thus receive the rewards that are the result of doing so. The rewards may not only be economic and social but also mental. The needs for self-actualization and self-fulfillment are never completely satisfied. One can always reach one step higher. Figure 14.2 lists several examples of each need level.

Maslow believed that at any given time only one need level serves as a person's primary motivation. He also believed that people start with the lower-order needs and move up the need hierarchy one level at a time as the lower-order needs become satisfied. Thus, until the physical needs have been

FIGURE 14.2

Examples of Needs

Physical Needs

1. Food and water
2. Sleep
3. Health
4. Body needs
5. Exercise and rest

Safety Needs

1. Security and safety
2. Protection
3. Comfort and peace
4. No threats or danger
5. Orderly and neat surroundings
6. Assurance of long-term economic well-being

Social Needs

1. Acceptance
2. Feeling of belonging
3. Membership in groups
4. Love and affection
5. Group participation

Esteem (or Ego) Needs

1. Recognition and prestige
2. Confidence and leadership
3. Competence and success
4. Strength and intelligence

Self-Actualization Needs

1. Self-fulfillment of potential
2. Doing things for the challenge of accomplishment
3. Intellectual curiosity
4. Creativity and aesthetic appreciation
5. Acceptance of reality

substantially satisfied, they tend to dominate all other needs. Once the physical needs have been satisfied, the safety needs become dominant in the need structure. Different needs emerge as each of the respective need levels is satisfied.

In our society, the physical and safety needs are more easily and therefore more generally satisfied than the other levels of needs. In fact, Maslow estimated the percentage of persons satisfying the various need levels as follows: physical, 85 percent; safety, 70 percent; social, 50 percent; ego, 40 percent; and self-actualization, 10 percent. Many of the tangible rewards (pay and fringe benefits) given by today's organizations are used primarily to satisfy physical and safety needs.

Although the needs of the majority of people are arranged in the sequence shown in Figure 14.1, differences can occur, depending on an individual's learning experiences, culture, and social upbringing.

It is important to note that the strength of an individual's needs may shift back and forth under different situations. For instance, an individual's behavior might be dominated by the physical and safety needs in bad economic times and by the higher-order needs in good economic times.

It is not necessary to completely satisfy one need before another need emerges. Meeting some needs partially can result in an opportunity for another need to present itself. For instance, it is possible to be motivated by the social and esteem needs at the same time.

Finally, different individuals can use different methods to satisfy a particular need. Two individuals may have to satisfy the same social need, but the ways in which each of them chooses to satisfy that need may vary considerably.

As far as the motivation process is concerned, the thrust of the need hierarchy theory is that a satisfied need is not a motivator. Consider the basic physical need for oxygen. Only when individuals are deprived of oxygen can it have a motivating effect on their behaviors.

Many of today's organizations are applying the logic of the need hierarchy. For instance, compensation systems are generally designed to satisfy lower-order needs—physical and safety needs. On the other hand, interesting work and opportunities for advancement are designed to appeal to higher-order needs. Thus, the job of the supervisor is to determine the needs of employees and then provide the means by which those needs can be satisfied.

Achievement-Power-Affiliation Theory

Closely related to Maslow's theory is the **achievement-power-affiliation theory,** developed primarily by David McClelland. This theory holds that all people have three needs: (1) a need for achievement, (2) a need for power, and (3) a need for affiliation.

The need for achievement is a need to do something better or more efficiently than it has been done before. The need for power is basically a need to influence people. The need for affiliation is a need to be liked—to establish or maintain friendly relations with others.

McClelland maintains that most people have a degree of each of these needs but that the level of intensity varies. For example, a person may be high in the need for achievement, moderate in the need for power, and low in the need for affiliation. This person's motivation to work will vary greatly from that of a person who has a high need for power and low needs for achievement and affiliation. According to the achievement-power-affiliation theory, it is the responsibility of supervisors to recognize the differences in the dominant needs of both themselves and their employees and to effectively integrate these differences. For example, an employee with a high need for affiliation would probably respond positively to demonstrations of warmth and support by the supervisor. An employee with a high need for achievement would probably respond positively to increased responsibility. Through self-analysis, supervisors can gain insight into how they tend to respond to employees. They may then want to alter their response to employees so that they can best fit the employee's needs.

Figure 14.3 shows the responses of employees to certain characteristics present in the organization related to the needs for achievement, power, and affiliation.

FIGURE 14.3
Need Responses to
Organization
Characteristics

Characteristic Present in Organization	Need for Achievement	Need for Power	Need for Affiliation
Warmth	No effect	No effect	Aroused
Support	Aroused	No effect	Aroused
Conflict	Aroused	Aroused	Reduced
Reward	Aroused	No effect	Aroused
Responsibility	Aroused	Aroused	No effect

Source: From *Management* by William F. Glueck. Copyright © 1977 by The Dryden Press. Reprinted by permission of CBS College Publishing.

Motivation-Maintenance Theory

4   LEARNING OBJECTIVES

Frederick Herzberg has developed a theory of work motivation that has gained wide acceptance in management and supervisory circles. His theory is referred to by several names: motivation-maintenance theory, dual-factor theory, and motivator-hygiene theory.

Herzberg's theory deals primarily with motivation through job design. The theory is based on the belief that the factors that demotivate or turn off employees are different from the factors that motivate or turn on employees. Herzberg maintains that the factors that tend to demotivate employees are usually associated with the work environment. These factors include such things as job status, interpersonal relations with supervisors and peers, the style of supervision that the person receives, company policy and administration, job security, working conditions, pay, and aspects of personal life that are affected by the work situation. Herzberg refers to these factors as **hygiene** or **maintenance factors.** He chose these terms because he perceived these factors as being *preventive* in nature. In other words, he believed that these factors would not produce motivation but could prevent motivation from occurring. Thus, proper attention to hygiene factors is a necessary but not sufficient condition for motivation. For example, Herzberg contends that pay will not motivate a person (at least for more than a short period of time) but that insufficient pay can certainly demotivate a person.

According to Herzberg, the factors that motivate people are factors related to the work itself as opposed to the work environment. These factors, which he calls *motivators*, include achievement, recognition, responsibility, advancement, and the challenges of the job. Herzberg maintains that true motivation occurs only when both the motivator factors and the hygiene factors are present. At best, proper attention to the hygiene factors will keep an individual from being dissatisfied but will not motivate the individual. Figure 14.4 lists some examples of hygiene and motivator factors.

As a solution to motivation problems, Herzberg developed an approach called **job enrichment.** Unlike job enlargement or job rotation, job enrichment involves upgrading the job by adding motivational factors such as increased responsibilities. (**Job enlargement** merely involves giving an employee more of a similar type of operation to perform. **Job rotation** is the practice of periodically rotating job assignments.) Designing jobs that provide for meaningful

FIGURE 14.4	Hygiene Factors (relate to the environment)	Motivator Factors (relate to the job itself)
Hygiene and Motivator Factors	Policies and administration	Achievement
	Style of supervision	Recognition
	Working conditions	Challenging work
	Interpersonal relations	Increased responsibility
	Factors that affect employee's personal life	Advancement
	Money, status, security	Personal growth

work, achievement, recognition, responsibility, advancement, and growth is the key to job enrichment. Herzberg's major contribution has been his emphasis on the relationship between the job content and the employee's feelings.

Preference-Expectancy Theory

5 LEARNING OBJECTIVES

The **preference-expectancy theory** is based on the belief that people attempt to increase pleasure and decrease displeasure. According to this theory, which Victor Vroom pioneered, people are motivated to work if (1) they believe that their efforts will be rewarded and (2) they value the rewards that are being offered.

The belief that efforts will be rewarded can be broken down into two components: (a) the expectancy that increased effort will lead to increased performance, and (b) the expectancy that increased performance will lead to increased rewards. These expectancies are developed largely from an individual's past experiences. For example, an employee may feel that working harder does not result in higher performance. Or an employee may believe that working harder does result in higher performance but that higher performance is not directly related to rewards. It should be pointed out that employee expectations are based on *perceptions*. These perceptions may or may not reflect reality—but whether or not they do, they represent reality to the employee.

The preference element of the preference-expectancy theory is concerned with the value that the employee places on the rewards that the organization offers. Historically, organizations have assumed that employees will value whatever rewards are provided. Even if this were true, certainly some rewards are less or more valued than others. In fact, certain rewards, such as a promotion that involves a transfer to another city, may be viewed negatively by some people. Figure 14.5 illustrates the preference-expectancy theory.

Supervisors can affect each of the components of the preference-expectancy theory. They can positively influence the expectancy that increased effort will lead to increased performance by providing proper selection and training and clear direction to employees. They can also affect the expectancy that increased performance will lead to rewards by linking rewards to performance. Of course, other factors such as the presence of a union can also affect how rewards are distributed. The employee's preference component, with regard to the rewards being offered, is often taken for granted by the supervisor. Supervisors should solicit feedback from their employees concerning the types

---

FIGURE 14.5

Preference-Expectancy Theory of Motivation

$$\text{Motivation} = \left(\begin{array}{l}\text{Expectancy that increased}\\\text{effort will lead to rewards}\end{array}\right) \times \left(\begin{array}{l}\text{Preference of the}\\\text{individual for the rewards}\end{array}\right)$$

$$= \left[\left(\begin{array}{l}\text{Expectancy that}\\\text{increased effort will}\\\text{lead to increased}\\\text{performance}\end{array}\right) \times \left(\begin{array}{l}\text{Expectancy that}\\\text{increased performance}\\\text{will lead to rewards}\end{array}\right)\right] \times \left(\begin{array}{l}\text{Preference of}\\\text{the individual}\\\text{for the rewards}\end{array}\right)$$

---

of rewards they want. Since an organization is going to invest a certain amount of money in rewards (salary, fringe benefits, and so on), it should attempt to get the maximum return from this investment.

The development of the preference-expectancy theory is still in its infancy, and many questions remain to be answered. Some critics attack the theory on the grounds that it is overly rational, that humans often don't act as rationally as the theory assumes they act. Others say that the theory ignores impulsive and expressive behavior. Despite these criticisms, the preference-expectancy theory is currently one of the most popular theories of motivation.

Reinforcement Theory

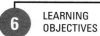

Reinforcement theory is closely related to the preference-expectancy theory. The general idea behind this theory is that reinforced behavior is more likely to be repeated than behavior that is not reinforced. For instance, if employees are given a pay increase when their performance is high, then the employees are likely to continue to strive for high performance in hopes of getting another pay raise. Reinforcement theory assumes that the consequences of behavior determine an individual's level of motivation. Thus, an individual's motives are considered to be relatively minor in this approach.

Basically, four types of reinforcement exist: positive reinforcement, avoidance, extinction, and punishment. **Positive reinforcement** involves providing a positive consequence as a result of desired behavior. **Avoidance,** also called *negative reinforcement*, involves giving a person the opportunity to avoid a negative consequence by exhibiting a desired behavior. Both positive reinforcement and avoidance can be used to increase the frequency of desired behavior. **Extinction** involves providing no positive consequences or removing previously provided positive consequences as a result of undesirable behavior. In other words, behavior that no longer pays is less likely to be repeated. **Punishment** involves providing a negative consequence as a result of undesired behavior. Both extinction and punishment can be used to decrease the frequency of undesired behavior.

The current emphasis on the use of reinforcement theory in supervisory practices is concerned with positive reinforcement. Examples include increased pay for increased performance and praise and recognition when an employee does a good job.

WHAT CAN THE SUPERVISOR DO?

In the light of the previously discussed motivation theories, a supervisor can do several things to affect employee motivation. Some of the most useful of these are to:

7   LEARNING
OBJECTIVES

Make the work interesting.
Relate rewards to performance.
Provide valued rewards.
Treat employees as individuals.
Encourage participation and cooperation.
Provide accurate and timely feedback.

Make the Work Interesting

Supervisors should carefully examine each job under their control. They should constantly ask, "Can this job be enriched to make it more challenging?" There is a limit to the extent that people can be expected to perform satisfactorily on very routine tasks. Doing the same simple task over and over again every minute of the workday can quickly lead to employee apathy and boredom.

The tendency of many supervisors is to say, "This job just can't be enriched." More often than not, however, jobs can be enriched without a total departmental reorganization. Take the example of a secretary. How often is a secretary treated as being incapable of doing anything other than typing and maybe a little filing? The usual result is that the secretary becomes bored and demotivated. With a little planning and thought, however, a secretary's job can

More often than not, jobs can be enriched without a total departmental reorganization.
Ron Chapple/FPG International

easily be enriched. He or she can be assigned such responsibilities as responding to certain correspondence, opening and sorting the mail, and making appointments. The key is to make the job challenging and interesting.

Relate Rewards to Performance

There are many reasons why supervisors are reluctant to relate rewards directly to performance. First and foremost, giving everyone an equal pay raise is much easier. Usually this approach requires very little justification and involves less hassle than relating rewards to performance. Second, union contracts generally require that everyone doing the same job be paid the same wage. Third, organizational policy may dictate that pay raises conform to guidelines that are unrelated to performance. Even in such instances, however, there are usually rewards other than pay that can be related to performance. These might include the assignment of preferred tasks or some type of formal recognition. The costs of failing to relate rewards to performance are great. The low performers are not motivated to do more, and the high performers are motivated to do less. Every supervisor should strive to relate rewards directly to performance.

Provide Valued Rewards

Most supervisors never stop to give any thought to what types of rewards are most valued by employees. Like all managers, supervisors usually tend to think of pay as the only reward at their disposal. Most supervisors truly believe that they have nothing to say about what rewards are offered. The common belief is that such decisions are made by upper management. However, employees may highly value many types of rewards other than pay. For instance, they may highly value being assigned to work on a certain project or being assigned a new piece of equipment. Supervisors should know what rewards are at their disposal and what rewards the employees value.

Treat Employees as Individuals

As discussed earlier in the chapter, different people have different needs. And different people want different things from their jobs. Treating everyone the same ignores these differences. In today's highly impersonal world, there is an increasing tendency to treat employees as if they were computer numbers. However, most people want to receive special attention and be treated as individuals. This raises their self-esteem and makes them feel that they are a part of the organization. It also results in more frequent and candid interaction between supervisors and employees. In such a climate, employees naturally feel more like talking over their ideas with the supervisor.

Encourage Participation and Cooperation

People like to feel that they are a part of their surroundings and that they contribute to their surroundings. People also tend to be committed to decisions in which they have participated. The motivation benefits of true employee participation are undoubtedly high. Despite the potential benefits of participation, however, many supervisors do little to encourage it. Most supervisors do not intentionally discourage participation. They simply fail to *encourage* it. Take, for instance, the familiar suggestion box. As soon as employees discover that their suggestions are not taken seriously, it becomes a collection point for jokes! The employee who makes several worthwhile suggestions to no avail soon quits making suggestions. The point is that active participation does not just happen, it requires commitment from the supervisor. Employees must feel that their participation is genuinely valued.

Closely related to the need to encourage participation is the need to sufficiently explain the reasons for certain actions. Employees are more motivated to do something when they understand why it is being done.

Provide Accurate and Timely Feedback

No one likes to be in the dark about his or her performance. In fact, a negative performance review may be better than no review. A person who receives such a review will at least know what must be done to improve. Lack of feedback usually produces frustration in employees and this frustration often has a negative impact on employee performance. Accurate and timely feedback involves more than just providing regularly scheduled performance appraisals (which were discussed in depth in Chapter 11). It also involves providing informal feedback on a regular basis.

It is easy for supervisors to fall into the trap of taking the performance of employees for granted. No one likes his or her work to be taken for granted. A simple verbal or written statement of appreciation can go a long way. A potential danger, however, is to become overly complimentary so that praise loses its impact.

Improperly used criticism can negatively affect motivation. Normally, criticisms should be communicated in private. There is often a strong urge to lash out verbally at a subordinate who does something wrong, but doing this very quickly turns the employee off. Feedback should include both the positive and negative happenings. All too often, supervisors focus only on the negative happenings. The goal is for the employee to know at all times exactly where he or she stands.

Supervision Illustration 14–2 shows the approach for motivating employees used at Lucent Technologies.

JOB SATISFACTION

Closely related to motivation is job satisfaction. In fact, many people view motivated employees as synonymous with satisfied employees. There are, however, important differences between motivated employees and satisfied employees.

Job satisfaction refers to an individual's general attitude toward the job. It can be affected by such factors as working conditions, pay and benefits, the individual's attitudes toward the organization and supervision and toward the work itself, and the individual's health and age. Therefore, job satisfaction is a general attitude that results from specific attitudes and factors. It is an individual's mind-set with regard to the job. That mind-set may be positive or negative, depending on the person's mind-set with regard to the major components of job satisfaction. Job satisfaction is not synonymous with organizational morale. Organizational morale refers to the individual's feeling of being accepted by, and belonging to, a group of employees through common goals, confidence in their

---

SUPERVISION ILLUSTRATION 14-2

MOTIVATION THROUGH INCENTIVES AT LUCENT TECHNOLOGIES

Joseph Freund took his wife, daughter, and mother-in-law on a two-week vacation to Florida. However, he didn't pay for the whole trip. His employer, Lucent Technologies, picked up the tab for the airfare and rental car. The reason that Lucent paid for those expenses was that Freund was part of a team that devised a way to reduce the costs associated with product-reliability testing. The idea was so valuable that the company gave Freund a percentage of the total cost savings in "points," which he then exchanged for travel vouchers. Under the terms of Lucent's employee incentive program, employees can redeem points for everything from pen-and-pencil sets to golf clubs to home appliances. Employees receive points for being recognized by a peer or a manager, or for being a top achiever in any given quarter. Employees also receive points for generating ideas on how to improve the business, with amounts ranging from 50 to 250,000 points, depending on the scope of the idea or its value to the business. The ideas must be implemented for the employee to receive points. The points accumulate in an account until the employee decides to redeem them for awards chosen from a catalog. The program is funded by a percentage of the cost savings and revenue generated by the employees' ideas.

Fifty-four percent of Lucent's workforce participated in the incentive program during its first year, and the level of participation continues to grow. During that first year, employees submitted 6,000 ideas, of which 2,100 were approved for implementation, including ideas for reducing recycling scrap, improving plant safety, reducing the costs of overnight mail, and improving the efficiency of the E-mail system.

Source: Adapted from Shari Caudron, "Spreading Out the Carrots," *Industry Week,* May 19, 1997, pp. 20–24. For more information on Lucent Technologies, visit its Web site at:
www.lucent.com

desirability, and progress toward them. Morale is related to group attitudes, while job satisfaction is more of an individual attitude.

As mentioned earlier, a wide range of both internal and external factors affect an individual's level of satisfaction. The top portion of Figure 14.6 summarizes the major factors that determine an individual's level of satisfaction (or dissatisfaction). The upper portion of the figure shows the organization behaviors generally associated with satisfaction and dissatisfaction. Individual satisfaction leads to organization commitment; individual dissatisfaction results in behaviors detrimental to the organization (turnover, absenteeism, tardiness, accidents, etc.). Employees who like their job design, supervision, and other job-related factors will probably be very loyal and devoted. But employees who strongly dislike their job design or any of the other job-related factors will probably be disgruntled and will often exhibit their disgruntlement by being late or absent or by taking other actions that disrupt the organization.

It must be remembered that satisfaction and motivation are not synonymous. Motivation is a drive to perform, while satisfaction reflects the individual's happiness with his situation. The factors that determine whether an individual is satisfied with the job differ from those that determine whether an individual is motivated. *Satisfaction* is largely determined by the comfort offered by the environment and the situation. *Motivation,* on the other hand, is largely determined by the value of rewards and by their relationship to

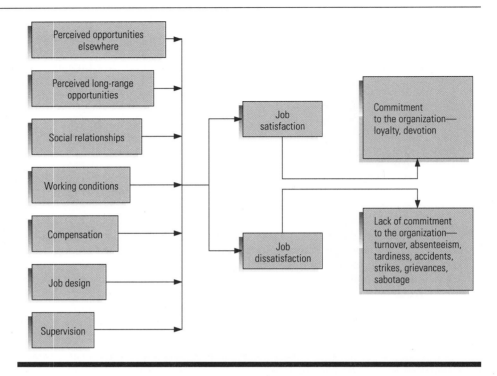

FIGURE 14.6
Determinants of Satisfaction and Dissatisfaction

performance. The result of motivation is increased effort, which in turn increases performance if the individual has the necessary ability and if the effort is properly directed. The result of satisfaction is increased commitment to the organization, which may or may not result in increased performance. This increased commitment will, however, normally result in a decrease in such problems as absenteeism, tardiness, turnover, and strikes.

SOLUTION TO THE SUPERVISION DILEMMA

Jane has learned that the motivation sequence is a continuous process that never ends. As one need is met, other needs arise that call for new actions by the supervisor. Several theories of motivation that should help Jane better understand her employees are discussed in this chapter. The need hierarchy theory (pp. 273–76) should be of particular interest to Jane in understanding her problem. The motivation-maintenance theory (pp. 277–78) should give her guidance in solving the problem. The account of what has been done for her employees (pay raises and the refurbishing of her department's facilities) indicates that the company has dealt with some of the maintenance factors of their jobs. However, Jane must remember that maintenance factors demotivate employees but don't motivate them. She must concentrate on the factors that motivate her employees. The suggestions offered on what a supervisor can do to affect employee motivation (pp. 280–82) should also be helpful to Jane.

SUMMARY

This chapter introduces the motivation process. It also presents and clarifies the relationships among the current theories of motivation. Several specific suggestions are presented to help the supervisor elicit high levels of motivation.

1. *Define motivation.* Motivation means getting people to exert a high degree of effort on their job.

2. *Define the traditional theory of motivation.* The traditional theory of motivation is based on the assumption that money is the primary motivator of people: If the monetary rewards are great enough, employees will work harder and produce more.

3. *Explain the hierarchy of needs.* The five levels of needs, in ascending order, are physical, safety, social, esteem, and self-actualization needs. The needs include food and water, sleep, exercise, clothing, and shelter. The physical safety needs are concerned with protection against danger, threat, or deprivation. Social needs are the need for love, affection, and belonging. The esteem needs include the need for both self-esteem and the esteem of others. The self-actualization needs are the needs of people to reach their full potential in applying their abilities and interests to functioning in their environment.

4. *Discuss the motivation-maintenance theory of motivation.* This theory postulates that all work-related factors can be grouped into two categories. The maintenance factors will not produce motivation but can prevent it. Factors in the other category, motivators, encourage motivation.

5. *Discuss the preference-expectancy theory of motivation.* This theory holds that motivation is based on a combination of the individual's expectancy that increased effort leads to increased performance, which leads to rewards, and of the degree of the individual's preference for the rewards being offered.

6. *Explain reinforcement theory.* This approach to motivation is based on the idea that behavior that appears to lead to a positive consequence tends to be repeated, while behavior that appears to lead to a negative consequence tends not to be repeated.

7. *State several things that the supervisor can do to affect employee motivation.* Some of the most useful things that a supervisor can do to affect employee motivation are to make the work interesting, relate rewards to performance, provide valued rewards, treat employees as individuals, encourage participation and cooperation, and provide accurate and timely feedback.

REVIEW QUESTIONS

1. What is motivation?
2. Are all employees motivated by the same things? Why or why not?
3. Describe the following theories of motivation:
   a. Traditional.
   b. Need hierarchy.
   c. Achievement-power-affiliation.
   d. Motivation-maintenance.
   e. Preference-expectancy.
   f. Reinforcement.
4. Briefly discuss several specific actions that supervisors can take to improve employee motivation.
5. What is job satisfaction?
6. What are the differences between motivation and job satisfaction? What results are obtained from motivated employees? What results are obtained from satisfied employees?

SKILL-BUILDING QUESTIONS

1. "In the final analysis, money and benefits are all that employees are concerned about." Discuss your views on this statement.

2. Many supervisors believe that they can have little effect on employee motivation because so many rewards are of a fixed nature. For example, a union contract might set pay raises. How would you respond to these supervisors?

3. A seasoned supervisor recently made the following statement: "A satisfied employee is one that is not being pushed hard enough." Do you agree? Why or why not?

4. The LMN Company has decided to throw a tremendous party for all of its employees to show its appreciation for the highly successful year that has just concluded. It plans to hold the party at a fancy place with live entertainment and expensive food. The affair will be quite a bash. In fact, it is expected to cost over $100 per employee. What is your reaction to this idea?

ADDITIONAL READINGS

Bielous, Gary A. "Why We Should Become a 'Can-Do' Supervisor," *Supervision*, December 1995.

Capozzoli, Thomas K. "Creating a Motivating Environment for Employees," *Supervision*, April 1997.

Dreyer, R. S. "Make Them Want to Be Motivated," *Supervision*, November 1996.

Gransbury, Pat. "Motivation of the Older Worker," *Supervision*, February 1995.

Pollock, Ted. "Six Keys to Improved Employee Motivation," *Supervision*, July 1995.

Ramsey, Robert D. "Are Ethics Obsolete in the 90s," *Supervision*, February 1996.

SKILL-BUILDING APPLICATIONS

Incident 14–1

No Extra Effort

You are the supervisor of nurses in the pediatrics section of a 700-bed hospital in a metropolitan area. You have been in your job for six months, having moved from a similar position in a much smaller rural hospital.

You: I just can't seem to get my people to perform. They're all extremely competent, but they don't seem to be willing to put forth any extra effort. Take last Saturday evening. I thought Sue was going to have a fit when I asked her to help tidy up the nurses' station. She was quick to explain that that was the janitor's job.

Friend: Exactly what are the duties and responsibilities of your nurses?

You: They don't really have much responsibility. That always seems to fall on me. Their duties don't vary much from those of the average nurse—make sure medicines are taken on schedule, perform periodic checks on patients, and provide general assistance to doctors and patients. Of course, pediatrics does require a certain disposition to deal with children.

Friend: How do you evaluate their performance?

You: Mainly based on complaints and my general feeling about how they are doing. It's hard to evaluate the quality of their work since most of it is fairly routine. However, if I receive several complaints on a nurse, I can be pretty sure that the nurse is not doing the job.

Friend: Do you receive complaints very often?

You: That's just the problem. Recently, complaints have risen noticeably. The number of complaints is much higher here than at my former hospital. The worst part is that the nurses don't seem too concerned about it.

Friend: What financial rewards does the hospital offer?

You: They're all well paid—when I think that I started 30 years ago at $25 per week! Base pay is determined mainly on the basis of longevity. They also get paid vacations, insurance plans, and all the other usual goodies. I don't know of any complaints about compensation.

Friend: How about the promotion possibilities?

You: Well, all I know is that I was brought in from the outside. I really don't think many of the nurses aspire for promotions.

Friend: Have you considered firing any of them?

You: Haven't you read about the nationwide shortage of nurses? Who would I replace them with? I figure that half a nurse is better than no nurse.

Questions

1. Reconsider the situation. Why do you think the nurses are not motivated? List possible answers.

2. What could you do to improve the situation?

Incident 14–2

The Secure Employee

Archie Banks is 53 years old and has been with Allgo Products for 27 years. For the last seven years, he has been a top-paid machine operator. Archie is quite active in community affairs, and he takes an interest in most employee activities. He is very friendly and well liked by all the employees, especially the younger ones, who often come to him for advice. He is extremely helpful to these younger employees and never hesitates to help them when called upon. When talking with the younger employees, Archie never talks negatively about the company.

Archie's one shortcoming, as Tom Williams, his supervisor, sees it, is his tendency to spend too much time talking with other employees. This causes Archie's work to suffer, and perhaps more important, it hinders the output of others. Whenever Tom confronts Archie with the problem, Archie improves for a day or two and then he slips back into his old habit.

Tom considered trying to have Archie transferred to an area where he would have less opportunity to interrupt the work of other employees. However, Tom concluded that he needed Archie's experience, especially since he had no available replacement for Archie's job.

Archie is secure in his personal life. He owns a nice house and lives well. His wife is a librarian, and their two children are grown and married. Although he has never specifically said so, Archie feels that he is as high as he'll ever go in the company. This doesn't seem to bother him since he likes his present job and feels comfortable in it.

Questions

1. What would you do to motivate Archie if you were Tom Williams?
2. Suppose Archie liked his job so much that he didn't want to be promoted even if offered a higher job. What would you do to motivate Archie in this situation?

Exercise 14–1

Money as a Motivator

Your instructor will divide you into groups of three or four. Your group will be assigned one of the two following statements:

1. Money is the primary motivator of people.
2. Money is not the primary motivator of people.

Your assignment is to prepare for a debate with another group on the validity of the statement that your group has been assigned. You will be debating a group that has the opposing viewpoint.

At the end of the debate, prepare a brief statement summarizing the key points made by your opposing group.

Exercise 14–2

Motivation-Maintenance Theory

This exercise is designed to illustrate the motivation-maintenance theory of motivation.

1. Think of an instance in which you found a job highly motivating. The instance could have taken place yesterday or several years ago. Write a two- or three-sentence description of the situation. After you have completed the description, list the reasons that this situation had a motivational effect on you.
2. Repeat the same procedure, but this time describe an instance which you found highly *demotivating*.
3. Hand in the unsigned papers.
4. To determine if the experiences described support or refute the motivation-maintenance theory, have someone read each description aloud and decide whether the response fits into the maintenance or motivator categories.

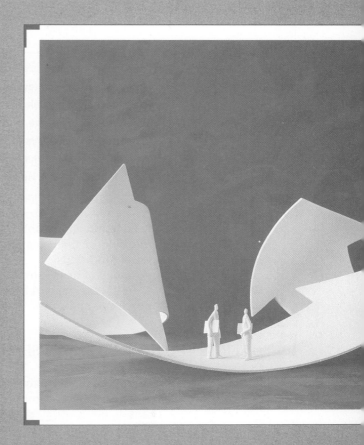

LEARNING OBJECTIVES

After studying this chapter, you should be able to:

1. Define leader.
2. Describe three basic styles of leadership.
3. Define supportive and directive leaders.
4. Discuss the Managerial Grid®.
5. Explain the contingency approach to leadership.
6. Describe Theory X and Theory Y.

SUPERVISION
DILEMMA

John Lewis has been a supervisor for over a year now, yet he still feels unsure of his ability to lead his employees. Oh, sure, he can order them around, but do they really follow his leadership? John can't help noticing Marlin O'Neal's group. Marlin has been a supervisor for over five years, and his group seems to operate like a well-oiled machine. Marlin's employees seem to trust him completely and never hesitate to follow his lead. On the other hand, John feels that he has to "sell his soul" to get his employees to follow his lead. He can't help wondering if Marlin knows something he doesn't.

Leadership is probably researched and discussed more than any other topic in the field of management. New suggestions, methods, and tips for improving leadership skills are offered each year. Everyone seems to acknowledge the importance of leadership to supervisory and organizational success. This chapter reviews the research on leadership and offers perspectives on leadership processes and styles.

POWER, AUTHORITY, AND LEADERSHIP

Before the undertaking of a study of leadership, a clear understanding must be developed of the relationships between power, authority, and leadership. **Power** is the ability to get others to respond favorably to instructions and orders. Put another way, power is a measure of a person's potential to get others to do what he or she wants them to do, as well as to avoid being forced by others to do what he or she does not want to do. Chapter 4 summarized several sources of power in organizations. The use of or desire for power is often viewed negatively in our society because power is often linked to the concepts of punishment, dominance, and control. However, power can have both positive and negative results. Positive power results when the exchange is voluntary and both parties feel good about the exchange. Negative power results when the individual is forced to change. Power in organizations can be exercised upward, downward, or horizontally. It does not necessarily follow the organizational hierarchy from top to bottom.

Authority, which is the right to issue directives and expend resources, is related to power but is narrower in scope. Basically, the amount of authority a supervisor has depends on the amount of coercive, reward, and legitimate power the supervisor can exert. Authority is a function of position in the organizational hierarchy, flowing from the top to the bottom of the organization. An individual can have power—expert or referent—without having formal authority. Furthermore, a supervisor's authority can be diminished by reducing the coercive and reward power in the position.

LEARNING
OBJECTIVES

Leadership is the ability to influence people to willingly follow one's guidance or adhere to one's decisions. Obtaining followers and influencing them in setting and achieving objectives makes a **leader.** Leaders use power in influencing group behavior. For instance, political leaders often use referent power. Informal leaders in organizations generally combine referent power and expert power. Some supervisors rely only on authority while others use different combinations of power.

Supervisors represent formal leaders in the sense that they are formally appointed by the organization. Other types of leaders may emerge who are not formally appointed by the organization.
Richard Pasley/Stock Boston

FORMAL VERSUS INFORMAL LEADERS

Supervisors represent formal leaders in the sense that they are formally appointed by the organization. Other types of leaders may emerge who are not formally appointed by the organization. These leaders, known as informal leaders, are chosen by the group itself. It is not unusual for a work group to have an informal leader in addition to the formally appointed leader. Informal leaders generally emerge because they are viewed by the group as filling its needs. A group's informal leader may change as the group's needs change. The following simple example illustrates this point. Suppose a group of people are shipwrecked on a desolate island. The group's first need would probably be to find food, water, and shelter, so the group would select as its leader the person viewed by the group as the one who could best help it acquire these essentials. After this had been done, other needs would emerge. The need to escape from the island would probably emerge rather quickly. The person originally selected as the leader may not be the person perceived by the group as the most capable in achieving the newly emerging needs. In that case, the group might select a new leader. Furthermore, the group might continue to change its leaders depending on the changes in its needs.

If a group has an informal leader in addition to the supervisor, this does not necessarily indicate that the supervisor is not a good leader. The informal leader may be fulfilling group needs that shouldn't be met by the supervisor. For example, an informal leader may be chosen because of a knack for telling jokes and keeping things on the light side. On the other hand, informal leaders may also cause detrimental behavior. For example, an informal leader might convince the group to restrict output. Successful supervisors do not try to over-power or eliminate informal leaders. Rather, they recognize them and learn to work through them to everyone's benefit.

LEADERSHIP CHARACTERISTICS

The first studies ever done in the area of leadership focused on looking at personal qualities and characteristics of successful leaders. These early researchers believed that leaders were different from ordinary people in terms of personality and physical characteristics. However, this approach has not produced any definitive findings. The end result has been that in over 50 years of study, no single set of personality traits or set of characteristics can be used to pinpoint a leader from a nonleader. At the same time, however, it is recognized that certain characteristics are desirable in most leadership situations.

Self-Confidence

Self-confidence stems from having precise knowledge and knowing how to use it. People with a high degree of self-confidence generally gain the confidence of those around them. Few employees want to follow a leader who appears not to know what he or she is doing.

Mental and Physical Endurance

Almost all leaders are subjected to situations that try their patience. The ability to control his or her temper and to be coolheaded can be very advantageous to the leader. Mental and emotional stress can be physically exhausting. Therefore, leaders should have enough physical endurance to withstand hardships and disappointments that might arise.

Enthusiasm

Enthusiasm is contagious! It is easy for group members to get excited about their work if the leader is excited about the work. On the other hand, no one wants to work for a dull and negative leader.

Sense of Responsibility

A leader should seek, not avoid, responsibility. Leaders who actively seek responsibility are admired by most followers. Followers like to feel that their leaders will stick up for them in difficult times. Leaders who attempt to avoid responsibility are quick to lose the admiration of their followers.

Empathy and Good Human Relations

Successful leaders are able to empathize with their followers. This means being able to see things from the followers' point of view. Because leadership involves working with others, good human relations skills are essential for leaders. A leader must be able to work with followers and understand their problems.

SUPERVISION ILLUSTRATION 15–1

CHARISMA AND LEADERSHIP

Whether it's Michael Jordan of the Chicago Bulls, Jack Welch of General Electric, Ted Turner of Turner Enterprises, the late Congresswoman Barbara Jordan, or President John Kennedy, the charismatic leader inspires followers in what he or she believes in, raises the followers' level of enthusiasm and productivity, and gets the team or the company to perform—if not to its best, at least better. These types of leaders are not always saints (for example, Adolph Hitler was charismatic) and can often lead their followers over the brink to disaster.

History has shown that charisma is an extremely important leadership trait in business.

The traits of charismatic leaders include the following: (1) simplify and exaggerate—leaders have a remarkable ability to distill complex ideas into simple messages; (2) romanticize risk—leaders relish risk (to many leaders, that may be what the game is all about); (3) defy the status quo—leaders are rebels who fight convention and their oddball image enhances their charisma; (4) step into another's shoes—leaders are able to see things from another person's perspective; and (5) spar and rule—leaders goad, challenge, poke, and prod (they test your courage and intellect). In the end, charisma can be learned and developed.

Source: Adapted from Patricia Sellers, "What Exactly Is Charisma?" *Fortune,* January 15, 1996, pp. 68–75. Reprinted by permission of Fortune © 1996 Time Inc. all rights reserved. For more information about *Fortune,* visit its Web site at:
www.fortune.com

It should be stressed that possession of the characteristics described above does not guarantee success as a leader. Many other factors may affect a leader's success. However, possession of these characteristics is certainly desirable and it usually increases the chances of success. Supervision Illustration 15–1 describes the traits of charismatic leaders.

BASIC STYLES OF LEADERSHIP

LEARNING OBJECTIVES

While there are numerous variations, there are three basic styles of leadership—autocratic, democratic, and laissez-faire. The main differences among these styles concern how decisions are made and who makes them. Generally, the autocratic leader makes all decisions for the group. The **autocratic leader** centralizes power and enjoys giving orders. Under this style of leadership, followers contribute little, if anything, to the decision-making process. The **democratic leader** wants the followers to share in making decisions. This type of leader guides and encourages the group to participate in making decisions. Even though the decision making is shared, the leader still has the final say. The **laissez-faire leader** pretty much allows the group members to do as they please. Such a leader allows the members of the group to make all the decisions. In effect, the laissez-faire leader only provides information to the group and does not direct or guide the group. A more detailed description of each of the three leadership styles is given in Figure 15.1.

While one of these styles (or a variation of one) tends to dominate, a supervisor can learn to develop various styles of leadership to fit different situations. This is discussed in detail later in this chapter.

FIGURE 15.1
Relationship between
Styles of Leadership and
Group Members

Autocratic Style
Leader
1. The leader is very conscious of his or her position.
2. The leader has little trust and faith in members of the group.
3. This leader believes that pay is a reward for work and the only reward that will motivate workers.
4. Orders are issued to be carried out, with no questions allowed and no explanations given.

Group members
1. No responsibility is assumed for performance, with people merely doing what they are told.
2. Production is good when the leader is present, but poor in the leader's absence.

Democratic Style
Leader
1. Decision making is shared between the leader and the group.
2. When the leader is required or forced to make a decision, his or her reasoning is explained to the group.
3. Criticism and praise are given objectively.

Group members
1. New ideas and change are welcomed.
2. A feeling of responsibility is developed within the group.
3. Quality of work and productivity are generally high.
4. The group generally feels successful.

Laissez-Faire Style
Leader
1. The leader has no confidence in his or her leadership ability.
2. This leader does not set goals for the group.

Group members
1. Decisions are made by whoever in the group is willing to make them.
2. Generally, productivity is low and work is sloppy.
3. Individuals have little interest in their work.
4. Morale and teamwork are generally low.

Source: Adapted from Leland B. Bradford and Ronald Lippitt, "Building a Democratic Work Group, *Personnel,* November 1945 (New York: American Management Association, Inc., 1945), pp. 143–45.

Supportive or Directive?

LEARNING OBJECTIVES 3

In addition to the three basic styles of leadership discussed above, leaders are often categorized as being supportive or directive. **Supportive leaders** are genuinely interested in the well-being of group members. Such a leader is sensitive to the employees as human beings. This leader wants to build morale, avoid conflict, and help the employees gain personal satisfaction. The supportive leader is usually very concerned about maintaining a good personal relationship with the employees.

Directive leaders focus primarily on successfully performing the work. Such a leader spends considerable time directing the employees in solving production problems. The emphasis is on getting the job done. The directive leader spends very little time providing emotional support and reassurance for the employees. A directive leader is not necessarily harsh or rude, but one who simply gives priority to work accomplishment over human feelings.

HOW DO THE DIFFERENT STYLES OF LEADERSHIP RELATE?

Directive leaders generally employ an autocratic style of leadership. Supportive leaders generally employ a more democratic style of leadership. Most leaders are not all directive or all supportive. A large middle ground is occupied by some mix of these two extremes. For example, a supervisor may actually be 70 percent supportive and 30 percent directive.

Robert Tannenbaum and Warren Schmidt have argued that there is a continuum of leadership behaviors that may be employed, depending on the particular situation. Figure 15.2 presents this continuum. The behaviors on the left are associated with the autocratic or directive leader. Those on the right are generally associated with the democratic or supportive leader. Tannenbaum and Schmidt suggest that three important forces must be considered in determining what leadership style is most effective: forces in the leader, in the subordinate, and in the situation. Figure 15.3 describes each of these forces in detail. The key to successful leadership, according to Tannenbaum and Schmidt, is for the supervisor to be keenly aware of these forces and to behave appropriately in light of them.

George Terry developed the leadership continuum shown in Figure 15.4. The continuum attempts to relate the different categories of leadership style, from very democratic on the left to very autocratic on the right. *Democratic, follower-oriented,* and *permissive* are terms commonly used to describe the supportive leader. *Autocratic, task-oriented,* and *restrictive* are terms commonly used to describe the directive leader. In general, the less structured the work, the more democratic is the required style of leadership. For example, a supervisor whose employees are engaged in very repetitive work will probably

FIGURE 15.2 Continuum of Leadership Behavior

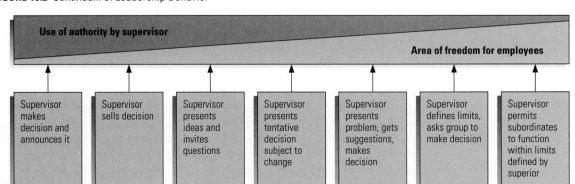

FIGURE 15.3 Forces in the Leadership Situation

Forces in the Leader	Forces in the Employees	Forces in the Situation
1. Value system How does the leader feel about delegating? Degree of confidence in subordinates. 2. Personal leadership inclinations. Autocratic versus democratic. 3. Feelings of security in uncertain situations.	1. Need for independence. Some people need and want direction while others do not. 2. Readiness to assume responsibility. Different people need different degrees of responsibility. 3. Tolerance for ambiguity. Specific versus general directions 4. Interest in and perceived importance of the problem. People generally have more interest in and work harder on important problems. 5. Degree of understanding and identification with organizational goals. A supervisor is more likely to delegate authority to an individual who seems to have a positive attitude toward the organization. 6. Degree of expectation in decision making. People who have worked under supportive leaders tend to resent directive leadership.	1. Type of organization. Centralized versus decentralized. 2. Work group effectiveness. How effectively does the group work together? 3. The problem itself. Does the work group have the knowledge and experience to handle the problem? 4. Time pressure. It is difficult to delegate to subordinates in crisis situations. 5. Demands from upper levels of managements. 6. Demands from government, unions, and society in general.

get the best results with a mostly autocratic style of leadership. The second series describes the characteristics of each style of leadership. The decision makers for the various leadership styles are listed in the last series.

The *Managerial Grid®*, developed by Robert Blake and Jane Mouton, uses a two-dimensional grid to identify and relate different styles of leadership. The vertical axis of the grid represents concern for people (supportive style). The horizontal axis represents concern for production (directive style). Figure 15.5 shows some of the more obvious styles that may be identified by means of the Managerial Grid. The Managerial Grid is intended to serve as a framework that enables supervisors to learn what their leadership style is and to develop a plan

4 LEARNING OBJECTIVES

FIGURE 15.4 Relating Different Leadership Styles

		Continuum of Leadership			
	Supportive ←		Leadership Style		→ Directive
	Very Democratic	**Democratic**	**Mixed**	**Autocratic**	**Very Autocratic**
Nature of work	Requires conceptualization of work; no procedure to follow	Nonroutine; modestly complex	Skilled machine work; difficult to write procedure for performing	Complex assembly work; somewhat routine	Repetitive; very simple; routine
Characteristics of leadership style	Group makes decision, shares data, analyzes data; leader is a thought stimulator and coordinator	Leader suggests what things to consider; group contributes its ideas; decision emerges as group and leader effort	Leader gives ideas to group; issues are discussed; modifications in what to do are made; decision is hammered out jointly; but leader has final word	Tentative decision is announced by leader who asks for and answers specific questions; decision may or may not be modified or changed by leader	Leader makes decision and announces it; rules are carefully followed
Who makes decision	Group	Leader and group	Leader	Leader	Leader

FIGURE 15.5

Blake and Mouton's Managerial Grid®

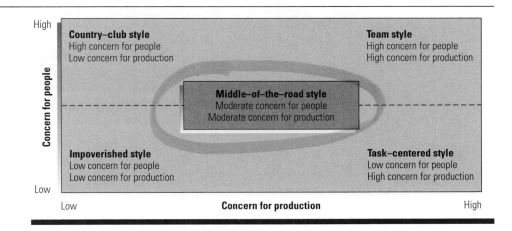

for moving toward a team-management style of leadership (upper right-hand corner of the grid). Blake and Mouton have developed a set of training experiences to help move supervisors more toward a team-leadership style. This approach has been criticized for assuming that a team-management style works best in all situations.

As one might expect, the majority of today's leaders do not fall at either extreme of the continuum or grid but rather somewhere in between.

When leadership styles are discussed, this question always surfaces: "Which style is best?" Research by Blake and Mouton concluded that the team style works best in all situations. Others believe that the most appropriate style of leadership usually depends on the situation.

PICKING THE BEST STYLE

Implying that a supervisor should be supportive rather than directive (or vice versa) does not offer much guidance for daily leadership situations. All of us can think of situations in which a task-oriented leader was very successful (for example, General George Patton). We can also think of situations in which a supportive leader was equally successful (General Dwight Eisenhower). Practice and research both have shown that *no one leadership style works best in all situations*.

Fiedler's Contingency Approach

5 LEARNING
       OBJECTIVES

Fred Fiedler has further refined the idea of a situational approach to leadership. He has attempted to identify the particular styles of leadership that are appropriate for particular situations. Fiedler identified three dimensions of the situation that he found to have an impact on the leader's effectiveness. These dimensions were (1) leader-member relations, (2) task structure, and (3) position power. *Leader-member relations* refer to the degree of the followers' trust and respect for the leader. *Task structure* is the extent to which the followers' tasks are structured—that is, routine and repetitive work versus unstructured work. *Position power* refers to the power and influence of the leader.

Using these three dimensions, Fiedler classified different situations as to the favorableness for the leader. For example, the most favorable situation for the leader is one in which there are good leader-member relations, a highly structured task, and a high degree of position power. The least favorable situation for the leader has just the opposite features. Figure 15.6 shows Fiedler's classification of situations. Using this scheme, Fiedler reported the following relationships:

1. When the situation is either highly favorable or highly unfavorable to the leader, directive leadership tends to result in the most effective group performance.
2. When the situation is moderately favorable to the leader, supportive leadership tends to result in the most effective group performance.

Thus, the overriding conclusion is that the most effective style of leadership depends on the situation! So it seems if the situation is highly favorable or unfavorable to the leader, adopt a directive style. If the situation is moderately favorable, adopt a supportive style. The key to success lies in matching one's leadership style to the situation.

FIGURE 15.6 Fiedler's Classification of Situations

Situation	1	2	3	4	5	6	7	8
Leader-member relations	Good	Good	Good	Good	Poor	Poor	Poor	Poor
Task structure	Structured	Structured	Unstructured	Unstructured	Structured	Structured	Unstructured	Unstructured
Position power	Strong	Weak	Strong	Weak	Strong	Weak	Strong	Weak
	Favorable for leader							*Unfavorable for leader*

←——→

LEADER ATTITUDES

LEARNING
OBJECTIVES

Douglas McGregor developed two attitude profiles, or assumptions, concerning the basic nature of people. These two divergent attitudes were termed *Theory X* and *Theory Y*. **Theory X** maintains that the average employee dislikes work and will do whatever is possible to avoid it. **Theory Y** states that people like work and that it comes as naturally as rest and play. (Figure 15.7 defines Theory X and Theory Y in greater detail.) McGregor maintained that many leaders basically subscribe to either Theory X or Theory Y and behave accordingly. Thus, it is more than likely that a leader subscribing to Theory X would use a more autocratic style of leadership than that used by a leader subscribing to Theory Y. The real contribution coming from McGregor's work was the suggestion that a person's attitude toward human nature has a large influence on that person's behavior as a leader. It should also be realized that the Theory X/Theory Y issue is not always a matter of choice by the supervisor. For example, if a supervisor inherits a group of Theory X employees who have been supervised under a Theory X style, an immediate switch to Theory Y style could cause problems.

Others have also investigated the relationship between a leader's attitudes and the performance of individuals within the group. Specifically, the relationship between a leader's expectations of an individual and the resulting performance achieved by the individual has received considerable attention.

J. Sterling Livingston has looked at the relationship between the supervisor's expectations and the performance of subordinates. If the supervisor's expectations are high, the subordinates' productivity is likely to be high. On the other hand, if the supervisor's expectations are low, the subordinates' productivity is likely to be poor. Livingston's findings are summarized as follows:

> What a manager expects of his subordinates and the way he treats them largely determine their performance and career progress. A unique characteristic of superior managers is their ability to create high performance expectations that subordinates fulfill. Less effective managers fail to develop similar expectations, and as a consequence, the productivity of their subordinates suffers. Subordinates, more often than not, appear to do what they believe they are expected to do.[1]

FIGURE 15.7
Assumptions about
People's Personalities

Theory X

1. The average person has an inherent dislike of work and will avoid it whenever possible.
2. Because of this dislike of work, most people must be coerced, controlled, directed, and threatened with punishment to get them to put forth adequate effort toward the achievement of organizational objectives.
3. The average person prefers to be directed, wishes to avoid responsibility, has relatively little ambition, and wants security above all.

Theory Y

1. To the average person, the expenditure of physical and mental effort in work is as natural as play or rest.
2. External control and the threat of punishment are not the only means for bringing about effort toward organizational objectives; people will exercise self-direction and self-control in the service of objectives to which they are committed.
3. Commitment to objectives is a function of the rewards associated with their achievement.
4. The average person learns, under proper conditions, not only to accept but to seek responsibility.
5. The capacity to exercise a relatively high degree of imagination, ingenuity, and creativity in the solution of organizational problems is widely, not narrowly, distributed in the population.
6. Under the conditions of modern industrial life, the intellectual potentialities of the average person are only partially utilized.

Source: Adapted from *The Human Side of Enterprise* by Douglas McGregor. Copyright by McGraw-Hill, Inc. Used with permission of McGraw-Hill Book Company, 1960, pp. 33–34 and 47–48.

LEADERSHIP AND MORALE

In addition to its obvious impact on employee performance, the appropriateness of one's leadership style can have an impact on many areas of the organization. The group's morale or team spirit is greatly affected by the type of leadership style employed. Morale usually refers to the general attitude of the group and to the group's overall level of satisfaction. Morale can have a very significant impact on many personnel-related variables, such as turnover, attendance, tardiness, and sabotage. Prolonged low morale can even contribute to poor mental health.

There are things that the leader can do to raise the morale of the group:

1. **Be a good communicator.** This involves good listening as well as clear directions.
2. **Be considerate.** Being considerate of the group members doesn't mean that production will slide.
3. **Encourage employee input.** Encourage the employees to take an interest and participate in what is going on.
4. **Maintain a clean and safe environment.** A sloppy and dangerous environment breeds low morale.

5. Keep your word. Don't say one thing and do another.
6. Be fair. Treat everyone equally, and don't play favorites.
7. Set a good example. Remember that the leader is constantly being watched.

IMPLICATIONS FOR TODAY'S SUPERVISORS

Can any general conclusions be drawn concerning leadership for today's supervisors? The following points can be made concerning effective leadership:

1. A combination of high-supportive and high-directive styles is often a successful leadership style.
2. Under emergency or high-pressure situations, emphasis on the work is desirable and often preferred by employees.
3. Since the supervisor is frequently the only information source for employees regarding their work, they often expect the supervisor to structure their behavior.
4. Higher management often has set preferences regarding the leadership styles employed by lower-level managers and supervisors.
5. Some leaders can adjust their behavior to fit the situation, while others appear to be fake and manipulative when they attempt to make such adjustments.[2]

Supervision Illustration 15–2 describes one successful supervisor's leadership style.

SUPERVISION ILLUSTRATION 15–2

TRANSFORMATIONAL LEADERSHIP

Jason replaced Ron, a solid, steady supervisor who had kept things under control and produced reliable results. Ron had a breadth of knowledge and was highly respected by his organization. As a result, his instructions were rarely questioned or challenged. He did not take risks, and little had been done to expand the unit for several years.

Shortly after Jason became supervisor, his new boss set a difficult challenge for the group. Jason called a meeting of the work group and laid out the challenge. The meeting started out badly. Everyone knew that the challenge was well beyond the current status and seemed out of reach. Jason said to the group, "Look, we might not meet the challenge, but let's see what we can do. You guys are the experts. How can I help?" One employee, John, said, "I've had some ideas in the past, but Ron didn't want to hear them." However, John laid out his ideas, others pitched in, and soon they developed an action plan. Then Jason took responsibility for ensuring that his team had the resources necessary to accomplish the plan.

Ultimately, the team met the challenge. After that, the team felt there was nothing they couldn't do. They set several more production records and improved safety levels. Jason exhibited the following leadership behaviors: clear goals, open communications and generation of team motivation, prudent risk taking, confidence building, shared responsibility, and winning together. These are also called transformational leadership behaviors.

Source: Adapted from "An Example of Transformational Leadership," *Business Quarterly,* Summer 1997, p. 63. For more information about *Business Quarterly,* visit its Web site at:
www.cmpa.co/b3.html

SOLUTION TO THE
SUPERVISION
DILEMMA

John has learned that being a successful leader means getting employees to willingly follow him. He now knows that self-confidence, mental and physical endurance, enthusiasm, a sense of responsibility, empathy, and good human relations are all admirable characteristics in most leadership situations (pp. 292–93). He has learned that there are three basic leadership styles—autocratic, democratic, and laissez-faire (p. 293). He has also learned that the most effective leadership style depends on the situation, that the key to success lies in matching one's leadership style to the situation (p. 298). He is now aware that his expectations play a big role in his employees' performance. If his expectations are high, the productivity of his employees is also likely to be high (pp. 299–300).

SUMMARY

This chapter defines leadership and shows its relationship to the supervisory process. Different approaches to leadership are presented, along with specific implications for today's supervisors.

1. *Define leader.* A leader has the ability to obtain followers and influence them in setting and achieving objectives.

2. *Describe three basic styles of leadership.* The autocratic leader centralizes power and enjoys giving orders. The democratic leader wants the followers to share in making decisions. The laissez-faire leader allows the group members to do as they please.

3. *Define supportive and directive leaders.* Supportive leaders are genuinely interested in the well-being of the group members. Directive leaders focus primarily on the work being successfully performed.

4. *Discuss the Managerial Grid.* The Managerial Grid uses a two-dimensional grid to identify and relate different styles of leadership. The vertical axis of the grid represents concern for people. The horizontal axis represents concern for production.

5. *Explain the contingency approach to leadership.* The contingency approach to leadership identifies the particular styles of leadership that are appropriate for particular situations. If the situation is highly favorable or highly unfavorable to the leader, adopt a directive style. If the situation is moderately favorable to the leader, adopt a supportive style.

6. *Describe Theory X and Theory Y.* Theory X maintains that the average employee dislikes work and will do whatever is possible to avoid it. Theory Y states that people like work and that it comes as naturally as rest and play.

REVIEW QUESTIONS

1. What is a leader?
2. What is power?
3. Describe five types of power.
4. What is the difference between power and authority?
5. What is the difference between a leader and a supervisor?
6. Name five desirable characteristics for a leader to possess.
7. Describe the following leadership styles.
   a. Autocratic.
   b. Democratic.
   c. Laissez-faire.
8. Compare and contrast a supportive leader with a directive leader.
9. What is the Managerial Grid?
10. Describe Fiedler's contingency approach.
11. Describe Theory X and Theory Y.
12. List seven things that a leader can do to improve group morale.

SKILL-BUILDING QUESTIONS

1. What do you think of the leader who says, "Do what I say, not what I do"?
2. Discuss the following statement: "Leaders are born, not developed."
3. How can you explain the fact that leaders who employ entirely different leadership styles may enjoy equal success? For example, two football coaches who use very different leadership styles may both be very successful.
4. Support or refute the following statement: "If a leader thinks that a certain follower is going to fail, then that follower will fail."

REFERENCES

1. Reprinted by permission of the Harvard Business Review. Excerpt from "Pygmalion in Management" by J. Sterling Livingston (July–August 1969). Copyright © 1969 by the President and Fellows of Harvard College; all rights reserved.
2. Adapted from Chester A. Schriesheim, James M. Tolliver, and Orlando Behling, "Leadership Theory: Some Implications for Managers," *MSU Business Topics*, Summer 1978, p. 39. Reprinted by permission of the publisher, Division of Research, Graduate School of Business Administration, Michigan State University.

ADDITIONAL READINGS

Bielous, Gary. "Seven Power Bases and How to Effectively Use Them," *Supervision*, October 1995.
Buhler, Patricia. "Are You a Transformational Leader?" *Supervision*, September 1995.
———. "Leaders vs. Managers," *Supervision*, May 1995.
Dreyer, R. S. "Do Good Bosses Make Lousy Leaders?" *Supervision*, March 1995.
Loraine, Kaye. "Leadership—Where Does It Come From?" *Supervision*, February 1995.

SKILL-BUILDING APPLICATIONS

Incident 15–1

Jealousy at the Bank

You have recently been promoted to supervisor of teller operations at the downtown office of the Fourth National Bank. Prior to this assignment, you held a similar position at one of the branch offices. Some of your initial gratification over receiving the job was taken away when you heard through the grapevine that many of the downtown tellers were upset about your appointment. Rumor had it that these tellers were infuriated that the head teller, Janice Adams, did not get the job.

You: I don't know what to do. I feel as though I've never had a chance in this job. Everybody seems to hate me from the start because I got this job instead of Janice Adams.

Your Boss: What has happened since you've been here?

You: When I arrived, I was full of energy and was committed to being a good leader. The very first thing I did was hold a group meeting and tell all the tellers that I welcomed their input and that my door was always open. That was about four weeks ago, and not one teller has come into my office yet. The next thing I did was send out a memo soliciting suggestions for improving the department. I did receive some suggestions, but no two were the same. In fact, many were in direct conflict with one another. For example, one suggestion was to implement more detailed procedures. Another suggestion was to relax the "overly rigid" procedures.

Your Boss: What have you done since you got the suggestions?

You: To be honest, nothing. As I said before, no clear trends or ideas emerged. Some people seemed to even resent my original memo. One response said that good supervisors could come up with their own ideas. Naturally, with the situation being as it is, I am reluctant to implement anything for fear

of making matters worse. At the same time, I know that the situation is deteriorating every day.

Your Boss: Didn't you just request a raise for several of your employees?

You: I sure did. That seemed like a good way to win them over. Anyway, several of them are definitely underpaid in comparison with the industry average. Of course, you know I don't have a lot of authority in this job. All I can do is make recommendations. At any rate, I'm frustrated by the situation and I don't know how long I can take it.

Questions

1. Do you think that giving the employees a pay raise will win them over?

2. How might you handle the situation now?

Incident 15–2

Promises You Can't Keep

Roy Radcliff was hired four years ago as supervisor of the order processing section of the Golden Platter Recording Company. Golden Platter has enjoyed overwhelming success in its seven-year history. Sales this year increased 38 percent over last year's sales. Several people in the company, including Roy, believe that Golden Platter will soon be in the $50 million category.

Roy's optimism spilled over to his employees. He constantly reminded them of Golden Platter's tremendous potential. In fact, Roy had most of his employees convinced that promotions would come automatically if they just stayed with the company and did as they were told. "Just keep your nose clean" was one of his favorite counsels. Almost everyone took him at his word and thought that he was a great guy to work for.

To even Roy's surprise, he was offered a job as sales representative for the company in what he described as a fabulous territory. David Wong was chosen to replace him. David had established an excellent reputation as an assistant supervisor in the maintenance department. Soon after David took over the order processing section, he discovered that Roy had made impossible promises to many of his employees. Two employees had been promised promotions that were obviously beyond their capabilities. Several had been led to believe that unrealistically high pay raises would be forthcoming. To top it all off, Roy had told all employees in the order processing section that they could take a coffee break whenever they wanted to.

Questions

1. What do you think of Roy's leadership style?
2. Why do you think that someone might resort to Roy's style of leadership?
3. What would you do if you were David?

Exercise 15–1

Insubordination?

Your company installed a new performance management system this year. You distributed the information and forms several weeks ago, and they were due to be completed two weeks ago. One manager reporting to you has not yet returned his forms. This morning, you ran into him in the parking lot and asked him about it. He reacted angrily. "I haven't had time to do it," he said. "I don't have enough time to get my job done as it is, much less take the time necessary to have my people write a bunch of meaningless information."

You ask him to stop by your office later to discuss the matter. As you think about how to handle the situation during the meeting, you consider several alternatives:

1. In view of his attitude and behavior, it is clearly appropriate to exercise your authority. Tell him in no uncertain terms that this task must be done if he expects to continue as a supervisor.
2. Tell him why this program is important, and use your best persuasion technique to sell him on carrying it out willingly.
3. Remind him that no salary increases, including his own, will be processed until the forms have been completed. Establish another deadline, and let him know that you expect the forms to be turned in by that date.

4. Explain to him that appraising employee performance is a part of every supervisor's job and that he is being evaluated on his performance in implementing this program.
5. Tell him that you understand the difficulties of his job and the shortage of time available to do it, but remind him that this is a mandatory program that has top management's backing.

Other alternatives may be open to you, but assume that these are the only ones you have considered. *Without discussion with anyone,* choose one of them. Be prepared to defend your choice.

Exercise 15–2

Situational Approach to Leadership

Under the situational approach to leadership, different situations call for different leadership styles. Assuming this approach is correct, outline specific situations in which you would employ an autocratic style of leadership. In addition, outline situations in which you would employ a participative style of leadership. Be very specific in describing the situation. Be prepared to present to the class your list of situations for both leadership styles.

Exercise 15–3

Test Your Leadership Style

Read both statements in each entry in the following list and circle either *a* or *b* to indicate which one best describes you—or is the least incorrect about you. You must answer every question to arrive at a proper score.

1. *a.* You are the person people most often turn to for help.
   b. You are aggressive and look after your best interests first.
2. *a.* You are most competent and better able to motivate others than most people.
   b. You strive to reach a position where you can exercise authority over large numbers of people and sums of money.
3. *a.* You try hard to influence the outcome of events.
   b. You quickly eliminate all obstacles that stand in the way of your goals.

4. *a.* There are few people you have as much confidence in as you have in yourself.
   b. You have no qualms about taking what you want in this world.

5. *a.* You have the ability to inspire others to follow your lead.
   b. You enjoy having people act on your commands and are not opposed to making threats if you must.

6. *a.* You do your best to influence the outcome of events.
   b. You make all the important decisions, expecting others to carry them out.

7. *a.* You have a special magnetism that attracts people to you.
   b. You enjoy dealing with situations requiring confrontation.

8. *a.* You would enjoy consulting on the complex issues and problems that face managers of companies.
   b. You would enjoy planning, directing, and controlling the staff of a department to ensure the highest profit margins.

9. *a.* You want to consult with business groups and companies to improve effectiveness.
   b. You want to make decisions about other people's lives and money.

10. *a.* You could deal with level upon level of bureaucratic red tape and pressure to improve performance.
    b. You could work where money and profits are more important than other people's emotional well-being.

11. *a.* You typically must start your day before sunrise and continue into the night six to seven days a week.
    b. You must fire unproductive employees regularly and expediently to achieve set targets.

12. *a.* You must be responsible for how well others do their work (and you will be judged on their achievement, not yours).
    b. You have a workaholic temperament that thrives on pressure to succeed.

13. *a.* You are a real self-starter and full of enthusiasm about everything you do.
    b. Whatever you do, you have to do it better than anyone else.

14. *a.* You are always striving to be the best, the tops, the first at whatever you do.
    b. You have a driving, aggressive personality and fight hard and tough to gain anything worth having.

15. *a.* You have always been involved in competitive activities, including sports, and have won several awards for outstanding performance.
    b. Winning and succeeding are more important to you than playing just for enjoyment.

16. *a.* You will stick to a problem when you are getting nowhere.
    b. You quickly become bored with most things you undertake.

17. *a.* You are naturally carried along by some inner drive or mission to accomplish something that has never been done.
    b. Self-demanding and a perfectionist, you are always pressing yourself to perform to the limit.

18. *a.* You maintain a sense of purpose or direction that is larger than yourself.
    b. Being successful at work is the most important thing to you.

19. *a.* You would enjoy a job requiring hard and fast decisions.
    b. You are loyal to the concepts of profit, growth, and expansion.

20. *a.* You prefer independence and freedom at work to a high salary or job security.
    b. You are comfortable in a position of control, authority, and strong influence.

21. *a.* You firmly believe that those who take the most risks with their own savings should receive the greatest financial rewards.
    b. There are few people's judgment you would have as much confidence in as your own.

22. *a.* You are seen as courageous, energetic, and optimistic.
    b. Being ambitious, you are quick to take advantage of new opportunities.

23. *a.* You are good at praising others and you give credit readily when it's due.
    b. You like people, but have little confidence in their ability to do things the right way.

24. *a.* You usually give people the benefit of the doubt, rather than argue openly with them.
    b. Your style with people is direct, "tell it like it is" confrontation.
25. *a.* Although honest, you are capable of being ruthless if others are playing by devious rules.
    b. You grew up in an environment that stressed survival and required you to create your own rules.

Find Your Score

Count all the *a* responses you circled and multiply by 4 to get your percentage for leadership traits. Do the same with *b* answers to arrive at supervisor traits.

Leader (numbers of *a's*)	____ × 4 =	____ %
Supervisor (number of *b's*)	____ × 4 =	____ %

Interpret Your Score

Consider yourself a supervisor if you score more than 65 percent in the supervisor tally above; consider yourself a leader if you score more than 65 percent in the leader tally. If your scores cluster closer to a 50-50 split, you're a leader/supervisor.

The Leader

Your idea of fulfilling work is to motivate and guide co-workers to achieve their best and to reach common goals in their work by functioning in harmony. You are the sort of person who simply enjoys watching people grow and develop. You are commonly described as patient and encouraging in your dealings with people and a determined self-starter in your own motivation. Since you have a natural ability for inspiring top performances, there's usually little turnover among your employees, and staff relations are harmonious. At times, however, you may be too soft on people or overly patient when their performance lags. Where people are concerned, you may be too quick to let emotions get in the way of business judgments. Overall, you're the visionary type, not the day-to-day grinder.

The Supervisor

You are capable of getting good work out of people, but your style can be abrasive and provocative. You are especially competent at quickly taking charge, bulldozing through corporate red tape, or forcing others to meet tough work demands. Driven partly by a low threshold for boredom, you strive for more complexity in your work. But you love the "game" of power and the sense of having control over others. Also, your confidence in your own ideas is so strong that you may be frustrated by working as part of a team. Your tendency to see your progress as the battle of a great mind against mediocre ones is not the best premise for bringing out the best in others. Therefore, the further up the corporate ladder you go, the more heavily human-relations problems will weigh against you.

The Leader/Supervisor Mix

As a 50-50 type, you probably do not believe in the need to motivate others. Instead, you maintain that the staff should have a natural desire to work as hard as you do, without needing somebody to egg them on. You do your job well, and you expect the same from your subordinates. This means that while your own level of productivity is high, you are not always sure about how to motivate others to reach their full potential. Generally, however, you do have the ability to get others to do as you wish, without being abrasive or ruffling feathers. You may pride yourself on being surrounded by a very competent, professional staff that is self-motivated, requiring little of your own attention. But don't be too sure: Almost everyone performs better under the right sort of encouraging leadership.

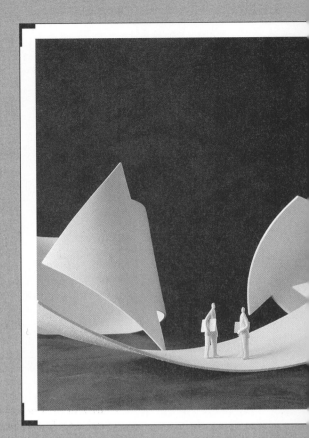

Handling Conflict

LEARNING OBJECTIVES

After studying this chapter, you should be able to:

1. Define conflict.

2. Outline the five stages of conflict.

3. Discuss the useful effects of conflict.

4. Explain the basic perspectives for analyzing conflict in organizations.

5. Define frustration.

6. Describe five strategies for dealing with interpersonal conflict.

SUPERVISION
DILEMMA

Jane Harris was in her office reflecting on a situation that had just occurred. She had just stopped an argument between two of her best employees. The argument had started with a discussion that the two employees were having about an upcoming political election. The discussion became rather heated, and Jane felt that the two employees were close to blows. Although this was an unusual situation, Jane felt that she was increasingly having to handle other types of conflict both in and out of her work unit. She wondered what was the best way to handle conflict situations.

Some conflict is inevitable in organizations. Supervisors are routinely faced with conflict situations and must learn how to deal with them. Too many supervisors view conflict as something that should be avoided at all costs. But conflict can have positive as well as negative results. Effective supervisors learn to curb the negative results of conflict and to guide conflict toward positive results.

WHAT IS CONFLICT?

LEARNING
OBJECTIVES

Conflict is a condition that results when one party feels that some concern of that party has been frustrated or is about to be frustrated by a second party.[1] The term *party* in the previous sentence may refer to individuals, groups, or even organizations.

Conflict is a dynamic process that does not usually appear suddenly. In fact, conflict generally passes through several stages, or cycles. The usual stages of conflict are as follows:

LEARNING
OBJECTIVES

1. *Latent conflict.* At this stage, the basic conditions for conflict exist but have not been recognized by the parties.
2. *Perceived conflict.* The basic conditions for conflict are recognized by one or both of the parties.
3. *Felt conflict.* Internal tensions begin to build in the involved parties, but the conflict is still not out in the open.
4. *Manifest conflict.* The conflict is out in the open, and the existence of the conflict becomes obvious to parties that are not involved.
5. *Conflict aftermath.* The conflict is stopped by some method. How the conflict is stopped establishes new conditions that lead either to a new conflict or to more effective cooperation between the involved parties.[2]

A particular conflict situation does not necessarily pass through all of these stages. In addition, the parties involved in the conflict may not be at the same stage at the same time. For example, it is entirely possible for one party to be at the manifest stage and the other to be at the perceived stage.

POSITIVE AND NEGATIVE ASPECTS OF CONFLICT

It has been estimated that managers spend at least 20 percent of their time dealing with conflict and that their ability to manage conflict has become more important in recent years.[3] Furthermore, it is safe to say that the manner in which a supervisor handles a conflict situation influences whether the conflict has a positive or negative impact.

The negative aspects of conflict are generally quite obvious. Most people can think of conflict situations in their organization that have diverted time, energy, and money away from the organization's goals. Moreover, it is entirely possible for such a situation to turn into continuous conflict and cause further harm to the organization. Conflict may cause one or more employees to leave the organization. It can adversely affect the health of the involved parties. Intense conflict can lead to sabotage, stealing, lying, distortion of information, and similar behaviors that can have a disastrous effect on the organization. Supervision Illustration 16–1 describes some suggestions for overcoming conflict.

On the other hand, when properly managed, conflict can have these very useful benefits:

3 LEARNING OBJECTIVES

1. Conflict usually causes changes. Attempting to determine the cause of a conflict and developing a solution to the conflict causes changes to occur.
2. Conflict activates people. It helps eliminate monotony and boredom in that it wakes people up and gets them moving.
3. Conflict is a form of communication. Recognizing a conflict may open up new and more effective channels of communication.
4. Conflict can be healthy in that it relieves pent-up emotions and feelings.
5. Conflict can be educational in that the participants often learn a great deal not only about themselves but also about the other people involved.
6. The aftermath of conflict can be a stronger and better work environment.

TYPES OF CONFLICT IN ORGANIZATIONS

4 LEARNING OBJECTIVES

Conflict can be either internal or external to the individual. Conflict *internal* to the individual is called **intrapersonal conflict.** Conflict *external* to the individual falls into one of three general categories—*interpersonal, structural,* or *political.*

Intrapersonal Conflict

Because intrapersonal conflict is internal to the individual, it is very difficult to analyze. Basically, intrapersonal conflict relates to the *need-drive-goal motivation sequence* (see Figure 16.1). In this sequence, needs produce motives leading to the achievement of goals. Needs are caused by deficiencies. These deficiencies can be either physical or mental. For example, a physical need exists when a person goes without food for 48 hours. Motives produce action. Lack of food (the need) causes the physical feelings of hunger (the motive), which produces eating (the action or goal). Achievement of the goal satisfies the need and reduces the motive.

SUPERVISION ILLUSTRATION 16–1

THE GENIUS OF SITTING BULL

What in the world would the American Indian icon Sitting Bull have to do with stress and conflict in modern corporate America? In his book *The Genius of Sitting Bull,* Emmett C. Murphy shows that not only did this great warrior chief defeat General George A. Custer in the epic Battle of Little Big Horn but he also provided great leadership advice to today's corporate warriors.

To overcome conflict and stress, the true leader, according to Sitting Bull, shapes policies and strategies accordingly:

1. Phase One: Assembly and Integration of Forces. "The leader creates commitment, builds trust, increases power, lives the experiences of the people, acts as a healer—and communicates on many levels, committing followers to a shared vision." By doing these tasks, the leader is able to channel energies away from conflict, reduce stress, and serve as the final and just arbitrator of diverse opinion and direction.

2. Phase Two: Projection and Application. "The leader thinks strategically, respects the competition, redefines the rules of battle, knows the terrain, rightsizes forces—overcoming obstacles and creating opportunity." Channeling dynamic forces, such as the aggressive portion of conflict, must become a part of the leader's thought process. From chaos and dissension can emerge opportunity and gain. Most great teams and

organizations have arguments. How to control the arguments is a mark of the true leader.

3. Phase Three: Adjustment and Reflection. "The leader welcomes crisis and measures results—continuously seeking improvement necessary for long-term success." Facing crisis head on shows the character of the leader. For example, when Johnson & Johnson faced the potential public relations disaster when poison was introduced into its pain-reliever capsules by an extortionist, it confronted the situation with boldness and concern for the public welfare by aggressively recalling all the capsules and reintroducing the product in tamperproof containers. A poll taken after the crisis showed that 93 percent of the public admired the way the company fulfilled its responsibilities and faced the crisis.

Since the emotion a crisis precipitates can cloud a manager's judgment, a manager should prepare for a crisis by anticipating and even practicing for it, taking charge of it (that's when you really know whether or not you are a leader) and learning from it (never repeat the mistakes of the past). Organizations, groups, or tribes that manage conflict and crisis well are those that succeed on the battlefield or in the marketplace. Those that do not become easy prey to their enemies and begin to dissolve their team and competitive spirit.

Source: Adapted from Emmett C. Murphy, *The Genius of Sitting Bull* (Englewood Cliffs, N.J.: Prentice Hall, 1993), inside cover and pp. 276–78. For more information on the book *The Genius of Sitting Bull,* visit its Web site at: **www.amazon.com/exec/obidos**

Intrapersonal conflict can result when barriers exist between an individual's drives or motives and the achievement of his or her goals. For example, employees who feel that they have not received a promotion because of race or sex are very likely to experience intrapersonal conflict. This situation leads to frustration on their part. Intrapersonal conflict can also occur when goals have both positive and negative aspects and when competing or conflicting goals exist. Figure 16.2 shows how intrapersonal conflict occurs in the motivation sequence.

FIGURE 16.1

FIGURE 16.1

The Motivation Sequence

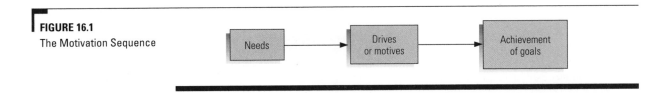

FIGURE 16.2

Sources of Intrapersonal
Conflict

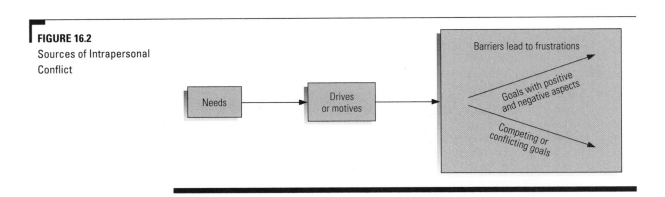

Frustration.   Frustration, which is one form of intrapersonal conflict, occurs when people feel that something is stopping them from achieving goals that they would like to achieve. The results of frustration in an organization are numerous and varied. Among the possibilities are sabotage, higher absenteeism, higher turnover, and poorer health.

Goal conflict.   Another form of intrapersonal conflict results from goal conflict. **Goal conflict** occurs when an individual's goal has both positive and negative aspects or when competing or conflicting goals exist. There are three forms of goal conflict:

1. *Conflicting positive goals.* This situation occurs when a person must choose between two or more positive goals. For example, say that a person is offered two equally attractive jobs. Suppose that a supervisor in Company A is approached by the personnel manager of Company B and offered a supervisory job in Company B. If the supervisor likes the present job but also thinks that the new job would be very good, he or she is faced with conflicting positive goals. This situation produces some intrapersonal conflict.

2. *Goals with both positive and negative aspects.* This situation occurs when a person is pursuing a goal that has both positive and negative aspects. A person who is offered a job in supervision may feel that the job has both positive and negative aspects. The positive aspects might include an increase in salary, more authority, and a higher status. The negative aspects might include having to listen to other people's problems and having to spend more time on the job.

Interpersonal conflict can occur between two of a supervisor's employees, between the supervisor and the boss, or between the supervisor and an employee.
Christopher Bissel/Tony Stone Images

3. *Goals that have only negative aspects.* This situation occurs when a person is confronted with two or more negative goals. For example, a person may be working at a job he or she dislikes but may consider quitting and looking for another job just as undesirable.

Goal conflict can generally be resolved by making a decision and eliminating the source of the conflict. Supervisors can help deal with intrapersonal conflict only if they can identify when and why it is occurring. Therefore, supervisors must learn to identify intrapersonal conflict not only within employees but also within themselves.

Interpersonal Conflict

Interpersonal conflict, which is external to the individual, can result from many factors. It can occur between two supervisors, between two of a supervisor's employees, between the supervisor and the boss, or between the supervisor and an employee.

One cause of interpersonal conflict is opposing personalities. Sometimes people just seem to rub each other the wrong way. For example, if a person who is constantly playing practical jokes and a person who is quiet and reserved are in regular contact with each other, these two people might experience interpersonal conflict because of their differing personalities.

Prejudices based on such characteristics as personal background can also cause interpersonal conflict. Everyone is familiar with the potential that exists for conflict based on racial, sexual, or religious differences. More subtle prejudices can also cause interpersonal conflict. Conflict based on such prejudices can arise between the college graduate and the person without a college degree, between the married person and the divorced or single person, or between the experienced employee and the new hire.

Jealousy and envy are also sources of interpersonal conflict. Supervisors sometimes experience such conflict when they are first promoted. Before the promotion, the supervisor is one of the gang. After the promotion, conflict can develop between the supervisor and some (former) friends because of envy and jealousy.

Structural Conflict

Structural conflict results from the nature of the organization structure. Such conflict is independent of the personalities involved. For example, the marketing department naturally wants the production department to produce every size and color that the customer could possibly imagine. The production department, of course, wants to limit the number of sizes and colors of the product. This type of conflict is a natural by-product of the organization structure and the outlook of the various departments. Various types of structural conflict are discussed below.

Differing goals.   Each department of an organization has its own goals. Ideally, all of these goals should contribute to the overall success of the organization. Unfortunately, different department goals often result in conflict. An example is the previously described conflict between the production and marketing department. Another example is the conflict that occurs between the marketing and finance departments. Most marketing departments like to keep a large stock of finished goods inventory so that customer demands can be instantly met. On the other hand, most finance departments like to keep inventories low because of the carrying costs. The result is conflict between these departments.

Mutual dependence of departments.   When two departments are dependent on each other, a potential for structural conflict exists. For example, marketing and production departments are often dependent on each other for their success. If marketing doesn't sell the product, production can't produce it. If production doesn't produce the product, marketing can't sell it. If either department fails to perform, the other is likely to have problems.

Unequal dependence of departments.   When one department is dependent on another department for its success, a potential for conflict exists. For example, staff departments such as the human resources department are generally dependent on the line departments. The human resources department must solicit the cooperation of the line departments, but the line departments don't have to accept the ideas of the human resources department. This can cause conflict.

Role dissatisfaction.   Certain departments or groups in organizations sometimes feel that they are not receiving enough recognition or status. When this occurs, they often generate conflicts with other departments or groups. For example, an internal auditing department may feel that it is not getting enough recognition. To show its importance and thus gain the recognition that it feels it deserves, this department may develop a conflict with other departments.

Ambiguities.   When the credit or blame for the success or failure of a particular assignment cannot be determined, conflict between the persons or groups that may deserve the credit or blame is likely to result. For example, changes in production techniques require the efforts of both the engineering department and the production department. However, credit for the success or failure of the changes is difficult to assign, and thus conflict between these departments can result.

Competition.   When two or more employees are competing against one another for a promotion or a preferred job assignment, conflict is likely to result. This conflict can be positive in that it may cause these employees to work harder and produce more. However, it must be supervised correctly to achieve positive results and avoid negative results.

Dependence on common resources.   When two departments share common but scarce resources, conflict often results. For example, conflict can result if two departments use the same printing facility and each department feels that its work should come first.

Communication barriers.   Conflict arising from communication barriers is often encountered in situations involving branch offices. The physical separation of branch offices from the home office has the potential for conflict. This form of conflict can also result from language and semantic differences. For example, conflict can arise between engineers and production people because the engineers use technical language to describe a production process, whereas the production people use less technical terms.

Political Conflict

Intrapersonal, interpersonal, and structural conflicts are usually not planned by the parties involved. They generally just happen, due to circumstances. On the other hand, **political conflicts** (sometimes called *strategic conflicts*) are planned and often intentionally started. Generally, such conflicts result from the promotion of self-interest on the part of an individual or a group. The individual or group that starts the conflict intends to get an advantage over the other party. For example, when control of a new project is viewed as being very worthwhile, managers within the organization often engage in political conflict to gain control of the project.

The participants in political conflicts are not necessarily unethical or dishonest. The reward structure of many organizations often encourages political conflicts. If such conflicts are managed properly, they can have the positive effects described earlier in this chapter. Unfortunately, conflicts of this type can easily become unfair and result in severe negative outcomes.

MANAGING CONFLICT

Supervisors most frequently deal with intrapersonal and interpersonal conflict. Therefore, these two forms of conflict are discussed in more depth in this section. As was stated earlier, intrapersonal conflict is very difficult to analyze. Supervisors should not go around looking for intrapersonal conflict in every situation. However, when an employee asks to discuss a personal problem with the supervisor, the supervisor should look for signs of *intrapersonal conflict*. The supervisor should be very cautious in giving advice relating to intrapersonal problems. In fact, the supervisor should normally refer the employee to the company's employee assistance program for advice in handling the problem (employee assistance programs are discussed in detail in Chapter 18). But if the intrapersonal conflict affects the employee's work performance, the supervisor must take action.

Supervisors can use these strategies in dealing with *interpersonal* conflicts:

6 LEARNING OBJECTIVES

1. Compromise.
2. Smoothing over the conflict and pretending that it does not exist.
3. Withdrawing.
4. Forcing the conflict to a solution.
5. Confrontation.

Compromise. Compromise is effective in dealing with interpersonal conflict when it benefits both parties. It can be used when the issue in question is not very important. It can also be used to expedite solutions under time pressures or to obtain temporary solutions to complex problems. Unfortunately, compromise often leaves the real cause of the conflict unsolved and provides the groundwork for future conflict.

Smoothing over or pretending conflict does not exist. A second strategy is to smooth over the conflict and pretend that it does not exist. The supervisor using this approach pretends that "we are all one big happy family." This approach rarely leads to long-term solutions and generally results in more conflict.

Withdrawal. A third strategy is withdrawal. If the supervisor has two employees who are engaged in interpersonal conflict, one of them can be moved or transferred. If a supervisor is involved in a conflict with an employee, with the boss, or with another supervisor, he or she can say, "I don't want to talk about it." Again, however, withdrawal does not address the underlying cause of the conflict and usually provides the basis for future conflict.

Forcing a solution. A fourth strategy is to force the conflict to a solution. For example, if two supervisors are engaged in an interpersonal conflict, their boss can say, "This is the way it is going to be, and that ends it." A supervisor can take the same approach to a conflict between two employees. Like the previous strategies, this one may only sow the seeds for future conflict.

Confrontation. The final strategy is confrontation between the participants. For this strategy to work, some basic guidelines must be followed:

1. Before the confrontation begins, review the past actions of the participants, and clarify the issues causing the conflict.

SUPERVISION ILLUSTRATION 16–2

TROUBLE AT THE UNITED STATES POSTAL SERVICE

Thirty-six killed. Twenty wounded. After one part-time worker learned of a future negative performance report, he killed 14 co-workers—the third worst case of mass murder by one person in history. All of this has occurred at a post office.

The United States Postal Service employs over 700,000 individuals. It has become apparent that the post office has become one of the most troublesome places to work. A troubled work environment commonly possesses the following characteristics:

- Chronic labor-management disputes.
- Frequent grievances filed by employees.
- Extraordinary numbers of injury claims, especially psychological injuries.
- Understaffing, or excessive demands for overtime.

- Many stressed workers.
- Authoritarian management.

The majority of these characteristics are present in the U.S. Postal Service; workers often complain of close supervision, high levels of pressure, and close monitoring of performance.

To accommodate employee grievances, the U.S. Postal Service is focusing on employee empowerment, in which workers and managers discuss problems. The service has set up a 24-hour 800 number for employees to report grievances. Until the U.S. Postal Service changes its entire workplace, it will remain a kind of laboratory case of the relationship between workplace culture and workplace violence—and remain a ticking bomb that could go off again at any moment.

Source: Adapted from "Murder at the Post Office: Until Culture Change Is a Reality, It's a 'Ticking Bomb,' " *Training and Development*, January 1994, p. 29. For more information on the United States Postal Service, visit its Web site at:

www.usps.gov

2. Encourage the participants to communicate freely. They should get their personal feelings out in the open and should not hold back grievances.
3. Don't try to place blame. This only polarizes the participants.
4. Don't surprise either party with confrontations for which either party is not prepared.
5. Don't attack sensitive areas of either party that have nothing to do with the specific conflict.
6. Don't argue aimlessly.
7. Identify areas of mutual agreement.
8. Emphasize mutual benefits to both parties.
9. Don't jump into specific solutions too quickly.
10. Encourage all of the participants to examine their own biases and feelings.

Confrontation has proven to be the most effective and lasting method for resolving conflict. On the other hand, forcing the conflict to a solution has been found to be the least effective means of resolving conflict. Therefore, supervisors should avoid that approach whenever possible.

Supervision Illustration 16–2 describes conflict problems encountered by the United States Postal Service.

SOLUTION TO THE
SUPERVISION
DILEMMA

First, Jane has learned that conflict is inevitable in organizations. In addition, she has learned that conflict can have both positive and negative consequences (p. 310). The conflict that Jane faced was a form of interpersonal conflict. Jane has learned that there are five strategies that a supervisor can use in dealing with interpersonal conflicts: compromise; smoothing the conflict over and pretending that it does not exist; withdrawing; forcing the conflict to a solution; and confrontation, or problem solving (pp. 316–17). Jane should probably use confrontation to resolve the conflict between her two employees. If she uses confrontation, suggestions that she should follow are offered on pp. 316–17.

SUMMARY

This chapter explores the causes of conflict in organizations. Several methods of resolving conflict are presented to aid the supervisor in resolving conflict in a constructive manner.

1. *Define conflict.* Conflict is a condition that results when one party feels that some concern of that party has been frustrated or is about to be frustrated by a second party.

2. *Outline the five stages of conflict.* The five stages of conflict are latent conflict, perceived conflict, felt conflict, manifest conflict, and conflict aftermath.

3. *Discuss the useful effects of conflict.* Conflict has these potentially useful effects: It energizes people; it is a form of communication; it often provides an outlet for pent-up emotions and feelings; and it may be an educational experience.

4. *Explain the basic perspectives for analyzing conflict in organizations.* Conflict in organizations can be analyzed from two basic perspectives. One perspective views conflict as a process internal to the

individual (intrapersonal conflict). The other perspective views conflict as external to the individual—individual versus individual, individual versus group, group versus group, organization versus organization, or any combination of these. External conflict is of three general types: interpersonal, structural, or political.

5. *Define frustration.* Frustration occurs when people feel that something is stopping them from achieving goals that they would like to achieve.

6. *Describe five strategies for dealing with interpersonal conflict.* There are five general strategies for dealing with interpersonal conflict: (1) withdraw one or more of the participants; (2) smooth over the conflict and pretend that it does not exist; (3) compromise for the sake of ending the conflict; (4) force the conflict to a conclusion by third-party intervention; and (5) have a confrontation between the participants in an effort to eliminate the underlying source of the conflict.

REVIEW QUESTIONS

1. Define conflict.
2. Describe the five stages, or cycles, of conflict.
3. Describe some positive and negative outcomes of conflict.
4. Define four types of conflict in organizations.
5. What is frustration?
6. Discuss some causes of interpersonal conflict.
7. Outline the causes of structural conflict.
8. Discuss the five strategies for solving interpersonal conflict.
9. What is the most effective method of handling interpersonal conflict?
10. What are some guidelines for using the confrontation approach to conflict?

SKILL-BUILDING QUESTIONS

1. "Supervisors should avoid conflict at all costs." Discuss.
2. Suppose you have two employees who just rub each other the wrong way. How would you handle this situation?
3. "Supervisors should smooth over any conflict that they have with their boss." Discuss your views on this statement.
4. Why do you think that some people try to avoid conflict at all costs, while others seem to seek it out?

REFERENCES

1. Kenneth Thomas, "Conflict and Conflict Management," in *Handbook of Industrial and Organizational Psychology*, ed. Marvin D. Dunnette (Chicago: Rand McNally, 1976), p. 891.
2. Louis Pondy, "Organizational Conflict: Concepts and Models," *Administrative Science Quarterly*, September 1967, pp. 296–320.
3. K. S. Thomas and W. H. Schmidt, "A Survey of Managerial Interests with Respect to Conflict," *Academy of Management Journal*, June 1976, pp. 315–18.

ADDITIONAL READINGS

Capozzoli, Thomas K. "Conflict Resolution—A Key Ingredient in Successful Teams," *Supervision*, December 1995.

Cousins, Roland B., and Linda E. Benitz. "Every Supervisor Needs Mediation Skills," *Supervision*, May 1994.

Nierman, Lyndy. "Managing Conflict without Conflict," *Food Processing*, March 1994.

Pollock, Ted. "Mind Your Own Business," *Supervision*, November 1996.

Ramsey, Robert D. "Conflict Resolution Skills for Supervisors," *Supervision*, August 1996.

Van Auken, Phillip M. "Conflict Diagnosis: Are You Hot or Cool?" *Supervision*, May 1993.

SKILL-BUILDING APPLICATIONS

Incident 16–1

Trouble in the Claims Department

Barbara Riley, supervisor of the claims section of the Reliance Insurance Company, really has a problem. She has been having trouble with two of her best employees. Ruth Gordon is 55 years old and has been with the company for 30 years. She started out as a secretary and has worked her way up to senior claims representative. She knows the claims procedures better than anyone, and she prides herself on the fact that many of the younger employees, most of whom are college graduates, come to her for help on their more difficult claims problems. She takes particular pride in the fact that she is of help to them even though she is not a college graduate.

Juan Perez is 24 years old and a recent business administration graduate from a large local university. Since joining the claims unit, he has made numerous suggestions for improving procedures. Just recently, he proposed an entirely new system for processing claims.

Barbara has decided to discuss the problem with her boss, Bill Rucker. The discussion goes as follows:

Barbara: I just don't know, Bill. Sometimes I feel like putting Juan and Ruth in a room and not letting them out until they agree to get along.

Bill: What do they argue about?

Barbara: Anything that comes up! You can count on it that if Juan proposes something, Ruth will be against it. Juan also contributes to the problem in that he acts like Ruth doesn't exist. If he would just ask for her advice every now and then, it would help.

Bill: How is it affecting everyone?

Barbara: For some time, most people sort of ignored it. Now, however, the arguments are getting out of hand and people are beginning to choose sides.

Questions

1. What is causing the conflict?
2. What method has Barbara been using in dealing with the conflict?
3. Recommend a solution to this conflict situation.

Incident 16–2

Ingram Manufacturing Company

Irene Hoyt has been extremely successful as training director of the Ingram Manufacturing Company, a position she has held for the past four years. She has helped develop some of the best prospects for handling the company's future, and she views "her graduates" somewhat like a parent. She is proud of them and very pleased that her help has been an important factor in enabling them to realize their potential.

One of her former trainees is Rodney Stone, who came from the factory assembly line about two years ago. Rodney proved to be an outstanding member of his training group and at its close was advanced to the job of associate trainer under her supervision. Rodney had two and one-half years of college before joining Ingram. He had to quit college for lack of funds and took the assembly-line job because it was the only employment he could find. He is extremely ambitious, has a very quick mind, and at times might be considered too aggressive by many.

Since being with Irene, Rodney has received several pay increases, has prepared several well-organized and well-written training manuals, and has become a productive but somewhat controversial trainer. Rodney is outspoken in his opinions and impatient with trainees who are ill prepared for discussion sessions.

Irene strongly feels that Rodney is aiming to take her job. He has occasionally disregarded procedures established for the training department and he takes certain matters that should be referred to Irene into his own hands. Morever, he doesn't tell Irene what he has done. On several occasions, ignorance of the status of such matters has caused Irene embarrassment and has raised some suspicion among her peers as to who is managing the training work. Several times, Irene has asked Rodney to be sure to keep her fully informed, but so far there has been no change in Rodney. If her suspicions are correct, Irene feels something must be done, but she doesn't want to act without reasonable basis.

Questions

1. Identify the types of conflict in this problem.
2. How would you handle the situation?

Exercise 16–1

Conflict over Quality

This morning, your department completed a large order and turned it over to quality control. The quality control supervisor has just come to tell you that she must tighten up on inspection standards because a number of complaints have been received from the field. She feels that the order must be reworked by your department to pass inspection. You try—but fail—to persuade her to impose the stricter standards only on future lots.

Reworking units will set you back a couple of days in your production schedule. You can explain this to your superiors. But the costs, which will be charged to your budget, will be much more difficult to explain.

As you reflect on what has happened, you are clearly annoyed. You decide that something must be done, and you see your alternatives as follows:

1. You can calm down, issue instructions to rework the units, and do the best you can with the budgeting and scheduling problems.
2. You can send the quality control supervisor a memo clearly outlining the cost considerations and ask her to help you find a solution.
3. You can call the quality control supervisor and ask her to meet with you to discuss the situation further at her earliest convenience.
4. You can go to the plant manager (to whom both you and the quality control supervisor report), point out the budget and scheduling difficulties, and request that the old standards be applied this one last time.
5. You can tell the quality control supervisor that if she does not go along with your suggestion to impose the stricter standards only on future production, you will no longer be able to lend her one of your operators for inspection work.

Other alternatives may be open to you, but assume that these are the only ones you have considered. *Without discussion with anyone,* choose one of the alternatives and be prepared to defend your choice.

Exercise 16–2

Secretarial Problems

Your secretary has been unusually irritable lately with several people in your department. You have purposely refrained from becoming involved because you believe that the parties involved should work out their difficulties. This approach has worked well in similar situations in the past. This morning, however, some unnecessary remarks were directed at you, and now it is apparent that you must act. Before you have an opportunity to discuss the situation, you hear through the grapevine that your secretary is having marital difficulties that obviously could be the source of the problem.

In handling the situation, your best approach is to:

1. Mention that you've heard about the marital problems and while you are sympathetic, you don't feel that personal problems should influence behavior toward co-workers or job performance.

2. Privately advise other staff members that your secretary is having some personal problems and ask for their understanding during this difficult period.

3. Approach the problem by using yourself as an example. Indicate that you sometimes have personal problems and irritations, but you try not to let them affect you on the job. Then suggest that an extra effort should be exerted to be less abrasive with others.

4. Ask questions and attempt to get a thorough understanding of your secretary's problem so you can give appropriate advice.

5. Mention that you have noticed the recent irritable behavior and listen to what your secretary has to say. Then, in an understanding way indicate that personal problems should not be allowed to affect job performance.

Other alternatives may be open to you, but assume these are the only ones you have considered. *Without discussion with anyone*, choose one of the alternatives and be prepared to defend your choice.

CHAPTER 17

Coping with Change and Stress

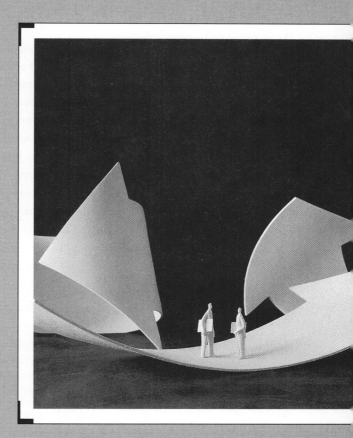

LEARNING OBJECTIVES

After studying this chapter, you should be able to:

1. Discuss the supervisor's role in introducing change.

2. Explain why employees tend to resist change.

3. Present several things that the supervisor can do to foster employee acceptance of change.

4. Describe a three-step model for implementing change.

5. Discuss the nature and sources of job-related stress.

6. Suggest several personal guidelines for managing organizational and personal stress.

7. Explain the Family and Medical Leave Act of 1993 and discuss how it is designed to reduce employee stress.

SUPERVISION
DILEMMA

It has been a stressful couple of weeks for John Lewis. Things had just begun to settle down from the yearlong task of reorganizing the department into five-person work teams when John received word that a new computer would soon be installed. John remembered when the record keeping had been done primarily by hand. The transition to the first computer over five years ago had been traumatic, to say the least. Now everything would have to be put on a new computer. John wondered if this meant that he would have to reorganize again. Would the new computer replace some of his employees? John also wondered if the company would eventually replace him with a computer expert. As he remembered the problems he experienced when they made the transition to the first computer, John wondered what he could do to make this transition less stressful.

In today's world, change is an everyday occurrence. The following excerpt emphasizes the increased rate with which change has been occurring:

> Let us suppose that we can reduce to one year of 12 months the total duration of the known period of the history of man: some 30,000 years. In these 12 months that represent the life of all our ancestors from the Age of Stone until our days, it is toward the 18th of October that the Iron Age starts. It is the 8th of December that the Christian era begins.
>
> It is on the 29th of December when Louis XVI ascends the throne of France. What mechanical power does mankind possess at that epoch?
>
> Exactly the same as that which the caveman had possessed plus whatever he was able to derive from draft animals after the invention of the yoke.
>
> By the 30th of December, in the first 18 minutes of the morning, Watt invents the steam engine. On the same day, the 30th of December, at 4:00 PM the first railway begins to operate.
>
> And thus we reach the last day of the year. The 31st of December.
>
> At 5:31 AM, Edison invents the first incandescent lamp. By afternoon, at 2:12 PM Blériot crosses the Channel. And not until 4:14 pm does World War I begin. At this date Western man disposes of 8/10 of a horsepower. This is notable and brutal progress because:
>
> During the whole year he has lived with only 1/10 of a horsepower. In one day he has multiplied it by 8, but only five hours suffice to bring this figure to 80.
>
> It is a fact that on the 31st of December at the 11th stroke of midnight Frenchmen dispose of 8 horsepower each. And at the same time, the Americans have 60 each, while the inhabitants of New York have 270 each.
>
> The following events take place during the last few minutes of the day: The first atomic bomb explodes, Neil Armstrong walks on the moon, and over 50 million computers are in use.[1]

CHANGE AND THE SUPERVISOR

1 LEARNING OBJECTIVES

Change can greatly affect the supervisor's job. Some changes occur gradually; others occur suddenly. In either case, change can have serious repercussions for the supervisor. Change as it applies to supervision can be classified in three major categories: technological, environmental, and internal to the organization.

In the scope of the known history of man, the rate of change is so fast that only a very short time has elapsed between the invention of the steam engine and the computerized world of today.
Hulton Getty/Tony Stone Images; Courtesy of Tektronix, Inc.

Technological change includes such things as new equipment, machinery, and processes. The technological advances since World War II have been dramatic. Automatically controlled machines and computers are common examples of technological advances that have greatly affected all of us.

Environmental change includes all of the nontechnological changes that occur external to the organization. New government regulations, new social trends, new political trends, and economic changes are examples of environmental change. Specific examples of such change include new tax rates, new laws, changes in interest rates, changes in fashions, and shifts in population. Ordinarily, changes of this kind have an indirect impact on the supervisor. However, there is very little that the supervisor can do to influence them.

Changes internal to the organization include such things as budget adjustments, methods changes, policy changes, reorganizations, and the hiring of new employees. These changes are the result of decisions made by the organization's management. It is not unusual for the supervisor to have an input into such decisions. Figure 17.1 summarizes the types of changes facing the supervisor.

The supervisor is often the focal point for implementing change. He or she is often the person responsible for introducing a change and seeing that it is successfully implemented. Thus, it is imperative that the supervisor know how to cope with change successfully.

REACTIONS TO CHANGE

How employees perceive a change greatly affects how they react to it. While many variations are possible, only four basic situations can occur:

1. If employees cannot foresee how the change will affect them, they will resist the change or be neutral, at best. Most people shy away from the unknown. An attitude often taken is that the change may make things worse.

FIGURE 17.1	Technological	Environmental	Internal
Types of Change Affecting the Supervisor	Machines	Laws	Policies
	Equipment	Taxes	Procedures
	Processes	Social trends	Methods
	Automation	Fashion trends	Rules
	Computers	Political trends	Reorganization
	New raw materials	Economic trends	Budget adjustments
		Interest rates	Job restructuring
		Consumer trends	Human resources

2. If employees clearly see that the change is not compatible with their needs and aspirations, they will resist the change. In this situation, the employees are certain that the change will make things worse.

3. If employees see that the change is going to take place regardless of their objections, they may initially resist the change and then resignedly accept it. Their first reaction is to resist. Once the change appears inevitable, they often see no other choice than to go along with it.

4. If employees see that the change is in their best interests, they will be motivated to accept it.

Obviously, the key here is for employees to feel confident that the change will make things better. It is the supervisor's obligation to foster an accepting attitude. Note that three out of the four situations result in some form of resistance to the change. The manner in which employees resist change can vary dramatically. At one extreme, for example, an employee may mildly resist by showing no interest in the change; at the other extreme, an employee may resist by sabotaging the change.

RESISTANCE TO CHANGE

LEARNING OBJECTIVES

While most people profess to be open minded, they still resist change. This is especially true when the change affects their jobs. Resistance to change is a natural reaction. It is not a reaction common only to troublemakers.

Resistance to change may be explicit or very subtle. The employee who quits a job because of a change in company policy is resisting the change in an open and explicit manner. The employee who becomes very sullen because of the change but does not quit is resisting the change in a more passive manner.

There are many reasons why employees resist change. Some of the most frequently encountered reasons, called *barriers to change*, are discussed below.

Fear of the Unknown

It is natural for people to fear the unknown. The problem with many changes is that their outcome is not always foreseeable. And even if the outcome of a change is foreseeable, the results of the change are not often communicated to all of the affected employees. For example, employees may worry about and resist the installation of a new machine if they aren't sure what the impact of the machine will be on their jobs. Similarly, employees may resist a new supervisor simply because they don't know what to expect from him or her. Another related fear is the uncertainty that employees may feel about operating under a change. Thus, employees may fully understand a change, yet have serious doubts about whether they will be able to handle it. For example, employees may resist a new procedure because of a fear that they won't be able to master it.

Threat to Job or Income

Employees fear any change that they think threatens their job or income. The threat may be real or only imagined, but in either case the result is employee resistance. For example, a salesperson will resist a territory change if he or she believes that the change will result in less opportunity. Similarly, production workers will oppose new standards that they believe will be more difficult to achieve.

Fear that Skills and Expertise Will Lose Value

Everyone likes to feel valued by others, so anything that has the potential of reducing that value will be resisted. For example, an operations supervisor might resist implementation of a new, more modern piece of equipment for fear the change will make him or her less needed by the organization.

Threats to Power

Many people believe a change might diminish their power. For example, a supervisor may perceive a change to the organization's structure as weakening his or her power within the organization.

Inconvenience

Many changes result in personal inconveniences to the affected employees. If nothing else, change often forces employees to learn new ways. This may require additional training, schooling, or practice, any of which will probably inconvenience the employees. A common reaction of employees is that the change "isn't worth the extra effort required."

Threats to Interpersonal Relations

The social and interpersonal relationships among employees can be quite strong. For example, the opportunity to have lunch with a certain group of employees may be very important to the employees involved. These relationships may appear insignificant to everyone but those employees. When a change, such as a transfer, threatens the relationships, the affected employees often resist. Employees naturally feel more at ease working with people they know well. Also, a group may have worked out a routine for accomplishing its work based on the strengths and weaknesses of its members. Any changes in the group would naturally disrupt that routine.

FIGURE 17.2

Suggestions for Reducing
Resistance to Change

Build trust.
Discuss upcoming changes.
Involve the employees in the changes.
Make sure the changes are reasonable.
Avoid threats.
Follow a sensible time schedule.
Implement the changes in the most logical place.

REDUCING RESISTANCE TO CHANGE

LEARNING OBJECTIVES

3

Most changes are originated by middle or upper management and passed down to the supervisor for implementation. As the last link between management and employees, the supervisor is responsible for seeing that these changes are successfully introduced. In this process, the supervisor must cope with employees' anxieties and fears that are related to change. Regardless of where or how a change originated, the environment created by the supervisor can greatly affect employees' acceptance of the change. Several suggestions for creating a positive environment for change are presented in Figure 17.2 and discussed in the following paragraphs.

Build Trust

If the employees trust and have confidence in the supervisor, they are much more likely to accept changes. Otherwise, they are likely to resist changes vigorously. Trust cannot be established overnight: it is built over a period of time. The supervisor's actions determine the degree of the employees' trust. If the employees perceive the supervisor as fair, honest, and forthright, they will trust him or her. If the employees feel that the supervisor is always trying to put something over on them, there will be no trust. Supervisors can go a long way toward building trust if they discuss upcoming changes with the employees and if they actively involve the employees in the change process.

Discuss Upcoming Changes

Fear of the unknown, one of the major barriers to change, can be greatly reduced by discussing any upcoming changes with the affected employees. During this discussion, the supervisor should be as open and honest as possible, explaining not only what the changes will be but why the changes are being made. The more background and detail the supervisor can give, the more likely it is that the employees will accept the changes. The supervisor should also outline the impact of the changes on each of the affected employees. People are primarily interested in how change will affect them as individuals. A critical requirement for success is that the supervisor allow the employees an opportunity to ask questions. This is the major advantage of an oral discussion over a written memo. Regardless of how thorough an explanation may be, employees will usually have questions. Supervisors should answer those questions to the fullest extent possible.

SUPERVISION ILLUSTRATION 17–1

ACTION FORUMS AT PG&E

In 1993, Pacific Gas & Electric Company (PG&E) implemented an approach for solving problems and introducing change. The San Francisco-based utility's success in implementing change is due largely to its action-forum process, which bites off problems in three-month, easy-to-digest portions. The process encourages anyone in the company to suggest areas for change. The only rules are that the change can be dealt with in 90 days or less.

Action forums usually last for two to three days and involve participation from employees and outsiders who might be appropriate (such as clients or vendors). The forums are usually held at PG&E's San Ramon Learning Center, which provides both room and board. The action forums use teams to evaluate suggested changes and to develop plans for their implementation.

By mid-1996, PG&E had hosted almost 80 action forums which had saved the company more than $270 million in cycle-time reduction, productivity and performance improvement, cost avoidance, revenue enhancement, and actual cost reductions.

Source: Gillian Flynn, "Think Tanks Power Up Employees," *Personnel Journal,* June 1996, pp. 100–108. For more information about PG&E visit its Web site at: **www.pge.com**

Involve the Employees

Another way to lower resistance to changes and to build employee trust is to actively involve employees in the change process. Employee involvement in change can be extremely effective. It is only natural for employees to want to go along with changes that they have helped bring about. A good approach is to solicit employee ideas and inputs as early as possible in the change process. In other words, don't wait until the last minute to ask the employees what they think about a change. Ask them as soon as possible. When affected employees have been involved in a change from, or near, its inception, they will usually actively support the change. The psychology involved here is simple: No one wants to oppose something that he or she has helped develop. Supervision Illustration 17–1 describes how Pacific Gas and Electric Company has implemented a very successful change program based on employee involvement.

Make Sure the Changes Are Reasonable

The supervisor should always do whatever is possible to ensure that any proposed changes are reasonable. Proposed changes that come down from upper levels are sometimes totally unreasonable. When this is the case, it is usually because upper management is not aware of certain circumstances. It is the supervisor's responsibility to intervene in such situations and communicate the problem to upper management. Figure 17.3 presents humorous examples of "unreasonable changes."

Avoid Threats

The supervisor who attempts to implement change through the use of threats is taking a negative approach likely to decrease employee trust. Also, most people resist being threatened into accepting something. A natural reaction is: "This

	CHANGE MEMO

FIGURE 17.3

Unreasonable Changes?

To: All personnel

Subject: New sick leave policy

Date: Today

Sickness — No excuse! . . . we will no longer accept your doctor's statement as proof, as we believe that, if you are able to go to the doctor, you are able to come to work!

Death — (Other than your own) . . . this is no excuse . . . there is nothing you can do for them, and we feel sure that someone else with a lesser position can attend to the arrangements. However, if the funeral can be held in the late afternoon, we will be glad to let you off one hour early, provided that your share of the work is ahead enough to keep the business going in your absence.

Leave of absence — (For an operation) . . . we will no longer allow this practice. We wish to discourage any thoughts that you might need an operation, as we believe that, as long as you are an employee here, you will need all of whatever you have, and you should not consider having anything removed. We hired you as you are, and therefore anything removed would certainly make you less than we bargained for.

Death — (Your own) . . . This we will accept as an excuse. But we would like two weeks' notice, as we feel it is your duty to train someone else to do your job.

Also, we feel entirely too much time is being spent in the rest room. In the future, we will follow the practice of going in alphabetical order. For instance, those whose names begin with A will go from 8:00 to 8:15, B will go from 8:15 to 8:30, and so on. If you are unable to go at your time, then it will be necessary for you to wait until the next day when your turn comes again.

---

must be bad news if it requires a threat." Even though threats may get results in the short run, they may be very damaging in the long run. They will usually have a negative impact on employee morale and attitude.

Follow a Sensible Time Schedule

As discussed previously, most changes are passed down to the supervisor for implementation. However, the supervisor can often influence the timing of changes. Some times are better than others for implementing certain changes. For example, the week before Christmas would ordinarily not be a good time to implement a major change. Similarly, a major change should ordinarily not be attempted during the height of the vacation season. The supervisor can often provide valuable insight regarding the proper timing of changes. If nothing else, the supervisor should always use common sense when recommending a time schedule for implementing a change.

Implement the Changes in the Most Logical Place

The supervisor often has some choice about *where* changes will take place. For example, the supervisor usually decides who will get a new piece of equipment. Common logic should be followed when making such decisions. Certain employees are naturally more adaptable and flexible than others. It makes good sense to introduce any changes through these employees. The supervisor who makes it a point to know his or her employees usually has a pretty good idea as to which of them are most likely or least likely to be flexible. Where possible, changes should be implemented in a way that minimizes their effect on interpersonal relationships. The supervisor should not attempt to disturb smooth-working groups.

The Five W's and an H

The preceding paragraphs suggest how to establish an environment that will readily accept change. Once a specific change has been singled out for implementation, the supervisor should always begin the implementation by explaining the five W's and an H to the employees—What the change is, Why the change is needed, Whom the change will affect, When the change will take place, Where the change will occur, and How the change will take place.

LEWIN'S THREE-STEP MODEL FOR CHANGE

In the late 1940s, psychologist Kurt Lewin presented a three-step model for successfully implementing change:

1. Lewin's first step, unfreezing, deals with breaking down the forces supporting or maintaining the old behavior. These forces can include such variables as the formal reward system, reinforcement from the work group, and the individual's perception of what is proper role behavior.

2. The second step, presenting a new alternative, involves offering a clear and attractive option representing new patterns of behavior.

3. The third step, refreezing, requires that the changed behavior be reinforced by the formal and informal reward systems and by the work group. It is in this step that the supervisor can play a pivotal role by positively reinforcing employee efforts to change.

Most of the suggestions offered in the previous section ("Reducing Resistance to Change") deal with the first two parts of Lewin's model: the unfreezing and the presenting of a new alternative.

Implicit in Lewin's three-step model is the recognition that the mere introduction of change does not ensure the elimination of the prechange conditions or that the change will be permanent. Unsuccessful attempts to implement lasting change can usually be traced to a failure in one of Lewin's three steps.

MANAGING STRESS

Stress is an arousal of mind and body in response to real or perceived demands or threats. Stress cannot be completely eliminated from anyone's life. In fact, some stress is desirable in many situations. For example, managed or controlled stress often contributes to personal growth and development. Also, many positive events—such as marriage, moving to a new city, or taking a new job—are accompanied by stress. Excessive stress, however, is generally harmful. Among employees, stress of this kind manifests itself in increased absenteeism, job turnover, lower productivity, mistakes on the job, and low levels of motivation. As a result of these and related problems, excessive stress has been estimated to cost U.S. industry more than $150 billion annually. It has also been estimated that one-third of all supervisors occasionally experience stress that impairs their ability to perform effectively.[2] In addition to its previously mentioned job-related manifestations, excessive stress can manifest itself in such health problems as high blood pressure, tension headaches, ulcers, insomnia, heart attacks, and even death.

Stress arises in situations in which an individual is unable to respond or perform adequately. In other words, a person is likely to experience stress when an imbalance exists between perceived demands and one's capacity to meet those demands. Conflict and change in an organizational setting are often accompanied by increased stress.

Types of Job-Related Stress

Stress can result from an imbalance of demand and capacity related to a person's job, physical condition, social environment, or personal problems. This section will deal specifically with job-related stress, which the supervisor's actions can directly affect. Some of the more frequently encountered sources of job-related stress are:

1. *Task stress.* The task or job is too difficult.
2. *Role stress.* The individual is not clear on exactly what he or she should be doing.
3. *Human environmental stress.* This condition is caused by overcrowding or understaffing.
4. *Physical environmental stress.* Poor physical conditions exist, such as extreme cold or heat or poor ventilation.
5. *Social stress.* Interpersonal conflict occurs among employees.
6. *Burnout.* Burnout occurs when an employee loses interest in and motivation for doing the job.

Because of its increasing prevalence in today's workplace, burnout is discussed further in the following section.

Burnout.   **Burnout** is one potential result of excessive job-related stress over a long period of time. It occurs when an employee loses interest in and motivation for doing the job. It generally takes place in three stages: (1) an increased feeling of emotional exhaustion, (2) a callous and dehumanized perception of others, and (3) a negative self-evaluation of one's effectiveness. Not all people who suffer from stress experience burnout. It has been found that burnout candidates have distinguishing characteristics that incorporate, but are not totally limited to, stress:[3]

1. Burnout candidates predominantly experience stress caused by job-related stressors.
2. Burnout candidates tend to be idealistic and/or self-motivating achievers.
3. Burnout candidates tend to seek unattainable goals.

The consequences of burnout are serious. Naturally, an employee who has lost interest and motivation is not going to be a good performer. As one would suspect, burnout is frequently accompanied by absenteeism, frequent job turnover, and even an increase in the use of drugs and alcohol. Because burnout usually results from stress, the same guidelines that have been offered for managing stress should be followed to reduce the potential for burnout.

Organizational Guidelines for Managing Stress

Many organizations have undertaken certain actions to reduce the amount of job-related stress experienced by their employees. Among these actions are:

- Shortening hours of direct contact with customers.
- Granting special leaves (sabbatical programs).
- Introducing early retirement programs.
- Installing on-site exercise facilities.
- Actively involving employees in the decision-making processes.
- Fulfilling the realistic expectations of employees.
- Clearly defining employee jobs.
- Introducing changes gradually.

Naturally, some of these actions are more appropriate in some situations than in others. For any of these actions to work, the organization must first have an awareness of its potential for dealing with stress-related problems. Supervision Illustration 17–2 discusses how Cable Midlands has introduced a stress management program that uses both conventional and nonconventional approaches.

Personal Guidelines for Managing Stress

LEARNING OBJECTIVES

Fortunately, supervisors and employees can do many things to reduce stress for themselves. Some of these are summarized below:

1. Pay attention to the physical needs of exercise, diet, and rest. Exercise should be regular (at least three times per week). Avoid large amounts of junk food and get enough sleep.
2. Don't create artificial deadlines. When deadlines are necessary, make them realistic and base them on normal working conditions.
3. Pace yourself. Try not to personalize everything about your job. Learn to step back and keep things in perspective. Take a breather when you begin to feel irritable.

SUPERVISION ILLUSTRATION 17–2

NONCONVENTIONAL STRESS MANAGEMENT

Cable Midlands has been supplying cable TV, telephone, and information services to the Black Country and Telford areas of the United Kingdom since the early 1990s. Employees are constantly under pressure because of frequent changes in working practices and advancing technology.

Aware of the increasing stress among its employees, management decided to offer a series of stress management workshops on topics such as time management, assertiveness training, and other traditional methods of dealing with employee stress. Initially the workshops were offered only to managers. However, the reaction was so overwhelmingly positive that it was decided to open the program to nonmanagers.

Building on the successes of the initial workshops, the company then implemented a range of other nonconventional therapies to help employees cope with stress. Clinical hypnosis, aromatherapy, and reflexology are now offered to employees at lunch times as well as in workshops. Clinical hypnosis teaches employees practical relaxation techniques. Aromatherapy involves the use of aromatic oils and massage to resolve muscular tension while reflexology uses pressure points to the feet to relieve stress. Conventional confidential counseling is also available to employees. Future plans call for yoga and exercise classes as well as sessions on healthy eating and creating a positive image.

Initial signs are that the program has helped reduce absences and turnover. It has also fostered the feeling among employees that the company genuinely cares about its employees.

Source: Siobahn Butler, "Alternative Ways to Take Out Stress," *People Management,* May 16, 1996, pp. 43–44. For more information about Cable Midlands and other telecommunication trends in the U.K., visit:
www.citresearch.com

4. Inject a change into your routine. List the things you have to do, and organize them according to priority and urgency. Then, as you complete them, your stress will ease as your feeling of accomplishment grows.

5. Periodically perform an emotional audit. Identify the pressure points in your life, and recognize the times when you are most susceptible to stress.

6. Share persistent problems with others. Don't let problems build up inside. Learn to share problems with your spouse, friends, colleagues, or a professional. Sometimes talking it out is a way of working it out.

7. Learn to relax away from the job. Develop non-work-related hobbies, and build time into your schedule for engaging in these hobbies on a regular basis.

8. Get away for lunch. It doesn't have to be every day, but you should get away from the office or plant for lunch on a regular basis.

9. Drink lots of water. Keep water at your workstation. Some people recommend drinking as many as eight glasses of water each day.

10. Utilize your mental and spiritual resources. Different forms of meditation and contemplation can help reduce stress.

The Family and Medical Leave Act of 1993

LEARNING OBJECTIVES 7

The Family and Medical Leave Act of 1993 (FMLA) went into effect in August 1993. One of the purposes of the FMLA is to reduce stress among employees who are experiencing certain changes in their lives. FMLA applies to employers who have 50 or more employees for 20 or more workweeks in the current or preceding calendar year. Under the FMLA, qualifying companies must grant employees up to 12 weeks of unpaid leave in any 12-month period for the birth,

Under the FMLA, qualifying companies must grant employees up to 12 weeks of unpaid leave in any 12-month period for the birth, adoption, or foster placement of a child.
Spencer Grant/Stock Boston

adoption, or foster placement of a child; the care of a seriously ill child, spouse, or parent; or a serious personal illness that prevents an employee from performing his or her job. The FMLA does not supersede state laws that are more generous to employees. Employees covered by a health care plan are entitled to coverage during FMLA leave.

SOLUTION TO THE SUPERVISION DILEMMA	**John is faced with implementing change in the form of a new computer system. Because of the uncertainties accompanying this change, he is experiencing anxiety and stress. In introducing the new system and related changes, John should first concentrate on creating a positive environment. He should discuss the upcoming changes with his employees and solicit their ideas (pp. 328–29). At this time, John should explain the five W's and an H to them: What the change is, Why it is needed, Whom it will affect, When it will take place, Where it will take place, and How it will take place (p. 331). John should also make sure that the implementation schedule is realistic (p. 330). He should be aware that the natural reaction of many of his employees is to resist change (pp. 325–26). John can overcome much of this resistance by carefully explaining what the new computer system will do and how it will affect each of his employees.**

     In addition, John should deal with his stress. John must first realize that he is experiencing stress, and then he must learn how to manage or reduce it. He should learn to pace himself and not set any unrealistic deadlines. He should also take care of his physical needs by resting, exercising, and eating properly (pp. 333–34).

SUMMARY

This chapter discusses the supervisor's role in introducing change in the organization. It offers several suggestions to help supervisors successfully deal with change. A three-step model for implementing change is presented. The nature and sources of job-related stress are explored.

1. *Discuss the supervisor's role in introducing change.* Although most changes are originated by middle or upper management, it is the supervisor who is usually responsible for implementing changes. To successfully implement changes, supervisors must constantly strive to create a positive environment for change.

2. *Explain why employees tend to resist change.* Some of the most frequently encountered reasons why employees resist change are (1) fear of the unknown, (2) threat to job or income, (3) fear that skills and expertise will lose value, (4) threats to power, (5) inconvenience, and (6) threats to interpersonal relations.

3. *Present several things that the supervisor can do to foster employee acceptance of change.* To foster employee acceptance of change, supervisors should build trust, discuss upcoming changes, involve employees in the changes, make sure the changes are reasonable, avoid threats, follow a sensible time schedule, and implement the changes in the most logical place. As the first step in implementing a change, supervisors should explain the five W's and an H—what, why, whom, when, where, and how—to affected employees.

4. *Describe a three-step model for implementing change.* In the late 1940s, psychologist Kurt Lewin presented a three-step model for successfully implementing change. The first step, unfreezing, deals with breaking down the forces supporting or maintaining the old behavior. The second step, presenting a new alternative, involves offering a clear and attractive option representing new patterns of behavior. The

third step, refreezing, requires that the changed behavior be reinforced.

5. *Discuss the nature and sources of job-related stress.* Stress arises in situations in which an individual is unable to respond or perform adequately—that is, when an imbalance exists between perceived demands and one's capacity to meet those demands. Some of the more frequently encountered sources of job-related stress are excessively difficult tasks, lack of clarity about what should be done, overcrowding or understaffing, poor physical conditions, interpersonal conflict, and burnout.

6. *Suggest several personal guidelines for managing organizational and personal stress.* Supervisors and employees can do many things to reduce their own stress. Some of them are paying attention to the physical needs of exercise, diet, and rest; not creating artificial deadlines; pacing yourself; changing your routine; periodically performing an emotional audit; sharing persistent problems with others; and learning to relax away from the job; getting away for lunch; drinking lots of water; and utilizing your mental and spiritual resources.

7. *Explain the Family and Medical Leave Act of 1993 (FMLA) and discuss how it is designed to reduce stress.* The Family and Medical Leave Act of 1993 applies to companies who have 50 or more employees for 20 or more workweeks in the current or preceding calendar year. Under the FMLA, qualifying companies must grant employees up to 12 weeks of unpaid leave in any 12-month period for birth, adoption, or foster placement of a child; the care of a seriously ill child, spouse, or parent; or a serious personal illness that prevents an employee from performing his or her job. The idea is that employee stress will be reduced if employees are allowed leave time when experiencing these changes.

REVIEW QUESTIONS

1. Name the three major categories of change that are of concern to supervision.
2. Describe the four basic reactions of employees to change.
3. Name six common barriers to change (reasons for resistance to change).
4. Discuss several methods or approaches for reducing resistance to change.
5. Describe a three-step model for implementing change.
6. Define stress.
7. Name and define six types of job-related stress.
8. Identify the three stages that generally accompany burnout.
9. Describe several actions that an organization might take to reduce employee stress.
10. Name several ways that a supervisor might reduce stress.
11. The Family and Medical Leave Act of 1993 applies to what companies?

SKILL-BUILDING QUESTIONS

1. Suppose that as a supervisor you received an order to implement a change that you personally opposed. What would you do?
2. Because of a recent OSHA (Occupational Safety and Health Administration) visit, you have been instructed to implement several changes relating to safety. You know that your employees are going to regard some of these changes as ridiculous. What might you do to get the employees to accept the changes?
3. Comment on the following statement: "Stress is inherent in every job, and employees must learn to cope on their own."
4. Do you agree with the following statement? "Burnout is just a new fangled notion that gives lazy people an excuse not to work." Why or why not?

REFERENCES

1. Adapted from Rolf Nordling, "Social Responsibilities of Today's Industrial Leader," *Advanced Management Journal*, April 1957, pp. 19–20.
2. Dorothy Schwimer, "Managing Stress to Boost Productivity," *Employment Relations Today*, Spring 1991, p. 23.
3. Oliver I. Niehouse, "Controlling Burnout: A Leadership Guide for Managers," *Business Horizons*, July–August 1984, pp. 80–85.

ADDITIONAL READINGS

"Are Managers under Stress?" *Management Services*, January 1997.

Flynn, Gillian. "Think Tanks Power Up Employees," *Personnel Journal*, June 1996.

Geber, Sara Zeff. "Pulling the Plug on Stress," *HR Focus*, April 1996.

Kaschub, William J. "Employees Redesign HR," *Human Resources Professional*, July–August 1997.

Weiss, W. H. "Coping with Work Stress," *Supervision*, April 1994.

SKILL-BUILDING APPLICATIONS

Incident 17–1

A New Boss

Jane McBride has been an accounting supervisor for Boland's department store for over 15 years. The previous store manager, Whit Calhoun, was originally hired as a junior accountant by Jane. Jane has always believed that her job is to see that the work gets out. She believes that work is work. Sometimes it is pleasant, and sometimes unpleasant. Any employee who doesn't like the work can adjust or quit. Jane believes that work is not a place for play.

As one might expect, Jane has a reputation for running things and of not standing for any nonsense. Yet her turnover is very low and almost all of her employees respect her. The employees also feel that Jane knows her business and will stand up for them.

Two months ago, Whit Calhoun retired and his replacement, Vincent Ball, took over as store manager. One of the first things Vincent did was call his supervisors together and present some major changes he hoped to make. These included (1) increasing employees' involvement in the decision-making process, (2) establishing a planning committee made up of three management representatives and three employees, (3) starting a suggestion system, (4) working out a new wage-incentive plan, and (5) installing an up-to-date performance appraisal system. Vincent stated that he would be active in the implementation of these changes.

Shortly after the meeting, Jane ran into Dan Driver, another supervisor who had been with Boland for many years.

Jane: It sure looks like Vincent is going to shake things up around here.

Dan: It sure does. Maybe it'll be for the good.

Jane: I can't see it if it is. He's going to stir things up that can only lead to trouble. We've got a good operation now. Why change it?

Dan: I agree we have a good operation, but it can still be improved. Maybe these changes will do just that. At any rate, I think we should support Vincent.

Jane: I'm not so sure things won't be worse.

Questions

1. Why do you think Jane is reluctant to accept Vincent's changes? Do you think Jane's reaction is unusual?
2. How would you suggest that Vincent go about implementing the desired changes?

Incident 17–2

Getting Rid of Bart

Bart had been with the QTZ Company for almost 20 years. QTZ is a large firm in the Southwest that manufactures high-tech products. By age 54, Bart had attained a nice salary with good benefits and pension. He had a superior work record and consistently positive performance appraisals.

As a result of a recent downsizing, Bart's boss was replaced by a younger manager. The new manager made it explicitly clear to Bart, without explanation, that Bart's days were limited at QTZ and that Bart should start looking for new employment. Immediately afterward, Bart was moved into a smaller office with no windows. His assistant was assigned to someone else and his last seven years of expenses were audited. Bart's next two performance appraisals were all below average. The new boss also became abusive and purposely belittled Bart in front of his peers and threatened him in private.

After almost one year of harassment, Bart was summarily fired without severance pay and no notice. By this time Bart had used up his sick leave and vacation pay trying to recover from a bout with ulcers and a severe sleep disorder. In addition, Bart was depressed, anxious, and despondent.

Questions

1. Is Bart's stress understandable? What could he have done to avoid it?
2. What would you do at this point if you were Bart?
3. In general terms, discuss the potential costs of this situation to QTZ.

Source: Adapted from C. Brady Wilson, "U.S. Businesses Suffer from Workplace Trauma," *Personnel Journal*, July 1991, p. 48.

Exercise 17–1

Preparing for Resistance to Change

One of the problems you face involves mistakes being made by employees who perform a particular operation. The same mistakes seem to occur in more than one department. You believe a training program for the people concerned will help reduce errors.

You are aware, however, that your supervisors may defend existing procedures simply because the introduction of training may imply criticism of the way they have been operating. You realize, too, that the supervisors may fear resistance by employees afraid of not doing well in the training program. All in all, you plan to approach the subject carefully.

You consider the following approaches for dealing with the situation:

1. Add to the agenda of your weekly staff meeting a recommendation that training be undertaken to help reduce errors.
2. Talk to all your supervisors individually and get their attitudes and ideas about what to do before bringing the subject up in the weekly staff meeting.
3. Ask the corporate training staff to come in, determine the training needs, and develop a program to meet those needs.
4. Since this training is in the best interests of the company, tell your supervisors they will be expected to implement and support it.

5. Appoint a team to study the matter thoroughly, develop recommendations, then bring it before the full staff meeting.

Other alternatives may be open to you, but assume these are the only ones you have considered. *Without discussion with anyone*, choose one of the approaches and be prepared to defend your choice.

Exercise 17–2

Truth and Misconceptions about Stress

Answer "True" or "False" to the following questions to see how much you know about stress and what you can and should do about it. Your instructor will discuss the answers with you after you have completed the quiz.

1. Stress is primarily an American disease.
2. Stress isn't always a negative condition; in fact, sometimes stress can be good for us.
3. The secret to escaping the damaging effects of stress is to avoid potentially stressful situations.
4. The more hours you work, the greater your stress.
5. A complex person suffers more from stress than one who has a simpler self-evaluation. Limit the facets of your personality and you'll improve your ability to cope with stress.
6. In the workforce, people in management positions with a great deal of responsibility feel the greatest amount of stress.
7. Putting aside time for leisure is one of the best ways to reduce the negative effects of stress; the harder you play, the better the results.
8. Don't put off solving your problems until tomorrow, even if you have to stay up half the night to work them out.

Source: A. Gaedeke, "The Truth and Misconceptions about Stress," *Manager's Magazine*, August 1989, pp. 29–30. Reprinted with permission of *Manager's Magazine*, a publication of LIMRA International, Inc., 300 Day Hill Road, Windsor, CT 06095.

Exercise 17–3

Measuring Your Level of Stress

The following quiz will enable you to determine how vulnerable you are to stress, how much stress there is in your life, and how well you han-dle its effects. Please respond to each question honestly by checking the answer that most accu-rately describes your situation as it *actually is*, not as you would like it to appear or as you think it should be. The scoring instructions are pro-vided at the end of the quiz.

Stress Quiz

Stress Experience	Times Experienced			
	Often	**Some-times**	**Seldom**	**Never**
1. During the past three months, how often were you under considerable strain, stress, or pressure?	___	___	___	___
2. How often do you experience any of the following symptoms: heart palpitations or a racing heart, dizziness, painfully cold hands or feet, shallow or fast breathing, restless body or legs, insomnia, chronic fatigue?	___	___	___	___
3. Do you have headaches or digestive upsets?	___	___	___	___
4. How often do you experience pain in your neck, back, arms, or shoulders?	___	___	___	___
5. How often do you feel depressed?	___	___	___	___
6. Do you tend to worry excessively?	___	___	___	___
7. Do you ever feel anxiety or apprehension even though you don't know what has caused it?	___	___	___	___
8. Do you tend to be edgy or impatient with your peers or subordinates?	___	___	___	___
9. Do you ever feel overwhelmed with feelings of hopelessness?	___	___	___	___
10. Do you dwell on things you did but shouldn't have done?	___	___	___	___
11. Do you dwell on things you should have done but didn't do?	___	___	___	___
12. Do you have any problems concentrating on your work?	___	___	___	___
13. When you're criticized, do you tend to brood about it?	___	___	___	___
14. Do you tend to worry about what your colleagues think of you?	___	___	___	___
15. How often do you feel bored?	___	___	___	___
16. Do you find that you're unable to keep your objectivity under stress?	___	___	___	___

Stress Quiz (*continued*)

	Yes	No
17. Of late, do you find yourself more irritable and argumentative than usual?	___	___
18. Are you as respected by your peers as you want to be?	___	___
19. Are you doing as well in your career as you'd like to?	___	___
20. Do you feel that you can live up to what top management expects from you?	___	___
21. Do you feel that your spouse understands your problems and is supportive of you?	___	___
22. Do you have trouble with any of your associates?	___	___
23. Do you sometimes worry that your associates might be turning against you?	___	___
24. Is your salary sufficient to cover your needs?	___	___
25. Have you noticed lately that you tend to eat, drink, or smoke more than you really should?	___	___
26. Do you tend to make strong demands on yourself?	___	___
27. Do you feel that the boundaries or limits placed on you by top management regarding what you may or may not do are fair?	___	___
28. Are you able to take problems in stride, knowing that you can deal with most situations?	___	___
29. Do you stay productive and seldom "lose your cool" under stress?	___	___
30. Do you feel neglected or left out in meetings?	___	___
31. Do you habitually tend to fall behind with your work?	___	___
32. During the last year, have you or anyone in your family suffered a severe illness or injury?	___	___
33. Have you recently moved to a new home or community?	___	___
34. During the last three months, have any of your pet ideas been rejected?	___	___
35. Is it difficult for you to say no to requests?	___	___
36. Do you generally work better under pressure?	___	___
37. Are you able to focus your concentration under pressure?	___	___
38. Are you able to return to your normal state of mind reasonably soon after a stressful situation?	___	___

Scoring: Add up your points based on the answer key below. See "What your score means" on p. 342.

	Often	Some-times	Seldom	Never		Yes	No		Yes	No
1.	7	4	1	0	17.	4	0	28.	0	3
2.	7	4	1	0	18.	0	3	29.	0	3
3.	6	3	1	0	19.	0	4	30.	4	0
4.	4	2	0	0	20.	0	5	31.	3	0
5.	7	3	1	0	21.	0	5	32.	6	0
6.	6	3	1	0	22.	3	0	33.	3	0
7.	6	3	1	0	23.	4	0	34.	4	0
8.	5	2	0	0	24.	0	3	35.	3	0
9.	7	3	1	0	25.	5	0	36.	0	3
10.	4	2	0	0	26.	4	0	37.	0	3
11.	4	2	0	0	27.	0	3	38.	0	4
12.	4	2	0	0						
13.	4	2	0	0						
14.	4	2	0	0						
15.	4	2	0	0						
16.	6	4	1	0						

Source: This quiz was drawn from Eugene Raidsepp, "Overcoming Job-Related Stress," *Supervision,* August 1987, p. 307. Reprinted by permission of © The National Research Bureau, P.O. Box 1, Burlington, Iowa 52601-0001.

What Your Score Means

90–167: A score in this range indicates not only that your troubles seem to outnumber your satisfactions but also that you are presently subjected to a high level of stress. You are, no doubt, already aware of your pressures, and you are rightfully concerned about your own psychological and physical well-being.

You should by all means do everything possible to avoid as many stressful situations as you can until you feel more in control of your life. It might be a good idea for you to go over the quiz to pinpoint the major sources of your present stress.

You might also need to develop more effective ways to manage how you respond to stressful situations. Your vulnerability to stressful events shows that you may be overreacting to problems or you may not be as willing to cope with adversities as you could be.

You might want to consider seeking professional help. Sometimes even a few hours of counseling can be of great help. You might also want to pay heed to the wise words of a cardiologist who offers the following three rules for combating stress:

Rule 1: Don't sweat the small stuff.

Rule 2: Everything is small stuff.

Rule 3: If you can't fight it, or flee from it, flow with it.

45–89: A score within this range indicates either that your stress seems to be moderate or that you are probably handling your frustrations quite well. You should, however, review various aspects of your daily life and try to relieve stress before it starts building up. Because you may have occasional difficulties in coping with the effects of stress, you might want to consider adding some new methods of dealing with disappointments.

Remember, we all have to face and live with occasional states of unwellness. We can ignore them, or we can turn situations of stress and pressure into an opportunity for further emotional growth. Life can either grind us down or polish us up—and the choice is largely our own.

0–44: A score in this range indicates that your stress is relatively low and that you probably are in great shape. In spite of minor worries and concerns, stress doesn't seem to be causing you any serious problem.

You have, no doubt, good adaptive powers, and you are able to deal quite well with situations that make you temporarily uptight. You seem to have been able to strike a good balance in your ability to cope with and control stress.

Exercise 17–4

Life Events Causing Stress

Research has shown that certain life events tend to be correlated with the onset of certain physical illnesses. In other words, people have a tendency to get sick (e.g., cold or flu) following certain events that require adjustment. Think back to the last time you were sick and determine which, if any, of the events shown in Exhibit 17.1 immediately preceded your illness. The mean values indicate the relative impact of each respective life event. Add up the mean values associated with each life event that you experienced. The higher the total value, the more these events probably contributed to your getting sick.

	Life Event	Mean Value
EXHIBIT 17.1 Life Events Causing Stress	1. Death of spouse.	100
	2. Divorce.	73
	3. Marital separation.	65
	4. Detention in jail or other institution.	63
	5. Death of a close family member.	63
	6. Major personal injury or illness.	53
	7. Marriage.	50
	8. Being fired at work.	47
	9. Marital reconciliation with mate.	45
	10. Retirement from work.	45
	11. Major change in the health or behavior of a family member.	44
	12. Pregnancy.	40
	13. Sexual difficulties.	39
	14. Gaining a new family member (e.g., through birth, adoption, relative moving in).	39
	15. Major business readjustment (e.g., merger, reorganization, bankruptcy).	39
	16. Major changes in financial state (e.g., a lot worse off or a lot better off than usual).	38
	17. Death of a close friend.	37
	18. Changing to a different line of work.	36
	19. Major change in the number of arguments with spouse (e.g., either a lot more or a lot less than usual regarding child rearing or personal habits).	35
	20. Taking on a mortgage greater than $50,000 (e.g., purchasing a home or a business).	31
	21. Foreclosure on a mortgage or loan.	30
	22. Major change in responsibilities at work (e.g., promotion, demotion, lateral transfer).	29
	23. Son or daughter leaving home (e.g., marriage, attending college).	29
	24. In-law troubles.	29
	25. Outstanding personal achievement.	28
	26. Wife beginning or ceasing work outside the home.	26
	27. Beginning or ceasing formal schooling.	26
	28. Major change in living conditions (e.g., building a new home, remodeling, deterioration of home or neighborhood).	25
	29. Revision of personal habits (e.g., dress, manners, associations).	24
	30. Troubles with the boss.	23
	31. Major change in working hours or conditions.	20
	32. Change in residence.	20
	33. Changing to a new school.	20
	34. Major change in usual type and/or amount of recreation.	19
	35. Major change in church activities (e.g., a lot more or a lot less than usual).	19
	36. Major change in social activities (e.g., clubs, dancing, movies, visiting).	18

(continued)

Life Event (*concluded*)	Mean Value
37. Taking on a mortgage or loan of less than $50,000 (e.g., purchasing a car or home improvement).	17
38. Major change in sleeping habits (a lot more or a lot less sleep, or change in part of day when asleep).	16
39. Major change in number of family get-togethers (e.g., a lot more or a lot less than usual).	15
40. Major change in eating habits (a lot more or a lot less food intake, or very different meal hours or surroundings).	15
41. Vacation.	13
42. Christmas.	12
43. Minor violations of the law (e.g., traffic tickets, jaywalking, disturbing the peace).	11

Source: Reprinted with permission from *Journal of Psychosomatic Research*, T. H. Holmes and R. H. Rahe, "The Social Readjustment Rating Scale." Copyright 1967, Elsevier Science, Ltd., Pergamon Imprint, Oxford, England. (The dollar figures used in this example have been adjusted for inflation.)

CHAPTER 18

Counseling Employees

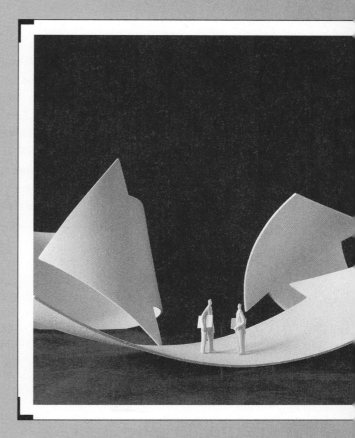

LEARNING OBJECTIVES

After studying this chapter, you should be able to:

1. Determine when it is appropriate for the supervisor to counsel employees.

2. Differentiate between directive and nondirective counseling.

3. Present a general approach for counseling employees.

4. Explain the supervisor's role in career counseling.

5. Define a "troubled employee."

6. Discuss ways to effectively supervise troubled employees.

7. Explain what employee assistance programs (EAPs) are.

8. Summarize the legal requirements for dealing with troubled employees.

9. Explain the difference between a "troubled" employee and a "problem" employee.

Jane Harris thinks that one of her employees, Ken Hall, has a drinking problem. Jane is almost certain that she has smelled alcohol on Ken's breath several times. On at least two occasions during the past month, other employees have told Jane that Ken drinks on the job. However, Jane has never caught Ken drinking during working hours. In an effort to get additional information, Jane has examined Ken's personnel file. The file showed that Ken had taken a considerable amount of leave on Mondays. Jane has also reviewed Ken's performance appraisals over the past few years and has noticed that Ken's ratings have been declining. Jane has never faced a problem of this kind as a supervisor. She wonders what the best way is to handle the problem.

Supervisors, by the nature of their jobs, work with people. Not all employees can be supervised in the same manner. The supervisor may have some employees who are easy to supervise and some who are difficult to supervise. Some employees are well-adjusted, "normal" individuals, and other employees have personal problems that affect their work. Some employees need assurance that they are doing the right things. Some employees need some assistance in planning their careers. As a result of such situations, supervisors are required from time to time to counsel employees.

WHEN AND WHY TO COUNSEL

1 LEARNING OBJECTIVES

Numerous situations require the supervisor to act in a counseling role. In some situations, an employee may voluntarily seek the supervisor's counsel on certain matters. In other situations, a supervisor may find it necessary to approach the employee. Usually, this happens when a supervisor observes a decline in an employee's performance. A supervisor should never counsel an employee if the employee's problem appears to be beyond the supervisor's ability. This is usually the case with an employee who has a severe personal problem. In such cases, the supervisor should refer the employee to a person professionally trained to deal with that problem. If a supervisor attempts to counsel an employee in areas where the supervisor is not qualified, this may only add to the problem and further hinder the employee's performance. The overwhelming majority of situations appropriate for supervisory counseling involve employee performance issues, not employee personal problems. How the supervisor should deal with employee personal problems is covered later in this chapter.

Many positive effects may result from effective supervisory counseling. From the employee's viewpoint, the positive effects of counseling may include reassurance, release of emotional tensions, and clarification of his or her thinking. From the viewpoints of both parties, a positive effect of counseling may be improvement of the employee's performance.

COUNSELING TECHNIQUES

Above all else, the supervisor must establish the proper climate for counseling. Supervisors must communicate that they are there to help the employee and that they have a genuine concern for the employee. Whenever possible, the counseling interview should take place in a private and quiet setting.

Directive versus Nondirective Counseling

2 LEARNING OBJECTIVES

When counseling with employees, the supervisor may use either a directive or a nondirective approach. In **directive counseling,** the supervisor takes the initiative and asks the employee pointed questions about a problem. When the supervisor feels that he or she has a good grasp of what is causing the problem, he or she suggests several steps that the employee might take to overcome it. In **nondirective counseling,** the employee assumes most of the initiative and the supervisor serves primarily as a listener. The employee is encouraged to discuss what he or she thinks is causing the problem and to develop solutions to it. Instead of asking pointed questions, the supervisor asks open-ended questions such as "Can you tell me more?" or "Would you elaborate on what you mean?" The nondirective approach is suggested for most situations because it tends to create an environment in which the employee is encouraged to come up with solutions and to focus on what he or she needs to change.

Steps in the Counseling Interview

3 LEARNING OBJECTIVES

Remember, most supervisory counseling involves employee performance issues. No one approach to counseling works best in all situations. The general approach outlined below for supervisors is a variation of the nondirective approach that should prove effective in most situations.[1]

Step 1. In a nonthreatening manner, describe what you have observed. Talk about actual performance and not about vague concepts such as attitude or motivation. Do not threaten or intimidate the employee.

Step 2. Ask the employee to comment on your observations. Encourage the employee to be open and honest. If you disagree with parts of the employee's response, do so in a gentle manner.

Step 3. If prior meetings have been held, briefly review what they accomplished.

Step 4. With the employee's input, identify the problem-solving techniques to be used. Do not attempt to solve the problem yourself, but guide the employee to resolve it alone. Be a good listener and let the employee talk.

Step 5. Once a solution has been agreed upon, restate the actions to be taken and reemphasize your concern about the problem.

Step 6. Always schedule a follow-up meeting, preferably in the near future.

Step 7. Document the meeting. While this is not always necessary, it is usually a good idea. The documenting should be done while the session is still fresh in your mind.

CAREER COUNSELING

4   LEARNING
OBJECTIVES

Every so often a supervisor is asked by employees for some type of career counseling. Just what is the supervisor's role in these situations? Many supervisors are reluctant to engage in any form of career counseling because they haven't been trained in this effort. However, it is not necessary to be a trained psychologist to be successful in career counseling. Supervisors who follow the counseling guidelines discussed earlier in this chapter can be successful. First and foremost, supervisors must realize that the primary responsibility for career planning rests with each individual employee. The supervisor's role is to assist the employee and to help the employee evaluate his or her ideas, not to plan or make decisions for the employee. It is of primary importance for supervisors to demonstrate a caring attitude toward employees and their careers. Being receptive to employee concerns and problems is another requirement. Some additional specific suggestions for helping supervisors become effective career counselors are:

1. *Recognize the limits of career counseling.* Remember that the supervisor serves as a catalyst in the career development process. The primary responsibility for developing a career plan lies with the individual employee.

2. *Respect confidentiality.* Career counseling is very personal and has basic requirements of ethics, confidentiality, and privacy.

3. *Establish a relationship.* Be honest, open, and sincere with the employee. Try to be empathetic and see things from the employee's point of view.

4. *Listen effectively.* Learn to be a sincere listener. A natural human tendency is to want to do most of the talking. It often takes a conscious effort to be a good listener.

5. *Consider alternatives.* An important goal in career counseling is to help employees realize that there are usually a number of available choices. Help the employees to expand their thinking and not necessarily be limited by past experience.

6. *Seek and share information.* Be sure the employee and the organization have assessed the employee's abilities, interests, and desires. Make sure that the organization's assessment has been clearly communicated to the employee and that the employee is aware of potential job openings within the organization.

7. *Assist with goal definition and planning.* Remember that the employees must make the final decisions. Supervisors should serve as "sounding boards" and help ensure that the individual's plans are valid.[2]

Supervision Illustration 18–1 discusses one way that Chrysler Corporation encourages career counseling among its supervisors.

SUPERVISION ILLUSTRATION 18–1

SUPERVISORS AND CAREER COUNSELING

Many companies believe that career development is much more important today than in the past. "Careers used to be like trains—the employee just sat down and went where it went," says Richard Knowdell, executive director of the Career Planning and Adult Development Network in San Jose, California. "Now careers are like all-terrain vehicles. The employee needs to know how to drive."

While there is no doubt that employees need to take more responsibility for managing their careers, successful companies realize that employees need assistance with the process. One of the more effective means of providing this assistance is through the supervisors who lead the teams or work groups.

To encourage supervisors to fulfill the role of career counseling and coaching, Chrysler Corporation offers intensive yet compact training for its supervisors. The first day of training requires supervisors to assess themselves in terms of their own careers and planning. The second day focuses on coaching and facilitation strategies. To further aid the process, Chrysler Corporation also offers training to nonsupervisors on how to develop a career network.

Source: Kathryn Tyler, "Prepare Managers to Become Career Coaches," *HR Magazine,* June 1997, pp. 98–101. For more information about Chrysler Corporation, visit its Web site at:
www.chrysler.com

SUPERVISING TROUBLED EMPLOYEES

5 LEARNING OBJECTIVES

6 LEARNING OBJECTIVES

All employees have personal problems that from time to time influence their motivation to work. Health, family, legal, and financial problems are common types of personal problems that influence performance on the job. Employees normally solve these problems privately or with help and encouragement from someone else. Some employees, however, have lasting or recurrent personal problems that are too difficult to solve in these ways.

Some employees are able to keep their personal lives separate from their work. They may manage personal problems while remaining fully productive members of the workforce. But many employees with personal problems cannot keep those problems from affecting their job performance. When the job performance of an employee is affected by personal problems that normal counseling or disciplinary measures cannot correct, the employee is usually diagnosed as a troubled employee.

The types of problems already mentioned (health, family, legal, and financial problems) may be serious enough to cause significant work problems for the employee. Family problems can lead to mental or emotional problems, which in turn can lead to drug dependence, illness, and financial and legal problems. Alcoholism, mental or emotional instability, drug dependence, and other illnesses are some of the common causes that create troubled employees.

How the Troubled Employee Affects the Organization

The troubled employee affects productivity and the work environment in many ways. A primary result of bringing personal problems to the workplace is reduced productivity. Absenteeism and tardiness tend to increase, and efficiency is reduced. Bringing personal problems to the workplace also increases the costs of insurance programs, including sickness and accident benefits. Some industrial theft is due to the need of drug addicts to support their habits. Lower morale, increased friction among employees and between supervisors and employees, and more grievances also result from the presence of troubled employees. The permanent loss of trained employees due to disability, early retirement, and premature death is a problem associated with troubled employees. Difficult to measure, but a very real cost associated with troubled employees, is loss of business and damage to the public image of the organization.

Each year, American business faces a loss of up to $150 billion because of personal problems that accompany employees to work and have a negative effect on their attendance and job performance. The average cost of a troubled employee to the organization is estimated to run between $1,300 and $3,000 per year. Drug and alcohol abuse alone have been estimated to cost U.S. business almost $130 billion a year due to decreased productivity and rehabilitation costs.[3] Studies show that drug and alcohol abusers have two to four times as many accidents as employees who do not use drugs and alcohol. These same studies report that drug and alcohol abusers are absent two and one-half more times than nonusers; they use three times the amount of sick leave as do nonusers; their workers' compensation claims are five times higher, and they are generally less productive.[4]

In addition to organizational costs, there are also personal and social costs. Studies have shown that alcohol abuse is related to increased suicide, homicide, accidents, and such ailments as heart disease and cirrhosis.

Similarly, there is a proven relationship between the use of illegal drugs and crime. The total cost to the families affected by the problems of troubled employees may never be known. Attempts to solve these problems are a service to the organization, the troubled employee, and society in general.

Help from the Organization

Until recent years, organizations attempted to avoid the employee's non-job-related problems. Although aware of the existence of these problems, organizations believed that they should not interfere with the employee's personal life. Instead, organizations tended to get rid of the troubled employees whose personal lives negatively affected their work. However, organizations have come to realize that it is often in their best interest to help rehabilitate troubled employees. At a minimum, salvaging the troubled employee saves the cost of hiring and training another employee. Most organizations have estimated the cost of hiring and training a new employee to be significantly greater than the cost of rehabilitating a troubled one. In addition, the increased productivity of an employee after treatment can be significant.

Today, many large organizations and a growing number of small organizations have implemented a variety of programs to help troubled employees. The supervisor plays a key role in these programs because it is the supervisor who is responsible for identifying and confronting the troubled employee. To handle this function, the supervisor must be properly trained.

Detecting the Troubled Employee

Personal problems do not necessarily make a person a troubled employee. Only when personal problems interfere with the employee's work performance should they become a concern to the supervisor. For a supervisor to hunt for personal problems and recommend help for all employees with such problems would be a violation of employees' right to privacy. Only when the problems affect the quality or quantity of work, when an employee becomes disruptive to the work environment, or when an employee asks for help should the organization concern itself with personal problems.

In some cases, employees with personal problems voluntarily seek help at work. This is much more likely to happen when the problems do not carry the stigma of social disapproval. Treating alcohol and drug dependency as illnesses rather than weaknesses should encourage employees to seek help voluntarily for these illnesses, as they would for any other physical illnesses.

Until recently, supervisors, along with family and friends, often attempted to help the troubled employee avoid detection. Rationalizing that the problem or the reasons for the problem will go away only prolongs treatment for the troubled employee. From the standpoint of both the troubled employee and the organization, overlooking rule violations and reduced productivity because the employee has personal problems may be the worst thing that the supervisor can do.

The supervisor must learn how to detect evidence of declining job performance. Through proper documentation, the supervisor can usually detect a deterioration in an employee's performance. The supervisor should make a habit of recording evidence of deteriorating relationships, unacceptable performance, and inability to follow rules.

Supervisors must be careful to be consistent in documenting performance problems. Noting inadequacies for one employee and not for others, just because the supervisor suspects that the employee has a serious personal problem, is unfair. Similarly, overlooking examples of poor performance because the employee gives a particularly sad or convincing excuse may only prolong the problem. Figure 18.1 provides a checklist to aid in detecting a troubled employee.

Confronting the Troubled Employee

Once a troubled employee has been identified, the supervisor must confront the employee. Most supervisors do not relish this responsibility. Sufficient documentation can greatly help the supervisor in this process. The confrontation between the supervisor and the troubled employee should consist primarily of three steps: (1) performance review, (2) referral to counseling and assistance, and (3) discussion of the consequences of the employee's actions.

The supervisor should first confront the employee with specific evidence of poor performance. Reviewing any available documentation with the employee is a good approach. It helps the employee realize that there is documented evidence of the poor performance. Be as specific as possible. For example, there

FIGURE 18.1

Detecting the Troubled Employee

1. Be alert to, and document, changes in personality that affect working relationships.
   a. Insubordination.
   b. Altercations with other employees or with the supervisor.
2. Be alert to, and document, changes in quality and quantity of work.
   a. Reduced output.
   b. Increased errors or defects.
3. Be alert to, and document, rule violations.
   a. Unexcused absences.
   b. Unexcused tardiness.
   c. Leaving workstation without permission.
   d. Dress code violations.
   e. Safety rules violations.
   f. Concealing or consuming drugs or alcohol on company premises.
   g. Involvement with law: garnishment of wages, drug traffic.
4. Be consistent.

is a big difference between "you have not been coming to work on time" and "you have been late to work 5 out of the past 12 workdays."

The supervisor should restrict criticism and discussion to job performance. Moralizing on the effects of drug abuse or other problems is not the supervisor's job. If the employee begins to talk about a problem, the supervisor should listen. However, it is not necessary for the supervisor to promote more discussion. The supervisor's advice to the employee should be limited to suggesting that the employee seek proper help. The supervisor should not try to act as a psychologist or medical doctor. He should not attempt to diagnose the cause of the employee's poor performance. He should make direct accusations only when there is specific evidence that the employee is breaking some rule on the job. For example, the supervisor should not accuse an employee of using drugs without specific evidence.

The second step in the confrontation is referral of the troubled employee to professional counseling and assistance. At this point, the employee may become defensive or hostile. The supervisor should not be influenced by an employee's excuses or stories. Employees with personal problems have had plenty of practice convincing themselves and others that their problems are caused by external forces beyond their control. The supervisor may sympathize with the employee and may wish that the poor performance could be overlooked. But acting on this wish is detrimental to both the organization and the employee. The employee needs help. Postponing that help will not ease the problem. The employee may attempt to blame the supervisor for the problem. This is a common reaction of a troubled employee, and it should not be taken personally. The supervisor should be prepared for it and try to remain calm. The supervisor must remain firm but supportive at all times.

During this second step in the confrontation, the supervisor should emphasize that the employee will not jeopardize his or her job by accepting assistance. The supervisor should point out that accepting assistance may, in fact,

FIGURE 18.2

Confronting the Troubled Employee

1. Performance review.
   a. Review documentation with employee.
   b. Restrict your criticism to job performance.
   c. Do not attempt to diagnose the cause of the poor performance.
   d. Do not attempt to counsel the employee concerning the nature of problem.
2. Referral to counseling and assistance.
   a. Be firm and supportive.
   b. Be prepared for excuses and hostility.
   c. Explain that seeking help will not jeopardize the employee's job.
   d. Emphasize the confidentiality of the program.
   e. Know and discuss insurance coverage or other financial assistance.
3. Discussion of consequences of employee action.
   a. Discuss the need for improvement.
   b. Discuss the possible consequences of the employee's not accepting help.
   c. Discuss past successes of the program or similar programs.

be the only way that the employee can continue employment with the organization. The supervisor should also emphasize that all aspects of the assistance program are confidential. Many organizations do not even record the assistance in the employee's personnel file.

Some organizations have company-based employee assistance programs, and some have insurance covering counseling and assistance programs. Other organizations use public assistance programs provided by the local, state, or federal government. Company-based programs, referred to as employee assistance programs (EAPs), are discussed later in this chapter. The supervisor should be aware of the options available for paying for this type of assistance and should communicate these options to the employee.

During the third step of the confrontation, the supervisor should also discuss the need for performance improvement. If the employee accepts help, most organizations agree to work with him or her on a schedule of improvement. If the employee does not accept help, he or she should be informed of the consequences. Usually, if an employee refuses assistance and his or her performance does not improve, the employee is subject to discharge. The employee should also be informed that to avoid discipline and discharge he or she must maintain improved performance.

It is helpful at this point for the supervisor to discuss the success of assistance programs in general. Once employees realize that the supervisor is aware of their poor performance and that assistance programs have a good chance of success, employees are much more likely to cooperate. Figure 18.2 outlines the necessary steps in the confrontation between a supervisor and a troubled employee.

Aiding and Evaluating Recovery

Troubled employees who have been referred for assistance are expected to be rehabilitated. The supervisor bears the primary responsibility for evaluating the extent of rehabilitation. That evaluation must be based on job performance.

Other criteria, such as abstinence for drug and alcohol abusers, certification of recovery by the assisting agency, or continued participation in the assistance program, are less meaningful to the organization than improved job performance. The overriding objective of the supervisor and the organization should be that the employee not only recover but also begin to function satisfactorily on the job.

EMPLOYEE ASSISTANCE PROGRAMS

In 1997, an estimated 20,000 company-based employee assistance programs (EAPs) were in existence in the United States.[5] A 1994 survey by TempForce, a temporary service company, found that 84 percent of the companies surveyed provide EAPs for alcohol and drug abuse, 68 percent offer EAPs for psychological services, 41 percent for marital problems, and 40 percent for financial difficulties.[6] There are several types of EAPs. In the rarest type, diagnosis and treatment of the employee's problem are provided by the organization. In a second type, the organization hires a qualified person to diagnose the employee's problem. Then the employee is referred to the proper agency or clinic. In the third and most common type, a coordinator evaluates the employee's problem only sufficiently to make a referral to the proper agency or clinic. Sometimes the coordinator is a consultant rather than a full-time employee of the organization.

For an EAP to be successful, it must first be accepted by the employees; they must not be afraid to use it. Experience has shown that certain elements are critical to the success of an EAP. Table 18.1 summarizes 10 of the most important characteristics of an EAP.

Studies have shown that company-based employee assistance programs can reduce absenteeism significantly. It has also been shown that EAPs help reduce on-the-job accidents and grievances. Workers' compensation premiums, sickness and accident benefits, and trips to the infirmary also tend to decrease when the company institutes an EAP. Knowledgeable people have estimated that EAPs return as much as $5 to $16 for every $1 invested.[7] Because of the obvious benefits to both the employees and the employers, it is estimated that EAPs will continue to grow in popularity. Supervision Illustration 18–2 describes a successful EAP at Levi Strauss and Company.

LEGAL AND UNION DEMANDS

Until fairly recently, organizations had the legal right to fire or refuse to hire employees who were drug or alcohol addicts. The Rehabilitation Act of 1973 was extended in 1977 to include alcohol and drug addicts. This act protects employable, qualified, handicapped employees (including alcohol and drug addicts) from discrimination in employment by federal contractors or subcontractors. It states that handicapped employees cannot be discriminated against

	Element	Significance
TABLE 18.1 Ten Critical Elements of an EAP	1. Management backing	Without this at the highest level, key ingredients and overall effect are seriously limited.
	2. Labor union support	The employee assistance program (EAP) cannot be meaningful if it is not backed by the employees' labor union.
	3. Confidentiality	Anonymity and trust are crucial if employees are to use an EAP.
	4. Easy access	For maximum use and benefit.
	5. Supervisor training	Crucial to employees needing understanding and support during receipt of assistance.
	6. Union steward training	A critical variable is employees' contact with the union—the steward.
	7. Insurance involvement	Occasionally, assistance alternatives are costly, and insurance support is a must.
	8. Breadth of service components	Availability of assistance for a wide variety of problems (e.g., alcohol, family, personal, financial, grief, medical).
	9. Professional leadership	A skilled professional with expertise in helping, who must have credibility in the eyes of the employees.
	10. Follow-up and evaluation	To measure program effectiveness and overall improvement.

Source: Adapted from F. Dickman and W. G. Emener, "Employee Assistance Programs: Basic Concepts, Attributes, and an Evaluation," *Personnel Administrator,* August 1982, p. 56. Reprinted with permission from the *Personnel Administrator,* published by the Society for Human Resource Management, Alexandria, Virginia.

in federally financed employment, education, and services. The Comprehensive Rehabilitation Service Amendments of 1978 state that the term *handicapped individual* does not include any individual who is an alcoholic or drug abuser whose current use of alcohol or drugs prevents the individual from performing his or her job duties or constitutes a direct threat to property or the safety of others.

Thus, a person may not be discriminated against with respect to employment *solely* because of alcoholism or drug addiction. However, an employer is not obligated to hire people whose use of alcohol or drugs prevents them from satisfactorily performing their job duties. In addition, an employer is not obligated to hire people whose use of alcohol or drugs results in a direct threat to the property or safety of others. Supervisors should realize that their organization can be held liable for injuries caused by a person who is under the influence of drugs or alcohol.

Organizations and unions are beginning to include employee assistance programs in their collective bargaining agreements. The supervisor may find that the contract restricts his or her actions in the handling of problem employees.

SUPERVISION ILLUSTRATION 18–2

LEVI STRAUSS EXPANDS ITS EAP

In 1979, Levi Strauss and Company was one of the first U.S. companies to establish an internal employee assistance program. Since that time, the company has added three major components to its EAP. In 1982, a component called corporate nursing was established to promote the importance of occupational health and a healthy, safe work environment. The second component to be added was the delivery of wellness programs by the EAP staff and corporate nursing. This component was designed to educate employees about a wide range of health issues. Furthermore, in 1989 the company went one step further and developed a work/family component of its EAP. This component deals with personal and family issues that may negatively impact an employee's performance and/or productivity.

Even though it is difficult for the company to measure its return on investment, it did note a $1.1 million savings in behavioral health care dollars in 1992 after it initiated its drug and alcohol education programs. Realizing that it is difficult for employees to separate their personal lives from their work, Levi's EAP has grown into a global health promotion program which provides counseling, health education, and training to employees, management, and family members.

Source: Shannon Peters, "Levi Strauss Promotes Health," *Personnel Journal,* May 1994, pp. 23–27, and "Return-to-Work Programs Essential," *Managed Healthcare,* April 1997, p. 76. For more information about Levi Strauss, visit its Web site at: **www.levi.com**

Some unions have assistance programs. These differ from employer programs primarily in the way the employee enters the program. The union program is voluntary, whereas employer programs usually demand participation for certain employees who are not performing satisfactorily.

In a unionized organization, the supervisor has the added responsibility of informing the union steward of the employee's participation in an assistance program. Keeping the steward informed helps ensure the union's cooperation. The steward can be very helpful in getting the employee to accept assistance.

PROBLEM EMPLOYEES

9 LEARNING OBJECTIVES

In addition to the troubled employees previously discussed, there are other categories of employees that can have a negative impact on the department's performance. The "flirter," the "evangelist," the "socializer," the "busybody," the "complainer," and "lovebirds" are all examples of employees who can cause problems. Such employees behave in a manner that disrupts normal operations. At the least, they set a poor example and distract others. If their behavior is not checked, they may negatively affect the climate of the entire department. When a problem employee of this type is detected, the supervisor should immediately counsel the employee, using the techniques described earlier in this chapter. If counseling is ineffective, the supervisor may be forced to invoke some type of disciplinary action. Discipline is discussed in Chapter 22.

SOLUTION TO THE
SUPERVISION
DILEMMA

Since Jane has detected a decline in Ken Hall's performance and suspects a drinking problem, she should attempt to counsel Ken, following the guidelines suggested in this chapter (p. 347). Specifically, she should present her documentation in a nonthreatening manner, and ask Ken to comment on her suspicions. If Ken acknowledges the problem, Jane should ask him for ideas on how to help overcome the problem. If Ken denies the problem, Jane should make sure that she has presented all of her evidence, warn Ken that she will be looking for evidence of a drinking problem, and point out that Ken's performance must improve. The next step is to wrap up the discussion and summarize what has been decided and what actions will be taken. Before dismissing Ken, Jane should set a time to follow up on the actions agreed upon. Immediately after Ken has gone, Jane should document what was decided.

Depending on what happens during her confrontation with Ken, Jane might suggest that Ken participate in the company's employee assistance program (p. 354). In any case, Jane would want to be sure that Ken is aware of what the company's EAP can do for him.

SUMMARY

Numerous situations require supervisors to act in a counseling role. This chapter discusses many of these situations and presents guidelines for counseling employees. It also offers guidelines for detecting, confronting, and managing troubled employees. Employee assistance programs (EAPs) are singled out for special attention.

1. *Determine when it is appropriate for the supervisor to counsel employees.*
   If the supervisor feels competent to offer counsel, he or she should counsel employees who voluntarily seek counsel or employees whose performance has declined. If the supervisor does not feel competent to offer counsel, he or she should refer such employees to a professionally trained person.

2. *Differentiate between directive and nondirective counseling.* In directive counseling, the supervisor takes the initiative and asks the employee pointed questions about a problem. When the supervisor feels that he or she has a good grasp of what is causing the problem, he or she suggests several steps that the employee might take to

overcome it. In nondirective counseling, the employee assumes most of the initiative and the supervisor serves primarily as a listener. The employee is encouraged to discuss what he or she thinks is causing the problem and to develop solutions to it.

3. *Present a general approach for counseling employees.* A general approach for counseling employees consists of these seven steps: (1) In a nonthreatening manner, describe what you have observed. (2) Ask the employee to comment on your observations. (3) If prior meetings have been held, briefly review what they accomplished. (4) With the employee's input, identify the problem-solving techniques to be used. (5) Restate the actions to be taken. (6) Set a time for follow-up. (7) Document the meeting.

4. *Explain the supervisor's role in career counseling.* The primary responsibility for career planning rests with each individual employee. The supervisor's role is to assist the employee and to help the employee evaluate his or her ideas, not to plan or make decisions for the employee.

5. *Define a "troubled employee."* A troubled employee is one whose job performance is affected by personal problems that cannot be corrected by normal counseling or disciplinary measures.

6. *Discuss ways to effectively supervise troubled employees.* A supervisor can effectively supervise troubled employees first by learning to detect them. Once a troubled employee has been identified, the supervisor should confront the employee. A part of the confrontation is to refer the employee to counseling and assistance. After a troubled employee has been through the necessary counseling and assistance program, the supervisor bears responsibility for evaluating the extent of rehabilitation based on the employee's job performance.

7. *Explain what employee assistance programs (EAPs) are.* EAPs are designed to provide assistance to employees with personal problems. There are several types of EAPs. In the rarest type, diagnosis and treatment of the employee's problem are provided by the organization. In a second type, the organization hires a qualified person to diagnose the employee's problem. The employee is then referred to the proper agency or clinic. In the most common type, a coordinator evaluates the employee's problem only sufficiently to make a referral to the proper agency or clinic.

8. *Summarize the legal requirements for dealing with troubled employees.* The Rehabilitation Act of 1973 and subsequent amendments protect employable, qualified, handicapped workers (including alcohol and drug addicts) from discrimination in employment by federal contractors or subcontractors. However, employers are not obligated to hire people whose use of alcohol or drugs prevents them from satisfactorily performing their job duties or presents a direct threat to property or the safety of others.

9. *Explain the difference between a "troubled" employee and a "problem" employee.* A "troubled" employee is one whose job performance is affected by personal problems that cannot be corrected by normal counseling or disciplinary measures. Alcohol and drug abusers are examples of troubled employees. A "problem" employee is one who has a negative impact on the organization's performance but whose problem can usually be corrected with counseling and/or discipline. "Flirters" and "socializers" are examples of "problem" employees.

REVIEW QUESTIONS

1. What are the differences between directive and nondirective counseling?
2. Outline the seven steps in a counseling interview.
3. Outline several suggestions for helping supervisors become effective career counselors.
4. Define a "troubled employee."
5. How do troubled employees affect the workplace environment?
6. What are some rules that the supervisor should observe when identifying troubled employees?
7. What are the three steps in the confrontation between the supervisor and the troubled employee?
8. What points should the supervisor emphasize when referring an employee to professional help?
9. What are some rules that the supervisor should follow to aid the troubled employee in the rehabilitation process?
10. What is an employee assistance program (EAP)?
11. What are three general types of employee assistance programs?
12. How do the Rehabilitation Act of 1973 and its amendments affect the supervisor's relationship with alcohol and drug abusers?
13. In addition to troubled employees, what other kinds of employees can have a negative impact on the work unit's performance?

SKILL-BUILDING QUESTIONS

1. "Employees with personal problems that affect their work performance are basically weak people." Discuss your views on this statement.

2. Should a supervisor try to give an employee advice on how to solve a personal problem? Why or why not?

3. "In order to help a troubled employee, the supervisor must get to the root of the employee's problem." Discuss your views on this statement.

4. Many supervisors believe that troubled employees deserve whatever they get. How do you feel about this?

REFERENCES

1. Much of this section is adapted from Steve Buckman, "Finding Out Why a Good Performer Went Bad," *Supervisory Management*, August 1984, pp. 39–42.

2. Adapted from N. T. Meckel, "The Manager as Career Counselor," *Training and Development Journal*, July 1981, pp. 65–69.

3. Elaine McShulskis, "Employee Assistance Programs," *HR Magazine*, May 1996, pp. 12–20.

4. "Substance Abuse in the Workplace," *HR Focus*, February 1997.

5. The Employee Assistance Professionals Association, 4601 N. Fairfox Drive, Suite 1001, Arlington, VA 22203.

6. "EAP Programs and Productivity," *Supervisory Management*, January 1994, p. 5.

7. Rhonda Cooke, "Hotline for Help," *Credit Union Management*, March 1997, pp. 23–24.

ADDITIONAL READINGS

Carey, Robert. "When Personal Becomes Professional," *Sales & Marketing Management*, June 1996.

Carney, Karen E. "Choosing an EAP," *Inc.*, July 1994.

Gill, Brian W. "Employee Assistance Programs," *American Printer*, June 1997.

McDonnell, Charles R. "Effective Employee Counseling for the First-Line Supervisor," *Health Care Supervisor*, September 1997.

McShulskis, Elaine. "Employee Assistance Programs Effective, but Underused?" *HR Magazine*, May 1996.

Stork, Diana. "The AMA Handbook for Developing Employee Assistance and Counseling Programs," *Personnel Psychology*, Winter 1993.

360   SECTION IV   HUMAN RELATIONS SKILLS

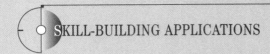

SKILL-BUILDING APPLICATIONS

Incident 18–1

Changes in an Employee's Behavior

Jack Sampson, a clerk in the human resources department of the Franklin County Hospital, had been with the hospital for four years. Until the last several months, he had been an ideal employee. He had always been excellent at answering other employees' questions. Furthermore, he was active in both community and church activities. He was married and had two children.

However, Mel Dillon, director of human resources for Franklin County Hospital, had noticed some significant changes in Jack's behavior during the last three or four months. Jack's work had become sloppy, and he had been very irritable and snappish when answering questions from employees. He had been absent from work on five occasions during the past two months. Before that, he had never missed a day of work. In addition, he had been late to work three times during the past month. This had never happened before. One day, Jack missed the weekly staff meeting. Afterward, he explained his absence by saying that he had forgotten about it.

Mel decided to talk to Jack about the change in his behavior. Jack explained he hadn't been feeling well lately. Mel suggested that he see a doctor, but Jack said, "I'll be OK. Just bear with me for a little while."

After another three weeks, Jack's behavior and performance did not improve. In fact, they seemed to be getting worse. During that time, Mel noticed that Jack was staying away from his desk for long periods. Since Jack's job didn't require him to be away from his desk for long periods, Mel decided to find out where he was going. As Jack was leaving his desk the next day, Mel followed him at a respectable distance. Jack went into one of the hospital's storage rooms and stayed there about 10 minutes. This storage room was for hospital supplies; as far as Mel could determine, Jack had absolutely no reason for being in it. A short time later, Mel thought he smelled alcohol on Jack's breath.

Questions

1. What should Mel do at this time?
2. How should Mel handle the overall problem?

Incident 18–2

Smoking in the Stockroom

Boyd Coleman was hired as a stock clerk 18 months ago. Until recently, Elena Ramirez, supervisor of the stockroom, had been very pleased with his work. She even talked him into enrolling in evening courses at a community college for which the company paid his tuition.

About two months ago, Elena noticed that Boyd had become very careless in his work. Two weeks ago, she had to give him a written reprimand for taking unauthorized leaves from the stockroom. Boyd's behavior improved for a week, but Elena felt that his work then again deteriorated. She called him into her office, where the following discussion occurred:

Elena: Boyd, I just don't know what I'm going to do about you. You started out so well. What happened?

Boyd: Nothing happened. You're just picking on me.

Elena: Picking on you! You know I've tried to help you. Remember, I was the one who got you to start school. That reminds me of something. The school called yesterday and said that you hadn't been in class for three weeks. Why?

Boyd: I just decided that the classes were useless. I don't need that stuff anyhow.

Elena: Boyd, something is bothering you. I don't know what it is, but I would like to help.

Boyd: Nothing is bothering me, and I want you to stop meddling in my personal life.

Elena: I'm not meddling. I would just like to help. As your supervisor, however, I must say that your performance on the job is my business, and it must improve. Do you understand?

Boyd: Yeah, I guess so.

Shortly thereafter, while walking through the stockroom, Elena heard two voices coming from behind a large stack of boxes. One of the voices said, "Don't smoke it all; let me have some of it." Elena recognized this voice as Boyd's. Elena also noticed a strange, sweet odor coming from the same area.

Questions

1. Would you confront the two people right now?
2. Should Elena walk away and discuss the problem with her boss?
3. How well did Elena handle the situation with Boyd before this incident?

Exercise 18–1

What Is the Problem?

Lately, one of your subordinates has been unusually irritable with several people in your department. You have purposely refrained from taking action because you believe that the parties involved should work out such difficulties. This approach has worked well in similar situations in the past. This morning, however, your subordinate directed some unnecessary remarks to you, and now it is apparent that you must act. Before you have an opportunity to discuss the situation, you hear through the grapevine that the subordinate is having marital difficulties, which obviously could be the source of the problem.

In handling the situation, you feel your best approaches are the following:

1. Mention that you've heard about the marital difficulties and that, although sympathetic, you don't feel that personal problems should influence behavior toward co-workers or job performance.
2. Privately advise other staff members that your subordinate is having some personal problems, and ask for their understanding during this difficult period.
3. Approach the problem by using yourself as an example. Indicate that you sometimes have personal problems and irritations but that you try not to let them affect you on the job. Then suggest that the subordinate exert extra effort to be less abrasive with others.

4. Ask questions and attempt to get a thorough understanding of your subordinate's problem so that you can give appropriate advice.
5. Mention that you have noticed the subordinate's recent irritable behavior, and listen to what the subordinate has to say. Then, in an understanding way, indicate that personal problems should not be allowed to affect job performance.

Other alternatives may be open to you, but assume that these are the only ones you have considered. *Without discussion with anyone,* decide which of these approaches you would take. Be prepared to defend your choice.

Source: Adapted from P. R. Jones, B. Kaye, and H. R. Taylor, "You Want Me to Do What?" Reprinted from the *Training and Development Journal,* July 1981, p. 62. Copyright 1981, *Training & Development,* American Society for Training and Development. Reprinted with permission. All rights reserved.

Exercise 18–2

How Do You Rate as a Career Counselor?

This quiz helps supervisors to examine their knowledge of the career counseling function and to discover those areas in which some skill building may be necessary. Rate your knowledge, skill, and confidence as a career counselor by scoring yourself on a scale of 0 (low) to 10 (high) on each of the following statements:

_____ 1. I am aware of how career orientations and life stages can influence a person's perspective and contribute to career planning problems.

_____ 2. I understand my own career choices and changes and feel good enough about what I have done to be able to provide guidance to others.

_____ 3. I am aware of my own biases about dual career paths and feel that I can avoid these biases in coaching others to make a decision on which way to go with their careers.

_____ 4. I am aware of how my own values influence my point of view, and I recognize the importance of helping others to define their values and beliefs so they are congruent with career goals.

_____ 5. I am aware of the pitfalls of "shooting behind the duck" and try to keep myself well informed about my organization, so I can show others how to "shoot ahead of the duck."

_____ 6. I know the norms existing within my own department as well as those within other departments and parts of the organization, so I can help others deal with them effectively.

_____ 7. I understand the organizational reward system (nonmonetary) well enough to help others make informed decisions about career goals, paths, and plans.

_____ 8. I have access to a variety of techniques I can use to help others articulate their skills, set goals, and develop action plans to realize their career decisions.

_____ 9. I am informed about the competencies required for career success in this organization in both the managerial and technical areas, so I can advise others on the particular skills they need to build on and how to go about developing that expertise.

_____ 10. I feel confident enough about my own skills as a career counselor that I can effectively help my people with their problems and plans and make midcourse corrections when necessary.

Scoring

Add up your score and rate yourself against the following scale:

0–30   It might be a good idea if you found *yourself* a career counselor.

31–60   Some of your people are receiving help from you. . . . However, do you know how many and which ones are not?

61–80   You're a counselor! You may not be ready for the big league yet, but you are providing help for your people.

81–100 Others have a lot to learn from you. You understand the importance of career counseling, and you know how to provide it.

Exercise 18–3

Who Is Right?

Because of his short temper and stubborn attitude, George was assigned to various jobs during his five years with the ABC Company.* When the quality of George's work declined along with his attitude, management began using progressive discipline. After getting suspended for insubordination, George was warned that another insubordination would result in discharge. At this same time, management urged George to seek counseling through the company's employee assistance program (EAP). George refused to seek the help of the EAP.

At one point, George's supervisor became so concerned about George's behavior that the supervisor temporarily removed him from his job. Management then offered George a "last chance" agreement which required George to seek counseling through the company's EAP. George signed the agreement only to announce later that he couldn't live up to its terms. After management suspended George, he insisted that he be terminated instead. Management obliged George by terminating him.

At this point, George withdrew his termination request and filed a grievance seeking reinstatement. He said that he objected to the "last chance" agreement because it required him to participate in the EAP, which was supposed to be voluntary. George stated that if he participated in the EAP, he would be admitting that he had done something wrong. Management replied that his insubordination and poor performance were sufficient grounds for discharge and that they had gone beyond the call of duty by offering him another chance. Management further stated that George's consistent refusal to get help left no alternative but termination.

1. Does George fit the definition of a "troubled employee"?

2. Do you think George should have been offered the "last chance" agreement? Why or why not?

3. How would you have handled the situation if you had been George's supervisor?

---

*This exercise is adapted from William E. Lissy, "Troubled Employees," *Supervision*, January 1996, pp. 17–18.

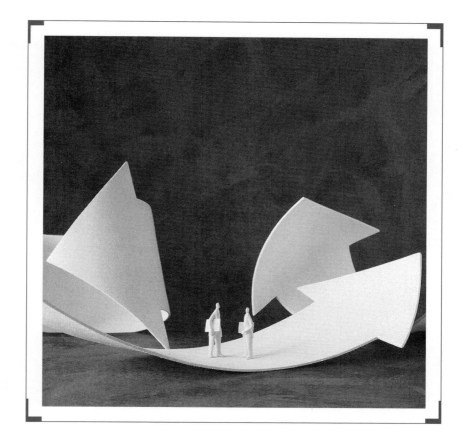

Controlling Skills

SECTION OUTLINE

19 Supervisory control and quality

20 Improving productivity through cost control

21 Safety and accident prevention

22 Discipline and grievance handling

chapter 19

Supervisory Control and Quality

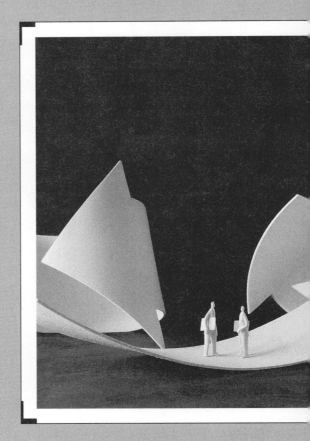

LEARNING OBJECTIVES

After studying this chapter, you should be able to:

1. Outline the three basic steps in the control process.
2. Identify tools and techniques most frequently used by supervisors to exercise control.
3. Define what quality means to a supervisor, and list several reasons for maintaining quality.
4. Define the concept of quality assurance.
5. Discuss Total Quality Management.
6. Summarize the thrust of ISO 9000.
7. Explain the purpose of a zero-defects program.
8. Define a quality circle.
9. Cite several guidelines that supervisors can follow to help build quality job habits among employees.
10. Differentiate between product quality control and process control.
11. Discuss the major types of inventories and explain the purposes for carrying inventories.
12. Explain the just-in-time approach to inventory control.

Since taking over as supervisor of the claims section, John Lewis has discovered that things often don't get done as they should. John has missed deadlines. In addition, his department has mishandled claims and made basic processing errors. On top of this, John's department ran out of claim forms last week. Much to John's dismay, it took three days to get some replacements.

John does not expect everything to go perfectly, and he understands why certain things can go wrong. What he doesn't understand is why he never finds out about a problem until it is too late to correct it. When John discussed this matter with a supervisor from another department, the supervisor suggested that John's supervisory controls might be inadequate.

The major purpose of supervisory controls is to ensure that things are progressing according to the supervisor's plans. Thus, controls should be designed to alert the supervisor to problems or potential problems before they become critical. Supervisors should use the controlling process to ensure success by detecting deviations early and therefore allowing time to take corrective actions. Controlling is similar to planning in many ways. The major difference between controlling and planning is that controlling usually takes place *after* the fact, whereas planning takes place *before* the fact.

STEPS IN THE CONTROLLING PROCESS

LEARNING
OBJECTIVES

Control is accomplished by comparing actual performance with predetermined standards or objectives and then taking action to correct any deviations from the standard. Thus, the control process has three basic requirements: (1) establishing performance standards, (2) monitoring performance and comparing it with standards, and (3) taking necessary corrective action. The first requirement is part of the planning process while the latter two are unique to the control process.

Establishing Performance Standards

When objectives have been set, they are generally used as standards. A standard outlines what is expected. **Standards** are used to set performance levels for machines, tasks, individuals, groups of individuals, or even the organization as a whole. Departmental objectives are types of standards. Usually, standards are expressed in terms of quantity, quality, or time limitations. For example, standards may deal with production output per hour, quality as reflected by customer satisfaction, or production schedules.

Performance standards attempt to answer the question "What is a fair day's work?" or "How good is good enough?" Although designed to reflect normal output, output standards take into account more than just work. Such standards include allowances for rest, delays that occur as part of the job, time for personal needs, time for equipment maintenance, and allowances for physical fatigue. Figure 19.1 lists several types of standards.

FIGURE 19.1
Major Categories and
Examples of Standards

Revenue standards—designed to reflect the level of sales activity.
Examples: dollar sales, average revenue per customer, per capita sales.
Cost standards—designed to reflect the level of costs.
Examples: dollar cost of operation, cost per unit produced, cost per unit sold.
Productivity standards—designed to reflect output per unit of time.
Examples: number of units produced per work hour, number of units produced over
a given time period.
Material standards—designed to reflect efficiency of material usage.
Examples: amount of raw material per unit, average amount of scrap per unit
produced.
Resource usage standards—designed to reflect how efficiently organizational
resources are being used.
Examples: return on investment, percent of capacity, asset usage.

Many methods for setting standards are available. Which method is most
appropriate depends on the type of standard in question. A common approach
is to use the judgment of the supervisor or other recognized experts. A limitation of this approach is that it is very subjective. A variation of this method is
for the supervisor and the person or persons performing the job to jointly set
the standard. With this method, the individuals actually performing the job provide input. The analysis of historical data, such as production data, is another
approach. A potential problem here is that things may have changed since the
data were collected. The most objective approach is the employment of industrial engineering methods. These methods usually involve a detailed and scientific analysis of the situation. Motion studies and time studies (discussed in
Chapter 9) are examples of this approach.

Monitoring Performance

The overriding purpose of monitoring performance is to provide information on
what is actually happening. The major problem in monitoring performance is
deciding when, where, and how often to monitor. Monitoring must be done
often enough to provide adequate information. If it is overdone, however, it can
become expensive and can result in adverse reactions from employees. The key
is to view monitoring as a means of providing needed information, not as a
means of checking up on employees. Thus, monitoring should be preventive
and not punitive. In this light, the reasons for monitoring should always be fully
explained to employees.

Timing is also important when monitoring performance. For example, raw
materials must be reordered before they run out so as to allow for delivery time.

Most control tools and techniques are primarily concerned with monitoring
performance. Reports, audits, budgets, and personal observations are methods
commonly used for this purpose.

Taking Corrective Action

Only after the actual performance has been determined and compared with the
standard can proper corrective action be determined. All too often, however,
managers set standards and monitor performance but do not follow up with ap-

propriate actions. If standards are not being met satisfactorily, the supervisor must find the cause of the deviation and correct it. A major problem in this step is determining when standards are not being met satisfactorily. How many mistakes should be allowed? Have the standards been set correctly? Is the poor performance due to the employee or some other factor? The key here is the supervisor's timely intervention. A supervisor should not allow an unacceptable situation to exist for long but should promptly determine the cause and take action.

The type of corrective action depends on the situation. If the performance meets or exceeds the standards, a supervisor might provide positive reinforcement such as commending an employee for a job well done or praising the work group as a whole. When performance is below standards, an approach that works well in most situations is for the supervisor to take increasingly harsh actions. For example, if an employee's productivity is unacceptable, the supervisor might first merely advise the employee of the problem. If the problem continues, the supervisor might take the more direct action of offering to work with the employee to identify difficulties. Once the problem has been clearly identified, the supervisor and the employee should agree on the actions necessary to make the employee's productivity acceptable. Then, if the employee's productivity is still unacceptable, the supervisor may have to take more dramatic action, such as transferring or terminating the employee. In almost all situations, the supervisor should help the employee overcome the deficiency before taking dramatic action. The style, finesse, and method used to take corrective action can greatly affect the results achieved. Supervisors should avoid talking down to employees when taking such action. Supervisors should also fully explain why the action is necessary. All too often, supervisors take corrective action without giving an adequate explanation. It is only natural for employees to resist something that they know very little about.

TOOLS FOR SUPERVISORY CONTROL

LEARNING OBJECTIVES

Many tools and techniques are available to help the supervisor exercise control. Among the tools and techniques most frequently used by supervisors are budgets, written reports, personal observation, and management by objectives.

Budgets

As defined in Chapter 6, a **budget** is a statement of expected results or requirements expressed in financial or numerical terms. Budgets express plans, objectives, and programs of the organization in numerical terms. While preparation of the budget is primarily a planning function, its administration is a controlling function.

Many different types of budgets are in use (Figure 19.2 outlines some of the most common). Although the dollar is usually the common denominator, budgets may be expressed in other terms. Equipment budgets may be expressed in numbers of machines. Material budgets may be expressed in pounds, pieces, gallons, and so on. Budgets not expressed in dollars can usually be translated into dollars for incorporation into an overall budget. Figure 19.3 presents an example of a simplified expense budget.

FIGURE 19.2

Types and Purposes
of Budgets

Type of Budget	Brief Description or Purpose
Revenue and expense budget	Provides details for revenue and expense plans
Cash budget	Forecasts cash receipts and disbursements
Capital expenditure budget	Outlines specific expenditures for plant, equipment, machinery, inventories, and other capital items
Production, material, or time budget	Expresses physical requirements of production, or material, or the time requirements for the budget period
Balance sheet budgets	Forecasts the status of assets, liabilities, and net worth at the end of the budget period

FIGURE 19.3

Simplified Expense
Budget

Product cost	$10,000
Advertising cost	5,000
Shipping cost	5,000
Sales commissions	2,500
Budgeted expenses	$22,500

While budgets are useful for planning and control, they are not without their dangers. Perhaps the greatest danger is inflexibility. Inflexibility is a special threat to organizations operating in an industry characterized by rapid change and high competition. Rigidity in the budget can also lead to a subordination of organizational goals to budgetary goals. The financial manager who won't go $5 over the budget in order to make $500 is a classic example. Another danger is that budgets can hide inefficiencies. Certain expenditures made in the past often become justification for continuing these expenditures when in fact the situation has changed considerably. Budgets can also become inflationary and inaccurate when supervisors pad their budgets because they know they will be cut by their bosses. Since the supervisor is never sure how severe the cut will be, the result is often an inaccurate if not unrealistic budget. The key to the successful use of budgets is to keep things in perspective. The budget should be used as a standard for comparison. However, it should not be inflexible. Cost budgets are described at length in the next chapter.

Written Reports

Almost all reports are designed to provide information for control. The supervisor may be a preparer or recipient of reports. Supervisors often prepare reports for use by upper management, and employees often prepare reports for use by supervisors. In both cases, the reports are designed to provide information on what is happening.

Written reports can be prepared on a periodic or as-necessary basis. There are two basic types of written reports. **Analytical reports** interpret the facts they present. **Informational reports** only present the facts.

The need for or the use of particular reports should be periodically evaluated. Reports have a way of continuing long past their usefulness. Unnecessary reports can represent a substantial waste of resources.

Personal Observation

Personal observation is sometimes the only way for a supervisor to get an accurate picture of what is really happening. Most supervisors regularly make personal observations. Besides providing information, such observations can communicate the supervisor's interest in the employees. Supervisors seldom seen by employees are often accused of spending too much time in their ivory towers. But supervisors may also be criticized for continually looking over the employees' shoulders. A potential inaccuracy of personal observation is that an employee's behavior may change while he or she is being watched. Another potential inaccuracy lies in the interpretation of the observation. The observer must be careful not to read into the situation events that did not actually occur. When observing the work of others, supervisors should concentrate on objective facts such as productivity, not on subjective opinions.

Management by walking around is a type of control based on personal observation. This type of control was popularized by managers at the Hewlett-Packard Company. When this method is used, supervisors are encouraged to walk around and mingle with one another and with the employees. Management by walking around is basically a hands-on approach to control.

Electronic Monitors

Today a number of different types of electronic devices can be used to monitor what is going on. Examples include electronic cash registers that keep a record of what items are sold and when; video cameras that record employee and customer movements; and phones that record how long each customer was engaged.

Management by Objectives

Management by objectives (MBO) was discussed in Chapter 6 as an effective means for setting objectives. The development of an MBO system is part of the planning function. However, once such a system has been developed, it can be used for control purposes.

SUPERVISORY CONTROL IN PRACTICE

Supervisors practice control in a number of the areas connected with their jobs. Which specific types of control supervisors practice depend on their areas of responsibility. However, quality assurance and inventory control are two types of control with which almost all supervisors are concerned. Quality assurance includes everything that an organization does to assure the quality of its products and services, such as the steps taken to prevent quality problems and to monitor the quality of products and services. Inventory control is concerned with monitoring inventory so as to maintain a supply of inventory adequate to meet customer demand but not greater than is necessary for that purpose.

QUALITY AND THE SUPERVISOR

3 LEARNING OBJECTIVES

Quality is a relative term. To a space engineer, it represents a million parts that have been carefully made, tested, and assembled so that they will function flawlessly. To the U.S. Department of Agriculture, it means uniformity and an absence of contamination in food. To a fancy restaurant, it may mean lobster flown in daily from Maine. Quality may not mean the same thing to the consumer and the supervisor. The consumer is concerned with service, reliability, performance, and appearance. The supervisor is concerned with the achievement of product or service specifications. The supervisor evaluates quality in relation to the specifications or standards that are set when the product or service is designed.

Why Insist on Quality?

What has caused all the recent concern about quality? Quality has always been important, but never more so than today. Rising labor and material costs, combined with the need to satisfy more demanding customers, have motivated organizations to become more quality conscious. When labor and materials were less expensive, remaking or scrapping an item wasn't nearly so costly. Also, America's leadership in quality has been eroding for years. In many instances, the quality of foreign products is viewed as better than that of American products. In the service fields, the public now demands higher quality at a lower cost. Historically, many other reasons have existed for maintaining quality. Figure 19.4 lists some of these.

Who Is Responsible for Quality?

In the final analysis, who is responsible for maintaining quality? Who causes quality problems? Most supervisors defend their positions on quality by saying, "If the material we get is good, then we'll send it on good." The obvious implication is that the material they get is often of poor quality. Taking this thought one step further, the supervisor might argue, "How can you expect me to produce quality products or services when I get such bad materials?" Any number of people can be blamed for a supervisor's quality problems. Purchasing, engineering, quality control people, and the human resources department are prime candidates. It is a natural tendency to blame someone else.

FIGURE 19.4
Steps for Maintaining Quality

1. Maintain certain standards, such as with interchangeable replacement parts or with service levels.
2. Meet customer specifications.
3. Meet legal requirements.
4. Find defective products that can be reworked.
5. Identify inferior services.
6. Find problems in the production process.
7. Grade products or services (such as lumber, eggs, or restaurants).
8. Provide performance information on individual workers and departments.

The supervisor should be one of the first to know what is going on! In other words, if *all* supervisors provided up-to-standard materials, there would be no quality problems. Every supervisor should first worry about his or her own area of responsibility. If all supervisors assumed responsibility for quality in their respective areas, quality would be a reality. In the final analysis, accountability for quality is spread across the entire organization.

Quality Assurance

For years the focus of industry was to ensure quality through the inspection process. The general approach was to produce a product or service and then inspect to ensure that the quality standards were being met. While this approach is still widely used, there has been a shift in philosophy toward placing the operator in charge of his or her own quality—while the product or service is being produced. Thus, *today* the emphasis is on the *prevention* of defects and mistakes rather than on finding and correcting them. The idea of "building in" quality as opposed to "inspecting it in" is known as **quality assurance.** With this approach, quality is viewed as the responsibility of all organization members rather than the exclusive domain of a quality control department.

While there have been many individuals who have championed the prevention approach to quality, W. Edwards Deming is perhaps most responsible. Deming was a statistics professor at New York University in the 1940s who went to Japan after World War II to assist in improving quality and productivity. While he became very much revered in Japan, Deming remained almost unknown to U.S. business leaders until the 1980s when Japan's quality and productivity attracted the attention of the world.

Total Quality Management

A major question facing today's supervisors is how to build quality into employee performance. How can supervisors get their employees to be concerned about the quality of their everyday work? Most successful attempts to improve quality have focused on the prevention of quality problems through employee involvement. **Total quality management (TQM)** is a management philosophy that emphasizes "managing the entire organization so that it excels in all dimensions of products and services that are important to the customer."[1] TQM, in essence, is an organizationwide emphasis on quality as defined by the customer. Under TQM everyone from the CEO on down to the lowest level employee must be involved.

TQM can be summarized by the following actions:[2]

1. Find out what customers want. This might involve the use of surveys, focus groups, interviews, or some other technique that integrates the customer's voice in the decision-making process.
2. Design a product or service that will meet (or exceed) what customers want. Make it easy to use and easy to produce.
3. Design a production process that facilitates doing the job right the first time. Determine where mistakes are likely to occur and try to prevent them. When mistakes do occur, find out why so that they are less likely to occur again. Strive to "mistake-proof" the process.

A major question facing today's supervisors is how to build quality into employee performance.
Ulrike Welsch/Photo Researchers, Inc.

4. Keep track of results and use them to guide improvement in the system. Never stop trying to improve.

5. Extend these concepts to suppliers and to distribution.

Continuous improvement and quality at the source are two terms that have particular relevance to TQM. **Continuous improvement,** in general, refers to an ongoing effort to make improvements in every part of the organization relative to all of its products and services. With regard to TQM, it means focusing on steady improvement in the quality of the processes by which work is accomplished. The idea here is that the quest for better quality and better service is never ending. **Quality at the source** refers to the philosophy of making each employee responsible for the quality of his or her work. In effect, this approach views every employee as a quality inspector for his or her own work. A major advantage of this approach is that it removes the adversarial relationship that often exists between quality control inspectors and production employees. It also encourages employees to take pride in their work.

As stated earlier, TQM is an organizationwide emphasis on quality as defined by the customer. It is not a collection of techniques but a philosophy or way of thinking about how people view their jobs and quality throughout the organization.

Some people confuse the concept of reengineering with TQM. **Reengineering,** also called business process engineering, is "the search for and implementation of radical change in business processes to achieve breakthrough results in cost, speed, productivity, and service."[3] Unlike TQM, reengineering is not a program for making marginal improvements in existing procedures. Reengineering is rather a one-time concerted effort, initiated from the top of the organization, to make major improvements in processes used to produce

Most successful zero-defects programs have the following characteristics:

1. Extensive communication regarding the importance of quality—signs, posters, contests, and so on.
2. Organizationwide recognition—publicly granting rewards, certificates, and plaques for high-quality work.
3. Problem identification by employees—employees point out areas where they think quality can be improved.
4. Employee goal setting—employees participate in setting quality goals.[5]

8 LEARNING OBJECTIVES

Quality circles approach.   This approach, which originated in Japan, has been transplanted to America. A **quality circle** consists of a supervisor and a group of employees who work together under that supervisor. Membership in a quality circle is almost always voluntary, and the basic purpose is to meet periodically to solve quality problems and identify ways of improving quality. These meetings are normally held once or twice a month and last for one to two hours. Usually, a quality circle begins by receiving specialized training relating to quality. It then proceeds to discuss specific quality problems which can be brought up by management representatives or by the circle members. Staff experts may be called upon by the circle as needed. There is evidence that hundreds, if not thousands, of U.S. companies are currently using some form of quality circles. As with zero-defects programs, the primary emphasis of quality circles is to get the employees actively involved. Research has shown that a key to quality circle effectiveness is properly training members to function in a quality circle.[6]

Quality Guidelines

9 LEARNING OBJECTIVES

As discussed earlier, the key to the prevention of quality problems is employee involvement. The following 10 guidelines are offered as aids for building quality job habits among employees:

Guideline 1: *Start new employees off right.* Make sure the new employee understands that high quality is expected. Set the quality standards high, and make sure they are clearly communicated.

Guideline 2: *Keep employee relations on an individual basis.* Talk with the employees individually. Tell them what they are doing that is good and what they are doing that is not so good with regard to quality.

Guideline 3: *Don't settle for less than desired.* Don't accept inferior work or reward an employee for it. Find the cause of inferior work and take the necessary corrective action.

Guideline 4: *Communicate the value of top quality.* Explain why high quality is necessary. Get down to dollars and cents. Explain the potential costs of inferior quality.

Guideline 5: *Perform thorough inspections.* Careful inspections help ensure high quality. This is another way for the supervisor to set the example. A careful inspection should not only find quality problems but also locate their causes.

Guideline 6: *Encourage suggestions.* Actively solicit suggestions from employees. Implement and give credit for good suggestions.

Guideline 7: *Learn from the past.* Investigate the areas that have historically caused quality problems. How could these problems have been prevented? What can be done to prevent these problems from recurring?

Guideline 8: *Solicit the help of other departments and supervisors.* Use individual accountability. Implement systems that make clear the quality responsibilities of each individual employee.

Guideline 9: *Assign individual responsibility wherever possible.* Use individual accountability. Implement systems that make clear the quality responsibilities of each employee.

Guideline 10: *Set the example.* If the supervisor strives for high quality in everything that he or she does, so will the employees. On the other hand, if a supervisor performs certain activities sloppily, so will the employees.[7]

The Malcolm Baldrige National Quality Award

In 1987, the U.S. Congress passed the Malcolm Baldrige National Quality Improvement Act. The purpose of this legislation was to inspire increased efforts by U.S. businesses to improve the quality of their products and services. The **Malcolm Baldrige Award** is named after the late Malcolm Baldrige who was a successful businessman and a former U.S. secretary of commerce. The award is administered by the National Institute of Standards and Technology and can only be awarded to businesses located in the United States. The purpose of the award is to encourage efforts to improve quality and to recognize the quality achievements of U.S. companies. A maximum of two awards are given each year in each of three categories: large manufacturer, large service organization, and small business (500 or less employees). Supervision Illustration 19–3 discusses how the Baldrige Award criteria have been used by Allied Signal, Inc., to implement its TQM program.

Types of Quality Control

In addition to a preventive approach to achieving quality, organizations also usually have some method for monitoring the quality of their products or services. This aspect of quality assurance is referred to as *quality control.*

While supervisors are usually not responsible for designing a quality control system, they are frequently responsible for implementing the system. They should therefore have a basic understanding of how quality control works.

10 LEARNING OBJECTIVES

Quality control relating to things (products, services, raw materials, etc.) is referred to as **product quality control.** Product quality control is used when quality is being evaluated with respect to a batch of products or services that already exist, such as incoming raw materials or outgoing finished goods. Product quality control lends itself to acceptance sampling procedures. With acceptance sampling, some portion of outgoing items (or incoming materials) is inspected in an attempt to ensure that the items meet specifications with regard to the percentage of defective units that will be tolerated. Under acceptance sampling procedures, the decision to accept or reject an entire batch of items is based on a sample or group of samples.

Quality control relating to the control of a machine or an operation during the production process is called **process control.** Under process control, machines and/or processes are periodically checked to ensure that they are oper-

---

SUPERVISION ILLUSTRATION 19-3

BALDRIGE CRITERIA GUIDE QUALITY AT ALLIED SIGNAL

Allied Signal, Inc., is a $14 billion Fortune 500 company that manufactures products for the aerospace, automotive, and engineered materials industries. Even though Allied Signal was under no corporate mandate to win the coveted Malcolm Baldrige Award, it decided to use the hundreds of procedures associated with the award to implement TQM across the entire organization. Management saw this as a way of getting its 87,000 employees and 3,000 teams in 30 countries marching to the same quality drummer.

Initially the company had no way to share quality information across the company. One result was that different quality teams operating in different areas would often spend time and energy solving prob-

lems that had already been addressed elsewhere. To eliminate this duplication of effort, Eric Singleton, information systems director at Allied Signal, introduced TQSoft, a client/server quality assurance program that consolidates the company's quality processes in a single repository to be shared throughout the company. TQSoft runs under Windows in tandem with Microsoft Corporation's Office and Mail, linked to Windows NT servers running SQL Server.

As a result of implementing the Baldrige Award criteria and TQSoft, Allied Signal appreciably cut the expected time necessary to come in line with its TQM goals. TQSoft is expected to eliminate redundant works by as much as 90 percent.

Source: Bronwyn Fryer, "Allied Signal Technical Services," *Computerworld,* August 1996, pp. 8–9. For more information about Allied Signal, visit its Web site at: **www.alliedsignal.com**

---

ating within certain preestablished tolerances. Adjustments are made as necessary to prevent the machines or processes from getting out of control and producing bad items. Process control is used to prevent the production of defects, whereas product control is used to identify defects after they have been produced.

Today considerable attention is also devoted to controlling the quality of *services* that are offered. Examples include supervisors calling customers to see how they would rate the quality of a service or asking customers to fill out a brief evaluation form regarding a service received.

INVENTORY CONTROL

 **11   LEARNING OBJECTIVES**

As mentioned earlier, inventory control is primarily concerned with monitoring and maintaining a supply of inventory adequate to meet customer demand but not greater than is necessary for that purpose. The costs of poorly managed inventories can be extremely high. If excessive inventory is carried, money is needlessly tied up and unnecessary storage costs are incurred. If too little inventory is carried, customers may be lost, production may be slowed, and employees may be laid off. In addition to determining what levels of inventory to maintain, inventory control systems determine when stock should be replaced and how large orders should be. Inventory management is one of the biggest responsibilities of many supervisors.

Inventories serve as a buffer between different rates of usage in the production system. Inventories can generally be classified as: (1) raw material inventories, (2) in-process inventories, or (3) finished goods inventories. *Raw*

FIGURE 19.5

Inventories as Buffers

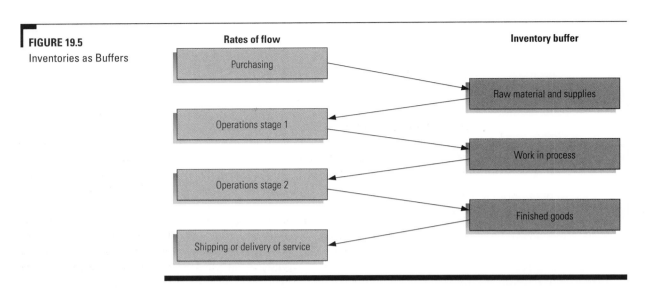

material inventories serve as a buffer between purchasing and operations. *In-process inventories* are used to buffer differences in the rates of flow through the various production processes. *Finished goods inventories* act as a buffer between the final stage of production and shipping or delivery of the product. Figure 19.5 illustrates the relationships of the three inventories.

Inventories provide added flexibility and efficiency to the production system by allowing the organization to:

1. Purchase, produce, and ship in economic batch sizes rather than in small lots.
2. Produce on a smooth, continuous basis even though the demand for the finished product or raw material may fluctuate.
3. Prevent major problems when forecasts of demand are in error or when there are unforeseen slowdowns or stoppages in supply or production.

When making inventory decisions, three basic questions must be answered: (1) what items to carry in inventory, (2) how much of the selected items to order and carry, and (3) when to order the items. Depending on the particular situation, supervisors may or may not be responsible for answering these questions.

If it were not costly, every organization would attempt to maintain very large inventories to facilitate purchasing, production scheduling, and distribution. However, as noted earlier, the cost of carrying excess inventory can be high. Potential inventory costs include such factors as insurance and taxes on the inventory, storage costs, obsolescence costs, spoilage, and the opportunity cost of the money invested in the inventory. The relative importance of these costs depends on the specific inventory being held. For example, when dealing with women's fashions, the obsolescence costs are potentially very high. Spoilage costs are potentially high in the food business.

Similarly, storage costs might be very high for dangerous chemicals. Thus, when making inventory decisions, the costs of carrying inventory must be weighed against the costs of running short of raw materials, in-process goods, or finished goods.

Just-in-Time Inventory Control

12   LEARNING OBJECTIVES

Just-in-time inventory control (JIT) was pioneered in Japan but has become popular in the United States. JIT systems are sometimes referred to as zero-inventory systems, stockless systems, or Kanban systems. JIT is actually a philosophy for production so that the right items arrive and leave as they are needed. Traditionally, incoming raw materials are ordered in relatively few large shipments and stored in warehouses until needed for production or for providing a service. Under JIT, organizations make smaller and more frequent orders of raw materials. JIT depends on the elimination of setup time between the production of different batches of different products. JIT can be viewed as an operating philosophy which has as its basic objective the elimination of waste.[8] In this light, waste is "anything other than the minimum amount of equipment, materials, parts, space, and employees' time which are absolutely essential to add value to the product or service."

The JIT philosophy applies not only to inventories of incoming raw materials but also the production of subassemblies or final products. The idea is to not produce an item or subassembly until it is needed for shipment. JIT is called a demand pull system because items are produced or ordered only when they are needed (or pulled) by the next stage in the production process. The appendix at the end of this chapter provides more technical information relating to inventory demand items.

SOLUTION TO THE SUPERVISION DILEMMA

From the material presented in this chapter, it appears that John has not given adequate attention to the basic steps in the control function. There is no evidence that he has clearly communicated what standards he expects in each of his problem areas (pp. 365–66). Even if his standards were clear, it is obvious that he does not do an adequate job of monitoring performance (p. 366). John needs to set up systems to alert him and/or his subordinates to problems before they get out of hand. Once problems have been identified, he should take swift and deliberate corrective action (pp. 366–67).

To avoid missed deadlines, mishandling of claims, and basic processing errors, John might set up daily reporting systems to help monitor what is going on. These systems should not be complex or time-consuming; they should simply report the production and quality status of claims. John might also consider implementing some type of quality assurance program as a means of "building in" quality. To avoid running out of claim forms, John might consider implementing some type of inventory control system for reordering.

SUMMARY

This chapter discusses the controlling function as it affects most supervisors. The chapter begins by defining the controlling function and its components. It then examines specific supervisory control techniques. Quality assurance and inventory control receive special attention.

1. *Outline the three basic steps in the control process.* Control is accomplished by comparing actual performance with predetermined standards or objectives and then taking corrective action to correct any deviations from the standard. Thus, the control process has three basic steps: (1) establishing performance standards, (2) monitoring performance and comparing it with standards, and (3) taking necessary action.

2. *Identify tools and techniques most frequently used by supervisors to exercise control.* Among the tools and techniques most frequently used by supervisors to exercise control are budgets, written reports, personal observation, electronic monitors, and management by objectives.

3. *Define what quality means to a supervisor, and list several reasons for maintaining quality.* Quality is a relative term that means different things to different people. A supervisor's primary concern with quality is that the product or service specifications be achieved to (1) maintain certain standards, (2) meet customer specifications, (3) meet legal requirements, (4) locate defective products, (5) identify inferior services, (6) find problems in the production process, (7) grade products or services, and (8) provide performance information on employees and/or departments.

4. *Define the concept of quality assurance.* Quality assurance refers to the idea of "building in" quality as opposed to "inspecting it in."

5. *Discuss Total Quality Management.* Total Quality Management (TQM) is a management philosophy that emphasizes "managing the entire organization so that it excels in all dimensions of products and services that are important to the customer." TQM, in essence, is an organizationwide emphasis on quality as defined by the customer.

6. *Summarize the thrust of ISO 9000.* ISO 9000 is a set of quality standards established in 1987 by the International Organization for Standardization (ISO). ISO 9000 focuses on the design and operations processes and not on the end product or service. ISO 9000 requires extensive documentation in order to demonstrate the consistency and reliability of the processes being used.

7. *Explain the purpose of a zero-defects program.* A zero-defects program attempts to create a positive attitude toward the prevention of low quality.

8. *Define a quality circle.* A quality circle consists of a supervisor and a group of employees who work together under that supervisor. Its primary purpose is to meet periodically to solve quality problems and identify ways of improving quality.

9. *Cite several guidelines that supervisors can follow to help build quality job habits among employees.* The following guidelines can be used by supervisors to build quality job habits: Start new employees off right, keep employee relations on an individual basis, don't settle for less than desired, communicate the value of top quality, perform thorough inspections, encourage suggestions, learn from the past, solicit the help of other departments and supervisors, assign individual responsibility wherever possible, and set the example.

10. *Differentiate between product quality control and process control.* Quality control relating to things (products, services, raw materials, etc.) is referred to as product quality control. Quality control relating to the control of a machine or an operation during the production process is called process control.

11. *Discuss the major types of inventories and explain the purposes for carrying inventories.* Inventories can generally be classified according to three categories: (1) raw materials, (2) in-process, or (3) finished goods. Inventories provide added flexibility to the production system and allow the organization to purchase, produce, and ship in economic batch sizes; to produce on a smooth, continuous basis even though the demand for the finished product or raw material may fluctuate;

and to prevent major problems when forecasts of demand are in error or when there are unforeseen slowdowns or stoppages in supply or production.

12. *Explain the just-in-time approach to inventory control.* The just-in-time (JIT) approach to inventory schedules materials to arrive and leave as they are needed. JIT can be viewed as an operating philosophy which has as its basic objective the elimination of waste.

REVIEW QUESTIONS

1. What is the major purpose of all supervisory controls?

2. Name and briefly discuss at least three tools used in supervisory control.

3. What determines the desired level of quality for the supervisor?

4. What is quality assurance?

5. What is the basic philosophy underlying Total Quality Management TQM)?

6. Describe the zero-defects and quality circles approaches to quality.

7. What is the difference between product quality control and process quality control?

8. What are the three major types of inventories?

9. List several reasons that inventories are carried by organizations.

10. List several other terms that are used to describe just-in-time (JIT) systems.

SKILL-BUILDING QUESTIONS

1. Why do you think that many supervisors are reluctant to take corrective actions when people are involved?

2. Since quality is a relative concept, how does a supervisor ever know if the quality level is optimum?

3. What do you think are the advantages of "building in" quality as opposed to "inspecting in" quality?

4. It has often been said that supervisory planning and supervisory control go hand in hand. Elaborate on this statement.

REFERENCES

1. Richard B. Chase and Nicholas J. Aquilano, *Production and Operations Management: A Life Cycle Approach*, 7th ed. (Homewood, Ill.: Richard D. Irwin, 1995), p. 163.

2 William J. Stephenson, *Production/Operations Management*, 5th ed. (Homewood, Ill.: Richard D. Irwin, 1996), p. 102.

3. Thomas B. Clark, "Business Process Reengineering," Working Paper, Georgia State University, November 1997, p. 1.

4. William Parzybok, Jr., "ISO 9000," *Industry Week*, June 6, 1994, p. 35.

5. Chase and Aquilano, *Production and Operations Management*, 3rd ed. (Homewood, Ill.: Richard D. Irwin, 1981), pp. 654–55.

6. Alan Honeycutt, "The Key to Effective Quality Circles," *Training and Development Journal*, May 1989, pp. 81–84.

7. These guidelines are adapted from Robert M. Sardell, "Building Quality into Employee Performance," *Supervision*, October 1979, pp. 13–14.

8. Nicholas J. Aquilano and Richard B. Chase, *Fundamentals of Operations Management*, (Homewood, Ill.: Richard D. Irwin, 1991), p. 586.

ADDITIONAL READINGS

Chase, Nancy. "MKS Fits ISO 9000 into Existing Systems," *Quality*, April 1997.

"From Quality Circles to TQM," *Government Executive*, July 1997.

Lackritz, James R. "TQM within Fortune 500 Corporations," *Quality Progress*, February 1997.

Smith, Bob. "A Proven Path to ISO 9000 Registration," *Industrial Distribution*, July 1994.

Van Horn, Lois H. "Improving Results through Total Quality Management," *American Agent & Broker*, June 1997.

Vogl, A. J. "Growing Pains," *Across the Board*, February 1997.

SKILL-BUILDING APPLICATIONS

Incident 19–1

The Assuming Supervisor

Nancy Keene is a supervisor of the children's clothing department for the Model Dress Company. Model Dress sells women's and children's casual fashions in the low-to-middle price ranges. Because of control problems related to many facets of the business, management decided to implement a management-by-objectives (MBO) system about 10 months ago. Shortly thereafter, Nancy, along with the company's 14 other supervisors, attended a company-sponsored seminar on MBO. After the seminar, Nancy's boss, Joan Chung, outlined what she thought should be Nancy's annual objectives in terms of sales, returns, and personnel turnover. Joan further suggested how these objectives might be passed down to Nancy's subordinates. All of Joan's suggestions seemed perfectly reasonable to Nancy, and she accepted them to the letter. A few days later, Nancy distributed a memo announcing just what the departmental objectives were and how they affected each member of her department. Much to her surprise, several of her subordinates reacted quite negatively and accused her of being "too bossy." After several meetings, Nancy was able to calm down these subordinates and assure them that she was not attempting to force anything on them. Things seemed to move along on an even keel for the next several months.

Then Joan called Nancy into her office, where the following dialogue took place:

Joan: Nancy, we're nine months into our MBO year, and you're running way behind on our agreed-upon objectives.

Nancy: What do you mean?

Joan: According to my records, your department's sales have averaged well below your goal, your returns have been running well over your goal, and your department has already exceeded your turnover goal for the entire year.

Nancy: I had no idea! Are you sure your records are correct? Since I hadn't heard anything from you, I just assumed everything was on target.

Joan: Haven't you been comparing your weekly figures with your goals?

Nancy: No, not really. Like I said, I just assumed everything was OK. And I've been extremely busy, as you know.

Questions

1. Who is most at fault for having allowed this situation to develop, Joan or Nancy? Why?

2. What do you think about Nancy's understanding of MBO?

3. What changes would you suggest to both Joan and Nancy?

Incident 19–2

High-Quality Toys

The Cutee Toy Company of Crossroads City makes all types of metal toys. Cutee has built a good reputation on the quality of its toys, which hold up much better than comparable toys made of plastic. Also, many parents are attracted to metal toys because they grew up with such toys. At the same time, because of the dangers inherent in metal toys, Cutee has to maintain very tight quality standards. Great care must be taken to ensure that no toys are shipped with sharp edges, protruding tabs, or any other hazards. The high price charged by Cutee also requires that the quality standards be kept high.

The basic production process is the same for all of Cutee's products. The parts for a particular toy are stamped out of sheet metal. The parts for the toy are then assembled by fitting small metal tabs on one piece through small slots on the matching piece and bending the tabs over (see Exhibit 19.1). To avoid scratches during the assembly process, the toy is painted after it has been assembled. A silk-screening process is often used to add details after the basic painting

EXHIBIT 19.1

Assembly of a Toy
Christmas Tree

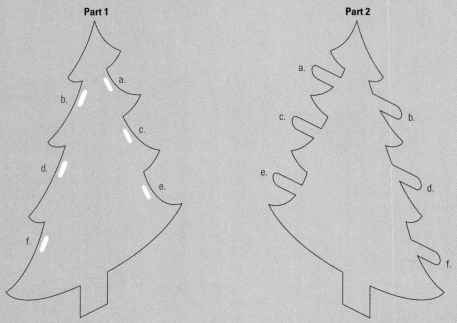

Part 1   Part 2

To assemble, put Tab a. on Part 2 into Slot a. on Part 1 and bend over; put Tab b. on Part 2 into Slot b. on Part 1
and bend over, etc.

process. All finished toys are carefully wrapped in kraft paper and put into boxes to be shipped or stored in inventory.

Questions

1. Assume you are the supervisor of the painting department. What do you think your responsibilities should be regarding the quality of the final product?

2. If you were a supervisor charged with inspecting the final products, what general type of inspection system would you set up? Support your answer with justifications.

3. If you were supervisor of the production department, what concerns might you have relating to raw material inventory?

Exercise 19–1

Controlling Production

The Gantt chart was introduced in Chapter 6 as a tool to help supervisors plan. Gantt charts are also frequently used for control purposes. The Cutee Toy Company, described in Incident 19–2,

uses the Gantt chart at the top of the following page to plan and control the production of toy Christmas trees.

1. Assuming that the vertical arrows indicate actual progress made to date, how would you describe Cutee Toy Company's present production situation? Is it ahead of or behind schedule?

2. Assuming that the following events take place, what actions would you take?
   a. The purchasing agent of the Top Mill Company calls and tells you that her order is not wanted until day 25.
   b. No work is done on the Carter Company order during the next two days.
   c. An order change from Keller, Inc., doubles its original order (thus requiring that each operation take twice the scheduled time).

3. If you were the production manager for the Cutee Toy Company, what additional information would you like for control purposes? Make specific recommendations for getting this information.

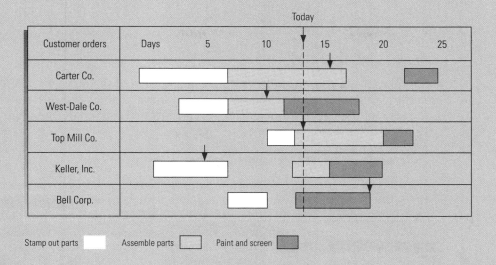

Customer orders	Days		5		10		15		20		25
Carter Co.											
West-Dale Co.											
Top Mill Co.											
Keller, Inc.											
Bell Corp.											

Stamp out parts [ ]   Assemble parts [ ]   Paint and screen [ ]

Exercise 19–2

Assessing Quality

Visit a local fast-food establishment and observe the service from the quality viewpoint. Make notes of the following specific things:

1. Was the facility and parking lot clean?
2. Were you greeted pleasantly and cheerfully by the person taking your order?
3. How long did you wait from the time you entered the facility until you received your order?
4. Was your order correct?
5. How would you rate the taste of the food?
6. Was the rest room clean?

After you have completed your visit and analyzed your notes, what suggestions do you have for improving quality? Can you think of anything that management might do to increase its employees' concern for quality?

APPENDIX

Managing Inventories

The purpose of this appendix is to introduce some of the more frequently used methods for managing inventories. While there are many models and techniques that are useful for managing inventories, an in-depth discussion of these is beyond the scope of this text.

Independent versus Dependent Demand Items

Which types of inventory systems are appropriate depends on whether the demand for the inventory items is independent or dependent. Independent demand items are finished goods or other end items. For the most part, independent demand items are sold or shipped out, as opposed to being used in making other products. Examples of independent demand environments include most retail shops, book publishers, and hospital supply firms. Dependent demand items are typically subassemblies or component parts that will be used in making finished products. The demand for such items depends on the number of finished products being produced. Wheels for new cars are an example of a dependent demand item. If a car company plans to make 1,000 cars next month, it knows that for that purpose it must have 5,000 wheels on hand (allowing for spares). With independent demand items, forecasting plays an important role in inventory stocking decisions. With dependent demand items, inventory stocking requirements are determined directly from the production plan.

Inventory Considerations for Independent Demand Items

ABC classification system. One of the simplest and most widely used systems for managing inventories is the ABC classification system. Under this system, inventories are managed in accordance with their value. Items that account for a large amount of inventory value are closely monitored. Items that account for a small amount of inventory value are monitored only occasionally.

Reorder point and safety stock. After it has been decided what items will be carried in inventory, a decision must be made concerning when to order each of these items. The two basic methods for determining when to order are the **fixed-order quantity method** and the **fixed-order period method.** Under the fixed-order quantity method, orders are placed whenever the inventory reaches a predetermined level, regardless of how long it takes to reach that level. Thus, the time between orders can vary, depending on the demand. Fixed-order quantity systems usually assume continual monitoring of inventory levels. This is not an unrealistic assumption today, since many organizations have computerized inventory records.

Under the fixed-order period method, restocking orders are placed at predetermined, regular time intervals, regardless of how much inventory is on hand. With this method, the amount ordered rather than the time between orders can vary, depending on the demand. The fixed-order period method requires that inventory be counted only at the designated review periods.

The fixed-order period method is easier to administer because when it is used, orders are placed on a regular basis and inventory does not have to be continually counted. Under this method, however, supplies are more likely to run out if demand goes up unexpectedly. The fixed-order quantity method has the advantage of making all orders equal and economic in size.

Most organizations maintain safety stocks to accommodate unexpected changes in demand and supply and to allow for variations in delivery time. The optimum size of the safety stock is determined by the cost of a stockout of the item versus the cost of carrying the additional inventory. The cost of a stockout of the item is often difficult to estimate. For example, it may include the lost profit if the customer goes elsewhere rather than wait for the product. If the product is available at another branch location, it may simply be the cost of shipping the item from one location to another.

The order quantity. Determining the amount to order is a decision that goes hand in hand with determining the reorder point. Most materials and finished products are consumed one by one or a few units at a time; however, because of the costs associated with ordering, shipping, and handling inventory, it is usually desirable to purchase materials and products in large lots or batches.

In determining the optimum number of units to order, the ordering costs must be balanced against the costs of carrying the inventory. Ordering costs include such things as the cost of preparing the order, shipping costs, and setup costs. Carrying costs include storage costs, insurance, taxes, obsolescence costs, and the opportunity costs of the money invested in the inventory. The smaller the number of units ordered, the lower the carrying costs (because the average inventory held is smaller) but the larger the ordering costs (because more orders must be placed). The optimum number of units to order is referred to as the **economic order quantity (EOQ).** There are mathematical formulas that can be used to calculate the EOQ.

Managing Inventories for Dependent Demand Items

Managing inventories for dependent demand items is basically a process of ensuring that the right numbers of items are available at the right times. Thus, in addition to determining the number of units needed, the timing of their need is also critical. Material requirements planning is a system designed to deal with these problems.

Material requirements planning (MRP). **Material requirements planning (MRP)** is a special type of inventory system in which the needed amount of each component of a product is figured on the basis of the amount of the final product to be produced. When each component is needed depends on when the final assembly is needed and the lead time required to incorporate the component into the assembly.

The basic purpose of MRP is to get the right materials to the right places at the right time. It does little good to have some of the parts needed to produce a product if the organization does not have all of them. Because carrying parts that are not being used is costly, the idea behind MRP is to provide either all or none of the necessary components. Almost all MRP utilizes a computer because of the need to store and manipulate large amounts of data. Many versions of MRP computer programs are available and can be purchased.

Improving Productivity through Cost Control

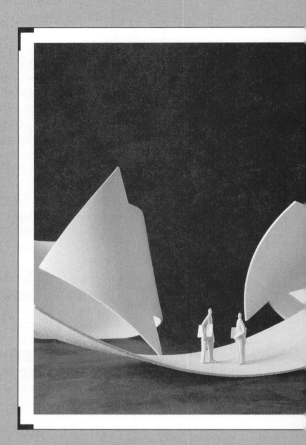

LEARNING OBJECTIVES

After studying this chapter, you should be able to:

1. Describe the supervisor's role in improving productivity through cost reduction and control.
2. Present several guidelines that supervisors might follow in establishing an environment conducive to continuous cost control and reduction.
3. Recount the major cost categories encountered by supervisors.
4. Discuss a supervisor's involvement with cost budgets.
5. Summarize several cost-reduction strategies that can be helpful to supervisors.
6. Outline a step-by-step plan for implementing a cost-reduction effort.
7. Identify several areas of concern to supervisors that tend to be especially susceptible to cost overruns.
8. Outline several guidelines for establishing a culture that supports employee honesty.
9. Discuss why employees may fear cost reductions.

Ever since Jane Harris took over as supervisor of the claims section, her costs have steadily risen. Until recently, she had attributed these cost rises to inflation. Not long ago, however, she overheard two supervisors talking about their successes with a cost-reduction program. Jane's only experience with a cost-reduction program had occurred before she became a supervisor, and that experience was mostly negative. All Jane could remember was a lot of talk, nothing happening, and the wave of fear that accompanied the program. The cost-reduction program had been presented as a threat: If you don't reduce costs, then . . . Jane wondered if her fellow supervisors knew something about cost reduction and control that she didn't.

Productivity may be defined as units of output per employee-machine hour. Productivity increases when more output is produced with a given amount of resources. Thus, one of the most effective ways for supervisors to improve productivity is by controlling and reducing costs. Reducing costs is also seen by most organizations as a way of gaining an edge over their competitors. Because of the universal emphasis placed on reducing costs, few supervisors escape the squeeze to cut costs.

Costs include everything that goes into making a product or providing a service. For example, they include everything directly and indirectly associated with personnel, materials, machines, and space.

THE SUPERVISOR'S ROLE IN COST REDUCTION AND CONTROL

The supervisor is a key person in any cost reduction and control program because he or she is in an ideal position to do something about costs. The supervisor can suggest means of cost reduction and control as well as oversee the implementation and measurement of cost reduction and control ideas. The supervisor also has a direct influence over many costs. Raw material, equipment, and labor costs can be significantly influenced by the supervisor. While many staff specialists such as cost accountants, budget analysts, and cost engineers devise plans to cut costs, they depend on inputs from supervisors; and it is usually the supervisor who implements these plans.

Establishing the Proper Environment

The concept of continuous improvement, which was introduced in the previous chapter, is directly applicable to cost reduction and control. Supervisors should establish a work environment in which employees are continuously looking for ways to reduce costs.

As is true for so many areas of supervision, the attitude of the supervisor toward costs sets the tone for the entire department. If the supervisor is constantly cost conscious, this usually rubs off on employees. The reverse is also true: If the supervisor has little or only periodic concern for costs, employees will seldom be concerned about costs. Additional guidelines for establishing an environment conducive to continuous cost control and reduction are presented next.

Cost reduction should be part of the normal routine. It should be viewed by supervisors and employees alike as a regular and continual, not a once-a-year, effort. The goal is to develop a constant awareness of costs. All too often, a brief, intensive campaign achieves some cost reduction. But once the campaign ends, costs again begin to increase.

Cost reduction should cover all areas. The idea is for cost control and reduction to be pervasive throughout the entire organization! It is both ineffective and unfair to permit costs to run wild in one area while rigorously controlling them in another.

A climate and format for encouraging employee suggestions should be provided. Employees often represent an organization's greatest potential for cost-reduction ideas! Usually, merely asking employees for cost-reduction ideas is not enough. Employees must feel that their ideas are genuinely desired and that they will be earnestly considered. Furthermore, far more cost-reduction suggestions are likely to be offered if a specific format for the submission of suggestion is provided. Suggestion boxes are used successfully by many companies. Another workable approach is to hold periodic staff meetings for the specific purpose of generating cost-reduction ideas. Electronic media and E-mail also provide means for employees to offer suggestions.

Cost objectives should be established and communicated. Knowing what costs to work on controlling means knowing what are and are not acceptable cost ranges. Employees who are held responsible for certain costs should also understand how those costs are calculated.

Individual responsibility for cost reduction should be made clear. One general problem with cost reduction is that when it's considered *everybody's* problem, it ends up being *nobody's* problem. Employees should be held responsible for the costs under their control. At the same time, they should be rewarded for controlling and reducing costs.

Incentives for cost reduction should be offered. Incentives are often the biggest factor in the success of a cost-reduction program. If employees believe that cost reduction is in their best interest, they are much more likely to participate actively in a cost-reduction program. Some organizations allow employees to share in the cost savings realized. Others give cash awards or time off to employees responsible for efforts that result in cost savings.

FIGURING COSTS

Before a supervisor can reduce costs, he or she must know how to figure them. Costs can be thought of as everything expended to provide the product or service. Generally, they can be broken down into several categories:

1. **Direct labor costs.** These are expenditures for labor that is *directly applied* in the creation or delivery of the product or service. (The more product or service provided, the more direct labor is used.) Examples

include expenditures for machine operators, claims processors, bank tellers, assembly-line workers, and salespeople.

2. **Raw material costs.** These are expenditures for raw material that is directly applied to the creation of the product or service. (The more product or service provided, the more raw material is used.)

3. **Indirect labor costs.** These are expenditures for labor that is *not directly applied* to the creation or delivery of the product or service. Examples include human resource specialists, quality-control personnel, housekeeping personnel, and public relations specialists.

4. **Operating supplies costs.** These are expenditures for necessary items that do not become a part of the product or service (items in addition to the product/service raw materials). Examples include brochures explaining a service, cleaning compounds, safety clothing, and office supplies.

5. **Maintenance costs.** These include labor and material costs incurred to repair and maintain equipment and facilities. Examples include expenditures for replacement parts, maintenance personnel, and repairs.

6. **Scrap or waste costs.** These include expenditures for products, parts, or services that cannot be reworked or reused and that do not meet quality standards. Examples include items damaged during manufacture, unusable scrap, and unused services.

7. **Energy costs.** These are charges for electricity, gas, steam, and any other sources of power.

8. **Overhead costs.** These include expenditures for physical space, staff services, research, advertising, and legal services. Generally, overhead costs are shared by several departments; an attempt is usually made to allocate them to each department on some equitable basis.

Depending on the degree of detail needed, each of the above major cost categories may be broken down further. For example, direct labor costs may be broken down by shift or by section within the department. However, this can be overdone; as a rule, cost information should be no more detailed than is necessary for making good decisions.

Supervisors may be provided with weekly or monthly cost reports for their department, based on the above cost categories (see Figure 20.1 for an example). Such reports are usually prepared by the accounting department, based on information provided by the supervisors. Naturally, the reports are no more accurate than the information provided. Therefore, supervisors should be sure they understand what information is being sought. Also, if a supervisor does not understand any of the information on the report, he or she should seek clarification from the accounting department.

COST BUDGETS

LEARNING OBJECTIVES

As defined in Chapters 6 and 19, a **budget** is a statement of expected results or requirements expressed in financial or numerical terms. Almost all supervisors must work with cost budgets. A supervisor's involvement with the cost budgeting process can vary. In general, however, a supervisor should know how to

FIGURE 20.1 Sample Cost Report

Weekly Cost Report   Department No. 33
Week ending: March 10, 199—   Supervisor: Janice Arnold

| | | | Variance | | | | |
| | | | For This Week | | Year to Date | | |
Account	Budget	Actual	Over	Under	Over	Under	Comments
Direct labor	$2,900	$3,140	$240		$1,780		
Raw materials	2,100	2,000		$100		$650	
Indirect labor	750	725		25		120	
Overtime	450	200		250		290	Made
Scrap	400	390		10		70	improvements
Supplies	500	405		95	220		this week but
Utilities	450	505	55		75		still over annual
Overhead	3,750	4,240	500		3,890		budget.

develop a cost budget, how to operate within a budget, and how to use a budget for control. Even when a cost budget is given to a supervisor, it is helpful for the supervisor to understand the general process. The second column in Figure 20.1 represents the weekly budget for supervisor Janice Arnold.

The preparation of a budget is a part of the planning function. The actual administration of a budget is part of the control function. Even when not required to do so by upper management, it is wise for the supervisor to prepare cost budgets for each of the major cost categories (such as indirect labor, direct labor, and operating supplies). Preparing a cost budget provides the supervisor with goals to work toward. Referring again to Figure 20.1, Janice Arnold can readily identify the areas in which she is experiencing cost problems in the year to date (direct labor, supplies, utilities, and overhead) and the areas that are in good shape (raw materials, indirect labor, overtime, and scrap).

Typically, the supervisor plays a role in the organization's budgeting system. Budgeting systems normally start at the top of the organization and cascade down. Usually, the supervisor participates in the preparation of his or her department's budget. Budgets of lower levels obviously must fit within the general constraints established from above. The common budget period is one fiscal year, with breakdowns for quarterly and monthly periods. How often a budget is revised depends on the system used. Under *periodic budgeting*, major revisions are made three times a year (March, June, and September). A *progressive budget* calls for revisions every two months for the following six-month period. For example, at the end of February, revisions are made for the six-month period from March through August. Under a *moving budget*, revisions covering the next 12 months take place every month. In effect, one month is dropped and another is added in each revision.

The budgetary process should not be viewed as punitive, and it should not be used punitively. The purpose of a budget is not to punish or restrict the supervisor but to provide the supervisor with guidance. Properly used, a budget helps accomplish realistic and specific goals within stated cost expenditures. Supervisors who master the budgeting process help both themselves and their departments.

COST-REDUCTION STRATEGIES

5 LEARNING OBJECTIVES

Where should cost-reduction efforts be focused? Logically, cost reduction should begin in the areas where the greatest savings can be realized. These areas are not always obvious. Locating them may require considerable effort, but that effort usually pays off. At the same time, small cost reductions are also important. This is especially true if they can be repeated frequently, thus adding up to sizable reductions. With this in mind, several general strategies may be used to cut costs.

Increase output.   Output may be increased by utilizing the same or fewer resources. This reduces the cost per item of product or service. The supervisor should always try to operate at the output level that results in the greatest efficiency. Unfortunately, the ability of supervisors to increase output is often drastically limited in unionized organizations.

Improve methods.   This means maximizing efficiency by eliminating any unnecessary activities or by introducing new methods. This may involve the establishment of work standards and the improvement of work methods. (Chapter 9 discussed the improvement of work methods.)

Regulate or level the work flow.   A regular, steady work flow with no bottlenecks and no equipment breakdowns is desirable. Work flows with many peaks and valleys are usually inefficient and often require costly overtime.

Minimize waste.   The creation of unnecessary services and the scrapping of partially processed or unused materials can be very expensive. Any effort to reduce such waste can pay big dividends. For example, the supervisor of a cafeteria should carefully plan the quantities of the different foods to prepare so as to minimize the amount of leftovers. Other types of waste include idle personnel, work on projects of little value, and the use of equipment at less than full capacity.

Reduce overhead.   While some overhead costs are not within the supervisor's control, certain items are. Seemingly small things such as lights burning in unused areas, increased janitorial costs due to poor housekeeping, and misuse of office supplies can add up to significant overhead costs.

Analyze all control points.   Adequate control is necessary. However, excessive control can interfere with the work and can run up costs. For instance, quality checks should be properly spaced to ensure the desired quality, but they should not be overdone to the point of interfering with accomplishment of the work.

Ensure adequate storage space.   Inadequate storage space can be very costly. This situation can cause unnecessary materials-handling and production delays. In a service-oriented organization, storage space would include such things as adequate waiting rooms and adequate space for storing supplies.

Minimize downtime.   Obsolete and worn-out equipment is one of the largest causes of downtime. Such equipment should be replaced. This not only increases the efficiency of the equipment used, but also has a positive effect on the operator. For example, one has only to look at the gains achieved by replacing a manual typewriter with a modern word processor. Another major cause of downtime is running out of materials. Proper inventory control can keep this from becoming a problem.

Invest in employee training.   Employees who properly understand how to do their jobs are more efficient than those who don't. Usually, any front-end investments in training are made up through increased job efficiency.

Work closely with suppliers.   Suppliers can be a good source for cost-saving ideas. Involve suppliers in the design process and keep communication lines open throughout the entire design process. Supervision Illustration 20–1 describes how Chrysler Corporation has reduced costs by involving suppliers early in the design process.

Cost-Reduction Resources

Supervisors seeking to cut costs will invariably spot some possibilities. The key is to look for them. At the same time, however, supervisors should not fail to enlist the aid of all available resources. Staff specialists can be very helpful: cost analysts, industrial engineers, and others on the staff can offer expertise in certain areas. As mentioned earlier, employees often represent the greatest potential for cost-reduction ideas. The person who does the job every day gener-

---

SUPERVISION ILLUSTRATION 20–1

COST REDUCTION AT CHRYSLER

The Becker Group of Sterling Heights, Michigan, supplied hard trim and door trim to Chrysler Corporation for the 1997 Dodge Dakota. Becker was involved early in the design phase of the vehicle development program, which took 24 months. As a result of its early involvement in the design phase, Becker submitted 10 Supplier Cost Reduction Effort (SCORE) proposals to Chrysler. One suggestion saved $10 and reduced weight by two pounds per vehicle by replacing metal with plastic for the interior door trim bolster. Several costly and labor-intensive steps were combined into one operation for a learner assembly process. Another SCORE proposal saved Chrysler $200,000 by modifying the door panel design.

Bob Crockett, Becker Group's vice president of the Chrysler Business Unit, attributes much of these cost savings to Becker's early involvement and to the close communication with the Chrysler product development team.

Source: "Supplier Cost-Reduction Efforts at Chrysler," *Manufacturing Engineering,* September 1997, pp. 107–8. For more information about Chrysler Corporation, visit its Web site at:
www.chrysler. com

FIGURE 20.2

Questions That Help
Uncover Useful Cost
Reduction Ideas

Top Management

1. Do top management members give full support and impetus for cost-cutting activities?
2. What policies being followed tend to keep costs at a relatively high level?
3. Will contemplated changes facilitate any future cost-reduction activity?
4. What items can be eliminated without impairing major objectives?

Materials Purchased

1. Can material specifications be liberalized so as to cut down on costs?
2. Are quantities purchased in the most economical amounts?
3. Can lower-priced substitute materials or supplies be used?
4. Would generically described materials or supplies be less costly than brand names?

Machines and Equipment

1. Can similar results be achieved by buying attachments or special devices for currently owned machines or equipment?
2. Can any machines or equipment be borrowed from another department?
3. Would a less accurate and smaller machine perform adequate work?
4. Can any equipment be built at less cost in the company's own facilities?

ally has some good ideas about how it can be improved. The key is to listen to and evaluate all suggestions. It is also important to implement worthwhile suggestions and to give recognition to the employees who make them. Yet another resource is a cost-reduction committee. A cost-reduction committee offers the benefits of group thinking. It also heightens its members' interest in cost reduction. Figure 20.2 presents some selected questions that are helpful in eliciting cost-reduction ideas.

A NINE-STEP PLAN FOR COST REDUCTION

LEARNING
OBJECTIVES

Even the supervisors who have established an environment that fosters continual cost control and reduction sometimes desire to implement a specific cost-reduction effort. Such an effort reinforces the climate of continual cost control and reduction and provides a means of transforming intentions into actions. The nine-step plan discussed below contains the essential ingredients for developing a specific cost-reduction effort.[1]

Step 1: Identify areas with high cost-reduction potential.   First, analyze the major categories (direct labor, raw materials, indirect labor, operating supplies, etc.) and see if any stand out. Such an analysis shows the relative values of each of the major cost categories. Each category should then be further divided. For example, direct labor could be broken down into regular-time and overtime costs. It may be desirable to divide these costs even further. For example, regular time could be divided by shift or by employee category. Step 1 is the point at which the ideas and suggestions of employees and staff experts, such as cost accountants and industrial engineers, should be solicited.

Step 2: Generate specific savings ideas.   Once the costs have been analyzed by categories, it is usually not difficult to generate specific savings ideas. The guidelines and strategies outlined in the previous sections of this chapter should be utilized in this step. Step 2 also includes the identification of what must be done to achieve the savings. For example, suppose one savings idea is to reduce the use of overtime. The actions necessary to do this must also be outlined.

Step 3: Develop a way to measure actual savings.   Savings must be measured before they can be evaluated. The specific method used will vary, depending on the savings idea. For example, cost per square foot might be used if the saving involves better utilization of the facility; cost per unit, if the saving involves materials; and cost per customer served, if the saving involves providing a service.

Step 4: Review your ideas with your boss.   The objective here is to obtain the active support and involvement of your boss. This can only be accomplished if he or she knows what is going on, is committed to support the ideas, and is kept informed of the progress of the program.

Step 5: Establish an implementation committee.   The main purpose of an implementation committee is to see that action is taken. All too often, good ideas fall through the cracks because no one is responsible for their implementation. An implementation committee also serves as a means for actively involving other employees. It is sometimes desirable to have upper management represented on the committee. This can ensure management's involvement and can help motivate others on the committee.

Step 6: Communicate the program.   The ideas of the cost-reduction program must be clearly communicated to all affected employees. If in doubt about informing an employee, it is usually best to include him or her. Many methods of communicating the ideas are available. Traditionally, the most used methods have been written memos and group meetings. Memos have the advantage of being less time-consuming than group meetings, but they do not allow the recipients an opportunity to ask questions. E-mail and other electronic media can also be used to communicate the program. Many available electronic media formats allow for user comments and thus provide direct feedback to the supervisor.

Step 7: Put the program into action.   Once the first six steps have been carried out, the program should be implemented. Ideas that result in the greatest savings should be implemented first. This gets the program off to a positive start and helps build up momentum.

Step 8: Make necessary revisions.   Most ideas require minor revisions after they have been implemented. The key here is to not hesitate to make necessary adjustments and to communicate those adjustments to the affected individuals. For some reason, many people think that revising or adjusting an idea is equivalent to saying that it won't work. Often the reverse is true; if the idea is *not* revised, it won't work.

Step 9: Periodically check the program's progress.   Many good cost-reduction programs run out of gas shortly after implementation, often because they were never checked for progress. A good approach is to monitor the program's progress at regular intervals. This way, nothing is left to chance.

A final recommendation is that the supervisor be persistent throughout all steps of the program. When things don't move as fast as one thinks they should, it is easy to become discouraged and to give up. The supervisor should always remember that cost reduction is part of the job and not an addition to it!

COST AREAS THAT FREQUENTLY CAUSE PROBLEMS

7   LEARNING OBJECTIVES

Certain areas that tend to be more susceptible to cost overruns than others have historically caused problems for supervisors. Overtime, absenteeism, tardiness, employee theft, materials handling, job methods, quality maintenance, and inventory control are potential contributors to cost overruns. Quality and inventory control were discussed in Chapter 19. Methods improvement was discussed in Chapter 9. Overtime, absenteeism, tardiness, employee theft, and materials handling are discussed in the following paragraphs.

Overtime

Overtime is a curious phenomenon. Some employees refuse to work overtime; others regard it as a gift from heaven. The attraction of overtime is, of course, that overtime pay rates are higher than normal pay rates. The federal law states that all hours over 40 worked in one week must be paid at least at the rate of time and a half. Some organizations pay double or even triple time for certain overtime. In addition to the obvious cost of higher wages, overtime often has other hidden costs. These include decreased employee efficiency, higher reject rates, and more absenteeism (all due to employee fatigue). In spite of these costs, there is a great temptation to resort to overtime whenever things get behind schedule. Certainly, there are times when the use of overtime is justified. But overtime should not be resorted to at the drop of a hat. Excessive overtime sometimes indicates poor supervision. The old saying "Something is wrong if you can't do your job in eight hours a day" has some validity. Furthermore, overtime can create other problems. Deciding who should work overtime can be difficult. Also, if overtime becomes habitual, employees tend to expect it as a part of regular wages. If it is discontinued, some employees become unhappy because they are "making less pay." Yet another problem is that employees will pace themselves in order to create overtime.

If overtime looks like it might be necessary, a supervisor should do certain things:

1. Determine the cause of the overtime. Is it poor planning, inappropriate organization, faulty equipment, or what? Can anything be done to avoid or minimize the necessity of overtime in the future?

2. Consider the alternatives. One alternative to overtime is to use the services of a temporary agency. Temporary agencies today can even provide part-time professional employees. The major advantage to using people from temporary agencies is that they do not have to be paid at overtime rates (assuming they work 40 hours or less) and that they usually do not receive benefits.

3. Explain why overtime may be necessary. All the facts should be made available as soon as possible. Tell the employees why and how they were selected for overtime and how long it will last.

4. Have sufficient raw materials and supplies on hand. Overtime is certain to be wasted if this is not done.

5. Include work breaks when overtime is utilized. Remember, employees have already worked a full day. Adequate breaks are essential.

6. Be alert as a supervisor. Because of the increased costs associated with overtime, make sure it is used wisely. Be available to answer employee questions and provide needed guidance.

Absenteeism

The costs associated with absenteeism can be large. Machines may be idle, schedules may slip, and temporary help may have to be hired. When someone fails to show up for work, it is usually the supervisor who must decide what to do. Should temporary help be hired? Should regular work assignments be altered? What other adjustments should be made?

Unfortunately, absenteeism cannot be completely avoided. Employees get sick, relatives die, accidents occur, and certain personal business must be tended to during normal work hours. However, there is an avoidable type of absenteeism—that of the employee who could come to work but stays out instead. Research has shown that absenteeism tends to be low when employees (1) are satisfied with their jobs and (2) are loyal to the organization. Both of these factors can be significantly affected by the supervisor.

Employees may stay out because they find their jobs boring. The jobs may be repetitive, may not use the employees' skills, or may have little responsibility. The challenge for the supervisor is to determine whether these conditions exist and, if so, what to do about them. The boredom in some jobs can be lessened through alternative work designs. Some employees want and seek responsibility; others do not. It is the supervisor's job to determine who does and who does not. Those desiring responsibility should be given it whenever possible. Those wishing to avoid responsibility should not be given any more than necessary. An employee who doesn't get along with his or her peers may also stay out. When this occurs, the supervisor should confront the problem directly and try to help resolve the differences. If this doesn't work, the supervisor may be forced to terminate the employee.

Loyalty to the organization occurs naturally if the employee feels good about the company. Of course, the reverse is also true. Employees who harbor ill feelings about the organization or the supervisor are rarely loyal. The general style of supervision employed by the supervisor affects employees' feelings about the organization. If employees feel that the supervisor is fair, openminded, and concerned, they are likely to develop good feelings and loyalty toward the organization.

Some tardiness is controllable and some is not. Severe weather, such as this snowstorm, may cause accidental tardiness.
Michael Dwyer/Stock Boston

Tardiness

An employee who reports late can run up costs in many of the same ways as the absentee. Tardiness also indicates a lack of job satisfaction and loyalty. In most situations, a small group of chronic offenders account for most tardiness. As with absenteeism, some tardiness is controllable and some is not. Accidental tardiness occurs because of flat tires, severe weather, or personal emergencies. Controllable tardiness relates to the habitual offender—the employee who is late on a regular basis.

Habitual tardiness should be dealt with directly. First, the habitual offender should be identified and verified through the attendance records. Second, the reasons for his or her tardiness should be determined, if possible. Third, a private conference should be held with the offender. During this conference, the seriousness of the situation should be discussed and a plan for eliminating the problems should be agreed upon. If the reason pertains to a condition of the job, steps should be taken to correct it. Fourth, if the tardiness continues, talk to the offender again. Emphasize that the tardiness must stop or disciplinary action will be taken. Fifth, if the tardiness continues, follow the formal disciplinary procedure and discipline the offender. It is essential that matters of this type be dealt with directly and consistently so that all employees receive the same message.

Employee Theft

As discussed in Chapter 4, employee theft has been estimated at $40 billion to $50 billion per year. Even the most conservative estimates place losses due to employee theft at $15 billion per year.[2] One recent study found that employee theft rose from $44.72 per employee in 1989 to $168.42 in 1992, a 376 percent increase.[3] Although many factors may be at the source of employee theft, major contributors are lax selection and hiring policies, readily accessible money and products, and managers and supervisors who project a callous and uncaring attitude. While specific steps can be taken to reduce each of these contributors to theft, building a corporate culture that supports an honest workforce is the most effective approach. The following guidelines should be followed to establish such a culture:

8 LEARNING OBJECTIVES

1. Establish a clear, explicit policy on corporate theft.
2. Set a good example in terms of not taking liberties at the expense of the company.
3. Watch for warning signs of abuse.
4. Be consistent in dealing with those employees who violate theft policies.
5. Do not become overly aggressive; conduct a thorough investigation before accusing an employee.
6. Do not police the workplace; be trustful of employees.[4]

Supervision Illustration 20–2 discusses one approach that some companies are taking to help reduce employee theft.

SUPERVISION ILLUSTRATION 20–2

WORKING TOGETHER TO REDUCE EMPLOYEE THEFT

Even with employee theft on the rise, many retailers deal with the problem by simply firing guilty employees and hoping it doesn't happen again. Other companies join special programs or mutual associations to share information to help employers weed out bad apples from the employment pool. While mutual associations have been around for over 75 years, traditionally they have existed only in large metropolitan areas and have focused on checking creditworthiness, virtually ignoring the potential applications for employment checks.

The way the concept works is that whenever someone is screened out at one location, it is reported to databases across the country. One reason why this concept works is that people tend to job-hunt in a familiar industry. One problem in getting good data is that nearly 60 percent of companies don't prosecute employees, largely because of the cost and time involved. Retailers who want to add names to the databases usually must provide tangible evidence such as a signed admission or a videotape.

The U.S. Mutual Associates and Employers Screening Services Inc. are two of the country's largest associations of this type.

Source: Cristina Adams. "Screening Program Targets Employee Crime," *National Petroleum News,* October 1997, p. 20. For more information about Employers Screening Services, visit:
www.employmentscreening.com

FIGURE 20.3

Questions to Help Reduce
Materials-Handling
Problems

1. Is the travel distance the absolute minimum?
2. Are storage areas convenient and of adequate size?
3. What alternative arrangement might be better?
4. Are components and partial assemblies often damaged in transit?
5. Are materials moved manually from one area to another?
6. Is materials handling performed by any of your skilled employees?
7. Do any loading or unloading operations take considerable time?
8. Are materials moved several times within the department before actually being used?

Materials Handling

Materials handling involves the movement of materials. These include raw materials, supplies, in-process materials, finished goods, and equipment. In a service organization, materials handling includes the handling of any materials and supplies that are used in creating and providing the service. The average cost of materials handling has been estimated to be as high as 35 to 40 percent in a manufacturing setting. Materials-handling costs are undoubtedly equally high in some service organizations, such as a post office. Associated with materials handling are not only the costs of physically moving things but also the costs of *not* moving them in a timely manner. Idle employees and machines waiting for materials, supplies, or customers can be extremely costly. The questions listed in Figure 20.3 suggest specific ways that materials-handling problems might be reduced. Many of the work methods presented in Chapter 9 can be applied to solving materials-handling problems.

WHY DO EMPLOYEES SOMETIMES FEAR COST REDUCTION?

LEARNING
OBJECTIVES

Employees not accustomed to an environment that fosters continual cost control and reduction are often threatened by any cost-reduction efforts. These employees often see cost reduction only in negative terms and as something that management is doing "to them." Loss of overtime, reduction of regular working hours, and the loss of jobs are some of the more obvious fears that employees might harbor.

On the other hand, when an environment of continual cost control and reduction has been established, employees not only expect but even promote initiatives in this area. These employees understand that continual cost control and reduction is a philosophy and not merely a technique. Unfortunately, cost reduction has gotten a bad name in many instances because supervisors have presented cost control and reduction in a punitive manner and not as a philosophy of managing.

SOLUTION TO THE
SUPERVISION
DILEMMA

It appears that Jane has never been exposed to a well-designed cost-reduction program. In Jane's only experience with such a program, an idle threat by a former boss about reducing costs caused Jane to fear the concept of cost reduction. At the very least, Jane should now have a heightened awareness of the possibilities for cost reduction.

Assuming that Jane understands basic cost categories and the budget within which she must work, she should design and implement a cost-reduction plan that follows the nine steps discussed in this chapter (pp. 395–97). In designing her plan, Jane should remember that her employees represent her greatest source of cost-reduction ideas. Keeping this in mind, she should build some incentives for her employees into her program. To make cost reduction a normal part of the routine, she might consider establishing a suggestion box system or a cost-reduction committee within her department. To emphasize her commitment to cost reduction, she should take advantage of every opportunity to set an example—even such small matters as turning out lights and not wasting supplies (pp. 393–94).

SUMMARY

The major purpose of this chapter is to emphasize the importance of cost reduction and control. The chapter discusses the supervisor's role in cost reduction and control and presents guidelines for achieving cost reduction. A step-by-step plan for cost reduction is outlined. Areas particularly susceptible to cost overruns are discussed.

1. *Describe the supervisor's role in improving productivity through cost reduction and control.* The supervisor is a key person in any cost reduction and control program because he or she is in an ideal position to do something about costs. The supervisor also sets the tone for the entire department and largely influences the attitudes of the employees with regard to cost reduction and control.

2. *Present several guidelines that supervisors might follow in establishing an environment conducive to continuous cost control and reduction.* In addition to setting the tone by their attitude and personal actions, supervisors should find the following guidelines helpful in establishing an environment that fosters continuous cost control and reduction: Make cost reduction a part of the normal routine; cover all areas of the organization; provide a climate and a format for encouraging employee suggestions; establish cost objectives; make it clear that each individual is responsible for cost reduction; and offer incentives for cost-reduction savings.

3. *List the major cost categories encountered by supervisors.* The major cost categories encountered by supervisors are direct labor costs, raw materials costs, indirect labor costs, operating supplies costs, maintenance costs, scrap or waste costs, energy costs, and overhead costs.

4. *Discuss a supervisor's involvement with cost budgets.* A supervisor's involvement with the cost budgeting process can vary. In general, however, a supervisor should know how to develop a cost budget, how to operate within a budget, and how to use a budget for control purposes.

5. *Summarize several cost-reduction strategies that can be helpful to supervisors.* Cost-reduction strategies that can be helpful to supervisors include the following: Increase output, improve methods, regulate or level the work flow, minimize waste, reduce overhead, analyze all control points, ensure adequate storage space, minimize downtime, and invest in employee training.

6. *Outline a step-by-step plan for implementing a cost-reduction program.* The following nine-step plan contains the essential ingredients for a successful cost-reduction program: (1) identify areas with high cost-reduction potential, (2) generate specific savings ideas, (3) develop a way to measure actual savings, (4) review your ideas with your boss, (5) establish an implementation committee, (6) communicate the program, (7) put the program into action, (8) make necessary revisions, and (9) periodically check the program's progress.

7. *Identify several areas of concern to supervisors that tend to be especially susceptible to cost overruns.* Areas that tend to be especially susceptible to cost overruns are overtime, absenteeism, tardiness, employee theft, materials handling, job methods, quality maintenance, and inventory control.

8. *Outline several guidelines for establishing a culture that supports employee honesty.* Guidelines for establishing a culture that supports employee honesty include the following: Establish a clear, explicit policy on corporate theft, set a good example in terms of not taking liberties at the expense of the company, watch for warning signs of abuse, be consistent in dealing with those employees who violate theft policies, do not become overly aggressive, and do not police the workplace, but be trustful of employees.

9. *Discuss why employees may fear cost reduction.* Employees not accustomed to an environment that fosters continual cost control and reduction are often threatened by any cost-control efforts. These employees often see cost reduction only in negative terms and as punitive measures taken by management. Loss of overtime, reduction of regular working hours, and even loss of job are some of the fears these employees experience.

REVIEW QUESTIONS

1. Why is the supervisor a key person in any cost reduction program?
2. What are the general cost categories with which most supervisors come in contact?
3. Briefly describe three types of cost-budgeting systems.
4. Name six major guidelines that should be followed when making attempts to reduce costs.
5. Name eight general strategies for reducing costs.
6. Outline a specific plan for implementing a cost-reduction program.
7. List several areas that tend to be more susceptible to cost overruns than others.
8. What are three major factors that contribute to employee theft?
9. Why do employees fear cost reduction?

SKILL-BUILDING QUESTIONS

1. Why do you think most employees are not enthusiastic about cost control? What can the supervisor do about this problem?
2. Why do you think overtime is abused in so many organizations?
3. In light of today's high standard of living, why do you think that employee theft is such a widespread problem in industry?
4. As a nation approaches full employment, the cost of labor increases. A recent news report stated that even though the nation was close to full employment, inflation had not been rampant because businesses had reduced other costs. Do you agree or disagree with this conclusion? Why? List some ways in which costs can be reduced.

REFERENCES

1. The basic plan presented here is adapted from James J. Semrodek, Jr., "Nine Steps to Cost Control," *Supervisory Management*, April 1976, pp. 29–32.
2. "When Employees Steal: How to Break the Pattern," *Supervisory Management*, July 1994, pp. 1–2, and Fred D. Miller, "Rising Employee Theft Wringing Out More Profits," *Nation's Restaurant News*, July 28, 1997, p. 36.
3. Deidra-Ann Parrish, "Controlling Employee Theft," *Black Enterprise*, June 1997, p. 46.
4. "Employee Theft: Prevention, Recommendations, Policy Making," *Supervisory Management*, July 1994, pp. 1–2.

ADDITIONAL READINGS

Albrecht, Steve. "Are Your Employees the Enemy?" *HR Focus*, April 1997.

May, Bess Ritter. "How to Cut Your Company's Costs," *Supervision*, October 1994.

Mintcloud, Buckley. "Money-Saving Ideas for the Profit-Minded Supervisor," *Supervision*, August 1997.

Parrish, Deidra-Ann. Controlling Employee Theft," *Black Enterprise*, June 1997.

SKILL-BUILDING APPLICATIONS

Incident 20–1

A Recommendation for Cutting Costs

Rumor had it that dramatic cost cuts would be ordered by top management. Although it was well known that sales had been below projections for the past two quarters, everyone had hoped that the rumors weren't true.

As had been feared, it wasn't long before all of the supervisors received a memo instructing them to submit recommendations for cutting their respective departmental costs by 7 percent. Tina Bates, supervisor of clerical operations, didn't know what to recommend. Unlike the workload in some of the other departments, her workload had not fallen off in the past six months. She decided to talk to her close friend, Jeri Snyder, a supervisor in the human resources department.

Jeri's answer to Tina's dilemma was simple— cut every cost in the department by 7 percent. Jeri reasoned that this was the fairest thing to do because it would affect everyone in Tina's department to the same extent.

Questions

1. What do you think about Jeri's recommendations for cost reduction?
2. What are some other approaches that Tina might take?

Incident 20–2

Here We Go Again

Word of a drastic cost-reduction program had just come down from top management. The memo read, "If Transistors, Inc., is to survive, it must trim costs significantly. The Japanese have already forced many electronics firms out of business, and there is no reason why Transistors, Inc., will be spared unless we take action."

Emory Sparks, supervisor of one of the assembly areas, responded by talking to all of the people on his line. He explained the dire circumstances and asked them "to get with it." Specific requests made by Emory to his employees included taking shorter coffee breaks, starting on time, and not quitting 15 minutes early. Emory stated that the plant's goal was to keep all machines and lines operating at near capacity. He cautioned that increased productivity did not mean reduced quality, as had been the case on some occasions in the past. All of his employees stated that they would fully cooperate with the cost-reduction program.

Cost-reduction programs were nothing new to Emory. He had seen a multitude of them come and go during his nine years as a supervisor. Although his employees had all agreed to cooperate in the latest cost-reduction program, Emory couldn't help wondering if Transistors, Inc., hadn't tried this approach once too often. As the old saying goes, "You can go to the well only so many times." Another thing that bothered Emory was the inevitable assault of the cost experts. Every time a cost-reduction program was implemented, management sent in a team of accountants to monitor costs. These cost experts rarely knew what they were talking about. They undoubtedly knew accounting, but they didn't understand the production process.

Emory felt that in the final analysis, his department's costs were not out of line. The real problem, in his opinion, was the marketing department. In Emory's words, "The marketing department couldn't sell a coat to an Eskimo."

Questions

1. Can costs always be reduced? Discuss.
2. How successful do you think Emory will be in reducing his departmental costs?
3. What provisions of a cost-reduction program do you feel are warranted in this situation?

Exercise 20–1

Preparing a Cost Report

Assume that your boss has asked you to prepare a cost report based on the information presented in Figure 20.1 on page 392. The boss has also requested that your report include recommendations that you would make as a result of your analysis. In two pages or less, prepare the requested report and be prepared to discuss it with the class.

Exercise 20–2

Cost Overruns

Assume that you are the supervisor in charge of running a small branch bank in the suburb of a major metropolitan area. Your branch has three tellers, a customer service representative, and a loan officer. The tellers handle normal transactions that occur at the teller windows. The customer service representative opens new accounts, approves credit card applications, and renders other customer-related services. The loan officer processes loan applications. Recently, your branch has been running over its cost budget in several areas, including overtime, supplies, and utilities. You have mentioned these problems rather casually to your employees, with no apparent results or even concern.

This morning one teller called in sick and your customer service representative reported an hour late. Normal procedure when an employee is absent is to report the problem to bank headquarters. Usually, headquarters then directs a "travel team" member to substitute for the day and charges the branch a fee for the use of that person. In the 10 A.M. interoffice mail delivery, you received a memo from your district manager expressing her concern about your cost overruns. The memo asked that you submit a written cost-reduction plan to her by the end of the next week.

1. Working by yourself, outline the different cost categories in which you think costs might be reduced. What cost-reduction guidelines should you implement? Formulate a plan for carrying out your ideas.
2. Get together with three or four of your fellow students and compare the ideas that each of you developed in question 1. As a group, design a cost-reduction plan for this situation. Be as detailed as time permits.

Exercise 20–3

Comparing Costs

The Que Company prints personal checks and is located in New York. The company has two options for serving its Washington customers. These options are outlined below:

Option 1. Maintain a sales and customer service office in Washington. Under this arrangement a clerk in the Washington office would receive orders through the mail and telephone them to the New York plant where the order would be produced and shipped directly to the customer. The following costs have been estimated for this arrangement.

Rent for office space	$400 per month
Salary for office person	$960 per month
Furniture and equipment (i.e., word processor rental)	$400 per month
Telephone expense (WATS line)	$200 per month
Production cost in New York plant	$175 per order
Capacity of this method	2,000 orders per month
Price	$3.25 per order

Option 2. Open a small plant in Washington. Under this arrangement, the following costs have been estimated.

Rent on plant space	$1,200 per month
Manager's salary	$1,600 per month
Materials cost	$0.40 per order
Depreciation on equipment	$200 per month
Labor cost:	
1 office clerk	$800 per month
1 typesetter/pressman	$1,000 per month
1 binding worker	$900 per month
Capacity of this method	3,000 orders per month
Price	$3.25 per order

A. For each of the options above, classify all of the costs according to the categories described on pages 390–91. Which of these costs are fixed (do not vary with the level of production), and which vary according to the level of production?

B. If Que expects approximately 1,500 orders per month from its Washington customers, should it implement Option 1 or Option 2? Which option should it implement if it expects to average 3,000 orders per month?

CHAPTER
21

Safety and Accident Prevention

LEARNING OBJECTIVES

After studying this chapter, you should be able to:

1. Discuss the supervisor's responsibility for safety.
2. Appreciate the costs associated with work-related accidents and illnesses.
3. Discuss the major causes of work-related accidents.
4. Measure safety in the workplace.
5. Explain the basic purposes of a safety program.
6. Outline several organizational strategies for promoting safety.
7. Outline several specific things that the supervisor can do to prevent accidents.
8. Identify several warning signs that can help supervisors learn to recognize potentially violent employees.
9. Understand the purpose of the Occupational Safety and Health Act (OSHA).
10. Explain the basic purpose of the Hazard Communication Standard.

John Lewis has just filled out an OSHA accident report concerning the second major injury in his department this year. Both of these injuries occurred when an employee was trying to reach something on a high shelf. In the first instance, Beth Harrison was trying to reach a box of claim forms on a storage shelf when the chair she was standing on slipped and she fell to the floor. She broke an arm and missed five days of work. In the second instance, Joe Evans was standing on the top step of a stepladder in the storage room when he lost his balance and fell. He was out for two weeks with a strained back. If John had talked to his employees once about being careful, he had talked to them a dozen times! John simply can't believe the stupid things his employees do. Why only yesterday he himself tripped over a Coke bottle someone had left on the floor. Fortunately, he was able to catch himself in time. What in heaven's name can he do to prevent more "useless" accidents?

Safety is an important concern of today's organizations. During 1995, approximately 8 out of every 100 American workers in the private sector suffered an injury or illness caused by exposure to hazards in the work environment. Although fewer than half of all instances of injury and illness result in lost workdays, approximately 6.6 million nonfatal injuries and illnesses were reported in the private sector in 1995.[1] In the same year, approximately 6,112 work-related deaths occurred in American industry.[2] For comparative purposes, in 1982 7.7 out of every 100 Americans in the private sector suffered a work-related injury or illness.[3] The costs of work-related accidents to American industry are known to be in the billions of dollars annually and are increasing in certain areas.

THE SUPERVISOR'S RESPONSIBILITY FOR SAFETY

**LEARNING
OBJECTIVES**

A successful safety program starts at the very top of the organization. The owners, top executives, and middle managers must all be committed to safety. However, because the supervisor is the one representative of management who has daily contact with the employees, the supervisor is the key person in the program. Even in organizations that have a safety engineer or a safety director, the supervisor is responsible for seeing that the safety directives are carried out. It is from the supervisor that the employees take their cues as to what is important. It is the supervisor who shapes the employees' attitude toward safety.

Because supervisors are responsible for the safety of their employees, they should listen attentively to employee complaints and suggestions relating to safety. Complaints should always be checked out and corrective action taken when necessary. The supervisor should also strive to develop a good working relationship with the safety engineer or safety director (if there is one). The supervisor should consult the safety engineer or safety director on any safety-related problems that come up. These actions can help to head off many accidents before they occur. When a safety committee (safety committees are discussed later in this chapter) exists, the supervisor should work to develop good relations with the committee.

Because safety committees often act in only an advisory capacity, the supervisor is responsible for carrying out its recommendations. Thus supervisors and safety committees are really dependent on each other.

Safety instruction should be an integral part of orienting and training employees. Employees cannot be expected to use safe methods if they don't know what those methods are. Clear instructions regarding safety methods and procedures should be a part of every orientation program.

In addition to the general responsibilities described above, supervisors may also be responsible for such things as accident investigation, first aid, maintenance of proper safety records, and the dissemination of changes in safety regulations and methods.

THE COST OF ACCIDENTS

As indicated in the introduction to this chapter, the costs of work-related accidents are high. The factors that contribute to these costs are many and varied. A major category of costs is directly related to lost production. This category includes costs incurred as a result of work slowdown, damaged equipment, damaged or ruined products, idle equipment, excessive waste, and the profit forgone due to lost sales. A closely related cost is the cost incurred for training new or temporary replacements.

Insurance and medical costs are increasing due to large claims and other costs that are incurred as a result of work-related accidents. This category includes the costs of workers' compensation insurance, health insurance, accident insurance, and disability insurance. **Workers' compensation** is a form of protection for the employee from loss of income and extra expenses associated with work-related injuries. Since 1955, several states have allowed workers' compensation payments for job-related cases of anxiety, depression, and certain mental disorders.

Currently, workers' compensation coverage is compulsory in all but a few states. In these states, it is elective for the employer. When elective, any employers who reject the coverage also give up certain legal protections. Although the specific requirements, payments, and procedures vary among states, the features outlined in Figure 21.1 are common to virtually all programs.

Before any workers' compensation claim is recognized, the disability must be shown to be work related. This usually involves an evaluation of the claimant by an occupational physician. One major criticism of workers' compensation concerns the variation in coverage provided by different states. The amounts paid, the ease of collecting, and the likelihood of collecting vary significantly from state to state. Figure 21.2 summarizes the types of work-related injuries covered by workers' compensation.

Health insurance covers such things as normal hospitalization and outpatient doctor bills. Some health insurance plans also cover prescription drugs and dental, eye, and mental health care. Most accident insurance provides funds for a limited period of time to the injured party. Usually, the amount of the benefit is some percentage of the victim's wages or salary.

FIGURE 21.1

Features Common to Most Workers' Compensation Programs

1. The laws generally provide for replacement of lost income, medical expense payments, rehabilitation of some sort, death benefits to survivors, and lump-sum disability payments.

2. The employee does not have to sue the employer to get compensation; in fact, covered employers are exempt from such lawsuits.

3. The compensation is normally paid through an insurance program financed through premiums paid by employers.

4. Workers' compensation insurance premiums are based on the accident and illness record of the organization. A large number of paid claims results in higher premiums.

5. An element of coinsurance exists in the workers' compensation coverage. Coinsurance is insurance under which the beneficiary of the coverage absorbs part of the loss. In automobile collision coverage, for example, there is often coinsurance in the amount of $100 deductible for each accident. In workers' compensation coverage, there is coinsurance because the workers' loss is usually not fully covered by the insurance program. For example, most states provide for a maximum payment of only two-thirds of the wages lost due to accident or illness.

6. Medical expenses, on the other hand, are usually covered in full under workers' compensation laws.

7. It is a no-fault system; all job-related injuries and illnesses are covered regardless of where the fault for the disability is placed.

Source: S. Ledvinka, *Federal Regulations of Personnel and Human Resource Management* (Boston: Kent Publishing, 1981), p. 144.

Disability insurance protects the employee during a long-term or permanent disability. Normally, a one- to six-month waiting period is required following the disability before the employee becomes eligible for benefits. Like accident insurance benefits, disability insurance benefits are usually calculated as a percentage of wages or salary. The rates paid by the organization for each of these insurance coverages are almost always a function of the organization's safety and health record. Organizations with a good safety and health record usually pay rates considerably lower than those paid by organizations with a poor record.

Less obvious costs are those associated with employee morale, employee relations, and community relations. It is only natural that employee morale will suffer in an unsafe environment. Employee reactions to a perceived unsafe environment can range from refusal to work to an unconscious slowdown. For example, a manufacturing company had failed for years to effectively guard a flywheel on a particular machine. On the few occasions when it broke, no one was hurt. However, the possibility of being hurt caused the operators to flinch at any suspicious sound. The result was a considerable loss in operator efficiency.[4] If word gets around that a certain organization is unsafe, prospective employees will often shy away from working there. This can result in having to pay higher wages. The morale of a group may be damaged considerably if a member of the group is injured, and the harmony of the group may be impaired by the absence of the injured employee. It is not unusual for a bad safety record

FIGURE 21.2

Work-Related Injuries
Covered by Workers'
Compensation

1. Accidents in which the employee does not lose time from work.
2. Accidents in which the employee loses time from work.
3. Temporary partial disability.
4. Permanent partial or total disability.
5. Death.
6. Occupational diseases.
7. Noncrippling physical impairments such as deafness.
8. Impairments suffered at employer-sanctioned events such as social events or during travel related to organizational business.
9. Injuries or disabilities attributable to an employer's gross negligence.

Source: Reprinted by permission from *Personnel Administration and the Law,* 2nd ed., by Russell L. Greenman and Eric J. Schmertz, pp. 190–91. Copyright © 1979 by The Bureau of National Affairs, Inc., Washington, D.C. 20037.

to be a major reason for poor employee relations with management. If employees perceive that management is unconcerned about their physical welfare, employee-management relations can deteriorate. In fact, safety is often a primary reason given for unionizing.

THE CAUSES OF ACCIDENTS

LEARNING OBJECTIVES

Accidents don't just happen! They are generally the result of a combination of circumstances and events. The circumstances and events causing accidents are usually unsafe personal acts or an unsafe physical environment, or both.

Personal Acts

Most experts believe that unsafe personal acts cause the bulk of workplace accidents. Such acts have been estimated to cause 80 percent of all such accidents. Acts of this kind include taking unnecessary chances, engaging in horseplay, failing to wear or use protective equipment, using improper tools and equipment, taking unsafe shortcuts, operating equipment too fast, and throwing materials.

It is difficult to determine why employees commit unsafe personal acts. There probably is no single reason. A desire to impress others or project a certain image, fatigue, haste, boredom, stress, poor eyesight, daydreaming, and physical limitations are all potential reasons. However, these reasons do not explain why employees intentionally neglect to wear prescribed safety equipment or don't follow procedures. Most employees think of accidents as always happening to someone else. This attitude can easily lead to carelessness or a lack of respect for what can happen. It is also true that some people get a kick out of taking chances and showing off.

An earlier section of this chapter pointed out that a poor safety record can adversely affect employee morale. Research studies have shown that employees with low morale tend to have more accidents than employees with high morale. This is not surprising when one considers that low morale is likely to be related to employee carelessness.

Physical Environment

Accidents can and do happen in all types of environments. They can happen in offices and retail stores, and they can happen in factories and lumberyards. However, they occur most frequently in certain kinds of situations. Listed in order of decreasing frequency, these locations are:

1. Wherever heavy, awkward material is handled, using hand trucks, forklifts, cranes, and hoists. About one-third of workplace accidents are caused by handling and lifting material. Improper lifting is also a frequent cause of accidents.

2. Around any type of machinery that is used to produce something else. Among the more hazardous are metalworking and woodworking machines, power saws, and machines with exposed gears, belts, chains, and the like. Even a paper cutter or an electric pencil sharpener has a high accident potential.

3. Wherever people walk or climb, including ladders, scaffolds, and narrow walkways. Falls are a major source of accidents.

4. Wherever people use hand tools, including chisels, screwdrivers, pliers, hammers, and axes. Hand tools also account for a good many household accidents.

5. Wherever electricity is used other than for the usual lighting purposes. Among the places where electrical accidents occur are near extension cords, loose wiring, and portable hand tools. Outdoor power lines have a high accident potential.[5]

Unsafe physical conditions.   Just as there are certain situations in which accidents occur more frequently, certain physical conditions also seem to result in more accidents. Some of these unsafe physical conditions are:

1. Serious understaffing or not having enough people to do the job safely.
2. Unguarded or improperly guarded machines (such as an unguarded belt).
3. Poor housekeeping (such as congested aisles, dirty or wet floors, and improper stacking of materials).
4. Defective equipment and tools.
5. Poor lighting.
6. Poor or improper ventilation.
7. Improper dress (such as clothing with loose and floppy sleeves worn when working on a lathe).

Figure 21.3 lists some specific safety hazards that also frequently result in accidents.

Accident-Proneness

A reason often given for accidents is that certain people are accident-prone. There is little doubt that due to their physical and mental makeup, some employees are more susceptible to accidents than are others. Accident-proneness may result from inborn traits, but it often develops as a result of the individual's environment. However, this tendency should not be used to justify an acci-

FIGURE 21.3

Some Specific Safety Hazards

1. Slippery floors.
2. Loose tile, linoleum, or carpeting.
3. Small, loose objects left lying on the floor.
4. Bottles, cans, and books on the floor or stacked on top of filing cabinets or windowsills.
5. Sharp burrs on edges of material.
6. Cluttered aisles and stairs.
7. Reading while walking.
8. Power and extension cords.

FIGURE 21.4

Formulas for Computing the Accident Frequency Rate and the Accident Severity Rate

$$\text{Frequency rate} = \frac{\text{Number of disabling injuries} \times 1 \text{ million}}{\text{Total number of labor-hours worked each year}}$$

$$\text{Severity rate} = \frac{\text{Days lost* due to injury} \times 1 \text{ million}}{\text{Total number of labor-hours worked each year}}$$

*The American National Standards Institute has developed tables for determining the number of lost days for different types of accidents. To illustrate, an accident resulting in death or permanent total disability is charged with 6,000 days (about 25 working years).

dent. Employees who appear to be accident-prone should be identified and receive special attention. Given the right set of circumstances, anyone can be accident-prone. For example, a "normal" employee who was up all night with a sick child might very well be accident-prone the next day. Thus, employees who are temporarily accident-prone should also receive attention.

HOW TO MEASURE SAFETY

 LEARNING OBJECTIVES

Frequency and severity are the two most widely accepted measures of an organization's safety record. A **frequency rate** indicates the frequency with which disabling injuries occur. A **severity rate** indicates how severe the accidents were and how long the injured parties were out of work. Only disabling injuries are used in determining frequency and severity rates. **Disabling injuries** are injuries that cause the employee to miss one or more days of work following an accident. Disabling injuries are also known as **lost-time injuries.** Figure 21.4 gives the formulas for calculating the frequency rate and the severity rate.

Neither the frequency rate nor the severity rate means much unless it is compared with similar figures. Useful comparisons can be made with other departments or divisions within the organization, with the rates of the previous years, or with the rates of other organizations. It is through such comparisons that an organization's safety record can be objectively evaluated.

THE SAFETY PROGRAM

LEARNING
OBJECTIVES

The heart of any safety program is accident prevention. It is obviously much better to prevent accidents than to react to them. A major objective of any safety program is to get the employees to "think safety"—to keep safety and accident prevention on their minds. Many approaches are used to make employees more safety conscious. However, four basic elements are present in most successful safety programs.

1. The safety program has the support of top and middle management. That support must be genuine, not casual. If upper management takes an unenthusiastic approach to safety, employees will be quick to realize it.

2. Safety is clearly established as a line organization responsibility. All line managers should consider safety an integral part of their job. Furthermore, operative employees also have a responsibility for working safely.

3. A positive attitude toward safety exists and is maintained throughout the organization. The employees must believe that the safety program is worthwhile and that it produces results.

4. One person is in charge of the safety program and is responsible for its operation. Typically, this is the safety engineer or the safety director, but it may also be a high-level manager or the human resources manager.

Organizational Strategies for Promoting Safety

LEARNING
OBJECTIVES

Many strategies are available for promoting safety within the organization. Some suggestions are provided below.

Make the work interesting.   Uninteresting work often leads to boredom, fatigue, and stress, all of which can cause accidents. In many instances, job enrichment (discussed in Chapter 14) can be used to make the work more interesting. Simple changes can often make the work more meaningful to the employee. Job enrichment attempts are usually successful if they add responsibility, challenge, and similar qualities that contribute to the employee's positive inner feelings about the job.

Incorporate Ergonomics.   Ergonomics, also called human engineering, is concerned with improving productivity and safety by designing workplaces, tools, instruments, and so on that take into account the physical abilities of people.[6] Major objectives of ergonomics are to reduce fatigue and accidents due to human error. Designing comfortable chairs for computer operators and designing scissors that are easier for left-handed people to use are examples of ergonomics. Thus, whenever possible, supervisors should encourage the use of equipment and facilities that have been ergonomically designed.

Establish a safety committee.   Include operative employees and representatives of management. The safety committee is a way to get employees directly involved in the operation of the safety program. A rotating membership of 5 to 12 members is usually desirable. Normal duties of a safety committee include inspecting, observing work practices, investigating accidents, and making recommendations. Figure 21.5 outlines typical safety committee

FIGURE 21.5
Typical Safety Committee
Activities

1. Make regular inspections of the work areas.
2. Sponsor accident-prevention contests.
3. Help prepare safety rules.
4. Promote safety awareness.
5. Review safety suggestions from employees.
6. Supervise the preparation and distribution of safety materials.
7. Make fire-prevention inspections.
8. Supervise the maintenance of first-aid equipment.

activities. The safety committee should hold a meeting at least once a month, and attendance should be mandatory.

Feature employee safety contests.   Give prizes to the work group or employee having the best safety record for a given period. Contests can also be held to test safety knowledge. Prizes might be awarded periodically to employees who submit good accident-prevention ideas.

Publicize safety statistics.   Monthly reports of accidents can be posted. Solicit ideas on how such accidents could be avoided in the future.

Periodically hold safety training sessions.   Have employees participate in these sessions as role players or instructors. Use such themes as "Get the shock (electric) out of your life." Audiovisual aids such as movies and slides might be used.

Use bulletin boards.   Make use of bulletin boards throughout the organization. Pictures, sketches, and cartoons can be effective if they are properly used and frequently changed.

Reward employee participation.   Provide some type of reward or recognition for people who are actively and positively involved in the safety program. One possibility is to recognize one employee each month as the "Safety Employee of the Month." Supervision Illustration 21–1 describes a program initiated by Seven Oaks General Hospital to reduce work-related injuries and costs.

How the Supervisor Can Prevent Accidents

7 LEARNING OBJECTIVES

Because supervisors are the link between management and the operative employees, they are in the best position to promote safety. As previously discussed, the supervisor's attitude toward safety often sets the tone for how employees view safety. In addition to fostering a healthy attitude toward safety, the supervisor can do several specific things to prevent accidents:

1. Be familiar with organizational policies that relate to safety. Make sure that the appropriate policies are conveyed to employees.
2. Be familiar with the proper procedures for safely accomplishing the work. See that each employee knows the proper method for doing the job (this is applicable to long-term employees as well as to new hires).

3. Know what safety devices and personal protective equipment should be used on each job. Ensure that the respective jobholders use the proper safety devices and wear the proper protective equipment.

4. Know what safety-related reports and records are required (such as accident reports and investigation reports). Be sure that these reports are completed and processed on a timely basis.

5. Get to know the employees. Learn to identify both the permanently and the temporarily accident-prone employees. Once these employees have been identified, be sure that they receive proper safety training.

6. Know when and where to make safety inspections. It is generally wise to develop a schedule for making safety inspections. This ensures that they won't be neglected.

7. Learn to take the advice of the safety director and the safety committee. Look at both of these groups as resources. Learn to work closely with these resources.

8. Know what to do in case of an accident. Be familiar with basic first aid. Know how to contact the doctor, emergency services, and the hospital.

9. Know the proper procedures for investigating an accident and determining how it could have been prevented. Know the proper procedures to follow during an investigation.

10. Always set a good example with regard to safety. Remember, employees are always watching the supervisor.

Figure 21.6 summarizes the accident process and the supervisor's role in that process.

FIGURE 21.6 The Accident Process and the Supervisor's Role in That Process

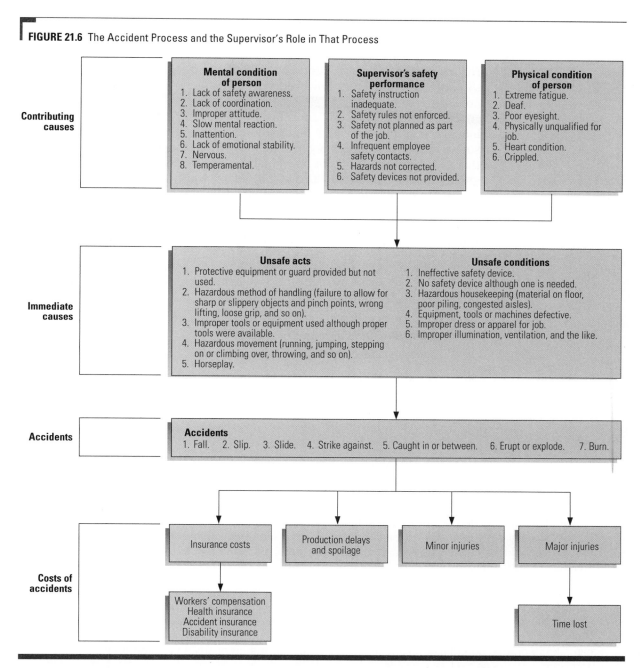

Source: Robert W. Eckles, Ronald L. Carmichael, and Bernard R. Sarchet, *Essentials of Management for First-Line Supervisors* (New York: John Wiley & Sons, 1974), p. 560.

VIOLENCE IN THE WORKPLACE

8   LEARNING OBJECTIVES

Historically, safety prevention has focused on the prevention of accidents in the workplace. Recently, however, violence in the workplace has become an increasing concern. Reports show that some form of violence has occurred in nearly one-third of all companies within the last five years.[7] These same reports indicate that approximately one million workplace incidences of violence result in some two million victims annually. While there is no way to guarantee that an organization will not be victimized, a violence-prevention programs can greatly reduce the probabilities of a problem. While most prevention programs contain many elements, supervisors always play a key role in making a program successful. Because most violent acts are not spontaneous, supervisors must learn to identify potentially violent situations. Specifically, supervisors should learn to spot the following warning signs:

- Employees making threats or being threatened.
- Employees who are suddenly terminated or anticipate being laid off.
- Employees with serious problems at home.
- Employees with a chemical dependency.
- Employees showing signs of paranoia.
- Employees fascinated by weapons.

Supervisors should also learn the proper organizational procedures for reporting and dealing with these different types of potentially violent situations. Supervision Illustration 21–2 describes a violence-protection program being used by Hardee's Food Systems, Inc.

SUPERVISION ILLUSTRATION 21–2

WORKPLACE VIOLENCE PREVENTION PROGRAMS

A poll of human resource professionals taken by the Society of Human Resource Management revealed that only 28 percent of companies have a formal plan aimed at preventing violence or dealing with its aftermath, and only 22 percent have plans to introduce such a strategy. Even though it may be impossible to completely prevent violence from happening in the workplace, there are steps that companies can take to defuse potentially violent situations and keep workers as safe as possible.

In 1990, Hardee's Food Systems, Inc., which operates 1,100 company-owned Hardee's and Roy Rogers restaurants and employs 35,000 people, created a comprehensive violence-prevention program. The program, which is run by a full-service loss prevention department, includes extensive training, a 24-hour hotline, and an intervention policy. The program's primary purpose is to reduce violent crimes within the restaurants. It also addresses threats, harassment, and domestic violence targeted toward any member of the company's workforce. Even though the company spends $3 million a year on prevention and safety, Francis D'Addario, director of loss prevention, believes "it's a small price to pay."

Source: Dawn Anfuso, "Deflecting Workplace Violence," *Personnel Journal,* October 1994, pp. 66–77, and S. Thomas Filippi, "Violence in the Workplace: Containing the Problem," *Professional Safety,* June 1996, pp. 37–39. For more information about the Society of Human Resource Management, visit its Web site at: **www.shrm.org**

OCCUPATIONAL SAFETY AND HEALTH ACT (OSHA)

9 LEARNING OBJECTIVES

In 1970, Congress passed the **Occupational Safety and Health Act (OSHA)**, which became effective on April 28, 1971. Its stated purpose is "to assure so far as possible every working man and woman in the nation safe and healthful working conditions and to preserve our human resources."

The Occupational Safety and Health Administration of the U.S. Department of Labor enforces OSHA, which covers nearly all businesses with one or more employees. (There are certain exceptions, such as businesses employing only family members.) Figure 21.7 shows a government poster explaining the basics of OSHA. Under OSHA, the Occupational Safety and Health Administration was created to:

- Encourage employers and employees to reduce workplace hazards and to implement new or improved existing safety and health programs.
- Provide for research in occupational safety and health to develop innovative ways of dealing with occupational safety and health problems.
- Establish "separate but dependent responsibilities and rights" for employers and employees for the achievement of better safety and health conditions.
- Maintain a reporting and record-keeping system to monitor job-related injuries and illnesses.
- Establish training programs to increase the number and competence of occupational safety and health personnel.
- Develop mandatory job safety and health standards and enforce them effectively.
- Provide for the development, analysis, evaluation, and approval of state occupational safety and health programs.[8]

Few laws have evoked as much negative reaction as OSHA. While few people would question the intent of OSHA, many have criticized the manner in which it has been implemented. The sheer volume of regulations has been staggering. Many have also criticized the vague wording of OSHA regulations. For example, the Occupational Safety and Health Administration developed the following 39-word single-sentence definition of the word *exit:*

> That portion of a means of egress which is separated from all other spaces of the building or structure by construction or equipment as required in this subject to provide a protected way of travel to the exit discharge.[9]

In addition, many OSHA regulations have been criticized as excessively petty. For example, one regulation states: "Where working clothes are provided by the employer and become wet or are washed between shifts, provision shall be made to ensure that such clothing is dry before reuse."

Because of definitions and regulations similar to the above examples, many organizations developed a negative attitude toward OSHA. As a result, legislation was enacted to soften some OSHA requirements. Also, many of the original OSHA standards have been subsequently revoked by the Occupational Safety and Health Administration itself.

FIGURE 21.7 Basic Requirements of OSHA

JOB SAFETY & HEALTH PROTECTION

The Occupational Safety and Health Act of 1970 provides job safety and health protection for workers by promoting safe and healthful working conditions throughout the Nation. Provisions of the Act include the following:

Employers

All employers must furnish to employees employment and a place of employment free from recognized hazards that are causing or are likely to cause death or serious harm to employees. Employers must comply with occupational safety and health standards issued under the Act.

Employees

Employees must comply with all occupational safety and health standards, rules, regulations and orders issued under the Act that apply to their own actions and conduct on the job.

The Occupational Safety and Health Administration (OSHA) of the U.S. Department of Labor has the primary responsibility for administering the Act. OSHA issues occupational safety and health standards, and its Compliance Safety and Health Officers conduct jobsite inspections to help ensure compliance with the Act.

Inspection

The Act requires that a representative of the employer and a representative authorized by the employees be given an opportunity to accompany the OSHA inspector for the purpose of aiding the inspection.

Where there is no authorized employee representative, the OSHA Compliance Officer must consult with a reasonable number of employees concerning safety and health conditions in the workplace.

Complaint

Employees or their representatives have the right to file a complaint with the nearest OSHA office requesting an inspection if they believe unsafe or unhealthful conditions exist in their workplace. OSHA will withhold, on request, names of employees complaining.

The Act provides that employees may not be discharged or discriminated against in any way for filing safety and health complaints or for otherwise exercising their rights under the Act.

Employees who believe they have been discriminated against may file a complaint with their nearest OSHA office within 30 days of the alleged discriminatory action.

Citation

If upon inspection OSHA believes an employer has violated the Act, a citation alleging such violations will be issued to the employer. Each citation will specify a time period within which the alleged violation must be corrected.

The OSHA citation must be prominently displayed at or near the place of alleged violation for three days, or until it is corrected, whichever is later, to warn employees of dangers that may exist there.

Proposed Penalty

The Act provides for mandatory civil penalties against employers of up to $7,000 for each serious violation and for optional penalties of up to $7,000 for each nonserious violation. Penalties of up to $7,000 per day may be proposed for failure to correct violations within the proposed time period and for each day the violation continues beyond the prescribed abatement date. Also, any employer who willfully or repeatedly violates the Act may be assessed penalties of up to $70,000 for each such violation. A minimum penalty of $5,000 may be imposed for each willful violation. A violation of posting requirements can bring a penalty of up to $7,000.

There are also provisions for criminal penalties. Any willful violation resulting in the death of any employee, upon conviction, is punishable by a fine of up to $250,000 (or $500,000 if the employer is a corporation), or by imprisonment for up to six months, or both. A second conviction of an employer doubles the possible term of imprisonment. Falsifying records, reports, or applications is punishable by a fine of $10,000 or up to six months in jail or both.

Voluntary Activity

While providing penalties for violations, the Act also encourages efforts by labor and management, before an OSHA inspection, to reduce workplace hazards voluntarily and to develop and improve safety and health programs in all workplaces and industries. OSHA's Voluntary Protection Programs recognize outstanding efforts of this nature.

OSHA has published Safety and Health Program Management Guidelines to assist employers in establishing or perfecting programs to prevent or control employee exposure to workplace hazards. There are many public and private organizations that can provide information and assistance in this effort, if requested. Also, your local OSHA office can provide considerable help and advice on solving safety and health problems or can refer you to other sources for help such as training.

Consultation

Free assistance in identifying and correcting hazards and in improving safety and health management is available to employers, without citation or penalty, through OSHA-supported programs in each State. These programs are usually administered by the State Labor or Health department or a State university.

Posting Instructions

Employers in States operating OSHA approved State Plans should obtain and post the State's equivalent poster.

Under provisions of Title 29, Code of Federal Regulations, Part 1903.2(a)(1) employers must post this notice (or facsimile) in a conspicuous place where notices to employees are customarily posted.

More Information

Additional information and copies of the Act, OSHA safety and health standards, and other applicable regulations may be obtained from your employer or from the nearest OSHA Regional Office in the following locations:

Atlanta, GA	(404) 562-2300
Boston, MA	(617) 565-9860
Chicago, IL	(312) 353-2220
Dallas, TX	(214) 767-4731
Denver, CO	(303) 844-1600
Kansas City, MO	(816) 426-5861
New York, NY	(212) 337-2378
Philadelphia, PA	(215) 596-1201
San Francisco, CA	(415) 975-4310
Seattle, WA	(206) 553-5930

Washington, DC
1997 (Reprinted)
OSHA 2203

Alexis M. Herman

Alexis M. Herman, Secretary of Labor

U.S. Department of Labor
Occupational Safety and Health Administration

This information will be made available to sensory impaired individuals upon request.
Voice phone: (202) 219-8615; TDD message referral phone: 1-800-326-2577

GPO : 1997 o – 429–604 QL 3

The Supervisor and OSHA

While OSHA has an impact on the entire organization, it also places certain responsibilities on the supervisor. It requires that the supervisor keep very specific records. One of these is OSHA Form 200 (Log and Summary of Occupational Injuries and Illnesses). Each occupational injury and illness must be recorded on this form within six working days from the time that the employer learns of the injury or illness. Furthermore, if fatalities occur, or five or more employees require hospitalization, the occurrences must be reported to OSHA within 48 hours. Another record that the supervisor must keep is OSHA Form 101 (Supplemental Record of Occupational Injuries and Illness). This form contains much more detail about each injury or illness that has occurred.[10] Form 101 must also be completed within six working days from the time that the employer learns of the accident or illness.

Occurrences that must be recorded are injuries and illnesses resulting in death, lost workdays, loss of consciousness, restriction of work or motion, transfer to another job, or medical treatment (other than first aid). Injuries requiring temporary first aid do not have to be recorded.

Supervisors are often asked to accompany OSHA officials while these officials inspect an organization's physical facilities. Because many organizations and supervisors feel threatened by OSHA officials, they may tend to behave antagonistically to these officials. However, it is in the best interests of the supervisor and the host organization for the supervisor to cooperate with visiting OSHA officials. An uncooperative supervisor could cause these officials to be more hard-nosed than usual. The end result could be stiffer penalties than would have been imposed otherwise.

Supervisors should be familiar with the OSHA regulations affecting their departments. They should constantly be on the lookout for safety violations. As previously discussed, it is the supervisor's responsibility to see that the employees follow all safety rules. Naturally, these include all OSHA rules and regulations.

Hazard Communications Standard

10 LEARNING OBJECTIVES

Approximately 32 million U.S. employees are potentially exposed to one or more chemical hazards in the workplace. There are an estimated 650,000 chemical products at present, and hundreds of new ones are being introduced annually.[11] Because of the threats posed by chemicals in the workplace, OSHA has established a Hazard Communications Standard. This standard is also known as the "right to know" rule. The basic purpose of the rule is to ensure that employers and employees know what chemical hazards exist in the workplace and how to protect themselves against those hazards. The goal of the rule is to reduce the incidence of illness and injuries caused by chemicals.

The **Hazard Communications Standard** establishes uniform requirements to ensure that the hazards of all chemicals imported into, produced, or used in the workplace are evaluated and that the results of these evaluations are transmitted to affected employers and exposed employees.

The Hazard Communications Standard specifically requires that employers maintain complete and updated Material Safety Data Sheets (MSDSs). MSDSs provide information on the nature of hazards, including appropriate handling and remedies for unexpected exposure. Employers, manufacturers, or importers of the hazardous material may prepare MSDSs.

OSHA has developed a variety of materials to help employers and employees implement effective hazard communication programs. Supervisors play a key role in these programs.

SOLUTION TO THE SUPERVISION DILEMMA

John's impromptu talks with his employees have had little effect on reducing accidents. He should attempt to implement a safety program in his department. Such a program has the best chance for success if it has the enthusiastic support of top and middle management. John could assume the responsibility for implementing the program, or he could assign the responsibility to one of his subordinates; the important thing is that somebody be responsible for the program (p. 414). Whoever is charged with responsibility for the safety program should remember that the main purpose of any safety program is to get the employees to "think safety." The safety program might incorporate such things as the establishment of a safety committee, a safety contest, the posting of safety statistics, and periodic safety meetings (pp. 414–15). Every effort should be made to seek and encourage employee input and participation in the program.

SUMMARY

This chapter is designed to heighten a supervisor's awareness of the costs of workplace accidents and illnesses and to suggest things that can be done to reduce the occurrence of such accidents and illnesses. The chapter also discusses the Occupational Safety and Health Act (OSHA).

1. *Discuss the supervisor's responsibility for safety.* Supervisors' primary responsibility toward safety is to establish an environment where safety is emphasized. Supervisors also have responsibilities to listen to employee complaints and suggestions, work closely with the safety engineer or director (if there is one), work closely with the safety committee (if there is one), and provide safety instruction. In addition to these general responsibilities, supervisors may be responsible for such things as accident investigations, first aid, maintenance of proper safety records, and the dissemination of changes in safety regulations and methods.

2. *Appreciate the costs associated with work-related accidents and illnesses.* The costs associated with workplace accidents and illnesses are many and varied, but they can usually be classified into three major categories: (1) costs directly related to lost production, (2) insurance and medical costs, and (3) costs resulting from the negative effects of workplace accidents and illnesses on employee morale, employee relations, and community relations.

3. *Discuss the major causes of work-related accidents.* The circumstances and events causing accidents are usually unsafe personal acts or an unsafe physical environment, or both.

4. *Measure safety in the workplace.* Frequency and severity are the two most widely accepted measures of an organization's safety record. A frequency rate indicates the frequency with which disabling injuries occur. A severity rate indicates how severe the accidents were and how long the injured parties were out of work.

5. *Explain the basic purposes of a safety program.* The basic purpose of any safety program is to prevent accidents. Since getting employees to "think safety" is one of the more effective ways to prevent accidents, this is a major objective of most safety programs.

6. *Outline several organizational strategies for promoting safety.* Many strategies are available for promoting safety within an organization. These include making the work interesting, incorporating ergonomics, establishing a safety committee, featuring employee safety contests, publicizing safety statistics, periodically holding safety training sessions, using bulletin boards, and rewarding employee participation.

7. *Outline several things that the supervisor can do to prevent accidents.* In addition to fostering a healthy attitude toward safety, the supervisor can do these things to prevent accidents: Make the work interesting; be familiar with organizational policies that relate to safety; be familiar with the proper procedures for safely accomplishing the work; know what safety devices and personal protective equipment should be used; know what safety-related reports and records are required; know the employees; know when and where to make safety inspections; learn to take the advice of the safety director and the safety committee;

know what to do in case of an accident; know the proper procedures for investigating an accident and determining how it could have been prevented; and always set a good example with regard to safety.

8. *Identify several warning signs that can help supervisors learn to recognize potentially violent employees.* Supervisors should learn to recognize the following warning signs of potentially violent employees: employees making threats or being threatened, employees who are suddenly terminated or anticipate being laid off, employees with serious problems at home, employees with a chemical dependency, employees showing signs of paranoia, or employees fascinated by weapons.

9. *Understand the purpose of the Occupational Safety and Health Act (OSHA).* The stated purpose of OSHA is to assure so far as possible every working man and woman in the nation safe and healthful working conditions and to preserve our human resources.

10. *Explain the basic purpose of the Hazard Communications Standard.* The basic purpose of the Hazard Communications Standard is to ensure that employers and employees know what chemical hazards exist in the workplace and how to protect themselves against those hazards.

REVIEW QUESTIONS

1. Name three major categories of accident costs to the organization.

2. What are the differences between workers' compensation and disability insurance?

3. What are the major causes of accidents? Which cause accounts for the majority of work-related accidents?

4. Name several unsafe physical conditions that frequently cause accidents.

5. What is accident-proneness?

6. What are the most widely accepted methods for measuring an organization's safety record?

7. List several things that a supervisor can do to promote safety.

8. State several specific things that a supervisor can do to prevent accidents.

9. What is the stated purpose of OSHA?

10. What does OSHA specifically require of the supervisor?

11. What are Material Safety Data Sheets (MSDSs)?

SKILL-BUILDING QUESTIONS

1. How would you answer this question: "How can I improve safety in my department since I don't have the authority to significantly alter the physical environment?"

2. Susan Baker has just been appointed the Que Company's director of safety, a newly created job. What are some of the more important safety thoughts that she should keep in mind?

3. Suppose many of your employees circumvent the safety regulations whenever possible because they feel that these regulations slow them down unnecessarily and keep them from making more money. What might you do in this situation?

4. Do you think that the overall benefit of OSHA has been positive or negative? Support your answer.

REFERENCES

1. Survey of *Occupational Injuries and Illnesses, 1995* (Washington, D.C.: U.S. Department of Labor, May 1997), pp. 1–2

2. "National Census of Fatal Occupational Injuries, 1996" (Washington, D.C.: U.S. Department of Labor, August 7, 1997), p. 1.

3. All of the 1982 statistics are from *Occupational Injuries and Illnesses in the United States by Industry, 1982* (Washington, D.C.: U.S. Department of Labor, April 1984), pp. 1–4.

4. Rollin H. Simonds and John V. Grimaldi, *Safety Management*, rev. ed. (Homewood, Ill: Richard D. Irwin, 1963), p. 30.

5. Garry Dressler, *Personnel Management: Modern Concepts and Techniques*, 3rd ed., 1984, p. 627. Reprinted with permission of Reston Publishing Company, a Prentice Hall Company, 11480 Sunset Hills Road, Reston, VA 22090.

6. James R. Evans, *Production/Operations Management: Quality, Performance, and Value*, 5th ed. (Minneapolis: West Publishing, 1997), p. 405.

7. Barry Brandman, "Fight Workplace Violence," *Transportation and Distribution*, September 1997, pp. 87–92.

8. *All about OSHA*, rev. ed. (Washington, D.C.: U.S. Department of Labor, 1995), p. 2.

9. *Code of Federal Regulations* (Washington, D.C.: U.S. Government Printing Office, 1988), p. 126.

10. Under certain conditions, substitute forms are allowed for both Form 200 and Form 101.

11. "OSHA to Revise HazCom," *Occupational Hazards*, December 1995, pp. 14–16.

ADDITIONAL READINGS

Berezin, Eric. "A New OSHA Focuses on the Big Picture," *Risk Management*, February 1996.

Peavey, Buck. "Building a Complete Incentive Program," *Occupational Health & Safety*, October 1997.

Ramsey, Robert D. "Violence on the Job: How Safe Is Your Workplace?" *Supervision*, August 1994.

Ruder-Finn Inc. "Employer Compliance with OSHA," *Supervision*, August 1992.

Sfiligoj, Eric. "The Need for Ergonomic Interventions," *Beverage World*, June 15, 1997.

SKILL-BUILDING APPLICATIONS

Incident 21–1

The Safety Inspection

Because of the risks associated with handling dangerous chemicals, Sam Armanetti was confident that his company would be inspected by the Occupational Safety and Health Administration in the near future. Sam's company, Star Compound and Chemical, processes and packages all types of industrial cleaning compounds and chemicals.

Sam decided to call a meeting of all his supervisors as the first step in preparing for the anticipated OSHA inspection. During the meeting, Sam stressed the importance of safety and the potential costs to the company if Star received a bad OSHA report. Sam handed out a new *OSHA General Standards Manual* (OSHA 2206) to the supervisors and announced that he was going to conduct a surprise mock OSHA inspection in about four weeks.

Joe Brooks is supervisor of the mixing department. His department is responsible for mixing all of Star's liquid compounds and chemicals. Joe, a conscientious supervisor, is committed to seeing that his department is completely up to OSHA standards. Shortly after the meeting with Sam, Joe outlined a three-week program for eliminating safety hazards. Among the actions taken were painting yellow lines to clearly mark the aisles, cleaning the filters on all the exhaust fans, ensuring that all chemicals were stored in their proper places, checking the groundings on all the electrical mixing motors, installing additional lights in the storage areas, and adding rails around the mixing drums.

By the end of three weeks, Joe felt ready for the inspection. In fact, he welcomed the opportunity to show Sam what had been done. Sam appeared for the inspection about a week later. The inspection was going great until the last few mixing drums were reached. No employee in this area was wearing the required safety glasses, two employees were seen smoking in an unauthorized part of the area, and several employees were not wearing the required protective gowns.

Joe couldn't believe his eyes! After all of the work that had been done to eliminate safety hazards, his employees were demonstrating almost no concern for the safety rules. Joe was naturally embarrassed.

As soon as Sam left, Joe went over and asked the employees why they had violated the safety rules. The explanations were basically all the same: the safety glasses, gloves, gowns, and so forth were bulky, and it was much easier to work without them.

Questions

1. Do you think that Joe's problem is unique?
2. Why do you think that employees are often lax with regard to safety rules that have been established for their own safety?
3. What would you do if you were Joe?

Incident 21–2

No One Listens

Several severe accidents have recently occurred in the 12-employee boiler room of City Hospital. Jackson Ward, the boiler room supervisor, is quite upset about the situation. Just yesterday, the hospital administrator called:

Administrator: Jackson, what in the world is going on down there? Are you trying to fill all of our empty beds with your employees?

Jackson: If I've lectured these people about safety once, I've done it 50 times. They just don't seem to listen.

Administrator: Accidents cost us money for repairs, lost time, and medical expenses, not to mention the human suffering involved. Your department's record is awful, and something must be done about it! Maybe you should try something new.

Jackson: I'm not sure what it will be, but I'll come up with something.

Administrator: Good. Please report back to me when you come up with something.

Jackson decided to discuss his problem with several other supervisors in the hospital to see what ideas they might have. One suggestion was that Jackson schedule a weekly 10-minute safety talk by one of his employees. These talks could be on such topics as "Good Housekeeping," "Using Proper Safety Guards on Equipment," "Following Procedures," and "Health Hazards." Another suggestion was that Jackson review his department periodically and that any unsafe act discovered during his review be punished by an immediate two-day suspension for the offender. The person making this suggestion obviously believed that what Jackson needed was to get tough. A third suggestion was that Jackson talk personally to each employee about the department's safety problems, let the employees know that he was personally interested in each of them. A final suggestion was that Jackson give the employee with the best safety record for the past four months a day off with pay.

Questions

1. Why do you think Jackson has been having safety problems?
2. Which of the suggestions given to Jackson would you attempt to implement?
3. What additional ideas might you try if you were Jackson?

Exercise 21–1

Potential Safety Problems

In groups of three to five students, examine the building in which your class is held and its immediate surrounding areas for potential safety problems and hazards. Pay special attention to the items listed in Figure 21.3 (page 413). For each potential hazard identified, address the following questions:

1. How long do you suspect the hazard has existed?

2. How would you correct the problem or remove the hazard?
3. Why do you think each of the identified problems or hazards has not been addressed?

Also identify any specific steps that appear to have been taken to make the building and its immediate area more safe.

Be prepared to report your findings to the class.

Exercise 21–2

National Safety

Almost everyone has an opinion about the Occupation Safety and Health Act (OSHA). Your opinion may be based on firsthand experience, on what others have told you, or on what you have read. The arguments in favor of OSHA center on the belief that most organizations, when left to their own volition, will not take adequate employee safety and health measures and that OSHA has in fact had a positive impact in reducing occupational injuries and illness. The arguments against OSHA include the belief that it has cost the country a large number of jobs (by causing certain companies to close down rather than comply with expensive OSHA rules), that it is an infringement on personal freedoms, and that it is being implemented by another poorly administered government bureaucracy.

1. All things considered, what is your opinion of OSHA? Without doing any additional research, prepare an outline of the points that you would use to support your position.
2. The instructor will divide the class into two teams. One team will take a pro position regarding OSHA and one will take a con position. Each team will be given equal time to prepare arguments supporting its position. The instructor may ask each team to orally present its arguments.

CHAPTER 22

Discipline and Grievance Handling

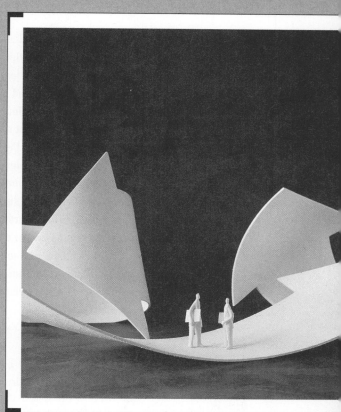

LEARNING OBJECTIVES

After studying this chapter, you should be able to:

1. Define discipline.
2. Explain the hot-stove rule for applying discipline.
3. Define grievance, union steward, and arbitration.
4. Discuss recommendations for pregrievance settlement.
5. Explain how to handle the first step of the grievance process.
6. Define employment at will in nonunionized organizations.

SUPERVISION
DILEMMA

While having lunch with her friend Bill Thomas, a supervisor in the underwriting de-partment, Jane Harris learned that Bill just had a grievance filed against him by one of his employees. Bill had suspended the employee for coming in late to work. The em-ployee had been late four times in the past five months, but Bill didn't say anything to him about it on the first two occasions. On the third occasion, Bill gave the employee a written reprimand. On the fourth, Bill suspended him.

The clerical employees of Global Insurance Company are unionized. The union contract has a disciplinary procedure that calls for an oral warning on the second oc-currence of tardiness during a six-month period, a written warning on the third, and a suspension on the fourth. The grievance filed against Bill Thomas stated that he had not followed the proper disciplinary procedure.

Jane had been a member of the union prior to her promotion. She hadn't paid much attention then to the discipline and grievance procedures because they didn't affect her. Now, as a supervisor, Jane feels she needs to know more about the disciplinary process.

When a member of management wants to take an action against an operative employee for violating an organizational rule, the organization's discipline pro-cedure is used to resolve the problem. When an employee has a complaint against the organization or its management, the organization's grievance proce-dure is normally used to resolve the problem. Some organizations have very formal discipline and grievance procedures; others have less formal proce-dures; still others have no formalized procedures. The purpose of this chapter is to outline typical discipline and grievance procedures and to suggest ways of handling disciplinary actions and grievances positively.

A POSITIVE APPROACH TO DISCIPLINE

**1   LEARNING
OBJECTIVES**

Discipline should be viewed as a condition within an organization whereby employees know what is expected of them in terms of the organization's rules, standards, and policies and what the consequences are of infractions. The basic purpose of discipline should be to teach about expected behaviors in a con-structive manner.

A formal discipline procedure usually begins with an oral warning and pro-gresses through a written warning, suspension, and ultimately discharge. For-mal discipline procedures also outline the penalty for each successive offense and define time limits for maintaining records of each offense and penalty. For instance, tardiness records might be maintained for only a six-month period. Tardiness prior to the six months preceding the offense would not be consid-ered in the disciplinary action. Less formal procedures generally specify the reasons for disciplinary action as being for just or proper cause.

Preventing discipline from progressing beyond the oral warning stage is ob-viously advantageous to both the employee and management. Discipline should be aimed at correction rather than punishment. If the behavior can be corrected by an open talk between the supervisor and the employee, there is less chance that the problem will become a source of bitterness. Formal oral or written warnings are less likely to cause animosity than a disciplinary suspension. It is obviously not in the supervisor's best interest to deprive employees of their income if their behavior can be corrected by an oral or written warning. A disciplinary suspension not only hurts the employee but also frequently deprives the supervisor and the organization of a needed employee. Of course, the most costly and least acceptable form of discipline is discharge. In most cases, supervisors should make every effort to avoid discharging an employee. Supervisors should view discipline as a means of encouraging employees to willingly abide by the rules and standards of the organization.

HOW DOES THE SUPERVISOR MAINTAIN GOOD DISCIPLINE?

One of the most important ways of maintaining good discipline is communication. Employees cannot operate in an orderly and efficient manner unless they know the rules. The supervisor has the responsibility of informing employees of the organization's rules, regulations, and standards. The supervisor must also ensure, when necessary, that employees understand the purpose of the rules and regulations. It is also essential that the supervisor remind employees in a friendly manner when their adherence to the rules has become lax. It is important to note that employees also have an obligation to become familiar with company rules and regulations. The sole responsibility is not on the supervisor. The supervisor should foster the overall atmosphere that encourages employees to become informed.

Whenever possible, counseling should precede the use of disciplinary reprimands or stricter penalties. Through counseling, the supervisor can uncover problems affecting human relations and productivity. Counseling also develops an environment of openness, understanding, and trust. This encourages employees to maintain self-discipline.

To maintain effective discipline, supervisors must always follow the rules that employees are expected to follow. There is no reason for supervisors to bend the rules for themselves or for a favored employee. Employees must realize that the rules are for everyone. It is a supervisor's responsibility to be fair toward all employees.

APPLYING THE DISCIPLINE PROCEDURE

Although most employees do follow the organization's rules and regulations, there are times when supervisors must use discipline. Figure 22.1 lists a number of frequent reasons for using discipline. Supervisors must not be afraid to use the disciplinary procedure when it becomes necessary. Employees may interpret failure to act as meaning that a rule is not to be enforced. Supervisory decisions to discipline after a period of lax enforcement contribute to poor morale and reduced productivity. Failure to act can also frustrate employees who are abiding by the rules. Applying discipline properly can encourage borderline employees to improve their performance.

Whenever possible, counseling should precede the use of disciplinary reprimands or stricter penalties.
Frank Siteman/Stock Boston

FIGURE 22.1
Reasons for Disciplining Employees

Absenteeism

Tardiness

Loafing

Absence from work

Leaving place of work (includes quitting early)

Sleeping on job

Assault and fighting among employees

Horseplay

Insubordination

Threat to or assault of management representative

Abusive language toward supervisor

Profane or abusive language (not toward supervisor)

Falsifying company records (including time records, production records)

Falsifying employment application

Dishonesty

Theft

Disloyalty to government (security risk)

Disloyalty to employer (includes competing with employer, conflict of interest)

Moonlighting

Negligence

Damage to or loss of machinery or materials

Incompetence (including low productivity)

Refusal to accept job assignment

Refusal to work overtime

Participation in prohibited strike

Misconduct during strike

Slowdown

Union activities

Possession or use of drugs

Possession or use of intoxicants

Obscene or immoral conduct

Gambling

Abusing customers

Attachment or garnishment of wages

Source: Adapted from Frank Elkouri and Edna Elkouri, *How Arbitration Works,* 3rd ed. (Washington, D.C.: Bureau of National Affairs, 1973), pp. 652–66.

FIGURE 22.2 Typical Union Contract Provision Relating to Discipline	ARTICLE XXI *Discharge, suspension or other disciplinary action* The EMPLOYER shall not discharge nor suspend any employee without just cause, but in respect to discharge or suspension shall give at least one warning notice of a complaint against such employee to the employee, in writing, and a copy of same to the UNION affected, excepting that no warning notice need be given to an employee before discharge if the cause of such discharge is unauthorized use of company vehicle, dishonesty, drinking of alcoholic beverages while on duty, use of narcotics (as described by the Pure Food and Drug Act), barbiturates, or amphetamines while on duty, or engaging in physical violence while on duty, to the employee who initiates such action, recklessness resulting in serious accident while on duty, the carrying of unauthorized passengers or failure to report a serious accident or one which the employee would normally be aware of flagrant disregard of reasonable instructions that do not conflict with the terms of this Agreement, willful destruction of EMPLOYER's or public property, becoming involved in a serious motor vehicle accident while driving the Company car as a result of negligence or recklessness. Discharge or suspension must be by proper written notice to the employee and the UNION affected. Warning notices shall have no force or effect after nine (9) months from the date thereof. Any employee may request an investigation as to his or her discharge or suspension. Should such investigation prove that an injustice has been done an employee, he or she shall be reinstated. The terms and conditions of such reinstatement may provide for full, partial, or no compensation for time lost. Appeal from discharge must be taken within five (5) days by written notice to the EMPLOYER and a decision reached within ten (10) days from the date of discharge. If no decision is reached between the EMPLOYER and the UNION within ten (10) days, the parties shall immediately proceed to the steps as set out in the grievance procedure for a final disposition of the matter.

Before supervisors use the discipline procedure, they must be aware of how far they can go without involving higher levels of management. They must also determine how much union participation is required. If the employee to be disciplined is a member of a union, the contract may specify the penalty that must be used. Other requirements may also be specified by the contract, such as who must be present during a disciplinary meeting and the length of time a record of the discipline can be kept on an employee's record. Figure 22.2 is an example of a union contract clause covering discipline.

Because a supervisor's decisions may be placed under critical review in the grievance process, supervisors must be careful when applying discipline. Even if there is no union agreement, most supervisors are subject to some review of their disciplinary actions. To avoid having a discipline decision rescinded by a higher level of management, it is important that supervisors follow the guidelines discussed below.

Predisciplinary Recommendation

Every supervisor should become familiar with the law, union contract, and past practices of the organization as they affect disciplinary decisions. Supervisors should resolve with higher management and the human resources department any questions that they may have about their authority to discipline.

The importance of maintaining adequate records cannot be overemphasized. Not only is this important for good supervision; it can also prevent a disciplinary decision from being rescinded. Written records often have a significant influence on decisions to overturn or uphold a disciplinary action. Past rule infractions and the overall performance of employees should be recorded. A supervisor bears the burden of proof when his or her decision to discipline an employee is questioned. In cases where the charge is of a moral or criminal nature, the proof required is usually the same as that required by a court of law (proof beyond a reasonable doubt). Adequate records by the supervisor and witnesses are of utmost importance in cases of this type. Written records of good performance and improvement can also be helpful, especially if the supervisor is defending himself or herself against a charge of inconsistency made by a disciplined employee.

Another key prediscipline responsibility of the supervisor is the investigation. This should take place before discipline is administered. The supervisor should not discipline and then look for evidence to support the decision. What appears obvious on the surface is sometimes completely discredited by investigation. Accusations against an employee must be supported by facts. Many decisions to discipline employees have been overturned due to an improper or less-than-thorough investigation. Supervisors must guard against taking hasty action when angry or when there has not been a thorough investigation. Before disciplinary action is taken, the employee's motives and reasons for the rule infraction should be investigated and considered. The employee's work record should also be a prediscipline consideration.

Furthermore, if the organization is unionized, the union should be kept informed on matters of discipline. Some organizations give unions advance notice of their intention to discipline an employee. Copies of warnings are often sent to the union.

Administering Formal Discipline

A supervisor is expected to use progressive, corrective discipline. As has been stated, it is to the supervisor's and the organization's advantage to correct the employee's behavior with a minimum of discipline. Sometimes, however, counseling and oral warnings are not sufficient and the employee must be formally reprimanded. A formal warning is less likely to be reviewed by higher management and less likely to produce resentment than a suspension or a discharge. Still, the supervisor should keep some key points in mind when issuing a formal warning.

2 LEARNING OBJECTIVES

The application of discipline should be analogous to the burn received when touching a hot stove. Often referred to as the **hot-stove rule,** this approach emphasizes that discipline should be directed against the act rather than the person. Other key features of the hot-stove rule are immediacy, advance warning, consistency, and impersonality. Figure 22.3 outlines the features of the hot-stove rule.

Immediacy refers to the length of time between the misconduct and the discipline. For discipline to be most effective, it must be administered as soon as possible, but without making an emotional, irrational decision.

FIGURE 22.3
Hot-Stove Rule for
Applying Discipline

1. The hot stove burns immediately. Disciplinary policies should be administered quickly. There should be no question of cause and effect.
2. The hot stove gives a warning, and so should discipline.
3. The hot stove consistently burns everyone who touches it. Discipline should be consistent.
4. The hot stove burns everyone in the same manner regardless of who they are. Discipline must be impartial. People are disciplined for what they have done and not because of who they are.

As has been discussed, discipline should be preceded by *advance warning*. The supervisor cannot begin to enforce previously unenforced rules by disciplining an employee as an example. The notation of rules infractions in an employee's record is not sufficient to support disciplinary action. An employee who is not advised of an infraction is not considered to have been given a warning. Noting that the employee was advised of the infraction and having the employee sign a discipline form are both good practices. Failure to warn an employee of the consequences of repeated violations of a rule is an often-cited reason for overturning a disciplinary action.

A key element in discipline is *consistency*. Inconsistency lowers morale, diminishes respect for the supervisor, and leads to grievances. Consistency does not mean that an absence of past infractions, long length of service, a good work record, and other mitigating factors should not be considered when applying discipline. However, an employee should feel that under essentially the same circumstances any other employee would have received the same penalty.

Supervisors should take steps to ensure *impersonality* when applying discipline. The employee should feel that the disciplinary action is a consequence of what he or she has done and is not a matter of personality or of relationship to the supervisor. The supervisor should avoid arguing with the employee and should administer discipline in a straightforward, calm manner. Administering discipline without anger or apology and then resuming a pleasant relationship aid in reducing the negative effects of discipline.

Ordinarily, the supervisor should administer discipline in private. Only in the case of gross insubordination or flagrant and serious rule violations would a public reprimand be desirable. Here a public reprimand helps the supervisor regain control of the situation. Even in such situations, however, the supervisor's objective should be to regain control, not to embarrass the employee. A good supervisor praises in public and reprimands in private.

Finally, the supervisor should warn the employee of the result of repeated violations. Sometimes suggestions to the employee concerning ways to correct his or her behavior are beneficial.

Supervisors should be very reluctant to impose disciplinary suspensions and discharges. Usually, discipline of this degree is reserved for higher levels of management. However, even though supervisors usually lack the power to administer disciplinary suspensions or discharges, they are nearly always the ones who must recommend such action to higher management. Since discipline of this kind is more likely to be reviewed, more costly to the organization, and more likely to affect overall morale and productivity than other kinds of discipline, it is very important for the supervisor to know when such discipline should be recommended. Observing the hot-stove rule is essential in administering suspensions and discharges.

The supervisor is expected to use corrective discipline whenever possible. Some offenses, however, may justify discharge. Among these offenses are stealing, striking a supervisor, and manifesting gross insubordination. The supervisor must be able to show, sometimes beyond a reasonable doubt, that the offense was committed. Attention to the points discussed in the prediscipline recommendations is especially important in supporting a decision to discharge an employee.

As with any lesser discipline, but even more essential in suspension and discharge, the employee has the right to a careful and impartial investigation. This involves allowing the employee to state his or her side of the case, to gather evidence supporting that side, and usually to question the accuser. If an employee's alleged offense is very serious, the supervisor may suspend the employee pending a full investigation. This may be necessary if an employee has been accused of a serious crime whose repetition would endanger others.

The suggestions outlined in the preceding paragraphs should help the supervisor maintain discipline in a positive manner and with minimal application of the harsher forms of discipline. When the supervisor needs to apply the discipline procedure, following these suggestions should reduce the chances of a grievance—or, if a grievance is filed, the chances of having the disciplinary action overruled. Figure 22.4 provides a checklist of rules that should be observed when applying discipline. Figure 22.5 outlines the formal discipline steps.

FIGURE 22.4
Supervisory Checklist for Applying Discipline

1. Be familiar with the law, union contract (if applicable), and past practices of the organization as they affect disciplinary decisions.
2. Maintain adequate records.
3. Investigate rule infractions and mitigating circumstances.
4. Keep the union informed (if applicable).
5. Administer discipline as soon as possible.
6. Precede formal discipline with a warning.
7. Be consistent among employees.
8. Relate the penalty to the offense rather than the person.
9. Administer discipline in private.
10. Warn the employee of the results of a future violation.

FIGURE 22.5
Formal Discipline Steps

1. Oral warning
2. Written warning
3. Suspension
4. Discharge

MINIMIZING GRIEVANCES

3 LEARNING OBJECTIVES

Employees have not always had the right to complain, especially formally, against the organization. With the advent and growth of labor unions, employees have gained in power, and the grievance procedure is a significant part of that power. A **grievance** is a formal dispute between management and an employee or employees over some condition of employment. The grievance procedure is a formal method for resolving grievances. Through the grievance procedure, complaints are aired, ambiguities in the labor agreement are identified for settlement in future negotiations, and organizational policy is further defined. Many nonunionized organizations also have grievance procedures.

A grievance usually begins with an informal complaint by an employee. Often this complaint will be talked out between the employee and the supervisor before it becomes a formal grievance. The supervisor should not be afraid of complaints. A reasonable number of complaints usually indicates a healthy atmosphere. Proper handling of complaints by the supervisor is extremely important. Once a complaint enters the formal grievance procedure, additional time, people, and cost will be needed to reach a decision.

The grievance procedure varies among organizations. Small organizations tend to have a less formal procedure with fewer steps—usually one or two. Large organizations have a more formal procedure with more steps—typically three or four. The first step usually involves the complaining employee (called the *grievant*), the supervisor, and, if there is a union contract, the union steward. The *union steward* is an operative employee whom the union members select to work with them on handling their grievances. Subsequent steps involve higher levels of management and the union hierarchy. Arbitration is usually the final step in the grievance procedure. **Arbitration** is a process by which both the union and management agree to abide by the decision of an outside party regarding the grievance. Supervision Illustration 22–1 describes an arbitration case. Figure 22.6 illustrates a typical grievance procedure.

Grievances arise for a wide variety of reasons. The most frequently grieved problems are disciplinary actions, promotions and layoffs, and distribution of work (including overtime). Some grievances are the result of failures to abide by the union contract, the law, or past practices of the organization. Other grievances result from failures of the union contract to address the unsure or the unclear nature of the contract and/or past practice concerning the issue. Regardless of the nature of the complaint, the grievance procedure provides a method for resolving the dispute.

There are many reasons for allowing the supervisor to settle a complaint before it enters the grievance procedure or at the lowest possible step of the grievance procedure. First, this saves time and money. Settling the grievance at the supervisory level saves the time of higher levels of management and the time of the union steward. Second, by achieving settlement before entering the formal grievance procedure or at the first level of the procedure, the supervisor develops the employee's confidence in the organization's ability to make decisions and solve problems. Many times, an employee's attitude about the job and the organization is based on his or her relationship with the supervisor. Early settlement also develops the confidence of higher levels of management in the supervisor's ability and confidence between the management and the union in

---

SUPERVISION ILLUSTRATION 22-1

WORKING IN THE RAIN

A dispute arose between Southwestern Electric Power Company and International Brotherhood of Electrical Workers Local 738. Southwestern Electric Power Company is a regulated public utility company serving some 900,000 persons in northwest Louisiana, northeast Texas, and western Arkansas. The company is organized into four geographical operating divisions, three of which are unionized. All the union divisions are covered by the same collective bargaining agreement, which in one form or another has existed for over 50 years. The dispute arose on Sunday, when the crew headed by senior lineman Lenny Ray and supervised by foreman Kincy reported for work at 8:00 AM on a prearranged overtime job scheduled at the Merritt Tool Company plant in Kilgore, Texas. It was raining, and the crew objected to working in the rain. Kincy told them that he had been told that when prearranged overtime had been scheduled, it was to be worked, rain or shine. The crew told him they would do the work only under protest, and would file a grievance, which they did.

Because the union and company were unable to resolve the grievance at the lower steps of the grievance procedure, it went to arbitration. The following union contract provisions were in effect at the time the grievance was filed:

Pertinent Contract Provisions
Article 14
GENERAL OPERATING RULES
Rule 10
INCLEMENT WEATHER

Only emergency line work shall be done out of doors by line crews when it is raining. For all the other Employees covered by this Agreement work in the rain shall be held to such minimum as is reasonably necessary for the protection and preservation of the property of the Company and for the rendition of safe, economical, and satisfactory services to the public. Employees on hourly rates of pay shall receive straight time on rainy days for such work as they perform, but in the event no work is performed, they shall be allowed one hour's pay for reporting to work at 8:00 AM and one hour's for reporting to work at 1:00 PM.

All Employees required to work outside in rainy weather shall be furnished rain coats or rain suits, hats, and rubber boots.

Arbitrator's Award

1. The Company did violate the Agreement when it required linemen to perform work in the rain on Sunday.
2. The Company will compensate all the men involved by paying them four (4) hours pay at time and one-half in addition to pay already received.

Source: 94LA444 (Washington, D.C.: Bureau of National Affairs, Inc.). For more information about the IBEW, visit its Web site at: www.compuserve.com/homepages/ibewnet/

their ability to settle differences and avoid costly arbitration. Early settlement also prevents minor problems from becoming major disturbances that upset morale and disrupt the entire organization.

Stressing pregrievance or early settlement of a complaint at the supervisory level does not mean that the supervisor should settle every complaint. Very unusual cases or decisions that could affect many employees are best referred to higher levels of management or the human resources department. An organization may be just as accountable for its supervisor's decisions as for decisions made by the plant manager, the president, or the owner. Grievances that result in the interpretation of broad general policies and union contract clauses are generally not settled at the supervisory level.

FIGURE 22.6

Typical Grievance Procedure

ARTICLE XI
GRIEVANCE PROCEDURE

Section 1. It is the intent and purpose of this article to provide for the presentation and equitable adjustment of grievances. The parties agree that in the interest of proper disposition of grievances there will be certified by the Union, two (2) grievance committeemen, and stewards who will aid in the disposition of grievances.

Grievances shall be presented within ten (10) workdays after the occurrence is known.

Step 1. The Employee and the designated department steward of the employee's department will discuss the problem with the employee's immediate supervisor, and these parties will attempt to resolve the grievance no later than the end of the shift.

Step 2. If the grievance is not settled in Step 1, the grievance stating the nature of the controversy shall be reduced to writing and submitted within ten (10) workdays to the assistant Plant Manager. He shall meet and give his answer in writing within five (5) workdays thereafter.

Step 3. In order for the grievance to be considered further, the committee shall serve notice of appeal on the Employer within five (5) workdays following the disposition of the grievance in Step 2. Such grievance shall be discussed thereafter between the Union's Business Manager or his representative, the grievance committee, and the plant manager within three (3) workdays after the date of notice of appeals. A written answer to the grievance will be made within three (3) workdays after the date of meeting. Either party may produce at the meeting any persons familiar with the facts involved to aid in a solution of the problem.

Step 4. In the event of any dispute or controversy which cannot be settled by mutual agreement under the foregoing procedure, either party may have the right, within ten (10) workdays following Step 3, to go to arbitration.

Section 2. The failure of the aggrieved party or his representative to present the grievance within the prescribed time limits in Step 1, 2, or 3 shall be considered a waiver of the grievance.

Grievances that arise out of suspension or discharge cases will be introduced into Step 2 within five (5) workdays after the company has notified the Union of the termination. If the grievance is unresolved after being treated in Step 2, it will be deemed to be waived to Step 3 of the grievance procedure. A Step 3 meeting will be convened and a written answer given within five (5) workdays from the date that the grievance is waived to Step 3.

The time limits in this Article may be extended by mutual agreement by both parties.

Section 3. Employees serving as stewards or witnesses in processing grievances under Article XI above shall suffer no loss in pay while attending meetings with the Company.

Under no circumstances should the supervisor attempt to obstruct the grievance procedure. Many times that procedure acts as a safety valve, preventing more costly employee actions.

RECOMMENDATIONS FOR PREGRIEVANCE SETTLEMENT

4 LEARNING OBJECTIVES

As was stated earlier, complaints should not be discouraged. It is how complaints are handled that is important. By effectively dealing with complaints, supervisors can reduce the number that turn into formal grievances.

Supervisors should give special attention to understanding the grievance procedure. By having knowledge of organizational policies and or the union contract, a supervisor may satisfy the grievant before a formal complaint is filed. If supervisors are not given formal training in this area, it is their responsibility to become familiar with pertinent material through study and through discussion with other members of management and the human resources department.

Developing a working relationship with the union steward can be especially helpful in working out problems before they become formal grievances. Although the union steward is an operative employee and should be treated the same as any other employee in the working relationship, the supervisor should treat the steward as an equal when handling complaints and other union business. The steward is less likely to push petty complaints if the supervisor is willing to listen and act in settling serious complaints. The union steward must be convinced of the supervisor's willingness to analyze the issues and settle them fairly and contractually. Power struggles between the supervisor and the union steward usually result in loss of time and very little constructive problem solving.

A supervisor who sees a problem should not wait for the employee to complain. It is better for a supervisor to admit an error and take action than to defend a wrong position. Waiting usually costs the organization more, results in loss of respect for the supervisor, and creates bitterness between the organization and the union.

Encouraging employees to voice their opinions and complaints works to the supervisor's advantage. Complaints often shrink in importance once they have been verbalized and grow in importance when they are not openly expressed. The supervisor must hear out the complaint rather than prematurely debate with the employee. Trying to understand the employee's point of view is one of the best ways to keep a complaint from becoming a grievance.

A supervisor is wise to investigate complaints that are expressed in nonverbal ways, such as excessive absences, high turnover, and low-quality work. Often an employee will complain about one thing when the real complaint is about something entirely different. A sensitive supervisor can head off potential grievances before they get out of hand by closely heeding nonverbal evidence of grievances. Developing a sensitivity to issues, working conditions, and attitudes that affect employee behavior is helpful in preventing grievances.

HANDLING THE FIRST STEP OF THE GRIEVANCE PROCESS

5 LEARNING OBJECTIVES

If the employee's complaint cannot be satisfied by an informal discussion with the supervisor, it becomes a formal grievance. Supervision Illustration 22–2 describes the importance of a quick response to employee complaints. In the first step of a formal grievance, the grievant and usually the union steward present the grievance to the supervisor. The grievance is usually described, in writing, on a grievance form. Written grievances not only establish a written record of the grievance but also tend to focus the discussion and investigation on the proper area. Written grievances also often result in the dropping of a grievance due to its lack of merit.

SUPERVISION ILLUSTRATION 22-2

EMPLOYEE COMPLAINTS

Corporate legal problems resulting from employee complaints are increasing. In addition, managers and supervisors can end up paying the price if they fail to take the right actions. However, when employee complaints are handled properly, managers and supervisors can prevent legal problems for their companies and for themselves.

The following example illustrates the proper way to handle complaints of sexual harassment. When a cook who worked in a Washington, D.C., museum restaurant accused her supervisor of sexual harassment and sued the supervisor, the company, and two executives of the company, the case was dismissed. The court found that because the company began investigating the charges the day they were made and because it took disciplinary action against the supervisor, neither the company nor the executives could be held liable. The case illustrates the value of quick action in response to employee complaints.

Source: Adapted from Geanne Rosenbert, "Employee Complaints 101: A Manager's Guide," *Investor's Business Daily*, July 10, 1997, p. A1. For more information about *Investor's Business Daily*, visit its Web site at:
www.investors.com

By the time the complaint has been formalized at the first step of the grievance procedure, the supervisor has usually had some discussion with the grievant. As in the pregrievance handling, the supervisor is advised to listen patiently and sympathetically to the grievant. If the supervisor does not have the time to listen to the grievance when it is first presented, he or she should schedule a time as early as possible to hear the grievant. The grievance should be treated seriously. The grievant should be given the opportunity to state the problem with no interruption other than occasional questions to help clarify the issue. Restating the complaint in summary and asking the grievant whether the restatement represents a fair presentation of the problem can be helpful in clarifying the issue. If necessary, the supervisor should ask the grievant and the steward for additional time to answer the grievance. However, every attempt should be made to abide by the time limits specified in the union contract. The supervisor's objective should be to get all the facts. The more facts obtained, the more effective any actions will be and the more receptive the grievant will be to those actions.

The supervisor must evaluate the facts objectively and attempt to determine the causes of the grievance. It is helpful for the supervisor to determine and evaluate the costs and possible side effects of alternative actions. It is extremely important for the supervisor to maintain adequate records of all meetings with the grievant.

Once the supervisor has made an evaluation of the grievance and arrived at a solution, the supervisor must plan the implementation of the solution. Before implementation begins, the grievant and the union steward should be informed of the solution and the reasons behind it. If management has made a mistake, the mistake should be admitted openly and a prompt settlement implemented. If the grievance is settled in management's favor, the supervisor should express confidence in the employee's willingness to abide by the decision.

FIGURE 22.7
Checklist for Minimizing Grievances

1. Gain an understanding of the labor law, union contract, and past practice as it pertains to decisions made at the supervisory level.
2. Develop a cordial relationship with the union steward.
3. Provide a work environment that is as fair as possible.
4. Encourage openness.
5. Try to understand the opposing point of view.
6. Investigate the cause of the complaint.
7. Determine the issue.
8. Evaluate the facts objectively.
9. Plan the implementation of the solution.
10. Before implementation, advise operative and union personnel who will be affected by the solution.
11. Check frequently on the results and side effects of the solution.

Finally, the supervisor should follow up with frequent checks on the implementation of the solution. The supervisor must ensure that the adjustment was fair and did not create other problems.

The suggestions discussed in the preceding paragraphs should help the supervisor minimize grievances and should aid the supervisor in settling them at the lowest possible level. The checklist provided in Figure 22.7 outlines the steps that should be followed.

HANDLING LATER STEPS IN THE GRIEVANCE PROCESS

If the grievant does not agree with the supervisor's decision in Step 1 of the grievance process, the grievance is processed through other steps. Figure 22.6, shown earlier, gives an example of the typical steps in the grievance process. The supervisor's actions taken before Step 1 come under close scrutiny from higher levels of management, union officials, and possibly an arbitrator. This is even more reason why the supervisor should follow the recommendations that have been outlined.

DISCIPLINE IN NONUNIONIZED ORGANIZATIONS

6 LEARNING OBJECTIVES

Until recently, management decisions on discipline or discharge in nonunionized organizations have been relatively free of judicial review. Courts intervened only in those cases violating legislation concerning equal employment opportunity. Generally, the concept of **employment at will** has applied. Employment at will means that when an employer hires employees to work for an indefinite period of time and the employees do not have a contract limiting the circumstances under which they can be discharged, the employer can terminate the employees at any time, for any reason, or for no reason at all. The majority of employees in organizations are employees at will.

This situation has been gradually changing as the courts have begun to hear discharge cases involving allegations of capricious or unfair treatment in nonunionized organizations. In some cases, the courts have ruled in favor of the discharged employees when the employee has been guaranteed due process under company procedures. Basically, the courts seem to be moving toward requiring nonunionized organizations to use a wrongful discharge standard, which is somewhere between the employment-at-will and just-cause positions.

In light of these developments, many organizations have established appeal procedures for disciplinary actions taken by management. The most common type of nonunion appeal procedure is an open-door policy that allows employees to bring appeals to successively higher levels of management. An open-door policy gives an employee the right to appeal a disciplinary action taken against him or her to the manager's superior.

SOLUTION TO THE SUPERVISION DILEMMA

Discipline is a serious matter in organizations, especially those that are unionized. It cannot be administered unless the established procedures are followed. Bill Thomas has obviously not followed the disciplinary procedure specified in the union contract. Thus, if the case is taken to arbitration, the company is more than likely to lose. Jane has learned how to handle complaints and how to handle grievances after they have been filed. Jane could tell Bill that it was a mistake not to follow the established procedure for handling discipline, and she could advise Bill to admit this mistake openly and implement a prompt settlement immediately. Jane could also advise Bill to follow the hot-stove rule in administering discipline (pp. 432–33).

SUMMARY

The purpose of this chapter is to outline typical discipline and grievance procedures and to present a positive approach to handling discipline and grievances.

1. *Define discipline.* Discipline refers to conditions within an organization whereby employees know what is expected of them in terms of the organization's rules, standards, or policies.

2. *Explain the hot-stove rule for applying discipline.* The hot-stove rule emphasizes that discipline should be directed against the act rather than the person. Other key features of the hot-stove rule are immediacy, advance warning, consistency, and impersonality.

3. *Define grievance, union steward, and arbitration.* A grievance is a formal dispute between management and an employee or employees over some condition of employment. A union steward is an operative employee whom union members select to work with them on handling their grievances. Arbitration is a process by which both the union and management agree to abide by the decision of an outside party regarding a grievance.

4. *Discuss recommendations for pregrievance settlement.* By showing knowledge of organizational policies and the union contract (in a unionized situation), the supervisor may satisfy the grievant before a

formal complaint is filed. Developing a working relationship with the union steward is also helpful. A supervisor who sees a problem should take action before an employee complains. Encouraging employees to voice their opinions and complaints works to the supervisor's advantage. A supervisor is wise to investigate complaints that are expressed in nonverbal ways, such as excessive absences, high turnover, and low-quality work.

5. *Explain how to handle the first step of the grievance process.* The supervisor should listen patiently and sympathetically to the grievant. The supervisor must evaluate the facts objectively and attempt to determine the cause of the grievance. After the supervisor has made an evaluation of the grievance and arrived at a solution, the grievant and the union steward should be informed of the solution and the reasons behind it.

6. *Define employment at will in nonunionized organizations.* Employment at will means that when an employer hires employees to work for an indefinite period of time and the employees do not have a contract limiting the circumstances under which they can be discharged, the employer can terminate the employees at any time, for any reason, or for no reason at all.

REVIEW QUESTIONS

1. What is discipline?
2. Give 10 reasons why an employee might be disciplined.
3. What are some actions that should be taken by the supervisor in the prediscipline stage?
4. What are the key features of the hot-stove rule?
5. What is a grievance?
6. What is a union steward? arbitration?
7. Give some recommendations for pregrievance settlement of complaints.
8. Give some suggestions on handling the first step of the grievance process.
9. Explain employment at will.

SKILL-BUILDING QUESTIONS

1. "Grievance procedures are only used by troublemakers and should be abolished." Discuss your views on this statement.
2. "A supervisor's disciplinary action against an employee should never be overturned." Discuss.
3. Can you think of any exceptions to the hot-stove rule?
4. Many people believe that after the first step of the grievance process the supervisor is placed on trial. Do you agree? Why or why not?

ADDITIONAL READINGS

Bielous, Gary A. "Five Ways to Cope with Difficult People," *Supervision*, June 1996.

———. "How to Fire," *Supervision*, November 1996.

Lissy, William E. "Probationary Employees," *Supervision*, April 1995.

———. "Troubled Employees," *Supervision*, January 1996.

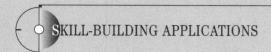
SKILL-BUILDING APPLICATIONS

Incident 22–1

You're Fired!

On September 30, 1990, John Arnold was hired as a mechanic by a large national automobile leasing firm in Austin, Texas. John, the only mechanic employed by the firm in Austin, was to do routine preventive maintenance on its cars. When he first began his job, he was scheduled to punch in on the time clock at 7 AM. On October 30, 1990, John's supervisor, Russ Brown, called him to his office and said, "John, I've noticed that you've been late for work seven times during October. What can I do to help you get here on time?"

John replied, "It would be awfully nice if I could start work at 8 AM, instead of 7 AM."

Russ then stated, "John, I'm very pleased with your overall work performance, so it's OK with me if your workday begins at 8 AM."

During the month of November 1990, John was late eight times. At the end of November, Russ and John had a conversation similar to the one that they had had at the end of October. As a result, John's starting time was changed to 9 AM. On January 11, 1991, Russ Brown posted the following notice on the bulletin board: **"Any employee late for work more than two times in any pay period is subject to termination."** On January 20, 1991, Russ called John into his office and gave him a letter that read, "During this pay period, you have been late for work more than two times. If this behavior continues, you are subject to termination." John signed the letter to acknowledge that he had received it.

John was late eight times during February 1991 and between March 1 and March 11 he was late five times. On March 11, 1991, Russ notified him that he had been terminated for his tardiness.

On March 12, 1991, John came to Russ with his union representative and demanded that he get his job back. John charged that another employee in the company, a woman, had been late as many times as or more times than he had been. John also charged that Russ had been punching the time clock for this woman because he had

been having an affair with her. The union representative then stated that three other people in the company had agreed to testify to these charges under oath. The union representative then said, "Russ, rules are for everyone. You can't let one person break a rule and penalize someone else for breaking the same rule. Therefore, John should have his job back."

Questions

1. Should John be reinstated in his job?
2. Was an effective disciplinary procedure followed?
3. What would you do about the charges against Russ if you were his boss?

Incident 22–2

Keys to the Drug Cabinet

John Brown, a 22-year-old African American, had been employed for only two and one-half weeks as a licensed practical nurse in the security section of a local hospital's alcohol and drug treatment center. He worked the 11 PM to 7 AM shift. Taking charge of the keys to the drug cabinet was one of his responsibilities.

One morning, at 1 AM, he became ill and the night supervisor, Margaret Handley, gave him permission to go home. A short time later, she realized that John had failed to leave the keys to the drug cabinet when he signed out. She immediately tried to reach him by telephoning his home.

More than a dozen attempts to reach John proved futile; all Margaret got was busy signals. Finally, at 3 AM, a man answered, but he refused to call John to the phone, saying that John was too ill to talk. Margaret became frantic and decided to ask the police to retrieve the keys.

The police arrived at John's home at 6:30 AM. They found John preparing to leave for the hospital so that he could return the keys. The police took the keys and returned them to the hospital. At 11 PM, John reported to work on his assigned shift, apologized for having failed to leave the keys, and questioned the necessity of calling the police.

Two days later, however, the unit director, Marcus Webb, informed John that he had been terminated. The reason cited for the discharge was that he had failed to turn in the drug cabinet keys before leaving the hospital and that he had them in his possession from 1 AM to 7 AM the following day. John learned that Margaret Handley had been verbally reprimanded for her handling of the case.

John filed an appeal regarding his dismissal with the human resources director of the hospital. However, the unit director's recommendation was upheld.

Following this decision, John filed charges with the EEOC that he had been discriminated against because of his race. (Both the night supervisor and the unit director were white.) He requested full reinstatement with back pay. He also requested that his personnel file be purged of any damaging records that alluded to the incident.

Questions

1. What would your decision be if you were asked to decide this case?
2. Should a supervisor and an employee be disciplined equally?

Exercise 22–1

Mock Arbitration

Summarized below is a situation in which you are to conduct a mock arbitration. The class will be divided into teams, five to six students per team. Each team will be assigned to represent either the union or the company. Your team must decide on the witnesses that you want at the hearing. Your opposing team must be given the names and job titles of your witnesses. During class time, two teams will conduct the mock arbitration.

BACKGROUND

General Telephone Company of the Southeast (Georgia), hereinafter referred to as "the company," provides local telephone service within certain areas of the state of Georgia. Its employees, as defined by Article 1 of the agreement, are represented by the Communications Workers of America, hereinafter referred to as "the union." The parties are operating under an agreement that became effective June 28, 1988.

The grievant, Cassandra Horne, was hired by the company as a service representative. On August 30, 1987, she was promoted to installer-repairer and was responsible for installing and repairing the equipment of residential and single-line business customers. The grievant's record is free of any disciplinary entries, and she is considered by her supervisor, Fred Carter, to be a satisfactory employee.

On May 19, 1989, the grievant suffered an on-the-job injury to her knee while attempting to disconnect a trailer from a company van. At some time after the injury, the grievant went on disability for approximately eight weeks. She then returned to work with a statement from the company physician allowing her to perform her normal work. After approximately three weeks, the grievant was still experiencing pain in her knee and was diagnosed by another physician as having a tear in the cartilage below her kneecap. She went back on disability and had surgery performed on October 19, 1989, to repair damage to the cartilage and ligament of her knee.

During the grievant's absence, her disability benefits expired and she agreed to take a six-month leave of absence beginning November 10, 1989. When the grievant's leave expired, on May 11, 1990, she was terminated from her employment with the company.

The company argued that according to the company physician the grievant could not perform installer-repairer work and that no other jobs were open that the grievant could perform. The union argued that the grievant had been cleared by her personal physician and that she felt she could do the work of installer-repairer. A grievance was filed at Step 1 on June 10, 1990, and was denied by the division human resources manager, Jerry L. Leynes. The grievance was submitted to arbitration, and it is now before the arbitrator for decision and award.

The company states that the issue before the arbitrator is as follows: Did the company violate the contract by terminating the grievant from her position as an installer-repairer, and, if so, what should the remedy be? The union states that the issue before the arbitrator is as follows: Is the discharge of the grievant for just or proper cause; if not, what should the remedy be?

PERTINENT PROVISIONS OF THE AGREEMENT

Article 1, Recognition

The company recognizes the union as the whole and exclusive collective bargaining agency with respect to rates of pay, hours of employment, and other conditions of employment for all employees within the exchanges coming under the operating jurisdiction of the above-named company. All supervisory and professional employees and those performing confidential labor relations duties are excluded from the bargaining unit.

Article 4, Work Jurisdiction

1. The company recognizes the right of its employees to perform its work and will make every reasonable effort to plan its work and forces to accomplish this end.
2. The company agrees that in its employment of contract labor to assist in the carrying out of its programs of construction, installation, removal, maintenance, and/or repair of telephone plant, it will not lay off or part-time, nor continue on layoff or part-time status, any regular employee performing the same work as that which is being performed by contract labor.

Article 11, Absences from Duty

1. Leaves of absence, without pay, not to exceed six (6) months will be granted by the company for good and compelling reason upon receipt of written request for such leave. Each such request will be approved or disapproved dependent upon the merit of the request. Such leaves may be extended for an additional period of not to exceed three (3) months.
   1.1 Working for another employer during leave shall constitute ground for termination of employment.
   1.2 Applying for unemployment compensation during leave may constitute grounds for termination of employment, except that this shall not be applicable where the employee has requested reinstatement in accordance with the provisions of this article and no work is available.

1.3 A leave of absence shall not carry a guarantee of reemployment, but the employee concerned, desiring to return from leave, shall be given opportunity for reemployment before any new employees are hired, provided the returning employee is qualified to perform the work.

Article 12, Paid Absences

4. In cases of physical disability resulting from compensable accidental injury while on the job, the company will pay the difference, if any, between the amount paid to the employee workers' compensation and the employee's basic rate in accordance with the schedule set forth below. No waiting period will be required.
   4.1 Up to five (5) years' accredited service, full pay not to exceed thirteen (13) weeks.

Article 23, Discharges, Suspensions, and Demotions

1. Requirement and limitations
   1.1 Any discharge, suspension, or demotion shall be only for proper cause and by proper action.
   1.2 Any employee who is discharged, suspended, or demoted shall, at the time of discharge, suspension, or demotion, be given a written statement setting forth the complete reasons for such action.

Exercise 22–2

Discipline in a Nonunionized Business

Assume that you are the office supervisor for a small business with 75 employees. You are not unionized. Lately, however, you have been receiving numerous complaints from employees about actions taken by some of the production supervisors. You feel that some system should be developed to handle these complaints.

Develop a formal procedure for handling complaints for your company. Be prepared to explain your system and answer questions regarding the advantages and the potential problems in implementing your system.

Glossary

achievement-power-affiliation theory: This theory holds that all people have three needs: (1) a need for achievement, (2) a need for power, and (3) a need for affiliation.

action planning: The phase of the planning process after the objective has been set, in which the supervisor must decide how the objective can be achieved.

activity: The work necessary to complete a particular event (usually consuming time).

administrative skills: Knowledge about the organization and how it works—the planning, organizing, and controlling functions of supervision.

affirmative action: Refers to an employer's attempt to balance its workforce in all job categories with respect to sex and race in order to reflect the same proportions as those of its general labor market in response to government requirements.

Age Discrimination in Employment Act of 1968: Prohibits discrimination against individuals over 40 years of age.

alteration ranking: Method in which a supervisor's employees are listed down the left side of a sheet of paper. The supervisor then chooses the most valuable employee, crosses this name off the list, and places it at the top of the column on the right side. The supervisor then selects and crosses off the name of the least valuable employee and places it at the bottom of the right-hand column. The supervisor then repeats this process for all the names on the left side. The listing of names on the right side gives the supervisor a ranking of his or her employees from most valuable to least valuable.

Americans with Disabilities Act (ADA): Gives the disabled sharply increased access to services and jobs.

analytical report: A report that interprets the facts it presents.

apprenticeship training: Supervised training and testing for a minimum time period and until a minimum skill level has been reached.

aptitude tests: Measure a person's capacity or potential ability to learn and perform a job.

arbitration: A process by which both the union and management agree to abide by the decision of an outside party regarding a grievance.

authority: The right to issue directives and expend resources.

autocratic leader: Leader who centralizes power and enjoys giving orders. Followers contribute little to the decision-making process.

avoidance: Giving a person the opportunity to avoid a negative consequence by exhibiting a desired behavior. Also called negative reinforcement.

brainstorming: Presenting a problem and then allowing the group to develop ideas for solutions.

brainwriting: Group members are presented with a problem situation and then asked to jot down their ideas on paper without any discussion.

budget: A statement of expected results or requirements expressed in financial or numerical terms.

burnout: A potential result of excessive job-related stress over a long period of time.

central tendency: The rating of all or most employees in the middle of the scale.

centralization and decentralization: Refer to the degree of authority delegated by top management.

chain of command: The principle that authority flows one link at a time from the top of the organization to the bottom.

changes internal to the organization: Changes that result from decisions made by the organization's management.

checklist: A performance appraisal method in which the supervisor does not actually evaluate, but merely records performance.

Civil Rights Act of 1991: Designed to reverse several Supreme Court decisions of 1989 and 1990 which had been viewed as limiting equal employment and affirmative action opportunity.

classroom training: The most familiar type of training, which involves lectures, movies, and exercises.

code of ethics: A written statement of principles to be followed in the conduct of business.

collective bargaining: Process by which a contract or an agreement is negotiated, written, administered, and interpreted.

communication: The process by which information is transferred from one source to another and is made meaningful to the involved sources.

computer-assisted instruction (CAI): A computer displays the material and processes the student's answers.

conciliator: A neutral person to help resolve the disputed issues during the bargaining process for a contract.

contingency plans: A plan made for what to do if something goes wrong.

continuous improvement teams: Another name for quality circles.

controlling: Comparing actual performance with predetermined standards or objectives and then taking action to correct any deviations from the standard.

critical-incident appraisals: The supervisor keeps a written record of unusual incidents that show both positive and negative actions by an employee.

cross-training: An employee learns several jobs and performs each job for a specific length of time.

delegation: Refers to the assigning of authority.

democratic leader: Leader who wants the followers to share in making decisions, although the leader has the final say.

departmentation: The grouping of activities into related work units.

dependent demand items: Typically subassemblies or component parts that will be used in making finished products.

direction: How well the person understands what is expected on the job.

directive counseling: The supervisor takes the initiative and asks the employee pointed questions about a problem. When the supervisor feels that he or she has a good grasp of what is causing the problem, the supervisor suggests several steps that the employee might take to overcome it.

direct labor costs: Expenditures for labor that is directly applied in the creation or delivery of the product or service.

disability insurance: Insurance that protects the employee during a long-term or permanent disability.

disabling injuries: Injuries that cause the employee to miss one or more days of work following an accident. Also known as lost-time injuries.

discipline: The conditions within an organization whereby employees know what is expected of them in terms of the organization's rules, standards, or policies.

dummies: Dashed arrows that show the dependent relationships among activities.

economic order quantity (EOQ): The optimum number of units to order.

Education Amendments Act: Prohibits discrimination because of sex against employees or students of any educational institution receiving financial aid from the federal government.

employment at will: When employees are hired for an indefinite time period and do not have a contract limiting the circumstances under which they can be discharged, the employer can terminate the employees at any time for any or no reason at all.

employment parity: When the proportion of protected employees employed by an organization equals the proportion in the organization's relevant labor market.

empowerment: Gives subordinates substantial authority to make decisions.

energy costs: Charges for electricity, gas, steam, and any other source of power.

environmental change: Includes all of the nontechnological changes that occur external to the organization.

Equal Employment Opportunity Commission (EEOC): One of two major federal enforcement agencies for equal employment opportunity. The other one is the Office of Federal Contract Compliance (OFCC).

Equal Pay Act: This requires that all employers covered by the Fair Labor Standards Act (and others included in the 1972 extension) provide equal pay to men and women who perform work that is similar in skill, effort, and responsibility.

essay appraisals: Requires the supervisor to write a series of statements about an employee's past performance, potential for promotion, strengths, and weaknesses.

esteem needs: These needs include both self-esteem and the esteem of others.

ethics: Standards or principles of conduct that govern the behavior of an individual or a group of individuals.

event: Denotes a point in time. The occurrence of an event signifies the completion of all activities leading up to it.

exception principle: States that supervisors should concentrate their efforts on matters that deviate from the normal and let their employees handle routine matters.

extinction: Provides no positive consequences or removes previously provided positive consequences as a result of undesired behavior.

fear of failure: Prevents many people from ever trying anything creative.

feedback: The flow of information from the receiver to the sender.

fixed-order period method: Restocking orders are placed at a predetermined, regular time interval, regardless of how much inventory is on hand.

fixed-order quantity method: Orders are placed whenever the inventory reaches a predetermined level, regardless of how long it takes to reach that level.

flow-process chart: A graphic representation of the steps in a task or job.

forced-choice rating: An evaluation method that requires the supervisor to choose which of two statements is either most (or least) applicable to the employee being reviewed.

forced-distribution ranking: The rater compares the performance of employees and places a certain percentage of employees at various performance levels.

formal work groups: Result primarily from the organizing function of government.

frequency rate: The number of times that disabling injuries occur.

functional departmentation: When organization units are defined by the nature or function of the work.

functional plans: Derived from the plans of higher levels of management.

functions of management and supervision: The functions are planning, organizing, staffing, motivating, and controlling.

Gantt chart: A diagram on which the activities to be performed are usually shown vertically and the time required to perform them is usually shown horizontally.

geographic departmentation: Occurs most frequently in organizations with operations or offices that are physically separated from each other.

good-faith bargaining: Interpreted as the sincere intention to negotiate differences and to seek an agreement acceptable to both parties.

grapevine: The informal communication system resulting from casual contacts between friends or acquaintances in various organization units.

graphic rating scale: The supervisor is asked to evaluate an individual on such factors as initiative, dependability, cooperativeness, and quality of work.

grievance: A formal dispute between management and an employee or employees over some condition of employment.

group cohesiveness: The degree of attraction or stick-togetherness of the group.

group norm: An understanding among group members concerning how those members should behave.

groupthink: When the drive to achieve consensus among group members becomes so powerful that it overrides independent, realistic appraisals of alternative actions.

halo effect: Occurs when the supervisor allows a single, prominent characteristic of the interviewee to dominate judgment of all other characteristics.

health insurance: Insurance which covers such things as normal hospitalization and outpatient doctor bills.

hierarchical idea filter: The more hierarchical levels an idea must pass through to be implemented, the greater the chances of its being distorted or lost.

hot-stove rule: Discipline should be directed against the act rather than the person. Other key features of the rule are immediacy, advance warning, consistency, and impersonality.

human relations skills: Knowledge about human behavior and the ability to work well with people.

independent demand items: Finished goods or other end items.

indirect labor costs: Expenditures for labor that is not directly applied to the creation or delivery of the product or service.

informal work groups: Not defined by the organizing function.

informational reports: A report that presents only the facts.

injunction: A court order to prohibit certain actions.

in-process inventories: Used to buffer differences in the rates of flow through the various operational processes.

input-output scheme: A technique developed by General Electric for use in solving energy-related problems. The first step under this method is to describe the desired output; the next step is to list all possible combinations of inputs that could lead to the desired output.

interest tests: Determine how a person's interests compare with the interests of successful people in a specific job.

interpersonal communication: Communication between individuals.

ISO 9000: A set of quality standards created in 1987 by the International Organization for Standardization in Geneva, Switzerland.

job analysis: Determines the pertinent information related to the performance of a specific job.

job bidding: Employees bid on a job based on seniority, job skills, or other qualifications.

job description: A written portrayal of a job and the types of work performed in it.

job enrichment: An approach that involves upgrading the job by adding motivating factors.

job knowledge tests: Measure the applicant's job-related knowledge.

job posting: The posting of notices of available jobs in central locations throughout the organization.

job rotation: An employee learns several jobs and performs each job for a specific length of time.

job satisfaction: An individual's general attitude toward his or her job.

job specification: The qualifications necessary to perform the job.

Kaizen: Means "good change" in Japanese.

Labor-Management Reporting and Disclosure (Landrum-Griffin) Act (1959): The act is primarily concerned with the protection of the rights of individual union members. For example, it permits union members to sue their unions and it requires that any increase in union dues be approved by a majority of the members (on a secret ballot).

laissez-faire leader: Leader who allows the group members to do as they please, thus allowing the group members to make all the decisions.

layout chart: A sketch of a facility that shows the physical arrangement of the facility and the major flow of work through it.

leader: Obtains followers and influences them in setting and achieving objectives.

leniency: The grouping of employee ratings at the positive end instead of spreading them throughout the performance scale.

line authority: Based on the superior-subordinate relationship. With line authority, there is a direct line of authority from the top to the bottom of the organization structure.

lost-time injuries: Injuries that cause the employee to miss one or more days of work following an accident. Also known as disabling injuries.

maintenance costs: Expenditures that include labor and material costs incurred to repair and maintain equipment and facilities.

Malcolm Baldrige Award: Administered by National Institute of Standards and Technology and can only be awarded to businesses located in the United States.

management by objectives (MBO): A style of supervising that has its roots in the planning function.

material requirements planning (MRP): A special type of inventory system in which the needed amount of each component of a product is figured on the basis of the amount of the final product to be produced.

materials handling: The movement of materials.

mediator: A neutral person to help resolve the disputed issues during the bargaining process for a contract.

methods study: Concerned with determining the most efficient way of doing a task or job.

motivating: Getting employees to put forth maximum effort while doing their job.

National Labor Relations Board (NLRB): Determines what the bargaining unit is (which employees the union will represent) and whether the authorization requirement has been fulfilled.

need hierarchy theory: Based on the assumption that employees are motivated to satisfy a number of needs and that money can satisfy, directly or indirectly, only some of these needs.

negotiation: The process by which a labor contract is produced.

nondirective counseling: The employee assumes most of the initiative and the supervisor serves primarily as a listener. The employee is encouraged to discuss what he or she thinks is causing the problem and to develop solutions to it.

nonverbal communication: Communication through body movements, facial expressions, gestures, or even silences that communicate messages. Nonverbal communication can totally change the meaning of verbal communication.

objective: A statement of a desired result or what is to be achieved.

occupational parity: When the portion of protected employees employed in various occupations in the organization is equal to their proportion in the organization's relevant labor market.

Occupational Safety and Health Act (OSHA): Its purpose is "to assure so far as possible every working man and woman in the nation safe and healthful working conditions and to preserve our human resources."

Office of Federal Contract Compliance (OFCC): One of two major federal enforcement agencies for equal employment opportunity. The other one is the Equal Employment Opportunity Commission (EEOC).

on-the-job training (OJT): Instruction given by the supervisor or a senior employee in which a new employee is shown how the job is performed and then actually does it under the trainer's supervision.

operating supplies costs: Expenditures for necessary items that do not become a part of the product or service.

organization politics: The practice of using means other than merit or good performance for bettering your position or gaining favor in the organization.

organizational communication: Communicating within the formal organization structure (committee meetings, reports, memos, etc.).

organizing: Distributing the work among employees in the work group and arranging the work so that it flows smoothly.

orienting: The process of introducing new employees to the organization and to the work unit and the job.

overhead costs: Expenditures for physical space, staff services, research, advertising, and legal services.

paired-comparison ranking: Method in which the supervisor lists employee names down the left side of a sheet of paper. The supervisor then evaluates the performance of the first employee on the list against the performance of the second employee on the list. If the supervisor feels that the performance of the first employee is better than that of the second employee, he places a checkmark by the first employee's name.

The first employee is then compared to each of the other employees. In this way, he or she is compared with all the other employees on the list. The process is repeated for each of the other employees. The employee with the most checkmarks is evaluated to be the most valuable employee, and the employee with the least checkmarks is evaluated to be the least valuable.

parity principle: States that authority and responsibility must coincide.

perception: How people view situations.

performance: How well an employee is fulfilling the requirements of the job.

performance appraisal: A process that involves communicating to an employee how well the employee is performing the job and also, ideally, involves establishing a plan for improvement.

physical needs: The basic needs for the human body that must be satisfied to sustain life. These needs include food, sleep, water, exercise, clothing, shelter, and so forth.

planning: Determining the most effective means for achieving the work of the unit.

policies: Broad, general guidelines to action.

polygraph: Also known as the lie detector, this device records physical changes in the body as the test subject answers a series of questions.

positive reinforcement: Providing a positive consequence as a result of desired behavior.

power: The ability to get others to respond favorably to instructions and orders.

preference-expectancy theory: A theory based on the belief that people attempt to increase pleasure and decrease displeasure. According to this theory, which Victor Vroom pioneered, people are motivated to work if (1) they believe that their efforts will be rewarded and (2) they value the rewards that are being offered.

problem-solving skills: The ability to analyze information and objectively reach a decision.

procedure: A series of related steps or tasks performed in sequential order to achieve a specific purpose.

process control: Quality control that relates to the control of a machine or an operation during the production process.

product quality control: Quality control that relates to things (products, services, raw materials, etc.).

productivity: Units of output per employee hour.

proficiency tests: Measure how well the applicant can do a sample of the work that is to be performed.

programmed instruction: Training method in which, after the material is presented in text form, the trainee is required to read and answer questions relating to the text.

protected groups: Classes of people identified by race, color, sex, age, religion, national origin, and mental and physical handicaps.

psychological tests: Measure personality characteristics.

psychomotor tests: Measure a person's strength, dexterity, and coordination.

punishment: Providing a negative consequence as a result of undesired behavior.

pygmalion effect: This concept refers to the tendency of an employee to live up to the supervisor's expectations.

quality circle: A voluntary group of employees who meet periodically for the sole purpose of solving quality problems and identifying ways of improving quality.

raw material costs: Expenditures for raw material that is directly applied to the creation of the product or service.

recruiting: Involves seeking and attracting qualified candidates for job vacancies.

Rehabilitation Act of 1973: Protects handicapped people by ensuring that people are not refused a job merely because of their handicap if the handicap does not affect their ability to do the job.

reinforcement theory: Reinforced behavior is more likely to be repeated.

resource allocation: The efficient allocation of people, materials, and equipment so as to successfully meet the objectives that have been established.

responsibilities: The things that make up the supervisor's job.

responsibility: Accountability for reaching objectives, using resources properly, and adhering to organizational policy.

right-to-work laws: A law passed by individual states prohibiting union shops.

routing: Determining the best sequence of operations.

rules: Require that specific and definite actions be taken or not taken.

safety needs: Needs concerned with protection against danger, threat, or deprivation.

scalar principle: States that authority flows one link at a time from the top of the organization to the bottom.

scheduling: The precise timetable that is to be followed in producing products or services.

scrap costs: Expenditures for products, parts, or services that cannot be reworked or reused and that do not meet quality standards.

selection: To choose the best person for the job from the candidates.

self-actualization: The needs of people to reach their full potential in terms of their abilities and interests.

semantics: The study of the meaning of words and symbols.

severity rate: Indicates how severe the accidents were and how long the injured parties were out of work. Only disabling injuries are used in determining frequency and severity rates.

sexual harassment: Unwelcome sexual advances, requests for sexual favors, and other verbal or physical conduct of a sexual nature are considered sexual harassment.

Sherman Antitrust Act of 1890: A law making it illegal to restrain trade.

sit-down strike: When employees stay on the job but refuse to work.

slowdown: Employees sometimes continue to work but reduce their output.

social needs: Needs that include love, affection, and belonging.

span of control principle: The number of employees a supervisor can effectively manage.

staff authority: Used to support and advise line authority.

staffing: Supervision function concerned with obtaining and developing qualified people.

standard operating procedures (SOPs): Well-established and formalized procedures.

standards: Used to set performance levels.

strategic management: The process of developing strategic plans and keeping them current as changes occur.

strategic or corporate plan: A plan developed by the top management of an organization.

structured interview: Supervisor knows the questions to be asked and records results.

strike: An action that occurs when employees leave their job and refuse to come back to work until a contract has been signed.

supervision: The first level of management in the organization, concerned with encouraging the members of a work unit to contribute positively toward accomplishing the organization's goals and objectives.

supervisory plans: Derived from the plans of higher levels of management.

systematic discrimination: Large differences in either occupational or employment parity.

Taft-Hartley Act of 1947: Spelled out rights of and restrictions on unions.

technical skills: Knowledge about such things as machines, processes, and methods of production.

theory X: Maintains that the average employee dislikes work.

theory Y: States that people like to work, and it comes as naturally as rest and play.

time study: The analysis of a task to determine the elements of work required to perform it, the order in which these elements occur, and the times required to perform them effectively. The objective of a time study is to determine how long it should take an average person to perform the task in question.

Title VI of the Civil Rights Act of 1964: Prohibits discrimination based on race, color, or national origin in all programs or activities that receive federal financial aid in order to provide employment.

Title VII of the Civil Rights Act of 1964: Amendments to this act make it illegal to hire, fire, pay, or take other management actions on the basis of race, color, religion, national origin, or sex.

Total Quality Management (TQM): A management philosophy that emphasizes managing the entire organization so that it excels in all dimensions of products and services that are important to the customer.

traditional theory: Based on the assumption that money is the primary motivator of people.

training: The acquisition by employees of the skills, information, and attitudes necessary for improving their effectiveness.

union organization drive: Started by the employees of the organization when, for one or more reasons, a group of employees determines that a union is desirable.

union shop: The union can require an employee who has been working for a specified period of time to become a member.

union steward: An operative employee whom the union members elect to work with them on handling their grievances.

unity of command principle: States that an employee should have one and only one immediate boss.

unstructured interviews: Have no definite checklist of questions or preplanned strategy.

vestibule training: The individual uses procedures and equipment similar to those of the actual job, but are located in a special area called a vestibule.

Veterans Readjustment Act: Requires federal government contractors and subcontractors to take affirmative action to hire and promote Vietnam War and disabled veterans.

wildcat strike: A strike in which employees leave their job and refuse to work during the contract period.

workers' compensation: Protection for the worker from loss of income and extra expenses associated with work-related injuries.

work-methods improvement: Used to find the most efficient way to accomplish a given task.

work-standards approach: Attempts are made to establish objective measures of an employee's work performance.

yellow-dog contract: An agreement between an employee and management that, as a condition of employment, the employee will not join a labor union.

zero-defects program: A program which tries to create a positive attitude toward the prevention of low quality.

Name Index

Ackerly, Leone, 273
Adams, Cristina, 400
Adams, Graham, Jr., 252
Ailes, Roger, 59, 62
Albrecht, Steve, 404
Anfuso, Dawn, 373, 418
Aquilano, Nicholas J., 381, 382
Armstrong, Neil, 324
Asch, Solomon, 158
Awad, Elias M., 179

Bakke, Allan, 239
Baldrige, Malcolm, 376
Barnes, Billy E., 195
Barnes, R. M., 170
Barnhart, Phillip, 68
Beaubien, Elaine, 40, 138
Behling, Orlando, 303
Bencin, Richard L., 40
Benitz, Linda E., 319
Benneyan, James C., 173
Berezin, Eric, 424
Bielous, Gary A., 16, 138, 286,
    303, 442
Bishop, James Wallace, 158
Bissel, Christopher, 313
Bistayi, Scott, 135
Black, Todd Gutner, 12
Blake, Robert, 296–298
Blériot, Louis, 324
Boring, Edwin G., 49
Bosler, Daniel, 3
Bradford, Leland B., 294
Brandman, Barry, 424
Brown, W. Stephen, 205
Buckman, Steve, 359
Buhler, Patricia, 16, 117, 158, 205
Butler, Siobahn, 334

Capozzoli, Thomas K., 286, 319
Carey, Robert, 359
Carney, Karen E., 359
Caudron, Sharon, 283
Chapple, Ron, 280
Chase, Nancy, 374, 382
Chase, Richard B., 381, 382
Chavez-Thompson, Linda, 256
Chute, Alan C., 173
Clark, Thomas B., 381
Coletti, John, 123
Cooke, Rhonda, 359
Costley, Dan I., 150, 151, 153
Cousins, Roland B., 319
Crockett, Bob, 394
Culpan, Refik, 175
Custer, George A., 311

D'Addario, Francis, 418
Darragh-Jeremos, Peggy, 59
Davis, Keith, 153

Delevingne, Lionel, 211
Deming, W. Edwards, 166, 175, 371
Deshpande, Satish P., 265
Dickman, F., 355
Doan, Amy, 32, 40
Douglas, Donna Niksch, 92
Douglas, Merrill E., 92, 95
Dressler, Garry, 424
Dreyer, R. S., 286, 303
Driscoll, Dawn-Marie, 74
DuBrin, Andrew J., 35
Dunnette, Marvin D., 319
Dwyer, Michael, 399

Eckles, Robert W., 417
Edison, Thomas A., 324
Eisenhower, Dwight D., 298
Elkouri, Edna, 430
Elkouri, Frank, 430
Emener, W. G., 355
Evans, Barbara Ryniker, 247
Evans, James R., 424
Faidley, Ray A., 225
Fairley, Peter, 265
Famularo, Joseph, 199
Farrant, Don, 92
Fessler, Clyde, 125
Fiedler, Fred, 298–299
Filippi, S. Thomas, 418
Flynn, Gillian, 329, 337
Freund, Joseph, 283
Fryer, Bronwyn, 377

Gaedeke, A., 339
Gamezy, Normal, 49
Geber, Sara Zeff, 337
Gertenberg, Richard C., 175
Getty, Hulton, 325
Gilbreth, Frank, 169
Gilbreth, Lillian, 169
Glass, Robert, 84
Glueck, William F., 277
Goddard, Robert W., 16
Gold, David S., 16
Gorman, Leon, 373
Gransbury, Pat, 286
Grant, Spencer, 335
Greenberg, J., 3
Greenman, Russell L., 411
Grimaldi, John V., 424

Haas, Robert D., 66
Hacy, John, 55
Hardy, Marc, 16
Hecht, Françoise, 117
Henderson, Richard L., 186
Herzberg, Frederick, 277–278
Hill, W. F., 49
Hobson, Gary W., 21
Hodges, Walter, 56

Hoevemeyer, Victoria A., 158
Hoffman, W. Michael, 74
Holmes, T. H., 344
Honeycutt, Alan, 382
Hook, Ethel, 416
Ireland, Karen, 68

Jackson, Phil, 156
Johnston, Judith, 107
Johnston, William B., 11, 16
Jones, John E., 43
Jones, Michael, 40
Jones, P. R., 361
Kaschub, William J., 337
Kennedy, John F., 293
Kimble, Gregory A., 49
Knot, Edward M., Jr., 181
Knowdell, Richard, 349
Kraushar, Jon, 59, 62
Kronemer, Alexander, 175

Laabs, Jennifer L., 89
Lackritz, James R., 382
Lebediker, Jeremy, 225
Ledvinka, S., 410
Lee, Chris, 9
Leeper, Robert, 49
LeJeune, Jean-Claude, 149
Level, Dale, Jr., 53
Levitt, Theodore, 167
Lewin, Kurt, 331
Libes, Stewart C., 205
Lieber, Ron, 156
Liemandt, Joseph, 125
Likert, Rensis, 144–145, 158
Lindo, David K., 59
Lippitt, Ronald, 294
Lissy, William E., 205, 222, 225, 247, 265,
    362, 442
Livingston, J. Sterling, 299–300, 303
Loraine, Kaye, 303
Lousig-Nont, Gregory M., 205

Madden, Kelly Hayes, 111
Magenau, John M., 265
Marchese, Marc, 210
Marcus, Amy Docker, 245
Maslow, Abraham H., 273–274
May, Bess Riter, 404
Maynard, Roberta, 175, 273
McClelland, David, 276
McConnell, Charles R., 138, 359
McGregor, Douglas, 299–300
McShulskis, Elaine, 359
Meckel, N. T., 359
Melrose, Kendrick, 125
Meyer, Herbert H., 221
Miller, Fred D., 404
Minehan, Maureen, 256
Mintcloud, Buckley, 404
Mixon, Malachi, 125

Moore, Jere N., Jr., 59
Morgan, Martha N., 225
Mouton, Jane, 296–298

Neuborne, Ellen, 193
Niehouse, Oliver I., 337
Nierman, Lyndy, 319
Nordling, Rolf, 337
Nussbaum, Karen, 256
O'Brien, Joseph D., 147

Painter, Charles, 16
Parker, Arnold E. H., 11, 16
Parrish, Deidra-Ann, 404
Parzybok, William, Jr., 381
Pasley, Richard, 291
Patton, George, 298
Peavey, Buck, 424
Pell, Arthur R., 225
Perican, John, 16
Peters, Shannon, 356
Pfeiffer, J. William, 43
Poisant, James, 126
Pollock, Ellen Joan, 245
Pollock, Ted, 138, 225, 286, 319
Pondy, Louis, 319
Porter, Elliott F., 40
Pulich, Marcia Ann, 247

Rahe, R. H., 344
Raia, Anthony P., 113
Raidsepp, Eugene, 341

Ramsey, Robert D., 59, 74, 286, 319, 424
Ray, Lennie, 436
Reigle, Daniel H., 243
Reynolds, James E., 92
Richles, Roger, 76
Robinson, Lois, 245
Rosenbert, Geanne, 439
Ross, Sherwood, 265

Samson, Barbara, 12
Sarchet, Bernard R., 417
Sardell, Robert M., 382
Schmertz, Eric J., 411
Schmidt, Warren H., 295, 319
Schonberger, Richard J., 181
Schriesheim, Chester A., 303
Schwimer, Dorothy, 337
Scott, K. Dow, 158
Sellers, Patricia, 293
Semrodek, James J., Jr., 404
Sfiligoj, Eric, 424
Sheridan, John H., 175
Shine, D. Bruce, 265
Simonds, Rollin H., 424
Singleton, Eric, 377
Siteman, Frank, 430
Smith, Bob, 382
Spragins, Ellyn E., 16
Stephenson, William J., 381
Stork, Diana, 359
Struebing, Laura, 164
Sullivan, F. L., 260
Sunderland, Margene E., 36, 40

Tannenbaum, Robert, 295
Taylor, Frederick W., 165, 272–273
Taylor, Glenn L., 225
Taylor, H. R., 361
Teerlink, Richard F., 125
Terry, George, 295
Thomas, Kenneth S., 319
Tilley, Kate, 117
Todd, Ralph, 150, 151, 153
Tolliver, James M., 303
Tschohl, John, 126
Turner, Ted, 293
Tyler, Kathryn, 349
Ulery, John D., 18

Van Auken, Phillip ., 158, 319
Van de Vliet, Anita, 92
Van Horn, Lois H., 382
Vasilash, Gary S., 175
Verespej, Michael A., 46
Vogl, A. J., 382
Vroom, Victor, 278
Wachtel, George S., 40
Waddell, Janet R., 59
Walker, Vivienne, 175
Watt, Isaac, 324
Weber, Steve, 110
Weiss, W. H., 59, 337
Welch, Jack, 293
Welsch, Ulrike, 372
Wenkman, Jackie, 247
Whitmer, Jim, 87
Williams, Bill, 158
Wolff, David Young, 233
Zachary, Mary-Kathryn, 247

Company Index

Accountemps, 84
Allied Signal, Inc., 376, 377
American Airlines, 46
AT&T, 12

Becker Group, 394
Bell-South, 12
Boeing 757, 46
Boeing Company, 193

Cable Midlands, 333, 334
Career Planning and Adult Development
    Network, 349
Chicago Bulls, 156
Chrysler Corporation, 349, 394
Citicorp, 68
Colorado Fuel and Iron Company, 252

Digital Equipment Corporation, 171, 173
Disney World, 125–126
Dodge Dakota, 394
Domino's Pizza, 111

Eateries, Inc., 135
Employers Screening Services, Inc., 400

Fayetteville Technical Community
    College, 36

General Electric, 37, 147
General Mills, 12
Grateful Dead, 156
GTE, 12

Hagberg Consulting Group, 193
Hardee's Food Systems, Inc., 418
Hard Rock Cafe, 123
Harley-Davidson Motor Company, 8,
    9, 125
Hewlett-Packard, 55
Honda, 125
Hudson Institute, 11

IdeAAs in Action, 46
Intermedia Communications, 12
Invacare, 135

Jacksonville Shipyards, Inc., 245
Janna Contact, 85
Johnson Controls, 237

Knowledge Networks, 32

L. L. Bean, Inc., 373
Levi Strauss and Company, 66, 356
Lotus Development Corporation, 85
Lucent Technologies, 282, 283

Martin Marietta Corporation, 68
Maximizer Technologies, 85
McDonald's, 165, 167, 177
Merrill Lynch, 12
Merritt Tool Company, 436
Microelectronic News, 194
MicroLogic, 85
Microsoft Corporation, 85, 377
Milagro Systems, Inc., 32
Mini Maid, Inc., 273

MKS Instruments, 374
Motivational Systems, 89

NEC Electronics, Inc., 194
Now Software, 85

Officeteam, 89
Olsten Corporation, 11

Pacific Gas and Electric Company, 329
Robert Hall International, Inc., 89
Roy Rogers restaurants, 418

Sanford Teller Communications, 84, 89
Southwestern Electric Power Company, 436
Southwest National Bank, 107
Suzuki, 125
Symantec, 85

TBM Consulting Group, 164
Toro Company, 135
TQ Soft, 377
Trilogy Development Group, 135

United States Mutual Associates, 400

Western Electric Company, 144

Yamaha, 125

Subject Index

ABC classification system, 386
Ability, 209
Ability of the supervisor, 129
Absenteeism, 398
Accident-proneness, 412–413
Accidents; *see* Work-related accidents
Achievable goals, 155
Achievement-power-application theory,
    276–277
Action forums, 329
Action planning, 105–106
Activity, 111
Administrative skills, 8
Admitting mistakes, 33
Advance warning of discipline, 433
Affirmative action programs, 198
    executive orders, 232, 235
    history of, 239–240
    positive approach to, 242–243
AFL-CIO
    recruiting campaigns, 256
    structure of, 254–255
African Americans
    glass ceiling, 12
    as protected group, 230
Age Discrimination in Employment Act, 197,
    232, 236
Aging workforce, 12
Alcohol addicts, 354–355
Alternation ranking, 217
Alternatives
    choosing and implementing, 29–30
    evaluating, 29
    gathering facts about, 28
    identifying, 27–28
Ambiguities, 315
American National Standards
    Institute, 373
Americans with Disabilities Act, 198,
    233–234, 236
Analytical reports, 368
Antidiscrimination laws, 230
    affirmative action programs, 239–240
    effect on supervisors
        in disciplinary action, 242
        in hiring, 240–241
        in job assignment, 241
        in performance evaluation, 241–242
    enforcement agencies, 237
    interpretation of Title VII, 237–238
    provisions, 231–236
Apprenticeship training, 201
Appropriated ideas, 37
Aptitude tests, 189
Arbitration, 259
Arbitration process, 435
Arbitrators, 259
Assigning work, 130–131, 134
Attitude profiles of leadership, 299–300
Authority, 9, 290
    centralized/decentralized, 125
    delegating, 129–135

line versus staff, 124–125
    principles based on, 127–129
    and supervisors, 123–124
Autocratic leaders, 293–297
Automated routing, 111
Avoidance, 279

Background checks, 192–193, 194
Bakke case, 239
Balance sheet budget, 368
Baldridge Awards Committee, 373
Barriers to change, 326–327
Bona fide occupational
    qualifications, 238
Boss
    attitudes toward, 70–72
    communication with, 54
Brainstorming, 36
Brainwriting, 37
Budget, 109
Budgeting systems, 392
Budgets
    cost budgets, 391–393
    for planning and control, 367–368
Building a team, 145
Burnout, 332–333
Business process engineering, 372

Capital expenditure budget, 368
Career counseling, 348–349, 361–362
Carrying costs, 387
Cash budget, 368
Centralization, 125
Centralized authority, 125
Central tendency, 219
Chain of command, 128
Change
    employee reactions, 325–326
    increased rate of, 324
    internal to organizations, 325
    reasons for resistance to, 326–327
    reduced resistance to, 328–331
    and supervisors, 324–325
    three-step model for, 331
    types of, 325
Charismatic leaders, 293
Checklist, 214–216
*City of Richmond v. J. A. Crosan
    Co.*, 239
Civil Rights Act of 1866, 231, 235
Civil Rights Act of 1870, 230, 235
Civil Rights Act of 1964, 237, 244; *see
    also* Title VII
Civil Rights Act of 1991, 198, 234,
    236, 239
Classroom training, 201
Clayton Antitrust Act, 252, 254
Closed shop, 253
Codes of ethics, 65–66
Coercive power, 69

Coffee talks, 55
Collective bargaining
    contract administration,
        258–259
    contract negotiations, 257–258
    contract provisions, 258
    definition, 257
    and supervisors, 261
College recruitment, 188
Common resources, 315
Communication, 45
    with boss, 54
    open, 154
    oral versus written, 53
Communication barriers, 315
Communication skills
    nonverbal, 52–54
    oral skills, 51–52
    writing, 52
Competition, 315
Complexity, 129
Comprehensive Rehabilitation Service
    Amendments, 355
Compromise, 316
Computer-assisted instruction, 201
Conciliator, 258
Conflict
    definition and types, 309
    interpersonal, 313–314
    intrapersonal, 310–313
    political, 315
    positive and negative aspects, 310
    structural, 314–315
Conflict aftermath, 309
Conflict management
    benefits, 310
    methods, 315–318
Conflict situations, 134
Confrontation, 316–317
Consistency of discipline, 433
Constructive discipline, 154
Contingency plans, 106–107
Continuous improvement, 372
    cost control tactic, 389
Continuous improvement teams, 146
Continuum of leadership
    behaviors, 295
Control, 365
Controlling, 7
Control process
    basic requirements, 365
    corrective action, 366–367
    cost reduction, 393–397
    discipline procedures, 429–434
    grievance handling, 435–440
    inventory control, 369, 377–379,
        386–387
    monitoring performance, 366
    performance standards, 365–366
    quality assurance, 369, 370–377
Cooperative Education
    Departments, 188

Co-op programs, 188
Corporate plan; *see* Strategic plan
Corrective action, 366–367
Cost areas
  absenteeism, 398
  employee theft, 400
  identifying, 395
  materials handling, 401
  overtime, 397–398
  tardiness, 399
Cost budgets, 391–393
Cost objectives, 390
Cost reduction
  employee fear of, 401
  and machines/equipment, 395
  and materials purchases, 395
  nine-step program, 395–397
  supervisor role, 389–390
  and top management, 395
Cost-reduction resources, 394–395
Cost-reduction strategies, 393–395
Costs
  categories of, 390–391
  related to productivity, 389
  of work-related accidents, 409–410
Cost standards, 366
Counseling
  career counseling, 348–349, 361–362
  directive and nondirective, 347
  employee assistance programs, 354,
    355, 356
  timing and reasons for, 346
Counseling employees, 134
Counseling techniques, 347
CPM; *see* Critical path method
Creating and obligation, 131
Creative climate, 35–37
Creative decisions, 34–37
Creative persons, 34–35
Creativity, isolated, 37
Crisis situations, 33
Critical incident appraisals, 216
Critical path, 112
Critical path method, 111–112
Cross-training, 201
Customer departmentation, 123

Daily log, 81–82
Data, failure to examine, 34
Decentralization, 125
Decentralized authority, 125
Decision making
  group participation, 154
  by groups, 30–32
  leadership styles, 293–295
  versus problem solving, 24
  traps to avoid, 32–34
Decision making process, 26–30
Decision making skills, 8
Decisions
  creative, 34–37
  delayed too long, 34
  expected and unexpected, 25
  recognition and timeliness, 25–26
  regretting, 33
  relative importance, 32
Delegating, 8, 86, 90, 129–135
  means of
    assigning work, 130–131
    creating an obligation, 131
    granting permission, 131
  practical tips for, 134–135

reasons for reluctance, 131–133
  tasks unsuitable for, 133–134, 135
Delegation, 129–135
Deming cycle, 166
Democratic leaders, 293–297
Departmentation, 122–123
Department of Agriculture, 370
Department of Commerce, 68
Department of Labor, 232
  Employment and Training
    Administration, 11
  Occupational Safety and Health
    Administration, 419
  Women's Bureau, 256
Department plans, 100
Dependent demand items, 386, 387
Detail work, 133
Dictating machine, 86
Direction, 209–210
Directive counseling, 347
Directive leaders, 294–295
Direct labor costs, 390–391
Disability insurance, 410
Disabling injuries, 413
Disciplinary action, 242
Discipline, 428–429
  administering, 432–434
  advance warning, 433
  consistency of, 433
  formal steps, 434
  immediacy of, 432
  impersonal nature of, 433
  maintaining, 429
  in nonunion companies, 440–441
Discipline procedure
  applying, 429–431
    administering discipline, 432–434
    checklist, 434
    formal steps, 434
    hot-stove rule, 432–433
    predisciplinary recommendation,
      431–432
  in labor contract, 431
  reasons for, 430
Discrimination
  effects of, 231
  in hiring, 240–241
  in job assignment, 241
  in performance appraisals, 241–242
Dishonest employees, 68–69
Distractions, 37
Diversity; *see also* Managing diversity
  and glass ceiling, 12
  guidelines, 12–14
Downtime, 394
Drug addicts, 354–355
Drug-testing programs, 192
Dummies, 111–112

Economic order quantity, 387
Education Amendments Act, 232
Effort, 209
Electronic monitors, 369
Empathy, 292
Employee assistance programs, 353, 354
  critical elements, 355
  at Levi Strauss, 356
Employee complaints, 439
Employee fears, 164–165
Employee feedback, 210, 282
Employee participation and cooperation,
  281–282

Employee Polygraph Protection Act, 192
Employee referrals, 188
Employee rewards, 114
Employees; *see also* Troubled employees;
  Unions
  absenteeism, 398
  causes of work-related accidents, 411–413
  conflict situations, 134
  cost-control suggestions, 390
  counseling, 134
  discipline procedure, 428–429
  dishonest, 68–69
  empowerment, 125–126
  fear of cost reduction, 401
  and grievances, 435–437
  job satisfaction, 282–284
  legal issues in hiring, 197–198
  morale, 300–301
  motivating, 134
  orientation programs, 198–199
  overtime, 397–398
  performance appraisals, 209, 212–223
  periodic progress reviews, 114
  poor performers, 222–223
  problem, 356
  protected groups, 230
  reactions to change, 325–326
  reasons for disciplining, 430
  reasons for resisting change, 326–327
  recruiting, 185–188
  reduced resistance to change, 328–331
  selecting personnel, 188–197
  span of control principle, 128–129
  steps in training, 202–203
  stress management guidelines, 333–335
  tardiness, 399
  training programs, 200–203
  treated as individuals, 281
  unity of command principle, 128
  warning signs of violence, 418
Employee safety costs, 415
Employee theft, 400
Employment agencies, 187–188
Employment application form, 190–191
Employment applications, 189
Employment at will, 440
Employment parity, 238
Employment tests, 189–192
  and antidiscrimination laws, 240–241
Empowerment, 125–126
Energy costs, 391
Enthusiasm, 292
Environmental change, 325
Envy, 314
Equal employment opportunity, 242
Equal Employment Opportunity Act, 231
Equal Employment Opportunity Commission,
  231, 237, 238, 244
Equal Pay Act, 232, 235
Equal Protection Clause of 14th Amendment,
  231, 235
Equipment design, 169, 170
Ergonomics, 414
Essay appraisals, 214
Esteem needs, 274–275
Ethics, 64
  and dishonest employees, 68–69
  questionable behaviors, 65
  setting the tone, 66
  values-based, 66
  in workplace, 64–65
Ethics board games, 68
Event, 111

Exception principle, 127–128
Excessive togetherness, 37
Executive Order 10988, 253, 254
Executive Order 11246, 232, 235
Executive Order 11375, 232, 235
Executive Order 11478, 235
Executive Order 11491, 253, 254
Expected decisions, 25
Expert power, 69
Extinction, 279

Failure to consult, 33
Fair Labor Standards Act, 232
Family and Medical Leave Act, 334–335
Fear of failure, 37
Fear of the unknown, 326–327
Federal employees, 253
Federation of Physicians and Dentists, 256
Feedback, 13, 48, 72
    from employees, 210, 282
    periodic progress reviews, 114
Felt conflict, 309
Fetal protection policy, 237
Fiedler's contingency approach to leadership,
    298–299
Filing, 86–87
Finished-goods inventories, 378
Fixed-order period inventory method,
    386–387
Fixed-order quantity inventory method, 386
Flow-process chart, 168, 178–179
Follower-oriented leaders, 295
Follow-up, 30
Follow-up filing system, 83–84
Forced-choice rating method, 216
Forced-distribution curve, 218
Forced-distribution ranking, 217–218
Forcing solutions to conflict, 316
Formal leaders, 291–292
Formal work groups, 144–146
Fourteenth Amendment, 231, 235
Frequency rate of accidents, 413
Frustration, 312
Functional departmentation, 122–123
Functions of management, 5–9
Functions of supervision, 5–9

Gantt charts, 111, 112, 113
Geographic departmentation, 123
Giving instructions, 56–57
Glass ceiling, 12
Goal conflict, 312–313
Goals
    achievable, 155
    compared to objectives, 103
Good example, 9
Good-faith bargaining, 258
Good work habits, 85–90
Granting permission, 131
Grapevine, 57
Graphic rating scale, 214
Grievance procedures
    arbitration process, 435
    first step, 438–440
    later steps, 440
    pregrievance settlement, 437–438
    steps, 435, 437
Grievances
    checklist for minimizing, 440
    definition, 435
    minimizing, 435–437
Group cohesiveness, 148–150, 151

Group conformity, 151–152
Group decision making, 30–32
Group norms, 148
Group pressures, 144, 151–152
Group rewards, 155
Groups, 144
Groupthink, 31

Halo effect, 194, 219
Handicapped individuals, 355
Hawthorne studies, 144
Hazard Communications Standard, 421–422
Health insurance, 609
Help wanted ads, 187
Hierarchical idea filter, 37
Hiring
    legal issues, 197–198
    methods, 186–197
    quotas, 239–240
Hot-stove rule, 432–433
Human body, use of, 169, 170
Human environment stress, 332
Human relations, 292
Human relations skills, 8, 67
Human resource needs, 109
Hygiene factors, 277

Illegal immigrants, 11
Immediacy of discipline, 432
Immigration Reform and Control Act, 236
Impersonality of discipline, 433
Implementation committee, 396
Improvement programs, 109
Incentives
    for cost reduction, 390
    motivation through, 283
Inconveniences, 327
Independent demand items, 386–387
Indirect labor costs, 391
Individual objectives, 113
Informal leaders, 291–292
Informal work groups, 146–148
    characteristics, 148–150
    group conformity, 151–152
    key factors in dealing with, 153
    leadership, 150
    potential benefits, 153
    supervision, 152–156
Informational reports, 368
Information availability, 10
Injunction, 252, 253
Injured Workers' Program, 416
In-process inventories, 378
Input-output scheme, 37
Insurance costs, 409
Interest tests, 189
International Standards Organization, 373
Internship programs, 188
Interpersonal communication, 45
    characteristics, 45–46
    differences in perception, 48–49
    feedback, 48
    lack of interest, 50–51
    misinterpretation, 49–50
    poor listening habits, 46–48
    process, 47
    supervisory failure, 50
Interpersonal conflict, 313–314
    strategies for, 316–317
Interpersonal relations, threats to, 327
Interruptions, 37
Interviews, 189
    guidelines, 196

interviews, 193–194
    pitfalls, 194–195
Intrapersonal conflict, 310–313, 316–317
Inventory control, 369
    ABC classification system, 386
    dependent demand/independent demand,
        386–387
    for dependent demand items, 387
    economic order quantity, 387
    for independent demand items,
        386–387
    just-in-time system, 374, 379
    materials requirements planning, 387
    purpose, 377–379
    reorder point, 386–387
    safety stock, 386–387
Inventory costs, 378–379
ISO 9000 standards, 373–374

Japan
    Deming's influence, 371
    kaizen philosophy, 163–164
    kanban system, 379
    quality circles, 146, 375
Jealousy, 314
Job advancement, 241–242
Job analysis, 185–187, 212
Job analysis questionnaire, 185–186
Job assignment discrimination, 241
Job bidding, 187
Job description, 187, 211–212
Job design, Herzberg's theory, 277–278
Job dissatisfaction, 284
Job enlargement, 277
Job enrichment, 277, 280–281, 414
Job-instruction training system, 200
Job interviews, 193–195
    and discrimination, 241
    guidelines, 196
Job knowledge tests, 189
Job posting, 187
Job rotation, 201, 277
Job satisfactions, 282–284
Job specifications, 187, 211–212
Job understanding, 81
Just-in-time inventory system, 374, 379

Kaizen philosophy, 163–164, 164–165
Kanban system, 379

Labor contracts, 257–259
    and discipline procedure, 431
    and supervisor responsibility, 261–262
Labor costs, 390–391
Labor law, 251–254
Labor-Management Relations Act, 253,
    254, 258
Labor-Management Reporting and Disclosure
    Act, 253, 254
Labor movement, 254
Labor unions; *see* Unions
Laissez-faire leaders, 293–297
Landrum-Griffin Act; *see* Labor-Management
    Reporting and Disclosure Act
Latent conflict, 309
Layout chart, 179–181
Leader-member relations, 298–299
Leaders
    charismatic, 293
    definition, 290
    formal versus informal, 291–292
    supportive versus directive, 294–295

Leadership, 290
  attitudes, 299–300
  behavior continuum, 295
  characteristics, 292–293
  of informal work groups, 150
  Managerial Grid, 296–297
  and morale, 300–301
  situational approach, 298–299
  and supervisors, 301
  transformational, 301
Leadership situation forces, 296
Leadership styles
  basic, 293–295
  contingency approach, 298
  relationship of, 295–298
Leading, 6
Legal Defense and Education Fund, 245
Legislation; *see* Regulation
Legitimate power, 69
Leniency, 219
Letters, 86
Line authority, 124–125
Listening habits, 46–48
Litigation
  over affirmative action, 239
  over job references, 194
Los Angeles Manufacturing Action
    Project, 256
Lost-time injuries, 413
Loyalty, 67, 71

Maine State Quality Award, 373
Maintenance costs, 391
Maintenance factors, 277
Malcolm Baldrige National Quality Award,
    373, 376, 377
Management
  and collective bargaining, 257–259
  at Harley-Davidson, 9
  and productivity, 162–163
  strategic planning, 99
  supervisor responsibility to, 259
  and union philosophy, 251
Management by exception, 127–128
Management by objectives, 112–115
  in control process, 369
  for performance appraisal, 218
Managerial Grid, 296–297
Managing diversity, 10–14
  guidelines for, 12–14
Mandatory protection policy, 237
Manifest conflict, 309
Martin v. Wilks, 239
Massachusetts Supreme Court, 252
Material budget, 368
Material Safety Data Sheet, 421–422
Materials handling, 401
Materials requirements planning, 387
Materials standards, 366
MBO; *see* Management by objectives
Mediators, 258
Medical examination, 197
Meetings, 55–56, 84
Memos, 86
Memphis fire department ruling, 239
Mental endurance, 292
Merit systems, 238
Methods; *see* Work methods improvement
Methods engineering, 164
Middle management, 4
Minorities; *see* African Americans
Misinterpretation, 49–50
Monitoring performance, 366

Morale
  and accidents, 410
  and leadership, 300-301
Moral standards, 64
Motion economy, 169, 170
Motivation
  basic theories
    achievement-power-application theory,
      276–277
    motivation-maintenance theory,
      277–278
    need hierarchy theory, 273–276
    preference-expectancy theory, 278–279
    reinforcement theory, 279
    traditional theory, 272–273
  definition, 271
  and job satisfaction, 282–284
  through incentives, 283
  understanding people, 272
Motivational problems, 134
Motivation-maintenance theory, 277–278
Motivators, 277
Movement chart, 179
Moving budget, 392

National Guild for Health Care Providers of
    the Lower Extremities, 256
National Institute of Standards and
    Technology, 376
National Labor Relations Act, 253, 254, 258
National Labor Relations Board, 235, 253,
    257, 258
National Organization of Women, 245
Need-drive-goal motivation sequence,
    310–312
Need hierarchy theory, 273–276
Needs
  and informal work groups, 147
  Maslow's theory, 273–276
  McClelland's theory, 276–277
  sensitivity to, 154
Negative reinforcement, 279
Negotiation, 257–258
New York City Central Labor
    Council, 256
Nonbehavioral assumptions, 13
Nondirective counseling, 347
Nonunion organizations, discipline in,
    440–441
Nonverbal communication, 52–54
Norris-La Guardia Act, 253, 254

Objectives, 103
  individual, 113
  measurable, 104
  priorities in, 104–105
  realistic, 104
  regularly updated, 104
  as standards, 365–366
  supervisory areas, 105
  understandable, 104
  written, 104
Objective-setting
  individual objectives, 113
  process, 101–103
  steps, 103–105
Observable behavior, 13
Occupational parity, 238
Occupational Safety and Health Act, 419
Occupational Safety and Health
    Administration
  basic requirements, 420

Hazard Communications Standard,
    421–422
Material Safety Data Sheets, 421–422
purpose, 419
and supervisors, 421
Office of Federal Contract Compliance,
    232, 237
On-the-job training, 200
Operating supplies costs, 391
Opposing personalities, 313
Oral communication skills, 51–52
Order quantity, 387
Organizational communication, 45
  characteristics, 54–55
  giving instructions, 56–57
  grapevine, 57
  handling meetings, 55–56
  suggestion system, 46
Organizational creativity, barriers to, 37
Organization charts, 122
Organization politics, 70–72
Organizations
  changes internal, 325
  discipline procedure, 428–429
  effect of troubled employees, 350
  help for troubled employees, 350–351
  planning by, 99–101
  policies, procedures, and rules, 107–108
  problem employees, 356
  safety strategies, 414–415
  stress management guidelines, 333
  types of conflict
    interpersonal, 313–314
    intrapersonal, 310–313
    political, 315
    structural, 314–315
Organization structure
  authority and supervisors, 123–124
  centralized versus decentralized
    authority, 125
  departmentation, 122–123
  line versus staff authority, 124–125
  organization charts, 122
  power and supervisors, 126
Organizing, 6, 122, 144
Orientation programs, 198–199
Orienting, 185
Orza, Vincent, 125
Output
  evaluation, 13
  increase in, 393
Overhead costs, 391
Overhead reduction, 393
Overtime, 397–398

Paired-comparison ranking, 217
Paperwork, 85–86
Parity principle, 127
PDCA (plan, do, check, act) cycle, 166–171,
    172, 173
Perceived conflict, 309
Perception, 48–49
Performance, 209–211
  confronting troubled employees, 351–353
  factors determining, 210
  and job analysis, 212
  and job description, 211–212
  and job specifications, 211–212
  monitoring, 366
  rewards related to, 281
  and troubled employees, 350
Performance appraisals
  definition, 212–213

discrimination in, 241–242
frequency of, 218–219
handling poor performers, 222–223
interviews
  conducting, 220–221
  preparation of, 221–222
methods, 213–214
  checklist, 214–216
  critical-incident appraisals, 216
  essay appraisals, 214
  forced-choice rating, 216
  graphic rating scale, 214
  management by objectives, 218
  ranking methods, 217–218
  work-standards approach, 216–217
overcoming biases in, 219
purpose, 209
supervisor biases, 219
Performance standards, 365–366
Periodic budgeting, 392
Periodic progress reviews, 114
Permissive leaders, 295
Personal actions, 67
Personal creativity, 35
Personal information managers, 84, 85
Personal observation, 369
Personal prejudices/preferences, 219
Personal problems; *see* Troubled
    employees
Personnel selection methods, 188–197
PERT, 111–112
Physical endurance, 292
Physical environmental stress, 332
Physical layout principles, 180
Physical needs, 274–275
Planning
  contingency plans, 106–107
  definition, 101–103
  at McDonald's, 167
  objective-setting process, 101–103
  organizational, 99–101
  steps, 6
  supervisory, 101–106
  for work-methods improvement, 166–169
Planning activities, 134
Policies, 107–108
Political conflict, 315
Polygraph tests, 189–192
Position power, 298–299
Positive reinforcement, 279
Power, 290
  definition, 69
  human attraction to, 132
  and supervisors, 126
  types of, 69
Power base, 69–70
Precedent and policies, 33–34
Predisciplinary recommendation, 431–432
Pre-employment tests, 189–192, 193
Preference-expectancy theory, 278–279
Pregnancy Discrimination Act, 236
Pregrievance settlement, 437–438
Prejudices, 313–314
Premature criticism, 37
Principles of motion economy, 169, 170
Prioritizing objectives, 104–105
Prioritizing work activities, 82–84
Private employment agencies, 188
Problem employees, 356
Problems
  identifying, 26–27
  indications and symptoms of, 26
  redefining, 27

Problem solving
  versus decision making, 24
  skills, 8
Procedures, 108
Process control, 376–377
Procrastination, 88–89
Production budget, 368
Production obstacles, 154
Production planning activities, 109–112
Productivity, 14, 162–163
  benefits of methods improvement, 165–166
  costs related to, 389
  flow-process chart, 168, 178–179
  kaizen philosophy, 163–164
  layout chart, 179–181
  PDCA cycle, 166–167, 172, 173
  principles of motion economy, 169, 170
  systematic methods improvement,
    166–171
  time study, 171–173
  work methods improvement, 164–165
Productivity peak, 84
Productivity standards, 366
Product quality control, 376
Product/service departmentation, 123
Proficiency tests, 189
Programmed instruction, 201
Progressive budget, 392
Promotion, 241–242
Protected groups, 230
Proximity, 129
Psychological tests, 189
Punishment, 279
Pygmalion effect, 272

Quality
  aspects of, 370
  continuous improvement, 372
  importance of, 370
  ISO 9000 standards, 373–374
  quality at the source, 372
  quality circles approach, 375
  reengineering, 372–373
  responsibility for, 370–371
  steps for maintaining, 370
  total quality management, 371–373
  zero-defects program, 374–375
Quality assurance, 369, 371
Quality at the source, 372
Quality circles, 146, 375
Quality control, 376–377
Quality guidelines, 375–376
Quality of the employees, 129
Quality of work life, 10
Quotas in hiring, 239–240

Ranking methods, 217–218
Raw material inventories, 377–378
Raw materials, 401
Raw materials costs, 391
Reading material, 84
Recruiting, 185
  co-op programs, 188
  employee referrals, 188
  employment agencies, 187–188
  help wanted ads, 187
  internship programs, 188
  job analysis, 185–187
  job posting, 187
  legal issues, 197–198
Reengineering, 372–373

Reference checks, 192–193, 194
  litigation over, 194
Referent power, 69
Regulation
  antidiscrimination laws, 230–236
  dealing with troubled employees, 354–356
  employment enforcement agencies, 237
  Family and Medical Leave Act, 334–335
  labor law, 251–254
  Occupational Safety and Health Act, 419
  protected groups, 230
  recruiting and hiring, 197–198
Rehabilitation Act of 1973, 197, 233, 236, 354
Reinforcement theory, 279
Reorder point, 386–387
Report writing, 86
Resource allocation, 110
Resource usage standards, 366
Respect, 71
Responsibilities, 126–127
Responsibility, 70
  delegating, 129–135
  and supervisors, 126–127
Restrictive leaders, 295
Revenue and expense budget, 368
Revenue standard, 366
Reverse-discrimination claims, 239
Reward power, 69
Reward systems
  related to performance, 281
  Taylor's theory, 272–273
  valued rewards, 281
  Vroom's theory, 278–279
Right-to-work laws, 253
Role change, 9
Role dissatisfaction, 314
Role stress, 332
Rolodex, 85
Routing, 110
Rules, 108

Safety
  measures of, 413
  supervisor responsibility, 408–409
  and workplace violence, 418
Safety committee, 408–409, 414
Safety hazards, 413
Safety needs, 274–275
Safety program
  basic elements, 414
  organizational strategies, 414–415
  supervisor role, 415–417
Safety statistics, 415
Safety stock, 386–387
Safety training sessions, 415
Sales departmentation, 124
Satisfaction; *see* Job satisfaction
Savings ideas, 396
Scalar principle, 128
Scheduling, 110–111
Scrap/waste costs, 391
Screening, 189
Self-actualization needs, 274–275
Self-confidence, 292
Self-fulfillment needs, 274–275
Semantics, 49–50
Seniority systems, 238
Sense of responsibility, 292
Sensitivity to individual needs, 154
Services, 162
Setting good example, 133
Severity rate of accidents, 413

Sexual harassment prevention, 244
Sherman Antitrust Act, 252, 254
Shewhart cycle, 166
Sit-down strike, 263
Skills, fear of loss in value, 327
Slow-down, 262–263
Smoothing over, 316
Socializing, 72
Social needs, 274–275
Social stress, 332
Society of Human Resource Management, 418
Span of control principle, 128–129
Span of management, 128
Staff authority, 124–125
Staffing, 6
    legal issues, 197–198
    orienting process, 198–199
    recruitment methods, 185–188
    selection methods, 188–197
        background/reference checks, 192–193
        employment tests, 189–192
        interviews, 189
        job interviews, 193–195
        medical examination, 197
        screening, 189
        supervisor decision, 195
    training programs, 200–203
Staffing function, 185
Standard operating procedures, 108
Standards, 365
    kinds of, 366
    methods of setting, 366
Standard time, 171–172
State employment agencies, 187
Status quo, 37
Stereotyping, 13
Stockout, 387
Storage space, 394
Strategic conflicts, 315
Strategic management, 100–101
Strategic plan/planning, 99, 100
    and supervisors, 100–101
Stress
    causes of, 342–344
    definition, 332
    job-related, 332–333
Stress management
    Family and Medical Leave Act, 334–335
    nonconventional, 334
    organizational guidelines, 333
    personal guidelines, 333–334
    questionnaire, 340–342
Strikes, 262–263
    United Mine Workers, 252
Structural conflict, 314–315
Structured interviews, 193
Subordinates
    socializing with, 72
    supervisor treatment of, 67
Suggestion box, 282
Suggestion system, 46
Supervision, 3
    functions, 5–9
    and informal work groups, 152–156
    key to productivity, 14
    management by objectives, 112–115
    periodicals, 22
    principles based on authority
        exception principle, 127–128
        parity principle, 127
        scalar principle, 128
        span of control principle, 128–129
        unity of command, 128

Supervision power base, 69–70
Supervisors
    affecting employee motivation, 280–282
    applying discipline, 429–434
    areas of ethical conduct, 67
    attitude toward ethics, 66
    and authority, 123–124
    biases in appraisal, 219
    and career counseling, 349
    and change, 324–325
    dealing with grievances, 435–440
    delegating authority, 129–135
    and dishonest employees, 68–69
    and effective leadership, 301
    effect of antidiscrimination laws
        in disciplinary actions, 242
        in hiring, 240–241
        in job assignment, 241
        in performance appraisals, 241–242
    employee selection decision, 195
    handling poor performers, 222–223
    at Harley-Davidson, 9
    human relations skills, 67
    job titles, 4–5
    loyalty, 67
    maintaining discipline, 429
    and motivation, 272
    and Occupational Safety and Health
        Administration, 421
    overt personal actions, 67
    and power, 126
    Pygmalion effect, 272
    reluctance to delegate, 131–133
    responsibilities to unions/
        management, 259
    responsibility, 126–127
    responsibility for quality, 370–377
    responsibility for safety, 408–409
    role in cost control, 389–390
    role in planning, 101
    and safety program, 415–417
    skills required by, 8
    socializing with subordinates, 72
    source of, 5, 6
    staffing function, 185
    and strategic planning, 100–101
    tasks not to be delegated, 133–134, 135
    and troubled employees, 349–354
    types of change affecting, 326
    understanding job, 81
    working with unions
        during collective bargaining, 261
        in contract administration, 261–262
        guidelines, 259–260
        during strikes, 262–263
        union stewards, 261
    work methods improvement, 164–165
Supervisor's environment
    information availability, 10
    outlook toward work environment,
        10–14
Supervisor's shadow, 37
Supervisory control
    practice of, 369
    process, 365–367
    purpose, 365
    tools
        budgets, 367–368
        electronic monitors, 369
        management by objectives, 369
        personal observation, 369
        written reports, 368–369
Supervisory failure, 50

Supervisory objectives, 105
Supervisory planning/plans, 100–106
    action planning, 105–106
    contingency plans, 106–107
    objectives versus goals, 103
    setting objectives, 103–105
Supervisory planning activities, 108–112
    developing budgets, 109
    human resource needs, 109
    improvement programs, 109
    information for high-level planning, 109
    production planning, 109–112
Supervisory success, 8–9
Supplier Cost Reduction Effort, 394
Suppliers, 394
Supportive leaders, 294–295
Systemic discrimination, 238

Taft-Hartley Act; see Labor-Management
    Relations Act
Tardiness, 399
Task analysis, 168–169
Task identification, 168
Task-oriented leaders, 295
Task stress, 332
Task structure, 298–299
Team-building, 145
Teamwork, 156
Technical skills, 8
Technological change, 325
Technology, 162–163
Telephone time, 87–88, 89
Tell-and-show training, 202
TempForce, 354
Theory X, 299–300
Theory Y, 299–300
Think time, 90
Threats
    avoiding, 329–330
    to interpersonal relations, 327
    to job or income, 327
    to power, 327
360-degree feedback, 210
Tickler filing system, 83–84
Time
    analyzing, 81–82
    organizing work routine, 84–85
    planning, 82–84
    prioritizing activities, 82–84
    productivity peak, 84
    scheduling production, 110–111
    for thinking, 90
Time budget, 368
Time caddy, 81–82, 83
Time inventory, 81–82
Time management, 81
Time or shift departmentation, 123
Time study, 171–173
Time wasters, 80
Title VII, 197, 232, 235
    disciplinary action, 242
    interpretation and application, 237–238
    provisions, 231, 235
To-do list, 82–83
Total quality management, 371–383
Traditional theory of motivation,
    272–273
Training programs, 185, 200–203
    for cost reduction, 394
    pitfalls, 201
    steps, 202–203
Transformational leadership, 301

Troubled employees
  aiding and evaluating, 353–354
  confronting, 351–353
  employee assistance programs, 353, 354–356
  identifying, 351, 352
  legal and union issues, 354–356
  organizational help, 350–351
Trust-building, 328
Try-out stage, 169–171

Unexpected decisions, 25
Unfair labor practices, 259
Union of American Physicians and Dentists, 256
Unions
  and collective bargaining, 257–259
  dealing with troubled employees, 354–356
  and discipline procedure, 431
  early illegality, 251–252
  grievance procedures, 437
  and labor law, 251–254
  and management philosophy, 251
  membership, 251
  minimizing grievances, 435–437
  in nontraditional industries, 256
  organization drives, 257
  reasons for joining, 256
  structure of, 254–255
  supervisor responsibility to, 259
  and supervisory responsibilities
    during collective bargaining, 261
    in contract administration, 261–262
    guidelines, 259–260
    during strikes, 262–263
    working with stewards, 261
  types of, 254
  unfair labor practices, 259
Union shop, 253
Union stewards, 260, 261
  grievance handling, 435
United Mine Workers, 252
United States Postal Service, 317
United States Register Accreditation Board, 374

United States Supreme Court, 239
Unity of command principle, 128
Unsafe physical conditions, 412
Unstructured interviews, 194

Validation, 240–241
Values-based ethics, 66
Variety, 129
Vestibule training, 201
Vietnam-Era Veterans Readjustment Assistance Act, 232–233, 236
Violence; see Workplace violence
Visitors, 88

Wagner Act; see National Labor Relations Act
Wards Cove v. Atonio, 239
Waste minimizing, 393
Wildcat strike, 263
Withdrawal, 316
Women
  glass ceiling, 12
  preventing sexual harassment, 244–245
  as protected group, 230
Work environment, 277, 412
  characteristics, 146–147
  managing diversity in, 10–14
  quality of work life, 10
  supervisor responsibility, 145–146
Workers' compensation, 409
  injuries covered by, 411
  program features, 410
Work flow regulation, 393
Workforce 2000, 11
Work groups
  formal, 144–146
  group pressures, 151–152
  informal, 146–156
  morale, 300–301
  quality circles, 146
  status of, 149
Work habits, 85–90
  dealing with visitors, 88
  delegating work, 90
  filing, 86–87
  letters and memos, 86

  meetings, 87
  paperwork, 85–86
  procrastination, 88–89
  reading material, 87
  report writing, 86
  telephone time, 87–88, 89
Work methods improvement
  benefits, 165–166
  and employee fears, 164–165
  flow process chart, 168, 178–179
  layout chart, 179–181
  proper climate for, 165
  systematic
    evaluating results, 171
    fine-tuning, 171
    planning, 166–169
    try-out stage, 169–171
Work-out program, 147
Workplace
  arrangement, 169, 170
  discipline, 428–429
  ethics, 64–65
  violence in, 418
Work-related accidents
  causes
    accident-proneness, 412–413
    personal acts, 411
    physical environment, 412
  costs of, 409–411
  disabling, 413
  frequency rate, 413
  lost-time, 413
  number of, 408
  prevention, 415–417
  severity rate, 413
Work routine, 84–85
Work simplification, 164
Work-standard appraisal approach, 216–217
World Wide Web, 85
Writing skills, 52
Written reports, 368–369

Yellow-dog contract, 252, 253
Zen Buddhism, 156
Zero-defects program, 374–375